ECONOMICS

Houghton Mifflin Company   Boston   Toronto

Geneva, Illinois   Palo Alto   Princeton, New Jersey

Economics

SECOND EDITION

Rodney H. Mabry

Clemson University

Holley H. Ulbrich

Clemson University

To Ida, Hattie, R.A., and Kay.

R.H.M.   H.H.U.

Sponsoring Editor: *Denise Clinton*
Editorial Assistant: *Kelly Faughnan*
Project Editor: *Susan Westendorf*
Production/Design Coordinator: *Caroline Ryan Morgan*
Senior Manufacturing Coordinator: *Marie Barnes*
Marketing Manager: *Michael Ginley*
Cover Designer: *Karen Gourley Lehman*
Cover Image: © *1993 ARS, New York/VG Bild-Kunst, Bonn*

Photo Credits:
P. 5, © M. Dwyer/Stock Boston; p. 35, NASA; p. 53, © Judy S. Gelles/Stock Boston; p. 93, © Hollis Officer; p. 109, © Barbara Alper/Stock Boston; p. 139, © Jeremy Ross/Photo Researchers; p. 149, Kim Sakamoto/*Sports Illustrated;* p. 197, © Michael Dwyer/Stock Boston; p. 211, © Lionel Delevingne/Stock Boston; p. 247, © Tim Ryan; p. 267, Donna Binder/Impact Visuals; p. 309, © Daemmrich/Stock Boston; p. 333, © Michael Weisbrot/Stock Boston; p. 354, © Michael Weisbrot/Stock Boston; p. 375, Photo Courtesy of the Washington, DC Convention & Visitors Association; p. 399, Photo Courtesy of the New York Federal Reserve; p. 421, © Spencer Grant/Photo Researchers; p. 449 © Charles Gupton/TSW.

Printed in the U.S.A.

Library of Congress Catalog Card Number: 93-78685

ISBN: 0-395-66996-0

23456789-DH-97 96 95 94

Contents in Brief

Contents

Chapter 2

. . . .

Chapter 3

· · · · · · · · · · · · · · · · · · · ·

Chapter 4

· · · · · · · · · · · · · · · · · · · ·

Chapter 5

. . . .

Demand and Supply: Extensions

Chapter 6
. . . .

Behind the Supply Curve: Cost and Production   121

Chapter 7
. . . .

The Market in Operation: Pure Competition   143

Chapter 8

· · · · · · · · · · · · · · · · · · ·

Imperfect Competition and Market Power   173

Chapter 9

· ·

Chapter 10

. . . .

The Economic Role of Government

P A R T   III   MACROECONOMICS CONCEPTS 257

Chapter 11
. . . .

Macroeconomic Goals and Their Measurement 259

Chapter 12

. . . .

Aggregate Demand and Supply: Determining the Levels of Prices, Output, and Employment

Chapter 15

. . . .

Fiscal Policy and Deficits   365

Chapter 17

. . . .

Money, the Banking System, and Monetary Policy   417

Chapter 19

. . . .

The Practical Economist: Using Your Economics   469

Preface

A second edition is always a joy to the authors. It is an affirmation of what we did in the first edition. At the same time, it provides an opportunity to repair the inevitable imperfections and improve the text after a great deal of "road-testing" in the classroom. As we noted in the preface to the first edition, a one-semester course is difficult to address in a textbook. Unlike the two-semester course in the principles of economics, the shorter course lacks a standard sequence or even a standard selection of topics. Its audience ranges from those needing remedial work to beginning MBA students, and the emphasis can vary from heavily micro to heavily macro to current issues. Whereas two-semester texts increasingly look as much alike as the major television networks, the offerings in the one-semester market are as diverse as a Chinese menu.

OVERALL GOALS

Our basic goals are the same in the second edition as they were in the first. In searching for a text for our students, we found that despite the variety there was an empty space in the middle, where we were looking. We wanted a text that neither assumed too much nor asked too little; that was neither all micro with a macro afterthought, nor vice versa; that had enough but not too much theory; that integrated current issues into the discussion of theory; and that gave the neophyte economist adequate pedagogical aids without spoon-feeding. We wanted a book that set a theme early on and followed it through, so that the pieces of economics fit together into a coherent whole. We wanted to give equal emphasis to both micro and macro, while providing some options about which of the two areas to stress.

As in the first edition, aggregate demand and aggregate supply are used as the foundation of the macroeconomic chapters, and the book is organized so that it is possible to teach the Keynesian model or to delete it.

Although in a text such as this one, authors must make some difficult decisions about what to include and what to omit, several "road maps" in the book should help the instructor in tailoring the course content to his or her particular preferences. Our own class experiences have attuned us to the challenges of trying to squeeze an adequate introduction to economics into fifteen weeks.

THEME

This book represents our best effort to design and redesign a text that meets the needs of balance, brevity, and coherence. The coherence of economics as a single melody with many variations is established in the first chapter, where we identify the characteristics of the PRACTICAL ECONOMIST—a person who engages in self-interested, maximizing behavior, responds to incentives and chooses at the margin, and weighs costs and benefits before making a decision. Your reaction to the theme of the practical economist led us not only to retain but to reinforce this device in the second edition. You will find this theme cropping up throughout the text and the end-of-chapter questions. In the final chapter, the interrelationships of economic ideas are reiterated through the practical economist concept. The initial description of the practical economist, with whom the student should easily identify, and the constant reminder of that behavioral model throughout the text should make it clear to the student that these assumptions about the behavior of individuals as practical economists underlie all of the economic theory. The theme of the practical economist also provides some continuity between macro and micro, since the behavioral assumptions are the same for both. Thus, the student will not see economics as a series of unrelated topics and chapters, but as a description of the various facets of economic behavior of individuals acting as practical economists.

PEDAGOGY

We have designed the text to aid students in comprehending and retaining important points. Each chapter begins with a preview, to set the stage, and ends with a numbered summary and thought-provoking questions and problems. We have paid special attention to those questions in the second edition, providing more problems and applications and fewer review questions. Key terms are defined in the margins for easy reference, and each chapter contains three or more boxed *Checklists*—brief, helpful summaries of key ideas from the preceding pages.

The boxed MYTH in each chapter, a feature strongly praised by users and reviewers, is retained in this edition. Students come to their first economics course with a great deal of acquired folk wisdom, much of which is simplistic, inaccurate, or just plain wrong. The myths identify and demolish some of these time-honored ideas that haunt economics—myths such as "the dollar is backed by gold," "all monopolists make profit," and "we can fine-tune the economy." Thus, the myths reinforce the efforts of the text and the instructor to teach students to approach economic questions in a systematic and thoughtful manner by challenging some of their previously acquired ideas. The IN PRACTICE feature in each chapter adds a longer current illustration of a chapter concept to the shorter examples in the text. These boxes reinforce the goal of our text: they show students how to use the basic tools of economics to understand their everyday experiences. The accompanying *Instructor's Resource Manual* provides some suggestions for using these MYTH and IN PRACTICE boxes.

MAJOR CHANGES IN THE SECOND EDITION

The second edition is much shorter than the first, a response to comments of users and reviewers. The number of chapters has been reduced from twenty-two to nineteen. We eliminated the chapter on labor, retaining some of the material about labor markets in the chapters on competition and monopoly, and the material about poverty in the chapter on market failure. We eliminated the final macro chapter, exporting relevant material to other chapters. The chapter on growth has been moved up from Chapter 18 to Chapter 13—a change that reflects current emphasis on economic growth. Every chapter has been thoroughly reviewed and edited for content, level, and presentation, as well as brought up to date with new examples, boxes, and data.

ORGANIZATION AND ALTERNATIVE OUTLINES

Macro and micro concepts receive approximately equal attention (seven chapters each) in this edition, in contrast to many books currently on the market, which strongly emphasize one or the other. Three introductory chapters present some basic ideas for both micro and macro. Micro precedes macro so that macro can be built on micro foundations. Most of the appendixes contained in the first edition have been deleted, but we did keep the appendix on using graphs. Other material from the appendices has been moved to the *Instructor's Resource Manual* for those who would like to address some of these supplementary topics. International examples are scattered throughout, in addition to the traditional chapter on international economics. The final wrap-up chapter is based on the practical economist model of economic behavior, with suggestions for continuing to use economics in daily life.

Instructors may take one of three paths through the course, one with a micro emphasis, one with a macro emphasis, or one with a balanced emphasis:

Micro Emphasis	Macro Emphasis	Balanced Emphasis
Introduction		
Chapter 1	Chapter 1	Chapter 1
Chapter 2	Chapter 2	Chapter 2
Chapter 3	Chapter 3	Chapter 3
Microeconomics		
Chapter 4	Chapter 4	Chapter 4
Chapter 5	Chapter 5	Chapter 5
Chapter 6	Chapter 9	Chapter 6*
Chapter 7	Chapter 10	Chapter 7*
Chapter 8		Chapter 8*

Chapter 9		Chapter 9
Chapter 10		Chapter 10
Macroeconomics		
Chapter 11	Chapter 11	Chapter 11
Chapter 12	Chapter 12	Chapter 12
	Chapter 13	
	Chapter 14	
Chapter 15	Chapter 15	Chapter 15
Chapter 16	Chapter 16	Chapter 16
Chapter 17	Chapter 17	Chapter 17
Chapter 18 (trade part)	Chapter 18 (finance part)	Chapter 18
Chapter 19	Chapter 19	Chapter 19

*Selected topics in each of these chapters

ANCILLARIES

For this edition we have thoroughly revised both the *Study Guide* and the *Instructor's Resource Manual and Test Bank with Transparency Masters*. The *Study Guide* includes, for each chapter, a chapter summary, chapter outline, completion exercises, discussion/essay questions, multiple-choice questions, true/false questions, and answers. The instructor's manual section of the *Instructor's Resource Manual and Test Bank with Transparency Masters* contains a chapter outline, applications and extensions, ideas for using IN PRACTICE and the MYTH, suggestions for further reading, answers to chapter questions and problems, and transparency masters taken from the main text. The test bank section includes more than fifteen hundred multiple-choice and true/false questions, including all those from the *Study Guide*. A *Computerized Test Bank* is available for IBM compatible and Macintosh computers and contains all the questions from the printed test bank. *Computer Tutorials* are also available for IBM compatible computers.

ACKNOWLEDGMENTS

We want to express our thanks to the editorial team at Houghton Mifflin Company: Denise Clinton, sponsoring editor, Kelly Faughnan, editorial assistant, and Susan Westendorf, project editor.

We would also like to thank those professors who provided their invaluable advice on the revised manuscript: Stephen R. Ball, Cleary College; Jim Betres, Rhode Island College; Jeffery Blais, Rhode Island College; Thomas W. Bonsor, Eastern Washington University; Thomas M. Carroll, Central Oregon Community College; James E. Clark, Wichita State University; Richard Crowe, Hazard Community College; Carl Dauber, Southern Ohio College; Tommy Georgiades, DeVry Institute of Technology; Katheryn Houck, Great Lakes Junior College; Bruce Roberts, Highline Community College; and Clay Smith, Stark Technical College.

In addition, we would like to thank our colleagues at Clemson University for numerous ideas and suggestions; our students, who were the inspiration for this effort; Carlton Ulbrich for the artwork in the supplements; Merle Mabry for her patience with the project; and Cindy McCullough for her word-processing skills and hard work in keeping track of details and preparing final materials for publication.

RODNEY MABRY
HOLLEY ULBRICH

About the Authors

Rodney H. Mabry

Rodney H. Mabry is Professor of Finance and Department Head at Clemson University. He received his Ph.D. in economics from the University of North Carolina at Chapel Hill, specializing in economics of the public sector.

Professor Mabry's research interests cross a wide range of topics. He has published articles and completed funded research projects involving regional differences in state and local taxation and expenditures, growth in crime, federal government spending, economies of scale in state court systems, the effectiveness of public employment projects, the advantages of "real dollar" mortgage instruments, the impact of technology on employment, and teacher fringe benefits. For several years he also served as a Field Research Associate for the Brookings Institution and for the Woodrow Wilson School at Princeton University.

Dr. Mabry lives in Clemson, South Carolina, with his wife, Merle, and has two children in college, Brad and Patty.

Holley Ulbrich

Holley H. Ulbrich is Alumni Professor of Economics at Clemson University, where she has been on the faculty since 1967. She is the author of three other textbooks in economics. She received her Ph.D. in Economics from the University of Connecticut, specializing in international economics and public finance. Professor Ulbrich's research interests are primarily in the areas of tax policy, local government, and intergovernmental fiscal relations. She has also published research in macroeconomic policy, water policy, women's issues, and the economics of religion.

For five years she served as the Director of the Center for Economics Education at Clemson University, winning a Freedoms Foundation Award for Excellence in Private Enterprise Education for her work. She has also served in Washington as a Senior Analyst at the U.S. Advisory Commission on Intergovernmental Relations and is currently a Senior Fellow at the Strom Thurmond Institute for Government and Public Affairs at Clemson.

Dr. Ulbrich and her husband, Carlton, a Professor of Physics, are the parents of three daughters, Christine, Carla, and Katrina.

I

The Framework: How Economic Decisions Are Made

1

Introduction to Economics

Economics is the study of mankind in the ordinary business of life.

ALFRED MARSHALL, *Principles of Economics* (1890)

Main Points

1. Economics is the study of how people allocate resources among competing uses to maximize their satisfaction. Microeconomics explains the choices made by individual households and businesses, whereas macroeconomics deals with choices made at the national level.

2. Economists' models are based on the idea that people are "practical economists"; that is, they confront the prob-

lems of scarcity and choice as self-interested maximizers making decisions at the margin according to their own preferences and responding to incentives.

3. Economists use models to describe economic behavior, the scientific method to analyze problems, and graphs and statistics to describe the economy and economic behavior.

In the nineteenth century, historian Thomas Carlyle labeled economics the "dismal science" in response to some economists of his day who made forecasts of gloom and doom, overpopulation, and starvation. While there are still some gloomy forecasters around, most economists are actually rather cheerful people, looking for ways to produce more out of existing resources, increase standards of living, and find new and better ways to respond to changing conditions and changing economic wants.

In this chapter, we address the most profound mystery surrounding economics: What is it? We also try to explain why you should study economics and how economists "do" economics—the kinds of questions they ask and the methods they use in searching for answers. ■

WHAT IS ECONOMICS?

Unlike history, mathematics, English, and chemistry, economics is a subject most students study only briefly—and sometimes not at all—before they begin college. If you came to this course with the common misunderstanding that you would learn to balance your checkbook or get rich in the stock market, you are about 90 percent wrong. Economics is a basic discipline like those just listed, not an applied subject like accounting or drafting in which specific skills are taught.

Economics is similar to mathematics in that it relies on logical reasoning and mathematical tools. It also has some common ground with history and sociology because economics studies people as they interact in social groups, often drawing on historical experience. Like chemistry and physics, economics employs the scientific method, although much of economics is descriptive rather than analytical. Finally, like English grammar, economics has a few simple rules and principles, but from these principles economists can derive many powerful conclusions.

Economics is the science of making choices. Individuals must decide whether to study another hour or eat dinner; buy a six-pack of Pepsi or a half-gallon of milk at the grocery; choose firefighting or nursing as an occupation; and play golf, go for a drive, watch television, or "pump iron" for an afternoon of recreation. As a group, people must also choose through their governments whether to build a dam or repair highways with their taxes; strengthen national defense or build public housing for the poor; and grant investment tax breaks to businesses or expand state and national park systems.

The common element in all these decisions is that every choice involves a cost. Choosing anything means that one must give up something else. (Reading this text means you are not enjoying a bike ride.) Since people want to get the most out of their choices—that is, maximize the benefit they receive from the

Myth 1-1

The Best Things in Life Are Free

Those words to an old popular song are appealing, but most economists would take issue with them. What *are* the best things in life? Love? Friendship? Both love and friendship take hard work to develop and sustain over the rough spots, and scarce resources of time, energy, and attention must be diverted from other uses. Love and friendship have an opportunity cost.

Fresh air? Ask the Environmental Protection Agency how much it costs. Fresh air for you requires that someone else give up using it as a convenient carrier of waste (cigarette smoke), as you will learn in Chapter 9.

Flowers? Someone has to plant and tend them, or you have to go somewhere to view them in the wild. In both cases, time and energy must be sacrificed to allow enjoyment of flowers; that is, an opportunity cost exists that requires a choice.

Truth? The sacrifices people have made to discover, defend, and proclaim truth include not only time and energy but often lives. Folk singer Pete Seeger recorded a German song, *"Die Gedanken Sind Frei"* ("Thoughts Are Free"). A nice idea, but not true. Thoughts, like truth, have a cost in the sense that alternative subjects for thinking must be given up.

Will you use your time, energy, and analytical skills in the next hour to think about economics, your favorite songs, or planting trees on campus? Even your beliefs are not free. They crowd out alternative views you might have held.

Think about it. While there are many things, like love, truth, and beauty, that we can't price in dollars, it's difficult to find anything that is free in an economic sense. ■

Opportunity cost The cost of a choice stated in terms of the next best alternative forgone.

sacrifices they make—understanding the process of making choices and the costs that go with them is an important and useful branch of knowledge. We discuss the costs associated with making choices, called **opportunity costs,** in detail in Chapter 2.

Why are choices necessary? Choices must be made because the resources needed to make goods and services are limited, but the competing uses for them are not. One limited resource is time. There are only 24 hours in a day, and people do not live forever. By choosing to study for another hour, you lose time for some other, competing activity such as playing tennis. Other resources, such as farm land, coal, welding machines, concrete, and human labor, are also limited relative to their possible uses. There are simply not enough resources to produce all the cars, college textbooks, computers, blue jeans, and food that people want. Thus, it is the scarcity of productive resources that makes choices necessary. We will examine the basic economic problem of scarcity and choice in Chapter 2.

Economics The study of how people allocate scarce resources among competing uses to maximize their satisfaction.

Making choices under conditions of scarcity is not only an occupational hazard of life but also the subject of economics. **Economics,** then, is the study of how individuals allocate scarce resources among competing uses to maximize their satisfaction.

While scarcity is a constraint that requires making choices, it is also a challenge. Think how dull life would be without choices! If people had no time constraints because they were immortal, it would be easy to procrastinate indefinitely because there would always be a tomorrow to do what one put off today. Life in a Garden of Eden with no responsibilities, no demands, and no decisions, where everything is handed out on a silver platter, may have some superficial appeal, but is doesn't sound very challenging. The need to make choices may be frustrating, but choices also make life exciting.

The Boundaries of Economics

Some economists like to confine the discipline of economics within narrow limits, focusing on such central subjects as production, markets, and exchange. Other economists prefer a broad definition that allows them to extend their research into areas that might be considered the provinces of psychology, statistics, political science, sociology, management science, or operations research. Sometimes such a broad definition leads economists far astray from their traditional preoccupation with markets and prices, production and exchange.

Economist Gary Becker, who received the Nobel prize for economics in 1992, has ventured into the realm of sociology, applying economic reasoning to decisions to marry and have children and decisions to commit crimes. Other economists, notably those in the area of public choice, apply the tools of economics to political processes such as those by which legislative committees set agendas and bureaucracies set priorities. These questions lie in the gray area between economics and political science. But economists generally feel somewhat at home whenever questions of choice arise, because choice implies competing uses for scarce resources.

Practical economist A model of the typical economic actor who knows his or her own preferences, responds to incentives, makes decisions at the margin, and engages in self-interested, maximizing behavior.

The Practical Economist

Economists—or, for that matter, psychologists—still have much to learn about the process by which people make these choices. Despite this imperfect information, however, economists have been able to predict a great deal about market outcomes from a few basic assumptions about human behavior. In this book, we call the typical individual who makes choices in economic models the **practical economist.** A practical economist is not necessarily a professional economist.

Practical economists are people in all walks of life in the process of making economic choices as consumers, workers, owners or managers of business firms, citizens, or public officials. You are already a practical economist, and you can expect to be a better one as a result of taking this course.

The basic problem the practical economist faces is scarcity, which requires making choices. Scarcity is a basic problem for both individuals and societies. Because time and resources are scarce, the practical economist cannot have everything he or she wants. Thus, choices must be made.

Following are the basic assumptions about the behavior of the practical economist in dealing with the problem of scarcity and choice.

Self-Interested Behavior   *The practical economist knows his or her tastes, preferences, and likes and dislikes, and acts to satisfy those preferences.* That is, the typical person knows where his or her self-interest lies and pursues that self-interest. The practical economist can tell you whether bowling is more fun than swimming (at a given moment), whether economics is more interesting than history, or whether living in a condominium is preferable to taking on the responsibilities of a single-family house. Economists pay relatively little attention to how these tastes and preferences are formed; they simply take tastes as given.

Self-interested behavior does not necessarily imply selfishness. Many people derive satisfaction out of helping others, serving the community, or making the world a better place in which to live. Those activities are a part of their preferences, and pursuing them is an expression of self-interest.

Maximizing   *The practical economist is a maximizer.* Individuals want to get as much satisfaction as possible out of the limited resources they have; that is, they want to **maximize** their satisfaction. Economists sometimes refer to maximizing as *rational behavior.* A household with a budget of $300 (or $3,000) a week will try to allocate that sum among housing, food, clothing, recreation, and other uses to obtain the highest possible level of satisfaction.

Maximize   To attempt to get the most happiness, satisfaction, or value of production out of available (scarce) resources.

Maximizing can also take the form of minimizing, or choosing from among several satisfactory alternatives on the basis of the lowest cost. Business firms often maximize profits by minimizing costs. A trip to the grocery store can be approached as getting the maximum satisfaction out of a given amount of spending (maximizing) or getting a particular level of satisfaction for the least possible expenditure (minimizing).

Incentives   The signals that encourage people to make one choice over another because the benefits are greater or the opportunity costs are lower.

Responding to Incentives   *The practical economist responds to incentives.* Change one incentive—the price of shoes, the hourly wage, or the movie rental fee—and the practical economist will process the new information and respond accordingly. Increase the reward, and the practical economist will try harder, other things being equal. Increase the cost of an item (a negative incentive), and the practical economist will use less of it and shift to something else. Tax cigarettes, for example, and smoking will decline; subsidize higher education, and more people will enroll in college. Usually the most important economic incentives are prices and profits.

Not every individual will respond to the same incentive at the same time or in the same way. Some smokers will not respond to higher cigarette taxes, whereas others will. Still others will make a delayed response. These characteristics of the hypothetical practical economist are *statistical* descriptions that apply to the behavior of "average" or "representative" persons rather than to each and every individual. But they do enable economists to predict the results of a change in the price of wheat, the number of workers in an area, the minimum wage, or the rate of sales tax. The experience of economists is that on the average, especially when given enough time to absorb new information, people do respond to changes in economic incentives.

Deciding at the Margin. *The practical economist chooses "at the margin."* Decisions individuals face are rarely all-or-nothing choices. The practical economist does not choose whether or not to study or whether or not to eat pizza. Marginal decision making involves deciding whether the benefits of an *extra* amount of a good is worth its cost. The practical economist decides whether to study one more hour or go to a movie or whether to eat one more slice of pizza rather than saving room for dessert.

Marginal thinking is very important in economics. It explains, for example, why people actually use less water when the price of water increases. Water is essential for human life, but the question isn't whether water is worth the higher price. Rather, the question is whether certain marginal uses of water are worth paying the extra amount to keep the lawn green or wash the car.

You can expect to see the practical economist at work throughout this book, making choices at the margin about allocating scarce resources among competing uses, calculating opportunity costs, engaging in self-interested, maximizing behavior, and responding to incentives. As you start to think like an economist, you will begin to observe yourself and others acting like practical economists in day-to-day decisions.

CHECKLIST: The Practical Economist

The practical economist embodies the economist's assumptions about how people behave in making economic decisions. The practical economist is the typical consumer and worker who

- Confronts problems of scarcity, choice, and opportunity cost
- Engages in self-interested behavior on the basis of his or her tastes and preferences
- Maximizes satisfaction or minimizes costs
- Responds to economic incentives
- Makes decisions at the margin

MICROECONOMICS AND MACROECONOMICS

Microeconomics The branch of economics that examines individual decisions and particular markets.

Economics consists of two broad subject areas. **Microeconomics** deals with individual decisions and specific markets. (The prefix *micro* means "small.") The market for wheat, the price of running shoes, the demand for restaurant workers, the supply of engineers, and the effect of the gasoline tax on gasoline sales are all microeconomic subjects. Microeconomists answer such questions as these: Will raising the tax exemption for dependents cause families to have more children? How much will the price of orange juice increase if a spring freeze destroys half the orange crop in Florida? Is it more efficient (less costly) to build a road with many road workers using shovels or with a few skilled workers using sophisticated earth-moving equipment? How many students will drop out when the university raises tuition by 25 percent? As you can see, microeconomics is concerned with very specific questions involving individual markets, firms, and consumers.

Macroeconomics The branch of economics concerned with aggregate questions such as the level of total national output, price levels, unemployment rates, and economic growth.

In contrast, **macroeconomics** deals with aggregates, or the sum total of actions in many separate markets. (The prefix *macro* means "large.") This branch of economics focuses on the macro, or large, economic elements of the economy as a whole. Macroeconomics is concerned with how total output in an economy is determined rather than the output of wheat, cars, or pizzas; with the average level of prices rather than particular prices for fish, or cat food, or telephone service; and with total employment or unemployment rather than the number of workers in the restaurant industry or in a particular McDonald's franchise.

While there are more microeconomists at work, macroeconomists get more of the headlines. They track the national and world economies, answering questions, making predictions, and recommending policy on such topics as recessions, inflation, unemployment rates, budget deficits, and economic growth. You will study microeconomics in Part II of this book and macroeconomics in Part III.

WHY STUDY ECONOMICS?

Why should you study economics? Chances are you have a simple answer to this question: Your curriculum may require it. If this course is an elective, we are glad you chose economics. But even if you have to take economics, there are good reasons why it is required.

First, understanding the marketplace, the economic system, the ways signals are sent, and the ways people respond are important to functioning effectively as an adult member of society. As a consumer, you need to understand the impact of economic events on your spending, saving, borrowing, and tax obligations. You need to be able to decide whether to buy a house now or wait until later on the basis of price and interest rate forecasts and other economic considerations. On a more abstract level, learning how to measure opportunity costs and to think very carefully about choices will help you make better decisions in everything you do, starting with what you eat for dinner tonight.

Second, as a worker, employer, producer, or owner of a firm, economics is important to you. Here too you need to understand the signals from the marketplace, the nature of costs, and the process of making decisions. You need to know the effects of competition on your income, whether you are an engineer competing for jobs against other engineers or a pizzeria operator worried about the new pizza joint down the street. You need to understand the role of government in providing services to your firm, setting the rules and regulations under which you must operate, and creating (or reducing) incentives for you to invest and develop new methods of production and delivery.

Finally, as a citizen you will have the opportunity to affect public sector decisions about taxing, spending, regulating, and borrowing. You may even wind up in charge of making some of those decisions! Here again you will need to understand price signals, opportunity costs, and maximizing behavior to make intelligent decisions about zoning, tax rates, funds for education, sign ordinances, and farm price supports.

A few of you may become professional economists, working in universities or business firms or as policy economists in some branch of government. Regardless of whether you become a professional economist, take more courses in economics out of other interests, or simply try to apply what you learn in this one course, economics will influence how you look at decisions.

You are probably already more of a practical economist than you realize. You have been making economic decisions from before you were old enough to talk. By the time you reached kindergarten, you were trading contents of lunchboxes and choosing among candy bars with your allowance. If your parents offered you a quarter to sweep the floor, you weighed the value of the quarter against the time and distastefulness of the task and thus made an economic choice. As you grew older, the choices became more complex, but they were still economic decisions based on self-interested behavior, incentives, and opportunity costs. By the end of this book, you should recognize that you have been a competent practical economist all along and in this course are on your way to becoming an even better one.

ECONOMIC METHODS AND TOOLS

Whether examining macroeconomic or microeconomic issues, economists have a standard kit of tools and a method for attacking problems that they use for virtually all economic questions. The method is based on a blend of traditional scientific method and a relatively new technique called *policy analysis*. The tools are models, graphs, and statistics.

The Economic Method

Suppose an economist were asked to try to develop solutions to the problem of inner-city teenage unemployment, a complex issue that has troubled public officials in our major cities for several decades. How would the economist's approach to this problem differ from that of the sociologist, psychologist, or average citizen?

The procedure an economist would follow would be to state the problem, apply an economic model, and use that model to identify solutions. Then, using economic tools and some set of criteria or goals, the economist would attempt to determine the various effects of each of those solutions (evaluation). At that point, the problem of choosing and implementing one or more solutions should be turned over to politicians or policymakers who make the final choice. In reality, economists often are involved in all stages of the process, helping to implement solutions and evaluating how well those solutions work when put into effect.

 **CHECKLIST** : **Steps in Analyzing a Policy Problem**

Step 1. State the problem.
Step 2. Apply the relevant economic model.
Step 3. Identify solutions.
Step 4. Evaluate solutions.
_____
Step 5. Select and implement a solution.

Step 1: State the Problem   This step sounds simple, but economists need to take care to state the problem in such a way that they don't prejudge the solution. Our hypothetical problem is how to lower a persistently high unemployment rate—30 to 40 percent—among inner-city youth. The side effects of high unemployment rates are poverty, high welfare costs, and high crime rates. Economists also worry about a wasted resource—labor—that could be used to produce more goods and services to raise the standard of living.

This problem is stated rather broadly, so we will focus on a narrower aspect of inner-city teenage unemployment. Suppose that as a result of interviews and surveys and examining data, the economist discovers that the average inner-city teenager is unemployed because she or he lacks marketable skills. Jobs are available, but the applicants for them are not qualified. Some youths may be high school dropouts, while the jobs available require not only a high school education but also such specific skills as plumbing, auto repair, or typing. This narrower focus defines the problem in terms of finding the appropriate incentives to get these youngsters to "invest" in themselves—to stay in school longer and/ or invest in some vocational skills to enhance their job prospects. Once the problem is expressed in terms of finding appropriate incentives, economists find themselves on familiar turf.

Step 2: Apply the Relevant Economic Model

This step is something you aren't prepared to do right now, but you will likely be able to at the end of this course. We will spend a good part of this course building and using **economic models.**

Economic model A simplified view of reality used to predict the effects of changes in one or more economic variables on other economic variables.

The purpose of an **economic model** is to predict, and most economic models are of the "if A, then B" (cause-and-effect) variety. To be useful, however, models must abstract and simplify reality. For example, on a model airplane, the gauges and passenger seats are omitted in favor of basic features such as wings and a rudder. The important thing about the model airplane is not that it is a precise duplicate of the real thing but that it can fly. An architect's model of an apartment complex does not include plumbing and window curtains, but it has sufficient details to allow planners to envision the development in relation to the site and the adjacent buildings. In the same way, the analytical models of professional economists leave out details that clutter the picture without adding significantly to understanding or solving economic problems.

Economists use a number of analytical models. The models used primarily in this text are the microeconomic supply and demand model to be developed in Chapter 4 and the macroeconomic aggregate supply and demand model developed in Chapter 12. For now, we will use a simplified version of the supply and demand model that identifies the incentives and disincentives the individual inner-city teenager faces. Let's assume these unemployed teens do not differ fundamentally from the practical economist we just discussed. They too engage in self-interested, maximizing behavior, know their own preferences, and respond to incentives. From this model, it is reasonable to conclude that potential solutions involve changing the incentives teenagers face.

Step 3: Identify Solutions

This step involves listing all the possible ways to obtain the desired result (more teenage employment) that the model implies. In the case of inner-city youth unemployment, possible solutions to the problem focus on changing incentives for youths to prepare themselves for employment. Positive incentives would increase the benefits (or lower the opportunity cost) of devoting more time and effort to improving marketable skills. Negative incentives would increase the cost of *not* devoting more time and effort to developing those skills.

Here are a few possible solutions that stress positive incentives (increasing the benefits of preparation or lowering its costs):

1. Guarantee a job after completing a training program.
2. Pay students some modest amount of support while in vocational training. This approach was actually used in several federal government programs, such as CETA (Comprehensive Employment and Training Act) and JTPA (Job Training and Partnership Act).

3. Provide better information to students on the benefits of staying in school and getting training.
4. Provide (through either government or private nonprofit organizations) day care for teenage mothers, transportation to programs, and other support services that would reduce the cost of staying in school or taking vocational training.
5. Lower the cost of finishing high school by providing alternative curricula for vocationally oriented students, including building vocational and technical education centers in inner-city areas to make such training more accessible to students.

There are also some possible solutions that use negative incentives, raising the cost of not acquiring marketable skills and education:

1. Strengthen existing school attendance laws with steeper penalties and stronger enforcement, or require a longer period of staying in school.
2. Supply information to make students more aware of the costs of dropping out; tell them about higher unemployment rates and lower lifetime earnings, which may give some teenage practical economists an incentive to stay in school.

This list is far from exhaustive, but all of the proposed solutions change in some way the perceived set of incentives to which at least some inner-city teens should respond.

Step 4: Evaluate Solutions You are probably aware of some of the real-life efforts to lower the number of school dropouts and reduce teen unemployment in recent years. Some of these efforts have worked better than others, and all of them differ in cost, effectiveness, and the kinds of persons they reach. How do we decide which solution to implement? Step 4 provides useful input to that decision by evaluating the effects of alternative solutions. It is at this point that the work of the economist, who builds models to identify solutions, begins to overlap with the work of the policy analyst, who evaluates solutions (and may get to recommend and defend a particular solution in the political arena). In Chapter 3, we will identify some specific goals we can use as benchmarks to compare solutions. For now we will just consider some of the more obvious advantages and disadvantages of various solutions.

One consideration is cost. Providing better information to teens is probably the least costly solution, but it may also be the least effective. The other solutions all involve tax dollars, and each has different costs per unit reduction in teenage unemployment rates. The tax dollars to support these programs have to come from somewhere. Devoting resources to these programs may mean spending less on other public goods and services. Eventually lower unemployment should result in reduced expenditures on welfare and crime prevention, saving future tax dollars.

In Practice 1-1

What Do Economists Really Do?

Usually a person does not claim to be an economist without a graduate degree in economics, either a master's degree or a doctorate. By this definition, there are about 100,000 economists in the United States. About half of them are academic economists who engage in teaching, writing, and doing research in colleges and universities. These economists teach economics to more than 1 million students enrolled in at least one economics course each year. They also write textbooks and journal articles, develop and test new theoretical models, provide consulting services to governments and businesses, and engage in other professional activities related to their teaching and research interests.

The rest of these 100,000 economists work for business or government. Business economists forecast sales and costs, help firms anticipate (or try to influence) government policy, and use economic tools in helping firms respond to incentives and manage scarce resources effi-

ciently. Some business economists work for private lobbying firms, helping them prepare their arguments in their attempts to influence tax laws, regulations, and other public policies important to particular industries.

Government economists at all levels (federal, state, and local) also perform a variety of useful tasks. As we have seen in this chapter and will see throughout this book, analysis of public issues requires economic tools and methods. Often the government economist wears a second hat as a policy analyst, developing the case for a particular policy. Economists forecast tax revenues and interest rates, analyze who gains and who loses from changes in farm price supports or airline regulations, monitor prices, compute total output, and perform a host of other useful tasks in the public sector.

All economists, whether academic, business, or government, use the tools they acquired in undergraduate and graduate school. While some of the work they do appears very sophisticated, underneath it all lie the basic graphs, concepts, and models you will learn in this course. The fundamental ideas of scarcity, opportunity cost, self-interest, maximizing behavior, and people responding to incentives as practical economists are the bread and butter of the entire economics profession. ∎

When evaluating solutions, it is important not to overlook possible side effects. For example, creating job opportunities for teens may increase unemployment among older workers in the same area. Adding vocational programs in high schools may come at the expense of academic programs for college-bound students. Requiring those who are not academically talented to spend more years in school makes the tasks of teachers more difficult. The average quality of schooling may suffer, or it may become more difficult to attract enough qualified teachers. These program costs in the form of side effects play an important role in making a policy choice.

Step 5: Select and Implement a Solution   In the preceding checklist, you may have noticed the line between step 4 and step 5, choosing and implementing solutions. Step 4 is where the economist's job should end and the politician or policy analyst takes over. In reality, many economists wear a second hat as policy analysts and are involved in choosing and implementing as well. The line makes

Positive economics
Economic analysis concerned with facts and predictions rather than with value judgments.

Normative economics
Economic analysis that uses positive economic models combined with value judgments to recommend actions or policies thought to be better than others.

Ceteris paribus The assumption in economic models that everything else remains unchanged.

an important point, however: It emphasizes that economics is a **positive** science, one that answers factual or predictive questions about "what is or what if?" rather than "what is better or what ought to be?" A positive statement tells you that if A occurs, B will follow. It does not pass judgment on whether result B is desirable or important. An economist makes a positive statement when he or she states, "Raising the gasoline tax 5 cents will result in 2 percent fewer miles driven by the American public."

Normative economics, in contrast, involves making judgments. "Raising taxes for schools is better than increasing social welfare spending" is an example of a normative statement. Economists are expected to leave those judgment calls to politicians or policy analysts, who are elected or hired to make normative judgments based on the analyses economists provide, together with the tastes and preferences of the public.

In fact, however, economics is not value free. The choice of which problems deserve the attention of our scarce supply of economic analysts is a value judgment! Sometimes the choice of analytical tools, or the way solutions are identified and the space devoted to evaluating a particular solution, will reflect the personal biases and values of particular economists. However, most economists make a conscious effort to separate their personal values and preferences from their professional analyses of economic problems.

Qualifications of Economic Models

You will find the models in this book—and those in most economics books—hedged with nearly as many warnings and cautions as a pack of cigarettes or a prescription drug. Models are extremely useful for focusing attention on the major aspects of a given problem, but they are limited by their assumptions, by the inability to hold other relevant factors constant, by the neglect of secondary effects, and often by important differences in short-run and long-run effects.

Assumptions   The economist's equivalent of an architect's scale model without plumbing, or a model airplane with no passenger seats, is the use of simplifying assumptions. Simplifying assumptions are needed to make models useful for several different applications, but they also open the door for error. For example, the prediction that higher gasoline prices would sharply cut gasoline consumption in the late 1970s was in error because it assumed no increases in population and income. We will spell out most of the important assumptions in the models in this book. As you work through these models, try to determine what assumptions are being made.

When economists look at any question, they assume everything else "stands still," or is held constant, while they analyze this one issue. This standing-still assumption is called *ceteris paribus,* which is Latin for "other things being equal." Ceteris paribus is the most important assumption economists make.

For example, suppose an economist wants to analyze the effect of a $1 increase in the price of beef on the number of pounds of beef sold per consumer. It will be necessary to hold consumers' incomes constant, as well as their tastes for beef and other foods. The economist will predict that a price increase will make consumers buy less beef, but this prediction could be quite wrong if other things did not remain constant. If consumer incomes happened to double at the same time, or if the surgeon general announced that consuming one pound of beef per day would prevent cancer, beef consumption would go up despite the price increase.

Secondary effects Additional effects of changes in economic variables beyond the immediate, direct effects.

Secondary Effects A second qualification of the usefulness of economic models deals with **secondary effects.** We identified some potential secondary effects of the proposed solutions to the unemployment problems of inner-city teens, such as an increase in adult unemployment rates in the same community. Other secondary effects might include fewer teen pregnancies, resulting in less demand for day care, or lower welfare payments. Another might be that additional demand for vocational education teachers drives up their salaries, forcing school boards to raise taxes or cut services elsewhere in the system. As you can see, secondary effects can be either positive or negative. Often a policy has both positive and negative secondary effects.

Although we took care to identify some secondary effects of policies aimed at reducing teenage unemployment, often (especially in the popular press) analysts tend to concentrate on the direct and immediate effects of any policy action and ignore important side effects or unexpected consequences.

The Short Run and the Long Run Finally, the predictions of an economic model may differ for the short run and the long run. Throughout this book you will see statements such as

> In the short run an increase in the money supply will lower interest rates, but in the long run the result may be higher interest rates.

or

> In the short run price controls may appear to reduce inflation, but in the long run the price level will rise.

Short run The time period that is not long enough to permit changes in some of the important economic conditions decision makers face.

The short run and the long run are concepts that have particular meanings in economics, meanings that often differ from everyday usage of the terms. In microeconomics, the **short run** is the time period in which one or more important conditions cannot be changed. A firm may make decisions "in the short run" because its building lease runs for another year or two or because its workers have a three-year labor contract. Workers may make decisions in the short run because they have a fixed commitment, such as wanting to stay put until their children finish high school. Thus, most of the firm's workers may accept a pay cut in the short run, but once they have met their fixed commitments, their long-run response may be very different. For some firms or individuals the short run may be only a week or a month, while for others it may be years. The exact duration of the short run depends on the length of the fixed commitments people face in a given situation.

The **long run** is the time period in which anything can be changed, that is, individuals and firms are fully able to respond to economic incentives and take advantage of economic opportunities. The long run has no specific time frame; it is simply the time period that is long enough to allow full response to changing incentives.

Long run The time period that is long enough for all relevant information and choices to be available to decision makers.

The Economist's Tools: Graphs and Statistics

Economists are famous for drawing pictures and quoting numbers, sometimes at the same time. Graphs and statistics enable economists to take some abstract ideas about economic relationships and put them in a form they can visualize and remember.

Graphs   If you flip through this book you will see many graphs, much like the ones you learned to draw in high school algebra or geometry. Economists use graphs to help them visualize their models and because "a picture is worth a thousand words." With a little practice, you should feel as much at home with the graphs in this book as the average economist does.

Like models, graphs make it possible to clear away some of the "clutter" and visually isolate important relationships. Just as a physicist can demonstrate principles and theories with blocks on inclined planes that can be expanded to describe what happens to cars driving downhill, an economist can use relationships expressed in graphs to demonstrate the principles and theories underlying what happens in real markets. If the graph-drawing skills you learned in high school algebra are rusty, you may wish to review the appendix to this chapter to brush up on plotting and using graphs.

Numbers and Measurement   Economists also like to describe what is happening in numbers. Strike up a conversation with an economist about current events and soon you will hear about the price of oil, mortgage interest rates, price indexes, unemployment rates, the size of the federal deficit, and the price of the dollar. One characteristic that distinguishes economics from other social sciences is that more of the relationships in economics can be measured than in sociology, psychology, or political science.

The most popular economic measure is price, which measures costs to the producer and value or utility to the buyer. Economists have even found that price gives an answer to the standard elementary arithmetic problem of adding apples and oranges. How do we add three oranges and five apples? To an economist, the answer is simple. If three oranges are 50 cents each and five apples are 25 cents each, we have $2.75 worth of fruit. How do we compare an apple and an orange? If an orange is "worth" 50 cents (that's what sellers will take for it and buyers will offer) and an apple is "worth" 25 cents, one orange is worth two apples.

Economists can't measure the value of everything, but they can get a reading on the value people place on anything that goes through the market. What is a high school class ring worth? When the price of gold went above $1,000 in the late 1970s, our own class rings (which probably contained about half of an ounce of gold) apparently were worth more than $500 to each of us, because we still have them. They were worth less to many others, because gold buyers were inundated with personal jewelry when the price of gold reached all-time highs.

One reason economists are so fascinated with prices is that price is a signal. When the price of a good goes up, it signals that the good is scarce and buyers should substitute other goods for it. It also signals that producers should try to produce more of the good. At the same time prices send signals from the market to individuals, individuals use prices to send signals to one another through the market—the prices at which they will sell their goods, rent their apartments, or buy another pair of shoes.

Price is not the only number that intrigues economists. In microeconomics, quantities are also important. In macroeconomics, economists look at a lot of indexes and percentages. These "thermometers" of the national economic weather include such statistics as the growth rate of national output, the unemployment rate, and the price index.

Summary

1. Economics is the study of how individuals allocate scarce resources among competing uses to maximize their satisfaction. Every choice has an opportunity cost in the form of the alternative not chosen.

2. Most of economics is concerned with production and the exchange of goods and services. However, economics is sometimes applied to other kinds of allocation decisions, such as preventing crime or choosing family size.

3. The basic premise of the individual economic decision maker is that each person is a practical economist, making choices in response to scarcity that maximize his or her satisfaction. Individuals pursue their self-interest on the basis of their own tastes and preferences, make decisions at the margin, and respond to economic incentives.

4. Economics is a useful field of study because all people are practical economists in their economic roles as consumers, workers, and citizens.

5. Economics is divided into microeconomics and macroeconomics. Microeconomics focuses on individual prices, markets, and consumer choices. Macroeconomics is concerned with aggregate economic outcomes such as the level of total national output, the price level, inflation, and employment.

6. Economists approach issues by stating the problem, applying economic models, identifying solutions, and evaluating solutions. Then policymakers choose and implement solutions.

7. Economics should be positive (value free) rather than normative (making judgments about the desirability of outcomes).

8. The most popular tools of economists are graphs, which are visual representations of relationships between two or more economic variables, and statistics, which measure and describe economic variables.

Key Terms

ceteris paribus
economic model
economics
incentives
long run

macroeconomics
maximize
microeconomics
normative economics
opportunity cost

positive economics
practical economist
secondary effects
short run

Questions and Problems

1. In which of your decisions do you act most like a practical economist? For what kinds of decisions do you gather the most information and weigh choices most carefully?

2. Full-blown economic models are not always needed to identify and evaluate solutions. Here are some problems to practice on:
   a. Choosing between a high-cost, high-traffic downtown location for your restaurant or a more out-of-the-way, cheaper location
   b. Spending your last $18 on a date or on a CD
   c. Considering taking a ten-hour-per-week job while in school "to make ends meet"

   Note that in each case you will have to make assumptions. Spell out your assumptions, identify solutions, and evaluate the alternative solutions.

3. Which of the following are macroeconomic issues? Which are microeconomic issues?
   a. A rising general price level
   b. The price of wheat
   c. How much to provide in benefits for medicaid patients
   d. The size of the federal budget
   e. Your income taxes
   f. Total federal income tax collections

4. Suppose you are operating under a personal economic model that predicts that a speeding ticket will cost you "only" $30. What assumptions might you make? What secondary effects might you want to consider? (Think about insurance premiums.) How might your behavior differ if the expected fine were $100?

5. Your simple economic model says that if there are fewer high school graduates in 1994, there will be fewer college freshmen in the fall semester of 1994.

What are your *ceteris paribus* assumptions, that is, what else are you holding constant?

6. What is the opportunity cost to you of taking this economics course?

7. Suppose you are a bright, athletic high school student who could play professional baseball right after high school or go to college on an athletic scholarship, majoring in philosophy. Weigh the opportunity cost of each decision.

8. Jane Doe has decided to take a job after college as a flight attendant at a salary of $18,000 a year plus unlimited travel. Her dad asks her to explain this decision. To what incentives did she respond? What was she maximizing?

APPENDIX: USING GRAPHS

Graphs play a very important role in economics. Some graphs show changes in certain economic data over time, such as the ups and downs of industrial production, the spread between short-term and long-term interest rates, or the change in the cost of living. These graphs appear in newspapers and business magazines and on the evening news to help people visualize what is happening to the economy. Some of the graphs in this book are of this descriptive variety. Most of them, however, are analytical graphs that reflect an underlying model of an economic relationship between two variables.

Either type of graph is a visual representation of the relationship between two quantities that could be written in table form. Consider the relationship between grade point ratio (GPR) and hours studied per week. Hypothetical data for six students, obtained from a random sample of undergraduates, might be something like the following:

Grade Point Ratio (GPR)	Hours Studied per Week (on average)
4.0	20
3.5	16
3.0	12
2.5	8
2.0	4
1.5	0

There seems to be a positive relationship between grades and average hours studied, since when one increases, the other also increases. Figure 1A-1 plots a graph of these numbers. The "theory" underlying this graph is that higher grades

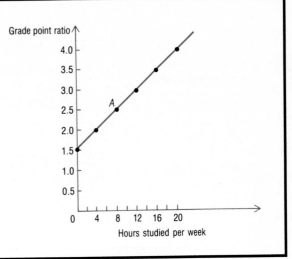

FIGURE 1A-1

This graph shows a positive relationship between the independent variable, hours studied (on the horizontal axis), and the dependent variable, grade point ratio (on the vertical axis). A higher grade point ratio is associated with an increase in average hours studied each week.

Independent variable
In a mathematical relationship, the variable(s) or factor(s) that influences the dependent variable but is not influenced by it in turn.

Dependent variable In a mathematical relationship, the variable whose value increases or decreases as the value of the independent variable(s) changes.

Positive relationship
A mathematical relationship between two variables in which they rise or fall together.

Negative relationship
A mathematical relationship between two variables in which an increase in one is associated with a decrease in the other.

and GPRs result from more hours of studying. Hours studied is the **independent variable,** because it is the cause of higher grades. Hours studied are plotted on the horizontal axis (Figure 1A-1). Grade point ratio is the **dependent variable,** because GPR (we think) depends on hours studied, holding intelligence and other factors constant. GPR is plotted on the vertical axis in the figure.

Economists are less consistent than mathematicians in observing the custom of plotting the independent variable on the horizontal axis and the dependent variable on the vertical axis. The demand curve, for example, shows the relationship between quantity and price. The usual statement of this relationship is that price is the independent variable and quantity the dependent variable. Demand curves (and supply curves), however, are always drawn with price on the vertical axis and quantity on the horizontal axis.

There is a **positive relationship** between GPR and hours studied, meaning that an increase in the independent variable (average hours studied) results from an increase in the value of the dependent variable (GPR). You can locate combinations from the table as points on the graph; for example, the combination of eight hours studied and a GPR of 2.5 is represented by point A (8, 2.5). The upward-sloping line through the points represents a visual version of the positive relationship between hours studied and GPR.

A **negative relationship** can be illustrated by the economist's demand curve, which you will study in Chapter 4. Economists have accumulated considerable evidence that the price of any good, such as a Coke, is the most important single influence (independent variable) on the quantity consumers choose to buy. Consumers buy smaller quantities at higher prices than at lower prices. The demand curve in Figure 1A-2 plots this negative relationship between the price of X and the quantity of X consumers wish to buy. At a price of $1 per Coke,

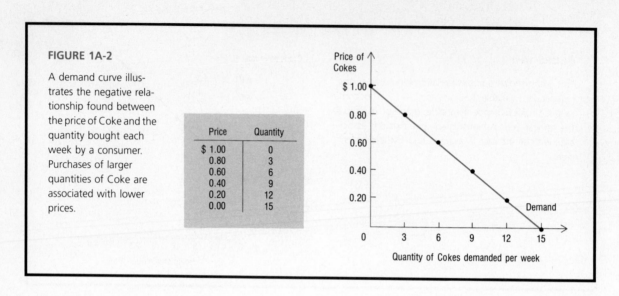

FIGURE 1A-2

A demand curve illustrates the negative relationship found between the price of Coke and the quantity bought each week by a consumer. Purchases of larger quantities of Coke are associated with lower prices.

Price	Quantity
$ 1.00	0
0.80	3
0.60	6
0.40	9
0.20	12
0.00	15

this consumer would buy only two Cokes a week; at 25 cents each, the consumer would buy eight. As you can see in the figure, downward-sloping lines on a graph represent negative relationships.

Key Terms   dependent variable   positive relationship   negative relationship
                     independent variable

Problem   Given the following information, plot the data on a graph and label the axes. Connecting these points should form a straight line.

Temperature (degrees)	Sales of Ice Cream (cones per day)
40	100
50	140
60	180
70	220
80	260
85	280
90	300

Is this a positive or a negative relationship? Which is the dependent variable? Which is the independent variable?

2

Scarcity and Choice

The most basic law in economics . . . [is] that one cannot get something for nothing.

SIR ROY HARROD, 1948

Main Points

1. The basic economic problem is scarcity, or the inability to satisfy unlimited human wants with limited resources.

2. Scarcity means we must make choices. Every choice has an opportunity cost. A production possibilities frontier shows the choices and opportunity costs an individual or a society faces.

3. The basic economic questions each society must answer are what to produce, how to produce, and for whom to produce.

4. Some of these questions are answered through the market, some through government, and some through a combination of the two. The entities through which decisions are made vary from one society to another.

5. The choice of an economic system and the ways the basic economic questions are answered reflect relative rankings of the economic goals of efficiency, equity, economic freedom, economic growth, full employment, and price stability.

How many times have you said, "If I had a million dollars, I would . . ."? The usual conclusion is "buy a Porsche, travel to a tropical island, or quit my job and play more." Even $1 million would not be enough to satisfy all your desires once you turned your imagination loose. Life could be even more exciting with $2 million or $20 million.

In Chapter 1, you learned that economics is the study of how people make choices in a world of scarcity. Everything of value is scarce—money, goods, time, even human skills—whereas the desire for goods and services is almost unlimited. With only limited resources available to satisfy these countless human wants, making choices is a fact of life.

At the level of the economy as a whole, the basic choices to be made are what to produce, how, and for whom. Different societies answer these questions in different ways. In some countries, markets play the largest role in economic decisions. Other countries make most of their choices through government. Still others develop partnerships between the private and public sectors to make choices. The different roles the market and government play in making decisions reflect different values in various societies, but all are designed to address the problem of choice in the face of scarcity. ■

SCARCITY AND OPPORTUNITY COST

Scarcity The basic economic problem resulting from the limited availability of resources to satisfy unlimited human wants.

Choices are necessary because we live in a world of scarcity. **Scarcity** means that although human wants are infinite, the resources available to satisfy those wants are limited. The variety of answers and ways people choose to cope with the problem of scarcity are the subject matter of economics.

Unlimited Wants

Are human wants really unlimited? You might think you want only a few things right now, such as a new car, a computer, or a bigger apartment. However, your imagination is probably wearing blinders in the form of price tags. Suppose your rich uncle gave you $1 million or you won a bundle on a television quiz program. How would you—a practical economist maximizing, choosing, and pursuing your self-interest—spend that windfall? Certainly you could buy the new car and the computer and rent a larger apartment. Would you also spend spring break in the Caribbean? Buy gifts for family and friends? Pay off the mortgage on the family home? Save a large sum and live off the annual interest, leaving time for leisure and working only when you wished and only at jobs you really enjoyed? Would you give to the needy?

When you come right down to it, most people have a long, if not infinite, list of wants. Although most of these lists include more goods and services of all kinds, they probably include some wants that are not strictly personal or selfish. Most people also want to help others or give to charity. Furthermore, not all wants are simply for greater amounts of goods and services. People also want better-quality goods. For example, they want shirts that last through more than 25 washings (the industry standard for wrinkle-free cotton shirts), homes with better insulation, cars with better gas mileage, stereo systems with less distortion, and lawns with fewer weeds. People also want more public goods such as clean air and safe streets. Once you start making such lists, you will find that the number of wants is endless.

Limited Resources

Resources The limited factors of production: land, labor, capital, and enterprise.

There are not enough productive resources to satisfy all the wants on people's lists. Productive **resources** are the inputs used to produce goods and services. These resources are scarce relative to the list of goods and services people want to enjoy.

Even though some resources or raw materials appear to be quite abundant, they may still be scarce in an economic sense. For example, there is a great deal of sand in the world, but it is not always available in the right places or in the right form. The sand needed to make plate glass can be found in the Sahara desert and along many coastal beaches, but its weight and bulk make it costly to ship. If glass factories were located on deserts to take advantage of the sand, other resources, such as labor, would have to move to where the sand was, and it would be expensive to ship the fragile glass to final consumers. Thus, using sand to make glass has an important cost: the cost of transporting sand to the glass factory. Shipping the sand from its source to where the other resources and the final markets are located uses scarce resources such as time, energy, machinery, and human effort. Sand in the Sahara may be free, but sand where it is needed for making glass has an opportunity cost.

Productive resources include coal, plastics, trucks, factories, laborers, teachers, managers, computers, machine tools, industrial diamonds, water, soil—the list is endless. To enable them to think about resources in an orderly way, economists classify productive resources into four basic categories: land, labor, capital, and enterprise.

Land All the physical resources occurring in nature, such as coal, timber, oil, water, and fish, that are used in production.

Land   In addition to soil or space on the surface of the earth, **land** includes all the raw materials available in nature—coal, timber, rivers, air, water, fish, rainfall, and even the energy from sunlight. Many of these natural resources can be considered fixed in supply because the amounts available cannot be increased very rapidly, or because supplies are difficult to locate or increase. For example, in many areas annual rainfall varies only within narrow limits. Mineral resources such as coal, oil, iron ore, and uranium renew themselves so slowly that they are often referred to as *nonrenewable resources*. Other kinds of natural resources can be increased or converted to a more usable form. Timber can be renewed fairly quickly with careful planting and harvesting. Even land in the usual sense can be augmented. The Dutch build dikes (known as *levees* in the American South) to push back the sea to expand their land supply. The U.S. Army Corps of Engineers creates lakes by building dams to develop water resources for recreation, flood control, and water supply.

Labor The human physical and mental skills used in production.

Labor Labor is another important input in production. **Labor** consists of all the human physical and mental skills used in the production of goods and services. People possess two important qualities that are useful in the production process. First, they have physical strength to dig, build, push, pull, and otherwise help produce goods and services. In the past labor accomplished some amazing feats, even though workers had access to only very simple tools. The pyramids of Egypt and the Great Wall of China were built with large amounts of physical labor over long periods of time.

The second type of labor resource consists of mental skills. The ability to think and solve problems, learn and develop bodies of knowledge to pass on to future generations, and apply that knowledge to new production problems is a very valuable resource. The difference between production in the Stone Age and production today is not the availability of resources such as oil, iron ore, timber, and other land but the missing ingredient of knowledge—how to use those resources to satisfy human wants.

Human capital Mental and physical skills created or enhanced by education and experience.

Human mental skills can be expanded just as some land resources can be enhanced or capital produced. More human skills result from experience (on-the-job training) and from applying scarce resources—teachers, classrooms, books—to the education of future workers. Mental skills are more like physical capital in that they are a factor of production created by human effort. For this reason, these acquired labor skills are sometimes referred to as **human capital.**

Capital The manufactured resources used in production, including tools, machinery, and buildings.

Capital **Capital** resources are the tools, machinery, and buildings created for use in the production of other goods and services. Computers, electrical generators, desks, textile machinery, and assembly lines are examples of capital. Unlike land and labor, capital resources do not occur naturally; rather, they are made by applying labor and other capital to raw materials.

Although much of the nation's capital is used by business firms, households also need capital to produce goods and services. Stoves, washing machines, and cars provide cooking, laundry, and transportation services to household members. Government and the nonprofit sector (including most colleges and universities) also need capital to provide services such as higher education. Classroom buildings are a form of capital, as are the books, tables, chairs, chalk, chalkboards, and other manufactured resources used in "producing" education.

Economists use the term *capital* in a specialized way, one quite different than its common use. Often *capital* refers to financial assets, such as the funds used to start and run a business, or the accumulated wealth of the household in the form of stocks, bonds, and bank deposits. However, money and financial assets are not capital in the sense that economists use the term to refer to a productive resource; rather, the productive resources that money can buy (or people can create) make up the factor of production called *capital*. Money serves other purposes, mainly as a convenient way to transfer ownership rights to goods, services, and assets from one person to another. Chapters 16 and 17 explore the roles of money and financial assets in a market system.

Technology The available knowledge of the techniques or processes of producing a good or service; production "know-how."

Technology, or the techniques and methods of production and the development of new and better products, is often included in labor and capital resources. Some technology takes the form of human capital because it is embodied in worker skills, such as assembling a product more efficiently or programming a computer. Other technology takes the form of newer and more sophisticated equipment, such as industrial robots. Often technology involves both worker skills and more sophisticated equipment.

Technology determines how much a society can produce with its available resources. An improvement in technology means more goods and services can be produced from society's scarce resources than before. The assembly line of the early twentieth century was a major advance in auto production technology. It is a concept rather than a physical resource like the machines and people that comprise an assembly line. It is technology because it represents a different way to combine existing resources to produce more efficiently.

Enterprise The scarce human ability to organize other resources to produce desired goods and services efficiently.

Entrepreneur A person who engages in enterprise by innovating, taking risks, and organizing production.

Enterprise The last resource, enterprise, is really a specialized kind of labor, but it is so central to the production process and so different from other kinds of labor resources that economists identify it as a separate resource. **Enterprise** is the combining of other types of resources to produce goods and services for the market. **Entrepreneurs** are people who engage in enterprise—innovating, taking risks, and organizing production.

Innovation consists of creating and developing new products or production processes. Edwin Land, creator of the Polaroid Land camera, certainly was an innovator when he conceived the idea of instant cameras. More recently, the innovation of computers that read handwriting developed a whole new segment of the computer industry.

The entrepreneur must also be able to carry an idea through to production. Many people have ideas of what products others need or might want, but few have the skill or special talent to organize a business. Even rarer is the courage to risk losing one's savings (or other people's savings) and years of one's time on a new venture.

Land, labor, capital, and enterprise include all the scarce productive resources available. If society wants to change the combination of goods being produced, resources must be shifted from one type of production to another. To increase total output, producers must find ways to increase the supply of resources or use existing resources more creatively and efficiently. At any given time, however, the problem of scarcity is defined by the quantity, quality, and variety of resources available in the forms of land, labor, capital, and enterprise.

CHECKLIST    Kinds of Limited Resources

The four kinds of scarce productive resources are:

Resource	Definition	Examples
Land	Natural raw materials	Coal, soil, trees, iron ore
Labor	Physical and mental abilities of people	Bricklayer, keyboarder, scientist, manager, teacher
Capital	Manufactured resources used to make other goods and services	Warehouse, train, office desk, drill, computer, electric motor, highway
Enterprise	Ability to innovate, take risks, and organize production	People who form or operate businesses successfully (Steve Jobs or Ted Turner)

Opportunity Cost

The practical economist, introduced in Chapter 1, decides how to use scarce resources on the basis of opportunity cost. The opportunity cost of using any resource, good, or service is the value of the next best alternative forgone. Entrepreneurs cannot obtain any resource without using other resources, such as miners to mine coal or camels to haul sand. The opportunity cost of mined coal or desert sand is the value of the next best alternative use of the resources used in mining and shipping. The opportunity cost of coal is the value of the final goods sacrificed to use scarce resources to remove coal from the earth and ship it to where it is wanted.

The concept of opportunity cost also applies to consumer decisions. What is the opportunity cost of a new, $500 mountain bike? You must give up the satisfaction you would receive from spending that $500 on some other good, such as a stereo system or a round-trip flight to the Caribbean for spring break.

Sometimes opportunity cost can be measured in terms of dollars. In other cases the opportunity cost is more subjective, such as the time you might have spent contemplating nature or thinking great thoughts, each of which is difficult to value in dollar terms. Whether or not the cost can be expressed in dollars, every scarce good has an opportunity cost, because every good or service produced requires resources that could have been used to produce something else.

The Opportunity Cost of a College Education   Consider the opportunity costs faced by Susan, who is thinking about entering Clemson University in South Carolina. She (and her parents) want to know the "full cost" of her four years at Clemson. Using the current university catalog and estimating her personal spending, Susan makes the following list of expenses for an in-state student attending Clemson and living on campus for four years:

Expense	Per Academic Year	Four Years
Tuition and fees	$2,500	$10,000
Medical fee	140	560
Dorm housing	1,800	9,600
Meal plan (7 days)	1,420	5,680
Books	400	1,600
Other expenses	1,000	4,000
Total for four years		$32,340

Has Susan included *all* the costs of going to Clemson, and has she included some that are not relevant opportunity costs? The $32,340 represents her out-of-pocket expenses, but an important item is missing. By going to school full time, Susan would give up what she could earn by working—the next best alternative use of her time. Average annual earnings for a recent high school graduate in South Carolina are about $10,500. Therefore, over four years Susan would forgo $42,000, increasing her estimated costs of going to Clemson to $74,340!

Susan also needs to think like a practical economist, measuring opportunity costs and making a sound self-interested decision. What expenses has she included in her list that are not really costs of going to college? There are some expenses she would have whether or not she enrolled in college. Susan needs to subtract her other expenses of $1,000 a year (personal items and recreation). She would have these expenses whatever she did or wherever she lived. She should subtract meal costs for the same reason. Whether she should subtract housing costs depends on whether she would live at home or in an apartment if she were working. If living at home is the alternative, the dorm rent is a true extra (marginal) cost. If she would live in an apartment otherwise, the dorm rental is not an opportunity cost of her education because she would pay rent anyway.

Let's assume Susan would live in an apartment and work if she did not go to Clemson. In that case, she should subtract both her other expenses and the cost of dorm rental and meals from her original estimate—a total of $19,280. Susan's opportunity costs to attend Clemson University for four years, then, are $55,060. Of that amount, $42,000 (or 76 percent) consists of forgone earnings.

THE PRODUCTION POSSIBILITIES FRONTIER

Production possibilities frontier (PPF) A curve showing the combinations of the maximum output of two goods that can be produced by fully using the limited resources available with the best technology.

A useful way to look at the choices individuals and societies face is the production possibilities frontier. The **production possibilities frontier (PPF)** is a simple model of an economy that uses its available resources to produce some combination of two goods. The PPF shows the maximum amounts of these two goods that can be produced using all available resources, including the best production technology. Thus, the PPF shows the practical economist the various possibilities for allocating scarce resources.

Consider an economy that produces only two goods: soybeans and cotton. Figure 2-1 illustrates a simple production possibilities frontier for these two goods. If all available resources are used to produce soybeans, this economy will produce at point *A*, an output combination of 80 tons of soybeans and no cotton. On the other hand, if all available resources are used to produce cotton, output will be at point *F*, 800 bales of cotton and no soybeans.

It is also possible to allocate resources to produce some of both goods at the same time. These combinations of both products are represented by points along the PPF between endpoints *A* and *F*. Thus, point *C*, with 40 tons of soybeans and 400 bales of cotton, is one possible combination of outputs that uses all available resources with the best available technology.

Scarcity and Attainable Combinations

The PPF in Figure 2-1 illustrates scarcity in a very concrete way. For example, it is not possible to produce the combination of soybeans and cotton represented

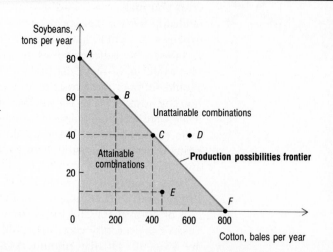

FIGURE 2-1

This straight-line production possibilities frontier for soybeans and cotton shows the maximum quantities of each good that can be produced using all available resources, including the best technology. Its negative slope illustrates opportunity cost, or the amount of one good that must be sacrificed to obtain more of the other.

by point *D* (40 tons of soybeans and 600 bales of cotton). There are not enough resources to produce that many soybeans and that much cotton at the same time. Thus, combinations that lie outside the frontier (above and to the right) cannot be produced. Given the amount of resources and technology available, this society's choices are limited to those combinations that lie on or inside the production possibilities frontier.

Opportunity Cost and the PPF

The production possibilities frontier also illustrates the concept of opportunity cost. The negative slope of the PPF means that some of one good must be given up to obtain more of the other. The opportunity cost of producing an extra 20 tons of soybeans, moving from *C* to *B* on the PPF in Figure 2-1, is 200 bales of cotton. Thus, the opportunity cost of 1 ton of soybeans is 10 bales of cotton, or the opportunity cost of 1 bale of cotton is 1/10 tons of soybeans. The slope of the PPF measures the opportunity cost of one good in terms of the amount of the other good forgone.

The Law of Increasing Cost

Along the simple, straight-line PPF in Figure 2-1, the amount of one good sacrificed (the opportunity cost) to get more of the other is a *constant* amount— 10 bales of cotton for 1 ton of soybeans. More commonly, however, the opportunity cost varies with the levels of production of the two goods, resulting in a PPF that curves outward. Along the PPF in Figure 2-2, the opportunity cost of producing more of either good changes as more of one good and less of the other is produced. Between *F* and *D*, the opportunity cost of 20 more tons of soybeans is 50 bales of cotton forgone. Between *D* and *C*, the cost of 20 more tons of soybeans is 100 bales of cotton. A further increase in soybean production—moving from *C* to *B*—would require an even larger sacrifice of cotton.

Law of increasing cost
The principle that the opportunity cost of producing an additional unit of a good increases as more of the good is produced.

The shape of the PPF reflects the law of increasing cost. The **law of increasing cost** says that the opportunity cost of producing more of one good increases as more units of that good are produced. Moving up the curve to production combinations that include more soybeans (from point *F* to point *D*, *D* to *C*, etc.) requires *ever larger* sacrifices of cotton per extra ton of soybeans produced. Moving down the PPF results in an increasing opportunity cost of cotton in terms of soybeans forgone.

As the economy becomes more specialized in the production of one good, opportunity costs increase because different resources are more suited to producing one good than another. Producing more cotton means some soybean farmers have to switch to making cotton and some farm machinery has to be put to use

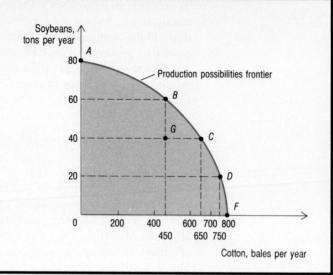

FIGURE 2-2

This production possibilities frontier bows outward to illustrate the law of increasing cost. Producing more of one good requires ever larger sacrifices of the other as more of it is produced. Combinations of soybeans and cotton inside or on the frontier are attainable, whereas combinations outside the PPF are unattainable given the resources and technology available. Only combinations *on* the frontier, however, represent efficient production.

in cotton production. To keep the opportunity cost of the extra cotton as low as possible, producers will first move those farmers (and that farm machinery) best suited to producing cotton and least productive in soybean farming. Further increases in cotton production will cost more, because the soybean farmers (and farm machinery) being shifted from soybeans to cotton will be better at soybean production and less suited to making cotton. Increases in cotton output come at the expense of larger and larger cuts in soybean output. The opportunity cost of cotton (in terms of soybeans) rises as more resources shift from soybean to cotton production.

Efficient Resource Use

The production possibilities frontier can show whether a society is fully using its resources. For instance, producing combination *G* in Figure 2-2 is possible but not efficient. If only 40 tons of soybeans are produced, enough resources are left to produce 650 bales of cotton (combination *C* on the PPF), not just the 450 in combination *G*. It certainly is possible to produce combinations that lie inside the PPF, like *G*, but *G* is wasteful. If society is producing at point *G*, it can obtain more output of either good (for example, at point *C* or *B*) without sacrificing any of the other good. Therefore, only combinations actually on the PPF curve reflect the maximum possible output, or the efficient use of society's scarce resources.

Economic Growth and the PPF

Finally, the production possibilities frontier can be used to show economic growth, which makes it possible to produce and consume more of *both* goods. Growth means an outward shift of the PPF due to either improved technology or more available resources. One way for an economy to grow is to produce fewer consumer goods in the present and use those resources to produce more capital goods. These extra capital resources allow a society to produce more consumer goods in the future.

To illustrate, suppose that at the beginning of 1993 Outland, a hypothetical society, is at point *A* on its production possibilities frontier (Figure 2-3), producing 50 units of consumer goods and 20 units of capital goods. These 20 units are just enough to replace the 20 units of capital that wear out each year. At *A*, then, there is no growth in Outland's capital resources. Now suppose the people of Outland decide to produce fewer consumer goods and more capital goods during 1993 to have more resources for future production than they have now. If they tighten their belts and cut consumer goods production from 50 to 30 units, they will be able to expand capital production from 20 to 40 units, represented by combination *B*. The reward for their sacrifice of current consumption in 1993 is an expanded PPF for 1994. Because the extra capital goods produced last year increases the resource base, the PPF shifts outward. Outland can now choose point *C* on PPF_{1994}, which allows more consumption

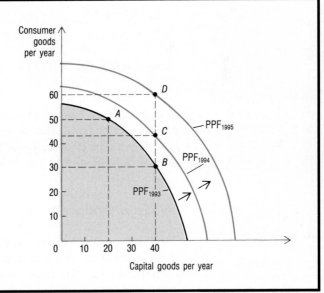

FIGURE 2-3

Outland can increase its ability to produce—expand its production possibilities frontier—by choosing to produce combination *B* instead of combination *A* in 1993. Combination *B* contains fewer consumer goods but more capital goods, which in turn increase Outland's resource base for 1994 and shifts its PPF outward for that year. In future years, Outland can use its expanded production capacity, if it chooses, to produce more of both consumer and capital goods, as shown by combinations *C* and *D*.

while still producing 40 units of capital goods. The extra capital goods produced in 1994 allow the PPF to expand again for 1995, so Outland arrives at point *D*. At *D*, residents can consume more consumer goods (a total of 60 units) than they could at point *A* in the years before 1993, while still producing extra capital goods for future economic growth!

However, expanding the production possibilities frontier in this way requires that Outland sacrifice some consumer goods in the present to produce extra capital goods. Sometimes such a sacrifice is difficult to make. In the 1990s, this issue—how to encourage more saving and investment—has been a focal point of public policy debates over the best way to speed up economic growth.

Another way to bring about economic growth (shift the PPF) is to develop new technologies that will allow more output from the same resources. However, to develop new technologies countries must spend heavily on education and research, again at the expense of current consumption. Economic growth, like almost everything else, has an opportunity cost.

CHECKLIST : **Production Possibilities Frontier**

The production possibilities frontier illustrates the following concepts:

Scarcity and choice	Attainable and unattainable combinations
Opportunity cost	The amount of one good that must be sacrificed to get more of another good
Increasing cost	A PPF that curves outward
Efficient resource use	Only combinations on the PPF
Economic growth	Shifts the PPF outward

THE BASIC ECONOMIC QUESTIONS

Basic economic questions The questions of what, how, and for whom to produce goods and services that every society must answer.

Scarce resources lead to scarce final goods and services, which requires people to make choices. Either individually or collectively through their governments, practical economists must choose what goods and services will be produced, how they will be produced, and for whom they will be produced. These are the **basic economic questions** every society faces.

What to Produce?

What to produce? The question of which combination of goods and services to produce with the limited resources available.

The first economic question is **what to produce** out of all the possible combinations of outputs. The PPF represents this question by showing the possible output combinations. Some combinations appeal more to some individuals, whereas different combinations are more satisfying to others, depending on their tastes. Some way must be found to select one particular combination.

Myth 2-1

If We Can Put an Astronaut on the Moon, We Can . . .

The phrase "If we can put an astronaut on the moon, we can . . ." has been popular ever since the first moon landing in 1969. If we can put an astronaut on the moon, then, why can't we wipe out illiteracy, or hunger, or AIDS, or crack?

The answer is very simple. It is precisely because we chose to devote very large quantities of our scarce resources to putting an astronaut on the moon that fewer resources were available for other public activities such as AIDS research, adult education, or fighting drug abuse. What is the opportunity cost of putting a person on the moon? It is the forgone benefits of billions of dollars that could have been allocated instead to these or other, equally deserving causes.

Nothing necessarily was wrong with the choice to use those resources for space research, which has generated all kinds of technical spinoffs and other benefits. But the premise "If we can put an astronaut on the moon . . ." is wrong. It is not true that if a nation has the resources to put a person on the moon, it should have the resources to provide all the other desirable programs too. If the United States chose to put an astronaut on the moon, its citizens must measure the opportunity cost in terms of the benefits of other programs forgone. ∎

Different societies make such choices in different ways. In the United States, the market plays an important role in making most of these choices. Consumers indicate what goods they want by "voting" in the marketplace with dollars. In other societies, government may influence the mixture of goods produced in various ways, including regulation, government production, or government purchases of goods and services.

How to Produce?

How to produce? The question of which mix of resources to use to produce particular goods and services at the lowest possible cost.

The second economic question—**how to produce**—is more technical than the first. Goods and services can be produced with many combinations of resources. For example, it is possible to cut the grass with a mower and one person. Another option is to have ten people cut the grass with grass shears. The first resource mix, using sophisticated capital and little labor, is "typical" in the United States and other developed countries. The second resource mix, using much labor and very little capital, sounds silly at first, but what if mowers were rare and very expensive, and labor were abundant and cheap? Using complex machines to mow grass, operated with little labor, seems reasonable only because capital is *relatively* less costly than labor in the United States.

The Great Wall of China is a monument to a production process that used very large amounts of labor and very little capital. It could be produced today with much less labor combined with a great deal of capital, such as bulldozers, giant earth movers, and forklifts. Similarly, a given quantity of corn can be produced with much land and a small amount of labor and fertilizer, for with half as much land combined with more fertilizer and more labor.

Answering the *how* question means choosing the "best" combination of scarce resources to produce the desired output at the lowest possible opportunity cost. Answers to this question vary around the world, not only because of the way the decisions are made but also because the "best" choice depends on the relative availability—or relative scarcity—of different productive resources.

For Whom to Produce?

For whom to produce?
The question of how to distribute goods and services among people.

The last basic question is **for whom to produce.** Who will get the output? Will those who work harder or longer receive a larger share of output? Or will everyone in the group (family, community, city, country, or world) share the output equally?

The question of for whom to produce is closely linked to the question of what to produce. If society decides, for example, that a larger share of output should go to elderly people, the output mix will reflect more medical care and travel and fewer children's toys and rock videos. If society decides that women are more deserving than men, more blouses and fewer men's shirts will be produced.

Usually, however, neither age nor sex is a basis for determining shares of output. Instead, shares of output may be determined on the basis of "need," or of how much output each person produces, or of how to provide equal shares for all. Answers to the *for whom* question, like those to the first two basic questions, vary among societies.

Americans answer all three basic economic questions partly through markets and partly through government. The mix of market and government varies greatly from country to country, although the range of variation is much smaller since the fall of communism in Central and Eastern Europe. Even China, a country that still calls itself communist, has shifted many of the *what* and *how* questions, and even part of the *for whom* question, to markets. The assignment of responsibilities between markets and governments, or sometimes to a third sector (see In Practice 2-1) determines the answers to these questions.

In Practice 2-1
. . . .

The Third Sector: Private Voluntary Organizations

Markets and government are not the only methods available to answer the basic economic questions. In many societies—but especially American society—there is a third sector that uses a blend of the methods of government and market to make certain economic decisions about what to produce, how to produce, and for whom to produce. This sector consists of private, not-for-profit organizations that include the United Way and its agencies, churches, homeless shelters, neighborhood associations, and thousands of other groups in which people join together to engage in production and consumption activities.

Although people are not coerced into giving to the United Way, attending church, or joining the neighborhood association, they often experience considerable social pressure to take part, particularly in smaller communities. Once you join, you accept a set of rules that probably involve your required contribution to production in some way. You also probably participate in redistribution—a hallmark of planned economies and also of the third sector. Services are not provided in exchange for a specific payment. You can attend a church service without making a contribution, enjoy the neighborhood beautification effort whether your contribution is small or large, and be either a contributor or a recipient of food from the local food bank. Big decisions are usually made in organizations on the basis of majority voting. Thus, in many ways the third sector is like government without the power to tax.

In other respects, activities in the third sector resemble market activities. People participate voluntarily. In many organizations, those who do not pay do not share in the benefits (a swimming pool club, a scout troop that requires parents to help out), just as in the market. Some services are sold for a fee, even though the organization is not supposed to make a profit. Museums charge admission, and many organizations charge dues for the benefits of membership. Individuals generally volunteer for the various tasks on the basis of their skills and opportunity costs. Like the market, volunteer organizations are very local or decentralized, so decisions are made by small groups.

The third sector exists all over the world, but historically it has played a particularly important role in American society since the days of quilting bees and barn raisings. Having a third sector to take care of some collective wants and provide for the poor makes it possible to work toward equity without expanding the role of government. ■

MARKETS, GOVERNMENTS, AND ECONOMIC SYSTEMS

Economic system A social framework of rules, goals, and economic incentives for answering the basic economic questions.

An **economic system** consists of a particular set of rules, goals, and incentives that govern economic relations among people in a society and provide a way to answer the basic economic questions. Any economic system must use one or more decision-making methods or rules. The bases for making decisions include tradition (families often decide to do something "the old way"); brute force (the strongest children get their way on the playground); first come, first served (people line up for concert tickets); authority or command (the boss, appointed or elected, decides what is produced and who gets it); and markets (individuals bargain with one another privately to obtain goods). In modern industrial societies, the answers to the basic economic questions come through the market, the government, or some combination of the two.

Although most modern societies rely on some combination of markets and governments to answer the basic questions, other methods of finding answers exist. Consider how the *for whom* question might be answered. Suppose your economics professor announces on the first day of class that the publisher of your textbook has provided ten free textbooks as part of its book promotion campaign. There are 40 students in the class, so textbooks are a scarce good that must be allocated among competing "consumers." How will your professor decide who gets the textbooks?

The professor could toss the textbooks "up for grabs." Those who moved fastest, sat near the front, or had the longest arms would win. The first ten students in the door could be rewarded with free textbooks. Lottery tickets could be passed out, with textbooks going to holders of lucky numbers. The professor might prefer to give textbooks to some arbitrary group, such as red-heads, left-handed students, or international students. Perhaps a "needs" test could be used, with textbooks given free to the neediest students. Or the professor could auction off the books to the highest bidders. Clearly there are lots of ways to answer the *for whom* question. The same is true of the *what* and *how* questions.

In practice, societies use a variety of methods in different combinations—need, tradition, first come, first served. For the most part, however, markets and government are the vehicles used to answer the basic three questions.

Planned Economies

Planned economy An economic system in which the government owns all resources and government authorities decide almost all economic issues.

Planned economies rely almost totally on government to make economic decisions through centralized authorities, and the government owns most of the major productive resources. The government has the power to coerce people into doing certain things. People who violate laws, fail to pay taxes, or refuse to work can be fined, jailed, or otherwise punished. This threat is a powerful incentive for people to cooperate.

Planned economies can be either democratic or dictatorial. Many Western European countries, notably Sweden, have highly planned economies but democratic, popularly elected governments. In these countries, some productive resources are owned by individuals and others by government, but the government owns a larger share than is the case in more market-oriented economies. Individuals have a fair amount of freedom, but governments redistribute some income directly from the rich to the poor, and many services (health care, child care, etc.) are provided for everyone through taxes rather than purchased by individual households.

Other planned economies, such as the nations of Eastern and Central Europe before 1990, offer examples of nondemocratic planned economies. When these countries were still planned economies, citizens were permitted only limited private ownership, generally of such personal items as clothes, household furnishings, and garden tools. Owning a sewing machine, for example, was discouraged because the sewing machine represented capital, or the means of production. In such a society, the government made major decisions about where individuals worked and lived, what consumer goods were produced and who received them, and how many resources were devoted to producing capital goods and military hardware relative to consumer goods.

As we have learned how these economies functioned, one lesson is clear, that planned economies answer certain big questions, such as how to reallocate resources from consumer goods to capital goods to promote economic growth, very well. However, a central authority that makes all economic decisions has little information about individual consumers' preferences. As a result, a planned economy usually fails to satisfy the variety of smaller wants of families and individuals. Efficient organization of production is also more difficult in a planned economy, because the central authority lacks the detailed information it needs to ensure that all the nuts, bolts, light bulbs, wire, and other materials show up at the right factory, at the right moment, and in the right quantities. The people at the factory or the store have this information, but they have neither the incentive nor the power to make the production decision. The people with the power to decide are far removed from where the goods are produced and sold.

Market Economies

Market economy An economic system in which individuals own resources and answer the basic economic questions through their private interactions as buyers and sellers in a bargaining process.

In **market economies,** most productive resources are owned by private individuals as households or through the businesses they own. In this case, the basic economic questions are answered by the actions of buyers and sellers as they trade in the market. People make economic decisions in response to market signals and on the basis of their own preferences. They decide what they will produce, for whom they will work, and to whom they will sell their other resources in exchange for income. They then decide what goods and services they will buy. If consumers choose to buy little of an item, its production will shrink, whereas production of goods in great demand will expand. If the price of a good is high, consumers will shift to another good. As a result, the answer to the *what* question is determined by tallying the dollar votes of thousands or even millions of individual consumers.

How goods are produced depends on another set of prices: the relative prices of resources. If labor is relatively plentiful and cheap, producers will use a lot of labor and conserve capital. If the prices of certain resources, such as oil, fall, those resources will be quickly substituted for other resources, such as coal, that have become relatively more expensive.

Even in a pure market economy, government plays at least one essential role. Government is a rule maker and a rule enforcer, called on to protect individuals and their property rights, enforce contracts, and serve as arbitrator when legal disputes arise.

Market economies answer the *what* to produce and *how* to produce questions very well. However, critics of the market argue that it fails to answer the *for whom* question efficiently. Extreme poverty can result when some people start with few resources or when the resources they own fall in value.

Mixed Economies

Mixed economy An economic system that relies on a mixture of markets and government to determine what, how, and for whom goods and services are produced.

The economic system in most countries lies between the extremes of planned and market economies. **Mixed economies** answer some economic questions solely through the market, other questions solely through government. For most questions, both markets and government play a role.

The U.S. economic system falls into the mixed category near the market end of the spectrum. Most decisions in this country are made by individuals and firms in private markets, but the government also plays a role. For example, anyone can open an ice cream store. But the store will need a business license, ice cream scoopers will have to receive the minimum wage, city building inspectors will check that the building meets fire and safety standards, the cream used will have to be graded and inspected, and the store will have to meet parking requirements and other local regulations. Countries like Sweden and France also have mixed systems, although their governments play a larger role than in the United States.

The governments of China, North Korea, and Cuba (the remaining communist countries at the present time) continue to own most of the productive resources, especially land and large, basic enterprises like steel plants, hospitals, and electric power plants. Even in these countries, however, markets play a role in certain smaller (but important) economic activities, such as dining in restaurants, repairing shoes, and selling garden produce. China has moved a long way toward individual ownership and the use of markets and has experienced rapid growth as a result.

Where citizens are free to choose, the design of a nation's economic system—and particularly the choice of the combination of market and government roles—will reflect citizens' basic social values. Some of those basic social values are embodied in the economic goals people want their economic systems to fulfill.

Economic goals The major objectives of societies: economic efficiency, distributional equity, economic freedom, economic growth, full employment, and price stability.

ECONOMIC GOALS

Every society has **economic goals**. While these goals are very similar the world over, different societies emphasize different goals on the basis of their own cultural values and level of economic development. Economic goals are categorized as microeconomic and macroeconomic goals, depending on whether the goals involve individual households or larger, economywide variables. Major microeconomic goals include economic efficiency, distributional equity, and economic freedom. Macroeconomic goals are economic growth, full employment, and price stability.

Economic Efficiency

Economic efficiency
The goal of producing the right mixtures and amounts of goods and services from limited resources.

A major goal of almost all societies is **economic efficiency**—using scarce resources to produce as much as possible of desired goods and services. This goal reflects the practical economist in action, confronting scarcity with self-interested, maximizing behavior. Economic efficiency means not only producing goods as cheaply as possible in terms of opportunity cost but also choosing the most desirable output combination on the production possibilities frontier. Economic efficiency is reflected in both the what to produce and how to produce questions.

Production efficiency
Producing as much as possible from limited resources and at the lowest possible cost.

Production efficiency involves answering the question of how to produce successfully. Production efficiency means producing a given amount of a good or service at the lowest possible opportunity cost (smallest sacrifice of resources). Thus, if a good can be produced with more than one combination of resources— for example, much capital and little labor or less capital and a lot of labor—the least costly resource combination should be chosen for production efficiency. In terms of a production possibilities frontier for combinations of two goods, production efficiency means producing any combination that is *on* the PPF rather than one that lies inside it.

Allocative efficiency
Producing the right mix of goods and services so that consumers get the goods they want most.

Allocative efficiency means distributing resources among all the possible goods and services that could be produced so that consumers get the products they want most. Allocative efficiency is the response to the desires of an entire society of practical economists. A society enjoys allocative efficiency if the answer to the what to produce question maximizes the satisfaction of its consumers. Allocative efficiency means using productive resources in such a way as to maximize the total value (to consumers) of all the goods and services produced.

Along the production possibilities frontier, each point represents a combination with different amounts of two goods, but all these points represent production efficiency. Picking the "right" combination on the PPF—the one that best satisfies consumers—means the society has achieved allocative as well as productive efficiency.

If the Great Wall of China were being built today, the productive efficiency question would be whether to use 1 million people with only a little capital (tools) to build the wall or use only 1,000 people equipped with earth-moving machinery and concrete trucks. Building it the cheapest way would be efficient production. The allocative efficiency questions are whether to build it at all (in preference to other goods and services that could be produced) or to build it half as high or half as long and use the remaining resources to produce other goods consumers value more highly.

Distributional Equity

Distributional equity
Apportioning income or output fairly among individuals in a society.

Is it fair for some people to be very rich and for many others to be very poor? Whatever your personal definition of a fair distribution of income or goods, most countries enjoy some degree of consensus about what is fair. **Distributional equity** describes a fair apportionment of income or output among the members of a society.

Distributional choices can range from a situation in which all families have the same amount of income (complete distributional equality) to one in which a few families have very large incomes and most others have much less. In most communes, for example, everyone shares equally in the income earned by the group. At the opposite extreme, feudal societies of the Middle Ages generated very unequal income distributions. The king and certain nobles might have received as much as 60 or 70 percent of a country's income, while the rest of the people barely made do with what was left.

What is the "correct" distribution of income? There is no simple answer to this question. Some people believe the income distribution in the United States is about right, whereas others think too much poverty exists. Those who argue for more equality generally believe everyone should have access to certain basic "necessities" (however defined) of housing, food, and medical care. Others argue that more equality will reduce the incentives to be productive, save, and invest if the rewards are taken from the winners to provide for the losers in the "market game."

One definition of distributional fairness defines the answer to the *for whom* question in terms of equal opportunity rather than a particular distributional outcome. That is, each individual should have an equal opportunity to produce and earn. After an "even start" (including basic education), whatever income distribution results would be fair under this definition. Fair distribution of income is a very controversial and value-laden (normative) topic. As a positive science, economics neither implies nor endorses any particular final income distribution. Many economists in the United States lean strongly toward using markets and prices to direct production and consumption, even though this approach will lead to some degree of unequal income distribution. Others argue that the distribution determined by the market should be changed by government intervention. Whichever the choice, economics can shed some light on efficient ways to achieve the desired distributional goal.

Economic Freedom

Economic freedom
Individuals' right to own and use property (resources) as they see fit to maximize their own satisfaction.

Another important issue in designing an economic system is the goal of economic freedom. **Economic freedom** means the right to own productive resources and use them as one sees fit in response to economic incentives and in accord with one's own tastes and preferences. The practical economist cannot pursue his or her self-interest effectively without some degree of economic freedom. Usually

Property rights The rules governing owner-ship of property, including whether individuals may buy and sell resources they own and whether they may keep and exchange their output.

economic freedom is subject to the limitation that others are not harmed by one's actions. The freedom to enjoy shooting does not include the right to use the neighbor's cow for a target. Even advocates of economic freedom realize that total freedom would result in total chaos. Those who place a high value on economic freedom would, however, keep the number of rules and limits on individual behavior to a minimum. They point out that the essential nature of government is the power to compel people to do what they might otherwise choose not to do—pay taxes, serve in the military, or drive within the speed limit.

All societies develop some rules for governing social behavior and economic activity—the "rules of the game." Although these rules vary widely, certain kinds of rules are necessary to permit economic activity. These rules take the form of property rights. **Property rights** determine whether individuals can own productive resources, such as land and even their own labor services, and what ownership allows them to do with their property. Can individuals hold parties in their backyards late at night? Can they plant tall trees that shade a neighbor's garden? Are people free to buy and sell their output to the highest bidder, or are there restrictions on to whom they can sell and what price they can charge? Most of these rules are embodied in constitutions, laws, and ordinances passed by legislatures and city councils. Practical economists need to know what the rules are to engage in production and exchange of goods and services.

In market economies, economic freedom means individuals are free to buy, sell, organize, produce, and consume with relatively little interference from others or from government. The self-interested, maximizing behavior of the practical economist requires a good deal of freedom to sell the services of his or her productive resources and to buy and use final goods and services.

Economic Growth

Economic growth A constantly increasing standard of living that re-sults when output or in-come per person increases each year; an expanding PPF each year.

Most Americans would like to see more output of goods and services over time, or **economic growth,** as long as growth includes quality as well as quantity. That is, growth should not come at the expense of leisure, the environment, or other desirable aspects of common life. The goal of economic growth is to raise a nation's standard of living, measured by income or output per person. This macroeconomic goal can be expressed as an outward shift in the PPF, meaning that more goods and services are available for consumption.

Essentially there are three ways to achieve economic growth. Discovering more natural resources is one way. The search for resources was a central reason behind the exploration of the New World by Europeans in the sixteenth, seven-teenth, and eighteenth centuries. It is also one reason for many past and present territorial wars.

Developing better technology is a second way to create economic growth. Better technology allows existing resources to produce more output. The last decade saw major breakthroughs in computer and robotics technologies. The increased knowledge and research that produce improvements in technology are a major purpose of higher education.

Increased capital resources—production of more capital goods or development of worker skills—is a third path to economic growth. This approach involves giving up present consumption to enjoy higher future consumption. Sometimes it is easier for those who control a planned economy to forcibly divert resources into capital goods. It may be harder to do so in a market economy, in which the output mix is dictated by consumer preferences for present versus future consumption.

Full Employment

Full employment The use of all resources available for production, especially labor.

A macroeconomic goal that reflects production efficiency—getting to the PPF—is **full employment** of *all* available resources, although the focus is most often on employing labor resources. While some labor is likely to be unemployed as resources shift among production of different goods and services in a dynamic economy, long periods of high unemployment are considered very undesirable. Loss of jobs and income during periods of unemployment cause a great deal of suffering and hardship for both the families directly involved and those whose income and jobs depend on the spending of those families. For example, closing an auto plant or a military base throws not only autoworkers or soldiers out of work but also workers in all the retail stores, restaurants, and other firms that provide services to the plant or base and its employees.

In addition, unemployment means that some scarce resources are not being fully used; society is producing inside the PPF. As a result, valuable output is lost forever. Thus, unemployment is costly to society as well as to individual workers.

Price Stability

Price stability A constant average level of prices of resources and goods as opposed to rising or falling prices.

Particularly in a market system, **price stability** is important because price signals guide production and exchange decisions. Households rely on those signals to tell them what is a good buy, where to sell their labor, where to lend their savings, and whether to buy now or wait until later. Unstable prices distort those signals and make it more difficult for producers and consumers to make sound decisions. When price instability takes the form of inflation, especially unexpected inflation, some people gain while others lose. That is, some people's incomes fall behind the cost of their spending, while others' come out ahead. This redistribution of income is likely to conflict with citizens' notion of equity or fairness in the distribution of income. Often the losers from steadily rising prices are the poorest groups with the least economic power.

CHECKLIST : **Economic Goals**

Microeconomic Goals

    Economic efficiency   Producing the maximum output possible given scarce resources (production efficiency) and producing the mix of goods consumers want (allocative efficiency)

    Distributional equity   Achieving a fair distribution of income and output among households

    Economic freedom   Being able to produce and consume according to one's own preferences

Macroeconomic Goals

    Economic growth   Moving the PPF outward over time

    Full employment   Ensuring that all available resources are being used productively

    Price stability   Keeping the average level of prices from either rising or falling

Conflict among Economic Goals

The pursuit of one economic goal is likely to make it more difficult to achieve one or more of the other goals. For example, the desire for economic freedom conflicts with policies to increase distributional equity. Greater equity would require that government intervene to take income from some groups and give it to others. Policies to promote full employment can sometimes create inflationary pressures (price instability). These and other conflicts will become more apparent in later chapters.

The choices and goals discussed in this chapter apply to all societies, whether they have market, planned, or mixed economic systems. All societies face the problem of scarcity that requires choices, each with an associated opportunity cost. In the next chapter, we explore how choices are made and how goals are ranked in a mixed market system such as that of the United States.

Summary

1. Scarcity is the universal, basic economic problem that arises from unlimited wants to be met with limited resources.

2. The limited resources or factors of production are land, labor, capital, and enterprise.

3. Scarcity means that choices must be made and that every choice has an opportunity cost.

4. The production possibilities frontier is a useful analytical tool that shows all the possible combinations of maximum output of two goods when all available resources and the best technology are fully used. The PPF separates the

attainable from the unattainable regions of output and reflects the economic concepts of choice, opportunity cost, efficiency, and the law of increasing cost. The PPF can also represent economic growth.

5. The basic economic questions arising out of scarcity that all societies must answer, are what to produce, how to produce, and for whom to produce.

6. The framework within which a society answers these basic questions is its economic system, which may be a planned, market, or mixed economic system.

7. Economic goals of all societies (with varying emphasis) are efficiency, distributional equity, economic freedom, economic growth, full employment, and stable prices. Efforts to achieve some goals may conflict with efforts to achieve others.

Key Terms

allocative efficiency
basic economic
  questions
capital
distributional equity
economic efficiency
economic freedom
economic goals
economic growth
economic system
enterprise

entrepreneur
For whom to produce?
full employment
How to produce?
human capital
labor
land
law of increasing cost
market economy
mixed economy
planned economy

price stability
production efficiency
production possibilities
  frontier (PPF)
property rights
resources
scarcity
technology
What to produce?

Questions and Problems

1. "Wants are not really unlimited; they are fictions created by Madison Avenue advertisers." Is this statement true? Could it be true for Double Bubble gum but not true for all goods and services?

2. What is (are) the primary opportunity cost(s) of
   a. Choosing to eat pizza tonight?
   b. Studying economics for one hour today?
   c. Doubling expenditures on Medicare?
   d. Hiring several people to plant shrubs and take care of the campus grounds?
   e. Producing a compact disc player?

3. Is using the latest high-tech equipment always the most efficient way to produce any good?

4. What does it mean to you if both a bottle of wine and bowling three games cost $6? In what way are these two goods equivalent?

5. If, among other things, prices direct resource allocation (what and how to produce), what do you think would happen over time to enrollment in agricultural departments at state universities if cheese prices rose to $8,000 per pound?

6. What economic goals are emphasized in the United States (or in your country if you are not a U.S. citizen)?

7. Which of the following represent land, labor, capital, or enterprise: (a) a two-ton drill, (b) a can of paint, (c) soft coal, (d) an autoworker, (e) swordfish steaks, (f) an inventory of diamonds, (g) a welder, (h) a scientist's knowledge, (i) Ross Perot?

8. There are two ways to attack the problem of scarcity. One is to try to increase output (by discovering more resources, producing more capital resources, or investing in education and research to develop new technology to get more from available resources). The other is to reduce the desire for goods and services. Would people be happier with one approach than with the other? Is either approach really likely to eliminate scarcity?

9. The opportunity cost of producing one book is four magazines. If all resources are used in producing books, this society can produce 100 books. How many magazines can be produced? If 50 books are produced, how many magazines can be produced? Draw the production possibilities curve representing the various output combinations of books and magazines.

10. Your opportunity cost calculations do not end when you decide to go to college. What opportunity costs do you encounter in making up your class schedule?

3

An Overview of the Market Economy

Political economy . . . proposes . . . first, to provide a plentiful revenue or subsistence for the people, or more properly, to enable them to provide such a revenue or subsistence for themselves; and secondly, to supply the state or commonwealth with a revenue sufficient for the public services. It proposes to enrich both the people and the sovereign.

ADAM SMITH, *Wealth of Nations*

Main Points

1. A market economy provides opportunities to increase individual and collective well-being through specialization and exchange based on comparative advantage.

2. A market economy consists of three groups of economic actors: households, businesses, and governments. Households and businesses exchange goods and services in product markets and productive resources in resource markets.

3. Households earn income from selling the services of land, labor, capital, and enterprise to business firms and use that income to buy goods and services from businesses.

4. The circular flow describes the economic relationships among households, businesses, and governments as they interact in markets to determine the size and composition of the flow of goods and services.

5. Business firms organize production and make decisions about what to produce, how to produce, and for whom to produce based on price signals from the product and resource markets.

6. Government provides services that the market cannot provide efficiently, redistributes income, tries to stabilize the level of economic activity, and collects taxes to pay for those services.

Now that we have explored the fundamental economic problem of scarcity and choice and identified the basic economic questions all economies face, we are ready to examine how those choices are made and those questions answered in market economies such as those of the United States, Canada, Japan, Australia, and the countries of Western Europe. We will largely draw on the United States as a model, but most of our discussion applies to any economy in which the market is the primary decision-making arena.

One of the primary ways individuals address the problem of scarcity is through specialization. When individuals work at jobs they perform relatively better than others and firms produce a few goods relatively better than other firms, more output can be produced from the same available resources. But specialization requires a way to exchange resources as well as goods and services. Exchange requires the existence of organized markets.

This chapter presents an overview of markets and the actors in the marketplace—households, businesses, and governments—as each group (and individuals within them) specializes in production and engages in exchange. We examine how specialization increases total output and how exchange takes place in markets. We also lay the foundations for addressing microeconomic questions (how product and resource markets work to determine prices and quantities) and macroeconomic issues (how the sum total of market decisions determines the levels of total output, employment, and prices). This foundation consists of the circular flow model of economic activity, in which households, businesses, and governments interact to exchange resources and products. ■

SCARCITY, SPECIALIZATION, AND EXCHANGE

Individuals such as bricklayers, teachers, secretaries, and doctors tend to specialize in certain kinds of productive activities. Likewise, business firms tend to produce just one or a few products or services. Even nations usually specialize in a limited range of products and exchange them with other countries.

Why do people, firms, and nations tend to specialize in particular kinds of production rather than produce for themselves all the goods and services they want? *They specialize because specialization enables them to produce more total output from the available resources.* Through exchange, both traders can enjoy the benefits of a larger total output, creating higher standards of living than they would enjoy if they did not specialize. Hence, specialized production provides a way to raise total output without increasing the quantity of scarce resources.

The Principle of Comparative Advantage

In a market economy with no one in charge, how do people decide who specializes in what, whether "who" is an individual, a community, or a nation? The answer lies in a very old and important idea in economics: the principle of comparative advantage. To understand this principle, we need to make some simplifying assumptions. We will begin with the assumption of two people who are the only producers and consumers and produce only two products.

Suppose two farmers, Mr. Johnson and Ms. Miller, are the only people in the country of Inland. Both grow various combinations of corn and wheat with their land and other productive resources, as shown by their respective production possibilities frontiers in Figure 3-1. Before they discovered each other, each had chosen a particular point (A for Johnson and A' for Miller) on his or her production possibilities frontiers. This point represents how much of each good each farmer produces for personal consumption. The amount of corn and wheat each farmer produces and consumes is as follows:

	Wheat	Corn
Johnson	10	45
Miller	15	15
Total	25	60

Johnson and Miller choose different output combinations for two reasons. First, their resources differ in quantity or quality, which gives them different production possibilities frontiers. The production possibilities frontiers in Figure 3-1 indicate that Johnson's resources are more suited to corn than wheat production compared to Miller's resources. Second, the two farmers have different tastes. The amounts each has chosen to produce and consume suggest that Johnson prefers corn to wheat, whereas Miller likes them about equally.

Total output for the two farmers is 25 bushels of wheat and 60 bushels of corn. Could they increase total output and make both better off if each specialized in producing one of the two goods? If you think they ought to try it, who should produce corn and who should produce wheat? This question can be answered using the concept of opportunity cost.

Which production possibilities curve shows a lower cost for producing wheat? Since there are only two goods, the cost of an extra bushel of wheat for either farmer must be the amount of corn given up. For Johnson, the opportunity cost of another bushel of wheat is one and one half bushels of corn, measured by the slope of the production possibilities curve. We can use a shortcut to calculate opportunity cost when the production possibilities curve is a straight line. If Johnson gives up corn production entirely and produces only wheat, the opportunity cost of 40 bushels of wheat is the 60 bushels of corn he could have produced with those resources. Thus, 60 bushels of corn = 40 bushels of wheat, or 1 bushel of wheat costs $1\frac{1}{2}$ bushels of corn.

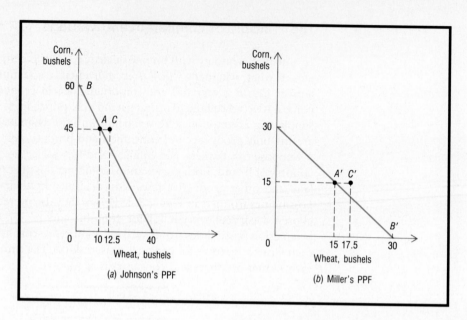

FIGURE 3-1

These two production possibilities frontiers show the various combinations of corn and wheat Johnson and Miller can produce. The slope of each frontier measures opportunity cost: how much of one good must be given up to produce more of the other. *A* and *A'* are the original output and consumption choices of the two farmers; *B* and *B'* are production with specialization; *C* and *C'* represent final consumption combinations of the two goods for each farmer.

Miller's opportunity cost of producing one more bushel of wheat is one bushel of corn. Therefore, her production cost for wheat is lower. Her opportunity cost of wheat is only one bushel of corn forgone, whereas Johnson's opportunity cost is one and one half bushels of corn. The way for both parties to gain from this difference in opportunity cost is for Miller to specialize in wheat and Johnson in corn.

We would have arrived at the same conclusion had we asked which farmer had the lower cost of production for corn. Calculate the opportunity cost of corn for each farmer and make sure you arrive at the same answer: a lower opportunity cost for Johnson than for Miller in corn production.

When the two farmers specialize, they move to points *B* and *B'* on their production possibilities frontiers in Figure 3-1, and output changes to the following:

	Wheat	Corn
Johnson	0	60
Miller	30	0
Total	30	60

··

Myth 3-1

··

I Win, You Lose

A game in which my winnings equal your losses (such as a game of poker or a simple bet) is called a *zero-sum game,* because the total winnings and losses of all the players add up to zero. Many people believe trade between individuals (or nations) is also a zero-sum game.

An important implication of the principle of comparative advantage is that trade based on specialization is a *positive-sum game:* One party benefits with no loss to the other, or (more often) both parties come out winners, as Johnson and Miller did. Trade is a positive-sum game because specialization and exchange allow output to increase, and the larger pie can generate positive gains for all.

The same is true of most other economic transactions. If Hardee's offers Joe a job and Joe accepts, both gain. Hardee's hires Joe because it expects that the firm will be better off with him, even after subtracting his salary. Joe accepts because he values the income more than the next best use, or opportunity cost, of his time. Likewise, if Sue sells her car to Bert for cash, both parties gain because Sue values the cash more than the car (or she wouldn't have sold it), whereas Bert values the car more than the cash.

Gambling and economics have some things in common, like risk taking. But buying and selling in the market will likely always be a positive-sum game for all the players. ■

Comparative advantage The principle stating that total output can be increased if each trading partner specializes in the product or service for which his or her opportunity cost is lower than the other party's.

Look at the startling result! There is more wheat as a result of specializing, without any increase in resources used. This specialization reflects the principle of **comparative advantage,** which states that total output can be increased if each individual (or business firm or nation) specializes in the production of that good or service for which their opportunity cost is lower.

The Gains from Exchange

The two farmers will be willing to specialize and increase output only if they can find some way to divide the gains so that both parties are made better off. In this case, *better off* means that each farmer still consumes some corn and some wheat, but now has more of at least one good.

There are many ways to divide the extra bushels of wheat between the two producers. One possibility occurs at points *C* and *C'* in Figure 3-1, where

Johnson has traded 15 bushels of corn for 12.5 bushels of wheat. Since he has 45 bushels of corn left, his consumption at point *C* is 45 bushels of corn and 12.5 bushels of wheat. This consumption mix is a clear improvement over the 45 bushels of corn and 10 bushels of wheat he consumed before specializing.

Miller is better off too. She receives 15 bushels of corn from Johnson. After trading 12.5 bushels of wheat, she has 17.5 bushels left. She also consumes more goods than before. Both farmers have been rewarded for behaving like practical economists, pursuing their own self-interest and responding to incentives. As a result, they were able to increase their consumption with no increase in effort or resources.

Farmers provide simple examples, but most people specialize on the basis of comparative advantage. Except for a few back-to-nature families, most of us produce one or just a few goods or services while consuming a great variety. Specializing in teaching, auto repair, meat packing, or software development allows us to become highly productive and use the earnings from that production specialty to consume more goods and services produced by others.

Sometimes the comparative advantage exists at the start; for example, Johnson may have soil better suited to corn than to wheat. More often, however, comparative advantage is acquired by learning a trade, acquiring a skill, buying specialized equipment, or developing sources of materials and markets. Whatever its source, the output and consumption gains from specialization are a basic source of the higher standard of living industrial countries enjoy. As other nations develop economically, individuals, households, and regions also become more specialized and enjoy the gains from trade.

The power of specialization and exchange to improve standards of living even without increased resources makes most economists strong advocates of free trade. When a nation restricts the flow of goods among countries, its citizens must give up some benefits of specialization and exchange. We will explore some of the reasons nations restrict trade in Chapter 18.

MARKETS

Market A setting in which buyers and sellers exchange productive resources or final goods and services.

Farmers Johnson and Miller, Ford and IBM, and New York and Pennsylvania can specialize only if they have a way to engage in trade. Any setting in which exchange takes place between buyers and sellers is called a **market**. Without markets, individuals could consume only what they were able to produce for themselves. Markets make it possible to specialize in producing just one or a few products while consuming a great variety of goods and services.

How Markets Work

Mention the word *market,* and your mind probably calls up visions of supermarkets, the stock market, or a flea market. Not all markets exist in a physical location, however. A large and growing mail order market works through correspondence or telephone. The labor market consists of many employment agencies, personnel offices, and individual contacts between employers and prospective workers. Two or more buyers or sellers operate in the same market if they sell or buy the same or similar products, even if they never have any direct contact or come to the same place.

Markets provide important information that buyers and sellers use in pursuing their self-interest. Sellers let potential customers know what they have to offer in terms of quality and quantity. Buyers provide information about what they want by either buying or not buying. The most important kind of information provided in markets is price information. Price signals whether two liters of Coke in a plastic bottle are "worth" more or less than the amount in a six-pack, how a can of Pepsi compares to the same amount of Coke, and how all of these items compare to movie tickets or a gallon of gasoline. Price is the incentive the practical economist needs to pursue his or her self-interest and maximize satisfaction.

Sellers often take the first step in the bargaining process by advertising their prices, putting price labels on packages, or quoting prices to prospective buyers. For markets to function well, information about product quality, quantities offered, and price must be widely and easily available. Buyers, in turn, supply information by bidding on products or by buying or not buying products at particular prices. In some markets, such as the New York Stock Exchange or a local antique auction, formal bidding takes place. Most of the time, however, buyers make their "bids" by rejecting a listed price and going elsewhere or waiting for a sale.

The Invisible Hand

Invisible hand The guiding force of self-interested behavior that directs the allocation of resources and the output mix in a market economy.

One of the most remarkable features of a pure market economy is that no one seems to be in charge. With no one to issue commands or provide direction, markets allocate resources to the production of different goods and services, determine what resource mix to employ, and distribute the goods and services among households. According to Adam Smith, whose 1776 classic the *Wealth of Nations* formed the cornerstone of economics, the **invisible hand** of self-interest is the only guiding force in the market. This guiding force is self-interested, maximizing behavior, with practical economists responding to incentives that appear in the form of changes in prices, wages, profits, and other rewards.

The invisible hand, guiding individuals in their pursuit of their own self-interest to use resources efficiently, is the market's answer to the question "Who's in charge here?" The market provides answers to the basic economic questions, but the show goes on with no director and no producer, just the actors. The practical economist does not need a stage manager!

Essential Elements: Property Rights and Competition

Not all markets succeed in providing information and matching up buyers and sellers. For markets to work effectively, two essential elements must be present: clearly defined property rights and competition.

Property rights The definition of who owns resources, goods, and services and the owners' rights to use, sell, or rent their property.

Property Rights **Property rights** define the ownership of goods, services, and resources and set limits on their transfer and use. For the buying and selling of resources or goods to occur, someone must clearly establish who owns them and what rights the owners have. When you buy a car, for example, the seller must prove her or his ownership rights with a clear legal title. Even after you buy the car, however, your rights to use it are restricted. You cannot drive it without a driver's license, and you must obey local noise ordinances, speed limits, traffic signs, parking restrictions, and emission control requirements. The title conveys a property right to own the car and the driver's license and other requirements the right to use it, but all are subject to regulations that limit your property rights to protect the rights of others.

Driving is not the only case of a property right that the government defines and limits. Most of us have the right to sell the services of our labor, but not if we are children under a certain age, non-U.S. residents without work permits, convicted felons trying to work in certain occupations, or professionals attempting to practice without the required licenses. Ownership of land conveys some rights to use it to build a house or plant a garden, but those rights are usually subject to restrictions such as zoning ordinances, prohibitions on using certain pesticides, and regulations governing the burning of refuse in one's yard.

In defining, protecting, and enforcing property rights, the government acts as an "umpire," an important role discussed later in this chapter and in Chapter 10. Without an umpire, market activities might be controlled by force or violence, with goods and services going to the strongest rather than to those who produce them for exchange. Thus, defining, protecting, and enforcing property rights are the most basic and essential function of government in a market system.

Competition A market situation characterized by a sufficiently large number of buyers and sellers so that no single buyer or seller can influence prices or quantities sold or bought in the market.

Competition The second essential feature of efficient markets is competition. To an economist, **competition** means the presence of a sufficiently large number of buyers and sellers in a particular market so that no single buyer or seller can significantly affect market prices and quantities. Without competition, a single seller, or a small number of sellers, could take advantage of its position to obtain higher prices for what it sells and lower prices for what it buys than would be the case if it had less market power. Strong competition from many buyers and sellers of the product helps prevent either side from having undue power to control the bargain.

Different markets enjoy different degrees of competition. Competitive markets are discussed in Chapter 7. The power of firms and individuals to control price when competition is weak or nonexistent and efforts by government to increase competition are described in Chapter 8.

In Practice 3-1

....

Social Infrastructure and Markets in Eastern Europe

The term *infrastructure* has become a part of American vocabulary, referring to roads, bridges, schools, and public buildings in need of repair, modernization, or replacement. The term is also commonly used to describe the nation's shared public sector capital. Along with our physical infrastructure, however, we share a social infrastructure that we take for granted but is essential to a modern market economy. That social infrastructure includes laws governing bankruptcy, inheritance, property transfers, enforcement of contracts, and resolution of property disputes; a banking system to provide convenient money transactions and a way to transfer funds from savers to lenders; stock and bond markets to transfer ownership rights and debt obligations among citizens; and a host of federal, state, and local regulations such as labeling requirements, safety rules, building codes, zoning regulations, parking rules, sign regulations, speed limits, and business licenses. These features are the social infrastructure of a market system. They spell out property rights and property responsibilities in considerable detail and keep an army of lawyers, judges, boards, and commissions busy interpreting, revising, and enforcing the rules of the game.

Central and Eastern Europe, from Poland to Bulgaria and throughout the successor nations to the former Soviet Union, had a very limited social infrastructure because citizens had little private property to bequeath, transfer, or use in productive ways that might have run afoul of government rules. With the transition to a market economy, the discovery of the need for such rules has come as a surprise to many citizens of formerly communist countries. In market economies, people accept the fact that such rules restrict one person's freedom to protect the rights of others. In Central Europe, however, the initial reaction was that a free market implies unrestricted rights to own and use property as one sees fit. Property rights hedged with rules, licenses, fees, and obligations are not these people's idea of a free market.

Most of these countries have absorbed the shock, however, and are now dealing with such pressing matters as developing banks and stock markets, defining property rights, selling off public property to private owners, writing contract and inheritance laws, and developing zoning regulations and building codes for the emerging private sector. The social infrastructure Westerners take for granted may be new to Eastern and Central Europe, but as markets and private property emerge, leaders in these countries are recognizing the need to more clearly define and enforce the rights of buyers, sellers, and owners in the marketplace. ■

CHECKLIST : **What Markets Are and How They Work**

Markets provide society with

- A forum for exchange
- Information, especially price information
- Direction for producing goods and services
- Answers to *what, how,* and *for whom* questions

To function efficiently, markets need

- Clearly defined property rights
- A property rights umpire (government)
- Competition

HOUSEHOLDS, BUSINESS FIRMS, AND GOVERNMENTS

The economy is one vast network of markets—particular markets for construction workers, pizza, running shoes, college educations, and all kinds of other goods, services, and resources. The sum total of all these microeconomic markets is the macroeconomy, or the aggregate level of economic activity. A useful way to visualize how these specific markets add up to the total market economy is the *circular flow*. This visual model offers a very broad, general view of an economy in which households and business firms interact in markets to determine the size and composition of output.

The idea of a circular flow diagram came from a group of French economists in the eighteenth century who saw an analogy between the flows in the economy and the flows of blood through the body. The original circular flow diagram was called the *tableaux économique*. The modern version is a useful descriptive tool for examining the economic relationships among households, businesses, and governments. The simplest circular flow describes a pure market economy in which all decisions are made by households and businesses; that is, there is no government.

The household sector consists of individuals living together in economic units. Economic decisions are made by both individuals and groups (families, communes, or roommates) that economists lump together under the term **households.** Households own all the productive resources in a purely market economy. General Motors "owns" factories, warehouses, and assembly lines, but GM itself is owned by its stockholders. In a market system with no government, households own all productive resources directly or indirectly.

Households sell or rent the services of their productive resources (land, labor, capital, and enterprise) to businesses to earn income. Firms purchase the services of productive resources, paying wages and salaries to owners of labor services, rent to landowners, interest to owners of capital, and profits to entrepreneurs.

The sale of resource services is the sole source of household income. On the other side, payments for those resources make up the total expenses of business firms. Buyers (firms) and sellers (households) come together to exchange resources and payments in the **resource market.** Most household income by far comes from wages and salaries (almost 80 percent in the United States). The income a household receives determines the share of total output that household can claim in the market. This distribution of income among households provides the answer to the question *for whom to produce*.

Households are populated by practical economists who try to get the maximum satisfaction (consumption and leisure) through the careful use of their available productive resources. Maximizing, minimizing, self-interested behavior, and response to incentives are all apparent in the circular flow.

Firms such as grocery stores, bike shops, steel producers, and oil refineries make up the business sector. **Firms** combine the services of the productive resources

Household An economic unit consisting of an individual or group of individuals (such as a family) who share ownership of productive resources and engage in joint consumption decisions.

Resource market The collection of markets in which households sell the services of their productive resources to businesses for use in production.

Firm An entity that organizes production by buying productive resources, combining them to produce output, and selling that output to customers (households, other firms, and governments).

Product market The collection of markets in which firms sell final goods and services to customers.

Circular flow A visual representation of how households and businesses (and governments) interact in resource and product markets to create corresponding flows of income and output.

they purchase from households to produce goods and services households desire. The mix of resources they use is the answer to the *how to produce* question.

The revenue firms receive from selling their products enables them to pay households for the resources firms use. The sale of goods and services by firms to households in exchange for revenue takes place in the **product market**. The mix of goods and services households choose to buy determines the answer to the *what to produce* question.

A Circular Flow Model of Economic Activity

The interaction of households and firms in resource and product markets creates a **circular flow** of economic activity. In resource markets (the lower half of Figure 3-2), firms pay wages, rent, interest, and profits in exchange for the services of households' resources. Resource markets consist of many individual markets, such as the markets for bricklayers, basketball players, factory buildings, machine tools, and farmland. Resource prices and quantities in those markets result from the individual decisions of buyers and sellers (practical economists) engaged in self-interested, maximizing behavior and responding to incentives.

The upper half of the circular flow in Figure 3-2 represents product markets. In these markets, households bid for goods and services in exchange for income. Like the resource market, product markets consist of many markets, such as the markets for bread, Nintendo video games, baseball tickets, rental housing, and pizza. The prices and quantities in these markets are the results of sales and purchases by many individual buyers and sellers (practical economists) acting in their own self-interest.

These individual markets and the prices and quantities they determine are the heart and soul of microeconomics. It is in these individual markets that society pursues the microeconomic goals of economic efficiency, distributional equity, and economic freedom.

The size of the total flow of resources and of goods and services represents total income (in resource markets) and total output (in product markets). Measuring and analyzing these aggregate flows and developing ways to control their size is the essence of macroeconomics. Managing the total flow of income and output is the key to pursuing the macroeconomic goals of economic growth, full employment, and price stability, which we discuss beginning in Chapter 11.

The Economic Role of Households

The household is really a minibusiness. Households earn income from selling the use of their productive resources to business firms and use that income to buy goods and services in the product market. Households themselves produce goods, combining labor with purchased "household capital" such as houses, cars, ovens, dishwashers, and lawn mowers to produce shelter, transportation,

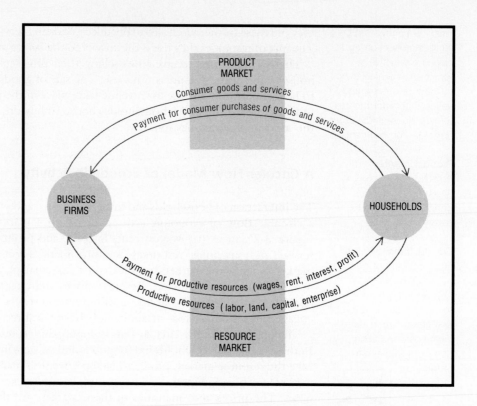

FIGURE 3-2

The lower half of this simple circular flow diagram shows the resource market, in which households sell their productive resources to firms. Households use the income they receive in the resource market to buy goods and services from firms in the product market.

meals, clean dishes, and attractive lawns for their own consumption. In more developed economies, household production tends to be undercounted in the circular flow because it does not pass through markets and create measured sales, jobs, and income, even though these home-produced goods and services are very important activities.

In many developing countries, an even larger share of production takes place within the household. When you consider the size of the flow in the circular flow diagram for such countries, keep in mind that much of the productive activity in those countries is not measured in official statistics because it does not pass through the resource and product markets. Thus, output and income statistics for developing countries may understate the actual levels of well-being, production, and consumption. Some understatement occurs even in U.S. statistics.

Household Income and the Resource Market   Most of the productive activity of households in developed industrial countries takes place outside the home, placing the services of the household's productive resources at the disposal of business firms. A household that owns a larger quantity of productive resources, or particular productive resources in great demand by those firms, can earn a higher income.

As we saw in Chapter 2, a household can increase its income in the same way a nation promotes economic growth. Households can divert resources from producing income for current consumption and use them instead to improve labor skills through education and training (increase their human capital) or to acquire additional capital or land resources with which to generate a larger income in the future.

Income depends not only on the productive resources households own but also on how much of those resources they offer in the resource market. Families with more than one earner have higher incomes, but they usually enjoy less leisure and less production occurs within the household. These families eat in restaurants more often instead of cooking at home and tend to use more day-care and house-cleaning services.

Household Spending and the Product Market While some sales occur among business firms, the primary customers for firms' goods and services are households. How households decide to divide their incomes between housing and clothing, food and recreation, and cars and boats, and what quality and variety of each commodity they want, answers the basic economic question of what to produce.

The U.S. Department of Labor gathers information at regular intervals on how consumers spend their incomes. Table 3-1 shows how the typical U.S. household divided its income among broad categories of competing uses as reported in the most recent survey of consumer spending patterns, conducted in 1987.[1]

As mentioned earlier, households are made up of practical economists who engage in self-interested, maximizing behavior in both resource and product markets. In resource markets, households attempt to maximize the income they earn from their productive resources by searching among competing firms for the one that will pay the highest price for their labor, land, capital, or enterprise. These prices provide incentives to which households can respond.

Households consider not only income (and consumption made possible from that income) but also leisure, working conditions, and job satisfaction in making decisions about allocating their productive resources. These considerations are part of the maximizing problem households face in resource markets.

In product markets, households allocate their income (earned in resource markets) among competing goods and services in a way that maximizes their consumption satisfaction. Again price signals play an important role. Consumers

[1]Data from the 1991–1992 survey will be available in 1995.

TABLE 3-1   Household Consumption Patterns, 1986–1987

| Category | Income Spent on Each Category | |
	Average Dollar Spending	**Percentage of Total Consumption**
Food	$3,914	19.4%
Housing*	6,030	29.8
Transportation	5,197	25.7
Clothing	1,061	5.2
Medical care	819	4.0
Entertainment	1,172	5.8
Other consumption	1,235	6.1
Total consumption	20,226	100
Savings and taxes	7,350	
Total income	27,576	

*Includes utilities and household operations.

Source: *Monthly Labor Review,* March 1990. The surveys on which these figures are based are conducted every five years.

choose the best combination of goods and services they can obtain from their limited incomes on the basis of the prices they face and given their preferences.

Households actually exchange the use of productive resources for consumer goods and services, but the process is more roundabout—and more efficient—because of specialization and the use of money income they receive in resource markets and spend in product markets. It would be difficult to imagine a society without specialization, without markets, and without money income. The use of money greatly increases the ability of households to specialize and make exchanges in markets.

The Economic Role of Business Firms

If households own all the factors of production and earn all the income, what is the role of the business firm? Firms organize production by purchasing resources and combining them to produce goods and services to sell in product markets. They contribute in a vital way to making specialization and exchange possible.

Firms allow an economy to take advantage of the principle of comparative advantage on a large scale. While households can easily acquire the needed capital and skills and organize their own labor to cook meals and do laundry, they would find it more difficult to produce a car or a washing machine. Obviously these goods are produced more efficiently by bringing together specialized skills and large amounts of capital equipment.

Even on a smaller scale, for many families it is preferable to rely on firms to provide food, transportation, laundry services, and other goods and services that could be produced within the household. Remember, households and individuals can gain more total consumption by specializing in those activities in which they have a comparative advantage and exchanging their output for other goods and services. Firms play an important role in facilitating such specialization.

The role of the business firm is the mirror image of the household's role in resource and product markets. Business firms are buyers in resource markets and sellers in product markets. Like households, businesses depend on market prices to signal which resources to use and which products to produce and offer for sale.

Forms of Business Organization   A smaller firm is usually organized in one of two relatively simple forms: the proprietorship and the partnership. A **proprietorship** has a single owner who has complete control; he or she need not account to any stockholders. However, a proprietorship has only the wealth of the owner plus whatever funds it can borrow to invest in capital, which can limit both its initial size and potential growth. In addition, the proprietorship lasts only as long as the owner does, whereas a corporation can last forever. Finally, if the business fails, the sole proprietor is liable for any debts of the firm out of his or her personal assets.

The **partnership** is similar to the proprietorship except that it involves a formal agreement between two or more owners. Both (or all) partners may provide capital, or one or more may put up capital while another brings special skills or know-how to the organization. The partnership requires a formal agreement and can be difficult to reorganize if a partner dies or decides to take his or her capital out of the firm. Partnerships and proprietorships exist mainly in service and retail industries and are typically very small.

Although the vast majority of U.S. firms are organized as partnerships and proprietorships, the greatest amount of output (about 85 percent) is produced by firms organized as corporations. A **corporation** is owned by stockholders. The corporation sells ownership shares to stockholders, which entitle them to voting rights in management and a share of the business's profits (what remains from sales revenue after paying for inputs or productive resources).

A corporation can acquire more capital than a partnership or proprietorship can because it can finance that capital by issuing ownership shares (stock) to a large number of people, as well as by borrowing from banks and other financial institutions. In addition, the corporation has an important advantage over other kinds of firms in the form of **limited liability**. This means that if the firm suffers

Proprietorship A form of business organization in which there is a single owner who supplies capital and enterprise.

Partnership A form of business organization in which two or more owners pool their capital, enterprise, and other resources and share any profits or losses.

Corporation A form of business organization in which the firm is owned by many stockholders who have limited liability.

Limited liability A feature of a corporation that limits the losses of owners (stockholders) to the amount they paid for their stock.

losses and goes out of business, the losses of the stockholders are limited to the amount they paid for the stock.

Decision Making in the Firm   Every firm continuously makes decisions about which products to produce, in what quantities, and with which combination of inputs—some of the basic economic questions raised in Chapter 2. Each of these decisions involves reading a host of market economic signals that direct the firm's actions. We will examine those signals more closely in the next few chapters.

The firm decides what to produce on the basis of signals from the product market as consumers spend their incomes on various products and services. It determines how to produce from signals from the resource market. Should the production process be labor intensive, or should the firm be heavily automated, with a lot of capital equipment and relatively few workers? What materials should it use? Market signals, especially signals about the relative prices of various inputs, determine the choice of technology or method of production.

ADDING GOVERNMENT: THE THREE-SECTOR ECONOMY

Although the household and business sectors are the primary actors in a mixed market economy, there is another important player—a minor character in some economies, a central one in others. This is government, which directly makes many economic decisions and influences many private decisions. We already considered government in its role as a definer and defender of property rights. Now we need to add its role in the circular flow of income and output.

Government in the Circular Flow

In a simple modification of the circular flow diagram, government receives income through taxes on business firms and households and uses that income to purchase goods and services from firms. This three-sector market economy is represented in Figure 3-3. In this model, a portion of household income is diverted (see the middle of the diagram) to government in the form of taxes. (For simplicity, we assume all taxes are paid by households.) In addition, with government now in the picture, businesses have an additional buyer for output. Governments buy not only tanks and missiles but also concrete for dams, asphalt for roads, automobiles for government agencies, and paper (lots of it!).

In reality, the relationship among government, households, and businesses in the circular flow is much more complex than the simple addition of tax collections from households and purchases of business output. First, governments are often major producers of goods and services. Examples of government production in-

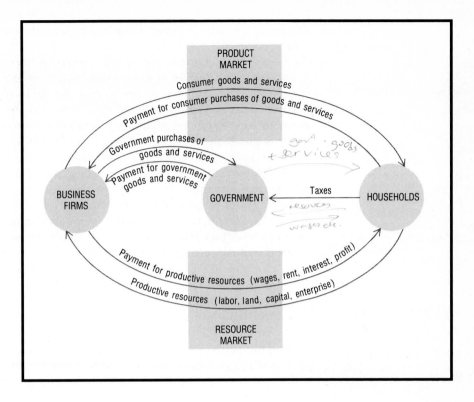

FIGURE 3-3

This circular flow model includes government. Government collects taxes from households, including business taxes, and purchases goods and services from business firms.

clude national defense, postal services, local subway transportation, public education, and police and fire protection. This production requires hiring the use of land, labor, and capital from households as well as buying inputs from business firms. Thus, there is a flow of both products from firms and productive resources from households to government and a flow of payments in the opposite direction.

Second, government makes payments to households for which no services or production is expected in return. These transfer payments include social security benefits, welfare, unemployment compensation, and veterans' benefits, all of which represent an additional income source for households. With the growth of the national debt, interest payments to households that have "lent" money to the government are another major flow of payments from governments to households.

To keep the circular flow diagram simple, we will ignore these complications for now. In Chapter 12, we will explore government production and transfer payments to households in more detail.

The Role of Government in a Market Economy

The need for government will become clearer in later chapters as we explore the workings of a market economy and learn what the market does well and where it fails. At a minimum, government needs to provide a framework of property rights and enforcement of those rights to give markets a set of rules by which to operate. In addition, government collects taxes, purchases and produces goods and services, borrows money, and engages in other economic activities. Government actively promotes all of the economic goals identified in Chapter 2, particularly distributional equity, economic growth, price stability, and full employment.

The functions of government are generally sorted out into three categories: allocation, redistribution, and stabilization. (These functions are the subject of Chapter 11.) **Allocation** activities of government relate to the question of what to produce and the goal of allocative efficiency. Included in its allocation function is the government's role in producing goods and services that private firms cannot produce easily, such as national defense, preventing monopolies when possible, and regulating certain industries in which the market fails in various ways. **Redistribution** includes government efforts to alter the distribution of income through welfare, social security, farm price supports, and other income redistribution programs. **Stabilization** refers to government actions to promote both stable prices (reduce inflation) and full employment (help prevent recessions or depressions). Closely related to stabilization are government activities aimed at promoting economic growth. Stabilization and growth are the main policy focus of Part III of this book.

In an ideal world, the two private sectors (businesses and households) and the public sector (government) would each carry out their clearly defined functions to maximize the satisfaction and well-being of citizens. The two private sectors would do those things they do well, operating through the resource market and the product market to match up resources with products consumers want. When the market was unable to function adequately, the government would intervene to correct its shortcomings.

In the real world, the division of responsibilities between governments and markets is much fuzzier. In addition, government as well as markets can fail. In the next few chapters, we will explore how the market works and when and how the government intervenes.

Allocation A function of government related to producing goods and services or changing the mix of goods produced by the private sector.

Redistribution A function of government related to changing the distribution of income determined in the resource market.

Stabilization A function of government concerned with limiting fluctuations in prices, employment, and output.

Summary

1. Firms and households specialize in production according to their comparative advantages, that is, according to which kind of product or service they can produce with a lower opportunity cost than others. Specializing on the basis of comparative advantage will increase total output.

2. Specialization is possible only in the presence of markets—settings in which

exchange takes place. Markets function best with clearly defined property rights, competition, and adequate information, guided by the invisible hand.

3. The circular flow represents the economic interactions among households, business firms, and government. The activities of buying and selling the services of production, resources, organizing production, and buying and selling goods and services are described by the circular flow diagram, which identifies the various markets and the sizes of the total income and output flows.

4. The household sector owns all productive resources and sells the services of those resources to firms to use in producing goods and services.

5. Households earn income from selling the services of their resources and use that income to consume goods and services purchased from the business sector. The size of a household's income is determined by the quantity and quality of resources it owns and how much of them it makes available to the market.

6. Firms organize production and make decisions about what to produce, how to produce, and for whom to produce based on signals from the resource and product markets. Firms may be proprietorships, partnerships, or corporations.

7. The government provides a framework of property rights and enforcement that enables a market system to work. Government also corrects for the failings of the market and collects taxes to pay for its services.

8. The functions of government can be divided into those that affect the output and input mix (allocation), those that change the distribution of income (redistribution), and those that attempt to influence the total levels of output, prices, and employment (stabilization).

Key Terms

allocation	household	property rights
circular flow	invisible hand	proprietorship
comparative advantage	limited liability	redistribution
competition	market	resource market
corporation	partnership	stabilization
firm	product market	

Questions and Problems

1. Try adding some of the omitted items to the circular flow (e.g., the foreign sector, which sells imports to households and buys exports from business firms) or some of the additional payments to and from government (e.g., purchase of labor services from households, transfer payments to households).

2. Many functions of government involve both allocation and redistribution. How does each of the following affect the mix of inputs and outputs? Who receives how much income?

   a. Using tax revenue to pay a subsidy for cotton production
   b. Requiring emission controls on automobiles, which raises the prices consumers must pay for cars
   c. Requiring a sixteen-year-old to stay in school instead of working (Hint: Think about his or her opportunity cost)

3. Investment in human capital is a major reason for going to college. Look up in the *Occupational Outlook Handbook* the starting salaries for your chosen occupation. Estimate how much more you would earn when you graduate than you would had you taken a job right out of high school.

4. The following situation is very similar to that of our two hypothetical farmers, Johnson and Miller:

   Fred can produce 100 apples and 0 oranges or 50 oranges and 0 apples. Before he discovers Sue and the possibility of specialization and exchange, he is producing 50 apples and 25 oranges. Sue, who owns less land but lives in a warmer climate, can produce 40 apples and 0 oranges or 40 oranges and 0 apples. Before Fred appears on the scene, she is producing 30 apples and 10 oranges.

   a. Draw the production possibilities frontiers for Fred and Sue.
   b. Determine who should specialize in which product.
   c. Measure the increase in total output that results from specializing on the basis of comparative advantage.

5. Crusoe and Friday can either fish or gather coconuts. If each works a four-hour day, he will produce the following output before meeting the other:

	Fish	Coconuts
Crusoe	10	15
Friday	15	15

   Assume each worked two hours at each task, so that if he specializes in either fish or coconuts, he will produce twice as much of one and none of the other. Solve their problem of specialization and distribute the output so that both gain.

6. Which of the following markets in which you operate has much competition and good information? Who are the competitors? Where and how is the information supplied?

    a. Off-campus housing

    b. Pizza

    c. Textbooks

    d. Telephone service

    e. Video rentals

7. Suppose you want to open a video rental store.

    a. Would you choose the proprietorship, partnership, or corporation form of business organization? Why?

    b. How and why might your answer differ if you were setting up a publishing firm instead of a video rental store. What if you planned to open a chain of video rental stores?

8. What property rights does an owner of a house enjoy? What restrictions does government place on the owner's property rights?

9. Explain how each of the following regulations is a form of protection of property rights:

    a. Residential zoning (no fast-food establishments in the neighborhood)

    b. Leash laws for dogs

    c. No burning leaves or trash inside city limits

    d. A limit of one-hour parking on Main Street

10. Often a college lacks enough openings in a particular course to meet all students' demand. Is price used to ration spaces at your school? If not, what methods are used to decide who gets into Economics 101 or an English or history course?

II

Microeconomics Concepts

4

Demand, Supply, and

Market Equilibrium

I am like any other man. All I do is supply a demand.

AL CAPONE

Main Points

1. **Market prices provide information essential for markets to work.** Prices reflect the relative values (scarcity) of both goods and resources. They also provide a way to ration scarce goods among consumers. Finally, changes in price signal consumers and producers to change consumption and production patterns.

2. **Demand describes how much of a good consumers are prepared to buy at various possible prices.** Other things equal, they buy more at lower prices and less at higher prices. The entire demand schedule shifts when any of the demand determinants change.

3. **Supply describes the amounts of a good firms are prepared to sell at various possible prices.** Quantity supplied is positively related to price. The entire supply schedule shifts when any of the determinants of supply change.

4. **Buyers and sellers determine prices and quantities sold in markets through the forces of demand and supply.** The equilibrium price in a market is the price at which the quantity consumers want exactly matches the quantity firms supply. Temporary shortages and surpluses are rapidly eliminated as markets move toward equilibrium.

Because goods and services are scarce, they must be rationed somehow among competing users. A variety of methods could be used to ration scarce apples, for example. If only 50 apples were available, they could be rationed by giving them only to children or brown-eyed people; distributing them only to apple pie makers; handing them out on a first-come, first-served basis at a local government office; or auctioning them off to the highest bidders. Markets use the last approach. Consumers who are willing and able to bid the most—offer the highest price—indicate they are willing to give up more command over other goods to get some apples than anyone else.

In this chapter, we focus on how the market price mechanism serves as a means to ration scarce goods and services. We explore how prices express information about the wants of buyers as well as the opportunity costs of producers; why prices rise, fall, and come to rest at "normal" levels; and why persistent shortages and surpluses of certain goods and services sometimes occur. Although the price system is a less than perfect rationing device, it uses buyer and seller information very efficiently and is no more—and probably much less arbitrary—than alternative rationing mechanisms such as those just described.   ■

MARKET PRICES AS SIGNALS TO GUIDE EXCHANGE

People exchange both goods and resources in markets primarily on the basis of price information. Prices are determined by the interactions of many buyers and sellers in these markets. Market prices reflect the relative values of goods and resources, ration goods and resources among competing consumers and competing producers, and signal consumers and producers to increase or decrease consumption or production of particular goods when the relative prices of those goods change.

Market prices are sometimes called *relative prices* because they represent the price of one good relative to another, or the rates at which goods and services exchange for one another. If the market price of a tennis racket is $60 and an economics textbook sells for $30, one tennis racket is worth two textbooks (or, equivalently, one textbook is worth one-half of a tennis racket). Prices also measure the relative value (scarcity) of resources used to produce goods and services in the long run. For example, the resources used to produce the $60 tennis racket are twice as valuable as those used to make the $30 textbook. If this were not the case, producers would see a profit opportunity in shifting resources to produce more of one good or the other. If tennis rackets sold for twice the price of textbooks but both had the same resource cost, textbook publishers would soon decide to use their labor, capital, and other resources to produce tennis rackets and earn twice as much using the same resources as before. Remember, publishers are practical economists too! Ultimately the market prices of goods reflect the relative costs of the resources used to make them. (This result is especially true in perfectly competitive markets, as you will see in Chapter 7.)

In addition to conveying information about scarcity, prices serve to ration goods among consumers and ration resources among producers. Consumers find that any good with a price above zero is scarce, and they must sacrifice other goods to be able to buy it. Goods are not free because they must be produced with scarce resources. Scarcity means BMW automobiles and boxes of Cheerios cereal must be rationed among competing consumers. The price mechanism is a rationing device that ensures that each product goes to those consumers wanting it most, that is, those willing to give up command over the largest amounts of other goods and services. One must be willing to spend $30,000 and up for a new BMW, which means sacrificing a great many other goods. Only those willing and able to make that sacrifice get such a car.

Relative price changes also perform an important signaling function. Price changes signal both consumers and producers to take some kind of action. When the price of a good increases, consumers buy less of it and they substitute other goods in its place. Thus, a higher price not only signals consumers to switch to substitutes but also results in conservation of the scarce resources used to make that good. A price decrease, on the other hand, acts like a green light: it signals that a particular good is now less scarce and can be substituted for other goods that are now relatively more expensive.

Suppose a nuclear reactor meltdown near a population center was of such a magnitude that power companies nationwide were forced to shut down all of their nuclear generating plants. Electricity prices would surely rise, and consumers could respond to that price signal with a variety of actions. In the short run (to save money), they would turn thermostats in their homes and offices down in winter and up in summer, switch off their backyard security lights, and buy more sweaters. Given more time in the long run, they might install gas furnaces in their homes and replace old refrigerators with new, better-insulated ones. A 1972 refrigerator used 1,500 kilowatt hours (kwh) of electricity each year, but 1992 models averaged about 900 kwh annually and one 1993 model uses only 540 kwh per year. In this and similar situations, consumers would behave as practical economists by making changes that were in their own self-interest (and the nation's as well).

Producers also respond to price signals. For example, IBM, Wang, Texas Instruments, Radio Shack (Tandy), Compaq, NCR, and Apple produced personal computers in a market that emerged less than 20 years ago. With so many competing producers facing continuous technological advances in computer chip design, computer prices have fallen steadily. These falling prices signaled some producers, including Texas Instruments, Wang, and NCR, to stop making personal microcomputers and shift their resources to making other products.

Thus, changes in product prices cause firms to respond by producing less of a product as its relative price falls and more when its price rises.

CHECKLIST : The Functions of Market Prices

Prices, determined by buyers and sellers in markets, serve to

- *Provide information:* Prices indicate the relative values of goods, services, and resources.
- *Ration goods:* Prices ration goods among competing consumers and ration resources among competing firms because both consumers and firms are unable to buy as much of every good or resource that they want.
- *Signal buyers and sellers:* Relative price changes cause consumers and producers to change their economic behavior, consuming and producing more or less of a good as its price falls or rises.

DEMAND: CONSUMERS' DESIRES FOR GOODS AND SERVICES

Just as it takes two to do the Texas two-step, it takes both the forces of consumer demand and producer supply operating in markets to determine prices. However, economists separate these two forces—the two sides of markets—and study them individually so that they may more easily understand the price mechanism. Following opportunity cost, the concepts of demand and supply are the most useful—and the most often used—tools in the economist's analytical kit.

The Demand Curve

Demand A schedule of the amounts of a good a consumer is both willing and able to buy at all possible prices in a given time period.

Demand curve A curve, sloping downward from left to right, that graphically represents a demand schedule.

Consumers express their desires for goods and services only by actually buying them. Wishful thinking doesn't count! For example, you might want a Lear jet, but the market price of these aircraft will not reflect your desire unless you purchase one. Market prices are influenced only by those consumer desires actually expressed through purchases.

The willingness of consumers to buy specific goods and services is represented by demand. **Demand** is a schedule (or table) showing the amounts of a good consumers are willing and able to buy at various prices during a particular period of time. A **demand curve** is a graphical representation of a demand schedule.

The demand for compact discs, given in Table 4-1, illustrates a demand schedule for a consumer named Anne. This schedule tells how many compact discs Anne would actually buy if any of those prices prevailed in the market. Anne obviously has a special love for recorded music, but even so the quantity she demands at a

TABLE 4-1   Anne's Demand for Compact Discs

Price per Disc	Quantity Demanded per Month
$ 0	20
6	16
12	12
18	8
24	4
30	0

price of zero is limited to 20 compact discs per month, not an infinite amount. If compact discs were free (as indicated by the zero price), she apparently would still find uses for only 20 new ones each month (or 240 per year)—to listen to, give as birthday presents, and so on. At a price of $30 each, however, Anne would buy no CDs at all; she would prefer to spend her money on other goods. Between these two extremes, Anne's demand schedule says she would buy a decreasing quantity of compact discs at each successively higher price.

Finally, Anne's demand for compact discs is valid only for a specific time period, in this instance each month. If a different time period, such as a week, a year, or a lifetime were specified, the quantity demanded at each possible price obviously would be quite different.

The Law of Demand

Law of demand The principle that the quantity demanded of a good is negatively related to the good's price.

Anne's demand curve for compact discs is drawn in Figure 4-1, which graphs her demand schedule from Table 4-1. As you can see, demand curves slope downward to the right, reflecting the law of demand. The **law of demand** says that the quantity demanded of a good is negatively related to the good's price. At higher prices, buyers demand smaller amounts per time period; at lower prices, they demand larger amounts. Anne's demand curve shows that she would buy only 4 compact discs each month at the $24 price but would increase her purchases to 12 discs per month if the price were $12.

Price and quantity demanded are negatively related for two reasons. First, price is an obstacle to consumption. It represents the other goods one must sacrifice to purchase a given good; thus, it represents opportunity cost. The higher the price of a good, the greater its opportunity cost in terms of other goods that must be given up, and the less consumers want to buy. This higher opportunity cost encourages consumers to substitute other goods. For example,

FIGURE 4-1

This demand curve repre-
sents Anne's demand for
compact discs. At a price of
$18, she buys 8 discs each
month. At $12 price, her
quantity demanded in-
creases to 12 discs per
month. Anne's quantity
demanded increases with
lower prices and decreases
with higher prices, illustrating the law of demand.

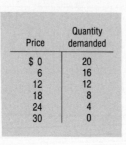

Price	Quantity demanded
$ 0	20
6	16
12	12
18	8
24	4
30	0

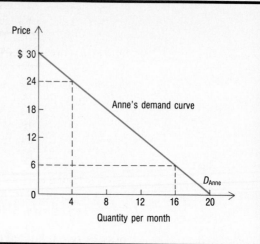

if the price of a movie ticket were $10 instead of $7, either bowling or renting a movie might be a more attractive substitute; thus, consumers would buy fewer movie tickets.

The second reason for the negative relationship between price and quantity demanded is that consumers' incomes will not go as far when they buy a good at a higher price. As a result, at a higher price consumers cannot afford to buy as much of it. One reason fewer movie tickets will be sold at a $10 price is that people who do buy at that price use up their entertainment budgets faster and thus cannot go to as many movies per month. In other words, paying a higher price for some amount of a good effectively reduces consumer income because it takes more dollars to buy a given quantity at a higher price. When the price of one good rises, consumers are forced to buy less of all the goods they usually buy, including that good.

Rising health-care costs dramatically illustrate the two-part foundation for the law of demand. As the prices of health-care services rise—higher doctor fees, higher charges for x-rays and diagnostic tests, and soaring hospital room charges—fewer units of health care are bought (per person per year). When the price of insurance also rises, consumers drop their insurance coverage and visit doctors less frequently, and then only for serious illness. They avoid going to hospitals if outpatient treatment and home recovery are possible alternatives. They buy more books on home remedies and substitute self-treatments for some illnesses. They also reduce health-care consumption partly because the higher prices for doctor and hospital services they still must use soak up more of their incomes. Thus, Americans simply cannot afford to purchase as much of everything, including health care, as they could before the prices of those services rose.

The law of demand is a "law" in the same sense that the universal attraction of two masses is called the law of gravity. As far as we know, it seems to work in all cases. Sometimes people deny the existence of the law of demand by describing exceptions. One obvious example is the "snob effect," which suggests that *more* can be sold at higher prices. Some people do buy designer dresses, trips to the Cayman Islands, Rolls Royces, or Rolex watches because they want others to think they have the income and good taste to buy such expensive goods and services. However, even Rolex watches obey the law of demand. Very few Rolexes are sold at $1,200 and up; wouldn't many, many more be sold if the price were lowered to $300 or $179? The fact that some people buy prestige as well as a timepiece when they buy a Rolex does not invalidate the law of demand.

Some people also deny that the law of demand applies to certain goods that are "needed" because consumers are expected to buy them at any price. In other words, they argue that quantities demanded of those goods do not fall as their prices rise. It is easy to confuse "want" with "need," however. Even heroin addicts respond to price increases by consuming less heroin and substituting methadone or alcohol part of the time. People want cheap electricity so they can heat their homes at low cost. However, higher prices will encourage consumers to reduce electricity consumption by substituting more home insulation, double-pane-windows, energy-efficient refrigerators and water heaters, and wood-burning fireplaces for more electricity, as well as by keeping thermostats lower in winter and higher in summer. Thus, like other goods, even an apparent "necessity" such as electricity obeys the law of demand: its demand curve slopes downward to the right.

Individual versus Market Demand

Market demand The sum of all individual consumers' demand schedules for a good in a particular market.

The **market demand** for a good or service is simply the sum of the demand of all consumers in a particular market at each possible price. Figure 4-2 shows a market demand curve for compact discs obtained by summing two individual demand curves horizontally (assuming a two-person market). Anne's and Bill's quantities demanded at each price are added together. Their combined quantity demanded in this market is six compact discs at a price of $24 and eighteen discs at $12.

SUPPLY: PRODUCERS' OFFERS OF GOODS AND SERVICES

Demand is only part of the story of how market prices are determined. How the quantities supplied by firms are related to price is the other component.

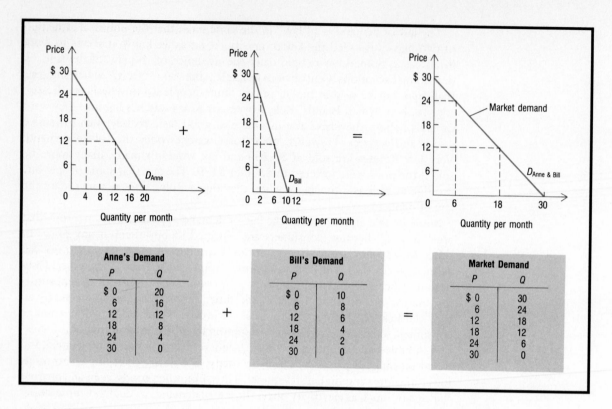

FIGURE 4-2

The market demand curve is the sum of the individual demand curves of all the consumers in a market. If Anne and Bill are the only buyers, the market demand curve for compact discs consists of the sum of the amounts each would buy at each possible price. At a price of $12, Anne buys 12 discs and Bill buys 6; thus, 18 is the total quantity demanded in the market at that price.

Supply A schedule of the amounts of a good a firm is both willing and able to offer for sale at all possible prices in a given time period.

Now let's consider the other side of the market by examining the behavior of producers as they supply the goods and services consumers want.

The Supply Curve

Supply curve A curve, sloping upward from left to right, that graphically represents a supply schedule.

The amount of goods and services firms make available in the marketplace depends on the prices those firms expect to receive. Supply expresses this relationship between amounts supplied and market prices. **Supply** is a schedule (or table) showing the amounts of a good producers are both willing and able to offer for sale at various prices during a particular period of time. A **supply curve** is simply a graphical representation of a supply schedule.

Like *demand*, the term *supply* refers to a schedule of price and quantity combinations. The quantity of compact discs Hot Sound, Inc., offers at different prices (Table 4-2) is an example of supply. Notice that Hot Sound is unwilling to offer any compact discs in the market when the price is $6 or less, but will rev up production to 24 CDs per month when the price is $30. Remember too that these quantities supplied at various prices represent what this recording company would actually do. Like demand schedules, supply schedules describe real action rather than wishful thinking. Further, supply is defined for a specific time period. Certainly the amounts Hot Sound offers at each price would be quite different if the time period considered were a week or a year instead of a month.

The Law of Supply

Hot Sound's supply curve for compact discs is drawn in Figure 4-3, which graphs the supply schedule given in Table 4-2. Unlike demand curves, supply curves slope upward to the right, reflecting the law of supply. The **law of supply** says that quantity supplied per time period is positively related to price. Firms offer smaller amounts for sale at lower prices, and larger amounts at higher prices in search of greater profits.

Law of supply The principle that quantity supplied of a good is positively related to the good's price.

Although price is an obstacle to consumption, it is the reward for production. Higher prices bring forth larger quantities in the market for two reasons. First, higher prices provide extra funds for producers to buy more productive resources to increase production. Recall the law of increasing cost from Chapter 2. It costs more per unit to produce additional amounts of a good in a given time period. It takes a higher price for a good to induce firms to bid increasingly expensive resources away from other uses to produce more of that good. Second, higher prices usually create profit opportunities that attract still more producers into the industry.

Consumers saw a good example of a supply curve that slopes upward to the right after Iraq invaded Kuwait on August 2, 1990. Following the invasion, the United Nations imposed sanctions on Iraq and prohibited other nations from buying oil from both Iraq and occupied Kuwait. The initial lost production in the world oil market amounted to 4.3 million barrels of oil per day. This initial

TABLE 4-2 Hot Sound's Supply of Compact Discs

Price per Disc	Quantity Supplied per Month
$ 0	0
6	0
12	6
18	12
24	18
30	24

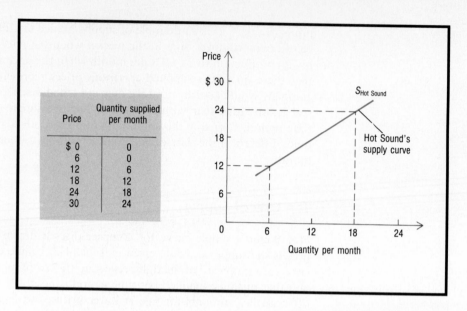

FIGURE 4-3

This supply curve represents Hot Sound's supply of compact discs. At a price of $12 the firm offers 6 discs for sale each month (quantity supplied = 6). At $18, Hot Sound increases its quantity supplied to 12 discs. Hot Sound's quantity supplied increases with higher prices and decreases with lower prices, illustrating the law of supply.

lost production, however, caused world oil prices to rise from $23 to $32 per barrel. The higher prices saved the day.

What do you think happened at the higher price? Other oil producers picked up the slack! On August 31 (just 29 days after the invasion), *The New York Times* reported that the actual amount of oil available in the world market remained almost the same. At the higher price, other large oil-exporting nations increased their production by 1.3 million barrels per day. Indian and Malaysian reserves contributed 0.4 million barrels daily, and Mexico and the industrial nations increased their production by 0.4 million barrels. Those who responded to the higher price added back 4.2 million barrels of the 4.3 million lost to the trade sanctions.[1]

At dramatically higher prices, many suppliers were willing and able to increase production from old oil wells and open up reserves and stocks put aside for this purpose. The higher price compensated them enough to bring less efficient wells "online" now and plan future expenditures to discover new wells to replace reserves and stocks drawn down now. At higher prices, firms can afford to use new recovery techniques and can drill deeper wells and explore more remote areas. The law of supply—that quantities supplied of any economic good increase with higher prices and decrease with lower prices—is a law in the same sense as Newton's laws of motion.

[1]Steven Greenhouse, "Filling the Void," *New York Times,* August 31, 1990, pp. D1 and D4.

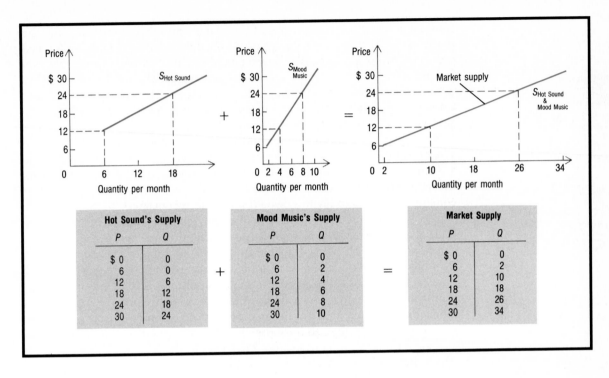

FIGURE 4-4

The market supply curve is the sum of the individual supply curves of all the producers in a market. If Hot Sound and Mood Music are the only firms producing compact discs, the market supply curve is the sum of the amounts each would offer at each possible price. At $24 Hot Sound supplies 18 discs and Mood Music offers 8; total quantity supplied at that price is 26 compact discs.

Firm versus Market Supply

Market supply The sum of all individual producers' supply schedules for a good in a particular market.

Market supply is the horizontal sum of the individual supply schedules of firms producing a particular good or service. The market supply curve for compact discs in Figure 4-4 is the result of adding together the amounts supplied at each price by two firms, Hot Sound and Mood Music. The quantity supplied in this two-firm market is 10 CDs per month at $12 and 26 CDs at $24.

Equilibrium The state of a market in which both price and quantity are at rest because quantity demanded and quantity supplied are equal at the current price.

EQUILIBRIUM: MARKET-CLEARING PRICES AND QUANTITIES

The two halves of the market—demand and supply—must be combined to determine equilibrium prices and quantities. A market is in **equilibrium** at that price at which the amount producers want to supply exactly matches the amount consumers want to buy. That price is known as the *equilibrium price,* and the *market-clearing amount*—the equal quantities demanded and supplied—is called the *equilibrium quantity.* The market tends to be "at rest" in equilibrium, making price constant because buyers are able to get exactly the amount they want at the equilibrium price and sellers are able to sell exactly their preferred amount. The equilibrium price (and the equilibrium quantity clearing the market) will stay the same until either demand or supply changes.

How are the equilibrium price and quantity established in a market? The adjustment toward market equilibrium is best described with an example. Table 4-3 combines the information from our previous compact disc examples, using the market demand and supply schedules derived in Figures 4-2 and 4-4. What equilibrium price and quantity would prevail in this market?

The compact disc market clears only at the equilibrium price of $15, where both quantity demanded and quantity supplied are equal at 15 compact discs per month. At prices below equilibrium, like $6, consumers demand more CDs than firms are willing and able to supply, creating a temporary shortage of 22 discs each month (24 demanded but only 2 supplied). Since CDs quickly disappear from store shelves under these circumstances, consumers offer store clerks more (bid the price up) to try to get a few more compact discs whenever the store has some available. As price rises, some consumers drop out of the market and some firms step up production. Price rises to the $15 equilibrium price, at which the temporary shortage no longer exists. At this higher price, consumers want fewer discs (15 instead of 24) and firms produce more (15 instead of 2). Thus, actions of both buyers and sellers serve to eliminate the temporary shortage and establish an equilibrium quantity that clears the market.

At above-equilibrium prices, on the other hand, the quantity firms supply exceeds the quantity consumers demand in the market, creating temporary surpluses. Again consumers and firms eliminate the problem over time. They behave as practical economists, simply pursuing their own self-interest and

TABLE 4-3 Equilibrium in the Compact Disc Market

Price	Quantity Demanded per Month	Quantity Supplied per Month	Temporary Shortage (−) Surplus (+)
$ 0	30	0	− 30
6	24	2	− 22
12	18	10	− 8
15	**15**	**15**	**0**
18	12	18	+ 6
24	6	26	+ 20
30	0	34	+ 34

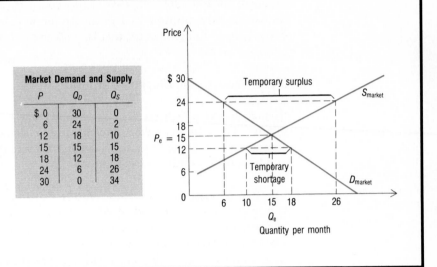

FIGURE 4-5

The equilibrium price in this market is $15, at which consumers want to buy 15 compact discs each month and producers want to sell exactly that number. At a price of $24, there is a temporary surplus of 20 discs because consumers want only 6 whereas firms supply 26. At a price of $12, there is excess demand, or a temporary shortage of 8 compact discs each month.

Market Demand and Supply

P	Q_D	Q_S
$ 0	30	0
6	24	2
12	18	10
15	15	15
18	12	18
24	6	26
30	0	34

maximizing. At the $24 price, firms want to sell 26 compact discs each month, but consumers want to buy only 6. The temporary surplus is the difference between quantity supplied and quantity demanded, or 20 compact discs. Firms will reduce their price to sell some of their surplus discs at the end of the month, causing firms to produce less and consumers to buy more. Actions on both sides of the market wipe out the temporary surplus as price falls, ultimately establishing the equilibrium price of $15 and the equilibrium quantity of 15 discs per month.

The demand and supply curves in Figure 4-5 correspond to the compact disc example in Table 4-3 and illustrate a market in equilibrium. The equilibrium price and quantity are represented by the intersection of the demand and supply curves. This intersection occurs at the same equilibrium price and quantity as in the table: $15 and 15 discs per month.

In most markets equilibrium is rarely achieved for very long, because demand and supply curves constantly shift. Still, this supply and demand model shows how prices and quantities adjust in markets and the equilibrium values toward which they move at any given moment.

HOW DEMAND AND SUPPLY CURVES SHIFT

Price is the primary factor affecting how much consumers buy and how much firms produce, but it is not the only factor. Demand and supply curves reflect the relationship between price and quantity demanded, or price and quantity supplied, while holding all other factors constant (*ceteris paribus*). What other factors affect the positions of demand and supply curves? What happens to either curve if other things change, that is, if all else is *not* constant?

Determinants of Market Demand

Determinants of demand Independent variables—number of consumers, consumer tastes, consumer income, prices of related goods, and consumer expectations—that shift market demand schedules when they change.

Changes in several factors can cause demand to increase or decrease *independently* of price. These factors, called **determinants of demand,** are (1) the number of consumers, (2) consumers tastes, (3) consumer income, (4) the prices of related goods, and (5) consumer expectations.

Number of Consumers   Since market demand is the sum of the separate demand schedules of individual consumers, increasing the number of consumers increases market demand for any good, shifting the demand curve to the right. The market demand for housing, newspapers, fast-food burgers, haircuts, and almost everything else increases with additional population in an area. Fewer consumers, on the other hand, cause market demand to decrease. The phrase *demand shifts* means that the entire schedule of quantities demanded changes for each possible price.

For example, the demand curve for apple cider in Figure 4-6 would shift to the right, from D_0 to D_1, if the number of cider consumers in a market increased. If population declined, demand for cider would decrease, illustrated by a leftward shift (D_0 to D_2) in the market demand curve.

Given a standard, upward-sloping supply curve like that in Figure 4-6, an increase in demand will tend to raise both the equilibrium price (P_0 to P_1) and

FIGURE 4-6

An increase in consumer income, or an increase in one of the other determinants of demand, increases the amounts of apple cider demanded at every price, shifting the demand curve to the right from D_0 to D_1. A decrease in one determinant, such as consumer tastes, decreases demand for apple cider and shifts the demand curve to the left from D_0 to D_2. Increased demand increases both the equilibrium price and the equilibrium quantity; decreased demand lowers price and the quantity, clearing the market.

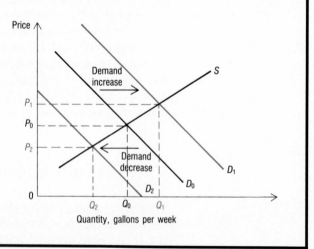

In Practice 4-1

. . . .

Nike Shoes, Body Building, and the Boot Scootin' Boogie

Really expensive basketball shoes, especially flashy-colored, high-top Nikes, captured America's youngsters in the early 1990s. Few urban (or rural) teenagers felt in style without a pair of these athletic shoes. Young adults carried on the fitness craze of the 1980s, but the early 1990s found them giving up Jane Fonda's aerobics lessons to pump iron in posh body-building gyms around the country. Currently, music consumers cannot get enough of Garth Brooks, Brooks and Dunn, and Billy Ray Cyrus, who have ushered in the phenomenal rise of country music, western dances, and silver belt buckles. Other fads have come and gone too: Cabbage Patch dolls, CB radios, hula hoops, and pet rocks.

Not all increases in demand for consumer products are fads, however. Fads are dramatic, short-run changes in consumer tastes in favor of certain products. Economists have no way to explain why certain products catch on and others do not, or why those that do eventually fade away. A fad causes demand for a particular product to increase significantly for a time, raising both prices and quantities sold as the rapidly shifting demand curve intersects the supply curve at higher points that are also farther to the right. Although output increases in response to higher prices, production typically cannot increase enough in the short run to keep prices from rising substantially. After the fad has run its course, demand begins to decrease, causing prices to fall back to (or below) prefad levels. The success of one such product spawns dozens of imitations, further reducing demand for the original product that initially started the fad.

Consider Billy Ray Cyrus and his hit song *Achy Breaky Heart,* which came out in early 1992. Cyrus captured the music charts with that song, but he was following on the heels of a country and western music revolution led by Garth Brooks. After *Achy Breaky Heart,* ticket prices for Cyrus concerts more than doubled to a nationwide average of more than $30 a seat. The Achy Breaky line dance also became popular, along with Brooks and Dunn's *Boot Scootin' Boogie.* More and more nightclubs around the country converted to western-style dance clubs. Many radio stations in major and minor markets switched from popular and rock programming to country and western formats.

During the Cabbage Patch doll craze of the 1980s, the dolls sold for as much as $100 each, but the price dropped to less than $20 two years later. Prices for albums, CDs, and personal appearances by some of today's country and western music stars can also be expected to fall as that craze fades. ∎

the equilibrium quantity (Q_0 to Q_1). A decrease in demand from (D_1 to D_2), on the other hand, tends to decrease both the equilibrium price and the equilibrium quantity (price falls to P_2 and quantity falls to Q_2). This will always be the case when demand curves shift (as long as supply slopes upward), regardless of what causes the shift in demand.

Consumer Tastes Economists include all consumer preferences for goods and services in the term *tastes.* Demand increases—greater amounts are demanded at each possible price—when consumer tastes for a particular good increase. For example, suppose consumers decide that apple cider is the "in" drink. When their tastes (preferences) change in favor of this beverage, the demand for apple cider increases and the good's demand curve shifts rightward from D_0 to D_1 in

Figure 4-6. At each possible price, consumers demand more apple cider than before the favorable change in tastes. This increase in demand causes the equilibrium price to increase to P_1 and the equilibrium quantity to increase to Q_1.

When consumer tastes change in the opposite direction for whatever reason, making a good less desirable, demand decreases. In Figure 4-6, D_2 represents the demand curve for apple cider after an unfavorable change in tastes for that good. The demand curve for apple cider shifts to the left, reducing the equilibrium price and quantity.

Consumer Income

More income indicates a greater ability to consume and therefore higher demand for most goods. Thus, demand curves for most goods shift to the right when consumer income increases. Similarly, lower consumer income reduces demand for most goods, shifting their demand curves to the left.

The shifts in demand for apple cider depicted in Figure 4-6 could result from changes in consumer income holding all the other determinants of demand constant. The shift to D_1 would be the result of an increase in consumer income, whereas the shift to D_2 would reflect a decrease in income.

Prices of Related Goods

Substitutes Goods that are similar in function or use so that when the price of one good changes, consumer demand for the other good changes in the same direction.

Consumer demand for a given item is affected by the prices of other, related goods and services. Goods may be related in consumption in two general ways. First, some goods may be **substitutes** for each other. Orange juice is a close substitute for apple cider, for example. What would happen to the demand for apple cider if the price of orange juice, a substitute, fell to just 10 cents per quart? Many people would want less apple cider, even though its price had not changed, because they would consume more orange juice instead. Demand for apple cider would decrease, shifting its entire demand curve to the left. Similarly, an increase in the price of a substitute good causes the demand for the other good to increase. If a winter freeze destroys the orange crop, forcing orange juice prices up, the demand for apple cider (as well as for lemonade, tomato juice, and other fruit drinks) will increase. In sum, increases (decreases) in the prices of substitutes cause the demand for related goods to increase (decrease).

Complements Goods that are consumed together so that when the price of one good changes, consumer demand for the other good changes in the opposite direction.

Second, related goods may be **complements** rather than substitutes. Complementary goods are goods that are consumed together. Examples are cereal and milk, gasoline and cars, and floppy disks and computers. What would happen to the demand for Cheerios if milk prices doubled? Demand for Cheerios would undoubtedly fall. On the other hand, when the price of a complementary good falls, demand for the related good increases. For example, the demand for automobiles (especially larger ones) increases as the price of gasoline falls.

Consumer Expectations

Consumers' expectations about future prices and their own incomes affect current demand for many goods and services. Suppose you expect the price of a product like apple cider to be much higher in a few months because newspapers report that apple borers have destroyed many orchards in Washington this month. Chances are you will stock up on apple cider right now to avoid the expected price increase. Thus, current demand for apple cider increases as you (and others) act on your expectations. Similarly, expectations that the price of a good will decline in the future can cause current demand to decrease.

The same is true for expectations about future income. If you expect your income to rise in the future (and most college students do), your current demand for goods and services increases. On the other hand, if you expect to be laid off next summer and earn a much lower income, you will reduce your demand for a variety of goods in the current period. Consumers' demand curves for most goods shift to the left as soon as consumers have reason to expect a lower future income.

CHEKLIST : **Determinants of Demand**

The primary determinants of demand—factors that cause shifts in demand curves when they change—are

- *The number of consumers:* More consumers mean increased demand, whereas fewer consumers cause demand to decrease.
- *Consumer tastes:* When tastes (preferences) change in favor of a good, demand for that good increases; when tastes for the good decline, demand decreases.
- *Consumer income:* Higher consumer income increases demand for most goods; lower income decreases demand.
- *Prices of related goods:* Higher prices for substitutes increase demand, and lower prices for substitutes decrease demand, for related goods; higher complement prices lower demand for related goods, and lower complement prices increase demand.
- *Consumer expectations:* Expectations of a higher future income increase demand now, whereas expectations of a lower income decrease demand; expectations of a lower future price cause demand to increase now, and expectations of a higher price increase demand.

Changes in Demand and Quantity Demanded

The distinction between changes in demand and changes in quantity demanded is one of the most important components of demand analysis. Demand is a schedule of price-quantity combinations. Thus, a *change in demand* means all the quantities in the schedule change for each price; that is, the demand curve shifts such that different quantities correspond to each possible price. This change in demand must be due to a change in one or more determinants of demand. For example, if purple shorts become popular (a change in tastes), the demand for purple shorts increases, resulting in an increase in the entire schedule of amounts demanded at each price. The shift in the entire demand curve from D_0 to D_1 in Figure 4-7 illustrates a change in demand.

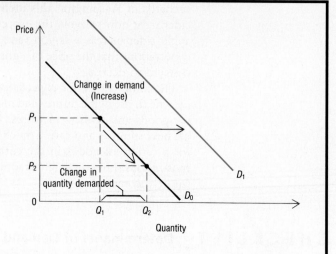

FIGURE 4-7

A *change in demand* refers to a shift in the entire demand curve. The movement of the demand curve from D_0 to D_1 represents an increase in demand in response to an increase in one or more determinants of demand. A *change in quantity demanded* refers to a movement from one amount demanded to another at a different price *on the same demand curve*. Quantity demanded increases from Q_1 to Q_2 along demand curve D_0 when price falls from P_1 to P_2.

A *change in quantity demanded*, however, occurs only when the *price* of a good changes. Fewer haircut-customers when barbers raise their prices is an example of a change in quantity demanded. Demand for haircuts (the schedule) has not changed, and the demand curve for haircuts has not shifted. Rather, changes in quantity demanded involve movements along the same demand curve from one price-quantity combination to another and are always the result of a change in price. Reducing price from P_1 to P_2 results in the change in quantity demanded indicated in Figure 4-7. Quantity demanded increases from Q_1 to Q_2 as price falls. Note that the curve is the same before and after the price change; thus, only quantity demanded changes, not demand.

Determinants of Market Supply

Price is the primary influence on quantity supplied as well as quantity demanded. The supply curve shows this relationship between price and quantities supplied while holding all other influences constant (*ceteris paribus*). Other factors, which affect quantities supplied independently of price, are called **determinants of supply**. These determinants are (1) the number of sellers, (2) resource prices, (3) prices of related goods in production, (4) technology, and (5) producer expectations.

Determinants of supply Independent variables—the number of producers, resource prices, prices of related goods in production, technology, and producer expectations—that shift market supply schedules when they change.

Number of Sellers   The number of firms supplying a particular good in a market affects market supply, since market supply is the sum of the supply schedules of individual producers. When additional firms enter a market, larger quantities of that good are available at all possible prices, shifting the market supply curve to the right. An increase in supply is illustrated by the shift from S_0 to S_1 in Figure 4-8. Similarly, supply decreases when firms leave a market, shifting the supply curve to the left from (S_0 to S_2 in Figure 4-8).

For example, suppose there are only two camera stores in Auburn, Alabama. If another store opens for business, more 35mm cameras will be available in that market than before, shifting the supply curve for 35mm cameras to the right. Given a standard, downward-sloping demand curve as in Figure 4-8, an increase in supply (S_0 to S_1) increases the equilibrium quantity (Q_0 to Q_1) clearing the market and lowers the equilibrium price (P_0 to P_1). In other words, combined camera sales of the three stores are up, but the price per camera is lower. A supply decrease (S_0 to S_2) raises equilibrium price but lowers the equilibrium quantity (Q_0 to Q_2).

Resource Prices When the prices of resources—land, labor, capital, or enterprise—used in a firm's production process increase, the supply of that firm's product decreases; that is, the entire supply schedule shifts to the left (from S_0 to S_2 in Figure 4-8) when resource prices increase. Higher production costs means firms are unwilling to offer as many units for sale as before at any given price.

Decreases in resource prices, on the other hand, reduce production costs, allowing supply to increase. Ever declining computer chip prices in the 1990s, for example, have reduced costs for firms that use computers and shifted their supply curves to the right in a variety of markets. Grocery stores of all sizes and even video rental stores can check out customers more rapidly using computers

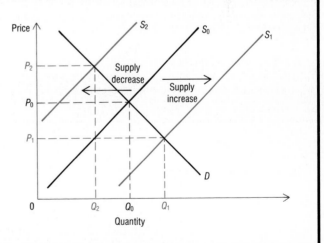

FIGURE 4-8

An increase in technology (or in one of the other determinants of supply) increases the amounts supplied at every price, shifting the supply curve to the right from S_0 to S_1. A decrease in the number of producers (or in another supply determinant) decreases supply, shifting the supply curve to the left from S_0 to S_2. Increases in supply (rightward shifts) lower equilibrium price and increase equilibrium quantity; decreases in supply (leftward shifts) raise price and lower equilibrium quantity.

······························

Myth 4-1

······························

"Middlemen Are Parasites"

Middlemen are regularly accused of unnecessarily driving up consumer prices. Farmers are fond of reporting that a $1.60 loaf of bread contains only $0.33 worth of wheat. But middlemen can actually *reduce* the opportunity cost of buying most goods.

Middlemen are wholesalers and retailers that buy goods from original producers and resell those goods to consumers in neighborhood stores. (Stockbrokers and real estate salespersons also fit in this category.) For example, an AC-Delco spark plug probably passes through several middlemen on its way to becoming part of your car's tune-up. After its manufacture in Flint, Michigan, or the Orient, it is sold for about 55 cents to a national warehousing and distributing firm. This distributor sells the spark plug to a regional jobber, another middleman, who goes on the road reselling it to independent auto parts stores, service stations, and auto repair garages. These final retailers then sell the spark plug (with or without installation) to you for about $2. Are these middlemen cheating you?

Here is the test: Do you pay more for goods when a middleman is involved? If you are a maximizing practical economist, of course you don't! You currently have the option of buying a spark plug directly from the factory where it was made by going to Flint or catching a plane to Korea. But this option would entail travel costs, the costs of acquiring supplier information in the first place, and the cost of your time. You could also buy from the West Coast distributor or the jobber traveling through

your state, but again the total costs would be too high. By choosing your local auto parts store or Wal-Mart, you demonstrate that your total opportunity cost of buying spark plugs through a series of middlemen is lower than it would be if you tried to bypass them. Middlemen—all those involved in our product distribution system—actually save you time and money!

Middlemen earn the amounts they add to a product's price because they add value to the product. They add the value of transportation to a retailer near your home and the value of the time and information search costs they save you. Buying a spark plug, when you consider the total opportunity cost of attempting to do so at the original source, is a lot cheaper because middlemen exist. ■

equipped with laser bar code scanners. They can keep track of their inventory at a much lower cost at the same time. Tax preparers now use cheaper computers to file tax returns for customers electronically. Book publishers typeset books from the disks sent in by authors. Because of the falling costs of computer resources, all these firms are able to increase their supply. This increased supply tends to lower price and raise the equilibrium quantities clearing each market.

Prices of Related Goods in Production   A firm can use resources to produce several goods and services other than the one it now produces, which we will call good *X*. When market prices of any of these related goods change, the supply of *X* changes (the supply curve for *X* shifts). Producers too are practical economists, responding to changing market signals in a self-interested way. For example, wheat farmers in Illinois can also use their labor and capital to produce a related good, corn. When the price of corn increases, the supply of wheat decreases because some wheat farmers switch to producing corn. Similarly, the supply of wheat increases if corn prices fall.

Technology   Changes in the techniques of production raise or lower production costs, which affect supply. An improvement in technology, like Henry Ford's assembly line, is a cost-saving innovation that enables firms to produce and sell more goods than before at any given price (refer back to Chapter 2). Thus, increases in technology shift supply curves to the right, such as the shift from S_0 to S_1 in Figure 4-8.

Examples of technological improvements (or increases) that shift supply curves rightward are easy to find, but what about decreases in technology that raise production costs? Although techniques of production are rarely forgotten or "lost," they can be restricted or even prohibited. For example, the government once required firms that used coal to switch from low-cost, high-sulfur-content coal to higher-cost, low-sulfur-content coal in the interest of improving air quality. This regulation meant those firms could not produce the same output at given prices as before (particularly in electricity generation). Their supply curves shifted to the left.

Producer Expectations   Producer expectations about future market prices affect the supply of any good. When firms expect the prices of their products to fall in the future, supply in the current time period increases, shifting supply curves to the right. Firms try to increase production now as well as sell off stored goods (inventory) at the current price, which they believe is a better price than they expect to get later. On the other hand, if producers expect prices of the goods they produce to rise in the future, they may hold current production off the market—reduce their supply—and store it for sale later. Farmers often store crops on the basis of forecasts that create expectations of higher future prices.

CHECKLIST : **Primary Determinants of Supply**

The primary determinants of supply, which cause shifts in supply curves when they change, are

- *The number of sellers:* More firms mean increased supply, whereas fewer firms cause supply to decrease.

- *Resource prices:* When resource prices increase, production costs rise, causing supply to decrease; falling resource prices increase supply.
- *Prices of related goods in production:* Higher prices of other goods firms can produce cause supply to decrease; lower prices of alternative goods cause supply to increase.
- *Technology:* Improvements in technology increase supply; decreases in technology cause supply to fall.
- *Producer expectations:* Expectations of higher future prices decrease current supply; expectations of lower future prices increase current supply.

Changes in Supply and Quantity Supplied

As with demand, it is important to distinguish between changes in supply and changes in quantity supplied. A *change in supply* results from a change in one of the determinants of supply, which causes the entire schedule of amounts offered at each price to change and the supply curve to shift. For example, the development of the transistor after World War II was a cost-cutting technological advance that increased the supply of radios, shifting the supply curve from S_0 to S_1 (see Figure 4-9).

A *change in quantity supplied* always refers to a movement along a given supply curve and is the result of a change in the price of the good. For instance, if the market price of home computers increased (P_1 to P_2 in Figure 4-9), a larger quantity would be supplied at the higher price (Q_2), but the supply curve itself would not shift.

You now have the basics of demand and supply analysis, which are powerful tools indeed. The next few chapters investigate demand and supply in greater detail and apply the analysis to a variety of interesting economic questions.

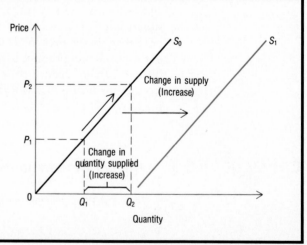

FIGURE 4-9

A *change in supply* refers to a shift in the entire supply curve. The movement of the supply curve from S_0 to S_1 represents an increase in supply in response to a favorable change in one or more determinants of supply. A *change in quantity supplied* refers to a movement from one amount supplied to another at a different price *on the same supply curve.* Quantity supplied increases from Q_1 to Q_2 along supply curve S_0 when price increases from P_1 to P_2.

Summary

1. The forces of demand and supply set prices in markets. Market prices reflect the relative values or scarcity of goods, serve as a rationing mechanism, and provide signals to guide production and exchange.

2. Demand is a schedule showing the quantities consumers are willing and able to purchase at each possible price during a specified time period. Since price and amounts demanded are negatively related, demand curves slope downward to the right. Changes in the determinants of demand—number of consumers, consumer tastes, consumer incomes, prices of related goods, and consumer expectations—shift demand curves.

3. Supply is a schedule showing the quantities firms are willing and able to sell at each possible price over a specified time period. Price and quantities supplied are positively related, yielding supply curves that slope upward to the right. Changes in supply determinants—number of suppliers, resource prices, prices of related goods in production, technology, and producer expectations—shift supply curves.

4. Equilibrium exists at the price at which quantity demanded just equals quantity supplied. There are no forces at work to change price or quantity.

Key Terms

complements
demand
demand curve
determinants of
   demand

determinants of supply
equilibrium
law of demand
law of supply
market demand

market supply
substitutes
supply
supply curve

Questions and Problems

1. Designer jeans are sold partly on the basis of their "snob appeal." Is it true that producers can sell more designer jeans by doubling the current price? If so, would sellers raise the price of this good without limit? Why or why not?

2. Do substitutes for everything exist at the margin? What about highly addictive drugs like crack cocaine? How do your answers relate to the law of demand?

3. Draw a demand and supply diagram for spiral-bound notebooks. Show what happens to the equilibrium price and equilibrium quantity if:
   a. Both demand and supply increase at the same time. (Hint: Try shifting both curves, but make the change for demand much larger than that for supply. Then see what you get if both increase but supply increases more than demand does.)

   b. Both decrease at the same time.

   c. Demand increases while supply decreases.

   d. Demand decreases while supply increases.

4. "Barbers in Chicago raised their regular haircut prices by $2 this week, and demand decreased immediately." What is wrong with this statement?

5. If a new breakthrough in tiremaking technology reduced the costs of producing tires by half, what would happen to

   a. The supply of tires?

   b. The demand for tires?

   c. The equilibrium price of tires?

   d. The demand for automobiles?

6. List several ways you might respond as a practical economist to an increase in the price of water to $1.50 per gallon.

7. To allocate scarce campus parking spaces to students for the semester, which of the following schemes do you prefer? Why?

   a. By class: first seniors, then juniors, and so on until available spaces are gone

   b. First come, first served each morning (no restrictions)

   c. Student government leaders, then athletes and cheerleaders, then fraternity/sorority members, then debaters and band members, then all other students

   d. Highest GPR and down until all spaces are assigned

   e. Rent spaces to students, faculty, and staff alike on a semester basis, varying rental rates according to parking space location

8. This textbook is printed in two colors (black plus several shades of another color). Some texts are printed in four colors (say, black, red, blue and yellow). By using four colors and several printing passes in which colors are laid on top of one another, any color under the rainbow can be produced. How might four-color printing affect the price of your textbook? Why?

9. Suppose equilibrium price = $8 and equilibrium quantity = 3,000 in the market for baseball caps. Sellers tell you they could sell 4,000 caps if they cut the price to $6; however, at $6 they would be willing to supply only 2,000 caps. Assuming both the supply curve and the demand curve are straight lines, draw those curves for baseball caps from the information given. (Hint: The equilibrium point lies on both the supply curve and the demand curve.)

10. An apartment rental firm wants to raise the rent on its standard two-bedroom apartment from $400 to $450 a month. At present, all 30 apartments are rented. Plot the demand curve from the schedule below, and

determine how many apartments would be vacant at the higher rent. What would happen if the rent were reduced to $350?

P	Q
600	22
550	24
500	26
450	28
400	30
350	32
300	34

5

Demand and Supply: Extensions

A thing is worth precisely what it can do for you, not what you choose to pay for it.

JOHN RUSKIN

Main Points

1. **If prices are not allowed to adjust in certain markets, the result will be persistent shortages or surpluses.** When price cannot rise to the equilibrium price due to a legal maximum price (price ceiling), a persistent shortage results. A persistent surplus occurs when sellers are forced to keep price above the equilibrium level (a price floor).

2. **Price elasticity of demand measures the responsiveness of quantity demanded to changes in price.** Elasticity determines whether the firm's total revenue increases, decreases, or stays the same when price changes.

3. **Consumers' wishes determine what to produce (the output mix) because firms, in their search for profits, re-** spond to consumer demand for different goods and services.

4. **Utility measures the want-satisfying power of goods and services.** Marginal utility is the extra satisfaction received from consuming one additional unit of a good. Marginal utility declines as more of a good or service is consumed in a given period of time.

5. **The law of demand—price and quantity demanded are inversely related—reflects the income and substitution effects of price changes.** The law of demand also reflects the law of diminishing marginal utility, because it helps explain the substitution effect.

I n Chapter 4, you saw how demand and supply determine equilibrium prices and quantities in markets. In this chapter, we extend that analysis by applying the demand and supply model to some specific situations.

One application is the idea of disequilibrium in markets. What happens when market prices cannot adjust upward or downward? Why are markets sometimes plagued with shortages or surpluses?

Another application is the concept of elasticity of demand, which helps explain why consumers' responses to price changes vary for different goods. When airline ticket prices fall by one-fourth during a fare war, will ticket sales increase a little or a lot? Would the extent of consumer response differ if, instead of airline travel, we considered how purchases of gasoline, pizza, salt, or newspapers respond to a change in price?

In this chapter, we will also further explore why the demand curve slopes downward. In Chapter 6, we will analyze costs and supply in depth. ∎

DISEQUILIBRIUM: PERSISTENT SHORTAGES AND SURPLUSES

Some markets do not achieve equilibrium with market-clearing prices and quantities even after allowing time for adjustment to the forces of demand and supply. Markets may not clear because the price adjustment mechanism is blocked, usually by law or other government action. Whether or not blocking the price adjustment mechanism is desirable or justifiable on some grounds, it always results in market disequilibrium. Whatever the reason, market disequilibrium takes the form of either a persistent shortage or a persistent surplus.

Persistent shortage
An excess of quantity demanded over quantity supplied that continues over time because price cannot adjust upward.

Price ceiling The legal maximum price; intended to keep the market price below its equilibrium level.

Persistent Shortages

When the market price is below equilibrium and is not allowed to adjust upward to the equilibrium price, market forces cannot eliminate excess quantity demanded. This excess quantity demanded is a **persistent shortage.** Suppose the state legislature sympathizes with the music lovers we encountered in the previous chapter and passes a bill to hold down the price of compact discs to a maximum of $12. Such a law establishes a **price ceiling,** or a legal maximum price. The diagrams in Figure 5-1 correspond to the hypothetical data for compact discs in Tables 4-2 and 4-3 in Chapter 4. What would be the result

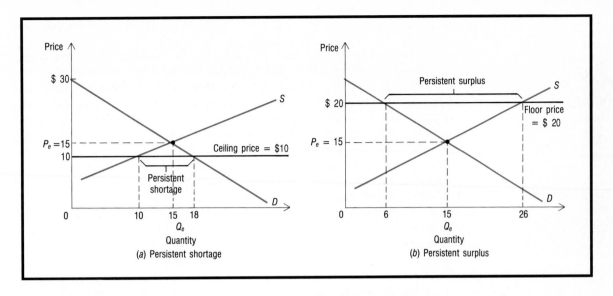

FIGURE 5-1

(a) Price ceilings (legal maximums) create persistent shortages because prices cannot adjust upward to the equilibrium price. The persistent shortage in this market for compact discs is 8 per time period at the price ceiling of $12. (b) Floor prices (legal minimums) create persistent surpluses when they are set above the equilibrium price. The persistent surplus in this market is 20 compact discs per month at a floor price of $20.

of setting a ceiling price of $12? The ceiling price would create an excess quantity demanded of 8 discs per month (see panel a of Figure 5-1). If the price could be bid up, the number of discs demanded by consumers would fall as the price rose and the number supplied by music companies would rise, eliminating the temporary shortage. However, it is now illegal for firms to raise price above the price ceiling. As a result, the market cannot clear (reach equilibrium). A persistent shortage of 8 compact discs will remain until the law is repealed, until the legal maximum price is raised to or above the equilibrium price, or until supply or demand shifts in response to other factors. Note that a price ceiling is effective only when it is set *below* the equilibrium price.

What happens in markets with price ceilings that create persistent shortages? Shelves are emptied early each month, so selection is poor. People wait in long lines to get compact discs whenever new shipments arrive. People with a low opportunity cost for their time (retired people, unemployed people, and students) often fill these lines. Perhaps taller, stronger buyers get to the counter first, leaving the slower or weaker people to try again. Over time, corruption enters the picture. Those with little time and larger incomes offer payments to clerks or managers (under the table) to get compact discs without having to stand in line. They bribe clerks to notify them when new shipments arrive so they can at least minimize their time in line (and maximize their success in obtaining goods).

Furthermore, shortages that result from price ceilings often encourage discrimination. Sellers can be choosy about buyers. They may offer compact discs only to friends, to people with brown eyes, or to those who agree to buy other goods from the store, such as three blank cassette tapes with each compact disc. Finally, if the price ceiling exists only in one geographic market, such as a state or a city, that area will receive only the lowest-quality goods. If only California controls the price of compact discs so that shortages develop, recording companies have no need to ship their hottest titles to California for sale.

Although the compact disc example is hypothetical, ceiling prices that result in persistent shortages are not. Rent controls that were supposed to be temporary were put into effect in New York City in 1943—and they still exist. Rent controls were designed to help low-income tenants keep their apartments as rents rose with the flood of returning soldiers after World War II. However, all of the side effects noted earlier have occurred in New York's rental housing market. Because there is a persistent shortage of rent-controlled apartments, landlords can discriminate among renters. Renters often have to "know somebody" to obtain a rent-controlled apartment. Furthermore, those lucky enough to get one of these apartments can sublet it to others for substantial payments called *key money*, often amounting to hundreds and sometimes thousands of dollars. Because the renters not the owners, get this extra money, owners have less incentive to fix faulty plumbing, replace broken windows, and make other repairs. As a result, these apartments are often allowed to deteriorate. This practice is not strictly a matter of greed. More than one-quarter of the dilapidated tenements in New York City are now owned by the city itself. Those tenements were abandoned by their owners because rents were too low to cover normal operating expenses, including taxes.

Most economists oppose laws that mandate ceiling prices, because such laws prevent the price mechanism from carrying out its rationing function. Controlling rents in San Francisco will not create new apartment housing. Rent controls simply change the way scarce apartments are rationed among competing users. Instead of price, the rationing method may be "first come, first served," an apartment lottery, or arbitrary discrimination by landlords who pick only friends, childless couples, or people of the "right" ethnic background.

If all these negative effects result from ceiling prices, why do officials insist on enacting price control laws? The answer to that question is complex. It will be easier to answer in Chapter 10, in which we discuss how individuals can influence government decisions. For now, we will simply assume such laws are passed with good intentions, such as helping low-income renters. Another reason is that politicians respond to voting power. There are many more renters who want controls than apartment owners who do not.

Those who actually get apartments at below-equilibrium rents come out ahead. Other groups, however, lose from rent controls. To see who gains and who loses, consider the rental price ceiling in Figure 5-2.

Without rent controls, the equilibrium price would be P_e and the equilibrium quantity would be Q_e. At the controlled price, P_c, however, only Q_1 apartments are supplied and occupied. Thus, Q_1Q_e is the number of apartments lost due to rent control, and the people who would have occupied these apartments lose. Furthermore, Q_eQ_2 is the number of extra apartments (beyond the equilibrium number) that people want at the artificially low controlled price. The renters would make other choices, such as moving to another city or living with relatives, if they did not hope to get an apartment at an artificially low price. But there are not enough apartments at the controlled price. These unsuccessful apartment hunters also lose because price controls encourage them to spend time looking for something that does not exist. The gainers are those renters who get apartments and pay controlled rents below the equilibrium prices that would otherwise be charged. Thus, those who get one of the few apartments now available are really smiling!

Price floor The legal minimum price; intended to keep market price above its equilibrium level.

Persistent surplus An excess of quantity supplied over quantity demanded that continues over time because price cannot adjust downward.

Persistent Surpluses

Just as governments can be persuaded to keep prices from rising to their equilibrium levels for certain goods, they are often persuaded to set price floors. A **price floor** is a legal minimum price designed to favor certain firms or groups. Price floors prevent prices from falling to their equilibrium levels, at which the market would clear. Thus, effective price floors create a **persistent surplus,** or

FIGURE 5-2

The controlled rental price, P_c, is a price ceiling set below the equilibrium price, P_e. Only Q_1 apartments are available at the controlled price (where P_c intersects the supply curve). The number of available apartments (quantity supplied) is less than Q_e, the number that would be available if the equilibrium price prevailed.

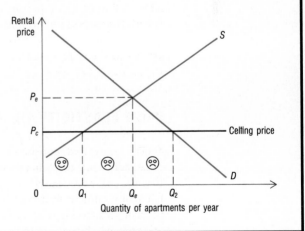

chronic excess quantity supplied. To have any effect, they must be set *above* the equilibrium price.

Suppose officials set a floor price of $24 for compact discs to discourage youths from wasting their lives listening to "degenerate" rock music. This floor price is shown in panel b of Figure 5-1. The legal minimum price blocks the normal price adjustment process, creating a persistent surplus of 20 units each time period (26 supplied − 6 demanded).

In reality, examples of price floors are everywhere. Minimum prices are set for many agricultural products, from milk to wheat. Hidden in a variety of farm support programs, these price floors are designed to help (transfer income to) farmers. In every case, however, these programs keep prices unnecessarily high for consumers and result in surpluses that cause headaches for government. In some cases, these surplus commodities are bought by government (meaning all taxpayers) to distribute through school lunch programs, store for "rainy" days, or distribute to needy people in other countries.

To maintain price floors, subsidies to the tune of $2 billion annually go to honey, wool, and mohair producers. The original rationale was that beeswax was needed to waterproof World War II military hardware, and wool and mohair were needed to produce uniforms. (To understand why these subsidies still exist, consider that Texas leads the nation in the production of all three products and a Texas congressman chairs the House Agricultural Committee that initiates legislation containing price supports.)

The minimum wage for basic, unskilled labor is also a price floor. The current federal minimum wage is $4.25 per hour. A simple demand and supply model suggests that a minimum wage above the equilibrium price of unskilled labor creates a surplus, thus contributing to unemployment. In Chapter 9, we discuss the full consequences of this price floor.

Like price ceilings, price floors prevent price from carrying out its rationing function. Whenever price is not allowed to adjust freely, scarce goods will be allocated among competing users in other ways. Furthermore, prices that are set arbitrarily provide no information about the relative values placed on goods by buyers or the production costs of firms. Thus, they no longer serve as accurate signals to guide production and exchange.

PRICE ELASTICITY OF DEMAND

Sellers know that consumers will buy less when price rises and more when price falls, but that information is not enough. Sellers also want to know the size of the change in quantity demanded. When the price of a good falls, how much more will consumers buy? If a firm lowers its price 10 percent to increase sales, will consumers increase their purchases by the same 10 percent, by more than 10 percent, or by less than 10 percent? The answer to that question is very important to firms, because it determines whether total revenue from sales increases, decreases, or remains the same after the price cut.

The measure of the responsiveness of quantity demanded to a price change is the **price elasticity of demand.** Price elasticity of demand *(PE$_d$)* is generally defined as the ratio of the percentage change in quantity demanded to the percentage change in price,[1] or

Price elasticity of demand A measure of the responsiveness of quantity demanded to changes in the price of a good; equal to the ratio of the percentage change in quantity demanded to the percentage change in price.

$$PE_d = \frac{\text{Percentage Change in Quantity Demanded}}{\text{Percentage Change in Price}}$$

Suppose a barber increases the price of his regular haircuts by 10 percent and finds that he gives 20 percent fewer haircuts each day. What is the price elasticity of demand for haircuts this barber faces? This solution is

$$PE_d \text{ for Haircuts} = \frac{-20\%}{+10\%} = -2.$$

The price elasticity coefficient is -2, or just 2. (Omitting the negative sign, or using absolute value, is standard practice since we know price and quantity demanded always move in opposite directions.) When price elasticity is 2, the change in quantity demanded is about twice the size of the percentage change in price. Therefore, this barber can expect the number of haircuts he gives to fall by 10 percent if he raises price by 5 percent or to rise by 20 percent if he lowers price by 10 percent.

Elastic demand Exists when quantity demanded is highly responsive to price changes *(PE$_d$ > 1).*

When the percentage change in quantity demanded is larger than the percentage change in price *(PE$_d$ > 1)*, demand is price **elastic.** Some of the products listed in Table 5-1 are examples of goods characterized by elastic demand. Quantities demanded of these goods are very sensitive to price changes.

Inelastic demand Exists when quantity demanded is only slightly responsive to price changes *(PE$_d$ < 1).*

On the other hand, when the change in quantity demanded is small relative to the change in price *(PE$_d$ < 1)*, demand is price **inelastic.** Water, jewelry, auto repairs, and medical care exhibit inelastic demand in the long run (see Table

---

[1]To obtain a value for price elasticity that is the same whether price rises or falls, we can refine this equation using percentage changes based on the average of the old and new quantities and the average of the old and new prices. That way, the elasticity coefficient is the same for changes in price either up or down the demand curve. The equation for price elasticity of demand becomes the midpoints equation:

$$PE_d = \frac{\text{Change in Quantity Demanded/Average Quantity Demanded}}{\text{Change in Price/Average Price}}$$
$$= \frac{(Q_2 - Q_1)/(Q_1 + Q_2)/2}{(P_2 - P_1)/(P_1 + P_2)/2},$$

where Q_1 is the original quantity demanded at the original price, P_1, and Q_2 is the new quantity demanded at the new price, P_2.

TABLE 5-1   Selected Long-Run Price Elasticities of Demand

Product	Long Run PE$_d$
Water	0.14
Auto Repairs	0.38
Jewelry	0.67
Medical Care	0.92
Tires	1.19
Houses	1.22
Electricity	1.89
Tobacco	1.89
Recreation equipment	2.39
China and glassware	2.55
Toilet articles	3.04
Movies	3.69

Source: Hendrick S. Houthakker and Lester D. Taylor, *Consumer Demand in the United States: Analyses and Projections* (Cambridge, Mass: Harvard University Press, 1970), pp. 166–167.

5-1). Prices for these goods can vary somewhat without causing people to change the amounts they consume very much.

Finally, if quantity demanded falls by exactly the same percentage by which price increases (PE_d = 1), demand exhibits **unitary elasticity** in that price range.

Unitary elasticity Exists when the percentage change in quantity demanded is exactly the same as the percentage change in price (PE_d = 1).

Price Elasticity and Total Revenue

Knowing the price elasticities of demand for particular goods and services can be extremely useful to sellers. Suppose the barber described earlier wants to raise his price for basic haircuts. He knows he is likely to sell fewer haircuts at a higher price (because of the law of demand), but he is not sure by how much his business will drop. If the number of haircuts he gives each day falls only a little, he will make more money because the effect of the higher price will be greater than the effect of selling fewer haircuts. On the other hand, haircut sales might drop by enough to more than offset any benefit from the higher price, and he will make less money. Because revenue and elasticity are closely related, knowing the price elasticity of demand for haircuts will answer the barber's question.

Total revenue The total amount received by a firm (or total expenditures by consumers); equal to price times quantity ($TR = P \times Q$).

Any firm's **total revenue (TR)** is simply price times quantity sold, or $TR = P \times Q$. A higher price (P) tends to raise total revenue because each unit sold goes for a higher price. At the same time, however, a higher price tends to reduce revenue because quantity sold *(Q)* declines. The opposite is true for a decrease in price. Therefore, the net effect of a price change on total revenue depends on whether the change in *Q* is relatively larger or smaller than the change in *P*. Changes in total revenue that result from price changes depend on price elasticity of demand.

If the barber increases price 20 percent, from $5 to $6, the quantity of haircuts sold might fall from 20 to 10—a 50 percent decline in quantity demanded. A 50 percent decrease in quantity sold resulting from a 20 percent increase in price means demand is price elastic, and the barber's total revenue will fall. Selling 20 haircuts at the old $5 price brings in $100, while selling only 10 haircuts at $6 yields total revenue of $60. Thus, when demand is price elastic, total revenue falls with a price increase and rises with a price decrease.

Now suppose that when price increases by 20 percent (from $5 to $6), quantity demanded falls only 10 percent, from 20 to 18 haircuts per day. Demand is thus price inelastic ($PE_d = 10\%/20\% = .5$, which is less than 1). Total revenue will increase from $100 ($5 × 20 haircuts) to $108 ($6 × 18 haircuts). Thus, when demand is price inelastic, total revenue increases with a price increase and TR falls with a price decrease.

When demand exhibits unitary price elasticity ($PE_d = 1$), total revenue will not change as a result of a price change. Unitary price elasticity means the extra revenue from a price increase is exactly offset by the revenue lost from selling fewer units. The product of a 20 percent higher *P* and a 20 percent smaller *Q* will yield the same total revenue as before.

 CHECKLIST : **Relationship among Price Changes, Elasticity, and Total Revenue**

Price Change	Change in Total Revenue	Elasticity	
	Opposite		
Increase	Decrease	Elastic	$(PE_d > 1)$
Decrease	Increase	Elastic	$(PE_d > 1)$
	Same		
Increase	Increase	Inelastic	$(PE_d < 1)$
Decrease	Decrease	Inelastic	$(PE_d < 1)$
	None		
Increase	Unchanged	Unitary	$(PE_d = 1)$
Decrease	Unchanged	Unitary	$(PE_d = 1)$

Comparing the Elasticity of Demand Curves

Although most demand curves have both elastic and inelastic segments, any demand curve can be described as relatively more elastic (or inelastic) than another. Since the two demand curves in Figure 5-3 cross each other, they have one point in common. Both curves are inelastic in the range of the two prices shown. However, D_A is *relatively* more elastic than D_B. Comparing the same percentage increase in price, from P_1 to P_2, along each of these demand curves results in a relatively larger quantity response along D_A (quantity falls from Q_1 to Q_A) than along D_B (quantity falls from Q_1 only to Q_B).

Determinants of Price Elasticity of Demand

Why is demand for some goods relatively elastic and demand for others relatively inelastic? The three main determinants of price elasticity of demand are (1) the availability of substitutes, (2) total spending on a good relative to consumers' budgets, and (3) the amount of time consumers have to adjust to price changes.

If a good has many close substitutes, it is easier for practical economists to respond to incentives, or price changes in either direction. For example, in Table 5-1 the price elasticity coefficient for movies is very high: 3.69. There are many substitutes for going to a movie—playing miniature golf, playing bridge, going for a drive, renting a video, water skiing, or reading

---

FIGURE 5-3

Demand curve D_A is relatively more elastic than demand curve D_B. The same relative increase in price from P_1 to P_2 causes a relatively larger quantity response along D_A (quantity falls from Q_1 to Q_A) than along D_B (quantity falls from Q_1 to Q_B).

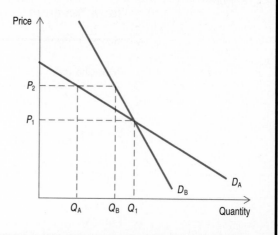

Most Demand Curves Are Vertical

The phrase *basic needs* implies that people have a very high demand for certain goods and services. The notion that people "need" such goods as water, clothing, housing, and even gasoline or heating oil implies that the demand curves for those goods are vertical. With vertical demand curves, consumers would buy a fixed quantity of such goods regardless of price. Price changes would not affect the amount bought; that is, demand would be perfectly inelastic ($PE_d = 0$).

Do vertical, or perfectly inelastic, demand curves really exist? Economists have had a hard time finding such goods. Even heroin users respond to price changes. A higher heroin price (perhaps the result of a large police "bust" of a smuggling ring) will cause abusers to use a little less or to substitute other drugs like cocaine or methadone, which are now relatively cheaper.

Apparently the vertical demand curve is a mythical beast. Consider water. People must have some water to survive, but does this mean the demand curve any city water company faces is vertical? Can the water company charge any price for water without affecting usage? The answer to both questions is no.

The demand curve for water slopes downward for several reasons. First, consumers use a great deal more water than the first few gallons they need each month for survival. Many substitutes for these extra units of water exist, such as not watering lawns, washing cars less often, dry cleaning clothes, and fixing leaky faucets and pipes. Consumers can (and do) adjust their purchases of water when its price changes.

Second, there may be substitutes even for the first few gallons of water from the city water company

that the human body requires to survive. If Dallas water prices rose to $100 per gallon, wouldn't people in that city decide that watermelons from Alabama are good substitutes for tap water? Or orange juice from Florida? Or milk from Tennessee, and Cokes from Oklahoma? Or water collected from downspouts (a common practice just a few years ago)? Or even digging wells or installing water recycling systems in homes?

Some water may be a necessity, but that fact has little economic relevance because there are so many ways to get water and so many substitute sources, especially for survival amounts. If water has substitutes, its demand curve will slope downward. Consumers will respond to changes in the price of water. Thus, even water is not an example of a good whose demand curve is vertical. If a necessity is a particular good that people must buy in certain quantities regardless of price, true necessities in the economic sense are hard to find. ■

a book. Thus, it is easy for consumers to change their consumption of movies in response to price changes. On the other hand, the price elasticity of demand for auto repair services is low—0.38 in Table 5-1. If your car breaks down, you have few good alternatives to getting it fixed, short of buying a new car or walking, regardless of repair prices. Demand for these repairs is relatively price inelastic. Thus, the larger the number of close substitutes, the greater the price elasticity of demand.

The total amount spent on the good relative to the size of the consumer's budget is the second factor influencing price elasticity of demand. Consider the price elasticity of demand for socks. At $3 a pair, a consumer might buy five pairs of socks each year, spending a total of $15. If the price of socks increases by 25 percent to $3.75, the consumer's total spending on socks will increase by only $3.75 if the consumer continues to buy five pairs. Since most consumers are not likely to notice an extra $3.75 expenditure over a year's time, they are unlikely to reduce their sock purchases very much. Thus, price increases (and decreases) for "small budget" items affect quantity demanded only slightly, making demand for those items relatively price inelastic.

However, consumers spend large fractions of their income on "big-ticket" items such as automobiles. If car prices increase such that monthly payments for a typical car increase by the same 25 percent as for socks, payments may rise from $400 per month to $500. This monthly increase in car payments pushes up annual car expenditures from $4,800 to $6,000, which is no small matter! Consumers are likely to respond to this 25 percent price increase with a large drop in quantity demanded, making demand for automobiles price elastic. Thus, the larger the fraction of a consumer's budget spent on a particular good, the more likely that good is to be price elastic, *ceteris paribus.*

The third determinant of price elasticity of demand is the amount of time consumers have to make adjustments to changes in price. For most goods, practical economists need enough time to seek alternatives and change their consumption patterns. Consequently, price elasticity will be lower in the short run than in the long run. If heating oil prices rise dramatically, consumers can do little over the short run but pay the higher prices and try to cut their consumption of heating oil somewhat by turning down their thermostats and wearing sweaters. Short-run demand for heating oil is price inelastic. The long run is another matter. Given enough time, consumers will respond to the price increase. They may buy more efficient furnaces as their old ones wear out, change to wood-burning or natural-gas furnaces to avoid buying any heating oil at all, or add attic insulation. All of these steps serve to cut consumption of heating oil significantly. In the long run, the price elasticity for heating oil is much higher, that is, more elastic. Thus, the longer the time period involved, the more price elastic is demand.

CHECKLIST : **Determinants of Price Elasticity of Demand**

Price elasticity of demand is *higher* if

1. The good has more or better close substitutes.
2. The proportion of a consumer's budget spent on the good is large.
3. The time period under consideration is longer.

Applying Elasticity: Excise Taxes

Price elasticity of demand has many applications in economics. One example of the kind of question elasticity can help answer is that of who actually pays taxes on goods—consumers or producers.

Governments levy particular taxes on the basis of factors such as which tax might raise the most revenue, which might disturb markets the least, and which are "fairer." To evaluate the fairness of and the market disruptions created by a particular tax, policymakers need to know who actually winds up paying the tax. Consider an **excise tax,** which is a tax levied on particular products such as gasoline, tires, tobacco products, alcoholic beverages, soft drinks, and long-distance telephone calls. How much of any excise tax falls on consumers of the taxed good in the form of higher prices, and how much falls on producers of the good in the form of reduced revenue (and profits)?

Suppose the surgeon general issues a health report revealing that U.S. consumers eat far too much ice cream, raising their fat intake and thus increasing their risk of a heart attack. Congress decides to levy an excise tax on each gallon of ice cream to reduce ice cream consumption (Congress knows about the law of demand!) and raise revenue at the same time. Figure 5-4 illustrates the effects of an excise tax of $2 per gallon of ice cream.

In panel a of Figure 5-4, the equilibrium price before the tax is imposed is $3 and the equilibrium quantity sold (quantity demanded and supplied) is 50 million gallons each year. The $2 excise tax per gallon shifts the supply curve upward by the amount of the tax. (An excise tax is similar to an increase in one of the costs of production.) It now costs $2 more to produce each gallon, because producers must send this amount of tax to the government for each gallon of ice cream sold.

The new equilibrium price—the price at which the demand curve intersects the new supply curve ($S_{\text{with \$2 tax}}$)—is $4.40, and sales fall to 36 million gallons. Consumers eat less ice cream than they otherwise would and have to pay more for it. Of course, this is exactly what the surgeon general wanted.

The total excise tax revenue is the shaded rectangle, or $72 million ($2 per gallon × 36 million gallons sold). How much is paid by consumers and how much by producers? The price of ice cream has increased, but not by $2, the amount of the tax. Price has increased only $1.40, from $3.00 to $4.40. In effect, consumers are not paying the entire $2 excise tax on each gallon they

Excise tax A tax levied on particular products such as gasoline and tobacco products.

In Practice 5-1

. . . .

Sin Taxes, Clintonomics, and Elasticity

President Clinton proposed several new taxes and tax increases on various goods to raise funds for health care and to reduce the annual federal deficit. *Fortune* (March 22, 1993, p. 30) reported that the president wanted to impose higher taxes on guns, alcohol, tobacco, and, most important, energy.

These particular goods were not chosen by accident. Taxes on the first three goods fall into the category of "sin taxes." Goods like guns, alcohol, and tobacco share two characteristics. First, their demand is relatively inelastic compared to other goods. Extra taxes would have the effect of raising their prices, but the quantity sold would not decline very much. Therefore, the tax revenue generated would be greater than it would be if the government chose to tax goods or services with elastic demand. Higher taxes on goods with elastic demand, like shoes or movies, would simply cause consumers to switch to other, substitute goods. In that case, the government would raise little revenue.

Second, many people regard the consumption of these goods as bad for people. Alcohol and tobacco are unhealthy, and guns are dangerous. If public officials agree with this view, the government is in a "win-win" situation. The sin taxes will raise revenue and, to the extent that sales and use of alcohol, tobacco, and guns declines, society will get the added bonus of reducing the use of harmful products.

Another belief, although less widely held, is that reducing energy consumption in the United States, either to reduce air pollution or to conserve resources, is a good idea. Thus, in a way President Clinton's proposed tax on most major forms of energy can be thought of as a sin tax. However, the major purpose of the energy tax was to raise revenue; it would raise about $400 annually from the "average" family.

Here again the economic concept of price elasticity of demand affects the choice of policy. Why did President Clinton's advisers choose to propose taxing a wide variety of energy sources based on their heat content? The reason is that the price elasticity of demand for all energy is surely much less elastic than the demand for any single energy source like coal, gasoline, heating oil, or natural gas. Taxing all sources would make it harder for consumers and industrial customers to substitute one for another. Therefore, demand elasticity would be lower, and tax revenues would be higher. ∎

---

buy. Consumers' share of the tax bill is the upper part of the shaded area, or $50.4 million ($1.40 × 36 million gallons).

Since producers must send the $2 excise tax to the government for each gallon sold, they are able to keep only $2.40 of the $4.40 they receive per gallon. Thus, the price they actually receive is now $0.60 lower than the original price of $3.00. Producers, therefore, are also paying part of the excise tax, $21.6 million ($.60 × 36 million gallons), represented by the lower portion of the shaded area. The $50.4 million of the tax consumers pay and the $21.6 million producers pay add up to the total $72 million of ice cream tax revenue the government receives.

The division of the tax between consumers and producers depends on the elasticity of demand (and supply). Panel b of Figure 5-4 shows the extreme case

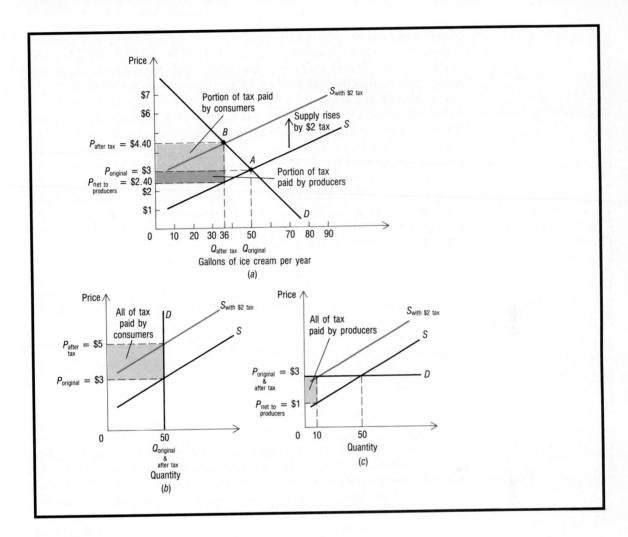

FIGURE 5-4

(a) An excise tax of $2 per gallon of ice cream shifts the supply curve upward by $2. The equilibrium price rises to $4.40; consumers pay $1.40 of the $2 tax. Producers pay the other $0.60 of the tax and receive a net price of only $2.40 per gallon. (b) In the case of perfectly inelastic demand, consumers do not respond to the change in price when the excise tax is added. Therefore, they pay the entire tax as the equilibrium price rises from $3 to $5, and quantity demanded is unchanged. (c) In the case of perfectly elastic demand, consumers respond to increases in price above $3 by substituting other goods and reducing their consumption of ice cream to zero. Since consumers will pay no price above $3, producers must pay the entire tax.

of perfectly inelastic demand for ice cream. Consumers demand 50 million gallons of ice cream regardless of price. (They are ice cream junkies, like one of the authors.) The $2 excise tax raises price to $5. Since consumers do not reduce their consumption at all, they will pay the entire tax bill of $100 million ($2 × 50 million gallons).

The other limiting case, perfectly elastic demand, is shown in panel c. After the supply curve shifts upward by $2, the quantity of ice cream sold decreases. There is no change in the price consumers pay. The tax is absorbed entirely by producers, who receive only $1 per gallon after paying the $2 tax out of the $3 price they still receive. They cut back their quantity supplied to only 10 million gallons, while consumers switch to other products to satisfy their desire for treats. The government's ice cream tax revenue falls to only $20 million ($2 per gallon × 10 million gallons). Thus, the higher the elasticity of demand, the lower the tax revenue to the government.

Typically, the proportions of the excise tax paid by consumers and producers lie somewhere between these two extremes. If you knew the actual price elasticity of demand for ice cream (and the price elasticity of supply of ice cream, discussed in the next chapter), you could calculate exactly how high the excise tax should be to reduce ice cream consumption by some desired amount and to raise a target amount of revenue. Elasticity is useful information for practical economists as buyers, sellers, and policymakers.

BEHIND THE LAW OF DEMAND

Most economists want to see markets free of price controls, because they know consumers are "in charge" in markets and generally get what they demand; that is, consumers make their wishes known through the market mechanism. This "consumer is king" attribute of market economies is known as **consumer sovereignty.** Consumers ultimately control production and exchange decisions when they are free to choose the products they want and when firms, in their search for profits, are free to produce goods and services they think consumers want. Consumer sovereignty exists in an economic system when production and exchange decisions respond primarily to individual consumer demand.

However, consumer sovereignty is not absolute in most societies. Even in market economies, governments limit consumer sovereignty by outlawing, regulating, or restricting certain economic activities determined not to be in consumers' own interests. Consumers are prohibited from buying certain goods (such as mind-altering drugs) and are forced to buy and use others (such as seat belts). Likewise, firms cannot offer some products (M-60 machine guns, jewelry made from black coral, or the services of prostitutes) and must offer others (cars with padded dashboards and apartment buildings with fire sprinkler systems).

Consumer sovereignty
The central role consumers play in directing market economies because firms produce and exchange goods and services primarily to satisfy consumer wants.

Despite these limits on consumer sovereignty, people in most market economies are free to choose how they will satisfy their own wants within broad limits, and producers are free to supply the goods and services they believe consumers desire. Consumers, acting as practical economists, can choose eggs and bacon for breakfast or cereal and fruit. For recreation, they can read a newspaper, go to a movie, or play bridge. Producers, who are also practical economists, can operate a fast-food restaurant, start a car wash, or make premium ice cream to satisfy consumer desires and make a profit.

The law of demand, introduced in the last chapter, states that quantity demanded is negatively related to product price. The explanation given for this law was that price represents the opportunity cost of consuming a particular good. The higher the price of bread, for example, the greater the amounts of other goods that must be forgone to consume a loaf of bread, making bread both less attractive and less affordable than other goods. The law of demand therefore is rooted in the self-interested, maximizing behavior of consumers as practical economists trying to satisfy their wants as much as possible.

The Law of Diminishing Marginal Utility

In the nineteenth century, economists developed a model of consumer choice based on the observation that consumers try to spend their incomes on goods and services in a way that will maximize their total satisfaction from consumption. That model was called the *utility theory of demand.* Just as wants differ greatly from person to person, the amount of satisfaction, or utility, received from consuming a particular good varies among individuals. Economists define **utility** as the satisfaction a consumer obtains from consuming a good or service.

Remember that practical economists make decisions "at the margin," buying one loaf of bread or pair of shoes at a time. The utility of marginal (extra) amounts of goods to potential consumers is the important determinant of consumer demand. The **marginal utility (MU)** of a good is the extra utility, or extra satisfaction, a particular consumer receives from consuming one extra unit of the good in a given period of time.

For most people, consuming a second slice of pizza at lunch is not quite as satisfying as consuming the first, and consuming the third is rarely as satisfying as consuming the second. Thus, economists say marginal utility falls with additional pizza consumption. Put another way, each additional pizza slice consumed adds less and less to a person's total utility. In fact, eating a fourth slice of pizza at lunch may add nothing to your satisfaction level (its marginal utility would be zero) or may even make you sick (its marginal utility definitely would be negative).

How the changing value of additional slices of pizza satisfies people illustrates the **law of diminishing marginal utility.** This law states that after some amount, marginal utility declines as extra units of a good are consumed in a given time period. Economists have found that human behavior consistently reflects this

Utility The satisfaction obtained from consuming a good or service.

Marginal utility (MU) The additional utility received from consuming one more unit of a good in a given time period.

Law of diminishing marginal utility The principle that after some level of consumption, the extra utility received from consuming each additional unit of a good declines.

principle. Extra amounts of any good consumed in a given period of time tend to yield less and less *marginal* utility to consumers.

Declining marginal utility affects consumers' decisions about what goods to buy and how much of each. Practical economists decide how many units of goods to purchase each period according to the marginal utility each good provides. Consumers start with those goods that provide the greatest marginal utility per dollar spent on them (marginal utility divided by price). Next, they choose those goods that give less utility per dollar, including extra units of the same goods. Consumers continue choosing goods in this fashion until they use up their incomes. They choose goods according to the marginal utility per dollar spent, from highest to lowest, until available income runs out. This process maximizes each consumer's total utility from consuming one mix of goods and services out of all the possible choices.

Do people go through stores calculating marginal utilities for the items they might buy, dividing by price, and determining which unit gives "the most bang for the buck"? They come very close to doing exactly that! While people do not make formal calculations, they do make reasoned choices by weighing the marginal satisfaction they expect from each possible purchase. Utility-maximizing theory is a descriptive *model* of consumer behavior. When people stand in front of the soft-drink case in a store trying to decide whether to take one more six-pack of Coke for $2.95, they are comparing the satisfaction they would get per dollar spent on the extra soft drinks relative to whatever else that money could buy—two bags of potato chips, a carton of ice cream, or more gasoline. Of course, consumers develop habits over time that reduce the time they need to make these decisions. As they develop these habits, however, consumers gain experience by comparing expected utility for the price (sometimes called the "best value") time and time again.

Explaining the Law of Demand

Recall from the last chapter that the law of demand can be explained in terms of the two ways price changes affect consumers, the substitution and income effects. First, a change in a good's price changes the quantity demanded because the good is now relatively more or less attractive than other goods whose prices remain unchanged. This effect of a price change is the **substitution effect.** A price decrease for one good causes the quantity demanded to increase because that good is now cheaper relative to all other goods than it was before the price decrease. As practical economists, consumers will choose to substitute more units of this good for some of the other goods they were buying. A price increase, on the other hand, makes the good relatively more expensive. Consumers demand a smaller quantity as they substitute other goods for this one.

The law of diminishing marginal utility helps explain the substitution effect and thereby helps explain the law of demand. Recall that consumers buy units

Substitution effect
The change in the quantity demanded of a good when its price changes that results from substituting that good for others when it becomes relatively cheaper or substituting other goods for it when it becomes relatively more expensive.

of goods according to the marginal utility they receive per dollar spent on each good, selecting units of goods with "more bang for the buck" before units of other goods. Thus, when the price of a particular good rises, its marginal utility *per dollar* spent on it falls for all consumers. This lower marginal utility per dollar causes consumers to buy less of the good and more of all other goods whose marginal utilities divided by price have remained constant. Consumers substitute other goods that are now *relatively* more attractive for the good with the higher price to maximize their utility.

Income effect A change in the quantity demanded of a good resulting from the change in the purchasing power of consumer income when the price of the good changes.

A change in the price of a good also creates an income effect. The **income effect** is that part of the change in quantity demanded that results from the slight change in the purchasing power of consumer income. Suppose Linda buys 10 regular McDonald's hamburgers each month when the price is 99 cents each. These hamburgers cost Linda a total of $9.90 (10 × $0.99). What would happen if McDonald's cut its hamburger price to 79 cents each? Linda would want more hamburgers, not only to substitute for other food but partly because she feels a bit richer. The lower hamburger price means, *ceteris paribus,* that she can buy the same 10 hamburgers as before and have some money left over. Ten hamburgers now would cost Linda only $7.90 instead of $9.90. This additional effective income of $2 from the decrease in the price of hamburgers allows Linda to purchase more goods than before, *including hamburgers.* Therefore, a price reduction leads to a larger quantity demanded partly because of the income effect. A price increase works in reverse: Consumers are effectively a little poorer, and they buy less of that good as well as of other goods in their market basket.

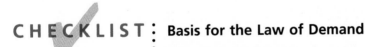

CHECKLIST : **Basis for the Law of Demand**

The law of demand reflects the two effects of a price change: (1) the substitution effect and (2) the income effect.

PRODUCER BEHAVIOR AND THE LAW OF SUPPLY: A PREVIEW

The law of supply states that the quantity supplied by producers increases when market price goes up and decreases when market price falls. This law depends primarily on the fact that costs go up as firms increase their levels of output in response to higher prices. The practical economists who operate firms want to maximize profit, and profit is the difference between revenue and cost for a given output level. If production costs rise with increases in output, higher product prices are required to entice firms to produce more.

The key to understanding the law of supply, then, is understanding *why* and *how* production costs tend to increase when output increases. In the next chapter, we examine how production costs increase with the level of output.

Summary

1. Persistent shortages or persistent surpluses mean that a market is in disequilibrium. Price ceilings result in persistent shortages. Price floors create persistent surpluses.

2. Consumer sovereignty is the driving force in market economies because firms undertake production and exchange primarily to satisfy individual consumer demand, (which in turn allows them to make a profit).

3. Price elasticity of demand measures the responsiveness of quantity demanded to changes in price. Elasticity determines whether the firm's total revenue increases, decreases, or stays the same when price changes. Total revenue and price change in the same direction when demand is price inelastic and in opposite directions when demand is price elastic.

4. Utility is the want-satisfying power of goods. Marginal utility is the extra satisfaction received from consuming each additional (marginal) unit of a good. The law of diminishing marginal utility expresses the principle that marginal utility declines as additional units of a good are consumed per time period.

5. Consumers want to maximize their total utility from consumption. They do this by purchasing units of goods that yield the highest marginal utility per dollar in descending order.

6. The law of demand can be explained in terms of both the income and substitution effects of price changes. The substitution effect is the incentive for the consumer to substitute a particular good for others when that good's price falls or to substitute other goods when its price rises, because the opportunity cost of the good changes when its price changes. The substitution effect can be explained using the law of diminishing marginal utility. The income effect means that a lower price enables consumers to buy more of a good with the additional purchasing power of their income that results from the price change. A higher price reduces the income available to spend on the good, so quantity demanded falls.

Key Terms

price ceiling	inelastic demand	price elasticity of
consumer sovereignty	law of diminishing	demand
elastic demand	marginal utility	substitution effect
excise tax	marginal utility	total revenue
price floor	persistent shortage	unitary elasticity
income effect	persistent surplus	utility

Questions and Problems

1. Suppose your state legislator led a campaign to convince the state government that a college education is so important today that tuition at all colleges (public and private) should be no higher than $50 per semester. If he succeeded in getting such a law passed, would your letter to him be a congratulatory one? What would be the major economic consequences and side effects of such a law?

2. Suppose that a year or so after observing the effects of the tuition law in question 1, another legislator decided that the state should ensure high salaries for college faculties to attract and hold the most esteemed professors. If she succeeds in convincing other legislators to pass a law requiring that tuition not be less than $3,000 per semester, would your letter to her be a congratulatory one? What would be the major economic consequences and side effects of such a law?

3. "Utility is in the eye of the beholder." Discuss this statement.

4. Does adhering to the consumer sovereignty premise of market economies preclude government action? (Hint: Could consumers express some of their desire for roads and national defense through the political process?)

5. Would you put an excise tax (sometimes called a "sin tax") on products that are price elastic or price inelastic? Why or why not?

6. Which of the following products do you think has relatively elastic or relatively inelastic demand? Why?

    a. Salt
    b. Hershey bars
    c. Socks
    d. Wendy's hamburgers

7. If the price of apples rises 10 percent and the quantity sold falls 50 percent, what is the coefficient of price elasticity? Is demand price elastic, inelastic, or unitary elastic?

8. Joe's record shop cuts the price of compact discs from $15 to $12. Sales increase from 100 to 150 per day. Using the total revenue test, is demand for Joe's compact discs price elastic, inelastic, or unitary elastic?

9. **a.** Fill in the blanks in the following demand schedule.

Price	Quantity	Total Revenue	Elasticity
$10	100	1,000	
9	120	1,080	2.0 (20%/10%)
8	140	_____	___
7	160	_____	___
6	180	_____	___
5	200	_____	___
4	220	_____	___

b. What happens to elasticity as price continues to decline?

10. An increase in the production of basic farm commodities like grain, corn, wheat, and soybeans usually lowers overall farm income. In fact, most farmers earn more income when a mild drought cuts grain production measurably. Draw a demand and supply diagram for one of these grains, and explain what happens when a drought reduces supply. What are you assuming about the price elasticity of demand for most grains?

6

Behind the Supply Curve:

Cost and Production

The real price of everything, what everything really costs to the man who wants to acquire it, is the toil and trouble of acquiring it.

ADAM SMITH, *The Wealth of Nations*

Main Points

1. Firms can increase or decrease all of their resources in the long run; thus, all costs are variable. However, since the quantity of one or more inputs is fixed in the short run, firms have fixed as well as variable costs. Because fixed costs are unavoidable in the short run, they have no role in decision making; only variable costs affect decisions at the margin.

2. Economic profit—the difference between revenue and total economic (opportunity) costs—provides firms

with the incentive to organize for production and to take risks.

3. Firms maximize profit or minimize losses by choosing the output level at which marginal revenue equals marginal cost.

4. Price elasticity of supply measures the responsiveness of quantity supplied to changes in price.

P roduction usually takes place within firms rather than individual households, because firms have certain advantages over households with re-
spect to large-scale or specialized production. Therefore, firms answer
the "how to produce" question discussed in Chapter 2. From among several
alternative combinations, firms decide which mix of resources to use to produce
particular goods and services at the lowest possible total cost.

Firms also determine how much of particular goods they plan to produce—
the answer to the "what to produce" question. They compare expected revenue
to the expected costs of producing different levels of output and choose the
single output level that will maximize profit. Since expected revenues will vary
at different market prices, firms generally choose a different profit-maximizing
output level to correspond to each possible market price. Thus, their output
decisions for each possible price determine supply curves.

In this chapter, we focus on costs and how they relate to output decisions
and supply curves. In later chapters, we will explore how output decisions are
made in specific market situations such as competition and monopoly. ■

ORGANIZING FOR PRODUCTION

Although a great deal of production takes place within households (from cleaning
and cooking to painting and mowing), most of this output never reaches the
formal markets in which prices are charged and money changes hands. When
households want certain goods and services that require more skills or more
resources than they possess, they rely on business firms to supply goods to satisfy
those wants. Most production in the U.S. economy is organized and directed
by the business firms introduced in Chapter 3—corporations, proprietorships,
and partnerships.

Choosing Inputs for Production

Production function A
function that describes the
mix of productive re-
sources needed to produce
a particular product.

Firms produce goods and services by combining productive resources in a certain
way. A **production function** describes the various combinations of resources
(the input "recipes") needed to produce a particular product. For example,
corn is produced with some mixture of seed, soil, labor, tractors, fertilizer,
pesticide, water, and sunlight. A production function for corn would tell how
much of each of these inputs is needed to produce given yearly output levels.

Suppose a farmer wants to produce 100 bushels of corn per acre. The farmer's
corn production function might say that 100 bushels can be produced on an

In Practice 6.1

···

Productivity and
Technological Change

Production functions are not constant over time. They change as technology improves. Technological progress—learning how to produce more from the same quantity of inputs—is incorporated into production functions through changes in the productivity of certain inputs. As economists put it, technological change is "embodied" in one or more of the resources used. One resource category, capital, includes machinery and equipment of which new versions appear each year that produce a little faster or a little better.

Consider the problem of storing data and files in an office. Today much information, from letters to statistical analyses, is created on microcomputers and stored magnetically on floppy disks. These thin plastic disks first came out in an 8-inch size. Next, 5¼-inch diameter disks with 160 kilobytes of storage arrived. Then the same 5¼-inch disk could store 320kb, then 360kb, then 1,200kb, all without increasing the size of the removable storage disks or the amount of plastic used to make them. In the early 1990s, 3½-inch floppy disks with 1,440kb (1.44 megabytes) of storage capacity

rapidly took over. Small optical/laser disk drives that write to the same 3½-inch floppy disks are now available. These disks can store eight times as much data as the current standard, or about 10 megabytes. New CD readers are available on many new desktop computers. Thus, greater information storage capacity has become increasingly possible from the same inputs—a technological change embodied in a more efficient disk.

Technological progress is also embodied in labor. People learn over time how to perform certain tasks faster, more easily, or with greater accuracy and less waste. Additional training and higher levels of education also make labor more productive each year. Learning to crack eggs in both hands at the same time is a productivity improvement for a short-order cook at a waffle restaurant. New methods of production that are simply new ideas also represent technological progress that is embodied in labor. Examples include discovering better methods of motivating workers or treating infectious diseases.

In each instance, technological advancement changes the production function for particular goods so that more output can be produced with the same quantity of inputs, or, equivalently, so that fewer resource inputs are needed to produce the original output level. In either case (more output for a given cost or lower cost for a given output), technological improvement shifts supply curves to the right. ■

acre by using one unit of labor (worker), one unit of capital (tractor), and three units of fertilizer, pesticides, and seed. However, many other combinations of labor, capital, and other inputs may also be used to produce the same 100 bushels per acre. For instance, it may be possible to substitute more units of labor to check for pests and hoe weeds for one or two units of fertilizer and pesticides.

It is possible to substitute some of one input for a little of another in the production of most goods. In recent years, industrial robots have taken over welding duties in most automobile factories. Laser scanners have reduced the need for many checkers in supermarkets. Both cases are examples of substituting capital for labor. Recall our discussion of the Great Wall of China in Chapter 2 (p. 26). The Great Wall could have been produced with thousands of workers and only a little capital (wagons, ropes, hammers, and chisels) or with a few hundred people and much advanced capital (jackhammers, bulldozers, earth-moving equipment trucks, and large cranes).

Production Efficiency

Production efficiency
Efficiency resulting from choosing a combination of inputs to produce a particular good at the lowest possible cost.

Because inputs can be substituted in production functions, firms can be practical economists too. That is, firms have an opportunity to maximize output for a given level of cost or to minimize cost for a given target level of output by responding to input prices. The total cost of a given level of output depends on the combination of inputs chosen to produce it, because each input comes with a different price. Thus, firms want to pick the combination of resource inputs with the lowest cost to produce a given level of output. Using the least-cost combination of inputs is known as **production efficiency**. (Recall from Chapter 2 that production efficiency is one component of the overall goal of economic efficiency.)

The choice of inputs used in production depends partly on the technology of production, as expressed in a production function, and partly on the relative prices of the different types of inputs. Given the various possible input combinations, relative resource prices determine which input combination is most efficient (least costly). For example, which combination of inputs—A, B, or C—in Table 6-1 would an auto repair shop choose to repair 100 cars each week? The combination that is least costly! At $20 per hour, each unit of labor costs $800 per week. At $16 per hour, each unit of capital equipment—diagnostic computers and wheel- and frame-straightening equipment—costs $640 per week. Combination A uses 12 servicepeople and only 1 unit of equipment. Combination C uses 6 units of each to repair the same number of cars each week. Assuming the amount of steel used is the same in any case, the least costly combination of inputs would be B, which uses 8 units of labor and 3 units of capital for a total cost of $7,320 per week.

TABLE 6-1   Least-Cost Input Combination to Repair 100 Cars per Week

Weekly cost of labor @ $20 per hour   = $800 per unit
Weekly cost of capital equipment @ $16 per hour = $640 per unit

Input Combination	Units of Labor	Units of Capital	Total Cost
A	12	1	$10,240
B	8	3	7,320
C	6	6	8,640

Since relative resource prices determine which input combination is most efficient, the actual mix of productive resources used to make a particular product will change as resource prices change. Here is another case of making decisions at the margin. If the price of one of the "ingredients" increases, firms will substitute a little more of other resources for a little less of the one whose price has risen. When a resource price decreases, more of it is used at the margin in place of some of the other resources. For example, in almost all banks one or more automatic teller machines have replaced some bank tellers (as well as counters and floor space). The reason is that in the mid-1990s, the prices of computer hardware and software have continued to fall sharply relative to the prices of skilled teller labor and bank counters and floor space.

COSTS AND PROFITS

The practical economists who operate firms want to maximize profit—the difference between total revenue and total costs. The last two chapters described how the price of the product and the quantity sold together determine total revenue. In this section, we will focus on what costs include and how costs change as output increases or decreases. Firms need to be able to measure and predict costs as well as revenue to maximize profit.

Economic Cost

Economic cost   All the opportunity costs of producing a good with scarce resources, regardless of whether money payments are made for those resources.

Explicit costs   Money payments for productive resources, such as wages, rent, and interest.

Implicit costs   The forgone benefits of using resources in production that are owned by the producers and for which no direct, monetary payments are made.

The **economic cost** of a good always equals the full opportunity cost of that good; that is, the true cost of producing any good is the value of what must be given up to obtain it. One part of economic cost includes the money payments—called **explicit costs** or sometimes *accounting costs*—for using productive resources. Explicit costs are the usual costs recorded by accountants in the firm's books: wages paid to labor, payments for raw materials, interest paid on debt, and other money outlays for inputs.

A second kind of economic cost is less obvious but equally important. **Implicit costs** are the value of alternatives given up (or benefits lost) to produce a good regardless of whether money payments are made. Implicit costs include forgone benefits of resources used in production that are owned by the producers and for which no direct, monetary payments are made. The true test of an opportunity cost is whether it affects decisions, and implicit costs certainly do.

For example, one implicit cost of a grocer who owns her store is the building's rental value. Although the store owner does not have to pay rent, the store could be rented to others. This forgone rent is an implicit cost of operating the grocery. The grocer is a practical economist. If she could rent out her building for more than the store's monthly accounting profit, she would go out of business and rent the store because doing so would maximize her income. Thus, the rental value of the building is a true (implicit) opportunity cost. It should be added to explicit costs to arrive at total economic cost.

A second implicit cost is the normal income or return an entrepreneur could earn in his or her next best alternative enterprise or other job. Payments for performing the entrepreneurial functions of innovating, taking risks, and incurring the headaches of organizing any business must be included as costs. As discussed in Chapter 2 enterprise, like land, labor, and capital, is a scarce resource.

Look at it this way: The owner of the grocery could use her entrepreneurial skills to start up some other business, such as making bicycles or selling mail-order retail goods. The normal return she could have earned in those other businesses is an implicit cost of undertaking the grocery concern. Suppose this grocer had been earning $2,000 monthly in her job as an accountant before going into business for herself. That amount would be an implicit cost of being in the grocery business. Why? Because the grocery must return at least $2,000 a month in profit, or the owner will close it to return to work as an accountant or operate an alternative business. Economists call this required normal return for enterprise a **normal profit.** Normal profit is a very real cost of doing business. Since an entrepreneur must receive at least a normal profit to stay in a particular business, that amount of profit is an opportunity cost and must be included in implicit costs.

Normal profit An implicit cost equal to the usual return for enterprise in alternative businesses; a firm earns a normal profit when its revenue just covers all of its economic costs.

CHECKLIST

Economic Cost

Economic cost includes both explicit and implicit costs:

Economic Costs	= Opportunity Costs		
	= Explicit Costs	+	Implicit Costs
	Wages, rent, expenses for electricity, supplies, insurance, etc.		Forgone rent, wages and income from alternative uses of owned resources such as buildings, owners' labor, and enterprise

Economic profit The difference between total revenue and economic cost for a firm; a firm incurs an economic loss when its economic profit is negative.

Economic Profit

Economic profit is the difference between total revenue and total economic cost for producing a given level of output. If revenue and economic cost are equal, the firm makes zero economic profit. If revenue exceeds economic cost, the firm earns an economic profit; if revenue is less than economic cost, the firm incurs an economic loss.

Suppose Allen Works, Inc., is a small firm that partially assembles bicycles for a major manufacturer and packs them in boxes for shipping to department stores. The owner, Bill Allen, supplies the following weekly total revenue and cost figures for assembling and packing 500 bicycles at $10 per carton:

Total revenue (500 bikes @ $10)		$5,000
Explicit costs		
Labor	$1,000	
Bicycle parts	2,500	
Total explicit costs		$3,500
Accounting profit (net revenue)		$1,500
Implicit costs		
Rental value of owned warehouse	$ 500	
Normal profit available in alternative business or former job	1,000	
Total implicit costs		$1,500
Total economic cost (explicit costs + implicit costs)		$5,000
Economic profit		$ 0

Accounting profit The difference between a firm's total revenue and its explicit costs.

Assembling and packing 500 bikes each week at $10 per carton means Allen Works' total revenue is $5,000. The firm's explicit costs for labor and bicycle parts total $3,500, leaving a net revenue of $1,500. Ignoring taxes and other costs, Allen Works is making a nice weekly accounting profit of $1,500. **Accounting profit** is simply the difference between total revenue and explicit costs. However, the firm is not making a profit in the economic sense; it has implicit costs of $1,500 that also must be "covered" by its revenue.

Allen Works is earning zero economic profit because its $5,000 revenue is just sufficient to cover its total economic costs of $5,000, including all implicit costs. Since the firm earns just enough to offset the amount that could be earned operating the next best alternative business, no more or less, Allen Works is making a normal profit.

Economic profit is an important concept because it is the primary criterion by which new firms decide to enter an industry and existing firms decide to continue to produce or leave the industry in the long run. When economic profit is zero (the firm is earning a normal profit), the firm has no incentive to change its price or output level. (Remember, we assume the firm is already doing all it can to keep costs low and revenue high.) Likewise, other firms have no incentive to enter this industry and compete with this assembler/shipper, since Allen Works earns only a normal profit.

When economic profit is negative, the firm is incurring economic losses and will eventually go out of business, switching its resources to other industries in which it can at least earn a normal profit. Note that accounting losses are not necessary for this to happen. A firm making a small accounting profit may still decide to go out of business if its dollar profit does not match the profit it could make in an alternative business (i.e., accounting profit is less than normal profit). Without making at least a normal profit, the firm will close in the long run.

On the other hand, a positive economic profit encourages other firms to enter this industry, just as the pain of economic losses signals existing firms to leave. This signaling function of economic profit (loss) will be very important in understanding the behavior of firms in the various market models we discuss in the next two chapters.

PRODUCTION IN THE SHORT AND LONG RUN

Short run   The period of time during which a firm cannot change the amount of one or more of its inputs.

To produce output at the lowest possible cost and respond to changes in resource prices, firms must be able to change the amount of one or more of the inputs they use. In the short run, firms can adjust some inputs but not all of them. In fact, the **short run** is defined as the period of time during which at least one of the firm's inputs—usually land or capital—is fixed.

Firms have both fixed inputs and variable inputs in the short run. A **fixed input** is an input whose amounts firms cannot reduce or increase to change output in the short run. Sometimes planning and building new manufacturing plants takes years. Automobile companies, for example, cannot simply develop new cars and build new factories overnight in response to a year of high prices. When BMW announced in 1992 that it would build a new plant in South Carolina, the firm predicted that the first car would roll off the assembly line in December 1995, two and one-half years later.

Fixed input   A resource, such as capital, whose amounts firms cannot reduce or increase to change output in the short run.

Variable input   A resource, such as labor or supplies, whose amounts firms can increase or reduce to change output in the short run.

Variable inputs, on the other hand, are those productive inputs whose amounts firms can increase or decrease in the short run. Typically, variable inputs include labor and materials. A McDonald's restaurant can increase its daily hamburger output by hiring additional workers and ordering more meat, buns, and lots of mustard and ketchup. On the other hand, it can reduce output by decreasing its variable inputs, laying off workers and canceling orders for supplies. The fixed inputs for a McDonald's franchise are the restaurant's building, counter space, cash registers, and cooking equipment.

Long run   The period of time in which firms can vary all their inputs to change output.

Only in the long run can firms adjust *all* of their resources. The **long run** is a planning period sufficiently long that all the firm's inputs are variable. If IBM's managers want to increase their output of microcomputers, they can do so in the short run only by adding more workers and materials. In the long run, however, they also have the option to build a larger plant and use more machines instead of (or along with) using more workers and raw materials.

The short and long run are not specific, measurable time periods but analytical concepts that help explain how firms make decisions about levels of output and costs. The length of the short run varies greatly from industry to industry. The short run for a steel company is much longer than the short run for a restaurant. It may take years for a steel plant's fixed inputs of blast furnaces and factories to become variable. But a fast-food restaurant may be able to change its fixed inputs of kitchen square footage, installed cooking equipment, and customer seating space in a matter of months or even weeks.

SHORT-RUN COSTS

Fixed costs (FC) Expenses that do not vary with increases or decreases in the level of a firm's output, corresponding to the expenses for fixed inputs.

In the short run, some costs are fixed, whereas others ave variable. **Fixed costs (FC)** do not vary with increases or decreases in the level of a firm's output over a certain time period. Fire insurance on buildings, lease contracts for equipment and warehouses, property taxes, and even normal profit are examples of expenses that must be paid in the short run whether the firm produces 60 units, 1,000 units, or no units of output. It is important to remember that firms cannot escape these fixed costs in the short run, even by shutting down.

Variable costs (VC) Expenses that vary with changes in the level of a firm's output, corresponding to the expenses for variable inputs.

Variable costs (VC) include expenses that increase and decrease with changes in the level of a firm's output. Payments of wages for labor, expenses for raw materials, and such inputs as electricity and boiler fuel usually vary with different output levels as more or fewer resource inputs are used. Increase output and variable costs rise. Reduce output and variable costs decrease. Stop producing altogether and variable costs fall to zero.

Total cost (TC) The sum of all fixed and variable costs, whether those expenditures are explicit or implicit.

Total cost (TC) for a given level of output in the short run is the sum of all fixed and variable costs, whether those expenses are explicit or implicit. In symbols,

$$TC = FC + VC.$$

Fixed, variable, and total costs for Jane's Picture Frames, Inc., are shown in Table 6-2. Various output levels (frames per day) are given in column 1. Columns 2, 3, and 4 show the associated costs. Fixed cost is constant at $10 for all output levels in the short run. Variable cost increases at an increasing rate after the first few output levels. Total cost is the sum of FC and VC.

Law of increasing costs The principle stating that beyond some output level in the short run, variable costs increase by progressively larger amounts as output increases.

Law of Increasing Costs

Variable costs in column 3 of Table 6.2 increase in a particular way as output increases. These costs change according to the **law of increasing costs,** introduced in Chapter 2. This law states that beyond some output level in the short

---

TABLE 6-2   Short-Run Costs for Jane's Picture Frames, Inc.

Total Product (Q) (1)	Fixed Cost (FC) (2)	Variable Cost (VC) (3)	Total Cost (TC) (4)	Average Fixed Cost (AFC) (5)	Average Variable Cost (AVC) (6)	Average Total Cost (AC) (7)	Marginal Cost (MC) (8)
0	$10	$ 0	$10	$—	$—	$—	$—
1	10	3	13	10	3	13	3
2	10	4	14	5	2	7	1
3	10	6	16	3.33	2	5.33	2
4	10	10	20	2.50	2.50	5	4
5	10	16	26	2	3.20	5.20	6
6	10	24	34	1.66	4	5.66	8

---

run, variable costs (and therefore total costs) increase by progressively larger amounts as output increases. At low output levels, before the law of increasing costs sets in, variable costs may increase by constant amounts or may even increase at a decreasing rate as output expands. But sooner or later, the law of increasing costs takes effect. Because some inputs are fixed in the short run, adding more variable inputs to those fixed inputs adds less and less to total output. Since each extra unit of output produced requires ever larger quantities of variable inputs, those extra units cost more and more to produce.

The law of increasing costs is an example of a broader principle called the *law of diminishing returns:* The return, or gain, from adding more of a variable resource to a given quantity of a fixed resource diminishes as the ratio of variable to fixed inputs gets larger and larger.

For example, applying more and more fertilizer to a fixed plot of land increases corn output, but at a progressively increasing cost. Only a little more fertilizer may be required at first to produce another bushel of corn per acre. However, larger and larger doses of fertilizer will be needed to squeeze additional bushels of corn from each acre of land, pushing costs per bushel steadily higher. Eventually, even massive doses of extra fertilizer will yield little or no extra output; in fact, they may even *reduce* output per acre. The cost of an extra bushel of corn per acre ultimately becomes very high—even infinite.

The variable costs given for Jane's Picture Frames at each output level (Table 6-2) reflect the law of increasing costs. At first, the law is not in effect. The first picture frame can be produced for a variable cost of $3, but the variable cost for two frames is only $4. An extra picture frame can be produced for only $1 more instead of the $3 the first one costs. After two picture frames, however, variable cost starts to increase by ever larger amounts with each increase in output.

Average and Marginal Cost

Columns 5 through 8 of Table 6-2 show average fixed cost, average variable cost, average total cost, and marginal cost for Jane's framing business. Each of these concepts will help Jane decide how many frames she will supply at various prices.

Average fixed cost (AFC) is fixed cost divided by the number of units produced:

Average fixed cost (AFC)   Fixed cost divided by the number of units produced, or fixed cost per unit of output.

$$AFC = FC/Q.$$

Average fixed cost continually declines as output levels increase, because a constant fixed cost is divided by larger output levels (Q). Average fixed cost (column 5) declines from $10.00 at a production level of one frame per day to $1.66 for six frames per day. The larger the level of output, the smaller the fixed cost component of each unit's average cost. This concept is known as "spreading your overhead."

Average variable cost (AVC) is computed like average fixed cost—variable cost at each output level divided by the number of units produced:

Average variable cost (AVC)   Variable cost divided by the number of units produced, or variable cost per unit of output.

$$AVC = VC/Q.$$

Average variable cost may decline, remain constant, or rise for the first few units of output, but it eventually increases in the short run because of the law of increasing cost.

Average total cost (AC) is total cost divided by total output. It is also the sum of average fixed cost and average variable cost for any given output level:

Average total cost (AC)   Total cost divided by the number of units of output produced, or the sum of average fixed and variable costs.

$$AC = TC/Q$$
$$= AFC + AVC.$$

Average total cost may decline at low output levels because the impact of declining average fixed cost is stronger than the weak (or nonexistent) effect of the law of increasing cost. Beyond some output level, however, average total cost increases because average variable cost rises by enough to more than offset declining average fixed cost. This pattern for average total cost can be seen in column 7 of Table 6-2. Average cost (AC) declines through the first four picture frames produced per day but rises for output levels of five and six frames.

Marginal cost (MC) is the extra cost per additional unit of output produced. Marginal cost is calculated by dividing the change in total cost by the change in quantity produced:

Marginal cost (MC)   The change in total (or variable) cost divided by the change in output, or the extra cost of producing one additional unit of output.

$$MC = \text{Change in } TC/\text{Change in } Q.$$

In Table 6-2, the extra or marginal cost of producing the first picture frame is $3 and declines to $1 for the second frame. After the second frame, however, marginal cost rises for each additional unit of output, once again reflecting the law of increasing costs.

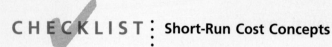

CHECKLIST : Short-Run Cost Concepts

- Fixed cost (FC)   Cost of fixed inputs in the short run
- Variable cost (VC)   Cost of inputs that vary with the level of output
- Total cost (TC)   Sum of fixed and variable cost at each output level
- Average fixed cost (AFC)   Fixed cost per unit of output ($AFC = FC/Q$)
- Average variable cost (AVC)   Variable cost per unit of output ($AVC = VC/Q$)
- Average total cost (AC)   Total cost per unit of output ($AC = TC/Q = AFC + AVC$)
- Marginal cost (MC)   Change in total cost per extra unit of output
                                     ($MC = \Delta TC/\Delta Q$)

Average and Marginal Cost Curves

The average and marginal cost curves that correspond to short-run costs such as those for Jane's Picture Frames, Inc., are drawn in Figure 6-1. The average fixed cost curve (AFC) declines over the entire range of output, since fixed cost (a constant number) is divided by ever larger levels of output. The average variable cost curve (AVC) declines at first, then increases thereafter because of the law of increasing costs. In most cases, the AVC curve is U shaped.

The average total cost (AC) curve is also U shaped, but it reaches its lowest point farther to the right. Average cost declines and then rises, but it does not take on exactly the same shape as the average variable cost curve because of the additional effect of declining average fixed cost. The AC curve is the vertical sum of the AFC and AVC curves ($AC = AFC + AVC$). (Costs are added vertically because costs are measured on the vertical axis, whereas the given output levels are on the horizontal axis.) Therefore, the vertical distance between the AC and AVC curves at any output equals AFC.

FIGURE 6-1

These are the general shapes of standard short-run cost curves that economists use most often. Both the AVC and AC curves are U shaped, and the MC curve cuts through the minimum points of each average cost curve.

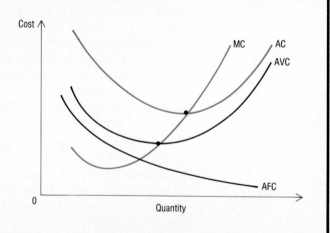

Economists are especially interested in the fourth curve in Figure 6-1, the marginal cost (MC) curve. Remember, practical economists make decisions at the margin! The MC curve has a special relationship to the AVC and AC curves: It intersects both curves at their minimum points. To see why this is so, think about your marginal and average test grades in any course. If your last test grade—your marginal grade—is lower than your average grade, your average grade in the course will fall. If your next test grade is higher than your average grade, it will pull your average up. Finally, when your marginal test grade equals your average grade, your average will not change.

Thus, when average variable cost is falling, marginal cost must be less than (or below) average variable cost to pull it down and greater than (or above) average variable cost when AVC is rising. Since the AVC curve is U shaped, MC must lie below its falling portion and above its rising portion. Since MC also must equal AVC at its minimum point, it will always cross the AVC curve at the bottom of the U.

The same relationship exists between marginal cost and average total cost. Marginal cost lies below the falling portion of the AC curve, crosses it at its minimum point, and lies above the rising portion of the U shaped AC curve. Figure 6-1 illustrates these general relationships among AFC, AVC, AC, and MC curves.

PROFIT MAXIMIZATION AND THE SUPPLY CURVE

Firms try to reduce costs and increase revenue whenever possible because their objective is to maximize economic profit. How does a firm determine which level of output is the one that maximizes profit for each possible price? The answer to this question is also the firm's supply curve.

The Profit-Maximizing Rule

Profit-maximizing rule
The principle that choosing the output level at which marginal revenue equals marginal cost (MR = MC) maximizes a firm's profit.

Marginal revenue (MR)
The change in total revenue divided by the change in output sold, or the extra revenue earned from selling one additional unit of output.

Firms choose what level of output to produce on the basis of both the costs and the demand they face. Firms try to get the greatest possible profit from their available resources by employing the **profit-maximizing rule.** This rule states that a firm will maximize profit (or minimize loss) in the short run by producing that output level at which marginal revenue equals marginal cost (MR = MC), provided it is worthwhile to produce at all. **Marginal revenue (MR)** is the extra revenue obtained from selling one more unit of output. For now, we will assume marginal revenue is equal to price. The profit-maximizing rule is based on the fact that an extra unit of output is worth producing and selling only if it adds at least as much to total revenue as it does to total cost; that is, the extra unit is worth producing and selling only if MR ≥ MC.

At output levels above the profit-maximizing output, marginal cost exceeds marginal revenue (MC > MR). The practical economist would choose to reduce output. The last unit is not worth producing because it adds more to cost than it adds to revenue. At output levels below the profit-maximizing level, marginal cost is less than marginal revenue (MC < MR). Since the last unit adds less to total cost than it adds to total revenue, it is a profitable unit. As long as MC < MR, extra output adds a positive amount to profit; thus, profit-maximizing firms will expand production. Therefore, the level of output that yields maximum profit occurs where output is expanded to the level at which marginal cost and marginal revenue are just equal.

Figure 6-2 illustrates the profit-maximizing rule using a horizontal demand curve for simplicity. The profit-maximizing level of output, Q_m, occurs where the marginal cost and marginal revenue curves cross, or where MC = MR. Producing any greater output, such as Q_b, would mean MC > MR. The marginal unit would add more to total cost than it would add to total revenue, thus reducing profit. At any output less than Q_m, such as Q_a, MR > MC. The firm could produce one more unit that would add more to revenue than it would add to cost, thus increasing profit. Therefore, Q_m, chosen where MC = MR, is the profit-maximizing level of output. Either a larger or a smaller output level would result in a lower profit for the firm.

CHECKLIST : The Profit-Maximizing Rule

For a given output level,	If	Then
	MC > MR	Reduce output
	MC < MR	Increase output
	MC = MR	Profit is maximized

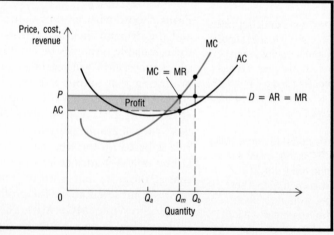

FIGURE 6-2

At output Q_b, MC > MR; the last unit produced and sold adds more to cost than it adds to revenue, thus lowering profit. At output Q_a, MR > MC; the last unit adds more to revenue than it adds to cost, hence raising profit. The profit-maximizing level of output is Q_m, where MR = MC.

Short-Run Supply

One useful property of cost curves is that they help explain where the short-run supply curve comes from. Consider the marginal and average cost curves for a typical firm such as those in Figure 6-3. The figure also shows two prices, P_1 and P_2. Assume this firm can sell as many units as it wants at each price, so price equals marginal revenue. The firm chooses the profit-maximizing level of output corresponding to each price at which MC = MR, or the intersection of the marginal cost and marginal revenue curves. When price is P_1, profit is maximized with an output of Q_1 and at P_2 with an output of Q_2. The firm supplies a larger quantity when the price is higher—a familiar result. These two price-quantity combinations on the marginal cost curve are also two points on the firm's short-run supply curve! Remember, the supply curve shows what quantities the firm will offer for sale at all possible prices. The profit-maximizing rule proves that the marginal cost curve determines those output levels.

Thus, this firm's supply curve is that portion of the marginal cost curve above the AVC curve (the thick line in Figure 6-3). The portion of the MC curve below the AVC curve is irrelevant. If faced with a price that did not at least cover the variable costs of production, the firm would produce nothing. The supply curve slopes upward because it is really part of the marginal cost curve. Since upward-sloping marginal cost curves depend on the law of increasing cost in the short run, *short-run supply curves slope upward due primarily to the law of increasing costs.*

Long-Run Cost and Supply

Because the long run is defined as the period in which firms have no fixed inputs in the long run but only variable inputs, the long run is considered

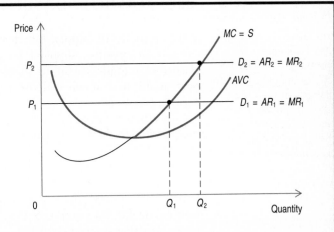

FIGURE 6-3

This firm maximizes profit (or minimizes losses) by choosing output Q_1 when price is P_1 or Q_2 when price is P_2. In each case, this quantity occurs where MR = MC. That portion of the MC curve above AVC (the thick line) represents the firm's supply curve, S.

to be firms' planning period. In the long run, firms plan for the most efficient plant size, or the least-cost overall scale of operations needed to produce each possible output level. Long-run average cost curves usually are U shaped, sloping first downward and then upward. It is often the case that average cost declines as firm size increases in the small to medium-size range. This initial decline in cost is due to **economies of scale,** production efficiencies encountered in the long run as firm size increases. These cost-reducing efficiencies usually result from the ability to use specialized labor and capital as firms move out of the small-size range. For example, a building contractor needs to be large enough to make use of a full-time accountant or an on-site crane.

After the firm reaches a certain size, however, long-run average and marginal cost increase with firm size, reflecting diseconomies of scale. **Diseconomies of scale** are cost-raising inefficiencies associated with poor information flows in large, bureaucratic firms. It becomes difficult to control the firm and make sound business decisions when there are multiple layers of management (senior associate vice presidents, associate vice presidents, assistants to the associate vice presidents) and far-flung divisions and plants. Average and marginal costs eventually rise with higher output obtained by creating ever larger and increasingly complex companies.

Like short-run supply curves, long-run supply curves usually slope upward, but for a different reason. (The law of increasing cost is not the reason, because it applies only when one of the resource inputs is fixed, and no resources are fixed in the long run.) Upward-sloping long-run supply curves are the result of increasing marginal cost in the long run, which reflects the inevitable diseconomies of scale associated with larger firm size.

Economies of scale
Long-run production efficiencies encountered as firms increase in size, enabling them to lower cost by using more specialized inputs.

Diseconomies of scale
Long-run production inefficiencies, encountered as firms increase beyond some size in the long run, that cause long-run average cost to rise.

PRICE ELASTICITY OF SUPPLY

Price elasticity of supply
A measurement of the responsiveness of quantity supplied to a price change; between two prices, it is equal to the ratio of the percentage change in average quantity supplied to the percentage change in average price.

Price elasticity of supply, like demand price elasticity, measures the responsiveness of quantity supplied to changes in price. Knowledge of supply elasticities is quite useful. If market prices for auto and truck tires fall 20 percent, by how much will tire producers like Goodyear and Michelin cut their production?

Between two prices (old and new), price elasticity of supply is the ratio of the percentage change in quantity supplied to the percentage change in price:

$$PE_s = \frac{\text{Percentage Change in Quantity Supplied}}{\text{Percentage Change in Price}}$$

Suppose tire prices fall by the 20 percent just mentioned. If tire producers respond by reducing output by only 5 percent, the price elasticity of supply for tires is less than 1, or inelastic:

$$PE_s = \frac{-5\%}{-20\%} = 0.25.$$

Supply is elastic if a change in price causes a relatively larger change in quantity supplied, or $PE_s > 1$. Supply is inelastic if the change in quantity supplied is relatively smaller than the change in price, or $PE_s < 1$. Finally, supply exhibits unitary elasticity where the relative change in quantity supplied equals the relative change in price, that is, when $PE_s = 1$.

Figure 6-4 illustrates relative price elasticity of supply. Supply curve S_B is relatively more elastic than supply curve S_A. If price rises from P_1 to P_2, the quantity response along S_B increases from Q_1 to Q_B. The same price increase would cause a smaller increase in quantity supplied along S_A, from Q_1 to only Q_A.

CHECKLIST : Price Elasticity of Supply

For a given percentage change in price,

If the Percentage Change in Quantity Is	Then Price Elasticity of Supply Is	
Larger	Elastic	$(PE_s > 1)$
Smaller	Inelastic	$(PE_s < 1)$
Same	Unitary	$(PE_s = 1)$

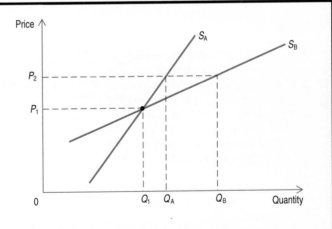

FIGURE 6-4

Supply curve S_B is relatively more elastic than supply curve S_A. The same increase in price from P_1 to P_2 causes a larger quantity response along S_B (quantity increases from Q_1 to Q_B) than along S_A (quantity increases from Q_1 to only Q_A).

To what extent does quantity supplied respond to price changes? It depends primarily on how much time the firm has to increase or decrease resource inputs to adjust the level of production. In the short run, when one or more inputs is fixed, it may be relatively difficult to increase output quickly in response to a price change. In the long run, however, output can be increased more easily because all inputs can be increased, allowing firms to obtain the most efficient input mix, which keeps costs lower. The greater the adjustment time available to the firm, the greater the quantity response to any given price change. Therefore, supply is relatively more elastic in the long run for any industry.

Figure 6-5 illustrates the impact of time on the price elasticity of supply for hamburgers. As price increases from P_1 to P_2, the quantity of hamburgers supplied in the present remains almost unchanged, and the present supply curve is nearly vertical, or nearly perfectly inelastic. Few additional hamburgers can be made available *in the next ten minutes* at any higher price! (If you have ever gone into a Burger King restaurant at the same time a high school band bus arrives, you know what nearly perfectly inelastic supply in the very short run means.)

Short-run hamburger supply, however, is likely to be more price elastic than that. At higher prices, a greater quantity can be made available in a few days or a week, which is enough time to hire one or two more workers and order more meat and buns. Long-run supply is even more elastic, because the firm has enough time to plan and to increase all inputs, including such things as the size of the building, grill space, and even the size of the parking lot. Since the firm can increase all these inputs in the "right" (efficient) proportions in the long run, it can increase output with smaller increases in

FIGURE 6-5

The price elasticity of supply for hamburgers (or any other good) varies with the time available for the firm to adjust to changes in price. Immediate supply is almost perfectly inelastic, or nearly vertical. The short-run supply curve has some elasticity, however, because the firm can vary certain inputs (labor, hamburger meat, and buns) to alter quantity supplied in response to a price change. The long-run supply curve is more elastic than any other because all inputs are variable, including the building and the cooking equipment.

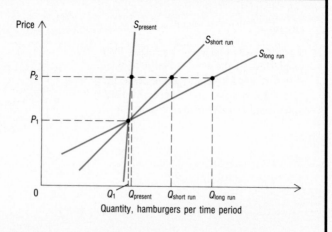

. . . .

Myth 6.1

. . . .

Most Supply Curves are Vertical

Many people suspect that most firms do not increase their output in response to higher market prices; rather, these greedy capitalists make "windfall profits." Many people expressed this belief during the oil crisis of the 1970s, when gasoline and heating oil prices rose dramatically in response to cutbacks in output by the Organization of Petroleum Exporting Nations (OPEC), an oil cartel.

The short-run supply curve for domestically produced oil is very price inelastic. It is difficult for firms to drill new wells and build new refineries overnight in response to higher prices. Thus, the quantity of oil supplied is not very responsive to price increases in the short run. However, in the 1970s oil companies did respond with *some* higher output in the short run. They used better techniques (such as pumping steam into wells to increase oil flow) to get more oil out of existing wells in a short period of time. They also "uncapped" old wells that had been closed because they produced too little oil per hour, making them unprofitable to operate at the old price.

In the long run, however, oil supply is much more price elastic. With higher oil prices, oil companies around the world increased their annual drilling operations more than tenfold, searching for oil in faraway places like Alaska's North Slope and in hostile environments such as the North Sea off the coast of Scotland. Such costly oil exploration activities could be undertaken only because the price of oil had risen significantly. Indeed, since OPEC could "turn the spigot back on" at any time and drive oil prices back down, oil prices had to rise a great deal before companies would undertake such risky exploration and production.

Given time to adjust (a six-to-eight-year long run), oil companies were very successful in their search for oil.

Great Britain began to produce enough from the North Sea to become an exporter rather than an importer of oil. Mexico became self-sufficient in oil and a major exporter. The former Soviet Union soon became one of the largest producers of oil in the world and began to supply European nations. The United States piped oil from Alaska and the Gulf of Mexico.

As supply increased from non–OPEC countries, prices fell in the 1980s and the OPEC price-fixing scheme fell apart. Oil prices (adjusted for inflation) dropped back to levels equivalent to those in the 1960s. Although the short-run supply curve for oil is somewhat inelastic (but certainly not vertical), the long-run supply curve for oil evidently is not inelastic at all.

Firms in all industries respond to price changes along their upward-sloping supply curves. Although short-run supply curves are steeper (more inelastic) than long-run curves, economists know of no instances where even those short-run curves are perfectly inelastic, or vertical. ■

cost. Thus, in the long run a larger quantity is supplied at each possible price, or price is lower for each possible quantity supplied.

In the chapters on microeconomics that follow, we will use these cost concepts, along with the concept of demand in Chapter 5, to examine the behavior of consumers and firms operating in particular kinds of markets. We will investigate more fully how different types of markets influence the behavior of firms and affect the equilibrium prices and quantities prevailing in those markets. In Chapter 7, we begin our study of these market models with pure competition.

Summary

1. Production functions describe the proportions, or "recipe," in which inputs can be combined to produce particular goods. Production functions also illustrate how amounts of some inputs can be substituted for one another in the production process.

2. Firms are interested in production efficiency. They try to produce any given level of output at the lowest possible cost. Therefore, the actual mix of productive resources used to produce a good depends on the prices of those resources.

3. In the short run, some inputs are fixed and firms may vary only a few other inputs to increase or decrease output. In the long run, all inputs in the production process are variable and firms focus on choosing the correct plant size, or scale of operations.

4. Production in the short run is subject to the law of increasing cost. Beyond some output level, marginal cost rises as output increases. Short-run supply curves slope upward because of the law of increasing cost.

5. Economic cost includes all the opportunity costs of production. It is the sum of all explicit and implicit costs. Economic profit is the difference between total revenue and total economic cost. Since economic cost includes a normal profit for entrepreneurs, a firm that makes zero economic profit still earns a normal profit.

6. To achieve the largest possible profit (or smallest possible loss) at each market price, firms employ the profit-maximizing rule, which requires that firms choose an output level at which marginal revenue and marginal cost are equal.

7. Price elasticity of supply measures the responsiveness of the quantity supplied by firms when product price changes. Supply is elastic (inelastic) when the percentage change in quantity supplied is greater (smaller) than the percentage change in price. Price elasticity of supply depends primarily on the time period involved. Elasticity is greater the longer the time period available for output adjustment.

Key Terms

accounting profit
average fixed cost
  (AFC)
average total cost (AC)
average variable cost
  (AVC)
diseconomies of scale
economic cost
economic profit

economies of scale
explicit costs
fixed costs (FC)
fixed input
implicit costs
law of increasing costs
long run
marginal cost (MC)
marginal revenue (MR)

normal profit
price elasticity of supply
production efficiency
production function
profit-maximizing rule
short run
total cost (TC)
variable costs (VC)
variable input

Questions and Problems

1. Suppose the production function for popcorn is $Q = 6K + 2L + 20FL$, where Q is tons of popcorn per season, K is units of capital equipment such as tractors and mechanical corn pickers, L is the number of farm laborers, and FL is acres of farmland.
   a. Find three sets of input quantities the firm can use to produce 28 tons of popcorn per growing season.
   b. If the price (yearly cost) of capital is $3,000 per unit, the price of labor is $16,000 per unit, and the rental price of land is $800 per acre, what is the cost of each set of inputs? Which input combination is most efficient? Do you think you have found the most efficient resource combination (the one with the lowest possible cost)?

2. Explain why the following definitions of economic efficiency must amount to exactly the same thing: (a) produce the most output for a given total cost, and (b) produce a given output level for the lowest possible cost.

3. Explain why increasing the level of output produced in the short run is likely to require a higher product price than if the same increase in output takes place in the long run.

4. Suppose you operate a bicycle shop near campus. Thinking in terms of a six-month short run for your business, list your major fixed inputs and major variable inputs. How would this list change if you planned to double your output in the long run?

5. Rank the following firms according to the likely elasticities of their short-run supply curves, and explain your reasoning:
   a. A wheat farmer
   b. A local Pizza Hut
   c. Lawn-care service
   d. A university
   e. A music teacher
   f. Ford Motor Company.

6. Why isn't there just one large burger restaurant on the fast-food strip in your town instead of three or four? Wouldn't costs (and prices) be lower if

the town council mandated that the area could have only one large burger restaurant (in the interests of aesthetics and lower hamburger prices)?

7. How would you describe the long-run average cost curve for the higher education industry? Is this industry dominated by many small firms (colleges), firms of very different sizes, or by just a few very large firms? Why?

8. When fluid milk prices increased from $80 per 100 pounds to $88, dairies statewide increased production from 1.2 million pounds per week to 1.44 million pounds. What is the price elasticity of supply for milk?

7

The Market in Operation:

Pure Competition

The price system will fulfill [its] function only if competition prevails, that is, if the individual producer has to adapt himself to price changes and cannot control them.

FRIEDRICH A. HAYEK, 1944

Main Points

1. Four basic market models exist: pure competition, monopolistic competition, oligopoly, and monopoly. These models describe the demand and cost conditions and the behavior of firms in different kinds of market structures.

2. Pure competition describes industries operating in markets that have a large number of sellers and buyers, a homogeneous product, free entry and exit by firms, and perfect knowledge of prices and technology. In purely competitive markets, neither firms nor consumers have any control over market prices, and no product advertising occurs.

3. In competitive markets, the "invisible hand" of self-interest directs both firms and consumers in their price and output decisions. Firms try to maximize profit, and consumers try to buy goods at the lowest possible price to maximize their utility.

4. In the short run, firms in competitive industries may make normal profits, economic profits, or economic losses. In the long run, short-run economic profits or losses are eliminated as firms enter or leave the industry.

5. In long-run equilibrium, firms in purely competitive markets produce at the lowest average cost (production efficiency) and produce those goods and services consumers want most (allocative efficiency).

6. Households are usually perfectly competitive sellers of the services of productive resources. Demand for resources, including labor, comes from the demand for a firm's products. Workers are paid according to the extra revenue their output adds to the firm.

M arkets for various goods and services—wheat, bonds, steel, rock concerts—differ greatly in terms of competitiveness. Some markets (wheat and corn) consist of thousands of producers, whereas others (automobiles and washing machines) are dominated by only a few firms. On the consumer side, some markets (bread and shoes) have thousands of competing buyers, and other markets (military equipment) have only a few (only governments buy tanks). Firms in some markets (a local water utility) are protected from competition by government; others are protected by patents or the fact that potential competitors would have to spend millions of dollars on advertising.

Firms react differently to changes in demand, cost, or technology when their industry is made up of many small firms instead of being dominated by only one or a few firms. When demand increases, the local power company may increase output very little, whereas a wheat farmer may increase production substantially during the next growing season. The structure of the industry in which a firm operates determines how much the firm changes output and price in response to changes in demand, supply, or other economic conditions. This chapter is devoted entirely to the most basic market model: pure competition. Other types of markets, characterized by less than pure competition, are the subject of Chapter 8. ■

MARKET MODELS AND FIRM BEHAVIOR

The desire to find the profit-maximizing level of output is the same for all firms regardless of the sturctures of the markets in which they operate. The rule they follow to maximize profit is also the same. As we saw in Chapter 6, profit-maximizing firms always choose the output level at which marginal revenue equals marginal cost. However, a given firm's profit-maximizing output and price differ in different market structures.

Some firms have many competitors that produce similar products (apple growers and gas stations), whereas other firms face few competitors (a local electrical utility). Still others sell a unique product (Nintendo Game Boy and Polaroid instant cameras). Firms in each of these markets respond differently to demand or cost changes depending on the structure, or characteristics, of their markets.

Market models De-scriptions of different market structures that enable economists to predict how firms will respond to changes in economic conditions.

Economists have developed four basic **market models** to predict how firms in different circumstances will react to technological changes, tax increases, and demand shifts. Pure competition, the model we will examine in this chapter, is the most basic market model. The three other models—oligopoly, monopolistic competition, and pure monopoly—apply to less competitive industries and are discussed in Chapter 8. The model of pure competition provides a frame of reference, or a benchmark of firm behavior, with which to compare the other market models.

PURE COMPETITION

How do firms in highly competitive markets determine the prices they charge and the quantities they produce and sell? How do such firms respond to changes in resource prices such as more expensive electricity or cheaper oil? Do they pass higher taxes on to customers in the form of higher prices, or are they forced to "eat" them by accepting lower profits? The model of pure competition provides answers to these and many other questions.

Assumptions of Pure Competition

Pure competition A market model characterized by a large number of buyers and sellers, a homogeneous product, free entry and exit of firms, and full knowledge of prices and technology.

The market model of **pure competition** applies to markets with (1) a large number of buyers and sellers, (2) a homogeneous product, (3) free entry and exit of firms from the industry, and (4) complete buyer and seller knowledge of all relevant prices and technology.

Large Number of Buyers and Sellers.   Because each buyer and each firm in a competitive market is very small relative to the total number of buyers and sellers, each is a minor player. No firm or buyer controls even 1 percent of the total amount of the product traded in the market. For example, no one would notice whether a single corn farmer (or corn buyer) doubled his corn output (or doubled her corn purchases). Neither action would measurably affect total corn output or total corn sales.

Homogeneous product An identical good or service produced by all firms in the market.

Homogeneous Product.   Competitive firms produce a **homogeneous product;** that is, the goods produced by each firm in the industry are all exactly the same. Examples of homogeneous products are class 1 tomatoes, light wool, number 8 nails, copper wire, 1 part–20 pound computer paper, and number 2 pencils. Since all firms in a purely competitive market produce exactly the same product, buyers do not care which seller supplies the goods they want. They are as willing to buy class 1 tomatoes from a farmer in South Carolina as they are from a grower in Southern California.

Free Entry and Exit (Free Mobility of Resources).   In pure competition, practical economists are free to organize a firm and enter any industry they choose, and they are free to leave anytime they please. For example, nothing can stop you from going into the cattle-raising business. If you can assemble the resources, you are free to enter that industry and to try to profit in that market. If you incur economic losses, you are free to leave the cattle-raising business and try something else. Free entry and exit simply means that resources of all kinds, including labor, are freely mobile. They may be bought or sold or be moved from place to place without restriction.

The freedom to enter and exit does not exist in all industries. Some noncompetitive markets have **barriers to entry (or exit)** that raise entry costs or stop firms from entering (and sometimes leaving) an industry. Barriers to entry include licensing requirements for lawyers, barbers, and certified public accountants; patents for products like Intel's computer chips and Polaroid's instant cameras; and even the large advertising budgets needed to enter certain markets like the ready-to-eat breakfast cereal industry (with products such as Kellogg's Corn Flakes and General Mills' Cheerios) and the beer industry (with brands like Anheuser-Busch's Budweiser and Miller Brewing Company's Miller Lite). We will examine industries with entry barriers in more detail in Chapter 8.

Barriers to entry (or exit) Artificial or natural restrictions on the ability of firms to enter (or leave) an industry.

Perfect Knowledge of Prices and Technology.

Perfect knowledge means firms and consumers know all input and product prices in the market. In this type of market, consumers are assumed to always know where to get the best deal and firms know the latest production technology and are aware of the prices of substitute inputs. This assumption ensures that the practical economists who operate firms have all the information they need to choose which products to produce and use the least-cost combination of inputs. It also ensures that practical economists as consumers are not at the mercy of firms because they are uninformed. They are able to look after their own self-interest because they are aware of their choices of products and prices.

Perfect knowledge A condition in which consumers and producers have all relevant information about product and input prices and production technology in the market.

Although the model of pure competition does not fit many (or any) industries exactly, it comes very close to describing the economic conditions of several important industries. Farmers, building contractors, financial services firms, and even workers selling their services in many labor markets all operate in markets that conform more or less closely to the model of pure competition.

Lack of Market Power and Advertising

As a consequence of these four assumptions, purely competitive firms have no market power. **Market power** is the ability of a particular firm or consumer to affect price by producing more or less or buying more or less. Small producers of an identical product, in an industry that potential rivals can enter readily and produce the same product, certainly have no individual control over the market. They cannot choose to raise price, because consumers can buy all they want of the identical product from a large number of competitive producers.

Market power The ability of one firm or consumer to affect market price by altering the amount of a good it produces or buys.

Similarly, individual buyers have no market power, or control over price. No one consumer can force price down, because each consumer buys too little of the total output to make a difference; firms can sell all they want to thousands of other consumers. Without market power, the actors in competitive markets

In Practice 7-1

. . . .

Barriers to Exit?

In recent years, some state legislators have introduced bills designed to reduce excessive entry and exit in competitive industries and thereby the social problems associated with high mobility of firms from one place to another. In particular, some state governments are trying to make it tougher to close plants in their areas and move them elsewhere.

Communities that feel threatened by the exit of firms want to pass laws that require firms to give notice of proposed closings well in advance to help displaced workers pay for retraining and find other work. Some proposals ask firms to compensate communities for the social problems created and tax revenues lost when they leave. In 1992, a federal court in Michigan required General Motors to repay a local government much of the tax revenue it lost by giving the firm several tax breaks as incentives to locate there. The reasons for this push for plant-closing laws were stated eloquently in a recent Conference on Alternative State and Local Policies report:

> The problems of capital mobility and major job losses are real and growing. . . . Massive job cuts often flood the labor market, overwhelming local employment opportunities. States and municipalities also face . . . fiscal difficulties as their tax base erodes and public spending rises to pay for the social costs of economic dislocation, which include rapid increases in juvenile delinquency, crime, divorce, mental illness, and despair.

These short-run problems are certainly very real. Some of the proposed laws would make plant closings less painful for individuals and communities by requiring firms to repay tax breaks if they leave. These proposed laws may force firms and governments to reconsider using these tax breaks as bargaining chips in attracting firms. However, such laws would also restrict both entry into and exit from industries. Firms would think twice about entering a potentially profitable industry in a new location, because it would be so much more expensive to get back out. Fewer jobs would be created, output would decline, and prices would rise. In other words, some of the benefits of competitive markets would be lost.

Especially stiff plant-closing laws would restrict resource mobility to a significant degree, reducing competition and making markets less responsive to changing conditions. How might such laws have affected the movement of the original wagon and buggy makers to Michigan when the automobile industry began to consolidate there in the early 1900s? How might such laws affect the decisions of firms like Wendy's restaurants and Hilton hotels if they could not easily close a restaurant or a hotel that proved unprofitable? Governments need to remember that plant-closing laws not only would keep existing firms in their current locations but also would tend to prevent new firms from moving to those same locations! Although some cities and states might cut their immediate losses by passing laws making it more difficult or expensive to shut down a plant, in the long run reduced resource mobility would mean lower output, higher prices, and slower economic growth. ■

Price takers Individual sellers and buyers in the competitive model who respond to the market price determined by market forces but cannot influence price on their own.

are necessarily **price takers:** Both firms and consumers take market price as given; it is entirely beyond their control. Farmers listen to radio and television "farm price reports" to learn what prices they can get for their products if they take them to market on a given day.

The assumptions of pure competition lead to a second special characteristic of competitive markets: an absence of advertising. In pure competition, there is no reason for an individual firm to advertise its product, since identical units of the product are available from a large number of competitors. Further, each firm is so small relative to the total market that it can sell all its output at the "going price" without having to pay for advertising.

CHECKLIST

Assumptions and Characteristics of the Model of Pure Competition

Assumptions

1. Large number of buyers and sellers
2. Homogeneous product
3. Free entry and exit
4. Perfect knowledge

Characteristics

1. No market power—neither firms nor consumers can influence price by their actions; they are price takers
2. No advertising—there is no payoff to advertising, since firms produce the same product and can sell all their output at the market price

Decentralized Decision Making: The Invisible Hand Once Again

As we noted in Chapter 3, in competitive markets no central authority guides sellers and buyers, telling them what to produce, how to produce, or for whom. For example, when you go to Denver on short notice, why can you expect to have eggs available for your breakfast, a cook in a restaurant to prepare them, a room in which to sleep, and a copy of a newspaper to read? Who directs the drugstore near your downtown hotel to stock enough "3×5" index cards in case you need them for your business meeting the next day? Who tells the taxi company to have enough cars and drivers available so you can get transportation to your meeting? In general, who directs the citizens of Denver to be ready for your visit?

Invisible hand The concept that the self-interest of producers and consumers guides and directs the production of goods and services in competitive markets.

The answer to these questions is that Denver's citizens, practical economists all, behave as though guided by an **invisible hand.** The concept of an invisible hand directing production and consumption according to self-interest was developed by Adam Smith more than 200 years ago. The desire of individual citizens to maximize their incomes to satisfy their own consumption wants guides them through millions of daily decisions as they produce goods and services for others. No central authority or government committee makes these decisions for individuals in competitive markets. Instead, decisions are made by the individuals who have the most to gain or lose from making correct or incorrect production decisions. The self-interest of individual producers drives them to gather sufficient information to make sound production decisions. Denver hotel restau-

Myth 7-1

"Somebody Needs to Be in Charge!"

It is a common belief that "things would be better" if someone were in charge of what and how to produce. Wouldn't prices be lower and quality higher if a public body operated a national trucking company, told airlines where to fly, or set hours for convenience stores? The answer generally is no. The invisible hand, operating in competitive markets and using price signals, directs firms to produce those goods and services that consumers want most at the lowest possible cost.

Would "someone" in charge eliminate the wasted resources—the costs illustrated by abandoned stores and displaced workers—associated with excessive entry and exit of firms from competitive markets? Controlling competitive entry and exit through some type of planning board would improve things only if the people in charge had greater insight into consumer wishes and were better able to predict future changes in market forces than practical economists operating in their own self-interest. However, there is no reason to expect that such a board would have a better crystal ball for predicting what will happen next to production costs, consumer tastes for goods, and changes in living patterns. Indeed, experience in planned economies like the former Soviet Union indicates the opposite is true. High-level planning boards in that country made far more mistakes in allocating resources than one would expect to result from market forces.

Having someone in charge means the values of a few regarding what and how to produce substitute for the impersonal control of competitive markets. Decentralized markets are able to cater to an almost infinite variety of tastes and values held by millions of individuals. Japan's Ministry of International Trade and Industry (MITI) is often cited as the best example of a successful public agency working as somebody in charge of industrial development. Most people are aware of Japan's "economic miracle" since World War II. What people don't know is that in some cases MITI may actually have slowed rather than accelerated Japan's industrial growth.

Although MITI has picked some winners, we don't often hear about MITI's mistakes. MITI's success in making Japan a leader in steel production (with subsidized loans) came at the expense of other industries it might have developed. For example, MITI encouraged Honda to stay out of the automobile market and stick to motorcycles. (MITI thought the market could support only two Japanese auto manufacturers!) MITI also assured Sony Electronics in the early 1960s that the transistor was an American fad and suggested the firm continue producing radios based on outdated vacuum-tube technology. Fortunately for both of these companies—and for millions of consumers—Honda and Sony ignored MITI's advice.

Carla Hills, former U.S. Trade Representative under President Bush, makes the point well ("The Fight for Free Trade," *Audacity,* Summer 1993, p. 21):

Today we're seeing some of the mistakes that the Japanese have made. When I took office, there was a raging debate as to whether our government should subsidize high-definition television. We resisted that, and now, as it turns out, the Japanese were altogether too ready to have their government spend a lot of money in that market. Our privately developed digital technology has jumped past high-definition television. I have never met a group of bureaucrats who do as well as a group of entrepreneurs at determining where the best chances of making a profit exist.

"Those in charge" cannot know all the pertinent information available to individual firms for each product in every market. Putting someone (like MITI) in charge of major industries (or of all industries) only reduces competition and ignores the benefits to society of relying on the invisible hand of self-interest. Markets not only do not need someone to be in charge but often work better when no one is. ∎

rant managers, for example, use their past experience and foresight (they make it their business to know when extra consumers will be in town for a convention) to order the quantity of eggs each believes will be needed the next day. If the restaurant orders too few eggs, *that manager's* income suffers from lost sales. If the hotel orders too many, *that manager's* pocketbook feels the effect when unsold eggs spoil.

Anonymous rivalry
Competition among sellers and buyers who are unknown to one another and thus depend only on price information for their decisions.

Competitive firms operate in an environment of **anonymous rivalry.** There are thousands of wheat farmers all over the world and millions of gasoline consumers in Los Angeles. Neither wheat farmers nor gasoline consumers know who their respective competitors are. Firms compete anonymously with other *firms* in the market, not with buyers. Anonymous competition among many producers keeps firms from getting together and conspiring to artificially raise prices. As a result, consumers get the best possible products at the least possible cost.

Even though each individual tries to make only himself or herself better off with each decision to buy, produce, or sell, competitive markets raise everybody's standard of living. In pure competition, one cannot make a profit without making consumers happy. In *The Wealth of Nations* (1776), Adam Smith stated this idea eloquently:

> . . . By directing that industry in such a manner as its produce may be of greatest value, he [the self-interested person] intends only his own gain, and he is in this . . . led by an invisible hand to promote an end which was no part of his intention. Nor is it always the worse for society that it was no part of it. By pursuing his own interest he frequently promotes that of the society more effectually than when he really intends to promote it.

COMPETITIVE OUTPUT DECISIONS IN THE SHORT RUN

Both price and cost play an important role in the firm's decision about what level of output to produce. Recall from Chapter 5 that total revenue (TR) is the product of price and quantity sold at that price: $TR = P \times Q$. The relationships among total revenue, average revenue, and marginal revenue are very similar to those among total, average, and marginal costs.

Average Revenue, Marginal Revenue, and Demand

Average revenue (AR)
Total revenue per unit sold, or *TR/Q;* the average revenue curve is the demand curve.

Average revenue (AR) is the total revenue per unit sold, or *TR/Q.* The average revenue curve is better known as the demand curve. This is because price always equals average revenue at each output level. If you sell 10 hats at a price of $5 each, total revenue is $50; average revenue is $50/10, or $5, which is the same as price.

Marginal revenue The change in total revenue resulting from selling an extra unit of output.

Marginal revenue (MR) is the change in total revenue resulting from selling another unit of output. Thus, marginal revenue is the amount added to total revenue for selling an extra unit, or

$$MR = \frac{\text{Change in } TR.}{\text{Change in } Q}$$

For downward-sloping demand curves, the marginal revenue gained from selling an extra unit is always less than the price of that unit. Again suppose you can sell 10 hats at $5 each for a total revenue of $50. If you face a downward-sloping demand curve, you will have to lower the price of all your hats to sell one more. If you can sell 11 hats by lowering your price to $4.75 each, what is your new total revenue? It is $4.75 $\times$ 11 hats = $52.25. Although the price of the 11th hat is $4.75, it adds only $2.25 to your total revenue (new $52.25 − old $50). Thus, the marginal revenue associated with producing and selling the 11th hat is less than its price. In fact, the marginal revenue for every unit after the first is always less than price. Thus, the marginal revenue curve associated with a downward-sloping demand curve must lie below the demand curve.

Horizontal Demand and the Purely Competitive Firm

Representative firm A typical firm among many firms in a competitive market.

In pure competition, the **representative firm** is one of many rival firms, each essentially identical to all the others in size and method of operation. Because competitive firms produce the same product and have identical knowledge of production technology and input prices, any one of them is representative of the others. For example, one corn farmer in the Midwest is very much like any other in terms of farming knowledge, production technology, and even size.

Representative firms in competition have one other important characteristic that distinguishes them from firms in most other markets: Each firm is very small relative to the total market, making each firm a price taker and a quantity searcher. Being a price taker simply means that the many relatively small firms selling in large competitive markets can sell all they want of their output at the market price. This price is the equilibrium price set in the total market for their product. Therefore, average revenue and marginal revenue equal the equilibrium price in the market. Individual, competitive *firms* face a horizontal price line, or horizontal demand curve, which shows that $MR = AR = P$. (Of course, *market* demand curves slope downward as always.) For example, the market for corn is very nearly purely competitive. The daily equilibrium price of corn is set in the total market for this grain, and it reflects the intersection of a downward-sloping demand curve for corn and an upward-sloping supply curve, as you learned in Chapter 4. However, an individual corn farmer simply hears the price per bushel on the radio and can sell as much as he or she wants at that price. In effect, the individual demand curve the farmer faces is a horizontal price line.

Market demand curves for a competitive industry as a whole, like D_{mkt} in panel a of Figure 7-1, are downward sloping. The price any competitive firm (or any competitive buyer) faces is the equilibrium market price set by the intersection of market supply and demand. Since each firm faces the same price determined by market demand and supply, each representative firm faces a horizontal (perfectly elastic) demand curve, such as *d* in panel b of Figure 7-1.

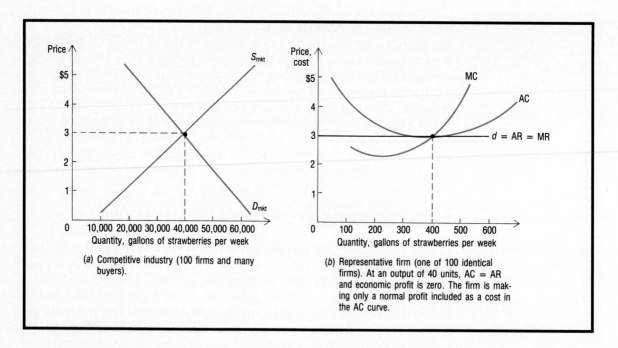

(a) Competitive industry (100 firms and many buyers).

(b) Representative firm (one of 100 identical firms). At an output of 40 units, AC = AR and economic profit is zero. The firm is making only a normal profit included as a cost in the AC curve.

FIGURE 7-1

(a) The equilibrium price and output for the strawberry industry are $3 and 40,000 gallons per week, determined by the intersection of market demand and market supply. (b) The demand curve for the firm, *d*, is horizontal because this representative farmer must take the $3 market price as given. Producing 400 gallons of strawberries per week (MC = MR when Q = 400) maximizes profit. Since average cost equals average revenue (AC = AR = P) at this output, the firm makes a normal profit (zero economic profit).

(We will use lowercase *d* and *q* for firm demand and output, respectively, and uppercase *D* and *Q* for market demand and output.)

The representative firm in this case is one of 100 strawberry farmers, each of whom can sell 100, 200, or even 600 gallons of strawberries per week at the market price of $3 per gallon. Thus, the firm faces a price line or horizontal demand, *d*, where $AR = MR = \$3$. This strawberry farmer is only one of 100 identical firms in the industry who can sell all of his or her output at the going market price of $3.

The driving force behind the decisions of a competitive firm, like those of any other firm, is the search for economic profit. Thus, competitive firms use the profit-maximizing rule (which also is the loss-minimizing rule) that you learned in Chapter 6 to choose their output level. Given their costs and the market price, they choose to produce that particular quantity of output for which $MR = MC$.

Maximizing Profit in the Short Run

To maximize profit, the representative strawberry producer in panel b of Figure 7-1 chooses to produce and sell 400 gallons of strawberries each week at $3 because marginal cost equals marginal revenue at that output level. (Since the other 99 farms are identical to this one, each of those farmers also produces 400 gallons per week. Their production totals 40,000 gallons, shown as market quantity in panel b.)

An output of 400 gallons is the equilibrium output for the representative firm in the short run, because at that price there is no incentive for individual producers to either increase or decrease output. Each producer is making the largest profit possible (zero economic profit), given the circumstances. A higher output level, such as 500 gallons, would mean the farmer's marginal cost per gallon would exceed marginal revenue, and profit would be lower. Producing fewer than 400 units would also reduce profit, because the farmer would forgo units for which marginal revenue exceeds marginal cost. This representative strawberry farm (and all others like it) is making a normal profit (economic profit is zero) because average cost equals average revenue, or $AC = AR = \$3$. Revenue per unit is "just covering" total cost per unit, including a normal return to the owner.

Changes in Market Price. Suppose market demand for strawberries increases to D_2, raising the equilibrium market price for strawberries to $4, as shown in panel a of Figure 7-2. How will competitive firms respond to this higher market price?

At the higher market price, the representative strawberry producer's horizontal demand curve (panel b) rises to d_2, where $d_2 = AR_2 = MR_2 = \$4$. The only choice available to the competitive firm in the short run is to use more variable inputs to increase output. The representative strawberry farmer increases output

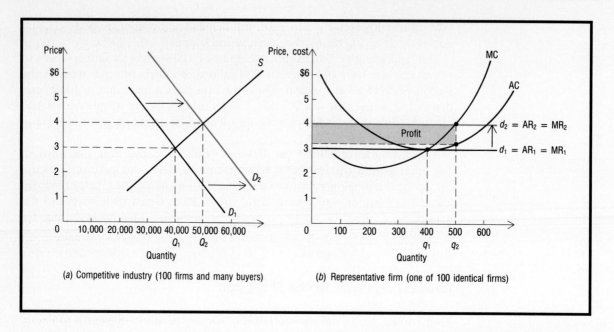

FIGURE 7-2

(a) When industry demand increases to D_2, the market price rises to $4 in the short run. Total industry output rises to 50,000 gallons of strawberries per week as each farmer expands output to maximize profit. (b) The representative firm increases output in response to the higher market price until marginal cost again equals the new, higher marginal revenue ($MC_2 = MR = 4). Each firm then produces 500 gallons per week and makes an economic profit (the shaded rectangle).

until *MR* and *MC* are again equal, at 500 gallons per week, and profit is again at a maximum.

Profit is equal to total revenue minus total cost. Total revenue in this instance equals average revenue of $4 times 500 units sold, or $2,000. Total cost equals average cost of $3.20 times 500 units sold, or $1,600. The difference of $400 is the total profit the representative farmer is making in the short run (the shaded rectangle in panel b). Another way to calculate this profit is to find profit per unit first: $4.00 − $3.20 = $0.80 each. Then we multiply that by the number of units sold, 500, for a total profit of $400. Each of the other 99 farmers makes the same profit.

The representative producer is again in short-run equilibrium. (The long run is discussed later in this chapter.) In the short run, there is too little time (by definition) for any of the current farmers to buy and plant more land to respond further to the higher $4 price. Nor is there time for others to enter the industry in response to the economic profits being made by each of the current 100 farmers.

A decrease rather than an increase in market price would result in reduced output and economic losses for the representative strawberry producer in the short run. (You should be able to verify that result on your own.)

Changes in Production Cost.
Suppose strawberry farmers are in equilibrium, making normal profits at a market price of $3. Now suppose production costs rise for all producers because fertilizer prices increase. How would the representative firm adjust to these higher costs?

Panel b of Figure 7-3 illustrates higher costs in the short run. The average and marginal cost curves shift upward, making the new average cost curve (AC_2) higher than the price line, or firm demand, d. All representative firms make losses at any chosen output level. Which output level minimizes this loss?

Once again the profit-maximizing rule comes to the rescue because it is also the loss-minimizing rule (as long as price at least exceeds average variable costs of production). The representative firm minimizes its loss by producing 300 gallons per week, where $MC_2 = MR$. The loss per unit is average cost ($4) minus

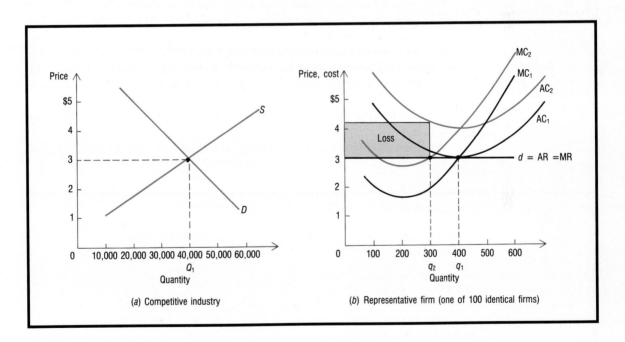

FIGURE 7-3

(a) Industry demand and supply determine an equilibrium price of $3 and an equilibrium quantity of 40,000 gallons of strawberries. (b) Higher costs shift average and marginal costs upward to AC_2 and MC_2, respectively. With the market price constant at $3, the firm decreases output to 300 gallons per week, which again equates marginal revenue with marginal cost ($MC_2 = MR = 3). This output minimizes the representative firm's loss, represented by the shaded rectangle.

average revenue ($3), and the total loss is 100 times that difference of $1, or the $100 represented by the shaded rectangle.

You should be able to redraw this diagram for a decrease in costs that result from improvements in technology or lower input prices. Lower costs mean competitive firms make economic profits in the short run.

The Short-Run Competitive Supply Curve

As you learned in Chapter 6, the short-run supply curve for an individual firm in pure competition consists of its marginal cost curve. Why? The representative firm always produces that level of output for which $MR = MC$. Since price is the same as marginal revenue for competitive firms, the profit-maximizing quantity to produce is always "read off" the marginal cost curve where price intersects marginal cost. Because the MC curve shows the profit-maximizing price-quantity combinations for the competitive firm, it is equivalent to the firm's supply curve, as illustrated in Figure 7-4.

Only that portion of the marginal cost curve above the average variable cost curve represents the representative firm's supply curve. Why? Because that firm will be better off producing no output, or shutting down altogether, in the short run if price is less than average variable cost. If market price falls below average variable cost, the firm cannot cover its variable costs on each unit. This means the firm would lose money on each unit produced *in addition to losing what it must pay in total for its fixed costs*. Thus, losses from operating would be greater than the firm's fixed costs. The firm would lose less money if it shut down.

When producing a few goods results in a total economic loss that exceeds

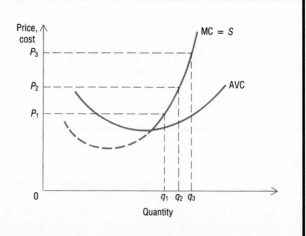

FIGURE 7-4

The MC curve (above average variable cost) is equivalent to the firm's supply curve. Each point on the marginal cost curve corresponds to a particular (profit-maximizing) price-quantity combination: At price P_1, output is q_1; at the higher price P_2, output rises to q_2; and at P_3, output is q_3. Only that portion of the MC curve that lies above the AVC curve is relevant, because firms would shut down if price were less than average variable costs.

fixed costs, practical economists realize the firm is better off not producing at all. Thus, the part of the MC curve below the minimum point on the AVC curve (the dashed portion in Figure 7-4) is not part of the firm's supply curve.

The short-run *market* supply curve for a competitive industry is the sum of all the quantities supplied by each firm at each possible price, or the horizontal sum of the short-run supply curves of all the firms in the industry.

COMPETITIVE OUTPUT DECISIONS IN THE LONG RUN

In the short run, competitive firms can be in equilibrium while making either economic profits or economic losses. The profit or loss signal has no effect because there is too little time in the short run for existing firms to change their fixed inputs or for new firms to enter the industry. The picture changes in the long run, however. In the long run, the number of firms in the industry can change as new firms enter (when firms are making economic profits) or existing firms exit (when there are economic losses).

Returning to the strawberry farm example (Figure 7-5), the representative firm sells strawberries at price P_1, determined by market demand D_1 and market supply S_1 (panel a). The representative firm maximizes profit at output q_1 and makes a normal profit (panel b).

Market Price Changes

Suppose market demand increases to D_2 in Figure 7-5. How will strawberry producers respond as market price increases? Market price rises initially to P_2, with a corresponding increase in the firm's demand curve (price line) to $d_2 = AR_2 = MR_2 = P_2$. Following the profit-maximizing rule, the representative strawberry farmer increases output to q_2, where marginal cost and marginal revenue are again equal ($MC = MR_2$). The representative firm now makes an economic profit, because price or average revenue exceeds average cost at the new output level ($AR_2 > AC$ at q_2). Total industry output is larger because each firm is producing more at the higher price. This is where the story ends in the short run. (Can you guess what happens to market supply in the long run with all those firms making economic profits?)

Long-Run Equilibrium

In the long run, however, economic profit (an above-normal return) attracts rival firms to the industry. Other "agrarian entrepreneurs" (farmers) decide to

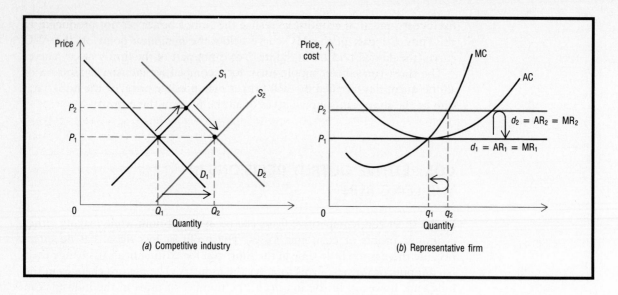

FIGURE 7-5

If demand increases from D_1 to D_2, market price rises temporarily to P_2. The representative firm increases output and earns a short-run economic profit, which attracts new firms. Supply shifts to the right in the long run, thus lowering price. Firms continue to enter until supply shifts to S_2 and price returns to P_1. Individual firms make no economic profit in the long run, and industry output increases solely because more firms are in the industry.

enter the strawberry business. Now here is the key: Although in pure competition *one* firm can enter (or leave) an industry without noticeably affecting supply or market price, entry or exit by *several* firms will have a sizable impact on supply and market price. Attracted by economic profit, many practical economists enter the strawberry business, shifting the industry supply curve to the right from S_1 to S_2. (Recall from Chapter 4 that "number of sellers" was one of the determinants of market supply.)

As industry supply increases with the entry of new firms, market price falls and so does the horizontal demand curve each individual farmer faces. Each of these competitive firms responds to the lower price by cutting output, but short-run economic profit also falls. New firms keep entering. Supply shifts farther to the right, and market price continues to fall as long as individual firms make *any* economic profit. Individual firms keep reducing their output and watching their economic profits decrease until all those extra profits are eliminated. The adjustment process stops only when supply has shifted far enough to the right that the new market price equals minimum average cost. Why? Because at any price above the minimum point on the average cost curve, firms make economic profit, and at any price below the minimum point on the average cost curve, firms incur losses. Thus, only when price equals minimum average cost will firms make a normal profit, and there will be no incentive for firms to either enter or leave the industry.

In Figure 7-5, the industry returns to equilibrium when supply has increased to S_2 and price has fallen back to the original P_1. At P_1, economic profit for each firm is again zero. After the market has adjusted, each strawberry farmer makes only a normal profit and produces the same output of q_1 as before at the same old market price. Total output, however, is larger at Q_2. This larger industry output is the result of having *additional firms* in the market. Each new firm produces the same amount that the representative firm produced in the beginning.

A Decrease in Demand

When demand decreases, the long-run adjustment to a lower market price is much the same. As market demand shifts leftward to D_2 in panel a of Figure 7-6, price falls temporarily to P_2. At this lower price, the representative firm produces less as it continues to maximize profit, but the best it can do is minimize its loss by producing q_2.

Since individual firms are incurring losses, some give up and leave the industry in the long run. As firms exit, the market supply curve decreases (shifts to the

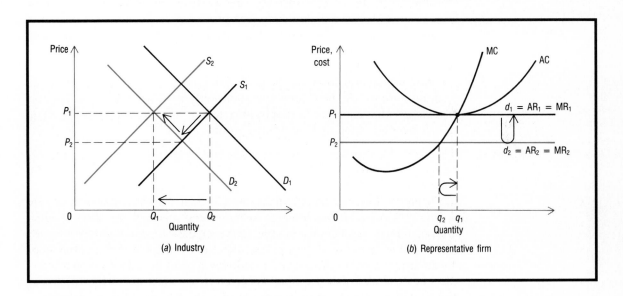

FIGURE 7-6

If demand decreases from D_1 to D_2, market price falls temporarily to P_2. The representative firm decreases output in the short run to minimize its loss. As some firms exit in the long run, supply shifts leftward, raising price. Firms continue to exit until supply shifts to S_2 and price returns to P_1. Firms make no economic profit in the long run, and industry output decreases solely because fewer firms are in the industry.

left) and price rises. Firms continue to exit and supply continues to shift leftward until market price rises enough to allow the remaining firms to once again make a normal profit. Thus, supply must continue to decrease until the curve shifts to S_2, where price again equals P_1 and minimum average cost.

When the long-run adjustment process is complete, industry output Q_2 is lower only because there are fewer firms in the industry. Since price returns to P_1 and costs are unchanged, each surviving firm produces its original output, q_1.

Cost Changes

The process of adjusting to cost changes in the competitive model is similar to the adjustment to price changes. Cost changes in pure competition affect all firms in the industry in the same way. All firms will make economic profits when costs decrease and economic losses when costs increase without market price changing first. Those profits or losses cause some firms to enter or exit the industry.

Suppose the strawberry farmer has to pay higher wages, but the market price is unchanged. The farmer will incur short-run losses. Some strawberry farmers leave the industry in the long run. As firms exit, supply shifts to the left and the market price for strawberries rises. As the price rises, the losses to the remaining firms become smaller. As long as there are losses, however, some firms continue to leave the industry. The process ends when market price rises to equal minimum average cost so that the remaining strawberry farmers again make normal profits. Exit from the industry stops, and industry output is lower because there are fewer firms in the industry.

Falling production costs, on the other hand, mean that firms reap short-run economic profits. As new firms enter the industry in the long run, supply increases. With an increase in supply, price falls in the long run until $P = AC_{min}$ and all firms are again making normal profits.

Long-Run Supply

In Chapter 6, long-run supply curves for individual firms were drawn as upward sloping. The reason is that long-run marginal cost inevitably increases as larger firms encounter diseconomies of scale. However, the long-run *industry* or *market* supply curves may not slope upward; they may be horizontal or even slope downward. The slope of the long-run industry supply curve depends on whether changes in total *industry* output affect costs (average and marginal) for all representative firms. A particular industry may experience increasing, decreasing, or constant costs in the long run as industry output expands. Input costs may rise when industry output increases because a larger number of firms producing a larger total output bid up input prices as they compete for resources. In that case, the long-run supply curve will be upward sloping. Input costs may fall as industry output expands because suppliers experience economies of scale as they

CHECKLIST : **Long-Run Adjustment in Pure Competition**

If	Firms	And in the Long Run	Until Finally
Market price rises (D↑)	increase output and make economic profits	new firms enter, increasing supply and driving price down	firms make normal profits at the original price, but industry output is larger
Market price falls (D↓)	decrease output and make economic losses	some firms exit, decreasing supply and driving price up	firms make normal profits at the original price, but industry output is lower
Costs increase	decrease output and make economic losses	some firms exit, decreasing supply and driving price up	firms make normal profits at the new, higher price, but industry output is lower
Costs decrease	increase output and make economic profits	new firms enter, increasing supply and driving price down	firms make normal profits at the new, lower price, but industry output is higher

supply more. In this case, the long-run supply curve will be downward sloping. In other industries, input costs are unaffected as total industry output increases. For those industries, the long-run supply curve is horizontal.

EVALUATING PURE COMPETITION

Few, if any, real-world industries exactly match the theoretical model of pure competition. Nevertheless, it is important to evaluate the benefits and costs of purely competitive markets before exploring other models. This model is a useful benchmark for comparison with the other less-competitive market models we will examine in Chapter 8.

Benefits of Pure Competition

Pure competition offers several important benefits. In the long run, pure competition offers both production and allocative efficiency, the two kinds of economic efficiency discussed under economic goals in Chapter 2. Competition also does not waste resources on advertising.

Production efficiency

Producing and selling output at the lowest possible cost ($P = AC_{min}$).

Production Efficiency ($P = AC_{min}$). Firms in competitive industries produce efficiently. **Production efficiency** means competitive firms produce and sell their output at the lowest possible cost in the long run; that is, price equals minimum average total cost ($P = AC_{min}$). A major benefit of this market structure is that goods are produced as cheaply as possible and consumers are charged a price equal to this lowest possible cost.

Figure 7-7 illustrates this important conclusion. The firm's demand curve, d_e, is just tangent to the minimum point on both the short- and long-run average cost curves, AC_{min}. The representative firm produces q_e, the profit-maximizing level of output at which average cost is at its minimum.

If price is above P_e—P_1, for example—the firm will produce output at a higher average cost in the short run (see point *a*). The firm will enjoy economic profits. These economic profits will attract other firms to this industry in the long run. The increased market supply that results from adding new firms will drive price back to $P_3 = AC_{min}$, wiping out economic profit. On the other hand, any price below P_e, such as P_2, results in lower firm output, q_2. Firms will have higher average costs (see point *b*) and economic losses. These economic losses ensure

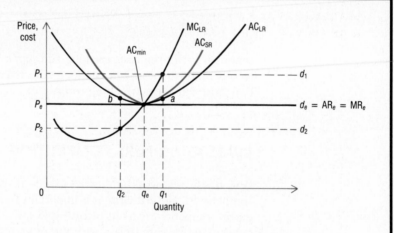

FIGURE 7-7

Firm demand, d_e, at the equilibrium price, P_e, is tangent to the minimum point on both the short- and long-run average cost curves, that is, at AC_{min}. A higher price, such as P_1, causes firms to increase output; firms make short-run economic profits even though average cost is higher (see point *a*). New firms enter in the long run and wipe out economic profit as they drive price back down to AC_{min}. A price below P_e, such as P_2, causes more output per firm, q_2, as firms try to minimize their losses. Some firms exit in the long run, raising price to $P_e = AC_{min}$ once again.

that some firms exit from the industry in the long run. As firms leave, the reduction in supply raises price to P_e and lowers average costs to AC_{min}.

In this model, consumers are guaranteed that price will equal the lowest possible production costs. Production efficiency, represented by $P = AC_{min}$, is a powerful and beneficial outcome of the purely competitive market model.

Allocative efficiency
Producing so that resources used reflect consumer preferences ($P = MC$).

Allocative Efficiency ($P = MC$). The model of pure competition also gives the economy **allocative efficiency,** meaning that resources are used in a way that reflects consumer preferences. Allocative efficiency exists when price and marginal cost are equal *($P = MC$),* which is true of pure competition in the long run.

In pure competition, consumers get the goods and services they demand *without giving up other goods of greater value.* The marginal cost of producing a good represents the value of alternative goods not produced with those resources (opportunity cost). When $P = MC$, consumers get the good for exactly what it is worth in terms of other goods forgone. When the price of a good is greater than its marginal cost ($P > MC$), too few resources are being devoted to it. Resources used to produce this good are producing something more valuable than the other goods those same resources could produce. Therefore, from the viewpoint of society, more resources should be used to produce this or any good whose price exceeds marginal cost.

When price is less than marginal cost, on the other hand, too many resources are devoted to producing that good. The value of forgone opportunities to produce more of other goods, reflected in the marginal cost of this good, exceeds the value of this good as measured by its price. In this case ($P < MC$), practical economists want resources to be reallocated to the production of other goods.

In the purely competitive model, $P = MC$ in the long run. Resources used to produce a certain good cannot be reallocated to produce any other good with greater value. Therefore, under conditions of pure competition, all resources are allocated efficiently in the long run; they are put to their highest-valued use.

No Advertising. One additional benefit of pure competition discussed earlier is the absence of advertising. No resources are spent on any form of nonprice competition, such as media advertising, salespeople, or special packaging. No practical economist would advertise a homogeneous product. What would be the point? The firm can sell all of its output at the going price without advertising. The ability of firms to completely satisfy customers without "wasting" resources to promote products is an important social benefit of pure competition.

Criticisms of Pure Competition

Purely competitive markets yield very desirable results, including production efficiency, allocative efficiency, and minimal advertising. Because of these benefits, competition is often used as a standard for judging actual markets and comparing the other market models developed in Chapter 8. However, pure competition does have some drawbacks.

Some criticisms of pure competition include (1) lack of product research and development, (2) lack of product variety, and (3) potential excessive costs of entry and exit.

Lack of Research and Development. Firms in pure competition have no resources to devote to research and development programs to improve product quality or production methods. They make no excessive profits in the long run with which to fund research and development. Any improvements would be copied immediately by other firms (the perfect information assumption); thus, the benefits would go to other firms that did not help pay for the research.

In most competitive industries, product improvements result from casual experimentation or by accident. In others, research and development comes from outside the industry. For example, much agricultural research for the almost purely competitive agricultural industry is undertaken by large seed, fertilizer, pesticide, and farm equipment companies (which are not in purely competitive industries) rather than by individual farmers. Even more agricultural research comes from agricultural experiment stations operated by universities in every state in the United States and funded by the federal government. Research results are then communicated to farmers through the Cooperative Extension Service with its nationwide network of county agricultural extension agents.

Lack of Product Variety. Since purely competitive industries produce a homogeneous product, they offer little variety to satisfy diverse consumer tastes. Popcorn is popcorn, right? At least it was until Orville Redenbacher launched his special "gourmet" popcorn, and his firm is no longer in a purely competitive market. Redenbacher's product is different, and his "brand" is a registered trademark. As a result, his firm has some control over the price of its popcorn.

Part of the satisfaction that practical economists maximize comes from variety, which is the reason you can buy cars in a rainbow of colors and many different styles, shapes, and optional equipment. Pure competition, in contrast, gives consumers products sold by the truckload, such as crushed rock, or sold in plain bags and sacks, like standard 10-10-10 fertilizer and bags of potatoes. Would you prefer one competitively produced, standardized car that came only in black with one engine size (Henry Ford's Model A!)?

Excessive Entry and Exit Costs. Another criticism of pure competition is that firms' constant entering and exiting competitive industries in response to changing demand and cost conditions wastes resources. New shops open in malls, increasing the need to pave parking lots and build new streets leading to the mall, while similar shops close downtown, leaving buildings idle for months or longer. Farmers have unused corn silos when changing prices signal them to grow a different crop or switch to raising cattle. You have certainly seen examples of both the strains of rapid entry into certain markets and the "leftovers" from competitive exit in your city or town.

CHECKLIST : Evaluating Pure Competition

Benefits

Production efficiency	Competitive output is produced and sold at the lowest possible cost ($P = AC_{min}$).
Allocative efficiency	Resources are allocated to produce the goods consumers value most highly, because the cost of the last unit produced equals exactly what it is worth to consumers ($P = MC$).
No advertising	Competitive firms produce identical products, making advertising unnecessary.

Criticisms

Lack of research and development	Competitive firms have no long-run economic profit to finance research, and perfect knowledge ensures that competitors realize the same advantage from new developments.
Lack of product variety	Competitive markets do not allow for variety and therefore fail to satisfy this important consumer desire.
Entry and exit costs	Free entry and exit is somewhat wasteful (e.g., new schools and roads are needed where new firms enter, and shops and factories may lie abandoned where firms have left).

SUPPLY AND DEMAND IN COMPETITIVE LABOR MARKETS

Derived demand Demand for a resource that depends on the demand for the goods and services it is used to produce.

The purely competitive firm is not only a seller of products but also a buyer of services. The forces of supply and demand in particular resource markets determine the amounts of resources firms use and the prices they pay. Any resource is demanded only because it can produce goods and services for consumption. Thus, labor demand is derived from the demand for the goods and services workers produce. This concept of resource demand coming from product demand is known as **derived demand.**

Labor Demand

A competitive firm's demand for labor depends on the additional revenue each extra worker brings to the firm. Since owners of firms are practical economists, they employ more labor (or any other resource) as long as each additional worker adds more to revenue than to cost. For example, a strawberry farmer decides how many pickers to hire by comparing what they cost to how much they add to the firm's revenue.

The additional revenue any firm receives from hiring an extra worker, called the **marginal revenue product of labor (MRP$_L$)**, depends on two factors: how much extra output that worker produces and how much the firm's revenue increases when the extra output is sold. The increased quantity of output from one more worker is called the **marginal product of labor (MP$_L$)**. For all firms, the marginal revenue product of labor equals MP$_L$ (the marginal worker's output) times marginal revenue:

$$MRP_L = MP_L \times MR$$

Since the maximum price the firm will pay for an extra unit of labor is the marginal revenue product of labor (MRP_L), the firm's labor demand schedule is simply its marginal revenue product schedule for labor.

In a competitive market, marginal revenue is constant and equal to the price because price is constant for the firm. Thus, the competitive firm's labor demand schedule slopes downward in the short run, because the marginal product of labor (MP_L) declines as workers are added. The marginal product of each additional worker (MP_L) declines in the short run because of the law of diminishing marginal returns discussed in Chapter 6. Each additional worker adds less to total output, because additional workers are combined with a fixed amount of capital. As a result, each extra worker is less productive than the last. In the equation above, MR can be replaced with P. If marginal product declines as output rises while product price remains constant, the quantity of labor demanded falls as more labor is hired. Labor demand for the competitive firm slopes down from left to right.

An example will help illustrate why labor demand, or the MRP_L schedule, slopes downward. Clock Works' demand curve for labor is d_L in Figure 7-8. It slopes downward to the right, reflecting the firm's declining marginal product of labor. The fifth worker, for example, is worth $12 per hour to the firm, whereas the ninth adds only $4 per hour to total revenue.

Clock Works must be a competitive firm (in the clock market), because its marginal revenue is constant; that is, its clock prices do not fall as output expands. Its labor demand curve therefore slopes down from left to right only because the marginal product of its workers declines as the firm adds more workers.

Labor Supply

Households supply labor resources to firms for a price: the wage rate. Many factors determine the quantities of labor households supply at various wage

Marginal revenue product of labor (MRP$_L$) The extra revenue resulting from selling the output produced by one extra unit of labor; equal to marginal revenue times marginal product of labor.

Marginal product of labor (MP$_L$) The extra output produced with one additional unit of labor.

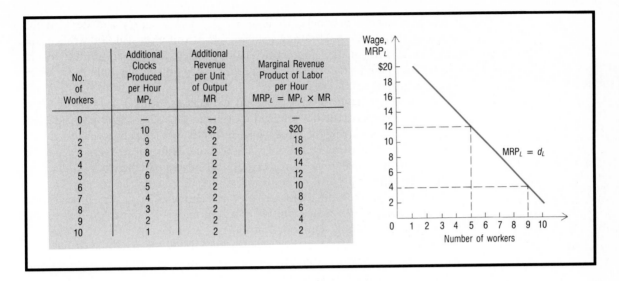

No. of Workers	Additional Clocks Produced per Hour MP$_L$	Additional Revenue per Unit of Output MR	Marginal Revenue Product of Labor per Hour MRP$_L$ = MP$_L$ × MR
0	—	—	—
1	10	$2	$20
2	9	2	18
3	8	2	16
4	7	2	14
5	6	2	12
6	5	2	10
7	4	2	8
8	3	2	6
9	2	2	4
10	1	2	2

FIGURE 7-8

The marginal revenue product of labor (MRP$_L$), which represents the value of employing additional workers, is the firm's demand for labor, d_L. The MRP$_L$ schedule for Clock Works is the product of the extra output from each marginal unit of labor and the price each unit of output brings when sold.

rates, but the most important is opportunity cost, or the value of the potential worker's next best alternative use of time. Your next best alternative to a particular job may be working for a different firm, running your own firm, or simply reading a book. You also have the options to loaf beside the lake, paint the house, grow garden vegetables, or build a garage. In general, firms "call forth" more labor when they offer wages to potential workers that equal or exceed those workers' opportunity costs. Therefore, *market* labor supply curves usually slope upward; the higher the wage rate, the greater the quantity of labor services offered.

Individual firms in competitive markets usually face a horizontal labor supply. A firm that is small relative to its labor market can obtain all the labor it needs at the "going" wage rate. Although the wage rate is always set by the intersection of total labor demand and supply in the market, an individual "representative firm" in a competitive labor market may hire a few extra workers without changing that equilibrium wage rate. Clock Works, for example, can hire all the workers it wants without affecting the going wage.

Equilibrium Wages and Employment

In a competitive labor market, the demand and supply for labor determine the equilibrium wage and total employment. The market for clock production workers is shown in panel a of Figure 7-9. Market supply and demand for workers set the $8 equilibrium wage rate, W_e. At this wage, 40,000 workers are hired by all firms in this competitive labor market. More than 40,000 people are willing to offer their services as production workers, but only if the wage rate is higher than $8 per hour.

On the other hand, several thousand workers are willing to work at wage rates below $8 per hour but are paid more than $8. Why? Firms pay the same wage to everyone doing the same work, and $8 is what they must pay to attract the "last" or "most reluctant" marginal worker. Thus, all workers receive the wage of the marginal worker, just as all bread buyers pay the price required to induce the marginal buyer to buy a loaf of bread.

How many workers does Clock Works hire, and what wage does it pay them? Because Clock Works is just one of a large number of similar manufacturing firms in its area hiring semiskilled production workers, it faces the horizontal labor supply curve. S_L^{firm}, at the going wage rate of $8 per hour (panel b of Figure 7.9). Clock Works can increase employment from 1 to 10 workers without affecting the market wage of $8.

The decision about how many workers to hire is similar to the decision about how much output to produce. Clock Works hires seven workers at

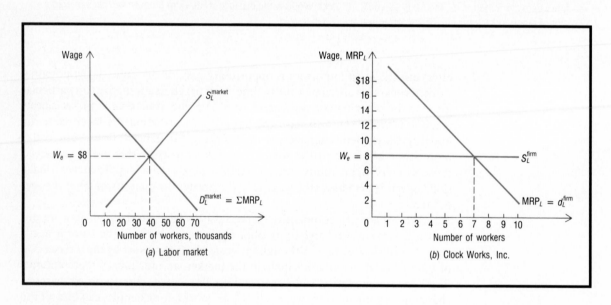

FIGURE 7-9

(a) At the equilibrium wage rate of $8 per hour, 40,000 workers are hired in total by all firms in this labor market. (b) Clock Works faces a horizontal supply curve for labor at the going market wage of $8. Given its demand for labor, d_L^{firm} Clock Works hires seven workers. Hiring fewer would reduce profit, because revenue would rise more than cost for each worker hired up to seven; hiring more than seven would also reduce profit, since the wage exceeds the MRP of these workers.

the market wage of $8. Each worker through the seventh adds more to revenue than to cost ($MRP_L > W_c$), thus increasing profit. Hiring the eighth worker would lower profit, because that worker's marginal revenue product is less than the wage rate.

No practical economist would pay more for a unit of labor than the additional revenue that unit generates. Since competition for labor keeps firms from paying workers less than their marginal revenue product, the competitive firm's wage rate is the same as the marginal revenue product of labor. The worker receives the value of his or her contribution—no more, no less. The allocation of workers (and other inputs) in pure competition is efficient just as the allocation of output is efficient.

In the next chapter, we will examine the price and output decisions of firms in less competitive markets: monopoly, oligopoly, and monopolistic competition. Firms in these less than purely competitive markets have an impact on prices and wages and may earn consistent economic profits. They may lack some of the benefits of pure competition, but they enjoy other advantages. The firms you encounter in the next chapter will be the more familiar sellers you encounter as a worker and consumer in daily life.

Summary

1. Economists have developed a few basic market models to describe and predict the behavior of firms in different types of industries. Pure competition is the model for markets that have the largest number of firms in competition and in which individual firms have the least control over price.

2. The basic assumptions of the purely competitive model are a large number of buyers and sellers, a homogeneous product, free entry and exit (resources are freely mobile), and perfect knowledge of prices and technology. These assumptions imply an absence of both market power and product advertising.

3. Competitive markets are directed only by "the invisible hand" of self-interest. Individual firms, trying to make a profit in an environment of anonymous rivalry, take prices as given and make choices about what to produce and how much, all without any central direction.

4. In the short run, competitive firms may make normal profits, economic profits, or economic losses.

5. The firm's short-run supply curve is that portion of its marginal cost curve that lies above the above average variable cost curve. The short-run industry supply curve is the (horizontal) sum of all the short-run supply curves of the competitive firms in the industry.

6. In the long run, competitive markets are in equilibrium when all firms make only normal profits. Economic profits in the short run encourage

entry, increasing supply and driving down the market price so that firms make only normal profits in the long run. Economic losses encourage exit, decreasing supply and driving up price, and the remaining firms make normal profits once again.

7. The long-run supply curve for an industry may be horizontal if costs are unchanged as the industry expends, slope upward if costs increase with expension, or slope downward if costs fall as industry output increases.

8. In long-run equilibrium, pure competition results in production efficiency ($P = AC_{min}$) and allocative efficiency ($P = MC$).

9. Individuals receive income by selling the services of their productive resources, especially their labor, to firms.

10. Supply and demand in resource markets determine the prices households receive for their resources. Resource demand in a particular firm or industry is derived from the demand for the firm's or industry's product.

11. The demand curve for labor reflects the value to the firm of the extra output the resource produces, or $MRP_L = MP_L \times MR$. Labor demand is downward sloping because the marginal product of labor declines as extra workers are hired in the short run.

Key Terms

allocative efficiency
anonymous rivalry
average revenue
barriers to entry (or exit)
derived demand
homogeneous product

invisible hand
marginal product of labor (MP_L)
marginal revenue
marginal revenue product of labor (MRP_L)
market models

market power
perfect knowledge
price takers
production efficiency
pure competition
representative firm

Questions and Problems

1. In what ways do the availability of street drugs and pornographic magazines and videos reflect competitive markets? Does this mean competitive markets are undesirable?

2. In earlier chapters, we said that demand curves slope downward. In this chapter, we saw that the representative firm in competition faces a completely horizontal demand curve. Explain how each of these apparently contradictory statements can be correct.

3. Suppose Susan's Bagel Bakery, Inc., operates in a competitive market. The bakery can produce the following quantities of 20-pound bags of bagels per day at the costs indicated:

Q/t	FC	VC	TC	AFC	AVC	AC	MC
0	20	0	20	—	0	—	—
1	20	2	22	20	2	22	2
2	20	4	24	10	2	12	2
3	20	7	27	6.7	2.3	9	3
4	20	12	32	5	3	8	5
5	20	20	40	4	4	8	8
6	20	34	54	3.3	5.7	9	14
7	20	56	76	2.9	8	10.9	22
8	20	88	108	2.5	11	13.5	30

    a. What will be the price of 20-pound bags of bagels in long-run competitive equilibrium? (Hint: What do you know is true about production efficiency in the long run for pure competition?)

    b. Plot the AC, AVC, and MC curves for this representative bagel bakery, and draw the firm's demand curve.

    c. Explain the process by which the firm adjusts to an increase in market demand for bags of bagels that raises the price to $14. What does Susan immediately do in the short run? Describe the long-run adjustment for this industry and for Susan's firm.

4. Referring to Problem 3, think about the bakery business, shopping malls (where Susan's firm is located), different kinds of bagels, and other market characteristics. Is Susan's bakery likely to be in a competitive industry? Which of the assumptions of the competitive market model are most likely to be satisfied? Which are not?

5. Do you think Susan's Bagel Bakery (Problem 3) is likely to be operating in an industry with horizontal supply (a constant-cost industry), with upward-sloping supply (an increasing-cost industry), or downward-sloping supply (a decreasing-cost industry). Why?

6. Explain why economists say that $P = MC$ means markets are allocatively efficient.

7. What will happen to a competitive firm's price and output in the short run if
    a. Labor costs rise.
    b. Business taxes are reduced.
    c. The firm's product becomes more popular.
    d. The industry's export sales fall sharply.

8. Answer question 7 for the long run.

9. From what is the demand for professors derived? What would happen to professors' salaries if college enrollments declined?

10. Explain carefully what is meant by the statement "A worker is paid no more and no less than what he or she is worth to the firm." What the two primary determinants of wage rates?

11. Return to Susan's Bagel Bakery, Inc. and assume it operates in a competitive market for bagels. The market price for wholesale bags of bagels is $4. Susan's also operates in a competitive labor market in which the wage is $10 per hour. Following is additional information about the firm's labor productivity:

Number of Workers	Hourly MP_L	Additional Revenue per Bag	MRP_L
1	9 bags	_____	_____
2	9 bags	_____	_____
3	7 bags	_____	_____
4	5 bags	_____	_____
5	3 bags	_____	_____
6	1 bag	_____	_____

a. Complete the above table.
b. How many workers will Susan's Bagel Bakery hire? Explain.

8

Imperfect Competition and
Market Power

It is probable that a considerable part of the monopolist's efforts and sacrifices will be devoted, not to increasing his output, but finding to what precise point he should restrict it.

J. R. HICKS, 1935

Main Points

1. The pure monopoly—an industry that has only one firm—is the market model at the opposite extreme from pure competition.

2. A monopoly sells a unique product (no close substitutes exist) and is protected from competition by high barriers to entry. These conditions are the source of its monopoly power over price and output; thus, a monopoly is a price searcher.

3. Unlike competitive firms, monopolies are neither allocatively nor productively efficient. Their monopoly power allows them to restrict output to raise price above the competitive level.

4. Monopolies' power to raise price is not absolute. Monopolies are limited by the buying public's ability to find substitutes (shown by the downward-sloping demand

curve monopolists face); by their desire to maximize profit, which requires them to select the profit-maximizing level of output and price; and by potential competition.

5. Oligopoly exists when only a few firms make up a market and each must take the behavior of its rivals into account.

6. Monopolistic competition describes markets in which many firms sell slightly different versions of a similar product, giving each firm a small degree of market power to control price.

7. Monopoly and oligopoly firms are usually large employers whose labor demand is a large share of a particular labor market. They face the upward-sloping market supply curve for labor and affect market wage rates when they hire or lay off workers.

I n pure competition, no individual seller or buyer has any control over the prices of goods, services, and resources. Everything is bought and sold for exactly "what it is worth." In this chapter, we focus on three additional types of markets, all of which exhibit some degree of imperfect competition. First, in monopoly, a one-firm industry stands at the opposite extreme from pure competition. Monopoly firms can restrict output to raise price (to whom else can consumers turn?) and can sometimes make long-run economic profits. In addition, they often affect labor market wage rates (and other resource prices) because they usually are large firms that face an upward-sloping labor supply curve.

Oligopoly and monopolist competition are market models that lie between the two extremes of competition and monopoly. Monopolistically competitive firms try to differentiate their products from those of other firms to obtain a small degree of market power over price. Oligopoly markets consist of only a few large firms, and market conditions may allow them to engage in illegal collusion and form cartels to increase their market power from time to time.

These three models of imperfect competition allow economists to analyze the behavior of firms in a variety of industries, thus helping them to understand and predict how firms in these kinds of markets respond to changes in economic conditions. ■

IMPERFECTLY COMPETITIVE MARKETS

Imperfect competition
Market models in which firms face downward-sloping demand and therefore have some control over price.

Pure competition represents the competitive extreme of the four basic market models. The other three models—monopoly, oligopoly, and monopolistic competition—are models of **imperfect competition.** Each of these models assumes the existence of conditions that allow firms (and sometimes buyers) to have some degree of market power, or control over price. Practical economists seek market power to increase their chance of earning economic profits in the long run and thus increase their ability to survive.

The most obvious difference among these three market models is in the number of sellers. The extreme opposite of pure competition is pure monopoly, in which only one firm exists. In monopolistic competition there are many firms in the market, but fewer than in pure competition. Oligopoly describes industries that are dominated by only a few large companies.

Since monopoly stands at the opposite end of the spectrum from pure competition, we begin our study of imperfect competition with that model.

THE MONOPOLY MODEL

Monopoly A market model in which a single firm, protected by barriers to entry, produces the entire industry output of a unique product.

The word *monopoly* comes from two Greek words meaning "one" and "seller." Thus, **monopoly** describes markets that consist of only one firm producing a unique product. How do changes in demand and cost conditions affect price and output decisions when only one firm exists in the industry? How do the outcomes of monopoly markets compare to the production and allocative efficiency of competitive markets? The monopoly model provides answers to these and other questions.

Assumptions of Monopoly

The monopoly model assumes (1) a single seller in the market, (2) a unique product, and (3) significant barriers to entry that protect the monopolist from competition.

A single monopoly firm produces the entire output of the industry. Since it controls the entire market, the monopolist faces the market demand curve. Thus, there is no distinction between individual competitive firms—illustrated by a representative firm—and the industry as there is in pure competition; instead, the firm and the industry are one and the same.

Whereas purely competitive firms produce identical products, a monopolist produces a unique product—one that has no close substitutes. For example, your local electric utility company is the only supplier of electricity to your home. Alcoa (Aluminum Company of America) was the only producer of aluminum until after World War II. Buyers who wanted that lightweight metal had to buy it from Alcoa.

Significant barriers to entry protect monopolists from competition. Entry barriers include exclusive government franchises (your local government probably authorizes only one cable TV company to operate in your area), patents, copyrights, control over the supply of specialized inputs, and size barriers resulting from economies of scale. These barriers keep other firms out of the monopolist's market, enabling the firm to exercise **monopoly power.** Monopolists can use their monopoly power to restrict output, raise price substantially above the competitive level, and earn persistent economic profits.

Monopoly power A monopolist's ability to restrict output and raise price the maximum amount possible relative to competitive firms; an extreme form of market power.

Whether or not a monopolist advertises depends on the type of product it produces and the source of its protective barriers to entry. The sole producer of a basic metal like aluminum has little need to advertise its product. On the other hand, a monopolist that produces a consumer product may advertise to increase demand or to reduce price elasticity so that it can raise price without having to reduce quantity substantially. If the source of its barriers to entry is a required government permit, as is the case for a public utility, the monopolist may also advertise to promote its "good neighbor" image.

Assumptions and Characteristics of the Monopoly Model

Assumptions

1. The industry has only a single firm.
2. The firm produces a unique product (no close substitutes exist).
3. Barriers to entry restrict or prohibit free entry and exit.

Characteristics

1. The firm enjoys monopoly power; it can restrict its output to drive price up. Thus, it is a price searcher rather than a price taker.
2. The firm may or may not advertise. A monopoly that produces a basic product like steel may choose not to advertise. A monopoly that produces a consumer product may advertise to make demand greater and less elastic or, if regulated by government, to create goodwill.

Monopoly in the Real World

Examples that fit all the assumptions of pure monopoly are rare. Familiar examples include local utilities that provide electricity, natural gas, water, sewer, and telephone service. Each of these utilities is the sole producer in its specific, local market. Another example of monopoly is Nimslo Corporation. If you want a 3-D camera, you must buy a Nimslo because that firm has the patent on 3-D cameras. At one time Xerox had a monopoly in electrostatic copiers, and Standard Oil of New Jersey, from which the Rockefellers made their fortunes, once came very close to being a full monopoly. The Duke family in North Carolina also did quite well with their cigarette monopoly, the American Tobacco Company.

Barriers to Entry

Monopolies depend on barriers to entry to protect them from competition. Not all barriers to entry lead to pure monopoly, but they all limit entry into an industry and create some degree of imperfect competition, whether monopoly, oligopoly, or monopolistic competition.

Barriers to entry may be either natural or artificial. Natural barriers include (1) the existence of large economies of scale in some industries, (2) exclusive ownership of resources, and (3) high fixed costs associated with advertising to establish and maintain brand names in certain consumer markets.

Artificial barriers to entry are often assisted or erected by the government. Artificial barriers include (1) exclusive government franchises (licensing), (2) patents and copyrights, and (3) import restrictions in the form of tariffs and quotas. Many barriers serve a useful purpose, but some are created solely to benefit particular groups of owners or workers (special interests).

Natural Barriers to Entry. One natural barrier to entry is large economies of scale. A very large output may be necessary to produce some goods at the lowest cost. The plant size needed relative to market demand may be so huge that it leaves room for only one firm. When average cost continues to decline as firm output increases over the range of market demand, the firm is called a **natural monopoly.** Electric utilities, local telephone service, water, natural gas, and railroads are examples of natural monopolies that result from economies of scale.

Natural monopoly A monopoly that results from the existence of large economies of scale in the industry.

Consider a local electric utility. Could two firms compete in the same city market? Not without higher average cost and a higher price. So much capital is invested in generating plants, transmission towers, poles, transformers, and lines that most of the cost of transmitting electricity is fixed rather than variable. The utility can transmit additional kilowatt-hours of electricity at a smaller and smaller cost per unit because fixed cost is spread over those additional units. Only one firm will survive in such a market, because one firm can supply all the electricity demanded at a lower cost (and price) than two, three, or more firms could. Even a practical economist would be willing to accept monopoly in these circumstances.

A second natural barrier to entry is exclusive ownership of resources. The Alcoa aluminum monopoly that existed before World War II owned all the sources of bauxite—the material containing aluminum—in the United States. Since one firm controlled all of the necessary resource, no other firm could enter the aluminum industry. In the 1940s, the federal government forced Alcoa to sell parts of the company and its bauxite resources, creating two more aluminum companies, Kaiser and Reynolds.

At one time, Nickel Company of Canada owned around 90 percent of the world's known nickel reserves. DeBeers Company of South Africa controls about 70 percent of the world's producing diamond mines. Large discoveries of diamonds in Australia in the 1980s threatened its monopoly, but DeBeers regained control with in bought some of the major Australian fields. These two firms are examples of near-monopolies resulting from almost exclusive ownership of necessary resources.

Well-known brand names, established over years of advertising, are the third type of natural barrier to entry in some industries. To compete with Coca-Cola or PepsiCo in the cola soft-drink market, you would have to prepare to lose money for several years spending millions on advertising to establish a new brand name. In such cases, entry is limited to firms with large amounts of capital to withstand long-term early losses.

Artificial Barriers to Entry. A patent or copyright, which confers the legal right to be the sole producer of a particular product, is an entry barrier created by government to encourage innovation and invention. A patent lasts for 17 years and often may be renewed for another 17 years. Polaroid Corporation has a patent monopoly in instant cameras (reaffirmed in the late 1980s when legal action forced Kodak to abandon its new instant camera). Intel has a patent on microprocessor chips (the 486 and other chips) used in most IBM microcomputers and their clones.

The authors of this text, through the publisher, have a copyright on this book that will last 50 years. Unfortunately, the copyright conveys little monopoly power, because the book does not meet the unique-product test; several close substitutes for this text compete all too well. Other copyrights, such as Garth Brooks's copyright for his *Ropin' the Wind* album, remain valuable for many years.

Another artificial entry barrier is created when governments give some firms the exclusive right to some markets. Cable television companies have no competition in many cities and subdivisions. The U.S. Postal Service has a legal monopoly in first-class mail. No other firm may deliver regular letters to homes and business firms. Other package delivery and overnight air delivery services, such as United Parcel Service (UPS), now carry most packages in the United States, but these firms still are not allowed to compete in the market for first-class letters.

New York City requires taxicabs to have a city license in the form of a medallion on the hood. Since the city has increased the number of medallions very little over the years, each medallion now sells for more than $100,000. Taxicab owners who purchase medallions buy a valuable privilege to operate in a market in which the local government restricts entry.

Governments also erect barriers that reduce or prevent foreign competition. One such barrier is a tariff, which is a tax imposed to restrict imports, thereby protecting certain U.S. industries from foreign competition. A quota limits the amount of a certain good that can be imported each year and serves the same purpose as a tariff. Tariffs and quotas are rarely high enough to create monopolies, but they do make domestic markets much less competitive in protected industries.

Price and Output in Pure Monopoly

Since the monopoly firm is the entire industry, it faces the downward-sloping market demand curve for its product. This means the monopolist must lower its price to sell a larger quantity, which is consistent with the law of demand. Lowering price to sell more requires the monopolist to reduce the price *on all units sold*, not just the last unit. Therefore, the change in total revenue from selling one more unit (MR) is lower than the price received for that extra unit (P). Selling an extra unit at the new, lower price adds to total revenue, but selling all the other units at that price subtracts from total revenue. Put another way, marginal revenue (the extra revenue obtained from selling one more unit) equals the revenue from the extra unit (its price) *minus* the revenue lost on each of the other units, which now must be sold at the new, lower price. Since marginal revenue is always less than average revenue when demand is downward sloping, MR curves must lie below AR curves. Any marginal values must be less than average values when those average values are falling.

The table in Figure 8-1 demonstrates why marginal revenue is less than price after the first unit sold. Since the firm must charge the same (lower) price on all units to sell one extra unit, it must reduce price from $8 to $6 to sell the third unit. How does this affect total revenue? Selling the third unit adds its price, $6, to total revenue. But now the first two units bring only $6 each instead of $8 each, meaning $4 less revenue is now taken in for these first two units. Thus, selling the third unit increases total revenue by only $2, not by the $6 received for the third unit. Therefore, marginal revenue is $2 for the third unit while price (AR) is $6, demonstrating that MR curves always lie below demand (AR) curves that slope downward.

Monopoly Profit and Loss.   Like competitive firms, monopolies may make economic profits, normal profits, or economic losses, or they may shut down in the short run. The primary difference between the two models lies in the long run. Unlike purely competitive firms, monopolies may make economic profits for long periods because barriers to entry keep potential competitors from entering the industry. The persistent economic profit earned by monopolists is called **monopoly profit.**

Monopoly profit The persistent economic profit earned by monopoly firms in the long run due to barriers to entry.

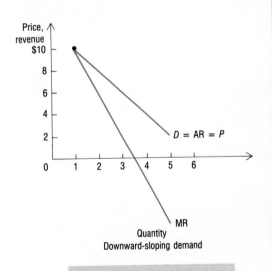

FIGURE 8-1

Demand curves slope downward when price must be lowered to sell more units. Price and average revenue are the same (*AR* = *P* always), but marginal revenue is less than price for downward-sloping demand curves.

Quantity	P	TR	AR	MR
1	$10	$10	$10	$10
2	8	16	8	6
3	6	18	6	2
4	4	16	4	−2
5	2	10	2	−6

Like other firms, monopolies maximize profit (or minimize losses) by producing that level of output at which marginal cost equals marginal revenue ($MC = MR$ at Q_m output). The monopoly in Figure 8-2 is making a monopoly profit in the long run, because price (on the demand curve) is higher than average cost at the profit-maximizing output level ($P_m > AC$ at Q_m). Note that the monopoly chooses the profit-maximizing output level, Q_m, then "reads" off the demand curve the price it can charge for that output.

Monopolies are not *guaranteed* monopoly profits in the long run, however. If the demand curve were lower while costs remained the same, this monopoly would make only a normal profit (zero economic profit) in the long run. In panel a of Figure 8-3, the profit-maximizing output, Q_m, sells at a price at which average revenue just equals average cost. An even lower demand curve or higher costs (panel b of Figure 8-3) may result in short-run economic losses for the monopolist. (Would you make an economic profit if you had a monopoly in slide rules or vinyl record albums?)

Changes in Demand and Cost.   Adjusting to changes in demand or cost in a pure monopoly is much simpler than in the competitive model. Unlike competitors that are price takers, monopolists are **price searchers.** Instead of adjusting quantity to a given market price, a monopolist adjusts price as well as quantity to find the profit-maximizing position.

What happens when market demand increases for a monopoly? The demand and marginal revenue curves both shift to the right (Figure 8-4). The monopolist increases output to Q_2, where marginal cost is again equal to marginal revenue, and raises price to P_2.

When cost per unit of output increases (Figure 8-5), the monopolist responds by reducing output from Q_m to Q_2 (where $MC_2 = MR$) and raising price from P_m to P_2. Note that price rises, *but by less than the vertical shift in the marginal*

Price searchers   A firm that has some control over price as well as output in an imperfectly competitive market.

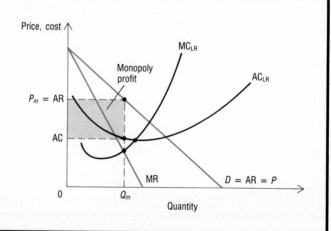

FIGURE 8-2

A monopolist makes an economic profit in the long run if demand is high enough. This monopolist maximizes profit at output Q_m. Total profit, represented by the shaded rectangle, is the difference between the firm's average costs, AC, and average revenue (price), AR, times Q_m units of output.

FIGURE 8-3

Monopolists are not guaranteed economic profits in the long run. If demand is just tangent to long-run average costs, as in panel a, the monopolist makes only a normal profit. If demand is even lower relative to costs, as in panel b, the monopolist will incur a loss and will go out of business in the long run.

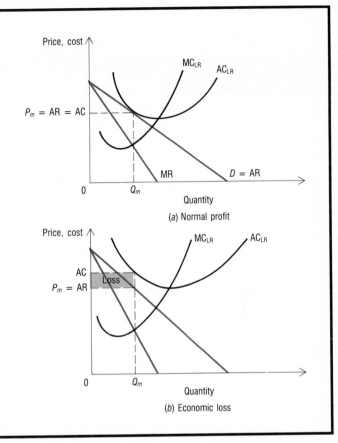

(a) Normal profit

(b) Economic loss

cost curve. As long as neither demand nor marginal cost is vertical (perfectly inelastic), profit-maximizing monopolists cannot raise price by enough to pass the entire cost increase on to consumers. In Figure 8-5, price would have to rise from P_m to P_1 to equal the amount of the cost increase. If the monopolist tried to raise price to P_1, it would be able to sell only Q_3, which would be less profitable than producing Q_2. Remember, practical economists (even monopolists) maximize profits when $MC = MR$. Output Q_2 and price P_2 comprise the profit-maximizing choice after the cost increase.

Price discrimination
Charging different prices to different customers for the same good or service.

Price Discrimination.   Monopolists can make more profit by charging different prices for the same product, a practice called **price discrimination.** Monopolists can discriminate when they can separate buyers into different submarkets. Physicians discriminate when they charge wealthy patients more than less affluent ones for the same service. College athletic departments discriminate when they charge students one price for seats at athletic events and nonstudents another price. Movie theaters discriminate by charging children less than they charge

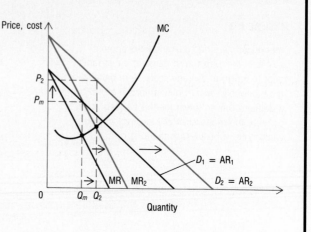

FIGURE 8-4

Monopolies adjust to demand increases by raising both quantity and price so that MC and MR are again equal.

adults to see the same movie and pharmacists by charging senior citizens less than other customers for the same medicine.

Why do monopolists charge different prices? Price discrimination allows them to increase profit. For example, some moviegoers, such as children, are very sensitive to price. Theaters can increase sales and profit from this class of customer by charging them a lower price. (Recall from Chapter 4 that if demand is price elastic, a reduction in price will raise total revenue.) Adults and teenagers on dates are less sensitive to movie prices (their demand is less price elastic), so they can be charged a higher price for the same movie tickets with little loss of sales. Thus, theaters (and ballparks, physicians, and airlines) increase their

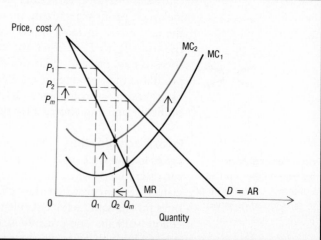

FIGURE 8-5

Monopolies adjust to cost increases by both reducing quantity and raising price. The increase in price from P to P_2 is less than the increase in cost per unit of output. Monopolists cannot increase price by the full amount of a cost increase. To make consumers pay the entire cost increase, the monopolist would have to raise price to P_1 and lower quantity to Q_1, but this price-quantity combination would not maximize profit.

revenue and profit by charging multiple prices, with higher prices for those customers with less elastic demand.

The ability to discriminate in price requires (1) market power over price, (2) different price elasticities of demand among customer groups, and (3) the ability to separate customers into groups according to their price elasticities. Grocery stores would like to charge tomato lovers a higher price than customers who just tolerate tomatoes, thereby increasing their profit from tomato sales, but they have no way to segment their customers. Tomato lovers can always get someone else to buy their tomatoes for them at the lower price. Services are often easier to segregate than goods. Physicians can enforce price discrimination because a wealthy patient with a bad heart cannot simply ask a friend to have heart surgery for him or her at the lower price. Adults cannot easily make themselves look like children to get into movies at a lower price. Athletic departments can check student ID cards at the gate to make sure those with cheaper student tickets are indeed students and not wealthy alumni.

Monopsony

Monopsony A firm (or a group) that is the sole buyer of a certain good or service; a monopoly buyer.

A **monopsony** is the sole *buyer* of a good or service. A monopsonist has power over the price it pays for reasons similar to those that give a monopoly its power over selling price: natural and artificial barriers limiting the number of buyers. Examples of monopsony include company towns (a single, large employer in a small, isolated town), local school districts that are the sole buyers of teachers' services in their areas, and the National Basketball Association (NBA), which has a monopsony in professional basketball talent as a result of its draft process. The NBA draft forces players to either negotiate and play with the team that drafts them, play in Europe, or sit on the sidelines. Professional sports leagues are exempt from the usual antitrust laws that govern other industries.

A monopsony imposes costs on its suppliers because it can use its monopsony power to force price down. Like a monopoly, a monopsony reduces the efficiency of resource allocation.

EVALUATING THE MONOPOLY MODEL

How does pure monopoly compare with pure competition? Does a monopoly yield the same production and allocative efficiency found in purely competitive markets? The answer is a strong no, but monopolies are not entirely without redeeming qualities.

Costs of Monopoly

Practical economists oppose monopolies because they expect those firms to overcharge consumers, enrich their owners, and engage in "dirty tricks" to keep their barriers to entry in place. At best, people are suspicious of monopoly power and believe monopolies should be regulated in the public interest. The unfavorable reputation of monopolies reflects their inefficient production and resource misallocation relative to competitive firms. Monopolies also result in an undesirable distribution of income.

Productive Inefficiency ($P > AC_{min}$). Monopolies sell their output at prices above minimum average cost ($P > AC_{min}$), even when they are making normal profits in the long run. Look back at panel a of Figure 8-3, which shows a monopoly making only a long-run normal profit. Unlike a firm in pure competition, the monopolist does not produce that quantity that minimizes average cost.

Resource Misallocation ($P > MC$). A monopoly produces less output and charges a higher price than does a purely competitive industry with the same demand and cost conditions. Because monopoly price exceeds marginal cost, monopolies misallocate resources. Additional units of the monopoly product would be worth more to consumers (measured by the price they are willing to pay) than the value or cost of other goods forgone. From the viewpoint of the practical economist as a consumer, this monopolist should expand output, which would cause price to fall and marginal cost to rise, until $P = MC$.

Suppose a monopolized industry somehow is organized as a competitive industry and the sum of all the marginal cost curves of the individual competitive firms is the same as the monopolist's marginal cost curve. Figure 8-6 compares the price and output results under the two models. In competition, long-run price and quantity are P_c and Q_c, respectively, determined by the intersection of

---

FIGURE 8-6

In pure competition, the intersection of market supply (ΣMC) and market demand (D) determines output (Q_c) and price (P_c) in the long run. Price is equal to marginal cost. The monopolist maximizes profit at output level Q_m, found at the intersection of marginal cost and marginal revenue in the market ($MC = MR$). The monopoly output, Q_m, is less than output Q_c under competition, and the monopoly price, P_m, is higher than the competitive price, P_c. The monopoly price also exceeds the monopolist's marginal cost, MC_m.

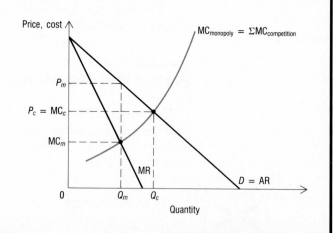

market supply and demand (the market MR curve is irrelevant in pure competition). The competitive output is sold at a price that equals marginal cost.

For the monopolist, the profit-maximizing output level is Q_m, found where $MC = MR$. The monopoly output, Q_m, is less than the Q_c output under competition, and it commands a higher price, P_m. High prices and restricted output are the two primary criticisms of monopoly.

Other Monopoly Costs.   Other costs or problems associated with monopoly include redistributing income, rent-seeking costs, costs of regulating monopoly, and general inefficiency.

Because monopolies produce less output and charge a higher price than competitive firms do, consumers suffer a loss. The difference between the total amount paid at the monopoly price for the monopoly output and the amount consumers would have paid at the competitive price for the same amount of output is the amount of income transferred from consumers to monopolists. For example, if a monopoly restricted output to 100 units to raise price from $4 (the competitive price) to $6 (the monopoly price), consumers would pay an extra $200 (100 units $\times$ $2). That $200 is an arbitrary transfer of income from consumers to the monopoly.

Rent seeking Efforts by any firm or person to earn above-normal profit or income by creating monopoly power.

To be able to raise prices, monopolies must erect barriers to entry and then maintain them. The costs of obtaining entry barriers from government are called **rent-seeking** costs. Economists use the term *rent* to describe any earnings in excess of opportunity costs. Monopoly profits are an example of rent.

Rent-seeking costs can be substantial. Consider the costs of lobbying Congress and the president to enact special import quota and tariff laws for a particular industry or to impose safety or environmental regulations that only one firm is prepared to meet. The lobbying costs to the firm, as well as the costs incurred by the government, are extra costs of monopoly and other imperfectly competitive industries.

Governments, on the other hand, are also in the business of preventing, breaking up, and regulating monopolies. The antitrust division of the Department of Justice, the Federal Trade Commission, and the Securities and Exchange Commission all investigate firms for illegal activities that eliminate competition and evaluate the competitive effects of proposed mergers of large firms. Governments also spend resources regulating natural monopolies such as electric utilities and regional airports. Public service commissions and other regulatory bodies must be created—at no small cost—to try to reduce the negative effects of monopoly.

X-inefficiency Extra costs (or lost output) resulting from the failure of large firms without strong competitors to produce efficiently and minimize costs.

A final cost of monopoly is due to the fact that monopoly firms are more likely than competitive firms to be inefficient, having higher than necessary costs or "output slippage." This failure of monopolies to produce efficiently and minimize costs is known as **X-inefficiency.** Recognized by economist Harvey Leibenstein in 1966, X-inefficiency differs from the conscious decision of monopolies to reduce output to raise price; it is the lost output and higher costs resulting from the firm's failure to operate efficiently on its production possibility frontier.

Monopolies are likely to be X-inefficient for two reasons. First, monopolies are large firms, and bureaucracy increases with organizational size, necessitating extra paperwork and quadruplicate forms to keep everyone in the firm informed. Controlling a firm this way is costly. Second, monopolies have less incentive to produce efficiently (to be "lean and mean"), because they are not disciplined by strong market competition. They are not forced to produce as much as possible at the least possible cost to survive. According to Leibenstein, X-inefficiency in large U.S. industries costs the country about 2 percent of its total output of goods and services each year.

Benefits of Monopoly

Monopoly, as you might expect, offers very few benefits to offset its negative characteristics. At least monopoly generally prevents the excessive entry and exit costs sometimes associated with pure competition. It may also be the only way to attain economies of scale in some markets. Some economists also suggest that monopoly firms advance technology more rapidly than competitive firms do, but that proposition is debatable. It is true that monopoly firms have a more certain life, have more resources, and can capture the benefits of research and development expenditures for themselves (due to their barriers to entry). Thus, monopolies may be more likely than competitive firms to engage in research to develop new production technology and new products. On the other hand, the very protection that barriers to entry offer also can have a "narcotic" effect on monopolies. Why work hard to develop new products to beat the competition when no competition exists? Consequently, monopolies may or may not develop new technology and products depending on the personal desires of managers and owners.

 **CHECKLIST** : **Costs and Benefits of Monopoly (Relative to Competition)**

Costs	Benefits
Higher price	Avoidance of industry entry and exit costs
Lower output	
Productive inefficiency ($P > AC_{min}$)	Economies of scale in some markets
Resource misallocation ($P > MC$)	
Income redistribution	Technological progress (sometimes)
Rent-seeking costs	
X-inefficiency	

Limits to Monopoly Power

Although pure monopoly is much less desirable than pure competition, monopoly firms are not always "ogres." There are important limits to monopoly power. Monopolies are limited by the market demand they face, by potential competition, by antitrust laws, and sometimes by powerful "single buyers" on the other side of their markets.

Like all firms, monopolies are constrained by consumer demand. They cannot charge any price they want for a given quantity of output. There is a maximum price (from the demand curve) that practical economists are willing to pay for any particular quantity. This price is limited by the buying public's ability to find substitutes. Furthermore, monopolists are profit maximizers: They charge the profit-maximizing price rather than the highest possible price on the demand curve.

Monopolies also do not always earn monopoly profits. Being a monopoly puts a firm in a better position to take advantage of its market power, but monopoly profits are not guaranteed. It all depends on how high demand is relative to costs. How much monopoly profit would you expect to make if you were granted an exclusive franchise in washboards, woolen T-shirts, or solar-powered vacuum cleaners?

In addition, even monopolies often face potential competition. Barriers to entry are seldom so secure that monopolies can fully restrict output and charge the profit-maximizing monopoly price. When barriers to entry are not absolute, firms operate in **contestable markets.** International markets are especially contestable. Many monopolies are national rather than global in scope, and the potential for foreign competition limits a firm's monopoly power at home.

In contestable markets, monopolies must restrain their exercise of monopoly power in the short run to avoid making it possible for potential competitors to become real ones in the long run. They cannot raise price too much or make monopoly profits so large that other large firms take steps to break down their barriers to entry. Other firms can overcome artificial barriers, like brand names, government franchises, or import quotas, if monopoly profits are large enough.

While government is often the culprit in establishing and supporting barriers to entry that create monopolies, governments in some countries also actively fight monopoly by enforcing **antitrust laws.** In the United States, such laws prohibit the formation of most kinds of monopoly (those that "restrain trade") and limit the use of monopoly power. They are called *antitrust laws* because a popular way to form a monopoly in the late 1800s was to create a trust. A trust was a combination of all the significant firms in an industry under a common board of directors that ran all the companies in the trust as though they were a single firm, thus reaping the benefits of monopoly. One famous example was the Standard Oil trust put together by John D. Rockefeller. Other trusts existed in wood, lead, sugar, tobacco, steel, rubber, canning, and even whiskey.

In response to popular protest, the U.S. government enacted antitrust laws at the turn of the century to reduce monopoly. The Sherman Act of 1890 was

Contestable markets An imperfectly competitive market in which barriers to entry are not absolute, causing firms to use less than their full market power in the short run.

Antitrust laws Laws prohibiting the formation of most kinds of monopoly and limiting the use of monopoly power by existing monopolies.

the first antitrust law. In forthright language, it outlawed monopoly:

Section 1.   Every contract, combination in the form of trust or otherwise, or conspiracy, in restraint of trade or commerce . . . is hereby declared illegal.

Section 2.   Every person who shall monopolize, or attempt to monopolize, or combine or conspire with any other person or persons, to monopolize any part of the trade or commerce . . . shall be deemed guilty of a misdemeanor, and . . . shall be punished [by fine and/or imprisonment]. . . .

Several other antitrust laws clarifying and extending the Sherman Act were passed in the years that followed. These laws, taken together, have substantially limited the ability of firms' to monopolize markets and to use monopoly power.

Finally, monopoly power can also be limited by the existence of monopsony, a single buyer. When powerful, single buyers bargain with monopolies, the power of the monopoly to raise price is substantially diminished. This effect is the reason consumers sometimes band together in cooperatives to buy goods, especially monopoly goods. Forming labor unions, which monopolize certain types of labor services (e.g., auto workers), can often reduce the monopsony power of large firms as buyers of labor.

OLIGOPOLY

Oligopoly and monopolistic competition are two other models of imperfect competition that lie between the extremes of pure competition and pure monopoly. Although each of these market structures contains elements of both monopoly and competition, oligopoly is closer to monopoly, while monopolistic competition has many similarities to pure competition. Almost all of the consumer durables you buy (cars, stereos, etc.) are produced and sold in oligopoly markets while most of everything else you purchase (from shoes to name brand shirts) is produced by monopolistically competitive firms.

Oligopoly A market model in which markets are dominated by a few firms that are protected by barriers to entry and produce a homogeneous product or slightly differentiated products.

Concentration ratio The percentage of industry output produced by the largest four (or eight) firms in a given industry; used to measure the degree of dominance of large firms in an industry.

Oligopoly Assumptions

The **oligopoly** model applies to markets that are (1) dominated by a few large firms, (2) protected by barriers to entry, and (3) characterized by either homogeneous products or slightly differentiated versions of a particular product.

What do we mean by "a few large firms?" The exact number is not fixed; it may be three or four, or even six or seven firms. The key feature of oligopoly is that the largest firms in the industry produce most of its output, leaving "scraps," or specialty products, for any other, smaller firms in the industry.

The dominance of large firms in an oligopoly industry is often measured with concentration ratios. A **concentration ratio** is the percentage of industry output produced by the largest four (or eight) firms in a given industry. The concentration ratios in Table 8-1 suggest that U.S. industries are dominated by a few large firms, whereas others are not. Interpret the ratios in Table 8-1 carefully,

TABLE 8-1   Concentration Ratios for Selected U.S. Manufacturing Industries, 1987

Industry	Four-Firm Concentration Ratio*	Total Number of Firms
Chewing gum	96	8
Automobiles	90	352
Cigarettes	92	9
Breakfast cereal	87	33
Beer	87	101
Aluminum	74	34
Tires	69	114
Soaps and detergents	65	683
Farm machinery	45	1,576
Bread and cake products	34	1,948
Petroleum refining	32	200
Newspapers	25	7,473
Soft drinks	30	846
Circuit boards	14	950
Commercial printing, lithographic	7	24,327

*Note: These ratios reflect U.S. sales by U.S. firms only. Including imports significantly lowers the concentration ratios for several industries, particularly automobiles and tires.

Source: U.S. Bureau of the Census, *1987 Census of Manufactures: Concentration Ratios in Manufacturing* (Washington, D.C.: U.S. Government Printing Office, 1989), pp. 7-6–7-51.

however; they include only sales by U.S. firms, which makes concentration in certain industries look much heavier than it really is.

Oligopolies exist because they are protected from competition by barriers to entry, including economies of scale. Local oligopolies are common. For example, a small to medium-size city may be able to support only two or three cement producers given the necessary investment in mixing plants and cement trucks. Advertising expenditures to establish brand names may also act as an entry barrier for oligopolies as well as for monopolies. Few practical economists would undertake the risk and expense of entering the breakfast cereal market against General Mills's Cheerios or Kellogg's Rice Krispies.

Some oligopolies produce homogeneous (standardized) products, such as steel, aluminum, paper, plate glass, cement, and fertilizer. Others produce **differentiated products,** which are similar but have certain distinctive characteristics that are important to consumers. For example, you may think Ford and Chevy sedans are not very different (both are cars, right?), but try telling that to a loyal Ford owner or a dyed-in-the-wool Chevy fan.

Firms try to differentiate their products to make demand less elastic. Through research and development, particular firms create antilock braking systems for their cars, make their cereals into the shape of small Os, or press their headache

Differentiated products
Goods that are similar (like cars) but have certain distinctive characteristics that make each firm's product slightly different (Fords, Chevys, Rolls Royces).

tablets into easier-to-swallow caplets. Whether real or imagined, these characteristics make each firm's product a little different, adding to brand loyalty, making demand less elastic, and giving the firm more market power over price.

Oligopoly Price and Output Behavior

Although no clear-cut theory of oligopoly behavior exists that allows economists to explain and predict exactly how oligopolists set price and output, one fact is clear: oligopoly firms must consider the reactions of rivals before taking any action to change price or output. This **mutual interdependence** plays an important role in price and output determination in oligopoly.

Suppose Ford lowers its car prices 10 percent in an attempt to sell more cars. What do you think GM and Chrysler will do? They are unlikely to let Ford get the extra sales and increase its share of the market. They are likely to match Ford's price cuts, and if they do, Ford will sell very few additional cars. Since Ford managers are bright enough to figure this out in the first place, they are not likely to lower prices without a strong reason (like a sagging economy) that also applies to the other automakers. Oligopolists are very careful not to cut prices too often on their own.

On the other hand, if Ford raises its car prices 10 percent to increase revenue, what are its rivals likely to do? They will probably let Ford price itself out of the market and laugh all the way to the bank! Ford customers will switch to Chevys, Chryslers, and Hondas. Since Ford is certainly aware that the other firms are unlikely to match its price increases, it will not increase prices very often (unless costs happen to be increasing for all automakers at the same time).

Because oligopolists are interdependent, they change their prices infrequently. Prices are considered "sticky" in such markets, usually changing only at a certain time of the year. In the case of autos, prices change when new models are introduced in the fall.

One way oligopolies deal with interdependence and solve their pricing problem is to let one firm in the oligopoly set the going price. The **price leadership** role is usually undertaken by the most efficient or the largest firm in the industry. The price leader changes price when its cost or demand conditions change, and the other firms follow its signal almost immediately. Price leadership behavior accounts for the fact that the big three cigarette producers had identical prices throughout the 1920s and 1930s, with R. J. Reynolds Tobacco Company playing the lead role. Today many basic industries, such as cement, tobacco, coal, copper, gasoline, plate glass, steel, and fertilizer, engage in some degree of price leadership.

Still another way for firms to deal with interdependence is collusion. Oligopoly firms have a better chance to make economic profits if they can avoid worrying about how rivals will react to price changes. Although illegal in the United States, oligopoly firms sometimes resort to **collusion,** or secretly agreeing to raise price or to stop offering some costly service.

In Practice 8-1

. . . .

How Profitable Are Large Corporations?

H ow much profit do most firms make on a dollar of sales? One opinion poll asked this question and came up with this average citizen estimate: 29 cents, or 29 percent of sales. Answers varied widely, but as the data below indicate, the vast majority of respondents overestimated corporate profits.

Following are the 1991 after-tax accounting profits of the 500 largest industrial corporations as a percentage of sales and as a percentage of the amount owners invested in the firm. The second figure is calculated in much the same way one would determine an interest rate on savings. These 500 *largest* industrial firms, many of which produce in imperfectly competitive markets, make profits far below what most people believe.

Are some of these firms making economic or monopoly profits? Surely that is the case for a few, but the average percentage return on owners' investment (10.2 percent) indicates such profits are close to normal or very little more than what investors could have earned on *their next best alternative.* Comparing corporate investor returns of 10.2 percent to interest of about 9.3 percent that could be earned on top-quality corporate bonds or on

Industry Category	1991 Profit as Percentage of Sales	1991 Profit as Percentage of Owners' Investment
Petroleum refining	3.2%	10.2%
Beverages	5.5	21.1
Chemicals	3.7	12.6
Metal manufacturing	1.5	5.2
Motor vehicles	0.4	1.0
Rubber, plastics	3.4	11.6
Aerospace	3.3	12.4
Electronics	2.7	10.7
Publishing, printing	5.1	10.7
Soaps, cosmetics	5.1	14.7
Average (including categories not shown)	3.2%	10.2%

Source: U.S. Bureau of the Census, *Statistical Abstract of the United States, 1992* (Washington, DC: U.S. Government Printing Office, 1992), p. 541.

safe, long-term U.S. government bonds in 1991 means that only the difference of about 1 percent could possibly be economic profit! However, much of that 1 percent difference was really a payment for the extra risk of investing in (owning) corporations rather than putting that money into safer bonds to earn interest. ∎

Cartel A formal (illegal) agreement among oligopoly firms to officially act as a monopoly, setting prices and allocating quantities to be produced by each firm.

Formal arrangements among oligopoly firms to set prices and allocate quantities to be produced by each firm are called **cartels.** Cartels are illegal in the United States but legal in many other countries, including Japan. The most famous cartel in recent years is the Organization of Petroleum Exporting Countries (OPEC), which ironically got its start with the support and encouragement of the U.S. government. State Department officials thought a little more oil revenue would help stabilize some of the less developed countries in the Middle East. Little did these officials realize just how well the OPEC countries would do! These nations were able to raise prices from $2.12 per barrel in 1971 to $35.00 by 1982 before

OPEC fell into disarray in the mid-1980s. By the 1990s, oil was selling in the $15-to-$20-per-barrel range.

Formal cartels try to get as close to the monopoly price as possible by acting together as a monopoly with formal agreements and contracts. The cartel sets the industry's marginal cost equal to marginal revenue corresponding to the market demand curve to find the profit-maximizing quantity and price combination. Then it allocates shares of the monopoly output to each firm to produce and sell at the monopoly price.

Cartels ultimately break up for two reasons. First, individual cartel firms have incentives to cheat, and other firms have incentives to enter the industry. Cartel members have an incentive to cheat on their share of the total cartel output because the monopoly price is so high. Producing a little extra and selling it "on the side" at or near the monopoly price can increase the firm's profits. Such a good deal is hard to pass up. Total output tends to creep upward as some firms cheat, and the cartel finds it difficult to maintain the monopoly price as output expands.

Second, although barriers to entry are high in oligopoly, they are not as insurmountable as monopoly barriers might be. Charging a monopoly price attracts other firms to the industry. Great Britain, a country that produced no oil before the OPEC–induced oil crisis, began producing large quantities of oil from the North Sea. Mexico became a major producer. The United States found oil in Alaska and built a formidable pipeline. Venezuela moved into the top ten oil-producing countries. Russia began exporting oil to European countries. As oil began to flood the market from new producers, OPEC's share of world oil sales slipped from about 56 percent in 1973 to less than 35 percent in 1985. Today that share has fallen below 27 percent.

The combined effect of the incentive for members to cheat and the incentive for other firms to enter the industry means that most cartels will be short-lived. This has been the fate of OPEC. While OPEC still exists and continues to influence oil prices from time to time, it has lost most of its control over world oil prices and output.

Evaluating Oligopoly

Because barriers to entry in oligopoly limit competition, oligopoly output clearly will be lower and price higher than in a purely competitive industry. Thus, oligopolies, like monopolies, are inefficient producers ($P > AC_{min}$) and misallocate resources ($P > MC$). What is not clear is by just how much oligopoly price exceeds the competitive price and to what extent oligopolies restrict output.

The answer to that question depends on the strength of each individual oligopoly's barriers to entry, or the degree to which its market is contestable. Oligopolies with weak barriers cannot raise price much above the competitive level. Those with strong barriers, and especially those that form tight cartels or otherwise collude, may be able to restrict output and raise price close to the pure monopoly level for a significant period of time.

CHECKLIST : **Special Features of Oligopoly**

Assumptions   Response to Mutual Interdependence

1. Few firms   1. Sticky prices
2. High barriers to entry   2. Price leadership
3. Homogeneous or slightly differentiated   3. Collusion
   products   4. Cartels

MONOPOLISTIC COMPETITION

Monopolistic competition A market model in which there are many small sellers, entry and exit are relatively free, and firms produce differentiated products.

Monopolistic competition is only "one step removed" from pure competition. **Monopolistic competition** is a market model in which (1) there are many small sellers in the market, (2) entry and exit are almost as free as in pure competition, and (3) firms produce differentiated products. Product differentiation is the source of the small amount of monopoly power.

In monopolistic competition, sellers face significant competition in the market—perhaps as many as 20, 30, 40, or even more firms. One firm can change its price and output without measurably affecting the sales of any other firm in the industry. Furthermore, there are enough firms that, unlike in oligopoly, no mutual interdependence exists.

Firms may enter and exit monopolistically competitive markets easily. Resource mobility in this model is almost as high as in pure competition. The only barriers to entry are those associated with product differentiation.

Product differentiation is the key characteristic of monopolistic competition. Each firm produces a product that is slightly different from those of other firms in the market. Brand names and advertising are especially important. For example, Kimberly-Clark Corporation makes Kleenex, which competes heavily with dozens of other brands of facial tissue nationwide. Kleenex, however, has its own package design, texture, weight, appearance, water-absorbing properties, softness, and aroma. In the pain reliever market, Bufferin is "buffered so it won't upset your stomach," but Bayer is "the aspirin most prescribed by doctors," and Anacin is "the extra-strength pain reliever." In effect, each firm making these differentiated products has a slight monopoly in its own product; no one else is allowed to produce Kleenex, for example. This fact gives each monopolistically competitive firm some control over price that pure competitors lack.

Monopolistically competitive markets are probably the most common and familiar market structure. Dishes, towels, jeans, magazines, shoes, hair spray, and facial tissue are all examples of products sold in monopolistically competitive markets. Grocery stores, dress shops, and gasoline stations (in fact, most retail outlets) are monopolistically competitive firms. Most cities have many dress shops, but each store differs slightly in terms of the product line it carries (junior, casual wear, price range, brand-name lines), as well as its atmosphere, salespeople, parking facilities, and location. These small differences allow retail outlets some control over their prices.

Price and Output in Monopolistic Competition

The price and output results of monopolistic competition are similar to those of pure competition. Because each product is slightly different, individual firms in monopolistic competition face a demand curve that slopes downward slightly, such as d_1 for the representative firm in panel a of Figure 8-7. This firm makes an economic profit in the short run. However, no barriers prevent other firms from entering this industry and making a very similar product. Short-run economic profits are a signal to practical economists to enter this industry, increasing market supply in the long run. In general, market price falls, shifting the representative firm's demand curve downward until it reaches d_2 (panel b). Thus, short-run economic profits are eliminated in the long run in monopolistically competitive markets.

If demand decreases or costs increase, the process just described is repeated: Firms incur economic losses in the short run, some firms exit, market price rises as industry output falls, and firm demand shifts downward until normal profits are made once again.

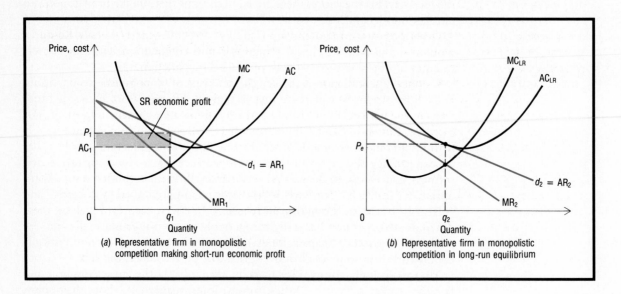

FIGURE 8-7

(a) This representative firm in monopolistic competition faces a slightly downward-sloping demand curve, d_1, due to product differentiation. It makes an economic profit in the short run because demand is sufficiently high (until new firms enter in the long run). (b) As new firms selling similar products enter this market in response to short-run economic profits, market price is driven down, shifting the representative firm's demand curve downward until it reaches d_2. The monopolistically competitive firm makes only normal profits in the long run, but price remains slightly higher than minimum average cost because the firm's demand curve is slightly downward sloping.

Evaluating Monopolistic Competition

In the long run, monopolistic competition results in normal profits (zero economic profits) due to easy entry and exit. Firms can make substantial economic profits in the short run. Equilibrium price and quantity in this model are close to competitive levels, because firm demand curves slope downward very little (they are nearly horizontal). The biggest difference from the competitive model is product differentiation, which makes firm demand curves less elastic (more steeply sloped) for particular firms. Advertising and other forms of nonprice competition to reduce demand elasticity are very important in monopolistically competitive industries.

In monopolistic competition, price is slightly above minimum average costs in the long run. These firms do not produce as efficiently as competitive firms do ($P > AC_{min}$), but the difference is not great. Monopolistically competitive firms also misallocate resources because price exceeds marginal cost $(P > MC)$, although by less than in oligopoly or monopoly. They produce too little because the value of the resources forgone to produce the marginal unit is less than the amount consumers are willing to pay for it.

Some economists point out that these inefficiencies of monopolistic competition are at least partly offset by the benefits of product variety. Prices would be lower if, for example, 1,000 firms produced identical blue jeans, identical typewriters, or identical cars, but would you prefer that result? Slight productive and allocative inefficiencies are the price practical economists pay for the benefits of variety in monopolistically competitive markets.

LABOR MARKETS AND IMPERFECTLY COMPETITIVE INDUSTRIES

Monopoly power also affects resource markets, especially labor markets. Recall that the demand for any resource depends on how much an extra unit of that resource adds to total output and, in turn, the net amount of extra revenue that increased output brings to the firm when it is sold. Therefore, the demand for labor is the marginal product of labor times marginal revenue, or $D_L = MRP_L = MP_L \times MR$. When product price and marginal revenue are the same, as in pure competition, each unit of labor hired receives exactly what it is worth to both society and the firm. The demand curve slopes downward only because marginal product falls as more workers are hired.

The economic value of a unit of labor, however, differs in imperfectly competitive industries, especially monopoly. In monopoly, product price and marginal revenue are not the same. Marginal revenue is less than price in a monopoly because the firm must lower price on all units to sell even one more unit of output than an extra worker would produce. Here there are *two* factors—falling marginal product and falling marginal revenue—for a downward-sloping

CHECKLIST

Comparison of the Four Basic Market Models

	Pure Competition	Monopolistic Competition	Oligopoly	Pure Monopoly
Assumptions				
	Large number of buyers and sellers	Many sellers	Few sellers	One seller
	Homogeneous product	Differentiated product	Homogeneous or differentiated product	Unique product
	Free entry and exit	Free entry and exit	Barriers to entry	Substantial barriers to entry
Characteristics				
	No market power	Slight control over price	Market power	Monopoly power
	No advertising	Considerable advertising	Advertising if products are differentiated	Some advertising of product to increase demand, reduce price elasticity, and improve the firm's image
Long-Run Results				
	No economic profit	No economic profit	Economic profit	Monopoly profit
	Productive efficiency $(P = AC_{min})$	$P > AC_{min}$ (slightly)	$P > AC_{min}$	$P > AC_{min}$
	Allocation efficiency $(P = MC)$	$P > MC$ (slightly)	$P > MC$	$P > MC$

demand curve for labor. As a result, monopolists hire less labor and produce less output than competitive firms do.

Figure 8-8 shows the demand for labor for a competitive firm (D_c) and for a monopoly (D_m). Because product price is greater than marginal revenue for every output level under monopoly, the competitive firm's demand curve lies above the monopolist's demand curve. Given the labor supply curve, S_L, the monopolist would hire Q_m units of labor. If this industry were a purely competitive one, the total amount of labor hired by all the competitive firms together would be Q_c. A competitive industry would hire more workers and produce more output, *ceteris paribus*.

Myth 8-1

All Markets Should Be Competitive

It is tempting to pick out pure competition as the ideal market structure and try to "install" it in all industries. However, each of the basic market models is appropriate for particular industries, and most consumers would be unhappy to see pure competition in every market.

Pure competition is "right" for agricultural markets from which consumers want generic goods (wheat, corn, soybeans, beef, and so on) produced at the lowest possible cost. But nobody wants firms to compete by stringing multiple local telephone lines to our homes or putting hundreds of different companies' water and sewer pipes under the streets. There is no way to break up natural monopolies into perfectly competitive firms without sacrificing valuable economies of scale. Such monopolies may need regulation in the public interest, but they should not be forced to fit the competitive model.

Most of us wouldn't want jeans to be sold in purely competitive markets either, because we like the variety of styles, designer labels, fabrics, and new colors available in monopolistically competitive markets. All of these extra choices make life interesting, and most consumers are willing to pay the slightly higher price required to have this variety.

Oligopoly is often the appropriate market structure for certain industries, too. It may provide the best blend of large-scale production, some degree of product differentiation, and a measure of competition in the automobile, home appliance, and pocket calculator markets. The efficient plant size relative to demand in certain oligopoly markets dictates that only a few firms should produce refrigerators, steel, and mainframe computers. Economies of scale are not so large in these industries that monopoly is likely, but neither are they small enough to allow competition among thousands of firms.

Thus, the *concept* of competition is ideal: Firms should strive to provide the best product at the lowest possible cost and price. The purely competitive market model, however, is not the ideal market structure for every industry. ∎

IMPERFECT COMPETITION AND MARKET FAILURE

Chapters 4 through 7 showed the market at its best. The case of imperfect competition described in this chapter is our first encounter with market failure, or some of the undesirable results of markets that are not perfectly competitive. In the next chapter, we will consider additional kinds of market failure. These failures include a distribution of income that some people consider unsatisfactory,

FIGURE 8-8

The monopolist's labor demand schedule is D_m. The firm will hire labor until the marginal revenue product of labor equals the marginal cost of labor, or the given wage rate in a competitive labor market. The monopolist hires Q_m units of labor. If the industry were a purely competitive one, the demand curve would be D_c and the quantity of labor hired would rise to Q_c. This curve is less steep because MR and product price would be equal.

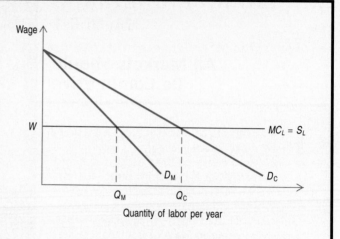

as well as the underproduction of certain desirable goods that are consumed jointly (like fire protection) and those that lack clearly defined property rights (clean air and water).

As you have seen, governments play a mixed role in market failure, sometimes creating problems by helping to erect barriers to entry and sometimes curing problems by enforcing antitrust laws and regulating natural monopolies. After examining other forms of market failure in Chapter 9, we will take a closer look at the economic role of government in Chapter 10.

Summary

1. Pure monopoly exists when a single firm sells a unique product in an industry protected from competition by high barriers to entry. Such a firm has monopoly power, which is the ability to raise price by restricting output.

2. Barriers to entry may be either natural or artificial, resulting from large economies of scale, exclusive ownership of raw materials, patents and copyrights, government franchises, high fixed costs of advertising to establish and maintain brand names, or protective legislation such as tariffs and quotas.

3. Natural monopolies are the result of large economies of scale. In a natural monopoly, only one firm can exist because it will have the lowest possible average cost of production when it expands to supply the entire amount demanded in the market.

4. Monopolies and other imperfectly competitive firms are price searchers. Purely competitive firms are price takers that adjust only their output when

demand or costs change. Imperfectly competitive firms search for the right combination of price and quantity to maximize profit.

5. Monopolies can make persistent economic profits in the long run given their monopoly power, but they are not guaranteed monopoly profits. Whether and how much economic profit monopolies make depends on how high demand is relative to costs and how contestable their markets are.

6. Monopolies do not produce efficiently ($P > AC_{min}$), nor do they produce enough of the monopoly good ($P > MC$). They also redistribute income to themselves, create rent-seeking and regulatory costs, and incur higher X-inefficiency costs.

7. Monopolies do not have unlimited market power. Their actions are limited by product demand, government antitrust laws, potential competitors (in contestable markets), and sometimes by the existence of monopsony on the other side of their markets.

8. Oligopoly is close to monopoly. In oligopoly, a few large firms dominate a market for either a homogeneous or a slightly differentiated product and are protected by barriers to entry. Mutual interdependence causes oligopoly prices to be "sticky." Oligopolies generally restrict output and raise price, thereby making economic profits in the long run. Cartels are oligopolies that make formal arrangements to restrict group output and set a monopoly price, but they are often short-lived.

9. Monopolistic competition is close to pure competition, with many firms and easy entry. However, each firm sells a differentiated product, which gives it some slight control over price. Monopolistically competitive firms make normal profits in the long run due to easy entry, but price exceeds both minimum average cost (inefficient production) and marginal cost (resource misallocation). These inefficiencies are the price consumers pay for product variety.

10. Imperfectly competitive industries, especially monopolies, hire too little labor (and other resources) and produce too little output.

Key Terms

antitrust laws	monopolistic	natural monopoly
cartel	competition	oligopoly
collusion	monopoly	price discrimination
concentration ratio	monopoly power	price leadership
contestable market	monopoly profit	price searcher
differentiated	monopsony	rent seeking
products	mutual	X-inefficiency
imperfect competition	interdependence	

Questions and Problems

1. Identify the barriers to entry in monopolies (or oligopolies) that engage in such illegal activities as gambling, drugs, and prostitution.

2. Given the following information for a monopoly, determine its profit-maximizing price-quantity combination. Does the firm make monopoly profit?

Price	Quantity	Total Cost
$10	4	28
9	5	31
8	6	34
7	7	37
6	8	40
5	9	43
4	10	46

3. Explain why, unlike a competitive industry, a monopolist restricts output to raise price. The monopoly firm charges a higher price, but it also cannot sell as much. How does it come out ahead?

4. Explain under what conditions antitrust action against many monopolies and near-monopolies is not desirable.

5. Economists claim most cartels are doomed to failure in the long run if they use their cartel power. Why?

6. Give two examples of price discrimination in imperfectly competitive markets, and explain in each case why firms are able to charge different prices to different customers.

7. If you owned a diner, which of the following customer groups would be good candidates for a discount on breakfast? Why?

    a. Senior citizens
    b. Students
    c. Commuters to a nearby major employer
    d. Truck drivers

8. Do you think the inefficiencies of monopolistic competition make that market structure less desirable than pure competition? Why or why not?

9. Explain how a monopolist decides how much labor to hire and why that amount is usually less than what a corresponding firm in a competitive industry would hire.

Market Failure: Externalities, Public Goods, and Poverty

One man's conservation is all too frequently another man's unemployment.

MIKE MCCORMACK, 1977

Main Points

1. **Producing or consuming some goods creates external costs or benefits for third parties.** Such externalities lead to market failure, because firms produce too much or too little of those goods.

2. **External benefits and costs arise when property rights are poorly defined.** Property rights must be assigned to external benefits and costs so that they can be bought and sold in markets, allowing resources to be allocated efficiently.

3. **Public goods are goods that are consumed by everyone at the same time and for which excluding nonpayers from consumption is too difficult.**

4. **Since consumers cannot be required to pay for the benefits they receive from public goods, markets fail to produce enough of them.**

5. **The distribution of income in the United States is unequal.** Some families earn a great deal more income than others. Government assistance programs and progressive taxes reduce U.S. income inequality.

6. **Minimum wage laws help those unskilled workers who keep their jobs, but higher minimum wages cause some workers to lose their jobs.**

7. **Differences in worker productivity, age, household size, labor mobility, amount and quality of resources owned, and discrimination on the basis of race and sex explain much of the inequality in household incomes.** Government programs and policies also create differences among household incomes.

8. **Poor families include African-Americans, European-Americans, and other groups rather than just one or two.** They also include both urban and rural families. Most poor people are also very young, unskilled, and/or living in one-earner households headed by women.

I n the last chapter, we discussed how imperfect competition may lead to lower output and higher prices than would occur in competitive markets. Such monopoly power is a form of market failure. Market failure leads to government intervention to try to make markets more efficient (e.g., antitrust laws, regulation of natural monopolies). In this chapter, we introduce another set of market problems that may also call for corrective government action.

In some cases, demand and supply for goods and services do not reflect all the relevant information. For example, producing or consuming some goods creates social costs, such as pollution. Producing other goods may create positive benefits that "spill over" to other parties not involved in the market transaction. Firms may produce too much or too little of such goods. These production "errors" are a form of market failure. Again, action by government may be needed to shift market outcomes in the right direction. Public goods, such as national defense and satellite navigation beams, also require government intervention to ensure adequate production.

In this chapter, we also examine the distribution of income among U.S. households that results from the workings of supply and demand in resource markets. Many economists consider a highly unequal distribution of income, especially poverty, to be a form of market failure. In this chapter, we look at the actual income distribution and the reasons for income inequality. In Chapter 10, we address the policy issue of whether and how government should alter the market-determined distribution of income. ■

EXTERNALITIES

Externalities Benefits or costs of production or consumption imposed on third parties rather than on producers or consumers of a good.

Sometimes production and/or consumption activities create side effects for people who are neither sellers nor buyers of a particular good. These side effects, or spillover costs or benefits for other parties, are called **externalities.** Externalities may be either negative (impose costs on third parties) or positive (benefit third parties).

Firms create production externalities. For example, a steel mill may create a negative production externality in the form of smoke pollution that settles on nearby houses and cars as well as in people's lungs. Houses must be painted more often, car finishes deteriorate, and cases of respiratory diseases increase. These costs of smoke damage, then, are borne by parties other than steel firms or steel buyers.

Firms can also create positive production externalities, or "spillover benefits," when they produce certain goods. For example, when a nuclear power company builds a lake for emergency cooling of reactors, it generates positive externalities along with electricity. Fishermen, swimmers, boaters, and lake house dwellers all benefit, whether or not they buy electricity from that power company. The firm can "capture" the value of some external benefits by selling lakefront property at a premium, but it cannot collect on all the benefits it provides.

Consumption externalities may also be either positive or negative. Your consumption of automobile travel imposes external costs on others in the form of exhaust fumes and highway congestion. If you use the full wattage in your stereo system with your window open late at night, you create another negative consumption externality. On the other hand, you generate a positive consumption externality when you spruce up your yard and paint your house. Your neighbors enjoy a nicer-looking neighborhood with no expense to themselves. Learning to read conveys private benefits, but that consumption activity also benefits others when the reader recognizes a stop sign.

Private markets have no method of accounting for externalities. Those who gain from positive externalities contribute nothing toward the cost of creating the benefits they receive. Those who put up with negative externalities receive no compensation. Markets respond only to the benefits and costs reflected in the demand and supply curves of buyers and sellers. When external costs or benefits fall on bystanders without affecting demand or supply, markets fail to allocate resources properly.

Resource Misallocation

Market failure
Resource misallocation and inequitable income distribution resulting from imperfectly competitive markets, poorly defined property rights, or the existence of goods that cannot be bought and sold in markets.

In the presence of externalities, private markets misallocate resources. Firms produce too much of goods that create negative externalities because the market does not force these practical economists to include all the true costs of producing their output. Private markets produce too little of goods with positive externalities. Because practical economists who run firms cannot collect for the external benefits they generate, private demand is less than total social demand, and equilibrium output is too small. The inability of private markets to deal with externalities is a major form of **market failure.**

Figure 9-1 illustrates market failure in the case of a negative production externality, a paper mill that pollutes a river. Paper mills sometimes create external costs for those downstream when they discharge waste wood materials into rivers. The result is unsightly foam or other serious problems for city water systems, swimmers, and fishermen. Thus, the true total cost, or social cost, of producing paper is the sum of the usual internal private costs to the firm (land rent, wages, expenses for materials) and the external public costs imposed on downstream users (the costs of installing water filtration devices, swimming elsewhere, and/or rescuing fish).

Adding these external pollution costs to its standard supply curve, the paper mill's true marginal social cost curve for producing paper is higher than its

FIGURE 9-1

In the absence of external benefits, market demand and marginal private benefit are identical, or $D = MB$. When the cost of the negative externality (damage from river pollution) is added to supply, the optimal price and output are P_s and Q_s. Instead of the optimal price and quantity, private firms overproduce at Q_p for a lower price, P_p.

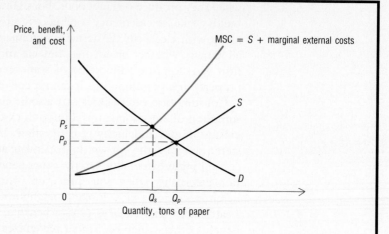

Marginal social cost (MSC) The total social cost of producing a good; the sum of marginal cost, or supply, and the marginal cost imposed by the externality.

Marginal social benefit (MSB) The total social benefit of producing a good; the sum of marginal benefit, or private demand, and the marginal benefit created by the externality.

private supply curve. **Marginal social cost (MSC)** is the total social cost of producing a good. It is the sum of the familiar marginal cost, or supply, plus the marginal cost of the externality (MSC = supply + marginal external costs). The demand for paper, D, in Figure 9.1 reflects the typical private benefits to paper consumers. In the absence of pollution control laws, the practical economists who operate the paper mill consider only their private supply along with demand to determine how much to produce. Therefore, the equilibrium quantity of paper produced is Q_p at price P_p, where private supply intersects demand.

However, society should be concerned with *all* costs in their production decisions. The intersection of the MSC and demand curves determines the socially desirable output level. That level reflects all costs and benefits. The social optimum calls for a smaller output, Q_s, and a higher price, P_s. Thus, ignoring negative externalities results in resource misallocation. Paper mills in private markets use too many resources to produce a larger than optimal amount of paper.

Firms in private markets produce too little when goods create positive externalities. When Jane is vaccinated against smallpox, she benefits from protecting herself against that disease, and she is willing to pay for that private benefit. But other people also benefit from Jane's vaccination. Her vaccination reduces the chances that they will get the disease (because Jane cannot be a carrier), even if they choose not to buy vaccinations for themselves. Thus, other people have some demand for Jane's vaccination.

Figure 9-2 illustrates how markets underproduce smallpox vaccinations. The standard supply curve reflects all costs of production, but external consumption benefits must be added to the demand curve. The **marginal social benefit** curve includes both private demand and the marginal external benefits of each vaccination (MSB = private demand + external benefits). Considering only

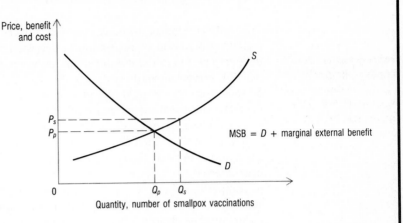

FIGURE 9-2

Total social demand for vaccinations is the sum of both private demand and the marginal external benefits of vaccinations. Consumers choose Q_p vaccinations where private demand equals supply. The socially desired number of vaccinations is Q_s, where total social demand equals supply.

private benefits would result in Q_p vaccinations, where private demand equals private supply. But a larger number of vaccinations, Q_s, is desirable from society's standpoint; Q_s is found where $S = MSB$.

In 1993, vaccinations became an important public issue. Because of rising vaccine prices (higher private cost) and cutbacks in funding for public health clinics (reducing subsidies for the positive externality), vaccinations of children for smallpox and tuberculosis have decreased. Outbreaks of these once eradicated diseases are occurring at an alarming rate, and public health officials have called for increased government spending for vaccinations.

CHEKLIST : **Externalities and Resource Misallocation**

Type of Externality	Example	Result
Negative production externality	Soot from steel mill	Too much steel produced
Positive production externality	Lake for nuclear power plant	Too little electricity produced, resulting in a smaller than desirable lake
Negative consumption externality	Tennis court lights	Too much night tennis
Positive consumption externality	Landscaped home	Too little area landscaping

Property rights Legally defined rights to enjoy specific goods, services, and resources, including the right to transfer their use to others for a price.

Property Rights Are the Problem

Practical economists, whether sellers or buyers, usually ignore externalities in making production or consumption decisions. Why? Often the reason is that **property rights** to the use of certain resources either do not exist or are poorly defined. For example, do your neighbors have the right to plant trees anywhere on their property? What if they plant trees near your joint property line, shading your favorite backyard garden plot? Which right is greater, the right to plant trees anywhere on one's property or the right to have good access to sunlight?

Without well-defined property rights, firms cannot make third parties pay for any external benefits they produce for those parties. Nor can third parties who bear external costs, like smoke from a neighbor's fireplace, force the originators to compensate them. Thus, externalities do not affect private market decisions about how much to produce or buy. For markets to work efficiently, property rights must be clearly defined so that practical economists can take account of external costs and benefits.

With poorly defined property rights, firms and consumers compete for the use of essentially "free" resources. Some firms compete with one another and with consumers to use the air to dispose of waste in the form of smoke. Scuba divers, shrimp boats, day sailors, and even city sewerage authorities all compete to use the same warm coastal waters for their own purposes. Consumers who want drinking water from western rivers compete with farmers who want to irrigate crops in arid area, with kayakers and rafters who love rushing white water, and with utility firms (and their customers) who want to dam those rivers to generate electricity. Again, without ownership and definitive property rights, competing users of "free" resources have no way to pay one another and cannot use the market to allocate those resources.

Internalizing externalities Causing those who create or receive externalities to bear the costs or benefits of them so that market prices will reflect those externalities.

SOLUTIONS TO EXTERNALITY PROBLEMS

To resolve externality problems, practical economists in the marketplace must include external costs and benefits in their decision-making process. Incorporating external costs and benefits into market demand and supply is called **internalizing externalities.** For example, the government could require steel firms to buy air filters for their smokestacks. Firms could also be required to buy (or rent) the right to emit smoke into the air from area residents, thus internalizing the firms' pollution costs. Steel firms would then have to include those costs, along with their normal private costs, in their production decisions. Adding this new, internalized cost to the usual production costs would shift the steel supply curve to the left, reducing quantity supplied of both steel and smoke.

External costs and benefits can be internalized in several ways. Approaches to the problem include (1) assigning or clarifying property rights when they are poorly defined, making it possible to buy and sell (or rent) those rights in private

In Practice 9-1

. . . .

Dirt Paths and Smog

Why do people walk across grassy areas, creating ugly dirt paths? Why would most drivers pollute the air with their cars if the government did not require pollution control devices? Are people uninformed or just thoughtless? Neither, really.

The explanation for this behavior lies in the special nature of some externalities. The negative externalities discussed in the text all have significant marginal effects. Swimmers (and city water authorities) would immediately recognize the harm from additional water pollution from the paper mill. When property rights are well defined, people have an incentive to bargain to reduce marginal units of negative externalities when they notice or feel the effects of the marginal pollution directly, as long as the benefit of doing so exceeds the cost.

Some externalities, however, like walking on the grass and polluting the air by driving, are different. These externalities have no measurable *marginal* effects; they have only cumulative effects. If marginal effects are so small that they are unnoticed or not considered important, individuals have nothing over which to bargain. You would waste your money to pay a neighbor to stop doing something that affected you only minimally. However, if you could get many people to stop the offending activity, you would be noticeably better off.

For example, one student can walk to class across the grass instead of the sidewalk without creating an ugly path. The marginal external cost of one extra trip across the grass is zero. This is because paths appear only after several students walk on the grass many times. With no damage at the margin (from one extra trip), students realize that one more trip across the grass won't hurt if no path exists. They also realize that avoiding one more trip if a path is already there won't help either.

Remember, students are practical economists who make decisions based on measurable costs and benefits at the margin. If they figure out that one extra trip has no marginal cost but does have a marginal benefit (saving walking time), all but the most socially conscious students will choose to take short cuts across the grass. Asking them not to walk on the grass will be ineffective, because taking short cuts is in their private interest! Thus, in the case of such cumulative externalities, only government intervention in the form of rules and fines will solve the problem.

The same is true for antismog devices such as catalytic converters. Would an individual Los Angeles driver voluntarily pay $340 for an optional catalytic converter for his or her car *if everyone else did?* The answer is no, because the pollution problem would already have been corrected without that person's participation. If no other driver bought a converter, would any individual buy one alone? No, because pollution would be severe whether or not one driver bought any antipollution device. Thus, under either circumstance, a catalytic converter would be a bad buy. In a city with millions of cars and trucks, one catalytic converter more or less would make no difference. The practical economist would consider buying such a converter a waste of money. That is why the government requires catalytic converters for cars rather than making such antipollution devices optional. ∎

markets; (2) prohibiting practices that create negative externalities; (3) regulating production or consumption to ensure that optimal quantities of goods (and their externalities) are produced; (4) taxing or subsidizing externality producers to reduce negative externalities or increase positive ones; and (5) creating markets in externalities.

Different solutions work better in different situations. We will consider each of these methods for internalizing externalities in turn.

Assigning Property Rights

For private markets to work properly on their own, someone must own all valuable resources and property rights must be clearly defined. Resource ownership and specifying which rights are attached to that ownership allow buyers and sellers to negotiate, or bargain, in private markets.

Every day legislators and courts are called on to define or assign property rights to one or another disputing parties. Do you have the legal right to play loud music on your deck or patio at night? If you do, your neighbors must bargain with you (pay or persuade you) to keep your music inside, purchase earplugs for them, or move. On the other hand, if you do not have the right to play loud music outdoors at night, you must negotiate with your neighbors before having an outdoor party on your property. Thus, defining property rights to solve externality problems is a major role of government in a market system.

In the paper mill example, the problem is that no one really owns the river or is sure about what rights to use the river exist. The river is a resource with several competing uses. Swimmers are unhappy because they cannot swim when the mill pollutes the river. The customers, owners, and workers of the mill would be unhappy if swimmers persuaded their legislators to pass an antipollution law that would reduce mill workers' wages and owners' profit and raise prices for consumers.

What should be done? Because practical economists want resources to be used efficiently, the river should be put to its highest-valued use. Suppose the mill currently uses the river for waste disposal but could put in a filtration system to clean its water discharge. Using the river to carry away waste is "free" (to the firm), but the filtration system would cost $1,000 annually. The alternatives for swimmers who live downstream are to continue to swim in the polluted river at no cost or join a private swim club in town at an annual cost of $600 for the group.

Giving the mill rights to use the river means the firm would use the river for waste disposal, which is the river's highest-valued use. It is cheaper for society to impose the $600 cost on swimmers than the $1,000 cost on the mill. Of course, swimmers will lose $600 each year for pool fees if the mill gets the property right to the river.

Now suppose the swimmers argue that rivers are national treasures and persuade the government to assign the rights to use the river to them. Will the river still be put to it highest-valued use? Yes. Now, the mill must approach the swimmers and try to buy or rent their rights to the river. The mill can offer up to $1,000 to use the river to carry away wood waste, the cost of its alternative filtration system. The swimmers will accept any offer above the $600 annual swim club fee to give up the river. With room for negotiation, the swimmers agree to let the mill use the river for a payment of, say, $700. They could use this money to join the swim club ($600) and have enough left over to throw an annual party ($100). The mill is better off spending $700 to use the river rather than $1,000 to filter wood waste.

If the swimmers agree to this bargain, everyone gains. Thus, *regardless of who gets the property right to the river,* the mill uses the river for waste disposal because that is the river's highest-valued use.

You should note three important points from this example. First, when property rights to a resource are assigned to either party, that resource will be put to its highest-valued use. The river is used as a waste disposal device when its opportunity cost for that use is higher ($1,000 filtration system versus $600 for swimming). You can verify that it would be used for swimming when its recreational opportunity cost is higher than its opportunity cost as a waste disposal system, regardless of which party gets the property right. Assigning property rights and encouraging negotiation to allocate resources is based on the **Coase theorem.** This theorem (named for economist Ronald Coase) says first that if property rights are well defined, the market will internalize externalities and eliminate market failure.

Second, this internalization will occur without government intervention as long as the number of people involved in the bargaining process is small. This is because the transactions costs of making decisions are relatively low when only a few people are involved. **Transactions costs** describe all the costs of making transactions and enforcing agreements, such as the costs of negotiating deals, hiring lawyers to write contracts, advertising to find buyers or sellers, and traveling to meetings.

Because the river pollution example involves only a single mill and a small group of swimmers, assigning a property right and simply allowing negotiation in the private market should work. However, when thousands (or even millions) of people live downstream and hundreds of factories operate along the river, transactions costs are so high that just assigning a property right will not cause the market to reach an efficient solution. With thousands of participants involved in such a decision, government will have to intervene.

Third, the Coase theorum states that even though the resource will be allocated efficiently when the number of participants is small no matter *who* receives the property right, assignment makes an important difference in the distribution of income and wealth. The person or group assigned the property right is wealthier as a result.

Coase theorem The rule that externality problems can be solved by assigning property rights when only a small number of parties is involved, allowing markets to internalize externalities and allocate resources efficiently.

Transactions costs The costs of conducting business or making any transaction, such as time, legal costs, and advertising costs.

Banning Negative Externalities

Oregon and Vermont have banned non-returnable beverage containers. New York, Connecticut, and other states have banned detergents containing phosphates. The federal government banned the use of lead and mercury in house paint several years ago. Outright bans on activities or products that create negative externalities are very appealing but generally very poor solutions to such problems.

Forbidding an activity or product altogether is a drastic alternative that fails to set benefits equal to costs at the margin. Banning externalities normally fails to result in the most efficient allocation of resources, because such a drastic step fails to take account of the benefits that led people and firms to produce that product or service in the first place. Thus, while the market may allow too much of a negative externality, banning externalities usually errs in the opposite direction. Banning products or manufacturing processes that create externalities may be appropriate when the damage is difficult to assess but evidence suggests it may be very high. When it is very costly or impossible to determine the optimal amount of a good to produce, government may choose zero pollution over the risk of too much.

Regulating Externalities

Firms and individuals are often regulated to control the negative externalities they produce. Users of coal are told how much sulphur dioxide they may emit into the atmosphere. Homeowners are told whether or not they may burn trash in their subdivisions and even how close to the street they may build a new garage. This regulatory approach to solving externality problems recognizes the fact that there are usually socially desirable, or optimal, amounts of particular externalities—even negative ones. Eliminating or reducing the externality means eliminating or reducing production of the primary good or service that comes with it. Rather than totally eliminating pollution, government regulations can be designed to achieve the optimal amount of production of goods or services with negative externalities.

How do you determine the optimal amount to produce of a good or service that generates a negative externality? You guessed it! Production of any good should be allowed as long is its marginal social benefit exceeds its marginal social cost, or until the marginal benefit of the last unit of the externality equals its marginal cost.

The marginal cost of a negative externality is the damage an extra unit does to third parties. The marginal benefit of a negative externality is less obvious, but very real just the same: It is the value of resources saved by avoiding the cost of reducing or eliminating the last unit of that externality. The marginal benefit of an extra unit of water pollution, for example, is the value of the resources that would have to be used to build a costly water filtration system. In other words, the benefit of pollution equals the resources saved by not disposing of waste in a more costly way. Practical economists would undertake cleanup operations only when the gains from reduced pollution damage exceeded the cost of cleaning up or preventing that amount of pollution.

Government regulatory bodies, specifically the Environmental Protection Agency, try to estimate the marginal benefits and costs of particular types of pollution to set optimal pollution standards. These agencies then regulate firms to ensure that they meet those standards, allowing them to produce only the optimal amount of certain types of pollution.

The regulatory approach has drawbacks, however. Regulation (in practice) creates substantial administrative costs. Also, most regulations fail to achieve

····························

Myth 9-1

····························

A Little Pollution Is a Dangerous Thing

DDT (dichlorodiphenyltrichloroethane) is a potent, general-purpose pesticide banned by the federal government. One of DDT's harmful side effects was a softening and thinning of birds' egg shells. DDT was reducing the populations of many birds, including eagles. On the other hand, banning DDT created serious problems for farmers in the South and Southwest, who depended on DDT to control fire ants. Fire ants cause significant damage for cattle raisers. Cattle unfortunate enough to step on a soft mound of fire ants may break a leg or be stung unmercifully. There were few satisfactory alternatives to DDT for controlling these pests.

Was it wise to ban DDT altogether? Rarely are externalities "all or nothing" situations in which negative marginal externalities exceed the positive private benefits from producing and using *any* amount of the product. Normally, private benefits outweigh external costs at the margin for at least some amount of the good. Using a small amount of DDT to control fire ants (as opposed to using it in widespread crop dusting for general insect control) might have had marginal benefits that exceeded marginal external costs. A little pollution may not be a dangerous thing.

What about banning horn honking on already noisy city streets? Such honking bans have appeared in many cities. A *little* noise pollution of this type might actually be very desirable. Automobile drivers need to blow their horns occasionally to warn pedestrians and others drivers to prevent accidents. Thus, banning horn honking would lower total *net* benefits for society. The goal should be an optimal amount of horn blowing rather than a total honking ban. Local authorities could levy fines for unnecessary honking in front of a girlfriend's apartment or honking impatiently at slower drivers, while allowing drivers to honk to warn others of impending disaster. In most cases, the objective is to find the optimal, or efficient, amounts of negative externalities, not eliminate all traces of them. ∎

the optimal (efficient) amount of pollution, because regulators usually set the same pollution standards for all firms.

Taxes and Subsidies

Another way to reduce negative externalities, or to encourage positive ones, is to tax or subsidize buyers or sellers. For example, Elm City decides it needs more elm trees in keeping with the town's name and tradition. The city council determines that payment of $20 per tree would encourage homeowners to plant the optimal number of residential trees for everyone to enjoy. It might elect to pay homeowners that subsidy for each tree they plant in their front yards. Alternatively, the town could tax residents who have no elm trees in their yards. The practical economists in Elm City who have no elm trees would then determine whether paying the tree tax would cost more than planting trees. If the tax were high enough, residents would plant elm trees rather than pay the tax. Thus, either subsidies or taxes ("carrot or stick" approaches) can be used to encourage production or consumption activities that create positive externalities.

Negative externalities (and positive externalities) can also be successfully internalized using either taxes or subsidies. If a firm must pay a tax per unit of pollution, it will reduce pollution to the point where the benefit of being allowed to dump the last gallon of waste water into a river is just equal to the tax. The tax will reduce pollution to the optimal level. If the firm receives a subsidy of the same amount for each unit of pollution removed, it will arrive at the same answer. Either the tax or the subsidy is an opportunity cost of polluting.

Both subsidies and taxes can effectively reduce negative externalities and encourage positive ones. The difference between them is a question of equity, or income distribution. Should firms be taxed for the pollution they produce, or should they be subsidized for reducing their pollution? Should homeowners be subsidized to improve the looks of their homes and yards or be taxed for letting them deteriorate?

Selling Pollution Permits

Pollution permit A certificate issued by government and bought and sold in markets that grants the right to pollute up to a specified amount, thereby limiting the total amount of pollution in an area.

In recent years, government agencies have begun to experiment with pollution permits. **Pollution permits** allow their holders to emit specified amounts of sulphur dioxide, carbon monoxide, or other pollutants. An agency determines the overall optimal amount of pollution for a given geographic area, that is, the amount at which the marginal cost of environmental damage equals the marginal benefit of pollution. Then the agency divides this amount of acceptable pollution into a number of fixed amounts, represented by individual permits. These permits are auctioned to the highest bidders. What will the practical economists who operate firms pay for these permits? They will bid the price up to the amount it would cost them to reduce pollution to that quantity.

Pollution permits ensure that the total amount of pollution in an area does not exceed the optimal, or acceptable, amount. This method also allows individual firms to sell or buy permits as the benefits of being allowed to pollute change over time or among industries. Thus, a market for these permits develops. New firms can come into an area and know what it will cost them to emit certain pollutants. They must buy enough pollution permits from other firms at the going market rate. Existing firms are willing to sell their pollution permits if they receive a price greater than what it would cost them to reduce or eliminate their pollution. At a high enough price, it may even pay a firm to shut down and sell its pollution permit!

A market in pollution permits provides opportunities for new firms and expanding firms. These firms can pollute more if the benefits of doing so are worth the cost of additional permits purchased from other firms. Total pollution remains at the optimal level, because the firms that sold the permits must reduce their pollution. A market in permits even gives environmental groups the opportunity to become directly involved in further reducing pollution levels. If such groups want less pollution than the amount a government agency decides is acceptable, they can buy permits from firms and then not use them.

This pollution permit approach may sound like a far-fetched, ivory tower approach to controlling pollution. In fact, however, it is one of the methods used to control some types of pollution in California, Pennsylvania, and other states.

CHECKLIST : Policy Approaches to Correcting Externalities

Method	Advantages	Drawbacks
Assigning property rights	Uses the market	Works best when only a few parties are involved
Banning negative externalities	Useful when there is much uncertainty and potential losses from damage are very high	Costs of the ban often exceed benefits
Regulation	Internalizes externalities	Difficult to tailor to different cleanup costs encountered by different firms
Taxes and subsidies	Uses market incentives Works for both positive and negative externalities Allows different firms to respond differently	High administrative and monitoring costs
Pollution permits	Greater flexibility Use the market	High administrative and monitoring costs

PUBLIC GOODS

Public good A good or service that does not lend itself to market allocation because it is collectively consumed and excluding consumers is impossible or too expensive.

Public goods are much like private goods that create positive externalities except that *all* the primary benefits of public goods are "external"; they cannot be captured by individual sellers in market transactions. Public goods have certain inherent characteristics that require government intervention to ensure that they are produced in sufficient quantities or produced at all.

Characteristics of Public Goods

Public goods differ from private goods in two important ways: (1) Public goods are collectively consumed, and (2) no one can be excluded from consuming the good once it is produced for at least one person. A pure public good possesses both of these characteristics.

Collective consumption A characteristic of some goods indicating they can be consumed simultaneously by several consumers; consumption by one person does not diminish the amount available for others.

    Collective consumption means that many people can consume *the same units* of a public good at the same time. Put another way, consumption of the good by one person does not reduce the amount available for anyone else. Private goods, in contrast, are consumed individually. When you eat an ice cream cone, no one else can enjoy that treat. The same is true when you consume shoes, auto tires, shirts, dry-cleaning services, car repair work, and all other private goods and services.

    National defense, on the other hand, is consumed collectively. More than one person enjoys protection by the military at the same time. The fact that Betsy is protected by the U.S. Navy does not mean John has any less protection available to him. A movie shown in a theater also can be consumed collectively. Up to the capacity of the theater, it makes no difference whether 10, 20, or 100 people watch the movie. One person's viewing does not make the movie any less available to others.

    Does the fact that both national defense and movies are collectively consumed mean that both are public goods? The answer is no. Public goods must also satisfy the second test: No one can be excluded from consuming the good once it is produced. This **nonexclusion principle** means there is no easy way to prevent people who do not pay for the good from consuming it. The costs of exclusion are prohibitively high. This is also true of national defense. Short of expelling citizens from the country, there is no way to exclude people from enjoying the benefits of national defense once it is produced for at least one person. Thus, national defense cannot be produced and sold in a private market.

Nonexclusion principle The inability to prevent additional people from consuming certain goods once they are produced.

    What about movies? Although movies pass the collective consumption test, they are not public goods because nonpaying moviegoers can be excluded. All this is necessary to exclude nonpayers is a doorway and a strong ticket taker. Therefore, movies are private goods that can be produced and sold in private markets.

    The fact that a good is a public good does not mean all consumers value its benefits equally. Preferences and demand curves differ for public goods just as they do for private goods. What is true is that units of public goods are *equally available* to all consumers.

Another example of a public good is broadcast radio signals. Once a signal is broadcast to one consumer, millions of other listeners can collectively receive the same signal. It is possible to scramble and unscramble the signal to exclude nonpayers, but the cost of doing so would be very high. City streets are another example. Many automobiles can use city streets at the same time (collective consumption). The costs of trying to charge each car to use each street would be very high (nonexclusion principle). The maze of city streets and intersections and the short trips involved make tollbooths an impractical means of excluding nonpayers from using them. On the other hand, exclusion with tollbooths is feasible for long-distance, limited-access highways.

Most goods and services actually fall along a spectrum from purely private goods to purely public ones. Figure 9-3 shows how various goods might be classified as private or public or somewhere in between based on the two characteristics of collective consumption and nonexclusion.

Free Riders and Public Goods

Free rider A person who consumes public goods (or positive externalities) without paying for them, causing underproduction of those goods.

Because public goods are collectively consumed and exclusion is not feasible, it is difficult to make people pay for them. Since they can enjoy the benefits of public goods without paying for them, most practical economists would choose not to pay; that is, they would be **free riders.** The free-rider problem means private markets fail to produce enough public goods. Since everyone hopes

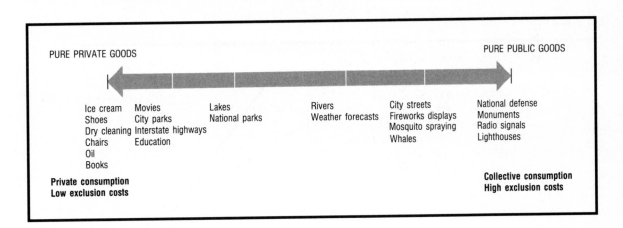

FIGURE 9-3

Goods and services lie along a spectrum from purely private to purely public ones. Many goods and services between the two extremes show some degree of collective consumption and problems in trying to exclude nonpayers.

someone else will pay for public goods, private markets will not allocate enough resources to the production of those goods.

Suppose a rainmaker can save a drought-ravished valley from disaster by "seeding" passing clouds (with silver dioxide crystals) to create rain. Assume the rainmaker approaches ten ranchers in the valley and tells them she can generate three inches of rain before the end of the month for a modest fee of $5,000. (She will deposit the money in the local Valley Bank and refund it if she fails, so there is no risk to the ranchers.) Suppose three inches of rain would be worth at least $1,000 to each rancher, or a total of $10,000. The rainmaker's proposal is obviously a good deal for each rancher. The benefits of success ($1,000 each) would far outweigh the costs ($500 each).

Will this rainmaking operation be undertaken? It may or may not be. Although the proposal will benefit each rancher, an even better deal is available: Each one could let the other ranchers pay and receive the rain benefits for nothing! Each rancher realizes that the $5,000 total fee could be paid by the other nine, if those others paid just $555.55 each, and the tenth, nonpaying rancher could ride free. Even six or seven ranchers would be enough to round up the $5,000 fee and still leave a profit for each. If too many ranchers behave as free riders and each has the incentive to do so, the deal will fall through. It is likely that the rainmaker will not be hired, *even though it would be efficient to produce the rain.*

Figure 9-4 shows the underproduction likely to result from the free-rider problem. It also illustrates how to determine the optimal amount of a public good to produce. For simplicity the supply curve is horizontal, implying constant marginal cost. The sum of the demand curves of individual consumers A and B, D_{A+B}, is the total demand for the public good.

The individual demand curves, D_A and D_B, are added vertically rather than

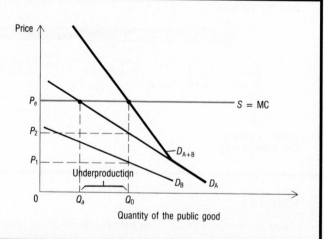

FIGURE 9-4

The social demand for the good, D_{A+B}, is the vertical sum of the two individual demand curves, D_A and D_B. The optimal quantity of the public good at price P_e is Q_o. If B decides to be a free rider, A will choose Q_a amount of the public good based on A's demand curve, D_A, and price P_e. Since Q_o is the optimal amount to produce, $Q_o - Q_A$ equals the amount of underproduction.

horizontally, as in the case of private goods. The curve D_{A+B} reflects total benefit per unit, because each unit of the public good benefits both consumers at the same time. For example, B is willing to pay P_1 and A is willing to pay P_2 for quantity Q_o, so the total value (or total price buyers would pay) for that quantity is $P_1 + P_2 = P_c$. Thus Q_o is the optimal quantity of the public good to be consumed collectively by A and B. Would Q_o be the outcome of private choices? Probably not.

Suppose consumer B is a free rider who decides to let A do the buying and "hides" his or her true preferences. Facing price P_c, A chooses quantity Q_a of the public good. Since Q_o is the optimal amount, leaving it up to A will mean too few resources are devoted to producing this public good. The difference between Q_o and Q_a is the amount of underproduction. The larger the number of consumers, the more likely it is that free riding will occur.

CHECKLIST : Public Goods

Public goods have two defining characteristics:

1. *Collective consumption*—more than one person can consume the same units of a good at the same time.
2. *Nonexclusion Principle*—It is impossible or too costly to prevent nonpaying individuals from consuming the good.

Public goods are underproduced because of the free-rider problem.

When large numbers of people are involved, some kind of government intervention is necessary to allocate the proper amount of resources to the production of public goods. Thousands of people drive on city streets, but voluntary contributions for street construction and upkeep will not work *even though individuals demand a network of such streets.* Most people would drive quickly by street improvement "contribution buckets" located at intersections without pausing to drop in a contribution. Some kind of government coercion is needed to raise enough revenue to produce the optimal quantity of this public good. Most often, governments use their ability to tax to force free riders to pay for public goods.

The central problem for governments is to determine the true (social) demand for a public good. Governments rely on the political process of voting to find out the amount of public goods people want. In the next chapter, we discuss problems in using the political process to reveal social demand for public goods.

Public production
Direct government production of some goods and services using resources or enterprises owned by government.

Public Production versus Public Provision

Governments may allocate resources to public goods either by producing them directly or by contracting with private firms to produce them. **Public production** occurs when governments actually produce public goods using government employees and other government-owned resources. For example, state, county, and city highway departments produce street and road services directly.

Public provision Government allocation of private resources to ensure the optimal production of certain goods and services.

Public provision means governments use other methods, such as subsidies, contracts with private firms, and even regulations, to ensure the optimal production of certain public goods. For example, the federal government does not produce missiles or fighter planes for national defense; rather, it provides for defense by contracting with private firms. McDonnell-Douglas, Lockheed, and Boeing actually produce the airplanes used as inputs in the production of national defense.

It is important to note that there is nothing about most public goods that requires public production. Private firms can (and do) produce city streets, elementary education, police protection, and other public (or near-public) goods. Nothing is different about the supply of these goods. The problem is on the demand side.

Whether governments actually produce public goods or simply provide for their production should depend on which approach is cheaper. Sometimes, for example, the costs of monitoring private contractors to make sure they comply with government standards are so high that direct government production is cheaper.

Privatization Shifting production of such traditional government goods as fire protection, prison, and park services to the private sector.

In recent years, many governments in the United States and elsewhere have explored the cost savings available from **privatization,** or the shifting of production of public goods to the private sector. Private firms are often (but not always) more efficient producers due primarily to existing or potential competition for government contracts. Such services as fire protection, garbage pickup, prison management, and even police services have been turned over to private firms.

Not all goods and services produced by governments are true public goods. Parks and recreation departments at the local government level provide services to consumers even though it is not difficult to exclude nonpayers from those programs. Furthermore, recreation services do not fit the collective consumption part of the definition of public goods. Public intervention in the form of subsidies (public provision or public production) for such goods may be justified in other ways. Public parks and recreation programs can help with both income redistribution (no one wants to charge poor people for summer baseball programs) and positive externalities (parks make a city attractive even for those who do not use them for recreation).

User charges Consumption fees charged by governments to finance part or all of certain goods and services such as campgrounds, car registration, and parks.

Recognizing the private benefit component of many government services, governments at all levels rely to some degree on **user charges** to obtain revenues to pay for many of the services they provide. User charges often cover most of the private benefit, leaving general tax revenue to cover the value of positive externalities. Fees are charged to launch boats at city- and county-owned ramps at lakes and rivers or to use local dumps (landfills). Citizens also often pay fees for residential garbage pickup, using city tennis courts, and fire protection services.

User charges are a good choice when government-produced services offer strong private benefits. In such cases, optimal resource allocation can be better attained by letting prices and the forces of demand and supply in markets play a larger role in rationing those services.

THE DISTRIBUTION OF INCOME

A distribution of income that many believe is too unequal often results from using markets to allocate resources. This result does not represent market failure in the same sense that underallocated public goods do, but it is still an unsatisfactory outcome of efficient markets. What share of all households can be considered rich or poor? How equal or unequal is the distribution of income? Why is income distributed unequally? In this section, we will measure the distribution of income among U.S. households and consider some of the reasons income is distributed unequally. We will address the question of what that distribution ought to be and how government can change it in Chapter 10.

Measuring Income Distribution

Table 9-1 gives the percentage distribution of U.S. households by income level. In 1990, 14.9 percent of U.S. households received less than $10,000, a smaller percentage than in 1980 (16.3 percent) and 1970 (15.7 percent) in real terms

TABLE 9-1   Distribution of Households by Real Money Income Level, 1970–1990

| Real Money Income (1990 Dollars) | Percentage of Households | | | | |
	1970	1975	1980	1985	1990
Under $10,000	15.7%	15.7%	16.3%	16.2%	14.9%
10,000–14,999	8.7	10.1	9.7	9.6	9.5
15,000–24,999	17.6	18.4	18.9	18.3	17.7
25,000–34,999	18.6	16.7	16.6	15.7	15.8
35,000–49,999	20.0	19.5	18.5	17.7	17.5
50,000–74,999	13.8	13.8	13.6	14.5	14.9
75,000 and over	5.6	5.8	6.4	8.0	9.7
	100.0	100.0	100.0	100.0	100.0
Median household income	$29,421	$28,667	$28,091	$28,688	$29,943

Source: U.S. Bureau of the Census, *Statistical Abstract of the United States, 1992* (Washington, D.C.: U.S. Government Printing Office, 1992), p. 445.

(inflation-adjusted dollars). The percentage of all households receiving higher incomes at the other end of the scale has grown over time—a favorable outcome. About 10 percent of all families received more than $75,000 in 1990, up from 6.4 percent in 1980 and only 5.6 percent in 1970 in inflation-adjusted dollars.

It is interesting to note that the median ("middle") household income in the United States, after adjusting for inflation, has changed only slightly over time, falling a little in the 1970s and "recovering" to a bit more than its 1970 real value by 1990. In 1990, half of U.S. households received less than $29,943 and half received more. Some of the gain in real income in the late 1980s and early 1990s at all income levels is masked by the use of households as the base unit. The number of single-person and single-parent households has increased in recent years, which tends to depress measured household income relative to earlier years, in which there were proportionately more two-earner family units.

One measure of income distribution is the fraction of total income received by income groups of equal size. In terms of income, all households can be divided into the bottom fifth, the next lowest fifth, and so on to the highest fifth. Each fifth is called a *quintile*. A perfectly equal income distribution would be one in which each quintile of families has exactly 20 percent of total income, since each quintile has 20 percent of all households.

The percentage of total income received by each quintile of U.S. households (Table 9-2) reveals that (1) the U.S. income distribution is relatively unequal and (2) the degree of inequality has remained remarkably stable over the years. The bottom 20 percent of all households receive about 5 percent of all U.S. income, whereas the highest fifth receives more than 40 percent, or about double its "proportional share." Some change in the distribution toward increasing inequality occurred between 1980 and 1990. The percentage of total income received by families in the lowest quintile fell from 5.2 percent to 4.6 percent. On the other hand, the share of total income earned by families in the highest quintile increased from 41.5 to 44.3 percent.

TABLE 9-2   Percentage of Total Real Income Received by Families by Quintile, 1950–1990

Family Quintile	1950	1960	1970	1980	1990
Lowest fifth	4.9%	4.8%	5.4%	5.2%	4.6%
Second fifth	11.7	12.2	12.2	11.5	10.8
Third fifth	17.6	17.8	17.6	17.5	16.6
Fourth fifth	23.7	24.0	23.8	24.3	23.8
Highest fifth	42.1	41.3	40.9	41.5	44.3

Sources: U.S. Bureau of the Census, *Statistical Abstract of the United States, 1980* (Washington, D.C.: U.S. Government Printing Office, 1980), p. 454; *Statistical Abstract of the United States, 1992* (Washington, D.C.: U.S. Government Printing Office, 1992), p. 450.

In-kind income transfer
A payment in the form of a free or subsidized good or service, such as free medical care and subsidized school lunches.

The stability of the U.S. income distribution over time shown in Table 9-2 is truly amazing, especially considering all the attempts to assist low-income families throughout the 1960s and 1970s. The family incomes used to make these calculations include money income transfers from government, such as social security and welfare payments. However, these figures do not take into account taxes paid and all of the in-kind income transfers of other government programs. **In-kind income transfers** include such nonmoney transfers as food stamps, rent subsidies, free school lunches, and free or subsidized medical care. Including the value of in-kind transfers to poorer groups would make the distribution of measured income more equal than it appears in Table 9-2. A second adjustment for taxes paid by middle- and upper-income groups would also reduce the inequality shown in Table 9-2. Although the distribution of income is still unequal after making these adjustments, government transfer programs and the progressive income tax together substantially reduce income inequality in the United States.

Factors Influencing the Distribution of Income

Earnings differ among individuals and households for several reasons. Some major factors that influence the distribution of income are (1) inborn differences, (2) human capital differences, (3) work and job preferences, (4) discrimination, (5) age effects, (6) labor mobility, (7) government programs and policies that alter the distribution of income (whether intended or not), and (8) luck.

Inborn Differences.   Human characteristics differ greatly from one person to another. Like it or not, not all people are created equal. Many individual human differences affect productivity. People do not have the same innate or natural abilities. They differ in strength, energy, stamina, mental capacity, natural skill, and motivation to produce, all of which combine to yield an infinite variety of productivity levels. Since market wages depend on productivity (as well as on the value of output), individuals earn a variety of incomes from their labor services. Vinny Testaverde, Shaquille O'Neal, Monica Seles, and John Scully certainly are endowed with special skills at football, basketball, tennis, and computer development, respectively.

Human Capital Differences.   People invest different amounts in their human capital. They build up their *physical* human capital through long hours of training and practice. They increase their *mental* human capital through education and related training. Both forms of investment in human capital can greatly increase productivity and raise earnings.

Dr. Albert W. Niemi, Jr., an economist and dean of the College of Business Administration at the University of Georgia, examined how educational attainment helps explain differences in income across different racial and ethnic groups.

He came to some forceful conclusions in a brief article published in *Georgia Trend* in March 1993. The rest of this subsection draws heavily or is borrowed from what he wrote, with some paraphrasing.

Despite some recent problems, America's quality of life is still the highest in the world. Unfortunately, this affluence is not spread equally across all racial and ethnic groups. Blacks have been on the bottom of the economic pyramid since the days of slavery. The picture of income inequality is bleak. In 1990, black income levels were 60 percent of the average for whites. The average income for black households ($18,680) was 84 percent of the average for Hispanics and only 49 percent of the average for Asian-Americans. As a group, Asian-Americans are now the wealthiest Americans, with an average income ($38,450) that is 23 percent higher than the average for whites.

What explains the large, persistent black-white income gap? Why have Asian-Americans become the wealthiest Americans? The answer is education. The education gap between blacks and whites persists, and Asian-Americans are far and away the most highly educated group in the United States. In 1970, only one out of three adult blacks had completed high school; today two out of three have high school diplomas. In 1970, only 4.5 percent of adult black population had a college degree; today the percentage is 11.4. However, 21.5 percent of adult whites and 36.6 percent of Asian-Americans have college degrees. Only Hispanics, with 9.2 percent completing college, have education levels comparable to those of blacks.

Differences in educational attainment explain a large part, but not all, of the earnings differential between blacks and whites. Black males with college degrees earn 80 percent of the average earnings of their white male counterparts. Among males with high school diplomas, the black-white earnings ratio is 76 percent.

Since older whites have much higher levels of education than older blacks, the education-adjusted earnings ratios just presented do not fully reflect the power of education to raise earnings. Young black males (ages 25 to 35) with college degrees have an earnings differential of only 12 percent. Black females with high school diplomas earn 94 percent of the average for their white counterparts. College-educated black females earn slightly more than white females with college degrees ($26,881 versus $26,822).

The message is clear: Education is really the most important way, if not the only way, for blacks or any minority group to achieve equality with the white majority. Asian-Americans are the best-educated racial/ethnic group, and they have the highest incomes. In recent years (and only in recent years), barriers to upward social and economic mobility for U.S. minorities have been substantially reduced. Today the only major obstacle to black-white parity in earnings is the education gap.

Work and Job Preferences.   Individuals differ in their preferences regarding the tradeoff between work and leisure. Very few people prefer work to leisure; if they did, they would be willing to work for nothing! Practical economists choose to work different amounts, or choose to supply different amounts of labor, even at the same wage rate, because some place a higher value on marginal income (the goods that extra income can buy) than others do. These people work more and receive higher total incomes. Others prefer more leisure at the cost of earning lower incomes.

People also prefer different types of jobs, because each job comes with a different set of characteristics in addition to different wage rates. Some jobs are indoors, others are outside. Some are risky and exciting (astronaut), others are quiet and safe (librarian). These specific job choices will affect the distribution of household income.

Discrimination.   Household income also varies because discrimination limits the earnings of certain groups. **Discrimination** in the workplace means treating people differently solely on the basis of factors unrelated to productivity. Minorities and women have long been kept out of some higher-paying occupations solely on the basis of their race or sex, reducing their opportunities to increase their earnings.

Discrimination Treating people differently solely on the basis of characteristics unrelated to productivity, such as skin color or ethnic background.

Firms cannot discriminate without cost, however. If managers of firms choose to hire only European-American males, for example, they limit their hiring options and must pay higher wages than they would otherwise. In effect, two wage rates prevail in segregated labor markets, as shown in Figure 9-5. Some firms hire the best available applicant without discriminating. These firms face the full labor supply curve for all workers. Discriminating firms, however, face a restricted supply curve, one for European-American males only. These firms must pay higher wage rates and incur higher production costs. In a purely competitive market, discriminating behavior could not continue in the long run, since discriminating firms would be driven out of business. But long-run discrimination can persist in imperfectly competitive industries.

FIGURE 9-5

Firms pay a price to discriminate when they hire. Hiring only European-American males restricts the supply of available workers, such as $S_{L\ for\ white\ males}$, forcing the firm to pay a wage rate higher than the equilibrium wage. Nondiscriminating firms face the full labor supply curve, S_L, pay a lower wage, and incur lower production costs.

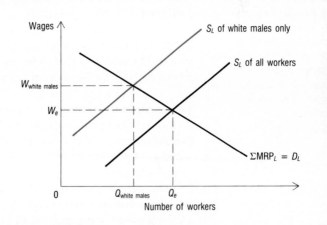

On average, women earn only about 71 cents for every dollar men earn (up from 59 cents 15 years ago). Certainly part of this difference is due to discrimination. Much of it, however, is due to other factors. Until recently, large numbers of women were relatively new to the labor force. Women still, *on average,* have less education and less work experience. They have higher turnover rates (change jobs more often) and a higher probability of leaving the work force for extended periods. They also work part time more often than men do. All of these factors lower women's productivity and account for a significant portion (but not all) of the earnings differential between women and men.

Another factor in the male-female earnings disparity is that traditional male-female roles, which may reflect past discrimination, used to concentrate women in certain occupations like teaching and nursing. As more women entered the labor force in the 1970s and 1980s, supply was very high in these occupations, keeping women's wages and earnings low. Now that traditional barriers to other occupations are lower, women have moved into construction, management, finance, engineering, military service, and even space exploration. The result has been increases in women's earnings and a continuing decline in the gap between male and female earnings. (A disturbing trend noted by the authors in the mid-1990s is the sharp decline in women business majors at colleges and universities around the country and the corresponding upturn in enrollment in traditional majors like nursing and education. The consequences for the "gender gap" in pay should be obvious.)

Age Effects.   For most individuals, earnings vary significantly at different ages. Most people earn little or nothing before age 18. After earning "starting" wages or salaries, incomes increase as workers gain experience and their productivity rises. Earnings often reach a peak for workers in their forties and early fifties. Those in their mid-50s to early 60s often experience constant income for several years, followed by a decline in earnings in the retirement years beyond age 65. This income pattern is called the **life cycle of earnings.**

Life cycle of earnings
A pattern of low earnings early in one's career, increasing earnings with age as experience leads to higher productivity, constant earnings in later work years, and decreasing earnings during retirement years.

Table 9-3 reports average family income by age of the primary earner. Family income varies significantly with age and reflects the life cycle earnings pattern. In 1990, workers in the 15-to-24 age group earned $18,002, whereas experienced workers peaked at $41,922 in the 45-to-54 group. Thus, the age distribution of the labor force heavily influences the distribution of household income.

Labor Mobility.   Mobility is another factor that affects earnings. It is costly to move, in both psychological and monetary terms. Thus, labor is not as freely mobile between either occupations or locations as the purely competitive model assumes. Immobility limits worker response to changing wage rates and can contribute to an unequal distribution of income.

Some people become attached to their locations, especially relatively isolated people who have lived in one location for a long period of time. Thus, for example, when some coal mines in Appalachia closed due to the increasing use of oil after the 1940s, poverty became the order of the day. Many mountain

TABLE 9-3　Average Household Income by Age of Primary Earner, 1990

Age of Primary Earner	Average Household Income before Taxes
15–24 years	$18,002
25–34	30,359
35–44	38,561
45–54	41,922
55–64	32,365
65 and over	16,855

Source: U.S. Bureau of the Census, *Statistical Abstract of the United States, 1992* (Washington, D.C.: U.S. Government Printing Office, 1992), p. 446.

families did not want to leave their region for higher-paying jobs in other parts of the country. The incomes of these families suffered as a result. It is worth noting here that college graduates who are unwilling to consider taking a job away from home, perhaps even one in another region, limit their opportunities and their incomes. Being willing to go where the jobs are or to move wherever the company needs you will enhance your income-earning potential.

Government Programs and Policies.　Some government programs and policies designed to reduce income inequality unintentionally *increase* inequality. As we noted earlier, government transfer programs such as social security, welfare, veterans' benefits, subsidized school lunches, free medical care, and subsidized housing increase the household incomes of poor families. The U.S. progressive income tax, which charges higher tax rates to higher-income families, also reduces income inequality. On the other hand, policies such as the minimum wage law may actually increase income inequality. (Specific income redistribution programs are discussed in Chapter 10.)

Minimum wage　The legal wage floor designed to raise incomes of unskilled workers; the minimum amount employers can pay for labor services.

The **minimum wage** law requires most employers to pay at least a minimum amount for labor services (at this writing, $4.25 per hour). It is designed to help unskilled workers at the bottom of the income ladder. Some workers are surely helped by this law, but others are hurt by it. Those who remain employed receive a higher wage than they might otherwise. Many workers, however, lose their jobs because their productivity is too low to justify paying the minimum wage. These workers, who are already at the bottom of the income scale, earn nothing because of the law!

The equilibrium wage without a minimum wage law would be W_e in Figure 9-6, and Q_e workers would be hired. Now add a minimum wage of W_m, which is above the equilibrium wage. Some workers (Q_m) remain employed and gain the amount of income indicated by the cross-hatched rectangle. Others

FIGURE 9-6

An effective minimum wage, W_m, must be set above the equilibrium wage, W_e. As a result, employment falls from Q_e to Q_m. Workers who retain their jobs at the higher minimum wage, Q_m, gain the income represented by the shaded rectangle. Workers who lose their jobs because of the minimum wage, $Q_e - Q_m$, lose the income indicated by the shaded rectangle. Whether the gains outweigh the losses depends on the relative elasticities of the demand and supply of unskilled labor. The minimum wage also frustrates a third group, $Q_s - Q_e$, the people who are attracted to the labor force by the higher minimum wage rate but are unable to find jobs.

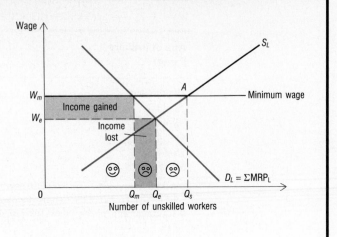

$(Q_e - Q_m)$ lose their jobs at the higher wage rate; the amount of income they lose is shown by the shaded rectangle.

In addition, more practical economists decide to seek work at the higher minimum wage rate even though fewer jobs are available. This extra labor supplied is the amount between Q_e and Q_s. Attracting some people into the labor force who would not be there otherwise increases reported unemployment rates.

The minimum wage makes it especially difficult for new workers to enter the labor force and increase their incomes. Jobs requiring few skills are eliminated when the minimum wage rate exceeds the relatively low marginal revenue product of unskilled workers. Gone are such entry-level jobs as store clerk, inventory stock clerk, sweeping and cleaning person, and loading dock worker. Poorly educated workers—and especially younger workers just starting out—lose important training opportunities in entry-level jobs that would prepare them to move into higher-paying positions later.

Luck.   Finally, luck can affect household income considerably. Mental capacity and physical ability are both randomly distributed in the population, and how much of either someone has depends on luck. In fact, it is tempting to attribute almost everything to luck—whether you were born rich or poor, strong or weak, and musically talented or with a "tin ear." Furthermore, tornadoes, hurricanes, fires, auto accidents, and diseases can wipe out all your resources, whereas winning the Illinois lottery or discovering oil on your land can make you wealthy.

On the other hand, you should not overlook the greater importance of the choices made at each point in your life. Is it luck that you have chosen to major in journalism rather than nursing or engineering, in general business instead of industrial marketing, or in economic forecasting or sociology rather than pre-med? You know (or could find out) the differences in salaries, working conditions, and prestige for each occupation. Is it bad luck if you choose to remain ignorant, make an uninformed occupational choice, and later regret it?

Likewise, is it bad luck when some students make mostly Cs in their courses rather than mostly Bs? Mental abilities differ, but "burning the midnight oil" (something students can control) also makes a difference—and a far larger one. Looking at it objectively, every choice leads toward either a higher or lower income, more or less job satisfaction, and reaching or failing to reach goals.

In general, people have more than enough mental and physical capacity to excel in one of the countless ways to earn a living. More often than not, individuals are responsible for where they head and for the incomes they receive as a result. Thus, although luck makes a difference and people "down on their luck" deserve assistance, individuals' choices play a major role in determining household income.

CHECKLIST : **Factors That Influence the Distribution of Income**

Factor	Effect on Household Income
Productivity differences	More natural ability or more human capital increases productivity and income.
Work/leisure preference	Those who prefer more goods relative to leisure at the margin work more and earn more.
Job preference	Jobs with more highly valued output and less attractive or riskier working conditions offer higher wages and thus yield more income.
Supply constraints	Extra training or licensing requirements restrict entry to some jobs, lowering labor supply and increasing wage rates and income.
Discrimination	Being a member of a favored group increases income.
Age	Experienced middle-aged workers earn more than either younger or older people.
Mobility	More mobile workers earn more than those less willing to change jobs or locations.
Government programs and policies	Benefit programs and the progressive income tax reduce income inequality. The minimum wage may increase income inequality.
Luck	Luck plays a role in determining the distribution of income, but choices are perhaps still the most important factor

Poverty

Poverty The condition of living with an income level below a certain minimum amount determined by government as satisfying only the basic needs for food and shelter.

Income inequality is not the urgent social issue that poverty is. In 1993, a family of four earning less than $14,350 was in **poverty** by government standards. This **poverty** level is based on the annual cost of a minimal, nutritious diet, which is then multiplied by three because families tend to spend about one-third of their income on food. Some 34 million people, or about 14 percent of the U.S. population, had incomes below the official poverty line in 1991. That is quite a large problem!

Admittedly, poverty is relative. The standard of living of some of the American poor is high relative to that for the poor in many less developed countries or to American families living in the not too distant past. Nevertheless, poverty usually means an inadequate diet, substandard housing, limited access to transportation, and a lack of many other amenities that middle-class Americans take for granted.

Who are the poor? Are poor people mostly "deadbeats" who refuse to work? Are the poor located mostly in urban areas, and are they mostly minorities suffering from discrimination? Looking at the facts reveals some interesting characteristics of poor families in the United States.

Poverty is not limited to just one or two groups; it is a problem for all races and ethnic groups. About 9.8 million African-Americans lived poverty in 1990 (around 32 percent of the African-American population), but so did 22.3 million European-Americans, Hispanics and others (about 11 percent of the white population). Put another way, while a greater proportion of African-Americans are poor, more than two-thirds of poor people belong to other racial and ethnic groups.

Poverty is not only an urban problem; it also exists in rural areas. Although most poor people (about 60 percent) live in cities, poverty is a *relatively* greater problem outside urban areas. Forty percent of the U.S. poor live in rural areas that have less than 30 percent of the nation's population. In 1990, the relatively rural South had almost as many poor (13 million) as the Northeast and Midwest regions combined (14 million).

Most poor people are not able-bodied individuals of working age who choose to be "on the dole." Of the 34 million poor in 1990, more than one-fifth (21 percent) were children and youths under 16 years of age, or more than one-third (37 percent) if the cutoff used is 21 years of age. More than one-tenth (11 percent) of the poor were over age 65. Therefore, nearly half (48 percent) of the poor in the United States are not within the normal working age range.

What about the 52 percent? Shouldn't they be working to get out of poverty? The answer is yes, when possible, but *half of all primary earners in poverty families did work in 1990!* These "working poor" hold part-time or part-year jobs (and some have full-time jobs) doing whatever they can, but they have very few skills and often can earn only the minimum wage. Even year-round, full-time work at the minimum wage translates into an annual income of only $8,840, which is not nearly enough to lift a family of three or four above the current poverty line. In addition, many of the working-age poor suffer from poor health or disability in any given year, making it difficult for them to support themselves.

Fully one-half of all poor families are headed by women who care for at least two dependents. Although a minimum wage income might enable a single individual to live in modest comfort, spreading that income over one adult and two or three children would make life very difficult. For that reason, the U.S. government defines poverty levels for families according to household size. As mentioned earlier, the poverty line for an urban family of four was $14,350 in 1993.

Primary earners in poor American families are generally poorly educated. More than half do not have a high school diploma. Poor families also have more children and other dependents and incur significant child-care expenses. Poor families also have fewer members in the labor force. Families with incomes below $10,000 average less than one earner per family (often a part-time worker), whereas families with incomes between $25,000 and $50,000 average nearly two workers per family and those families with more than $50,000 in income average more than two workers.

One encouraging observation offsets all these bleak numbers. Often the poor are not the same people each year. The typical family receiving welfare stays in the program about 18 months. Many families living just above the poverty line are likely to fall below it when problems such as divorce, illness, injury, layoffs, or additional dependents arise. Remarriage, recovery from illness, and getting back to work are often quick cures for temporary poverty.

CHECKLIST : Characteristics of the Poor in the United States

- In 1993, a family of four was considered poor if income was below $14,350.
- A significant proportion (14 percent) of the population lives in poverty
- Poverty strikes all races and groups (about 11 percent of European-Americans, Hispanics, and others combined and 32 percent of African-Americans).
- Poverty exists in all areas (60 percent of poor people are urban, 40 percent are rural).
- Nearly half the poor are either very young or very old (21 percent are under age 16, 37 percent are under 21, and 11 percent are over 65; thus, only 48 percent of the poor are between 21 and 65 years of age).
- Many of the working-age poor
  - Actually work, but part-time or full-time work at the minimum wage still leaves them in poverty.
  - Suffer from disabilities that keep them from working.
  - Are women who head households with one or more dependents.
  - Have low value in the workplace because they are poorly educated.
  - Are not the same people from year to year.
- Poverty is relative. Many poor people in the United States live better than those just 25 or 50 years ago and better than many people in most other countries today.

Summary

1. The activities of producers and consumers can impose external costs and benefits, called *externalities*, on other people. Externalities cause markets to misallocate resources because goods with positive externalities are under-produced and those with negative externalities are overproduced.

2. The optimal amount of a negative externality is rarely zero. The optimal amount is that quantity for which the damage from the last unit (marginal cost) equals the avoided costs of cleaning up or preventing the last unit (marginal benefit).

3. Externalities exist primarily because property rights are sometimes not clearly defined.

4. Externality problems sometimes can be resolved by defining property rights so that sellers and suppliers internalize all the external costs and benefits of their actions. According to the Coase theorem, assigning property rights and allowing private negotiations to solve externality problems can work if the number of persons affected is small.

5. Government intervention may be needed when affected groups are large and transactions costs high, such as banning certain goods, regulating, using taxes or subsidies, or creating markets in pollution permits.

6. Public goods also lead to market failure (underproduction). Public goods differ from private goods in that they are collectively consumed and nonpay-ers cannot be excluded from their consumption. These two characteristics create free-rider problems for public goods.

7. Governments need not actually produce public goods. Governments may contract with private firms to produce them, paying for them out of tax revenue to avoid the free-rider problem.

8. The U.S. income distribution is unequal. The lowest fifth of households receive about 5 percent of total household income; the highest fifth receive a little more than 40 percent of the total. While this distribution appears to have been roughly constant over the last four decades, inequality is much less severe when in-kind transfers from government and progressive income taxes are taken into account.

9. Factors that affect the distribution of household income include (1) produc-tivity differences, (2) preferences for work versus leisure, (3) job preferences, (4) supply constraints, (5) discrimination, (6) age, (7) labor mobility, (8) government programs and policies that alter the distribution of income, and (9) luck.

10. Minimum wage laws raise the incomes of some workers who retain their jobs at artificially higher wages, but lower the incomes of the least capable unskilled workers and reduce training opportunities as the number of entry-level jobs declines.

11. Poverty occurs among young and old people, urban and rural families, and all races. The working-age poor are likely to be uneducated, female heads of households, ill or disabled, or unable to earn much at part-time or low-wage jobs.

Key Terms

Coase theorem
collective consumption
discrimination
externalities
free rider
in-kind income transfer
internalizing
   externalities

life cycle of earnings
marginal social cost (MSC)
marginal social benefit
   (MSB)
market failure
minimum wage
nonexclusion principle
pollution permit

poverty
privatization
property rights
public good
public production
public provision
transactions costs
user charges

Questions and Problems

1. List and discuss several ways to resolve externality problems. When will a simple assignment of property rights be most likely to solve externality problems?

2. Is it possible for government to correct every externality problem that exists? Why or why not?

3. Suppose your area has a problem with water pollution. Would you support a citizen movement to require factories to discharge only pure water into streams? Why or why not?

4. Consider an electric utility that produces power with coal-fired plants that emit some air pollution. Draw the "private" demand and supply curves for electricity. Then draw the marginal social cost curve (total supply curve). Determine the socially desirable price and output levels for this utility. If left entirely to market forces, why would this utility produce too much electricity (and smoke)?

5. Explain how resources are misallocated when externalities are associated with some goods. Does it matter whether the externalities are positive or negative?

6. Which of the following are public, private, or in-between goods to which some externalities are attached? (Hint: Remember to look for natural characteristics associated with goods rather than whether they are currently provided by governments.)

   a. A concert in the park
   b. A fire truck
   c. Fire protection services
   d. A white-water river
   e. A scientific discovery

7. Do goods ever change from the public to the private category? If so, how and why?

8. Why are public goods not produced in sufficient quantities by private markets? Must government produce such goods?

9. Give three examples of privatization of government goods. What makes it possible to privatize some kinds of government production but not others?

10. What are the major reasons for income inequality in the United States? Has the U.S. distribution of income become more or less unequal over time? Why?

11. Are the poor mostly deadbeats who could work but will not? How does your answer affect the way you would deal with poverty?

12. **a.** Explain which groups of workers benefit and which lose as a result of minimum wage laws.
   b. Unions often support legislated increases in minimum wages. How might union workers benefit from such increases? (Hint: Most union labor is highly skilled labor.)

10

The Economic Role of Government

Government is emphatically a machine: to the discontented a "taxing machine," to the contented "a machine for securing property."

THOMAS CARLYLE, 1829

Main Points

1. Even a market economy needs government to define and enforce the basic rules of economic life (property rights); allocate goods and services when markets fail; ensure an equitable distribution of income; and try to promote economic growth, stabilize the price level, and reduce unemployment.

2. Government's allocation function includes regulating monopoly, providing public goods, and helping to internalize externalities.

3. Government's redistribution function consists of using its taxing and spending powers to reduce poverty and inequality in the distribution of income. Two concepts of fairness are equality of results and equality of opportunity.

4. Government's stabilization function includes using its powers to tax, spend, and change the money supply to achieve the macroeconomic goals of growth, full employment, and no inflation.

5. Government can also fail to allocate resources efficiently. Public choice theory suggests that majority voting, pressure from special-interest groups, and bureaucracy may all contribute to government failure.

6. Governments spend to provide goods and services and to transfer income. These expenditures are financed primarily with taxes, although for the federal government borrowing has become an increasingly important revenue source.

In this chapter, we examine the economic role of government in market-oriented economies. Since markets function properly only when property rights are well defined, one very important function of government is to set these basic "rules of the game." Another government function is to correct for the failures of private markets that result from monopoly or the existence of public goods and externalities.

Government's role can also include modifying the distribution of income that results from the market. Another function is to address macroeconomic problems such as slow growth, unemployment and inflation. This stabilization role of government is the principal subject of Part Three of this book.

In this chapter, we also look at what governments at all levels in the United States actually do as reflected in their budgets. These budgets show how governments spend their money and how they raise revenue.

Finally, we will see that government intervention in markets to allocate resources, redistribute income, and stabilize aggregate economic variables like employment does not ensure more favorable outcomes. Public choice theory suggests that government outcomes are sometimes no better than market results. ■

THE FUNCTIONS OF GOVERNMENT

Government plays an important but secondary role in a market economy. It intervenes only to "fill the gaps" when market failure occurs by altering market outcomes to make them more favorable. This notion that markets are primary and government is secondary is a valid assumption in market economies like those of the United States and other industrial nations. In the past, the reverse was true in many parts of the world. Until recently, in many countries government owned most resources and answered most of the basic economic questions of what, how, and for whom to produce. The collapse of communism in Eastern and Central Europe means that today this is true for very few countries.

In market economies, competitive markets are expected to serve households fairly well most of the time. The primary functions of government are to (1) define and enforce property rights, (2) allocate resources when markets fail, (3) modify income distributions as desired, and (4) stabilize macroeconomic variables (national output, employment, and the price level).

Making the Rules: Defining and Enforcing Property Rights

Recall from the last chapter that markets will fail if goods, services, and resources lack well-defined property rights. Markets depend on ownership of what individual buyers and sellers bring to (and take away from) markets. The first function of government is to decide who can own resources and goods and clearly define what rights go with ownership. A legal structure of courts and police is also needed to enforce rights when disputes arise.

Individuals might try to define basic property rights and settle inevitable disputes on their own, that is, without a government or the force of group law. However, that approach will be more expensive than using government. The history of earlier civilizations, or even the American West of the 1800s, illustrates the problems and costs associated with using a system of rights in which people "own" only what they can protect. Such a system gives an unfair advantage to those who are the strongest or the most skilled with a gun. Using brute strength to enforce property rights is costly because it forces everyone to be a part-time police officer, judge, and jury!

 Practical economists know that collective rulemaking with government as the enforcer reduces transactions costs. When laws defining property rights exist, households have less need to constantly define rules for every exchange. Moreover, professional law enforcement can protect property rights for many people at the same time (like a public good); thus, households enjoy better protection at a lower cost than they would if each household tried to protect itself. Finally, government can apply and enforce its laws over wider regions than rules made by individual households cover, thus facilitating trade among widely separated households.

Therefore, a major role of government at all levels, from local to national, is to (1) define property rights (legislate civil and criminal laws); (2) create contracts to recognize and establish ownership (deeds to land, automobile titles, labor and business contracts); and (3) set up legal systems (police, courts, and prisons) to clarify, refine, and enforce property rights.

Allocation

Allocation (function)
The government's role of correcting market failure by promoting competition, regulating natural monopolies, providing public goods, and internalizing externalities.

In its **allocation function,** government tries to assist markets when they fail, or to replace them when necessary, to ensure that resources are allocated properly. Government's allocative activities include those discussed in Chapters 8 and 9. Government tries to limit monopoly with antitrust laws. Government regulates the output and pricing policies of natural monopolies. Government also regulates, taxes, and subsidizes firms and individuals to solve externality problems. Finally, government provides public goods such as national defense, navigational aids (e.g., marking public waterways with buoys), and disease control and research.

An opportunity cost always arises when government diverts resources from the private to the public sector. The cost of public provision of certain goods is the cost of the private goods forgone. For example, the steel and labor used to make a tank or a bridge for the public sector mean the private sector cannot produce as many toasters and automobiles. How much public resource allocation is enough? As you saw in Chapter 9, public provision of goods and services should continue to expand as long as the marginal benefit of the last unit provided exceeds the marginal benefit of the private goods forgone.

There are always gainers and losers in government allocation decisions. Another way to state the guiding economic principle for government is that it should provide services as long as the gain to gainers exceeds the loss to losers. Additional government services are desirable if it would be *possible* for those who gain from the services to completely compensate those who lose (from paying higher taxes) and still be better off. Whether gainers actually *must* compensate losers is an income distribution question.

Distribution

Recall from Chapter 9 that household income is determined by the quantity and quality of resources households own (including human capital) and the prices those resources bring in resource markets. Because resources are distributed unevenly and command very different prices, and because individuals make different choices about education and type of work, household incomes are distributed unequally. Many people believe the market-determined distribution of income is unfair or inequitable and call on government to modify that distribution. Changing the income distribution that results from the market to make it more equitable is government's **distribution function.**

Distribution (function)
The government's role of altering the market's distribution of income to make it more equitable.

If you consider the actual income distribution unfair, what distribution would you prefer? Does equity require exactly equal incomes for everyone? Does fairness require a distribution such that every household can obtain at least adequate housing, food, and medical care? What fairness rule should government follow to establish and maintain a fair distribution of income?

In most market-oriented economies, the principal concept of distributional fairness is **equality of opportunity.** According to this concept, individuals should have equal amounts of resources "at the beginning of the game" and have equal opportunities to make the most out of their resources in the marketplace. Having people start out equally implies that education (for acquiring human capital) and medical care (for maintaining body and mind) should be free, or equally available to all.

Equality of opportunity
The concept that any income distribution is fair as long as everyone has the same economic opportunity and the rules of the game apply equally to all.

This fairness concept also calls for substantial inheritance taxes to prevent some people from starting out with far more resources than others. It suggests that a fair income distribution is any distribution that results from "an equal start and a fair game," regardless of the actual degree of equality or inequality of the resulting distribution.

Making all property and contract laws and the rules of exchange apply equally to all is the easy part. The main problem associated with the equal opportunity concept is the difficulty of putting everyone on an equal footing at the start. Although land and capital resources could be apportioned equally for everyone as they begin their productive lives, substantial differences in labor and enterprise ability would remain. No one would suggest tying one of Michael Jordan's arms behind his back to make his basketball skills comparable to those of mortal players! Given the luck of the draw, then, even access to basic resources such as education and medical care can only approximate equality. Still, this concept of economic justice has strong appeal as a means of guiding government's distribution role.

This first concept of equity—equal opportunity—works for a very large percentage of society, but not for everyone. There will always be some people who are unable to participate in the market and satisfy their basic needs. Such people are too old, too sick, or too severely handicapped. Only some kind of redistribution program that focuses on **equality of results** will keep this group out of poverty. This second concept requires the government to change the distribution of income in a direct way, giving directly to the poor out of tax revenues taken from those who have more.

Equality of results The concept of redistributing income directly based on some criterion such as need in order to achieve a fair income distribution.

Today's U.S. income distribution policies reflect elements of both forms of redistributional fairness. On the equal opportunity side, much government effort is devoted to writing and clarifying the "rules of the game" to ensure that opportunities are equal. Programs such as free public education, subsidized public health care, free and subsidized food and nutrition for children, and inheritance taxes represent an effort to allow people to enjoy a more equal start on their economic lives than they might otherwise.

Although the U.S. income distribution is determined primarily by the market, it is also substantially modified in some cases according to need—the equality of results concept. Considerable effort and revenue go into directly changing the final income distribution to make it more fair. The poorest families are eligible for Aid to Families with Dependent Children (AFDC) and the food stamp program. These two programs, along with supplemental security income (SSI) for people with disabilities, make up the major welfare programs in the United States. In 1992, more than 18 million children and adult relatives received AFDC assistance totaling more than $19 billion, or $1,055 per recipient. Food stamps assisted more than 20 million people in 1992, amounting to more than $12 billion. The same year, SSI payments for 4.84 million Americans with disabilities totaled more than $14.9 billion, or $3,088 per recipient.

The United States has several food assistance programs other than the food stamp program. In 1992, these programs included the National School Lunch Program ($3.1 billion with 23.4 million children participating); the School Breakfast Program ($0.514 billion); the Women-Infant-Children Program ($1.614 billion with 4.1 million participants); the Child Care Feeding Program

($0.567 billion with 1.3 million children participating); the Summer Feeding Program ($0.118 billion); and five smaller programs for elderly persons, needy families, child nutrition in Puerto Rico, special school milk, and donated federal food commodities (together totaling $2.689 billion).

Social security—known formally as the Old Age, Survivors, and Disability Insurance program (OASDI)—also alters the distribution of income. Federal law requires almost all workers to pay into the system during their working years. In 1993, this amounted to more than 15 percent of wages up to $55,600. Revenues from this payroll tax are used to pay social security benefits to currently retired persons, surviving spouses and children, and workers with disabilities. This program redistributes a substantial amount of income from young and middle-aged people (current workers) to elderly citizens (current retirees). In 1992, more than 39 million Americans received social security benefits totaling more than $233.6 billion. The average amount paid annually to each beneficiary was just under $6,000.

Progressive income taxes—taxes for which the percentage paid rises with income—also directly affect the resulting U.S. income distribution by reducing the degree of income inequality at both ends of the distribution. Those with low incomes pay no federal or state income taxes in most cases. Those with middle incomes pay progressively higher percentage rates. The highest-income families pay the highest tax rates and pay the most tax dollars per family. Progressive income taxes thus tend to level after-tax spendable incomes. However, tax rates on property at the local level, excise taxes on products like gasoline, cigarettes, and alcohol, and user charges for parks and roads (tolls and gasoline taxes) make the overall U.S. tax system much less progressive. In fact, it is closer overall to a proportional tax system, one in which individuals pay about the same percentage of their incomes in taxes regardless of their income levels.

Stabilization

Stabilization (function)
The government's role of reducing fluctuations in aggregate output, employment, and the price level.

A role of government at the federal level that has developed since the 1930s is **stabilization.** The government has a strong interest in achieving the macroeconomic goals of stable growth in aggregate output (no recessions or depressions), stable prices (no inflation), and full employment of the labor force and other productive resources. The government carries out its stabilization function through its powers to spend, tax, and control the nation's supply of money. To give the economy a boost, the government might increase its spending, cut taxes, or expand the money supply. On the other hand, reducing government spending, raising taxes, or contracting the supply of money should help cool down an economy that is "overheating" and experiencing inflation.

This stabilization function of government plays an important role in the next seven chapters. Those chapters are devoted to macroeconomics—the study of how the economy as a whole behaves and how government can intervene to influence the levels of prices, total output, and employment.

In Practice 10-1

....

Progressive Tax Rates and the Underground Economy

The *underground economy* is the term given to the cash transactions and barter exchanges made by individuals and firms to avoid income taxes (and sometimes to avoid the police, as in the cases of gambling and illegal drugs). To the extent the underground economy exists so that citizens can avoid being taxed at high marginal tax rates, it represents another form of government failure.

The underground economy includes doctors who exchange free medical care for services from lawyers, accountants, and even brick masons to avoid reporting that "income" and paying extra taxes at the upper end of the progressive income tax. Of course, failing to report the equivalent value of barter income to the IRS is against the law—but the chances of being caught are low.

Unreported cash transactions are another important part of the underground economy. Many workers hold second jobs for cash payments. Farmers cut trees and sell firewood for cash. Teachers tutor students in the evenings and on weekends for cash. In fact, estimates from a Louis Harris poll concerning the underground economy suggest that about $500 *billion* escapes taxation by way of hidden barter and cash income. The IRS says that in 1992 the taxes lost on this underground income could be $127 billion, enough to put a nice dent in the deficit.

Why is the underground economy so large? Part of the cash economy reflects illegal activity, but another important reason is the U.S. progressive tax system, especially the high marginal tax rates of the past. The top federal income tax bracket alone was 90 percent before the early 1960s, when it was reduced to 70 percent. In 1982 the top marginal tax rate was reduced to 50 percent, and the 1990 Deficit Reduction Act reduced it again to 31 percent. (The downward trend in marginal tax rates was reversed with the tax increases passed in 1993.)

Lower marginal rates should cause some of this underground economy to surface and pay taxes. So why hasn't the underground shrunk? Even a 31 percent marginal rate (plus any state and local income taxes) makes it profitable for workers to go underground. It is worthwhile to take odd jobs at cash wage rates below regular or overtime pay, or to make inefficient barter exchanges of professional services, as long as citizens can avoid reporting that extra income to the IRS. A dollar earned in the underground economy is a full dollar available for spending. ∎

Relationships among Government Functions

While it is helpful to sort the activities of government into categories, the rule-setting, allocation, distribution, and stabilization functions of government are really less distinct than they might seem at first. In fact, they are interrelated; it is difficult for government to pursue one of these goals without affecting another.

Changing the distribution of income will alter consumption patterns and the mix of output produced, or allocation. For example, taxing the rich and giving to the poor means producing fewer symphony concerts and yachts but more subsidized apartments, hamburgers, and baseball gloves. Similarly, stabilization efforts change both the allocation of resources and the distribution of income. Increasing government spending to boost the economy will send more income to workers producing health care, roads, and schools. Expanding the money supply (stabilization) may cause interest rates to fall, benefiting borrowers at the expense of savers (distribution) and encouraging purchases of houses and cars instead of other goods (allocation).

Policymakers therefore must keep in mind all the effects of the actions government might take. They must recognize that trying to meet one goal may require compromising other goals. It is difficult to successfully address all elements of government's role at the same time.

CHECKLIST : The Economic Role of Government

The four primary functions of government in a market-oriented economy are

1. Defining and enforcing property rights
2. Allocating resources
   a. Providing public goods
   b. Internalizing externalities
   c. Controlling monopoly
3. Redistributing income
   a. Equality of opportunity
   b. Equality of results
4. Stabilizing the economy
   a. Stable prices (no inflation)
   b. Full employment
   c. Steady growth of output

GOVERNMENT EXPENDITURES AND REVENUES

To carry out their allocation, distribution, and stabilization roles, governments must allocate, or budget, their revenues among competing uses. One way to describe local, state and federal government budgets is to sort government expenditures by function or program (defense, welfare, science research) and revenues by source (primarily income, payroll, sales, property taxes, and borrowing). Looking at how governments spend their money and where they get it helps us better understand the current economic role of government and how various levels of government emphasize different functions and rely on different revenue sources.

How Governments Spend Money

The federal government spends the largest share of its budget on income security, or income redistribution (see Table 10-1). This redistribution role accounted

Table 10-1   Federal Expenditures

Spending Category	1980		1985		1993*	
	Amount Spent (billions)	Share of Budget (percent)	Amount Spent (billions)	Share of Budget (percent)	Amount Spent (billions)	Share of Budget (percent)
Social security, welfare, health, medicare, veterans' benefits, farm support	$290.4	49%	$468.0	49%	$807.1	55%
Defense, general science, space, international affairs	152.5	26	277.6	29	325.1	22
Education, commerce, community development	73.8	12	67.1	7	120.9	8
Net interest on federal debt	52.5	9	129.5	14	202.8	14
Energy and natural resources	24.0	4	19.0	2	26.3	2
Administration of justice and general government	17.6	3	17.9	2	30.0	2
Offsetting receipts and other adjustments	−28.0	−3	−32.7	−3	−37.2	−3
Total	$582.8	100%	$946.4	100%	$1475.0	100%

*1993 figures are government estimates and include both "on-" and "off-budget" spending items.

Sources: *Economic Report of the President, 1989* (Washington, D.C.: U.S. Government Printing Office, 1989) p. 398; *Economic Report of the President, 1993* (Washington, D.C.: U.S. Government Printing Office, 1993), pp. 436–437.

for an estimated 55 percent of total federal expenditures in 1993. Income is redistributed as direct cash transfers and as in-kind transfers, which include transfers of goods and services as discussed in Chapter 9. Examples of cash transfer programs are social security, unemployment compensation, some veterans' benefits, food stamps, welfare payments, and farm support payments. In-kind transfers include such goods and services as free or subsidized medical care, school lunches, and public housing.

Most economists suggest that redistribution should take place at the federal level so that practical economists in poor families are not encouraged to migrate to states or local jurisdictions that provide higher benefit levels. State and local governments have some flexibility in setting benefit levels under the federal AFDC program, and many state and local governments have their own income transfer programs.

The federal government's largest expenditure for public goods is on national defense and related general science, space, and international activities. About $325 billion was spent on national defense and related functions in 1993, or about 22 percent of all federal spending (see Table 10-1). Both the dollar amount and fraction of the federal budget spent on defense are very large. The proportion of the federal budget spent on defense and science increased significantly until the Soviet Union collapsed at the beginning of the 1990s. From a peak of 29 percent of the budget in 1985, defense and science spending declined to 22 percent in 1993. With the end of the Cold War, defense spending is expected to fall steadily throughout the rest of the 1990s.

One other component of federal spending deserves special emphasis: interest paid on the national debt. Net interest paid (interest paid on borrowings minus some interest received by government) grew from 9 percent of the budget in 1980 to about 14 percent in 1985 and also in 1993. Thus, more than one out of every seven federal dollars collected go to pay interest on *past* spending that was not fully funded with tax revenues.

The trend in federal government spending has been to increase the redistribution function's share of federal expenditures. Income security expenditures reached 55 percent of federal expenditures in 1993 but represented only 24 percent of the federal budget in 1960, 36 percent in 1970, and 49 percent in 1980. With defense and science spending down to just 22 percent of the budget in 1993, the redistribution function of the federal government is now considerably larger than its role of allocating funds to public goods, producing or providing goods and services such as defense, roads, parks, and even consumer tips.

State and local governments spend their funds somewhat differently than the federal government, because they provide a different array of public goods and services. Table 10-2 shows the general expenditures of these governments for 1970, 1980, and 1993. Most state and local government spending is for allocation—education, health programs, highways, and police and fire protection.

Education, which receives more than one-third of state and local government expenditures, is by far the largest state and local government expenditure category. However, the share of state and local government spending for education declined from 40 percent in 1970 to 35 percent in 1993. Welfare and housing expenditures for the poor, like the redistribution expenditures of the federal government, have grown since 1970 (from 13 percent of expenditures to 15 percent in 1993). Highway spending declined the most during the period, from 12 to 7 percent of total state and local government spending.

Each of these state and local government spending categories involves providing goods with significant externalities, redistributing income, or a combination of both. For example, education (especially at the lower grades) confers valuable external benefits, such as basic reading skills that create better workers for employers and better voters for everyone. But this good is also publicly provided, in part, for its redistributional benefits for lower-income families.

Table 10-2   State and Local Government General Expenditures

Spending Category	1970		1980		1993*	
	Amount Spent (billions)	Share of Budget (percent)	Amount Spent (billions)	Share of Budget (percent)	Amount Spent (billions)	Share of Budget (percent)
Education	$53	40%	$133	36%	$367	35%
Welfare and housing	17	13	52	14	159	15
Health and hospitals	10	8	32	9	95	9
Highways	16	12	33	9	73	7
Police and fire protection	7	5	19	5	55	5
Sanitation	3	2	13	4	38	4
Other	26	20	85	23	276	25
Total	$132	100%	$367	100%	$1,063	100%

*1993 figures are authors' projections from 1990 data.

Source: U.S. Bureau of the Census, *Statistical Abstract of the United States, 1993* (Washington, D.C.: U.S. Government Printing Office, 1993), p. 284.

How Large Is Government?

As Figure 10-1 indicates, government spending has grown significantly over time for all levels of government. In 1929, all governments combined spent $10.3 billion; this grew to $2,247.8 billion by 1993, or about 218 times as much! However, the growth in spending after adjusting for inflation is much less dramatic, although still substantial. Inflation-adjusted government spending was about 24 times as large in 1993 as it was in 1929. Adjusting further for growth in population, real government spending (in 1993 dollars) grew from about $3,240 per person in the labor force in 1929 to about $17,260 for every worker in 1993.

The size of government can also be measured in terms of the proportion of the population governments at all levels employ. Just before the Civil War, about 1 worker out of 800 was employed by government. By the 1940s government employment had increased to 1 in 70, and now that figure is more than 1 in 7. In 1993, all governments combined employed 15 percent of the civilian labor force. Eighty-four percent of all government employees worked for state and local governments.

Another useful way to measure the size of government is to compare government spending over time as a percentage of the total value of goods and services

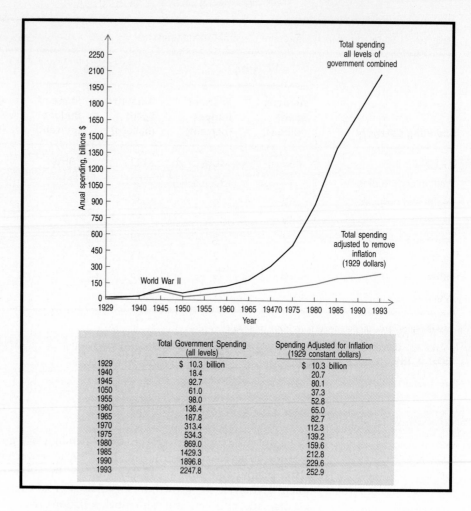

FIGURE 10-1

Total government spending in the United States has grown dramatically since 1929, increasing 218 times in dollar amount and about 24 times after correcting for inflation.

produced each year, or the percentage of gross domestic product (GDP). Figure 10-2 illustrates federal, state, local, and combined government spending in the United States since 1929 as a percentage of GDP. Total government spending has taken a steadily increasing share of national output, with a temporary large jump during World War II. Today all levels of government together account for nearly 40 percent of total income spent in the United States.

Most of the growth in the state and local government expenditures since the 1970s has been split evenly between purchases of goods and services and transfer

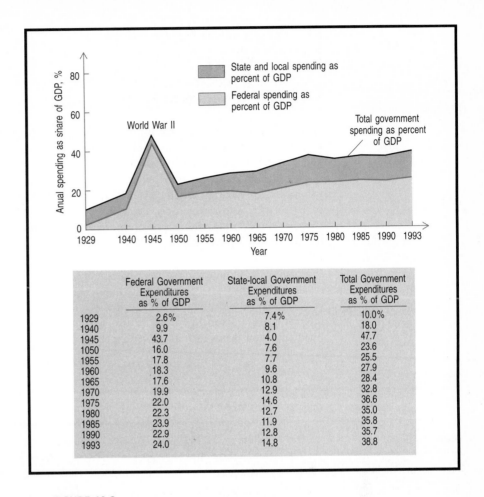

FIGURE 10-2

Total government spending as a proportion of gross domestic product (GDP) increased from around 10 percent in 1929 to about 39 percent in 1993. Although state and local governments' share of GDP has doubled since 1929 (7 to 15 percent), the federal government's share has grown much more, increasing from less than 3 percent of GDP to 24 percent.

payments to individuals. Most of the growth in federal expenditures during that period, except for a portion of the 1980s, was concentrated in redistribution programs. Part of that federal redistribution benefited individuals directly and part went to state and local governments in the form of grants for such programs as building major highways, installing water and sewer systems, and hiring disadvantaged workers. These federal transfers simply represent funds "passing through" the federal government rather than "exhaustive" expenditures (like purchasing labor and concrete to build highways) that use up resources. Federal purchases of goods and services as a proportion of GDP have grown very little since the 1970s.

Sources of Government Revenue

Where do governments get the funds to make all these expenditures? They obtain revenue primarily from taxes, which account for some two-thirds of both federal and state revenues and about half of local government revenue (see Table 10-3).

The major revenue source at the federal level is the individual income tax (35 percent of total revenue in 1993), followed closely by payroll taxes for social security and other social insurance taxes (30 percent of 1993 revenue). Perhaps surprisingly, the corporation income tax is not a large revenue source for the federal government; only 7 percent of federal revenues came from this tax in 1993.

Because the federal government has spent far more than it has received in tax revenue over the past 25 years, borrowing is now very important at the federal level. Borrowing is not really a revenue source, since these funds plus annual interest must be repaid in the future with tax revenue. Still, this source of financing cannot be ignored given that the federal government financed at least

Table 10-3   Government Revenue Sources, 1993*

Federal		State		Local	
Individual income tax	35%	Sales tax	28%	Federal and state grants	35%
Social insurance payroll tax	30	Federal grants	23	Property tax	30
Borrowing**	22	Individual income tax	19	User fees and enterprise receipts	25
Corporation income tax	7	User fees and enterprise receipts	19	Sales tax	6
Other taxes, user fees, and enterprise receipts	6	Other taxes	7	Other taxes	2
		Corporation income tax	4	Individual income tax	2
Total	100%	Total	100%	Total	100%

*Federal revenues for 1993 are government estimates from Table B-75 of the 1993 *Economic Report*. State and local revenue percentages for 1993 are the authors' estimates from the 1992 *Significant Features*.

**Borrowing is not really a revenue source, but it is an important "temporary" method of financing current expenditures against future tax revenues at the federal level.

Sources: *Economic Report of the President, 1993* (Washington, D.C.: U.S. Government Printing Office, 1993), p. 437; *Significant Features of Fiscal Federalism, 1992* (Washington, D.C.: U.S. Government Printing Office, 1992), pp. 117, 119.

Myth 10-1

Corporations Should Pay Their Fair Share

The Tax Reform Act of 1986 shifted some of the federal tax burden from individuals to corporations. While the top marginal tax bracket was reduced from 46 percent of corporate income to 34 percent, many corporation tax deductions were eliminated, raising both corporation taxable income and the average corporation tax rate. The tax increases included in President Clinton's economic package passed in 1993 raised the corporation marginal tax rate slightly. Thus, total corporation tax collections are increasing substantially after reaching low levels in the mid-1980s. For example, corporation tax payments were $96 billion in 1985, $137 billion in 1990, and about $148 billion in 1993.

Do corporations really pay taxes? The answer is no; only people pay taxes, because households are the ultimate owners of all resources, and the ultimate recipients of all income. Corporation taxes are hidden taxes. These taxes are borne by consumers in the form of higher prices, by workers in the form of lower wages or smaller raises, and/or by owners in the form of lower dividend payments. Revenues from the corporation income tax come from some combination of these three groups.

Economists know little about how the burden of the corporation income tax is divided among consumers, workers, and owners. As a result, there is no way of knowing whether the tax is fair. Does it ultimately fall on stockholders, who may be wealthy individuals, poor widows, or pension funds guarding retirement savings? If it comes out of wages, does the tax fall more heavily on low-wage janitors or on high-wage engineers? If consumer prices rise, are buyers who pay the tax wealthy or struggling to pay their bills? Since the burden of corporation taxes falls on a variety of people and in ways that are hard to determine, most economists give the corporation income tax low marks when it comes to equity. A fair share for corporations does not necessarily mean a fair distribution of taxes among citizens. ∎

22 percent of its total expenditures with borrowed funds in 1993. When ranked as a revenue source (see Table 10-3), at the federal level borrowing is second in revenue-raising importance only to the individual income tax.

At the state level, sales taxes are the most important revenue source (28 percent of state revenue in 1993), but substantial revenue also comes from federal grants (23 percent), individual income taxes (19 percent), and user fees (e.g., auto license fees) and receipts from state-owned enterprises (19 percent).

Local governments continue to depend heavily on grants from both state governments and the federal government (35 percent of local revenue in 1993), even though federal grants to local governments dropped sharply after 1982. The property tax is still the most important revenue source under the direct control of local governments. This tax accounted for 30 percent of all local revenues in 1993 and 75 percent of local *tax* revenues. Local governments use the property tax rather than the income tax or sales tax because people cannot easily avoid a tax on immobile property. If local governments relied more on income taxes or local sales taxes, people could move outside the locality or buy from stores located elsewhere to avoid paying local taxes.

Federal, state, and local governments exhibit very different expenditure patterns and revenue sources, as Tables 10-1 through 10-3 show. These differences reflect the concept of fiscal federalism. **Fiscal federalism** means government responsibilities and revenue sources are divided among the levels of government according to the different functions they perform. Thus, the federal government handles national defense and most transfers and relies on the individual income tax and payroll taxes. State governments provide education and roads and use sales, income, and other taxes to raise most of their revenues. Local governments rely on the property tax and grants from other levels of government to provide water, sewer, police, fire, and health services. This division reflects the taxes that each level of government is best equipped to collect, the primary role of the federal government in income redistribution, and the division of responsibility for public goods according to how widespread their benefits are.

Fiscal federalism The division of government into different levels (federal, state, and local), each with different responsibilities and revenue sources.

CHECKLIST

Government Expenditures and Revenues

Major categories of government expenditures are as follows (in order):

Federal	Combined State and Local Governments
1. Redistribution (social security, health care, welfare, etc.)	1. Education
2. Defense, general science, space, and international affairs	2. Welfare and housing
3. Net interest on federal debt	3. Health and hospitals
4. Education, commerce, and community development	4. Highways
	5. Police and fire protection

Major revenue sources are as follows (in order):

Federal	State	Local
1. Individual income tax	1. Sales tax	1. State and federal grants
2. Social insurance payroll tax	2. Federal grants	2. Property tax
3. Borrowing	3. Individual income tax	3. User fees and receipts
4. Corporation income tax	4. User fees and receipts	4. Sales tax

GOVERNMENT FAILURE AND THE THEORY
OF PUBLIC CHOICE

How do governments determine what public goods people want and how much to provide? How do citizens tell their governments what kind of income distribution they want? Transmitting this information from consumers to government is the most difficult problem in the political process. Government must somehow discover "the public interest," or consumer demand for public goods and redistribution. The primary mechanism government uses to discover consumer demand is voting.

If the political process does not succeed in directing government to fulfill its economic role efficiently in accordance with consumer wishes, there is government failure, the counterpart to market failure in the private sector, has occurred.

Government Failure

An effective political process should reveal consumers' true preferences for government-provided goods and services and result in the provision of optimal amounts of public goods (and optimal amounts of goods that have externalities). Specifically, government should provide that quantity of a public good (or one with externalities) for which marginal social benefit and marginal social cost are equal. This quantity is the one that private, competitive markets would produce if all costs and benefits were completely internalized.

Government failure

The misallocation of resources that results when government overprovides or underprovides public goods or otherwise causes a nonoptimal amount of output to be produced.

In the last chapter, we defined market failure as the production of nonoptimal quantities of certain goods and services. This failure provides the basis for the allocation role of government. However, **government failure** can also occur if government provides too much or too little of the goods and services under its control. This potential misallocation of resources through the political process can be as serious a problem as market failure.

For example, goods with negative externalities (such as steel and associated air pollution) may be overproduced in private markets (see Chapter 9). However, if the government solution is to ban the production of steel to reduce air pollution, resources still will be misallocated, but in the opposite direction (too little steel produced). Which outcome would be worse? The federal government also provides national defense, but if one of its agencies pays $800 for coffeepots on military aircraft and $200 for ordinary hammers, resources are surely misallocated. If government provides too much national defense, is that outcome better than the insufficient amount private markets would produce?

One concrete example of government failure concerns the production of milk. The federal government subsidizes dairies supposedly to ensure an adequate supply of milk. These subsidies amount to more than $1 billion each year, or $5 to $6 per year for each U.S. citizen. It is likely that subsidies of this size cause more than the optimal amount of milk to be produced—a clear case of resource misallocation. Why do you suppose these milk subsidies are so large? The answer lies in how political choices are made.

Public Choice

Public choice theory A theory that applies the model of self-interested, maximizing behavior to the political process to explain and predict whether government is likely to achieve the proper allocation of resources to goods and services under its control.

In recent years, economists attempting to understand the political process and describe how that process leads to government failure (resource misallocation) have developed a body of thought called **public choice theory.** This theory seeks to explain how citizens communicate their desires to government and how the economic incentives of the political decision process affect the government's allocation of resources.

At the heart of public choice theory is the idea that elected representatives and other government officials are practical economists like everyone else. They try to maximize their own utility and respond to the incentives around them. Government has no magic that causes people to exchange their normal, self-interested behavior for statesmanlike altruism when they enter government service.

In using this model of individual behavior to examine how public decisions are made, public choice economists suggest several important ways government failure may occur:

1. Majority voting may not accurately reveal true consumer preferences.
2. Voters may be uninformed.
3. Special-interest group preferences may count more than those of the majority of individual citizens.
4. Legislative techniques such as logrolling lead to expansion of programs beyond optimal levels.
5. Bureaucrats may be responding to incentives that have little to do with consumer wants.

Majority Voting.   The primary mechanism government uses to discover consumer demand is voting in elections, and the winning proposal or candidate is the one that receives a majority of the votes. A majority voting rule means 50 percent of the votes plus one vote decide an issue. Minority votes do not count, because the will of the majority is decisive. The fact that 47 percent of voters voted against building new city tennis courts does not matter. Majority rule yields an "all or nothing" result, which frustrates minority voters since they must accept, and help pay for, tennis courts (or a higher level of defense spending or more redistribution) that they do not want. It is possible to use "supermajority" decision rules. Juries must often attain 100 percent agreement to reach a decision, and it takes three-quarters of the states to amend the federal constitution. Such rules help protect minority interests but may frustrate the majority.

Majority voting also fails to reflect the intensity of voter preferences. A proposal may pass (or fail) because most voters slightly favor it even though a sizable minority of voters passionately dislike it. If voters were allowed to register the strength of their desires (perhaps marking ballots with one of several possible responses, such as "strongly agree/slightly agree/slightly disagree/strongly disagree") and if heavier weights were attached to stronger responses, election results might be different in many cases.

Contrast the "all or nothing" outcome of majority voting and its failure to account for preference intensity with the proportional results of private markets. Outcomes in private markets are proportional to dollar "votes." Dollar votes allow firms to supply a greater variety of goods to satisfy differing tastes, based on the proportions spent on each type of good. Wooden, fiberglass, steel, aluminum, boron, and graphite tennis rackets are on the market to suit almost every tennis player's preference in proportion to the dollar "votes" cast for each.

Uninformed Voters.   When only a small percentage of the electorate votes, election outcomes do not reflect true citizen demand. Around election time, newspaper editorials appear calling for more voter participation. They cite evidence of voter apathy, such as low voter registration and low participation in recent elections, to "prove" citizens care little about their government. Many studies show that only 20 or 30 percent of eligible voters actually elect their political representatives. For example, suppose 60 percent of eligible citizens register to vote and only 70 percent of those registered turn out to vote in an election (a very high participation rate). That would mean only 42 percent of citizens actually participate in the election, and a candidate could win with support from just over 21 percent of the potential voters.

Rational ignorance

The explanation that low voter registration and election turnout occurs because voting costs exceed the expected benefits from voting.

However, low voter participation is not necessarily an indication of apathy or an uncaring attitude on the part of nonvoters. Rather, low participation may indicate **rational ignorance** on their part: It is rational, or in one's best interest, to be uninformed and not vote if the *expected* benefit of participating in the political process (the probability that one's vote will determine the election times one's gain if the proposal wins) is less than the total costs of voting.

Since some election issues are routine and boring (e.g., electing the dogcatcher or the tax assessor) and candidates are often similar, little can be gained by studying carefully for such elections. More important, since most elections are not decided by one vote, the probability of any individual voter affecting the outcome is negligible. Therefore, the expected benefit for any particular voter in most elections is quite small. Consequently, voter turnout is low in most elections, except those in which the issues are "hot" ones or the vote is expected to be very close. Voting has characteristics of a public good, and free riding is as likely to occur here as with any public good.

Special-Interest Groups.   The process of finding out what the public really wants is further complicated by the pressure of special-interest groups.

Special-interest group
A group that seeks gain from government on a narrow issue that may come at the expense of other groups or of society as a whole.

Special-interest groups seek rent (profit or benefits in excess of opportunity costs) through special legislative favors. Although their arguments are often couched in terms of "the public interest," these groups usually seek benefits for themselves. When influential citizens ask the city to build a concert hall for the local symphony, do they represent the public interest or their own? What about truckers who want the government to set minimum rates for hauling, or milk producers (or sugar producers, wheat producers, tobacco producers, mohair producers, etc.) who request subsidies to "ensure adequate production" for the future?

In Chapter 8, we discussed rent seeking in relation to monopoly and other imperfectly competitive markers. Rent seekers try to create situations where they can receive returns higher than their opportunity costs. Because government has the power to coerce (to regulate, tax, subsidize, and grant exclusive contracts), it is especially fertile ground for creating rents.

Why are special-interest groups so successful in obtaining rents from government? The few people who form a special-interest group stand to reap large, direct benefits from special legislation, while its costs are spread over large numbers of taxpayers. Thus, on one side, special interests are highly organized and can marshal large campaign contributions and hire professional lobbyists to get what they want from legislators. (They can afford to spend on lobbying any amount up to the value of the expected benefits of the special legislation they seek.)

On the other side, taxpayers are loosely organized at best, and often unsuspecting. Even if they are fully aware of pending special-interest legislation, taxpayers have little incentive to block it because their *individual* tax burden would increase very little. If proposed special legislation imposes small extra costs *per taxpayer*, perhaps only a few cents or a few dollars in extra taxes annually, it is not rational for practical economists to go to much trouble and expense to try to defeat the pending legislation. Writing hundreds of letters to legislators or hiring expensive lobbyists is likely to cost more than simply accepting the extra taxes.

Hundreds of special-interest bills pass each year because in each case a few people benefit significantly while the bulk of taxpayers foot the bill, each paying only a little more tax. Special-interest pressures (coupled with legislators' need for campaign contributions) lead to expansion of many government programs to nonoptimal levels—an important form of government failure.

Logrolling. In a referendum, citizens may vote directly on certain major issues especially at the state and local levels. Examples of issues that might come up in a referendum are property tax limits, restricting the sale of pornography, borrowing to build a new civic center, and changes in state constitutions. Most issues, however, are settled by elected representatives using a majority voting rule.

The behavior of elected representatives resembles that of brokers. Even the most selfless legislator must first get elected before he or she can serve constituents, and to be reelected legislators must "deliver the goods" back home. One way to get projects passed that are important to the people back home but not too important to anyone else is to trade support. This "you vote for mine and I'll vote for yours" process is known as **logrolling.** A North Carolina representative might offer to vote for a "pork barrel" water bill that is important to a Nevada representative in exchange for support for federal funding of a coastal beach erosion program. As a result of such logrolling, government is quite a bit larger than it might otherwise be.

Logrolling   A legislative process in which representatives trade support for each other's proposals.

Legislators also broker their programs and votes outside the halls of Congress and state legislatures to national special-interest groups that can contribute to reelection campaigns or can help deliver reelection votes back home. Sometimes the results are quite different from consumers' wishes.

Sam Peltzman, an economist at the University of Chicago, has documented the fact that senators who receive most of their funds from business vote for business benefits and those who receive most of their financial support from labor have strong pro-labor voting records. Those with mixed contributions from special-interest groups split their votes in almost identical proportions to the mix of financial support they receive from different groups.

Bureaucrats and Bureaucracy.   Individuals who work in government as appointed officials or as civil servants are called *bureaucrats*. Bureaucrats administer or work for agencies responsible for carrying out government programs and providing public goods. Examples of bureaus are the Bureau of Land Management (manages public lands), the Bureau of Indian Affairs, and the Occupational Safety and Health Administration (makes safety rules for workplaces).

Bureaucratic behavior can also lead to resource misallocation, or government failure. Bureaucrats do not face reelection, nor must their agencies or bureaus "show a profit" like their counterpart firms in private industry. What incentives guide the behavior of bureaucrats? Most economists believe that bureaucrats, like all other practical economists, seek to maximize their own utility. Rather than acting in some vaguely defined public interest, they act in their own self-interest. This means carrying out policies that maximize their salaries and prestige. Bureaucrats' salaries, prestige, and power almost always reflect the size of the bureau's budget and the number of its employees. Thus, bureaucrats have strong incentives to make their agencies grow and to increase congressional or legislative funding regardless of the fact that costs may increase without corresponding increases in benefits. In fact, budget size can increase partly *because* of increased inefficiency and result in additional rewards for bureaucrats. When a larger program and more funding happen to be what the public wants, this behavior serves the public interest. However, when the public wants a particular program to be smaller or less costly, bureaucratic behavior can lead to government failure in the form of overproduction.

CHECKLIST  : **Two Kinds of Failure**

Kinds of Market Failure	Kinds of Government Failure
Underproduce public goods	Under- or overproduce public goods
Underproduce goods with positive externalities	Under- or overproduce goods with positive externalities
Overproduce goods with negative externalities	Under- or overproduce goods with negative externalities
Poverty/income inequality	Redistribution to special interests
Monopoly	Bureaucracy

A Final Word on Public Choice and Government Failure

Although monopoly and oligopoly markets, an unequal distribution of income, and the existence of externalities and public goods may lead to market failure, government efforts to resolve these problems will not always provide a better outcome. It is possible that government will also fail to allocate resources optimally according to consumer wishes. Is there no one consumers can trust outside of competitive markets?

The picture of government is not as bleak as it seems, however. First, competitive or nearly competitive markets allocate a substantial share of goods and services in the United States. Second, when governments decide to assist or replace markets, government failure occurs in some cases and not in others. Politically determined output levels for public goods may be close to optimal levels. Third, there is hope. Economics can raise awareness of both market and government failure. Citizens who are aware of these risks will seek better solutions, monitor government (as well as market) performance, and insist on improvements. Despite the predictions of public choice economists, Americans have experienced significant reductions in trade barriers in recent years (against the wishes of some public-interest groups), decreased regulation of airlines and telephone companies, sharp reductions in grants to state and local governments in the 1980s, and tax reform eliminating many special-interest provisions. None of these changes would have been predicted by public choice theorists. Thus, it is possible to uncover government failure, perhaps after an accumulation of special-interest legislation over time, and make corrections. If this is so, government failure in the long run may be less pervasive then the public choice model apparently leads us to believe.

Summary

1. The economic role of government includes four basic functions: defining and enforcing property rights (the rules of the game); allocating resources

to correct for market failure; redistributing income to achieve greater equity; and stabilizing total output, income, employment, and the price level.

2. Government's distribution function can aim at redistributing income directly (equality of results) or establishing a fair set of rules and having everyone start off with similar access to basic resources such as education and training (equality of opportunity).

3. The functions of government are interrelated. Taking corrective action in one area will affect the other functions.

4. Government spending at all levels has grown faster than inflation, faster than the population growth warrants, and faster than private-sector spending. Thus, combined governments at the federal, state, and local levels allocate a rising share of GDP. Most federal government growth since 1970 reflects rapidly growing transfer programs rather than direct purchases of goods and services.

5. The bulk of government revenue comes from taxes. The most important revenue sources at the federal level are the individual income tax and social insurance taxes, followed closely by borrowing. States rely on the sales tax, federal grants, and individual income taxes, as well as user fees and enterprise receipts. Local governments rely most heavily on grants from higher levels of government, property taxes, and user fees.

6. The different tax sources used at each level of government reflect the concept of fiscal federalism—dividing the responsibility for both spending and revenue raising among the three levels of government. Each level has somewhat different expenditure priorities and tends to rely on a different mix of revenue sources.

7. Just as market failure can occur, so can government failure. Public choice theory suggests that government may misallocate resources when it intervenes to correct market deficiencies because the majority voting process may not reveal true consumer preferences, voters may be informed, special-interest groups may be able to obtain rents because costs are spread over large numbers of citizens, logrolling increases the number of pork barrel projects accepted, and bureaucratic behavior may lead to government waste.

Key Terms

allocation (function)	fiscal federalism	rational ignorance
distribution (function)	government failure	special-interest group
equality of opportunity	logrolling	stabilization (function)
equality of results	public choice theory	

Questions and Problems

1. What is the economic role of your local government in terms of the four government functions mentioned in the text?

2. In terms of who benefits, why is defense provided at the federal level and landfills at the state and local levels?

3. Contrast the distributional equity concepts of equality of results and equality of opportunity. Describe federal redistributional efforts that make use of each concept.

4. Which function(s) (defining property rights, allocation, distribution, or stabilization) that comprise the economic role of government are illustrated by the following?

   a. Stimulating employment with more defense spending
   b. Making tax rates more progressive and giving the extra tax revenue to the poor
   c. Relaxing zoning regulations to promote more low-income housing
   d. Giving federal funds to states for building more highways

5. Local governments are in a competitive "market" to attract firms and residents, whereas the federal government is more like a monopoly. How does this difference help explain the fact that local governments rely more heavily on property taxes and the federal government on income taxes?

6. Is it really possible to tax corporations? Why or why not?

7. Suppose coal-burning industries created a problem of excessive acid rain. Suggest two ways the government might try to resolve the problem.

8. How are market failure and government failure alike? What does public choice theory say about the success of special-interest groups?

9. Contrast "dollar voting" in markets with majority voting in the political process.

III

Macroeconomics Concepts

11

Macroeconomic Goals and

Their Measurement

Unemployment is rarely considered desirable except by those who have not experienced it.

JOHN KENNETH GALBRAITH

Main Points

1. The goals of macroeconomic policy are economic growth, stable prices, and full employment of labor and other resources.

2. Increases in gross domestic product (GDP) measure economic growth, which provides a higher standard of living and absorbs new workers into the labor force.

3. Gross domestic product (GDP) is the sum of consumption expenditures, gross private domestic investment, government purchases, and net exports of goods and services.

4. National income (NI), the sum of the incomes of productive resources, provides an alternative measure of the level of economic activity.

5. Price instability (inflation or deflation) redistributes income and arbitrarily distorts market price signals. The consumer price index (CPI) measures changes in the price level.

6. Unemployment means wasted resources. The unemployment rate measures the proportion of the labor force that is not working but is actively seeking work.

The last seven chapters described particular markets and the determination of specific prices and quantities, such as bushels of wheat, numbers of autoworkers, prices of pizza, wages of labor, and rental prices of housing. Those prices and quantities reflected the workings of supply and demand in individual markets for goods, services, and productive resources that made up the circular flow in Chapter 3.

Now we shift our attention from the component parts of the economy to the economy as a whole. In the next seven chapters, we explore what determines the level and rate of change of the flow of output and income in the economy, the level of prices and the rate of inflation, and the level of employment and unemployment of labor and other resources.

In Chapter 2, we identified six economic goals that societies pursue in varying combinations. Three of these goals—efficiency, distributional equity, and economic freedom—are primarily microeconomic in nature. In the last seven chapters, we saw the extent to which a market system succeeds in attaining those three goals. In chapter 10, we discussed what the role of government should be in promoting those goals by improving on, or sometimes interfering with, the market decision-making process.

The other three goals—economic growth, stable prices, and full employment—are primarily macroeconomic in nature. The nature and measurement of these three goals and why they are important are the subject of this chapter. ∎

MACROECONOMIC GOALS

The last 20 years have seen much debate over the ranking of the various goals that macroeconomic policy should pursue. Should Americans pursue all-out economic growth, zipping past Japan and Hong Kong? What would it cost to do so? Which groups would gain, and which would lose? Or should America's goal be zero inflation at any cost, even if the cost turns out to be lost output, slow growth, and unemployment? Or should full employment be at the top of the list, even if it means less efficiency or greater inflation?

Politicians and their economic advisers must wrestle with these questions daily. The 1992 presidential election campaign focused on both economic growth and unemployment as major public concerns, because unemployment was higher than in the past and economic growth was very slow. President

Clinton saw concerns about growth and unemployment as the most pressing issues his administration faced when he took office in 1993.

These issues are of concern to practical economists as well as public officials. The decisions politicians make about which goals to emphasize and what tools to use in pursuing them affect each of us as workers, consumers, and citizens. Thus, practical economists need to know not only the price of eggs but what is happening to the price level, and not only what their incomes are but how rapidly total income (output) is growing and how long it is likely to continue to grow at that pace.

The Economic Growth Debate

Economic growth is an increase in the size of the flow in the circular flow model of the macroeconomy. This flow is measured in real terms, that is, adjusted for changes in the price level. The other two goals, price stability and full employment, are closely linked to performance in economic growth. Slow growth is often accompanied by high unemployment and sometimes by high inflation as well. More rapid growth creates more jobs and often also means less inflation. Thus, of the three goals, the one that gets the most attention is economic growth, or a sustained increase in output per person.

Many economists look back to the 1950s and 1960s as a sort of macroeconomic "golden age." Prices were relatively stable. From 1959 through 1965, the inflation rate never reached even 2 percent, although inflation rates started to rise in the late 1960s during the Vietnam War. Unemployment rates (3 to 5 percent) were much lower than those of the 1970s and 1980s. Economic growth was in the 3 to 6 percent range for most of the 1960s. The only recession during those 20 years was a relatively mild drop in output and employment at the end of the 1950s and again in 1969–1970.

During the 1960s, there was much disagreement about the value and the costs of economic growth. Pro-growth economists argued that it is easier to absorb new workers (and reduce unemployment) and control inflation in a steadily growing economy than in an economy that is growing very slowly or not at all. Other economists at that time, however, questioned whether a continued growth in income and output was necessary or desirable. Critics of the economic growth goal pointed out that growth is not costless. Costs of rapid economic growth include resource depletion (using up less easily renewable energy resources, such as oil) and environmental problems, including water and air pollution, nuclear waste disposal, and acid rain. Both kinds of problems worsen when an economy is growing rapidly. As the U.S. economy sought more energy to fuel rapid growth, for example, there was more acid run-off from coal mines in West Virginia and greater damage to the permafrost and wildlife habitats near the oil pipeline in Alaska.

The terms of the economic growth debate changed during the 1970s and

1980s as the United States and many other countries experienced slower rates of economic growth, higher levels of unemployment, and episodes of double-digit inflation. In the 1970s, the average growth rate was 2.8 percent, compared to 3.8 percent in the 1960s. The 1980s saw an average growth rate of only 2.3 percent per year. Instead of turning in a comfortable performance on all three primary goals, the United States was failing to reach any of them. The 1980s began with a recession that set new records in unemployment. A period of moderate growth from 1983 on ended with a short recession beginning in 1990, followed by a weak recovery and continued unemployment of more than 7 percent of the labor force. During this period, the antigrowth voices softened, then faded almost to silence as Americans became aware of some of the costs of *not* growing.

Two important discoveries about economic growth emerged from the experience of the 1970s and 1980s. One lesson was that less social conflict over the use of resources occurs during periods of faster economic growth. The other was that the three major macroeconomic goals are closely connected; thus, good performance in one area tends to be associated with better numbers for the other two goals.

When the economy is growing, there is less conflict over how to use scarce resources, especially for public programs such as health care, welfare, highways, and education. Rapid economic growth makes more resources available for both public and private programs. Rising incomes generate more tax revenues; thus, increases can occur in one area of public spending without having to make budget cuts for other programs. New spending or new programs can come out of the **growth dividend,** or the extra income or output being produced each year. With little or no growth, increased spending for health care, public education, or transfers to elderly citizens must come at the expense of other public spending or at the cost of higher taxes and reduced private spending.

Growth dividend The additional output resulting from economic growth that can be used for various public or private purposes.

The second benefit of economic growth, discovered anew in the 1970s and 1980s, is that growth can be a fairly painless way to promote both full employment and stable prices at the same time. From 1975 to 1980, slow economic growth was accompanied by both high inflation and high unemployment. The somewhat faster growth from 1983 to 1989 was accompanied by much lower inflation rates, as well as some decline in unemployment.

This shift in attitudes toward economic growth in the last two decades does not mean elected officials during that period ignored the concerns about resource depletion and environmental quality that received so much attention a decade earlier. These decision makers learned, however, that opportunity costs are as real in macroeconomics as in microeconomics and that the opportunity cost of not growing can be very high indeed.

Thus, as the United States looks forward to a new century, the search continues for an appropriate balance between the benefits of growth, with lower unemployment and greater price stability, and some of the costs of rapid growth in terms of environmental quality.

Price Stability

Inflation A rise in the general or average level of prices.

Inflation—a rise in the general or average level of prices—has no fans in its corner. Favoring inflation would be political suicide! Yet many elected officials in fact endorse inflation when they pursue policies that increase the demand for total output without increasing the total supply. Similarly, citizens who want tax cuts without spending cuts, or workers who strike for higher wages when their productivity is stagnating, are voting for inflation whether they realize it or not.

What is so bad about inflation? Two problems arise from inflation, especially unexpected inflation. One problem is unplanned redistribution of income and wealth. Workers whose wages more than keep pace with inflation come out ahead. Workers who live on relatively fixed incomes from pensions or interest on bonds or are employed in low-wage, low-skill jobs lose purchasing power when the price level rises. The cost rises for the market basket of food at the grocery store, the electric bill, the rent, and all the other daily items that households consume, but their incomes do not rise fast enough to keep pace.

Another group that loses from inflation is lenders. Suppose that Larry lends Betsy $100 for a year at 5 percent interest, anticipating zero inflation. Events show that Larry guessed wrong: Inflation the following year turns out to be 10 percent. At the end of the year, Betsy cheerfully repays the loan with interest, $105, but its purchasing power has fallen by 10 percent ($-$10.50) to only $94.50. Betsy the borrower bought a $100 vacuum cleaner at the beginning of the year that would now cost $110, so she benefits. Larry the lender is now Larry the loser, suffering a $10.50 loss in purchasing power due to unexpected inflation.

There are many Larrys, including owners of bonds and depositors in banks that make consumer and business loans. There are also many Betsys. Because a major borrower is the federal government, inflation benefits the U.S. Treasury at the expense of owners of treasury bonds. The value or purchasing power of the bonds falls, making them worth less to owners but less painful for the Treasury (and the taxpayer) to repay.

Real, tangible assets, such as land, gold, houses, machinery, classic cars, stamp collections, and antiques, tend to increase in value during inflation. Owners of such assets gain from inflation. Owners of nominal assets (anything whose value is fixed in dollars, such as cash value life insurance, savings accounts, pension fund accounts, or certificates of deposit) will suffer a loss of purchasing power from inflation.

When the state or federal tax system is progressive, another "winner" is government and another loser is the taxpayer. A 10 percent increase in salary with a 10 percent inflation rate translates into the same real income. With a progressive income tax, however, the government will collect a higher percentage of that income in taxes than before.

In addition to gainers and losers from redistribution, everyone loses from inflation, for two reasons. First, all practical economists must expend extra effort to make adjustments for inflation—gather more information, protect their assets more carefully, and make sure they get the appropriate adjustment in their wages or other payments. Second, it is more difficult for practical economists to make intelligent maximizing decisions if the signals from the marketplace are unclear. It is difficult enough for a consumer to recall last week's prices and recognize that beef is now cheaper relative to chicken than before—a signal to substitute. It is even more difficult to keep those signals straight when all prices are rising at the same time, because people have difficulty sorting out which price changes are relative price changes and which are merely keeping pace with inflation.

CHECKLIST  : **Gainers and Losers from Inflation**

Gainers from Inflation	Losers from Inflation
Borrowers	Lenders
Earners whose wages adjust rapidly	People on fixed income
Governments that have bonds outstanding	Bondholders
Governments with progressive taxes	Taxpayers
Owners of real assets	Owners of nominal assets
	Everyone who depends on price signals

Full Employment

What is wrong with unemployment? To answer this question, recall from Chapter 2 the production possibilities curve, redrawn for consumer goods and producer goods in Figure 11-1. An economy with unemployed resources is inside the production possibilities curve at a point such as *A,* producing 60 units of consumer goods and 100 units of producer goods. It is possible to have more of either good with no sacrifice of the other. A combination of 60 consumer goods and 300 producer goods, or 85 consumer goods and 100 producer goods, is possible when all available resources are being used. This economy could even produce more of both goods, as at point *B* (80 consumer goods, 200 producer goods). Unemployment is wasteful. Scarce resources, which could be used to satisfy more of those unlimited wants, are sitting around idle. No practical economist would approve of wasted resources. They are a problem not only for society but also for the unemployed worker, who needs to find another source of income.

FIGURE 11-1

This production possibilities frontier shows how it is possible to increase output of producer goods with no loss of consumer goods production (or vice versa) when there are idle resources. It is even possible to produce more of both goods, as at point *B*. At point *A*, the opportunity cost of either good in terms of the other is zero.

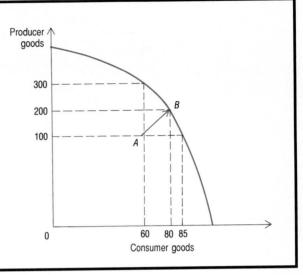

Who Is Unemployed? Table 11-1 presents some data on unemployment rates for various groups in the economy. Until about 1982 women had higher unemployment rates than men, but since that time the two rates have been nearly equal. In 1991, the unemployment rate for women was considerably lower than that for men. The lowest unemployment rates are for adult workers of both sexes. The highest unemployment rates are for teenagers, especially African-American teens. Race, sex, and age all appear to play an important role in unemployment. Other direct factors (not shown in the table) that relate to the likelihood of being unemployed are education and region of the country. The unemployment rate difference by age actually reflects the lack of experience for younger workers. Investing in education or getting some experience will resolve this problem over time. However, even if the unemployment rates for African-American and European-American workers are adjusted for differences in education and experience, there remains an unexplained difference in unemployment rates. Some of this smaller difference is due to discrimination.

Unemployed Capital   When you think of unemployment, you probably do not envision an idle machine or a vacant lot. Unemployment means idle labor to most people, but other resources can also be unemployed. For example, capital employment is measured by the **capacity utilization rate.** A capacity utilization rate of 90 percent translates into 10 percent unemployment for capital. Owners of capital are frustrated because their income from capital resources is less than it could be if it were being fully used. This figure, however, receives much less attention than the latest labor unemployment figures.

Capacity utilization rate   The percentage of the capital stock currently being utilized.

TABLE 11-1   Unemployment Rates for 1992 By Age, Race, and Sex

Category	Unemployment Rate
All workers	7.4%
Teenagers (ages 16–19)	20.0
White males	18.4
African-American males	42.0
White females	15.7
African-American females	37.2
Adults (age 20 and up)	
White males	6.3
African-American males	13.4
White females	5.4
African-American females	11.7

Source: *Economic Report of the President, 1993* (Washington, D.C.: U.S. Government Printing Office, 1993).

Costs of Unemployment   The focus on labor unemployment reflects concern not only about society's wasted resources but also about lost work experience and the impact on human capital. Most machines can sit idle for long periods without "forgetting" how to do the job. An unemployed machine can usually get up to speed fairly quickly when pressed back into service. Labor is another matter. A large part of a worker's human capital is on-the-job experience. Idle workers not only lose current income but also let their skills deteriorate when they could be sharpened and expanded by working. This loss of human capital is a major cost of unemployment of labor.

Policy Targets for Growth, Inflation, and Unemployment

To formulate an appropriate macroeconomic policy, policymakers must be able to measure output and growth, employment and unemployment, the price level, and the rate of inflation. Attaching numerical values to the basic economic goals will occupy most of the remainder of this chapter. In addition to measures, policymakers also need some standard of what is a "good" growth rate, an "acceptable" rate of inflation, or a "tolerable" level of employment; that is, they must make some normative judgments about goals or targets. Recent experience can suggest some values for these important numbers that might be reasonable targets for policymakers to adopt.

Economic Growth   The rate at which an economy can grow without straining its resources depends on how rapidly those resources grow. Historical experience

....
Myth 11-1
....

A Rising Tide Lifts All Boats

The statement "A rising tide lifts all boats" first became popular during the Kennedy administration in the 1960s and regained popularity in the Reagan and Bush administrations in the 1980s. It means that economic growth raises everyone's standard of living, including the poor. Thus, those who oppose much direct redistribution of income are far more willing to support pro-growth policies with benefits "trickling down" to the poor.

But does growth help everyone? One flip reply to "A rising tide lifts all boats" is "Not the ones that are already under water." Two groups are likely to be left out when society relies solely on economic growth rather than direct redistribution to raise everyone's living standards.

One group left behind by the rising tide owns the resources that are least in demand. Economic growth is an uneven process. Demand for some goods and some resources grows very rapidly; for others, demand grows more slowly; and for still others, it falls. Owners of resources that are specialized in declining industries do not share in the immediate gains of economic growth unless there is also some direct redistribution. Pipefitters, oil rig workers, and captains of tankers have lost jobs as the oil industry fell on hard times in the early 1980s, whereas computer repair and programming skills and medical workers have been in great demand. Workers at the bottom of the pay scale will be in poverty if they are trying to raise a family. For example, the minimum wage of $4.25 an hour comes to $8,840 for full-time, year-round work. This sum was much less than the poverty threshold for a family of four in 1993, which was defined as an income of less than about $14,350.

A second group that does not automatically gain from economic growth consists of those who are unable to work or unable to find work, even during boom times. They may be too old, too young, disabled, or otherwise unemployable. They own no productive assets. With no way to "plug in" to the market, they cannot claim a share of the growth dividend. Without a team of divers and a winch to raise their leaky boats, they will stay submerged in high and low tides alike. ■

suggests that it is possible to sustain a growth rate in real output of about 3 to 4 percent a year for long periods. The United States achieved a 3 percent growth rate in the 1950s and a higher rate in the 1960s. With a recession at the beginning of the 1980s, the average growth rate in that decade was about 2.3 percent.

A stable growth rate has some great benefits. Periods of slow growth or even falling GDP (for example, the 1980–1982 and 1990–1991 recessions) experience high unemployment and lost output. Periods of very rapid growth are often accompanied by very high rates of inflation.

Inflation Finally, what is an acceptable rate of inflation? The past two decades have seen periods of 1 to 3 percent inflation, as well as spells of double-digit inflation. In the late 1960s, people were appalled when the inflation rate rose to 4 percent; in 1984 and 1985, they applauded when it fell to "only" 4 percent. During the Great Depression of the 1930s and for long stretches in the nineteenth century, the price level actually fell.

There is no magic number for an acceptable rate of inflation. Some policymakers, including Federal Reserve Board chair Alan Greenspan, want to work toward a zero rate of inflation. Most economists would regard inflation in the 1 to 4 percent range as acceptable. They would also argue that a stable and predictable rate of inflation is at least as important as the actual inflation rate.

Unemployment The target rate of unemployment is not zero. There will always be some workers between jobs or just entering the labor force at any given time. While they are looking for work, they are counted as unemployed. It takes time for workers to find the "right" job, and for employers to find the "right" worker. This kind of unemployment is called **frictional unemployment.**

A second reason the target unemployment rate is not zero is that there will always be some workers whose skills do not match current job openings, a problem called **structural unemployment.** If there is a need for nurses in Florida, a surplus of coal miners in West Virginia will not help to solve the problem.

The combined effect of frictional and structural unemployment is that labor force analysts expect that about 5 to 6 percent of the labor force is unemployed for one of these two reasons. This figure is higher than the 3 to 4 percent figure from the 1960s, but still below actual unemployment for most of the last ten years.

Macroeconomic policymakers focus their attention on employment above this "normal" level resulting from frictional and structural unemployment. This excess unemployment, which results from fluctuations in the level of output, is called **cyclical unemployment.**

Frictional unemployment Unemployment due to new workers entering the labor force and workers temporarily between jobs; unemployment that reflects the time the search process requires to place workers in jobs.

Structural unemployment Unemployment due to a mismatch between worker characteristics, such as skills or geographic location, and job characteristics.

Cyclical unemployment Unemployment resulting from downturns in the level of economic activity; measured by changes in total output.

CHECKLIST : Setting Economic Policy Targets

The economy is performing well if

The goal of	Measured by	Is about
Real output growth	Change in real per capita output	3 to 4 percent per year
High employment	Unemployment rate	5 to 6 percent of labor force
Price stability	Inflation rate	1 to 4 percent per year

The Global Economy and Macroeconomic Goals The unemployment rate, inflation rate, and economic growth rate in a particular country are not determined by the actions of residents alone. Even a country as large and affluent as the United States is influenced by developments elsewhere. If growth is slow in the rest of the world, U.S. exports will be sluggish, affecting output and employment in the United States. If inflation is high in the rest of the world, American goods will look relatively cheap, and increased demand for U.S. exports will transmit inflation here from the rest of the world. The American economy is particularly sensitive to what happens in Canada, Mexico, Japan, and Western Europe, because these countries are our major trading partners.

The fact that this country (or any country) operates in a global environment places a significant limit on the power of policymakers to influence the level of output, employment, and prices in one country without also affecting, and being affected by, events throughout the rest of the world.

The Central Role of Output and Income When policymakers try to influence employment and unemployment rates, they usually try to expand the demand for output or speed up the rate of output growth. When policymakers work at reducing inflation, they try to restrain the demand for output or hold the rate of output growth down to a target that is attainable given the resources available. Thus, although all three goals are important for macroeconomic policy, the central goal on which the other two depend is the level of output and the rate of economic growth. The first and most important task in measuring goals, then, is to determine these two variables.

MEASURING OUTPUT AND ECONOMIC GROWTH

The essence of economic activity is captured in the circular flow diagram in Chapter 3, reproduced in Figure 11-2. This diagram shows how households, business firms, and government interact in resource and product markets to determine the size and composition of the flow of output and the amount of resources used. The resource market determines not only how specific resources are used and at what prices but also the level of resource use. Total resource use is determined in the sum of resource markets. Resource markets determine how much labor is employed and how much is unemployed, and how many idle machines, factories, and acres of land exist.

Likewise, the product market determines what mix of goods and services is produced, to whom those outputs are sold, and at what prices. The sum total of product market decisions by the practical economists who run households and business firms determines the size of the total flow of goods and services produced and the average level of prices. Thus, product markets, like resource

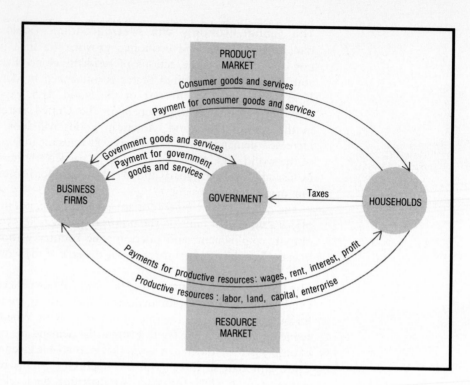

FIGURE 11-2

This circular flow diagram is the same as that in Chapter 3. Here the focus is on the size of the flows of output and income rather than on the workings of individual markets for resources and final goods and services.

Consumption (C) Expenditures by households for consumer durables, consumer nondurables, and consumer services in a given year, valued at market prices.

Saving (S) The part of income received by households that is left after consumption and taxes.

markets, provide both microeconomic and macroeconomic information. In macroeconomics, product markets and resource markets provide information about the size of the flow of income and output and whether it is growing; about the price level and in what direction it is changing; and about the level of employment and unemployment of productive resources. Thus, the circular flow is a visual image of how the economy is performing on the three macroeconomic goals of economic growth, price stability, and full employment.

The circular flow diagram is a good starting point for measuring the size of the economy's output and income. However, one element needs to be added. Most of the income households receive returns to the spending flow as **consumption (C),** or purchases of goods and services for household use. Part of the income flow, however, is diverted to government, which collects taxes from households and uses those revenues to buy goods and services (see Figure 11-3). Another leakage out of the flow is household savings. **Savings (S),** is any income received by households that is not spent on consumption or paid to the government in taxes.

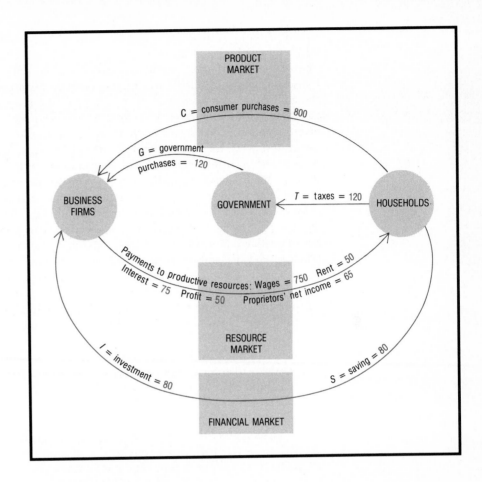

FIGURE 11-3

This circular flow diagram adds leakages in the form of saving and taxes, and injections in the form of government purchases and investment to the previous model. A financial market channels saving into investment. Numbers in this hypothetical example show how leakages must equal injections, or how the size of the flow will change.

If saving, like taxes, merely leaked out of the income and output stream, and there was no offsetting injection of nonconsumption spending into the income stream (such as government purchases or investment), the size of the flow would shrink. However, such injections do occur. Business firms make purchases from one another. Some of these purchases are simply incorporated into final goods—microchips into computers, flour into bread, leather into shoes. Others are for long-lasting business plants and equipment, such as machines or factories. These purchases, called *business investment,* are financed by borrowing through the financial market.

Households put their savings into certificates of deposit, stocks, bonds, pension funds, and other financial assets. The financial market (banks, stockbrokers, mutual fund providers, insurance companies, and credit unions) makes these household savings available to business firms to finance investment. Some of these funds are also borrowed by governments if tax revenue is insufficient to pay for government purchases. As long as the injections in the form of business investment and government purchases are equal to the leakages in the form of saving and taxes, the size of the flow will neither grow nor shrink.

Figure 11-3 shows a more nearly complete circular flow, with saving passing through the financial sector to business firms for investment purposes and to government to finance government purchases in excess of tax revenues. (A complete circular flow would also include a foreign sector, with exports and imports.) Figure 11-3 also includes some hypothetical numbers to measure the size of the flows. Note that the sum of household purchases ($800), government purchases ($120), and investment purchases ($80) is $1,000. This total is equal to the sum of the income flows from businesses to households, also $1,000. Getting the same number both ways is no accident. It should be possible to measure the size of the flow of goods and services in either half of the circular flow: the flow of output in the market for goods and services or the flow of income in the resource market.

The size of the flow through product markets represents the sum total of activity in the market for goods and services. The level of income (and output) can also be computed as the flow of incomes earned in the resource market. Remember, all the factors of production belong to households; thus, all the income business firms earn from selling goods and services accrues to households (with a few exceptions noted later on). Thus, the sum of either total sales or total incomes of resource owners should give roughly the same measure of total output.

The levels of output and income are indicators of economic well-being, or how much a nation's citizens have available to consume and invest. The rate at which the flow increases from year to year is the economic growth rate—one of the three macroeconomic policy targets.

Final and Intermediate Goods

A measure of total output was developed only in the twentieth century, after much struggle over exactly how to go about it. The biggest problem in computing the value of total output for a given year is to make sure some items are not counted twice. A numerical example will make this problem clear.

Suppose Mary owns a shoelace factory. She sells some shoelaces directly to consumers, but others go to a shoe factory, which incorporates them into shoes. The national income accountant does not want to count that second group of shoelaces twice—once when Mary sells them to the shoe manufacturer and again when the shoe manufacturer sells them to the consumer as part of a pair of shoes. To get an accurate measure of output, the accountant includes only final goods in the count. **Final goods** are those sold to the final buyer, who does not normally resell them or incorporate them into other goods to be sold. Thus, measured output should exclude semifinished goods and raw materials to avoid counting them twice.

Final goods Goods that will not be used as inputs into further production.

You may think of other kinds of economic activities that do not fit this definition of final goods and should therefore not be counted in final output. Sales and purchases of stocks and bonds and other financial assets, for example, do not represent any new current output. Such sales would not be counted in total income and output, although the efforts of stockbrokers in carrying out the sales would count as a service. Output also excludes sales of used goods, such as old cars or the odds and ends people sell at garage sales. Those items were already counted in the year they were produced.

Computing Gross Domestic Product

Gross domestic product (GDP) The market value of all final goods and services produced by the residents of an economy during a year; equal to consumption plus investment, government purchases, and net exports.

The most widely used measure of total output is gross domestic product. **Gross domestic product (GDP)** is the market value of all final goods and services produced by the residents of an economy in a year. Until 1991, the measure used was *gross national product (GNP)*, which measures production by a nation's *citizens* rather than by its *residents*. For some countries, there is a big difference. For the United States, the difference between GDP and GNP in 1992 was only $11.2 billion, or about two-tenths of 1 percent. Because GDP has replaced GNP in the newspapers and government reports, we will concentrate on GDP in this chapter.

Note carefully the words in the definition of GDP. Only *final* goods and services count, and they are counted in the *year* they are produced. The other important term is *market value*. To add together apples and oranges, cars and boats, or pizza and beer, these goods are valued at market prices.

The need for a market price means sales or purchases are not counted unless they take place in the market. Household production (child care, cooking, cleaning, sewing, repairs, mowing lawns, gardening) counts only if someone is paid to perform these tasks. Even then, a lot of these payments are missed. National income accountants cannot track all the payments made to teenage baby sitters, especially since they rely heavily on such data sources as sales data from firms and tax returns.

Underground economy The economy that consists of goods and services that are sold but are not sold in markets, usually to avoid paying taxes or other consequences.

Some exchanges are deliberately hidden from the government to avoid taxes (not to mention getting arrested if the transactions involve illegal activities such as drugs, prostitution, or gambling). These kinds of transactions make up the **underground economy,** which is neither taxed nor counted in GDP.

The output of the "aboveground" market economy is sorted by categories of purchasers of business output identified in the circular flow diagram—households (or consumers), other business firms, and government. Missing from the diagram is a fourth sector, the rest of the world, which purchases exports and sells imports to households, firms, and governments.

The reason for breaking down output flows into these four components is that the motives and rewards for each group are quite different. Although practical economists are at work in all four sectors, their objectives differ, as do the incentives and opportunities to which they respond. Business firms seek profit, consumers seek satisfaction or a higher standard of living, and governments seek to satisfy citizens. For purposes of predicting the course of GDP in response to a change in taxes, the price level, interest rates, or other influences, it is helpful to break down GDP into categories of actors who respond differently to changes in each of these influences.

Net exports (X − M)
Sales of goods and services to other countries less purchases by Americans from abroad; a component of GDP that can be positive or negative.

The variables C (consumption) and G (government purchases) stand for the sales of goods and services to households and government, respectively. The quantity $X - M$ (exports minus imports) is **net exports** and represents net sales to people in other countries. Purchases by businesses are represented by I (investment). Thus, in shorthand

$$GDP = C + I + G + (X - M).$$

Consumption   Consumption is the largest single component of GDP, as Table 11-2 indicates. In 1992, consumption accounted for 69 percent of GDP, followed in order by government purchases, investment, and (with a negative value) net exports. Consumption consists of all purchases of final goods and services by households—pizzas, haircuts, education, T-shirts, diapers, groceries,

TABLE 11-2   Gross Domestic Product, 1992 (billions)

GDP	$5,950.7
Consumption	4,095.8
Consumer durables	480.4
Consumer nondurables	1,290.7
Consumer services	2,324.7
Gross private domestic investment	770.4
Plant and equipment	548.2
Change in inventories	4.4
Residential construction	217.7
Government purchases	1,114.9
Federal	449.1
State and local	665.8
Net exports	− 30.4
Exports	636.3
Imports	665.7

Source: *Survey of Current Business*, March 1993.

cars, laundry services, and thousands of other items. Consumption falls into three main categories:

- *Consumer durables* are purchases by households of goods with a long useful life, such as cars and appliances.
- *Consumer nondurables* are purchases of goods that are used up fairly quickly, such as food and clothing.
- *Consumer services* are intangible purchases such as medical care, entertainment, haircuts, and auto repairs. This category also includes the rental of housing.

Government Purchases   Government purchases in GDP are much less than the sum total of budgets of federal, state, and local governments. The difference between the GDP number and the budget number consists of transfer payments of income to individuals, including interest on the national debt as well as social security, veterans' benefits, food stamps, and welfare payments. These payments are certainly important to recipients, who use them for consumption. However, remember that GDP is a measure of *production*. Transfer payments are made without requiring the recipient to offer any production of goods and services in exchange. Government spending is counted as part of gross domestic product only when the government produces services (roads, education, defense, courts) or purchases goods and services (printing services, defense contractors' services, and the services of the president, Congress, and the 50 governors).

Net Exports   As mentioned earlier, the term $X - M$ is net exports. The items U.S. producers sell abroad (exports) count as part of U.S. output, but it is necessary to subtract goods and services already counted in C, I, and G that were purchased from abroad (imports). For convenience, these two items are grouped together as net exports. Net exports can be negative if Americans spend more on imported goods than non–Americans spend on U.S. goods and services, as has been the case for the last 12 years.

Although net exports are a relatively small share of GDP, exports and imports taken separately are quite large. In 1992 exports accounted for 10.5 percent of total sales of goods, whereas imported goods accounted for 11.2 percent. Looking only at net exports tends to understate the importance of international trade in the U.S. economy.

Investment

Part of the definition of GDP is the phrase "final goods and services." The sharp reader may wonder about the inclusion of investment as a part of final product, because these investment goods will be used to produce other goods and services. In that sense, they are intermediate rather than final goods. However, these investment goods will be used up in the process of producing goods and services over many years. In the national income accounts, output is counted in the year it is produced. Not counting investment goods would understate output in the year in which investment goods are produced and overstate output in the years in which the investment goods are used up.

Plant and Equipment   Plant and equipment refers to buildings, machinery, and equipment used in production. Total expenditures on these items is called **gross investment.** However, some existing plant and equipment is used up each year, along with additions of new plant and equipment. Simply counting new capital produced and ignoring the fact that old plant and equipment are being used up or becoming obsolete, overstates the real amount of increase in the stock of capital equipment. Subtracting capital used up during the current period from gross investment yields **net investment.** The difference between gross investment and net investment, or the amount of capital equipment used up or worn out that must be replaced in any given year, is called **depreciation.**

Inventories   Another kind of business investment is changes in inventories. The shoelace manufacturer may have produced $100,000 worth of shoelaces. Of that total, $50,000 worth of shoelaces was sold directly to households and $20,000 to shoe manufacturers. The shoe manufacturers used up $15,000 in making shoes, leaving $5,000 worth of shoelaces on the shelves of shoe manufacturers and $30,000 on the shelves of the shoelace factory.

    In the process of producing the shoelaces, the shoelace maker generated $100,000 in income in the lower half of the circular flow. Where is the corresponding sale of output in the upper half? Some of it shows up in the sales of shoes with laces ($15,000), and some of it ($50,000) in direct sales to households. The remaining $35,000 is sitting on the shelves of business firms, waiting to be used or sold in a future year. Remember, GDP counts what is produced, not what is sold. Those unsold shoelaces are counted this year as **changes in inventory.** Note that inventory changes can be negative if firms draw down on inventories and do not fully replace them.

Housing   Housing, or residential construction, consists of new houses, apartments, townhouses, and condominiums. Much of this construction is ordinary business investment by firms that build apartments and sell the use of those apartments each year to consumers. However, many families own their own homes. Although they enjoy the same housing services that renters do, there is no market payment for the services. If national income accountants ignored this fact, they would treat owner-occupied houses as purchases the year they were built, with no payments thereafter. Since both the business firms with apartments and the homeowners are really engaging in investment and producing services, the accounts treat these families as business firms that own a "housing services factory" that they rent to themselves. Their houses are counted as investment. That investment, like the investment by business firms that build apartments,

---

Gross investment (*I*)
Total new spending on investment without correcting for capital used up during the current year.

Net investment Net addition to the capital stock; gross investment less capital used up during the current year.

Depreciation The amount of capital stock used up or worn out during a given year.

Changes in inventory
The component of gross private domestic investment that measures changes in the holdings of final product for future sale by business firms.

yields a stream of housing services each year that counts as part of consumption, regardless of whether the purchase of housing services occurs within the household or passes through the market.

National Income

National income (NI)
The sum of the incomes of productive resources—wages plus rent, interest, profit, and proprietors' net income; should equal GDP after adjusting for depreciation and indirect business taxes.

Proprietors' net income Net earnings of small, one-owner firms that cannot easily be separated into the component parts of wages, rent, interest, and profits.

GDP is a measure of output, or the product market side of the circular flow. The flow of economic activity can also be measured along the lower half of the circular flow by adding the incomes of productive resources. If GDP is measured accurately, the two numbers should be the same. Thus, an important function for **national income (NI)** is to provide a cross-check on GDP statistics.

When the services of productive resources (land, labor, capital, and enterprise) are sold in resource markets, they earn, respectively, rent, wages, interest, and profit. There is also a separate income category, called **proprietors' net income,** that represents the net earnings of small firms owned by a single individual. This income is listed separately because it is not easily broken down into its component part of wages (to the owner-worker), rent (to the owner-landowner), interest (on the owner's invested capital), and profit (to the owner as entrepreneur). Adding this category to the other four kinds of resource income gives this measure of national income (NI):

NI = Wages + Rent + Interest + Profit + Proprietors' Net Income.

National income should equal GDP, because every dollar received from the sale of output is also income earned by a firm that belongs to someone. Most of the firm's revenue is paid out in incomes to owners of productive resources in the forms of wages, rent, interest, and profit (or proprietors' net income). Some of the firm's revenue is paid to other firms for raw materials, semifinished goods, and capital equipment, but those other firms in turn pay out the proceeds in the form of incomes of productive resources. Thus, national income is simply the mirror image of output, or gross domestic product.

However, a few differences exist between GDP and NI that require correction before the two are equal. The first correction converts GDP to GNP by subtracting income earned by non–U.S. residents and adding income earned by Americans abroad—a difference of $11.2 billion.

The second, and largest, correction is for depreciation charges on capital equipment. These charges amounted to $653.4 billion in 1992. The cost of equipment used up in production is reflected in the prices of products, but does not result in income for productive resources.

Indirect business taxes
Taxes, such as sales taxes, that are part of what consumers pay for goods but do not represent income to productive resources.

The third adjustment is for **indirect business taxes.** When you buy a $20 sweater, in most states you will pay more than $20—perhaps $20.80 or $21.00, or, in New York City, $21.65. The difference is sales tax. Sales taxes and other taxes on particular products are grouped together as indirect business taxes. These taxes are part of the prices of products, so they are counted in consumption, but the proceeds go to the government instead of going to the firm to be paid out in factor incomes.

These three adjustments give this relationship:

$$\text{GNP} - \text{Depreciation} - \text{Indirect Business Taxes} = \text{National Income.}$$

In 1992, GDP was $5,951 billion, GNP was $5,962 billion, and national income was $4,744 billion. The gap of $1,218 billion was almost entirely accounted for by depreciation of $653 billion and indirect business taxes of $504 billion, leaving a gap of $61 billion. After a few other small corrections (including business transfer payments of $30 billion), there remained an unaccounted-for difference, called a **statistical discrepancy,** of $33.4 billion.

Statistical discrepancy
The gap remaining between GDP and national income as a measure of the level of economic activity after subtracting depreciation and indirect business taxes.

If you have ever taken accounting, you would probably love to be able to solve your accounting problems—or balance your checkbook—by simply tossing in a statistical discrepancy. However, remember that the government lacks access to all the information it needs to draw up accurate national income accounts. It is actually quite impressive that the gap between NI and GDP after making the necessary adjustments is so small—less than one-half of 1 percent. Thus, adding up national income by payments to productive resources is a useful way to verify the GDP numbers.

National Income, GDP, and Economic Well-Being

Neither gross domestic product nor national income is a satisfactory measure of the well-being of a nation's citizens, although changes from one year to the next may be a good indicator of the extent to which economic conditions have improved. Several important elements of economic well-being do not appear in any of these measures. For example, people may have more leisure, but the extra leisure is not counted in GDP. Households may produce goods and services for their own use, cooking meals, baking bread, cutting trees, repairing cars, and sewing curtains. If these activities do not go through the market, they are not measured and counted.

On the other hand, economic "bads" may increase—more noise, congestion, pollution, crime, and stress as a by-product of increased output. All of these "bads" should be subtracted to arrive at a "true" measure of the change in economic well-being. A rise in measured GDP, for example, may reflect an increase in protection services (police) when in fact that increase is a barely adequate response to a higher crime rate. The net change in economic well-being from more crime and more police may be zero or even negative!

Economists James Tobin and William Nordhaus attempted to create a measure of economic well-being that makes some of these corrections. Tobin and Nordhaus called their version of the GDP accounts the *measure of economic welfare (MEW).* They found that at least for the 1960s and 1970s, MEW tended to grow more slowly than GDP.

Despite such flaws, GDP and national income are the most widely used measures of economic well-being. Even after allowing for the problems of measuring depreciation, omitting the value of goods and services not sold in the market (home production and the underground economy), and failure to correct for increases in noise, congestion, pollution, and other ills of an industrial society, these indicators are the best tools available for measuring macroeconomic performance.

MEASURING INFLATION

National income accountants do make an effort to correct one particular problem in GDP: separating changes in real output of goods and services from an apparent increase that reflects only higher prices. This correction is the most important single adjustment in trying to determine how much the economy actually improved (or worsened) from one year to the next.

Between 1990 and 1991, GDP rose from $5,513.8 billion to $5,671.8 billion, an increase of 2.9 percent. That sounds impressive, but that number mixes increases in real output with increases in prices. If 1991 GDP had sold at 1990 prices, GDP would have been only $5,473 billion—a *decrease* of 3.5 percent. Between 1990 and 1991, all of the increase in GDP, and then some, was due to rising prices.

It is not possible to measure real economic growth directly. Instead, economists measure what is happening to the market value of output, or nominal GDP, and then correct for price changes by dividing by a price index. The **price index,** or the measure of price changes, also measures how the economy is performing on the goal of price stability.

Price index   A measure of the change in the price level between two time periods, with the price level in the second period expressed as a fraction of the price level in the first period times 100.

Computing a Price Index

The idea behind a price index is really very simple. Economists at the Bureau of Labor Statistics measure the cost of a particular market basket of goods in a base year, in this case 1990. Each good enters the basket as base year price (P_0) times base year quantity purchased (Q_0). The total value of the basket for the base year is the sum of the values of these goods at market prices, or $\Sigma P_0 Q_0$. For example, if the basket contains 10 pounds of ground beef and the 1990 price of ground beef is $1.89, the value of $P \times Q$ for ground beef is 1.89×10, or $18.90.

The following year, the cost of the same market basket of goods is measured again, valuing the base year quantities at the current year prices. The value of this basket is written as $\Sigma P_1 Q_0$. If the price of ground beef has risen to $2.10, its market value will now be $21.00 ($2.10 \times 10$), since Q_0 is unchanged.

Finally, the second number (the value of the basket in the second year) is divided by the first (the market value of the basket in the base year), and the result is multiplied by 100 to obtain a price index. In symbols,

$$\text{Price Index} = \frac{\text{Basket Value in Year 1}}{\text{Basket Value in Year 0}} \times 100 = \frac{\Sigma P_1 Q_0}{\Sigma P_0 Q_0} \times 100.$$

The price index is multiplied by 100 to make it a whole number. For example, if a market basket that cost $100 in 1991 was priced at $103 in 1992, the price index would be 1.03. However, it is normally stated as simply 103, meaning in either case that prices have risen by 3 percent.

To correct GDP for inflation by using this index, one simply divides 1992 GDP by 1.03 to obtain the value of 1992 GDP at 1991 prices. Table 11-3 makes this calculation using a price index called the *GDP deflator*. This index reflects all of the items in GDP. In the table, the base year for the price index is 1987; that is, the value of the index for 1987 is set equal to 100. Other years are a multiple or a fraction of that number. For example, in 1989 the figure of 108.4 for 1989 indicates that the price level rose 8.4 percent from 1987 to 1989.

Consumer price index (CPI) The most widely used measure of changes in the price level; measures changes in the cost of a representative market basket of consumer goods and services.

The Consumer Price Index (CPI)

Although Table 11-3 uses the GDP deflator to correct GDP for inflation, this index is not as widely known or quoted as the **consumer price index (CPI)**.

TABLE 11-3   Converting Nominal GDP to Real GDP (billions $)

Year	Nominal GDP	Price Index	Real GDP (= Nominal GDP/Price Index)
1981	$3,030.6	78.9	$3,776.3
1982	3,149.6	83.8	3,843.1
1983	3,405.0	87.2	3,760.3
1984	3,777.2	91.0	3,906.6
1985	4,038.7	94.4	4,148.5
1986	4,268.6	96.9	4,279.8
1987	4,539.9	100.0	4,540.0
1988	4,900.4	103.9	4,718.6
1989	5,244.0	108.4	4,836.9
1990	5,513.8	112.9	4,884.9
1991	5.671.8	117.0	4,848.4
1992	5,950.7	120.8	4,922.6

Sources: *Economic Report of the President, 1993* (Washington, D.C.: U.S. Government Printing Office, 1993); *Survey of Current Business,* March 1993.

TABLE 11-4 A Hypothetical Price Index

| | Year 1 | | | Year 2 | |
Item	Number	Price	Total Spent	Price	Total Spent
Jeans	2	$18.00	$36.00	$21.00	$42.00
Orange juice	8	0.90	7.20	0.85	6.80
Bread	15	0.75	11.25	0.85	12.75
Gasoline	10	1.25	12.50	1.40	14.00
Apples	5	0.30	1.50	0.25	1.25
Total			$68.45		$76.80

Also known as the *cost of living index,* CPI is based on a market basket of more than 400 items and measures changes in the prices of consumer goods. The mix of items in the basket is determined on the basis of periodic surveys of consumer spending patterns. Table 11-4 computes a very simple hypothetical price index, using the same method by which the CPI is computed. The price index for year 2 is (76.80/68.45) × 100, or 112.2. The average price of items in the basket rose 12.2 percent. Some rose more and some (orange juice and apples) actually fell slightly, but the cost of the total market basket increased 12.2 percent. Note, too, that some items count more than others; their weight in the basket is greater. There are only two pairs of jeans, but fifteen loaves of bread. This reflects how many of each item the consumers in the survey typically buy each year.

The CPI is probably the most widely quoted price index. It is very important to the practical economists who run business firms or make consumption decisions, because it is used to adjust wages, social security benefits, and tax brackets to correct for inflation. The CPI must be used with care, however, because it is based only on the goods consumers buy; thus, it does not reflect changes in the costs of investment goods or government services. A broader index, the GDP deflator, measures changes in the average price level of all components of GDP.

EMPLOYMENT, UNEMPLOYMENT, AND LABOR FORCE PARTICIPATION

Unemployment rate
The percentage of the labor force that is actively seeking work but is not currently employed.

The final economic goal, full employment, is measured using the **unemployment rate,** or the number of people who are currently not employed but are actively seeking work. An unemployment rate that is too high and/or rising too rapidly usually calls for some kind of macroeconomic policy response, typically more urgently than the call signaled by slow output growth or a high rate of inflation.

Unemployment is difficult to measure accurately. Some unemployment is seasonal. In some areas, farm workers are idle in the winter. More retail clerks are employed in November and December for the holiday season. The flood of high school graduates every June temporarily increases unemployment. Statisticians at the Bureau of Labor Statistics try to adjust measured unemployment for such expected seasonal variations. They are less successful in adjusting for two other aspects of employment, underemployment and discouraged workers.

Underemployed workers work fewer hours than they want to, or at jobs less skilled than those for which they were trained. Many are in temporary jobs when they would like to find something more permanent. Others are college graduates working in jobs for which a high school diploma would be adequate training. *Discouraged workers* are not counted among the unemployed because they have given up searching for work. Underemployed and discouraged workers mean that measured unemployment may understate the extent of the problem, especially during recessions.

The unemployment rate is expressed as a percentage of the labor force. To measure the unemployment rate, it is necessary to measure both the size of the labor force and the number of unemployed people. The Bureau of Labor Statistics calculates the unemployment rate each month on the basis of household surveys.

Labor Force Participation

Labor force participation rate The fraction of the population that is counted in the labor force, that is, those working or actively seeking work.

The size of the labor force depends on the population and the labor force participation rate. The **labor force participation rate** is the percentage of the population (outside of prisons or other institutions and excluding the military) that is either currently employed or actively seeking work. Table 11-5 gives the labor force participation rate in the United States for selected years from 1950 to 1992. It shows that a much higher percentage of the population is in the labor force today than was the case in the 1950s and early 1960s. Note that the percentage of the population in the labor force rose from 59 percent in the 1960s to 66 percent in the 1990s. This increase reflects two changes. First, over this period women went to work outside the home in increasing numbers. In 1960, 37 percent of women ages 18 to 64 were in the labor force; by 1990, 54 percent were working or seeking work. Second, the "baby boom" generation—the large number of persons born between 1946 and 1962, before the birth rate tapered off—came of working age in the period from 1964 to 1984.

TABLE 11-5 Employment, Unemployment, and Labor Force Participation, 1950–1992

	Employed	Unemployed	Unemployment Rate	Labor Force Participation Rate
	(thousands of persons)			
1950	58,918	3,288	5.3%	59.2%
1955	62,170	2,852	4.4	59.3
1960	65,778	3,852	5.5	59.4
1965	71,088	3,366	4.5	58.9
1970	78,678	4,093	4.9	60.4
1975	85,846	5,156	8.5	61.2
1980	99,303	7,637	7.1	63.8
1981	100,397	8,273	7.6	63.9
1982	99,526	10,678	9.7	64.0
1983	100,834	10,717	9.6	64.0
1984	105,005	8,539	7.5	64.4
1985	107,550	8,312	7.2	64.8
1986	109,597	8,237	7.0	65.3
1987	112,440	7,425	6.2	65.6
1988	114,968	6,701	5.5	65.9
1989	117,342	6,528	5.3	66.5
1990	117,914	6,874	5.5	66.4
1991	116,877	8,426	6.7	66.0
1992	117,598	9,384	7.4	66.3

Note: Data exclude resident armed forces.

Source: *Economic Report of the President, 1993* (Washington, D.C.: U.S. Government Printing Office, 1993).

A labor force that was larger, younger, and contained more female workers also meant higher unemployment rates. The economy successfully created new slots, but the labor force grew very rapidly in a short period of time, making it difficult to absorb such a large influx of new workers. Furthermore, there was more structural unemployment, or mismatch between the skills available and the skills required by vacant jobs. Many women entered the labor force in traditional women's occupations—teaching, nursing, secretarial, and clerical work. Those fields became overcrowded, keeping wages low and driving unemployment rates up. Some of these structural problems were resolved by the end of the 1970s as workers were gradually absorbed and more women shifted to nontraditional occupations, but unemployment has not yet returned to the low levels of the 1960s.

In Practice 11-1

. . . .

The Baby Boomers Leave Their Mark

One-third of the present population (74 million Americans) were born between 1946 and 1964, a generation nicknamed the "baby boom." Births during those years were 49 percent higher than in the two preceding decades. Baby boomers have had a great impact on the mix of consumer goods, the demand for public services, the unemployment rate, the demand for housing, and the growth of colleges and universities. As this generation ages, its members will continue to dominate the nation's patterns of production and consumption.

The end of World War II is credited with starting the baby boom. The first wave, born in 1946–1955, hit the schools, the toy market, and the orthodontists' offices with a bang. As the nation caught up with training teachers and building schools, colleges experienced the same surge. Classrooms were added, faculty salaries rose, and college fads and fancies caught the national attention, from goldfish swallowing to more serious matters like antiwar protests and environmental concerns.

Then the baby boom generation hit the job market. With a larger share of the population in the labor force, employment and unemployment rose together. Employ-

ment effects were painful for the last half of the baby boom, following an unprecedented crop of high school and college graduates competing for jobs just ahead of them. Too few jobs existed for an outsized generation, and real wages for new entrants dropped between 1973 and 1980 as stiff job competition pushed earnings downward.

In the 1970s, baby boomers hit the housing market. Skyrocketing housing demand drove up house prices far more rapidly than other prices. Again, the younger brothers and sisters were hit harder. Their (lower) average family incomes meant the majority of boomers could not qualify for mortgages on the average new house in 1980. Smaller houses, smaller lots, and more condominiums and mobile homes were yet another response to the generation bulge.

The baby boom moves on, approaching middle age and retirement. The first wave of the boomers reaches age 50 in 1996; if they retire at age 65, the first wave of boomer retirements will begin in 2011. Social security faces a smaller working generation following behind to pick up the cost. Expect the next effects of the boomer generation to show up in demand for investment services and travel, retirement villages, and nursing homes instead of the soft rock music, fashionable clothes, and kitchen gadgets favored by the middle class and middle-aged. The baby boom has left behind no longer needed public schools, excess space in college classrooms, bankrupt toymakers, and other abandoned facilities that catered to these consumers' wants as they grew up. ■

The Unemployment Rate

As mentioned earlier, the unemployment rate is the percentage of the labor force that is not employed but is actively seeking work. For example, if 100 million are working and 10 million are not working but are actively seeking work, the labor force is 110 million and the unemployment rate is 10/110, or about 9 percent.

The unemployment rate can be an inaccurate measure of actual unemployment for two reasons. First, if discouraged workers drop out of the labor force after searching in vain, they will no longer be counted in the labor force, and the unemployment rate will understate the seriousness of labor market conditions. Second, unemployed workers have to make some effort to find a job to be able to collect unemployment compensation benefits. Some of these workers may actually be interested not in employment but in staying eligible for unemployment benefits. These workers are counted as unemployed members of the labor force when they are really not looking for work; thus, unemployment is overstated. The net effect of these two opposing sources of error is difficult to determine.

A final problem in measuring unemployment is the large number of self-employed people. The labor department uses three sources of data for measuring employment and unemployment. One source is business firms' reports on the number of workers. The second source is state unemployment compensation claims. The third is household surveys. Household surveys pick up people who are self-employed, whereas business figures do not. These three sources gave very different estimates of unemployment in the 1990s, with business data suggesting higher unemployment rates because they ignored the self-employed.

Summary

1. The macroeconomic goals of growth, stable prices, and full employment are interrelated. Each goal receives greater emphasis at different times. In the 1990s, growth is the major concern.

2. The measure of economic growth is changes in real income or output. Output is measured by gross domestic product (GDP), the sum of consumer purchases, gross private domestic investment, government purchases, and net exports.

3. GDP is not a perfect measure of economic welfare, but it does give some indication of the standard of living of a nation's citizens and changes in their economic well-being. National income, an alternative measure of the income flow, provides a cross-check on the accuracy of GDP figures.

4. The most widely used measure of prices and changes in price (inflation) is the consumer price index (CPI). The CPI measures year-to-year changes in the cost of a fixed market basket of consumer goods and services.

5. The unemployment rate equals the number of unemployed divided by the labor force. Unemployment rates change due to changes in GDP (cyclical), to changes in labor force participation (frictional), or to mis-

matches between workers' skills and the skill requirements of available jobs (structural).

Key Terms

capacity utilization rate
changes in inventory
consumer price index (CPI)
consumption (C)
cyclical unemployment
depreciation
final goods
frictional unemployment

gross domestic product (GDP)
gross investment (I)
growth dividend
indirect business taxes
inflation
labor force participation rate
national income (NI)
net investment

net exports (X − M)
price index
proprietors' net income
saving (S)
statistical discrepancy
structural unemployment
underground economy
unemployment rate

Questions and Problems

1. Use the data in Table 11-3 to calculate the rate of real economic growth in 1985, 1986, 1987, and 1988.

2. Use the following data to calculate inflation rates for each year from 1985 to 1991. Note that the CPI is given as an index. To find the rate of inflation, simply divide the index for the current year by the index for the previous year and subtract 1. For example, if the index for year 2 is 121 and the index for year 1 is 110, inflation from year 1 to year 2 is (121/110) − 1 = 1.10 − 1, or 10 percent.

Year	CPI (base = 1982–1984)
1984	103.9
1985	107.6
1986	109.6
1987	113.6
1988	118.3
1989	124.0
1990	130.7
1991	136.2

3. The following data, from the 1993 *Economic Report of the President*, show the major components of GDP for 1984 through 1991. Compute each component as a percentage of GDP for each of those years. Over time, which component seems most stable? Least stable?

Year	GDP	Consumption	Investment	Government Purchases	Net Exports
1984	3,777.2	2,460.3	718.9	700.8	− 102.7
1985	4,038.7	2,667.4	714.5	772.3	− 115.6
1986	4,268.6	2,850.6	717.6	833.0	− 132.5
1987	4,539.9	3,052.2	749.3	881.5	− 143.1
1988	4,900.4	3,296.1	793.6	918.7	− 108.0
1989	5,224.0	3,517.9	837.6	971.4	− 82.9
1990	5,513.8	3,742.6	802.6	1,042.9	− 74.1
1991	6,571.8	3,886.8	745.6	1,086.9	− 27.1

4. Who gains and who loses from economic growth? From stable prices? From full employment? Do the gains to those who benefit outweigh the losses to those who lose?

5. Given the following data, compute a price index.

Item	Number of units	Price Year 1	Price Year 2
Apples	8	$0.20	$0.25
Soap	2	0.38	0.35
T-shirts	3	3.00	3.75
Gasoline	10	1.10	1.20
Ground beef	5	1.25	1.40

6. Explain in your own words what each of the following newspaper statements means in terms of the measures you learned in this chapter.

   a. The cost of living is rising at an annual rate of 3.5 percent.
   b. The unemployment rate for December was 6.9 percent.
   c. Real growth is currently at a rate of 1.9 percent per year.

7. Draw a production possibilities curve with public goods on one axis and private goods on the other. Sketch the effects of an increase in the capacity to produce private goods only (i.e., show how the curve shifts). Explain why economic growth makes it possible to consume more of both goods even when the growth occurs in only one good.

8. Suppose national income accountants find that machinery and equipment wears out much more rapidly than they used to think it did. They adjust the depreciation estimates. What happens to measured gross domestic product? To measured national income? To gross investment? To net investment?

In this case, which is a better measure of economic well-being, gross domestic product or national income?

9. In 1990, per capita GDP was as follows for a variety of countries:

India	$350
Bolivia	630
Argentina	2,767
Ireland	9,550
Canada	20,470
United States	21,790
Switzerland	32,680

Based on what you learned in this chapter, why might you be cautious about saying that Ireland's standard of living is 15 times Bolivia's or that the average American is more than twice as well off as the average Irish citizen but not as well off as a citizen of Switzerland?

12

Aggregate Demand and Supply:

Determining the Levels of Prices,

Output, and Employment

Economics from beginning to end is a study of the mutual adjustment of consumption and production.

ALFRED MARSHALL

Main Points

1. Aggregate demand is a graph, or schedule, showing the relationship between the quantity of real output demanded and the price level.

2. Aggregate supply is a graph, or schedule, showing the relationship between the quantity of real output produced (and offered for sale) and the price level.

3. Aggregate supply and aggregate demand interact to determine real output and the price level. Employment and unemployment are closely related to the level of real output.

4. Shifts in aggregate demand can come from household or business decisions. Government can attempt to influence aggregate demand with taxing and spending policies. Rising aggregate demand will drive up output and prices in various combinations.

5. Shifts in aggregate supply result from changes in technology, the size of the labor force, productivity, or the availability of natural resources. An increase in aggregate supply raises real output while lowering the price level.

In microeconomics, the tools of supply and demand explain how the market matches what people want to buy with what firms are willing to offer for sale. Macroeconomics also has a supply and demand model, which explains how total real output and the price level are determined. This model is the aggregate supply and demand model, which offers an organizing framework to viewing macroeconomic theory and policy. As in the chapters on microeconomics, we will go behind the aggregate demand and aggregate supply curves to examine their slopes and what makes them shift, in order to explain changes in the price level and in real output and employment. ∎

THE CONTEXT OF MACROECONOMICS

Macroeconomics focuses on the way market forces determine the values of various economic aggregates, including total real output, the price level, and the overall level of employment and unemployment. Although macroeconomics is concerned with aggregate values rather than with individual prices and quantities, it is very closely related to microeconomics, especially in the underlying assumptions about people's economic behavior. The practical economist of the microeconomics chapters becomes a whole nation of practical economists in the macroeconomics chapters.

Microeconomics and Macroeconomics Revisited

Macroeconomics and microeconomics are alike in that both use a supply and demand framework, both attempt to explain the equilibria resulting from market forces, and both are based on the assumption that people respond to incentives according to their own self-interest. Microeconomics and macroeconomics also differ in some very important respects.

First, microeconomics is much more *concrete*. In microeconomics, it is easy to cite examples of individual economic decisions about using time, spending money, choosing a job, or deciding which product to produce. Macroeconomic events also affect individuals personally, but the relationship between the individual and the macroeconomy is much more abstract and therefore more difficult to see.

Second, macroeconomic variables are harder to measure and sometimes difficult even to define. For example, it is relatively easy to measure the number of cars sold by Ford or Chrysler, or even the average price of pizza. As you learned in the last chapter, it is much more difficult to measure total real output or to compute the aggregate price level.

One reason this book began with microeconomics is that microeconomics is more concrete and its variables are more measurable. In learning microeconomics, you learned to think like an economist. You began to approach decisions or issues from a perspective of scarcity and opportunity cost, equilibrium and disequilibrium, maximizing and self-interested behavior. You should have discovered that the actions of people you know are described quite accurately by the model of the practical economist. All of these concepts underlie macroeconomics as well as microeconomics. Now you need to draw on your newfound ability to think like an economist to develop an understanding of the economic forces that operate on the sum total of all markets at the same time.

Classical and Keynesian Macroeconomics

Most economists in the late nineteenth and early twentieth centuries were more interested in microeconomic questions than in macroeconomic questions. These economists (called *neoclassical economists*) developed most of the theory of prices and costs presented in the preceding chapters. Macroeconomics received relatively little attention between 1850 and 1920. However, the preceding period from 1770 to 1850 was the heyday for a group of economists known as *classical economists.* This group included two of the most famous names in the history of economics, Adam Smith and David Ricardo. Classical economists were interested in both microeconomic and macroeconomic questions. Adam Smith's 1776 book *The Wealth of Nations* emphasized economic growth and development, a macro issue. Ricardo was concerned with growth through international trade, among other issues.

Economists and the Business Cycle.

Some economists of the classical period, including Karl Marx and Thomas R. Malthus, focused on fluctuations in output, employment, and prices. They observed a regular pattern in these economic fluctuations. Periods of falling output, employment, and prices alternated with periods of expanding output and employment and rising prices. This pattern of fluctuations was called the **business cycle.** Figure 12-1 sketches a typical business cycle. The period of declining output, employment, and prices is called a *recession* (or if severe enough, a *depression*). The part of the cycle with rising output, employment, and prices is called the *expansion phase.*

Every ten years or so, journalists and even economists proclaim that the business cycle is dead. The recessions of 1980–1982 and 1990–1991, however, suggest that the business cycle is alive and well. Many economists make a comfortable living forecasting and analyzing business cycles by looking at trends in leading indicators. **Leading indicators** are certain economic variables that turn up before the business cycle turns up and turn down before the business cycle turns down. Leading indicators include building permits, factory orders, the money supply, and other factors. Because they move ahead of the output and employment cycle, they can be used to predict that cycle. Watch for changes

Business cycle   Regular, cyclical fluctuations in output, employment, and prices, consisting of a recession phase and an expansion phase.

Leading indicators   Economic variables, such as building permits and factory orders, that turn up before the business cycle turns up and turn down before the business cycle turns down; can be used to predict business cycles.

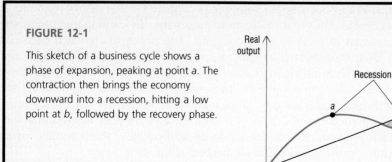

FIGURE 12-1

This sketch of a business cycle shows a phase of expansion, peaking at point *a*. The contraction then brings the economy downward into a recession, hitting a low point at *b*, followed by the recovery phase.

in the index of leading indicators at the beginning of each month to see the direction in which the economy is moving.

The Short Run or the Long Run?   Malthus, Marx, and other early economists were very interested in explaining why such fluctuations occurred and why an economy did not simply grow at a steady rate. Many other economists during the nineteenth and early twentieth centuries, however, believed that in properly functioning markets, output would always tend toward the level at which the labor market had full employment. They regarded the ups and downs of the business cycle as short run or temporary problems, just as in microeconomics a temporary shortage or surplus in the market for wheat might persist until the prices have had time to adjust and clear the market. These economists paid relatively little attention to the determinants of the level of output and employment, because they believed that in the long run the economy would tend toward the level of output associated with full employment of resources. Just as shortages and surpluses are self-correcting in individual markets, so would they correct themselves in aggregate markets.

The best-known economists of the eighteenth and nineteenth centuries include both those interested in business cycles and those who paid little attention to fluctuations because they believed the economy would return to the full employment level without government action. Among the most famous early economists were

- *Adam Smith,* who wrote *The Wealth of Nations* in 1776, advocated minimal government involvement in the economy, and stressed that the prosperity of a nation lay in the quantity and quality of its productive resources. Smith was a professor of moral philosophy at the University of Edinburgh.

In Practice 12-1

·····································

Dating the 1990–1991 Recession

A recession is a period of declining output and high unemployment. The beginning and the end of a recession are declared by the National Bureau of Economic Research (NBER), based on what is happening to real GDP as well as to employment, retail sales, industrial production, and other measures of economic activity. In December 1992, NBER officially declared an end to the recession that began in July 1990. It put the end of the recession in March 1991, making that period only nine months long. Encouraging signs finally began to appear in late 1992, with a modest drop in unemployment and strong retail sales, but these events occurred a year and a half after the recession ended. If the recession was so short, why did it take so long for economists, politicians, and the general public to conclude that it ended?

Two important factors made it difficult to declare this recession over. One was the very slow and weak growth of real output at the end of the recession. In the last nine months of 1991, economic growth averaged an annual rate of only 1.1 percent, very slow for a recovery. In the previous 1980–82 recession, the economy dropped sharply in 1980, recovered, and then returned to recession. The weak recovery in 1991 and 1992 made economists at NBER fearful that the economy would return to recession before a recovery actually began.

The second factor was persistent high unemployment. Normally unemployment rises during a recession and begins to fall after a recovery is under way. As the economy begins to recover, firms expand output by making better use of the workers they have kept on during the recession. They are reluctant to incur the costs of hiring and training new workers until they are sure the increased demand will last. Usually, however, about six months into the recovery, employment begins to rise and unemployment falls.

During the recovery that began in April 1991, unemployment remained high; in fact, it even rose a little, from 6.7 percent in March (the last month of the recession) to 7.1 percent in December 1991. Unemployment remained stubbornly over 7 percent throughout 1992. When the economy was relatively prosperous in 1988 and 1989, unemployment was in the range of 5.3 to 5.5 percent. The combination of slow growth and high unemployment made it very difficult to determine that the recession was indeed over.

A number of factors contributed to the weak recovery. One was the financial condition of many firms, which borrowed heavily in the 1980s to finance buyouts and expansions and were now keeping payrolls lean to improve their financial positions. Another was the shift from industrial jobs to service jobs, which has increased structural unemployment. A third factor was a reduction in defense spending, including fewer orders for military hardware and shutdowns of military bases, which created regional unemployment, especially in California and Connecticut. The average rate of more than 7 percent obscures the fact that there were pockets of prosperity with unemployment rates under 5 percent, offset by double-digit unemployment in defense-dependent California. Finally, the very weak recovery made many firms reluctant to commit to hiring until they were certain the new orders and sales would last.

Workers and the media, forgetting that the unemployment rate was only 5.4 percent at the beginning of the recession, were convinced that high unemployment was permanent. As economic growth picks up, the number of new workers remains low, government spending shifts to other areas, and workers retrain and relocate, unemployment should fall. Lower interest rates over the past few years have enabled many firms to gradually reduce their debt burdens, and they should be able to hire more workers. Based on past experience, the unemployment rate should follow the economic growth indicator as the economy climbs out of a short recession and a slow recovery, so that the public—not just economists—are convinced the recession is indeed over. ∎

- *Jean Baptiste Say,* who identified the connection between aggregate supply and demand in Say's law, "Supply creates its own demand" (discussed next).
- *Alfred Marshall,* whose 1890 *Principles of Economics* was the standard text for a generation of students. Marshall developed new insights into the role of money and also made many contributions to microeconomics.

Say's Law.   Jean Baptiste Say offered the most concise explanation of why the economy would always tend toward the level of output associated with full employment of labor and other resources. **Say's law** states that in the process of producing output, the economy also creates enough income for consumers to purchase that output; simply put, supply creates its own demand. This law should remind you of the circular flow diagrams in Chapters 3 and 11. In the language of the last chapter, "supply" is gross domestic product and "demand" is national income. The logic of Say's law is linked to the circular flow diagram, in which the income earned from selling productive resources in the resource market is used to purchase goods and services in the product market.

Say's law The argument that persistent unemployment should not occur because the process of producing output always creates enough income to purchase that output ("supply creates its own demand").

Say's law directed the attention of other early economists to supply rather than demand, because it implied that if the supply were there, enough purchasing power would be created to buy it. If economists assume there will always be enough demand to buy what is produced, the important economic questions center around the resources and technology that determine how much can be produced. Say's law encouraged economists to focus on the quantity and quality of labor, capital, and land and the ways the economy uses those resources. At the same time, Say's law seemed to imply that the problems of declining output and unemployment are temporary and self-correcting. A macroeconomist who believes in the validity of Say's law would be less likely to address such problems.

Keynes and the Study of Recessions.   John Maynard Keynes turned the classical view upside down, shifting economists' attention from supply to demand. A British economist, Keynes published his major macroeconomic work, *The General Theory of Employment, Interest and Money,* in 1936, in the midst of the Great Depression.

Keynes stood the classical view on its head simply by starting from the observation that it is possible for unemployment and low levels of output to occur and to persist. The pre–Keynesian view recognized that unemployment occurs, but did not expect unemployment to last very long. That view, however, did not square with the experience of the 1930s.

To explain persistent low levels of output and employment, Keynes stressed the role of demand. When idle resources exist (as they did in the 1930s), producers can be counted on to expand output only if they know it can be sold, that is, if there is adequate demand. In his model, aggregate supply played a passive role.

This debate may sound strange after what you have already learned about supply and demand in individual markets. You saw that in those markets, both supply and demand play an active role in determining equilibrium quantities and prices. It seems that both supply and demand should also play an active role in aggregate economic activity. In fact, most economists have adopted that view in the last few decades, after shifting emphasis from the role of aggregate supply to aggregate demand and back to aggregate supply.

These controversies over the relative importance of aggregate supply and aggregate demand are not merely intellectual debates. Different viewpoints about how the macroeconomy works lead to different policy recommendations. For example, one school of thought might recommend a tax cut to stimulate output and employment, whereas another would argue that the tax cut will be ineffective in stimulating the economy. After exploring the workings of aggregate supply and demand, you will better understand why different economists make different policy recommendations.

Macroeconomic Measures and Policy Tools

The measures of national income, gross domestic product, and the price level developed in Chapter 11 provide numerical values for two very important economic variables used in this and later chapters. One variable is real income or output, written as Y. Real income is the value of output adjusted for changes in the price level. The other variable is the price level, written as P. This quantity is measured in the form of an index such as the consumer price index or the GDP deflator. If P stands for the price index and Y for real GDP, then

$$GDP = P \times Y,$$

which says that nominal GDP equals the price level times real output. Another way to write this relationship is

$$\text{Real Output} = \frac{\text{Nominal Output}}{\text{Price Index}}$$

or

$$Y = \frac{GDP}{P}.$$

This way of writing the relationship shows that the value of real output is found by dividing nominal output by a price index.

Target variables

Measures of performance on macroeconomic goals, such as real output (measuring growth), the price index (measuring inflation or deflation), and the unemployment rate.

P and Y, along with the level of employment *(N)*, are **target variables.** That is, the numerical values and changes in the values of these variables measure progress toward the goals of economic growth (an increase in Y), a low inflation rate (i.e., a slow rate of change in P), and full employment (a low unemployment rate). The model in this chapter explains what determines the price and output levels and what makes them change, that is, what causes inflation, deflation, and growth in real output.

Policy variables Macroeconomic quantities that
measure the values of policy instruments used to
influence target variables,
such as the money supply
(M_s), government spending (G), and taxes (T).

Later chapters will introduce some other important macroeconomic variables
called **policy variables,** or *policy tools.* The most important policy variables are
taxes *(T),* government purchases *(G),* and the supply of money *(M_s).* Government purchases already appeared in Chapter 11 as a component of gross domestic
product, while taxes were a leakage out of the circular flow. Although the money
supply *(M_s),* will not formally appear until Chapter 16, it is also a policy variable.
The size of the money supply is controlled by the U.S. central bank, called the
Federal Reserve System, which is a somewhat independent arm of the federal
government. Governments attempt to use these policy variables to guide the
economy toward a more desirable level of output and prices.

AGGREGATE DEMAND

The starting point for aggregate demand is the GDP calculations from Chapter
11. Recall that economists compute GDP by adding the purchases of consumers
(C), business firms (gross investment, or *I),* government *(G),* and the rest of
the world (net exports, or *X − M).* In symbols,

$$GDP = C + I + TG (X - M).$$

Aggregate demand
The sum total of the real
quantities of output that
economic agents (house-
holds, business firms, and
governments) wish to pur-
chase at various alternative
price levels.

GDP gives a measure of one quantity and one price level that was actually
purchased; thus, it represents one price-quantity combination on the aggregate
demand curve. To go from a point to a curve, we need to have a series of real
quantities that would be purchased at various price levels. **Aggregate demand**
consists of various combinations of *P* and *Y* that represent the real quantities of
output that households, business firms, and governments wish to purchase at
various alternative price levels.

Like a demand curve for a particular good, an aggregate demand curve should
reflect not what people have spent in the past but what people *want to, intend
to, or plan to spend* on consumption, investment, government purchases, and
exports and imports. In Chapter 14, we will look more closely at the factors
that influence consumption and investment spending. Aggregate demand is the
sum of planned spending for not only consumption *(C),* and investment *(I)*
but also for government purchases *(G)* and net exports *(X − M)* at various
possible price levels.

Aggregate Demand and Individual Demand Curves

Like individual demand curves, the aggregate demand curve slopes downward
from left to right; that is, buyers will demand less total real output at higher
price levels and more total real output at lower price levels. Figure 12-2 shows
a demand curve for pizza in panel a and an aggregate demand curve for total
real output in panel b. The two curves look remarkably similar.

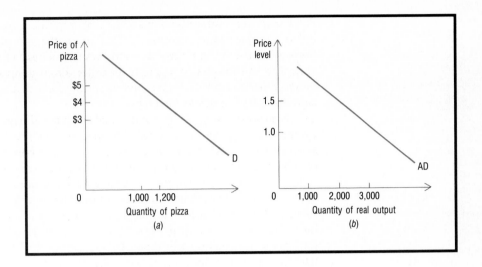

FIGURE 12-2

(a) On this demand curve for pizza, each point represents a price-quantity combination that buyers would choose.
(b) This aggregate demand curve shows the various price level–total output combinations that buyers (households, business firms, government, and consumers abroad) would choose.

A quantity of 1,000 pizzas at $5 per pizza and of 1,200 at $4 are two of the many points on the demand curve for pizza. A quantity of 2,000 units of real output at a price level of 1.50 and a quantity of 3,000 units at a price level of 1.00 are two of several points on the aggregate demand curve.

Gross domestic product (GDP) represents the combination of a particular price level and real output, or $P \times Y$. A price level of 1.0 would correspond to a price index of 100, while a price level of 1.5 would correspond to a price index of 150. Each point on the aggregate demand curve corresponds to a particular level of GDP, just as the quantity and price of pizzas sold in Denver in May represent one point on the demand curve for pizzas in that time and place. However, neither one GDP number nor one data point for pizza sales tells much about the rest of the demand curve on which that point lies.

The demand curve for pizza shows the relationship between the quantity of pizza and the price, because price is the most important single influence on quantity demanded. A change in anything else that may influence the price of pizza—the price of hamburgers, population, consumers' incomes, or tastes—can shift the demand curve. Similarly, the aggregate demand curve shows the relationship between total real quantity demanded and the price level as the most important single relationship. Other factors that affect real aggregate demand are incorporated into the model as factors that shift the curve when they change.

These two kinds of demand curves, however, are not as similar as they look. The reasons why particular demand curves slope downward help little in explaining why the aggregate demand curve slopes downward from left to right.

Pizza may have diminishing marginal utility, and movie tickets and loaves of bread definitely have substitutes. Neither of these explanations works for a downward-sloping aggregate demand curve, which is a demand curve for goods in general. Although people may experience diminishing satisfaction with more of one particular good, there is no reason to expect that satisfaction falls as they consume more goods in general.

The explanations for shifts in individual product demand curves are also of little use in explaining shifts in aggregate demand curves. The demand for a particular good or service will shift when a change occurs in consumers' incomes, prices of related goods, expectations, or other factors. Some of the influences that shift aggregate demand, such as expectations and population, are the same as those for individual demand curves. Other factors that influence demand for shoes and pizza, however, are no longer important when looking at demand for goods and services in general. Prices of substitute and complement goods, for instance, will shift individual demand curves, but they are very unimportant for aggregate demand. If the price of socks rises, the quantity of shoes demanded will fall. But a rise in the price of socks will have little effect on the demand for most of the other goods in Y and therefore on total or aggregate demand. At the same time, variables that matter very little in demand for pizza or shoes, such as the interest rate or the money supply, can have a significant effect on aggregate demand.

Why Aggregate Demand Slopes Downward from Left to Right

Despite these differences, the aggregate demand curve in Figure 12-2, like demand curves for individual products, still slopes downward from left to right. Why? One explanation relies on the effects of price level changes on the value of household assets. If the price level rises, the real value of a household's financial assets (bonds, savings accounts, certificates of deposit, even cash) will fall; that is, those assets will purchase less in the way of real goods and services. With the real value of their assets falling, practical economists feel poorer; thus, they spend less. Of course, debtors feel better off, because the burden of their debts is falling. However, households as a group own more financial assets than they owe to others. Thus, the net effect of general price rise is to lower real asset values and reduce consumer spending. The biggest debtor is the government, whose spending is relatively insensitive to price level changes. As a result, a higher price level will reduce consumption but have little impact on government purchases.

On the other hand, if the price level falls, the real value of household assets increases. Consumers feel wealthier, and (other things equal) they spend more. Thus, the effects of prices on consumption through changes in the value of consumer assets can explain why consumption spending (an important part of aggregate demand) falls when the price level rises and rises when the price level falls.

A second link between prices and real output demanded is through exports and imports. International trade is an exception to the "no substitutes" rule for the aggregate demand curve. Substituting one domestically produced good for another does not change the aggregate demand curve. Purchasing foreign goods instead of domestic goods changes the demand for output along the aggregate demand curve, because the quantity measured on the horizontal axis for the aggregate demand curve is *domestic* output. When U.S. prices rise, consumers abroad want to buy fewer (relatively more expensive) U.S. exports, whereas Americans want to substitute relatively cheaper foreign goods for higher-priced U.S. products. That may not sound very patriotic, but practical economists, who are concerned with getting the most out of their limited resources, respond to these price incentives. The loss of export sales and substitution of foreign for domestic goods means less real (U.S.) output is demanded at higher price levels.

The third link between prices and real output is through interest rates, which we will explore more thoroughly in Chapter 16. When the price level increases, interest rates rise. Higher interest rates mean both consumers and business firms will borrow less to purchase consumer durables and investment goods. Thus, at higher price levels both investment demand *(I)* and consumer demand *(C)* for real output will decrease.

The precise slope of the aggregate demand curve depends on how sensitive the various components of aggregate demand are to changes in the price level. Most economists draw a fairly steep aggregate demand curve, suggesting that consumption, investment, government purchases, and net exports are not very sensitive to price levels. Recall that the availability of substitute goods is the most important factor in making individual demand curves flat, or elastic. Since substitutes play a much smaller role in aggregate demand, it is easy to understand why this curve would have a fairly steep slope.

Shifts in Aggregate Demand

Some causes of shifts in aggregate demand are the same as those for individual demand curves, whereas others are not. Prices of substitutes and complements drop out when considering demand for aggregate output. However, some familiar demand shifters remain and some new ones appear. Shifts in the aggregate demand curve result from changes in economic conditions in the business and household sectors. Aggregate demand can also be shifted by the government's policy tools, such as the money supply, taxes, and government spending.

Households and business firms may experience large total changes in their expectations or their wealth, or the size or age distribution of the population may change enough that the effect is felt on the demand for total output at all possible price levels. When practical economists have positive expectations about future income levels, they will increase their current spending, shifting aggregate demand to the right. An increase in aggregate household or business wealth (financial assets such as bonds, stocks, or savings accounts, or real assets like houses, cars, and factories) will have the same effect. A decline in wealth or negative expectations will shift aggregate demand to the left. A larger or younger population will spend more at every price level than will a smaller or older population, shifting aggregate demand upwards.

In the early 1990s, as interest rates fell, interest rates and spending received a great deal of attention. Lower interest rates enabled many practical economists to reduce their debt, or at least their monthly payments, as they refinanced loans at lower interest rates. Many business firms that had taken on large debt burdens during the 1980s did the same. Other households that depended on interest income saw their monthly receipts fall and had to cut spending. Overall, however, the effect of lower interest rates was to stimulate spending by business firms on investment and by households on housing, cars, and consumer durables.

The aggregate demand curve may also shift in response to certain actions of government, specifically changes in the money supply, taxes, or government spending. A larger money supply, more government spending, or lower taxes will shift aggregate demand to the right. Less government spending, increased taxes, or a fall in the money supply will shift aggregate demand to the left.

CHECKLIST : **Shifts in Aggregate Demand**

The aggregate demand curve will shift in response to changes in

The household or business sector:
   Expectations
   Wealth
   Interest rates
   Population (size and age distribution)

Government policy:
   Money supply
   Taxes
   Government purchases

In sum, aggregate demand can shift due to either changes in the behavior of households and/or business firms or deliberate policy changes in taxes, government spending, or the money supply. A change in the price level does *not* shift the aggregate demand curve. Rather, as you should recall from your study of individual supply and demand curves, a change in the price level results in a movement along the aggregate demand curve.

Aggregate supply The sum total of real quantities of output that producers are willing and able to sell at various alternative price levels.

AGGREGATE SUPPLY

Aggregate supply consists of the various quantities of total real output that producers are willing and able to supply at various price levels. Like individual supply curves, the aggregate supply curve may be horizontal, vertical, or upward sloping, but is never negatively sloped. Also like individual supply curves, the aggregate supply curve isolates the relationship between quantity (real output) and price (the price level), holding other factors constant. When one of the other factors that influence aggregate supply changes, the aggregate supply curve shifts.

The Slope of the Aggregate Supply Curve

Although most economists agree on the negative slope of the aggregate demand curve, they disagree somewhat about the slope of the aggregate supply curve. The aggregate supply curve has three possible slopes: upward sloping, vertical, and horizontal. A fourth possibility is a curve with horizontal, upward-sloping, and vertical segments. All but the last of these shapes should be familiar to you from the description of individual supply curves in Chapter 6. The first three shapes correspond to upward-sloping, perfectly elastic (horizontal), and perfectly inelastic (vertical) supply curves for individual markets.

An Upward-Sloping Aggregate Supply Curve. Panel a of Figure 12-3 shows a rather ordinary-looking supply curve that slopes upward from left to right. This aggregate supply curve implies that higher prices result in more output, or perhaps that increases in output lead to a higher price level. It is not clear whether changes in total output cause price level changes or price level changes lead to changes in total output.

Each of these two directions of cause and effect offers a possible reason for the upward-sloping aggregate supply curve. According to the "price causes output" approach, as prices rise, more sellers are attracted into the market to take advantage of the rising prices (and profits in most cases). Rising prices thus call forth additional output.

The opposite view—"output causes prices"—stresses rising opportunity cost. To compete successfully for resources, producers will have to offer higher wages to labor or higher prices for more raw materials and intermediate goods. Producers will be willing to pay more for inputs only if they can charge a higher price for their output. Thus, increasing total output drives up the price level.

Both these views would appear to explain the reason for upward-sloping individual supply curves. There are important differences, however, between individual and aggregate supply curves. Whereas a market supply curve for wheat may be the sum of the individual firms' wheat supply curves, the aggregate supply of all goods and services is not simply the sum of all the individual supply curves in the economy.

How does aggregate supply differ from individual supply curves? Consider the first explanation, leading from higher prices to higher output. If the price of a particular product such as wheat rises, more wheat is produced, but at the expense of less output of corn, soybeans, or other products. Market forces will transfer productive resources from those products to wheat. Thus, a rise in the amount of wheat produced implies a fall in the output of other products whose prices have not risen. On an aggregate supply curve, this increased wheat output more or less offsets the fall in the output of corn or soybeans, and total real output *(Y)* remains about the same. Thus, saying that a higher price level will result in more aggregate output is very different from saying that a rise in the price of wheat will result in more wheat production. It is possible to produce more output of *all* goods and services only if additional resources can be called forth, particularly more labor.

Where do the extra resources come from? For a particular product, resources are bid away from producing other goods. That explanation does not work for the aggregate supply curve, however. Rather than just a shift from one product to another, more total resources are needed to produce more total output. The additional resources may be unemployed labor, land, and capital that are put to work when it becomes profitable for some firms to expand output. Consider unemployed labor. Eventually, as all unemployed workers seeking work at the going rate are absorbed, firms will need to offer higher wages to attract more workers into the labor market to increase total output further. Firms are willing to pay higher wages only if they can get higher prices for their output.

Recall from Chapter 9 that the labor supply (or the supply of any other productive resource) is not some magic number, such as 100 million workers. The supply of labor depends on the wage to some extent. Individuals who are not willing to work at $5 an hour may be willing to work at $7 an hour, because they will earn enough to give up their next best alternative, say, housework, leisure, or going to school. Other workers may be willing to put in extra hours at a higher wage. A higher wage will attract more workers into the labor market, or get current workers to put in more hours, and make a larger output possible. This positive link among prices, wages, and resource availability results in an upward slope for both individual and aggregate supply curves. For individual supply curves, a higher price for the product makes it possible to bid resources away from other uses by paying more for them. For aggregate supply, higher returns call forth more worker-hours or other inputs, resulting in more total output at higher prices.

Another explanation for the upward slope of the aggregate supply curve lies in bottlenecks and market imperfections. This explanation also applies to some individual markets, but it is much more important in the aggregate. As output expands, producers encounter shortages of particular resources, such as electricians, pilots, aluminum, or machine tools. Competition for those scarce resources drives up their prices. Higher resource prices are reflected in higher prices for output. This competition gets more intense and spreads to other kinds of resource inputs as the economy gets closer and closer to the full employment level of output. In this view, the aggregate supply curve is not a straight line but a curve that becomes steeper as output increases, as in panel b of Figure 12-3.

A Vertical Aggregate Supply Curve. This sequence of events from higher prices to higher wages to more workers available sounds reasonable. However,

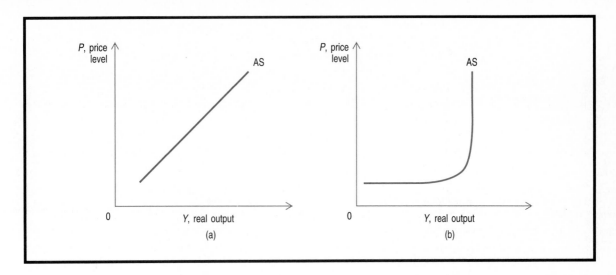

FIGURE 12-3

(a) The aggregate supply curve in this panel looks like most supply curves, sloping upward from left to right. Higher levels of total real output are associated with higher price levels.

(b) The aggregate supply curve in this panel also slopes upward, but is very flat at low levels of output, rising as firms experience shortages of resources, and finally becoming vertical as the economy reaches capacity or full employment.

Real wage The nominal or money wage divided by a price index; a measure of the purchasing power of wages.

a worker who fits the description of the practical economist should decide whether and how much to work based on the real wage rather than the money wage. The **real wage** measures the amount of goods and services a particular money wage will buy. The real wage corrects the money wage *(w)* for changes in the price level, *P;* real wage is *w/P.* For example, if your hourly (money) wage remained $10 while the price level doubled from 1.00 to 2.00, your real wage would fall from $10 to $5.

The real wage is the value of goods and services one can purchase in exchange for a unit of labor time and is the opportunity cost of working instead of doing something else. If money wages and the price level rise together, the real wage or opportunity cost of working does not change. No more labor should be supplied unless the money wage rises by more than the increase in the price level. Workers who are practical economists are not fooled by a change in money wages unless it represents a change in real wages.

Economists who believe that workers as practical economists respond only to changes in the real wage in deciding to work or to work more hours would expect the aggregate supply curve to be vertical rather than upward sloping. Rising money wages and rising prices of goods would simply offset each other, leaving real output unchanged. This view of the aggregate supply curve is shown in panel a of Figure 12-4.

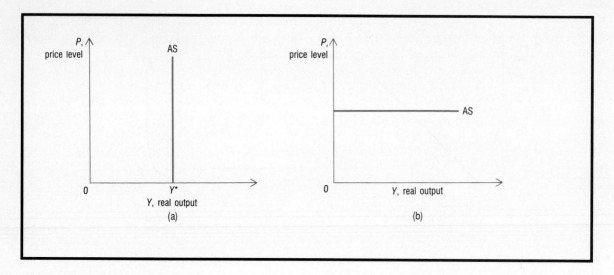

FIGURE 12-4

(a) Along this aggregate supply curve, the level of output is the same (Y*) regardless of the price level.

(b) Along this aggregate supply curve, the level of prices is the same (P_0) regardless of the level of real output.

Many economists believe both these aggregate supply curves are relevant but that the upward-sloping supply curve in Figure 12-3 describes the economy only in the short run. Recall that the short run is the period in which some factors are fixed or some contracts cannot be easily changed. The short run may also mean the time horizon during which workers, producers, and households have been unable to acquire and process all the relevant information they need to make good decisions as practical economists. In macroeconomics, the short run also plays an important role. In macro, the short run is the period in which markets may fail to function efficiently, both because imperfect information exists and because contracts may create obstacles to rapid change.

Many economists argue that in the short run, wages will rise more slowly than prices. The reason is that workers are slow to realize that higher prices mean the purchasing power of their wages has fallen, even though their money wage is unchanged. In addition, even if workers are aware of rising prices, they may have to wait until the next raise period, or the next scheduled contract negotiation, to get a wage adjustment. In the long run, however, wages will catch up with prices as workers process information and have an opportunity to negotiate a new contract. The long-run aggregate supply curve will look like the vertical aggregate supply curve in panel a of Figure 12-4.

A Horizontal Aggregate Supply Curve.   Still another possible slope for the aggregate supply curve is horizontal, as in panel b of Figure 12-4. If there is an ample supply of idle resources, the opportunity cost of additional output is zero. The economy is operating inside the production possibilities curve of Chapter 2. Under these circumstances, it is possible to attract more workers at the going wage, acquire more capital with no increase in the interest rate, or purchase raw materials and other inputs without driving up their prices or the general price level. Real output could increase with no rise in the price level, making the aggregate supply curve horizontal, at least in the short run. This is most likely to occur only when the economy is in a recession. The horizontal segment in panel b of Figure 12-3 comes from the same reasoning: Because there are idle resources at low levels of output, it is possible to expand production without driving up the price level. Aggregate supply can be horizontal for some time periods under depressed economic conditions, but few economists would argue that aggregate supply is ever horizontal in the long run.

In fact, much of the apparent conflict between classical economists (a vertical supply curve) and Keynesian economists (a horizontal or upward-sloping curve) disappears when one realizes that classical economists focused on the long run, whereas Keynesians were more concerned with the short run. Where they disagree is on just how long the short run is. In later chapters, we will largely compromise between these two views by using an upward-sloping supply curve.

CHECKLIST : ## Shapes of the Aggregate Supply Curve

Aggregate supply is more likely to be

Horizontal:
   In the very short run
   During periods of substantial unemployment

Upward sloping:
   In the short run
   As the economy approaches full employment and encounters bottlenecks
   When information is gathered and processed slowly
   When markets do not function smoothly

Vertical:
   In the long run
   At full employment
   When information is readily available and spreads quickly
   When markets adapt rapidly

Shifts in Aggregate Supply

In looking at the relationship between the price level and total real output, other factors are held constant. When these other factors change, the aggregate supply curve shifts. Some of these supply shifters are similar to the influences that shift individual supply curves, especially changes in the cost and availability of resource inputs, technology, and expectations. Policy variables, particularly tax policy, can sometimes influence both individual and aggregate supply curves. Other factors important in shifting individual supply curves, such as the prices of other products that can be produced with the same resources, do not affect aggregate supply.

A rise in the price of an individual product, such as wheat, relative to the price of another product, like corn, may mean that more wheat and less corn is produced. Total real output, however, is affected little, if at all, by the change in the output mix. Relative prices are very important for individual supply curves, but not for the aggregate supply curve.

A technological improvement specific to only one product will also have relatively little effect on total output supplied. Only major technological changes affecting a broad range of goods or services, such as computer-assisted production, would result in an outward shift in the aggregate supply curve.

An increase in the amount of labor or its productivity or an increase in the supply of capital, land, or raw materials will shift the aggregate supply curve to the right. Expectations of improved future economic conditions should result in more output, whereas negative expectations will shift aggregate supply to the left.

Lower tax rates will increase the net earnings of firms and individuals and should stimulate practical economists to supply more output (an issue we explore further in the next chapter). Broad-based incentives to invest (such as the investment tax credit or special tax treatment of investment income) should shift aggregate supply to the right, because they will result in an increase in the capital stock. Removal of such incentives will shift aggregate supply to the left.

Debate over the best ways to shift aggregate supply to the right played an important role in the 1992 presidential election. One candidate argued for reducing the federal budget deficit and reforming taxes. Another offered tax cuts to stimulate private investment. A third stressed public investment in infrastructure (such as roads and bridges), research and development, and worker training. In the next chapter, we will look more closely at policies intended to shift aggregate supply.

CHECKLIST : ## Factors that Can Shift the Aggregate Supply Curve

Shifts originating in households or business firms:
    Changes in resource quantity or quality—labor, capital, land, raw materials
    Changes in technology (broad-based)
    Changes in expectations

Shifts originating in public policy (government):
    Changes in tax rates
    Changes in regulations, subsidies, other incentives

PUTTING AGGREGATE SUPPLY AND AGGREGATE DEMAND TOGETHER

Figure 12-5 combines an aggregate demand curve with an upward-sloping aggregate supply curve to determine an equilibrium level of total real output, Y_0, and an equilibrium price level, P_0. The matching of what producers are willing to supply and what purchasers are willing to buy at various price levels determines the equilibrium level of prices and total real output.

The figure shows how the values of two macroeconomic target variables, real output and prices, are determined. The third target variable, employment, does not appear in the diagram. However, you know that employment and real output are very closely related. An increase in real output means a demand for more workers and, for any given size of the labor force, a fall in the unemployment rate. A decrease in real output, other things equal, will drive the unemployment rate up.

Shift in Aggregate Demand

Suppose an increase in population shifts aggregate demand to the right, from AD_0 to AD_1 in Figure 12-6, resulting in a higher price level (P_1) and a higher output level (Y_1). This shift in aggregate demand should also result in higher employment if no change occurs in the labor force. The rise in aggregate demand has increased output and reduced unemployment, but at the expense of some increase in the price level.

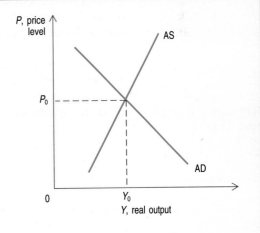

FIGURE 12-5

Putting aggregate supply and aggregate demand together determines an equilibrium level of real output (Y_0) and an equilibrium price level (P_0).

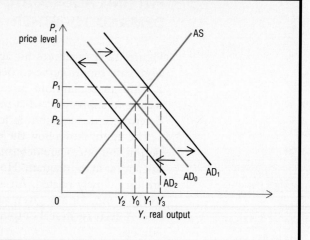

FIGURE 12-6

A rightward shift (increase) in aggregate demand will drive up both real output and the price level if the aggregate supply curve slopes upward, as it does in this diagram. A leftward shift will drive down both real output and the price level.

Now suppose aggregate demand shifts to the left to AD_2. This shift might result from a fall in exports, consumers cutbacks on purchases while they pay off their debts, or a reduction in the money supply. The leftward shift in aggregate demand leads to a lower price level (P_2) but also to lower real output (Y_2). Employment falls and unemployment rises.

Shifts in Aggregate Supply

Figure 12-7 shows a shift in the aggregate supply curve while holding aggregate demand constant. The initial equilibrium is represented by the curves AD_0 and AS_0, with real output as Y_0 and the price level at P_0. Suppose aggregate supply shifts to the left (AS_1) due to declining productivity or shortages of raw materials. Such a shift represents the dilemma of the late 1970s. The price level rises (to P_1), while output falls (to Y_1). As output (Y) decreases, employment falls and unemployment rises. A rising price level with falling real output and rising unemployment is a condition known as **stagflation.** *Stagflation* was coined from the two words *stagnation* (slow economic growth accompanied by high rates of unemployment) and *inflation* (a rising price level). This term became popular in the mid-1970s, when the U.S. economy experienced rising unemployment and a rising price level at the same time.

This unfavorable shift in aggregate supply in the 1970s has been variously blamed on the rising price of oil and other energy sources, a decline in labor productivity due to insufficient capital investment and/or less experienced work force, and other factors. Regardless of the cause, it is clear that a shift in aggregate supply can account for the economic events of the late 1970s. A leftward shift

Stagflation A combination of rising unemployment, slow economic growth, and inflation.

FIGURE 12-7

A rightward shift (increase) in aggregate supply will increase real output and reduce the price level. A leftward shift (decrease) in aggregate supply will decrease real output and raise the price level.

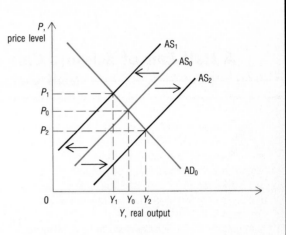

in aggregate supply can result in a higher price level and lower levels of output and employment.

When aggregate supply shifts to the right, however (AS_2 in Figure 12-7), the result is the best of all possible worlds. The price level falls, while output and employment rise. This rosy possibility led many economists and policymakers to turn their attention in the last 15 years to finding ways to shift the aggregate supply curve to the right. We will look more closely at policies for shifting aggregate supply in Chapter 13.

Moving from One Equilibrium to Another

When aggregate demand shifted from AD_0 to AD_1 in Figure 12-6, the economy did not instantaneously move from price level P_0 and output level Y_0 to P_1 and Y_1. The immediate effect of the shift in aggregate demand was to create a shortage in the amount $Y_0 - Y_3$ at the old price level, P_0. As consumers bought more goods, inventories fell. Producers found that they could not keep up with demand without increasing the level of output. However, as the practical economists in these firms responded to this sales opportunity, they began to run into bottlenecks—shortages of materials, overtime pay, costs of hiring new workers, or more frequent breakdowns of machinery. These higher costs would be reflected in higher prices for goods, moving upward along the aggregate supply curve. As the price level begins to rise, some would-be buyers drop out of the market, moving upward along the new aggregate demand curve. This process continues until the economy reaches the new, market-clearing price level P_1, at which buyers and sellers agree on a quantity of real output of Y_1.

Myth 12-1

A Half-Pair of Scissors Can Still Cut

Alfred Marshall, a nineteenth-century British economist who is credited with developing supply and demand curves, compared this famous economic model to a pair of scissors. It takes two blades for a pair of scissors to cut. Yet economists and noneconomists alike tend to forget this simple truth and keep having to relearn it.

Aggregate supply and demand offer a good example of this forgetfulness. For long periods, economists will focus on aggregate demand and ignore aggregate supply. Then the other half of Marshall's famous scissors, supply, takes the spotlight and the role of aggregate demand is cast aside.

Aggregate demand was "discovered" (or rediscovered) during the Great Depression. The Keynesian model of Chapter 14 ignores aggregate supply by assuming the curve is horizontal so that demand alone determines the level of output. Classical economists before Keynes (and some monetarists afterward) took the opposite tack: Their aggregate supply curve was vertical. In this case, shifts in aggregate demand have no effect on real output.

In the last 20 years, economic attention returned to aggregate supply, especially in looking for policy tools to shift it to the right. Economists who focused on aggregate supply tended to assume there would be enough aggregate demand to buy whatever the economy produced.

When first learning economics, it is convenient to look at supply and demand separately, but it is dangerous to attempt to dissect economic problems with only half a pair of scissors. Both supply and demand, at both the microeconomic and macroeconomic levels, contribute to determining prices and quantities in an important way. ∎

Price Level Changes and Real Output Changes

When aggregate supply shifts, how much will the shift affect the price level and how much will it affect real output and employment? The answer depends on the steepness of aggregate demand. If aggregate demand is very steep, most of the effect of an aggregate supply shift will be felt in prices, because it takes so much inflation to choke off much real demand or such a big drop in the price level to stimulate spending. On the other hand, if aggregate demand is rather flat (total demand is very sensitive to the price level), most of the effect of a shift in aggregate supply will show up as changes in real output and very little change in the price level. Panel a of Figure 12-8 illustrates these two possibilities.

Likewise, the relative effects of a shift in aggregate demand on output and prices depends on how steep the aggregate supply curve is. A shift in aggregate demand that occurs with a fairly steep aggregate supply curve, such as AS_1 in panel b of Figure 12-8, has more effect on prices than on real output. A rather flat aggregate supply curve, such as AS_2 in panel b, means increased aggregate demand will lead to mostly output changes with little effect on the price level. If the long-run aggregate supply curve is vertical, a shift in aggregate demand will change only the price level. Obviously, it is important that policymakers have some idea of how steep aggregate supply is before they try to use policy tools to shift aggregate demand.

LOOKING AHEAD: BEHIND THE AGGREGATE SUPPLY AND DEMAND CURVES

In the next chapter, we take a closer look at the aggregate supply curve. We begin with aggregate supply because it is a major policy focus in the 1990s and

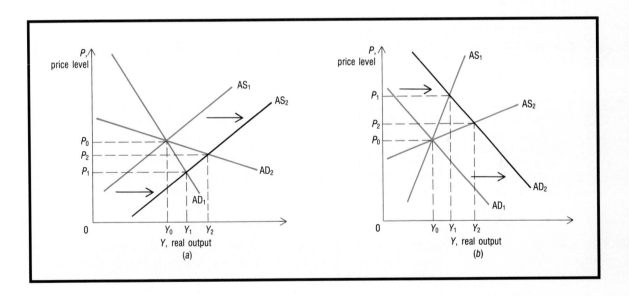

FIGURE 12-8

(a) When the aggregate supply curve shifts, the impact is divided between the price level and the real output level. The relative impact depends on the steepness of the aggregate demand curve. If aggregate demand is steep, most of the effect falls on prices. If aggregate demand is relatively flat, most of the effect falls on real output.
(b) When the aggregate demand curve shifts, the impact is divided between the price level and the real output level. The relative impact depends on the slope of the aggregate supply curve. If aggregate supply is relatively steep, most of the effect of a demand shift is on the price level. If aggregate supply is relatively flat, most of the impact is on real output.

also is less complicated. Following that chapter, we turn to the aggregate demand curve, developing a simple Keynesian model based on the behavior of consumers and business in determining the components of demand. In Chapter 15, we explore ways to influence aggregate demand using the fiscal policy tools of taxes and government spending. Finally, we add money and interest rates and examine their influence on aggregate demand.

Summary

1. Aggregate quantity demanded depends on the price level, expectations, assets, population, interest rates, the money supply, and government spending and taxes. Holding all other factors constant, aggregate demand shows the relationship between real output (Y) and the price level (P).

2. Among the factors that can shift the aggregate demand curve are changes in policy variables—the money supply, government spending, and taxes—as well as such traditional demand shifters as expectations, wealth, and population.

3. Aggregate demand slopes downward from right to left because of the effects of the price level on demand for real output through changes in wealth, imports and exports, and interest rates.

4. Aggregate quantity supplied depends on the price level as well as on technology, the labor force, the capital stock, productivity, and the cost and availability of natural resources. The aggregate supply curve shows the relationship between real output supplied and the price level, holding all the other factors constant. A change in one of the other factors, including resource quality and quantity, expectations, technology, and certain kinds of tax policies, will shift aggregate supply.

5. Aggregate supply curves may be horizontal, vertical, or upward sloping. Many economists believe aggregate supply curves are closer to vertical in slope in the long run and/or as the economy approaches the full employment level of output. Some economists think aggregate supply may be close to horizontal during periods of recession or depression.

6. Aggregate supply and aggregate demand together determine the levels of prices and real output. The level of employment is closely related to the level of real output.

7. The effects of shifts in aggregate demand on real output and prices depend on how steep the aggregate supply curve is. A steeper aggregate supply curve means a greater effect on prices and a lesser effect on real output.

8. If aggregate supply shifts to the left, output falls while prices rise (stagflation); if aggregate supply shifts to the right, more real output occurs at a lower price level.

Key Terms

aggregate demand
aggregate supply
business cycle

leading indicators
policy variables
real wage

Say's law
stagflation
target variables

Questions and Problems

1. Try to infer what combinations of shifts in aggregate supply and demand could be the cause of each of the following outcomes.

   a. Price level rises, real output rises
   b. Price level falls, real output rises
   c. Price level rises, real output falls
   d. Price level falls, real output falls
   e. Price level stays about the same, real output rises
   f. Price level stays about the same, real output falls
   g. Price level falls, real output stays about the same
   h. Price level rises, real output stays about the same

2. Consider the effect of each of the following—that is, decide whether it shifts aggregate demand, aggregate supply, both, or neither and what effect it will have on real output, prices, and employment.

   a. A cut in income taxes
   b. A major crop failure
   c. Doubling spending for the space program
   d. Discovery of new energy sources
   e. A reduction in consumer debt
   f. Depressed business expectations

3. How would your answers to problem 2 differ if the aggregate supply curve had a horizontal or a vertical slope?

4. Would each of the following shift aggregate supply, aggregate demand, or both? In what direction?

   a. Discovery of a new production technique
   b. A stock market crash that reduces consumer wealth
   c. A reduction in taxes on corporations that invest in new capital equipment

5. You are a government policymaker. If you could choose a slope for the aggregate supply and demand curves that would be most helpful to you in pursuing stable prices, economic growth, and full employment through policies that shift aggregate demand to the right, how steep would you want the aggregate supply curve to be? Do you care about the slope of the aggregate demand curve?

6. Suppose an increase in U.S. exports occurs for some reason other than a change in the U.S. price level—for example, a crop failure abroad that

increases demand for U.S. wheat. Does this event shift aggregate demand or aggregate supply? How will it affect output, prices, and employment?

7. The nation of Inland experiences a severe recession. The government increases spending. Output rises, employment rises, but the price level does not change. What does the aggregate supply curve look like?

13

Growth, Employment, and

Aggregate Supply

We will never question whether we want a big pie or a little pie of national wealth to divide, or deviate from our conviction that the big pie is always the easiest to split.

WALTER REUTHER (PRESIDENT, UNITED AUTO WORKERS), 1955

Main Points

1. The aggregate supply curve shifts when changes occur in the labor force (either quantity or quality), the stock of capital, or the amount of natural resources available. Improvements in technology can also shift aggregate supply.

2. Policy tools to shift aggregate supply include various kinds of tax incentives, improvements in infrastructure, subsidies to investment in human capital, and deregulation of selected industries and markets.

3. The slope of the aggregate supply curve is much flatter in the short run than in the long run. The slope of this

curve and the length of the short run determine whether policies to shift the aggregate demand curve have any effect on output, employment, and the price level.

4. When markets work efficiently and expectations adjust rapidly, the short run is very short and the long run aggregate supply curve is vertical.

5. When markets and expectations adjust slowly to changing conditions, the short-run aggregate supply curve is flatter and the short run is a longer time period.

In this chapter, we examine the aggregate supply curve more closely. As a result of economic conditions, the aggregate supply curve has gradually replaced aggregate demand as the central focus for macroeconomic policy over the last 15 years. In the late 1970s, the unfortunate combination of slow growth, high unemployment, and high rates of inflation suggested that the aggregate supply curve had shifted to the left, or at least had shifted to the right much more slowly than had the aggregate demand curve. In the 1980s, falling inflation rates, more acceptable economic growth rates, and a modest decline in unemployment rates suggested that aggregate supply had shifted to the right.

Before the late 1970s, macroeconomics meant the study of aggregate demand. Since that time, shifts in aggregate supply seem to have had a greater impact on output, employment, and the price level. As a result, emphasis on policies to shift aggregate demand has given way to greater concern for the sources of shifts in aggregate supply that create economic growth. The policies that can promote such shifts are the primary focus of this chapter. A secondary focus is the slope of the aggregate supply curve, which determines the impact of demand management policies on the levels of output and prices. ■

MEASURING PERFORMANCE: PRICES, OUTPUT, AND EMPLOYMENT

The "performance test" for the economy considers three important variables that reflect the three major macroeconomic goals. The first variable is the rate of economic growth, which measures the annual percentage increase in real output *(Y)*. The second variable is the price index, which measures changes in the price level. The third is the rate of unemployment. Practical economists use these three measures of macro performance to decide how to vote for president, assess their employment prospects, or make decisions about borrowing, lending, or investing.

When aggregate supply shifts, the price level, real output, and the rate of unemployment all change. A rightward shift results in the best of all possible worlds: higher real output (and employment) and a lower price level. A leftward shift results in the worst case: lower real output, fewer jobs, and a higher price level. Thus, it is important to know what causes aggregate supply to shift and to develop policies to encourage rightward shifts and cope with the undesirable effects of leftward shifts.

It is important to have some idea about the slope of the aggregate supply curve as well as what determines its position. As you learned in the last chapter, when aggregate demand shifts, the size of the changes in real output and the price level depend on the slope of the aggregate supply curve. When you read about the impact of shifts in the aggregate demand curve in later chapters, you will need to know what kind of aggregate supply curve exists to be able to anticipate how the effects of the shift will be divided between output and the price level.

SHIFTS IN AGGREGATE SUPPLY

In the last 15 years, the United States and other industrial nations have been fairly dissatisfied with their macroeconomic performance. U.S. growth rates have been below historic levels, and unemployment has remained quite high for almost two decades. In fact, the only thing that prevented double-digit unemployment during the 1990–1991 recession was the very slow growth of the labor force.

Table 13-1 shows the performance of the U.S. economy since 1960. As you can see, growth rates were generally higher in earlier years and unemployment was lower, especially in the 1960s. Although the last two decades saw a few good years, in most years the growth rate was consistently under 3 percent. The unemployment rate has rarely dropped below 6 percent and has been as high as 9.5 percent. The only bright spot in the last decade was the low inflation rate.

Some nations are doing even worse. GDP per capita has been falling in the nations of Eastern and Central Europe since the end of communism in 1990. In many cases, especially in the former Soviet Union, per capita GDP has been falling for several years before the revolution. Much of Africa is stagnating at very low levels of per capita GDP. India's population is in a race with growth in total output, with little gain in output per person when GDP increases.

While the United States, Canada, and Western Europe remain in the doldrums and much of the Third World is barely treading water, some countries are turning in spectacular economic performances. Most of them are in Eastern Asia, and a few are in Latin America. China has combined some elements of a market system—limited economic freedom and profit incentives—with a totalitarian government. In recent years, China's per capita output has grown at rates as high as 12 percent annually. Although these gains have been possible due to a low starting output level, China appears to have achieved a reasonable standard of living for its 1 billion citizens. Taiwan, Singapore, South Korea, and Thailand have all made significant strides in output per person while holding down inflation and operating close to full employment. In the Western Hemisphere, Mexico has made

TABLE 13-1   Changes in Output, Employment, and Prices in the United States, 1960–1992

Year	GDP Growth	Inflation Rate	Unemployment Rate
1960	2.2%	1.5%	5.4%
1961	2.7	0.7	6.5
1962	5.2	1.2	5.4
1963	4.1	1.6	5.5
1964	5.6	1.2	5.0
1965	5.5	1.9	4.4
1966	5.9	3.4	3.7
1967	2.6	3.0	3.7
1968	4.2	4.7	3.5
1969	2.7	6.1	3.4
1970	0.0	5.5	4.8
1971	2.9	3.4	5.8
1972	5.1	3.4	5.5
1973	5.2	8.8	4.8
1974	−0.6	12.2	5.5
1975	−0.8	7.0	8.3
1976	4.9	4.8	7.6
1977	4.5	6.8	6.9
1978	4.8	9.0	6.0
1979	2.5	13.3	5.8
1980	−0.5	12.4	7.0
1981	1.8	8.9	7.5
1982	−2.2	3.9	9.5
1983	3.9	3.8	9.5
1984	6.2	4.0	7.4
1985	3.2	3.8	7.1
1986	2.9	1.1	6.9
1987	3.1	4.4	6.1
1988	3.9	4.4	5.4
1989	2.5	4.6	5.2
1990	0.8	6.1	5.4
1991	−1.2	3.1	6.6
1992	2.1	2.9	7.3

Source: *Economic Report of the President, 1993* (Washington, D.C.: U.S. Government Printing Office, 1993).

substantial gains in output growth while reducing its inflation rate. Even Argentina is seeing economic growth again after decades of decline.

Is there a magic formula for such successes? Are any policy tools available to shift the aggregate supply curve to the right? Aggregate supply will shift

In Practice 13-1

. . . .

The Wonder of Compound Interest

Economic growth is not just an immediate concern. Growth now also affects the levels of output and prices far into the future. Suppose GDP was $5 trillion in 1993. If it grows at 1 percent each year over the following decade, in the year 2003 GDP will be $5.53 trillion. If GDP grows at 4 percent each year, in the year 2003 it will be $7.4 trillion, or one-third larger. In 2004, each 1 percent growth would mean additional output of $55 billion given a decade of 3 percent annual growth and $74 billion after a decade of 4 percent annual growth. In the latter case, growth would take place on a larger GDP base. Not only would consumption levels be higher in the year 2003, but the economy would have more capital, more skilled workers, and more power-generating capacity

with which to produce future output. The growth rate indeed matters.

Compounding applies to other forms of growth as well. Consider inflation. At 2 percent inflation, the price level will double in approximately 36 years; at 10 percent inflation, the price level will double in only 7 years!

A shortcut answer to the question "How long does it take output or prices to double?" is given by the rule of 72. Divide the number 72 by the rate of growth of real output or prices. The answer is the number of years it will take for output or prices to double. At 1 percent annual output growth, the output level will double in 72 years; at 4 percent, it will double in only 18 years. If China could sustain its present growth rate of 12 percent, its GDP would double in only six years.

When the growth rate of real output slows down, it affects the economy's future as well as its immediate welfare. Any policy that can increase the growth rate just a little will affect economic well-being, not only in the first year but in all the years that follow. ■

to the right if it becomes more profitable for the practical economists who run business firms to produce additional output. Production will become more profitable if the quantity or quality of resources available increases, or if an improvement in technology makes it possible to produce more output from the same inputs. These same factors shifted the production possibilities frontier introduced in Chapter 2, and most of them shifted individual supply curves as well. Most of these sources of shifts originate in the private sector, although public policy can play a role. Public policy such as changes in taxes or regulations can also affect profits. Since profits are the incentive for the practical economist as entrepreneur or investor to expand output and improve products, any policy that affects profits will also influence economic growth.

Aggregate supply will shift to the left if resources become scarcer, more expensive, or less productive, or if costs of production rise relative to output prices for other reasons, such as changes in government regulations and taxes on business income. Leftward shifts are fairly uncommon, however. A more common problem is that the aggregate supply curve is shifting to the right more slowly than the growth of population, so that real output is rising slowly while per capita output is falling.

The Labor Force

One factor that can shift the aggregate supply curve is a change in the labor force. In Chapter 11, we defined the labor force as all individuals who are working or actively seeking work. A larger labor force out of a given population is known as an increased *labor force participation rate*. In the 1980s, labor force participation rates were very high. The percentage of the population in the labor force increased steadily from about 59 percent in the early 1960s to more than 65 percent in the early 1990s. An increase in the labor force should shift aggregate supply to the right, because more workers mean more resources to employ in production. Greater competition for jobs will keep wages relatively low, providing firms with an incentive to hire more workers. During the 1970s, when the labor force was growing rapidly but its growth was having little effect on output and employment, economists began to consider the composition as well as the size of the labor force as a factor in economic growth. Recall that much of the rise in labor force participation was due to baby boomers, who were relatively young and inexperienced. Also, recall from the microeconomics chapters what happens when the marginal unit is below the average: It pulls the average down. Average productivity fell in the 1970s until new workers acquired some on-the-job training and experience to make them more productive.

A second source of labor force growth in that period was the return of women to the labor force after a long absence and the entrance of many women for the first time. Women with previous experience often concentrated in those skills that already had an excess supply of trained workers, particularly secretaries and teachers. A large supply of such workers depressed wages and increased unemployment in those occupations.

A third source of labor force growth has been an increase in worker hours. Workers can work overtime, shift from part-time to full-time employment, or work at more than one job. As the nation emerged from recession in 1993, one of the more striking developments was that the workweek increased while employment stagnated. Instead of hiring and training new workers, firms made more intensive use of their existing workers.

The relationship between the labor force and the aggregate supply curve is not simple. It consists of both a quantity aspect—more workers can produce more output at every price level—and a quality dimension.

Quantity.   An increase in the labor force can come from a higher birth rate in the past, immigration, or a higher labor force participation rate. Since the turn of the century, many factors have combined to limit the size and growth of the labor force. Compulsory schooling and child labor laws kept children out of the labor force. Mandatory retirement, social security, and private pensions pushed older workers into retirement. Before the late 1960s, large families and social pressures encouraged women to stay out of the labor force. Immigration restrictions limited the inflow of new workers from other countries.

The last two decades, however, have reversed the historical trend of falling labor force participation rates. Since the 1960s, labor force participation has risen steadily. Contributing influences have included the maturing of the baby boomers, the larger number of single-person and single-parent households, smaller families, a higher divorce rate, and changing attitudes toward women working outside the home. Immigration (most immigrants are of working age) has also added to the labor pool, particularly an influx of Asians on the West Coast and Hispanics from Central and South America in the Southwest.

Quality and Human Capital. The productivity of the labor force increases with the quality of the work force. Quality depends on experience and on-the-job training as well as education. The acquisition of useful skills and knowledge, through either on-the-job training or formal education, increases workers' human capital and makes them more productive.

Americans make substantial investments in human capital both privately and through government. Because becoming more educated and more productive benefits society as well as the individual, society (through government) has offered various incentives and subsidies to obtaining education. U.S. citizens generally are entitled to 13 years of free public education (including kindergarten), but increasingly this figure is becoming the minimum rather than the average. In 1990, more than half the adult population had some education beyond high school.

Publicly supported vocational schools, technical schools, and colleges share with private schools and colleges the effort to enhance the nation's human capital. The federal government's role in providing higher education began in the nineteenth century when the Land Grant Act provided funds for higher education with an emphasis on agriculture. After World War II and the Korean War, veterans were able to attend college with funds provided under the G.I. Bill of Rights. When the Soviets put the first satellite into space in 1957, the United States responded with the National Defense Education Act to increase the nation's supply of scientists and engineers. Since that time, the government has made low-cost loans and grants available to reduce the financial burden for students who qualify. Students still have to absorb the opportunity cost of earnings forgone while in school, and their families usually pick up part of the direct cost of higher education.

A substantial part of education is directed toward consumption skills (such as enjoyment of literature and the arts) or toward citizenship skills. A large part of education spending, however, goes toward increasing the productivity of labor. Thus, education spending should shift the aggregate supply curve to the right. Post–high school education in particular increases productivity and earnings. One recent study indicated that the average college graduate earns more than $1,000 a month more than the average high school graduate, or from $250,000 to $500,000 more over a lifetime.

Another important source of human capital is training in the workplace. Historically, the private market in the United States provided some such investment in the form of indenture and apprenticeship. Many early immigrants came to this country through indenture. Indenture was an arrangement in which a sponsor paid for the cost of an immigrant's passage across the Atlantic; in return, the immigrant agreed to work for that person for a specified number of years. In an apprenticeship, parents signed an agreement stating that their child would work for a specific person for a given period in exchange for room, board, and training in particular skills. Paul Revere learned his skills in silver work that way, and Ben Franklin trained as a printer's apprentice.

Apprenticeships have survived primarily in the U.S. military services. All branches of the armed forces offer training and future schooling benefits in exchange for a fixed time commitment to military service. Co-op programs for college students are another form of apprenticeship. Germany has a highly regarded apprenticeship program that combines supervised work experience in a specific skill with traditional high school programs. Today there is considerable interest in reviving apprenticeship in some form in the United States, perhaps along the lines of the German model.

Indenture also survives in a modified form. Young people often depend on loans to finance their training, to be repaid out of higher future earnings. The government has subsidized these loans with lower interest rates and a deferred payment schedule, because human capital has some aspects of a public good. The government also subsidizes higher education by providing public colleges and technical schools. The nation as a whole benefits from the more productive work force and higher level of output, as well as from more informed citizens and better educated consumers. President Clinton has proposed a national service plan that will forgive a portion of college loans in exchange for low-paid work in areas of national need. Many states have a similar program for students who plan to be public school teachers. Since most of the benefits of investment in human capital go to the person being educated or trained, however, the student (or the student's family) is still expected to shoulder a large share of the cost.

Work Incentives.   It is possible to both increase the size of the labor force and make workers more productive with appropriate **work incentives.** One important incentive for most practical economists is the amount of disposable income received in exchange for a day's work. Lower income taxes and payroll taxes are an incentive for individuals to work harder and earn more. (For some workers, there may be an incentive to work less because their take-home pay for the same number of hours is larger. Economists generally expect the first effect to be more significant, however.)

Prior to the 1980s, the United States had a very progressive income tax. A

Work incentives Government policies that affect the number of hours workers are willing to supply, primarily taxes on labor income.

progressive tax imposes increasingly higher tax rates on the extra or marginal hours of work of highly paid persons. At the end of World War II, the highest rate paid on the last dollar of income earned by high-income families was 94 percent! Such high rates particularly discouraged self-employed practical economists in the highest tax brackets, such as doctors, lawyers, and accountants, from taking on extra clients or cases because the after-tax return was so low. Instead, high marginal rates encouraged them to devote resources to searching for tax breaks, tax dodges, and tax shelters.

Since that time, the top bracket rate was reduced to 70 percent in 1964, 50 percent in 1981, 33 percent in 1986, and finally 31 percent in 1990. The reasoning in each case was that lower marginal rates would encourage greater work effort by the highest-paid, most productive workers. At the same time, rates were reduced at the lower end of the scale, encouraging work effort at all income levels.

At the other end of the income scale, the welfare system has been criticized for discouraging work because it too involves some high implicit tax rates. Persons on welfare who are able to work and find jobs may turn down work because they would lose more in benefits than they would gain in earnings, especially if they can find only minimum-wage jobs. Welfare clients not only lose cash benefits when they become self-supporting but may also lose their eligibility for Medicaid benefits, food stamps, and subsidized housing. The implicit tax rate, which measures the total loss of benefits per dollar of additional earnings, may exceed 100 percent! One of the biggest problems in reforming the welfare system is finding a way to provide adequate benefits for those in need without discouraging work due to loss of benefits when welfare recipients take jobs.

Along with improved work incentives, government can make it possible to better utilize the available work force through policies to reduce frictional and structural unemployment. State employment services, along with private employment agencies, help place workers in jobs and provide leads and other employment and training information. Information of future job opportunities is provided in the *Occupational Outlook Handbook,* published annually by the Department of Labor. This guide describes job opportunities, salaries, and training requirements in a vast array of occupations.

Capital and Investment

A second source of shifts in the aggregate supply curve is investment in additional physical capital by business firms. Firms, managed by practical economists, will purchase plant and equipment if the expected rate of return on such investments is higher than the opportunity cost of other uses of those funds. The opportunity cost is measured by the market interest rate on assets of comparable risk. Interest rates are high in a society that saves very little, since saving provides the funds with which business firms borrow and invest. The United States has had a lower saving rate (percentage of income saved) than many other industrial countries over the last 15 years. The result has been high long-term interest rates. The average yield of a high-grade corporate bond at the end of 1992 was 8.2 percent. Although that figure has come down considerably from its peak of 14.2 percent in 1981, it was high compared to the average rates of 4 to 6 in the 1960s and early 1970s.

These high interest rates have discouraged investment. Partly due to the low saving rate and high interest rates, the United States has invested less relative to GDP than some other industrial countries. As a result, the U.S. capital stock is older than that of most other developed nations. An older capital stock poses two problems. First, it breaks down more often and requires more maintenance. Second, since new technology is often embodied in new equipment (i.e., new techniques require new machines), the older U.S. capital stock means firms are not using the latest, most productive manufacturing methods. Thus, the slow growth of the U.S. economy in the last 20 years can be at least partly explained by older, less productive, less sophisticated capital equipment.

Public Capital.

Infrastructure   The capital available to society as a whole, such as roads, schools, and hospitals; usually supplied by government.

Along with private capital, certain kinds of public sector capital have an important influence on the level of output and thus on the position of the aggregate supply curve. The system of highways, schools, hospitals, fire stations, parks, parking lots, water and sewer systems, and other public sector capital is called **infrastructure.** In the 1980s, the worsening condition of the U.S. infrastructure received a lot of attention. Although infrastructure is not always used directly in production, components such as a healthy water and sewer system and access to safe, reliable transportation are important inputs into production in the private sector.

Public Policy toward Investment.

Investment tax credit   A reduction in tax liability equal to a percentage of the amount spent on new capital equipment.

Because after-tax profits determine investment, taxes also influence investment decisions. Lower tax rates encourage investment of all kinds, because the after-tax return on investment is higher. Higher after-tax returns make saving more attractive to the practical economist relative to consumption, thus making more funds available in the credit market. Interest rates fall, and investment increases. Lower corporate taxes have the same effect.

Tax laws can also encourage certain kinds of investments. The **investment tax credit** is a special tax break a firm receives for buying new capital equipment. It is intended to encourage business firms to invest and modernize their plants. This credit has been in and out of tax laws over the past two decades. It was removed in the 1986 Tax Reform Act, but will probably be restored in the 1990s.

Deregulation of business received much attention as an investment incentive in the 1980s. Chapters 8 and 10 discussed the role of the government in restricting monopoly and correcting externalities through regulation. Such regulations are not costless, however. The federal government may require a firm to put detailed labeling information on its packages, make equipment foolproof, reduce noise in the workplace, or pay higher wages for overtime. These regulations increase production costs and discourage investment and increased output.

Recognizing that the costs of the regulation may have exceeded the benefits in many cases, the federal government has tried to reduce and simplify regulations in recent years. Deregulation has freed some resources formerly devoted to compliance with regulations to be used to produce more goods and services. The result has been a shift in aggregate supply to the right.

Natural Resources

Depletion Using up natural resources more rapidly than they can be replaced.

Unlike capital and labor, natural resources are "givens." The relative scarcity of natural resources such as soil, climate, rainfall, mineral resources, and forests can limit growth. Finding new natural resources, such as the discovery of oil in the mid-nineteenth century, can enhance the capacity to produce. **Depletion**—drawing down the currently available stock of raw materials—raises the prices of these resources and encourages conservation as well as development of synthetics and shifting to substitutes. The last half of this century has seen a race between depletion and development of substitutes and synthetics for many natural resources, including copper, rubber, and oil.

A nation can greatly improve its productive capacity by increasing the quantity and quality of its natural resources. It is possible to use tax incentives or better technology to slow the process of depletion of less renewable resources or to increase the amount recovered. Methods include recycling metals, glass, paper; reclaiming land, or enhancing its productive capability through irrigation; and managing forests so that the stock or wood available for harvest is steady or even growing. Investments in research and development and in implementing new techniques of recovery can expand or at least maintain the stock of natural resources.

Technological Change

Research and development (R&D) Expenditures designed to improve product quality or develop new production technology.

Technological change is the development of new and improved products or new and better ways to produce old products. It does not occur by accident; rather, it requires investing resources in **research and development (R&D)**. R&D is another area in which the United States has traditionally been very strong. However, in recent years the relative amount of investment in R&D has been lower in the United States than in other developed countries.

Research and development carried on by private firms as part of their production activity is usually narrowly directed at particular products and immediate commercial applications. More general research, in which the potential commercial applications are less certain, usually takes place in universities and private research laboratories. This kind of research and development depends on a mixture of business, government, and foundation support. Public funding of general research is another potential policy tool for shifting aggregate supply by encouraging the development and application of technological improvements with broad applications.

Some technological changes are embodied in physical capital (more sophisticated equipment) or in human capital (new skills). Other changes simply use existing resources in different ways or in different combinations. Technological change occurs in two distinct steps:

Invention   The discovery of new products or new ways to produce or improve existing products.

1. **Invention**—the discovery of new products or new ways to produce old products.
2. **Innovation**—recognizing the commercial value of an invention and putting it to use in an actual production process.

Innovation   The process of putting inventions into commercial production.

Although financial support can help the invention process along, market incentives play an important role in the innovation stage. Practical economists are more likely to engage in innovation in industries in which competition pressures them to retain and expand their share of the market. Thus, oligopolies and monopolistic competition are more likely than either purely competitive or monopolistic firms to actively seek and implement innovations.

Technology transfer   The bringing of new ideas from the laboratory to the marketplace.

An important current policy issue is **technology transfer,** or getting new ideas from the laboratory to the marketplace. Universities, private firms, and government agencies in partnership can sometimes speed the process along. This kind of technology transfer partnership helped the United States regain its competitive position in microchips after a long period of losing market share to Japanese firms.

CHECKLIST : **Sources of Shifts in Aggregate Supply**

The aggregate supply curve will shift to the right with

More resources:
   Labor—quantity and quality
   Capital—private and public (infrastructure)
   Natural resources

Better technology, which requires:
   Investment in research and development
   Incentives to innovate

OTHER APPROACHES TO AGGREGATE SUPPLY POLICY

Two aggregate supply policy buzzwords that have captured a great deal of attention are privatization and industrial policy. These two policies have different advocates, but both are used at all levels of government in an attempt to increase production and create jobs.

Privatization

Privatization Turning some public sector production activities over to the private sector in an effort to increase production efficiency.

Privatization involves shifting some government activities back to the private sector, thus reducing the role of government. Privatization takes many forms and involves many different kinds of activities. Some of the activities transferred from the public to the private sector involve the production of goods and services for which the user pays a fee, not unlike the typical private business transaction. The U.S. Postal Service is an example of this kind of privatization. In other forms of privatization, private firms play a role in producing public services for which users pay little or nothing. Private paving firms build public roads. Private firms collect garbage, manage prisons, or provide fire protection. These goods and services may require public financing or public subsidy, but they need not be *produced* by government. Public financing can be combined with private production for greater efficiency through increased competition.

The privatization movement has gone much further in the United Kingdom than in the United States, primarily because the U.K.'s public sector is much larger. Among the government entities sold to the private sector have been a car manufacturer, electric utilities, steel mills, and other production facilities that Americans would expect to find in the private sector. Other nations have also been experimenting with privatizing, including Mexico and other developing countries, China, and the nations of Central and Eastern Europe that are just emerging from communism.

Privatization occurs for many reasons, including reducing pressure on government budgets. As a growth strategy, privatization is expected to shift aggregate supply by making more efficient use of existing resources and encouraging innovation. Although reports from Mexico look very promising, in general it is somewhat early to evaluate whether privatization increases efficiency and reduces costs. For small towns, it may be possible for a single private supplier to serve several communities and therefore achieve economies of scale. In other cases, competition, among several potential suppliers of a service such as trash collection, may help keep costs down. Public services that best lend themselves to collecting fees (such as water, sewer, fire protection, trash collection, and recreation services) may be the best candidates for privatization.

Industrial Policy

Industrial policy
Actions by government to promote economic growth by offering special assistance to promising industries.

One ongoing suggestion for promoting economic growth is some form of comprehensive planning and direction to ensure that industries with growth potential receive the appropriate kinds of government assistance and encouragement. This approach, known as **industrial policy,** helps such industries develop and compete internationally.

In a broad sense, the United States has always had an industrial policy. Tax deductions have benefited the housing and other construction industries. Until 1986, special tax treatment of capital gains favored risky ventures and rapidly growing firms. Federal subsidies to human capital have encouraged those industries that use highly educated workers, whereas the minimum wage has discouraged industries that rely heavily on unskilled labor. Heavy government investment in agricultural research and development, along with commodity price supports and export subsidies, has promoted agricultural development.

In a narrow sense, however, industrial policy calls on the government to select particular industries (or regions) to encourage and to devise policies to help them grow and develop rapidly. These policies might include tax breaks, research support, provision of certain kinds of infrastructure particularly important to those industries, import restrictions, or training programs for workers.

Various kinds of industrial policies are pursued in other developed countries, including Great Britain and Japan. Success stories in other countries have led many U.S. policymakers to consider industrial policies. However, those countries also report some failures. Japan's MITI, that nation's industrial policy agency, may never live down its recommendation that Honda stick with motorcycles instead of branching out into cars.

Industrial policy also creates some problems. One problem is identifying the "candidate" industries or regions. In this area the market can probably do a better job than the government. The industries with rapid growth, high profits, and promising innovations are those with the most immediate growth potential—and also the ones that have the least need for government help!

A second problem is that industrial policy often means helping one industry at the expense of others. Since resources are scarce, a tax break for industry A means citizens must make do with lower government services, pay more taxes, or find ways to make other industries bear more of the tax burden. Research and development funds earmarked for industry A have an opportunity cost, which may be other research activities that would benefit industry B or government spending programs to help other groups. There is simply no way to discriminate in favor of industry A without discriminating against other industries or taxpayers.

One very positive role for government in industrial policy is also a very general role. This policy calls for government to (1) create a tax system that encourages work and investment, (2) limit regulation by carefully weighing the costs and benefits of each proposed regulation, and (3) provide the necessary infrastructure. Such public policy will encourage industrial development of all kinds, leaving to the market the task of identifying and encouraging the most promising industries.

THE SLOPE OF THE AGGREGATE SUPPLY CURVE

The position of the aggregate supply curve is very important for achieving growth without inflation. The slope of the aggregate supply curve helps determine what happens to output and the price level when aggregate demand shifts. Recall from Chapter 12 that the aggregate supply curve can take several alternative shapes. Classical economists and their modern descendants regard it as vertical. Keynesians often treat it as horizontal. In Chapter 12, the aggregate supply curve sloped upward. A fourth possibility is the composite aggregate supply curve, with horizontal, upward-sloping, and vertical segments, which many economists regard as a realistic alternative.

Most economists today regard the horizontal aggregate supply curve, or the horizontal segment of that curve, as a special case that would occur only under extreme circumstances, such as the Great Depression of the 1930s. The disagreement over the slope of the aggregate supply curve centers on whether it is vertical or upward sloping.

Is the Aggregate Supply Curve Vertical?

The slope of the aggregate supply curve determines how much of a shift in aggregate demand is reflected in a change in the price level and how much shows up as a change in real output. A steep aggregate supply curve means shifts in aggregate demand affect the price level much more strongly than real output. A flatter aggregate supply curve causes output rather than the price level to bear most of the impact of shifts in aggregate demand. In panel a of Figure 13-1, aggregate demand shifts to the left along a steep aggregate supply curve. The result is a sharp decline in prices and a very small drop in real output. In panel b, with the same shift in aggregate demand, real output changes more than the price level because the aggregate supply curve is much flatter. Whether the shift in demand is due to private sector decisions or to public policy actions, the impact on real output and employment clearly depends on the slope of the aggregate supply curve.

Recall from Chapter 12 that some economists think aggregate supply is vertical at the level of output associated with full employment. A vertical aggregate supply curve means shifts in aggregate demand affect only the price level and do not change real output. In this case, the only way to change real output would be to shift the aggregate supply curve. This shift could be brought

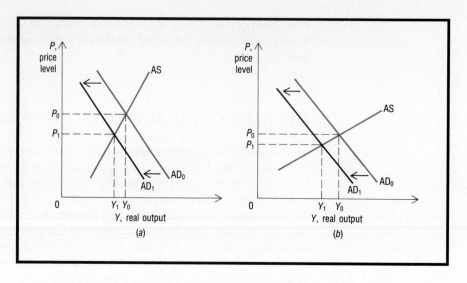

FIGURE 13-1

If aggregate supply is relatively steep, as in panel a, a decline in aggregate demand (AD_0 to AD_1) will fall mainly on prices, which fall from P_0 to P_1, rather than on real output (Y_0 to Y_1). In panel b, however, with a relatively flat aggregate supply curve, a decline in aggregate demand is reflected mainly in falling real output rather than in falling prices.

about by either increasing resources or finding more efficient ways to use those resources (improved technology).

The view that the aggregate supply curve *in the long run* is vertical at full employment or capacity output is quite widespread. Economists disagree, however, over the steepness of the short-run aggregate supply curve and the length of time that defines the short run.

How Short Is the Short Run?

Recall the discussion of the long run and the short run for the firm and the industry from Chapters 6 and 7 on costs and competitive firms. In microeconomics, the long run for a particular industry is long enough to allow firms to enter and exit and to change their contracts involving costs that are fixed in the short run. A lease or a labor contract could expire and be renegotiated; existing debts could be paid off; new buildings could be built. Nothing is fixed in the long run.

The short run and the long run also have an information aspect in microeconomics. Especially under conditions of imperfect competition, information may not be immediately and costlessly available. It takes time for producers (or consumers) to acquire and process the price, cost, and profit signals coming from the market and decide on a course of action. Until information is acquired and processed, firms (or consumers) are in the short run. Thus, from the standpoint of the household or firm, the long run is the period of time that is long enough for practical economists to acquire all the relevant information they need to make decisions.

No precise time period, such as six months, two years, or a decade, defines the short run in microeconomics. Undoubtedly it will vary among industries. It is much easier to get in and out of the retail used-car business than it is to enter and exit auto manufacturing! For the economy as a whole, however, choosing a time period that divides the short run from the long run is very important for policy purposes.

Many economists argue that policies to shift aggregate demand affect output and employment only in the short run, because aggregate supply is vertical or nearly vertical in the long run. However, using demand-shifting policies to shift aggregate demand may still be of great value if the short run is ten years rather than six months. The central question is: How long does it take the economy to move from the upward-sloping short-run aggregate supply curve to the vertical long-run aggregate supply curve? The answer to this question centers around two important issues: how people form expectations about prices and output and how markets adjust to new information.

Rational or Adaptive Expectations

Rational expectations
The viewpoint that market participants quickly and costlessly acquire and process all the relevant information they need to make decisions.

According to the **rational expectations** view, individuals search out economic information and incorporate it into their planning and decision making. In particular, workers cannot be fooled into offering more hours because of higher money wages that come with inflation. As practical economists, they are interested in real wages rather than money wages. Similarly, entrepreneurs are not likely to be misled. Higher product prices will not convince them to expand production (at least for very long) when they know that wages and prices of raw materials are rising at the same rate. They respond to real profit. Recall the profit equation:

$$\text{Profit} = \text{Total Revenue} - \text{Total Cost.}$$

If the price level doubles, total revenue, total costs, and total profit all will double, but the value or purchasing power of that profit will be exactly the same. With no increase in *real* profit, there is no incentive to expand real output.

If workers do not offer to work more hours in response to higher money wages (because with higher prices, the real wage is unchanged) and entrepreneurs do not increase output when prices (and costs) rise but profits are unchanged, the aggregate supply curve will be vertical. The level of output will be independent of the price level. An increase in aggregate demand will change only the price level.

Thus, if expectations are rational, we would expect a very brief short run. Those who support this view argue that real output is independent of the price level. Only the available supply of real resources affects real output. Under these conditions, the only way to change real output is to shift the aggregate supply curve.

This view of how workers and entrepreneurs think and make decisions is not universally held. Other economists, and also many psychologists, suggest that the process of acquiring information about prices and wages is gradual rather than instantaneous. This view of behavior, called **adaptive expectations,** implies an upward-sloping short-run aggregate supply curve and a short run that represents a longer period of time.

Adaptive expectations
The viewpoint that acquiring and processing relevant market information is neither instantaneous nor costless so that it takes time for markets to respond to new information.

Economists who support the adaptive expectations viewpoint out that even information has opportunity costs. To find out about wages, the practical economist must read ads, make phone calls, and apply for jobs, all of which takes time. Faced with problems in acquiring and interpreting information, people can easily confuse a rise in wages (and prices) in general with an increase in wages for plumbers, secretaries, or shoe sellers. When one lacks all the relevant market information, it is difficult to realize that all prices are rising.

Furthermore, information is often not available immediately. Suppose you find out that the wages of plumbers have risen 10 percent. Until you know how much the consumer price index rose—by 10 percent, more than 10 percent, or less than 10 percent—you have no way of knowing whether the real wage has risen, fallen, or stayed the same. In addition to the lag in getting the relevant price information, the information is often less than perfect, because the consumer price index or plumbers' wages may differ for your region, income level, or family size.

This slow process of acquiring and processing information means buyers, sellers, and markets may also not react quickly to changed price signals. During the interim, it is very possible that many households and firms will mistakenly assume higher prices for their products and services as a *relative* price change rather than simply a reflection of general inflation. They may respond with more labor supply or more output produced than they would if their information were more nearly correct. Under these conditions (adaptive expectations), higher price levels would, in the short run, call forth more output; that is, the aggregate supply curve would slope upward.

Eventually, of course, the information becomes available and is processed, and buyers and sellers respond. Because this process of acquiring, processing, and acting on price information and price expectations is gradual, this view of how information is transmitted and used is that of adaptive expectations.

Competitive or Monopoly Markets

Another influence on the short-term aggregate supply curve is the speed with which particular markets can change prices. If markets adjust rapidly to new

· ·

Myth 13-1

· ·

We Can Fine-Tune the Economy

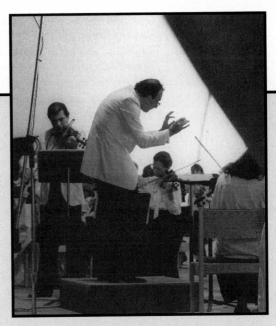

Although this chapter emphasizes aggregate supply policy tools to promote economic growth and the next few chapters look at aggregate demand policy tools to promote stability, in reality these tools are less powerful than economists once thought. The myth that government can fine-tune the economy was one of the most popular beliefs in recent economic history. It was discarded only reluctantly after the experience of the 1970s. People believed this myth in the 1950s and 1960s because they wanted to believe it, since fine-tuning suggested that the nation could control its economic destiny.

The term *fine-tuning* was popularized by Walter Heller, chairman of the Council of Economic Advisers under Kennedy and Johnson in the mid-1960s. The term, which comes from "piano tuning," refers to making continuous minor adjustments until the instrument is precisely in tune. In macroeconomics, fine-tuning meant directing policy tools toward attaining a particular growth rate and a given inflation-unemployment combination out of a set of attainable combinations. At 2 percent growth, 3 percent inflation, and 7 percent unemployment, the economy could move toward some more acceptable combination, such as 4 percent growth, 4 percent inflation, and 5 percent unemployment. This combination would then be attained through small, careful adjustments in the government's various policy tools.

Unfortunately for this appealing myth, the set of at-tainable combinations does not sit still. While policymakers are still trying to get the best combination in their gun sights, changes abroad or in the private sector shift the aggregate supply and demand curves, and the chosen target for growth, unemployment, and inflation may no longer be among the possibilities.

Fine-tuning is possible only if there is a stable, upward-sloping aggregate supply curve. Economists have learned, to their sorrow, that they cannot count on the aggregate supply curve to remain stable while they use it for aggregate demand policy target practice. Fine-tuning is an idea whose time has come and gone and will not be likely to return. ■

conditions and new information (like the competitive markets in Chapter 7), and if prices are flexible and resources are mobile, the short run is very short and the aggregate supply curve is nearly vertical in the short run as well as the long run. If these conditions do not hold, the aggregate supply curve is flatter and the short run is a longer time period.

The post–Keynesians, a group of economists who built on the work of Keynes, point to several factors that would make the aggregate supply curve relatively flat. They stress the presence of rigidities (such as long-term contracts and immobile labor) and market power in the economy. Post–Keynesians believe these factors would make the aggregate supply curve relatively flat and the short run quite long. They also tend to believe expectations are formed gradually rather than rapidly and that expectations play a significant role in decisions of practical economists to produce, work, and spend. This view would make demand management policies, which we will discuss in the next few chapters, much more effective than rational expectations economists would expect.

To understand this viewpoint, recall from Chapter 8 that prices tend to change less often in monopoly or oligopoly markets. Oligopolists are very reluctant to make price changes. They fear their rivals will not increase prices when they do (meaning they will lose a lot of sales) but will match their price cuts (thus, they will gain very few sales from price reductions). Therefore, facing a shift in demand, oligopolists are more likely to adjust the quantity of output than they are to adjust price.

If quantity changes a lot but price changes a little in a large number of oligopoly markets, the aggregate supply curve will be flatter; that is, there will be a greater quantity change than a price change when demand shifts, at least in the short run. Aggregate supply will look more like panel b than panel a of Figure 13-1.

In the perfectly competitive model of Chapter 7, resources are highly mobile. Small differences in wages for labor or rates of return on capital induce workers and investment capital to move among regions or industries. In reality, all factors of production are somewhat imperfectly mobile, especially in the short run. Post–Keynesians argue that this immobility is another reason the aggregate supply curve is fairly flat.

Since it is costly for a worker to relocate both financially and psychologically, it will take a very attractive opportunity to induce the practical economist to make such a move. A small wage difference will not be enough. Over time, new workers (and new capital) will gravitate to those industries with higher wages (or rates of return), but existing labor and existing capital will be much less willing or able to move, especially in the short run. Such structural problems are another reason the aggregate supply curve may slope upward. Structural problems (mismatch of resources demanded and resources available) arise when an increase in real output involves major changes in the output mix. Along with producing more total output, there may be more oil and less electricity, or more computers and fewer automobiles. To shift resources around to produce a different as well as larger output mix, resources must be lured into the growing industries with higher wages and rates of return. It may take rather large increases in wages and interest payments to induce resources to move. These increases in resource payments will be reflected in higher prices. Imperfect resource mobility is yet another reason the aggregate supply curve may be upward sloping rather than vertical.

CHECKLIST : **Determining the Slope of the Aggregate Supply Curve**

Aggregate supply will be

Relatively flat if:	*Vertical or nearly vertical if:*
Expectations are adaptive	Expectations are rational
Markets are sluggish	Markets adapt rapidly
Market power exists	Markets are competitive
Information spreads slowly	Information spreads rapidly
Resources are immobile	Resources are mobile

Implications for Demand Management Policy

A relatively flat aggregate supply curve helps ensure that demand management policies designed to shift aggregate demand to the right (or left) will be very effective. Effective means most of the impact will fall on output and employment rather than on prices. On the other hand, such an aggregate supply curve (panel b of Figure 13-1) suggests that it may be difficult to get prices to fall when aggregate demand shifts to the left, that is, from AD_1 back to AD_0. Instead, output and employment will bear most of the burden of a decline in aggregate demand. If the government tries to reduce inflation by shifting aggregate demand to the left, the process will be painful. Citizens can expect falling real output *(Y)* and employment and sharp increases in the unemployment rate.

British economist John Maynard Keynes, who wrote during the Great Depression of the 1930s, was concerned about the problems of the short run. To Keynes, the short run is the period when falling aggregate demand is reflected mainly in rising unemployment and falling prices (or declining inflation). His famous statement "In the long run we are all dead" reflects his belief that these adjustment processes could be very long and very slow. In the interim, shifting aggregate demand to the right could alleviate unemployment and increase output. In the next two chapters, we will explore Keynes's ideas about how government can shift aggregate demand to influence output, employment, and the price level.

Summary

1. The aggregate supply curve can be shifted by changes in the size of the labor force, improvements in the quality of the labor force, investment in physical capital, improvements in technology, or increases in natural resources.

2. The size of the labor force depends on the size of the population and on

the labor force participation rate. The quality of the labor force depends on the amount of investment in human capital.

3. Investment in physical capital responds to changes in the interest rate, opportunities for innovation, and tax policy.

4. Technological change is more rapid when there is greater investment in research and development by either private firms or the government.

5. Natural resources can be enhanced by reclamation, irrigation, technological improvements, development of substitutes, and other techniques.

6. Policy tools to affect aggregate supply include tax and welfare policies that offer work incentives, tax policies that affect saving and investment incentives, government investment in human capital and research and development, and changing regulations that affect production costs.

7. Industrial policy calls for identifying promising growth industries and regions and targeting tax policies and spending programs to encourage their development.

8. If the aggregate supply curve is upward sloping rather than vertical, shifts in aggregate demand will affect output and employment as well as the price level.

9. The aggregate supply curve will be vertical in the long run and the short run will be fairly brief if expectations are rational, markets are competitive and efficient, and resources are mobile. If expectations are formed more gradually (adaptive expectations) and markets are oligopolistic or slow to adapt, the short-run aggregate supply curve will slope upward, and the short run may be a very long time period.

Key Terms

adaptive expectations	invention	research and
depletion	investment tax credit	development (R&D)
industrial policy	privatization	technology transfer
infrastructure	rational expectations	work incentives
innovation		

Questions and Problems

1. Imagine yourself in charge of "getting the economy moving again," that is, increasing the rate of economic growth. What policies would you use? Under what conditions would your policies have the greatest impact?

2. You have decided to ask a famous economist about the slope of the aggregate supply curve. What is her answer likely to be if she believes expectations are rational and markets work rapidly and efficiently? What if she believes expectations are adaptive and markets are sluggish?

3. How do changes in the size and composition of the labor force affect the aggregate supply curve?

4. How would each of the following affect the slope and/or position of the aggregate supply curve?
   a. An increase in the size of the labor force
   b. Reduced costs of getting market information
   c. An increase in monopoly power
   d. Discovery of new raw materials
   e. Improvements in production processes
   f. Elimination of the investment tax credit

5. a. What is the role of the private sector in providing each of the following kinds of services in your community?

   1) Fire protection
   2) Garbage collection
   3) Education (pre-college)
   4) Recreation

   b. What other local public services in your community can you think of in which the private sector plays an important role?

6. Which of the following market situations is more likely to adjust quickly to changing conditions? Why?
   a. A garage sale
   b. A flea market
   c. A unionized labor market
   d. Sale of new aircraft to Israel
   e. Buying retail milk at the grocer
   f. Buying wholesale milk from the farmer

7. Aggregate demand shifts to the right as a result of increased sales of exports. Explain what happens to real output, the price level, and employment if
   a. Aggregate supply is vertical.
   b. Aggregate supply is horizontal.
   c. Aggregate supply is upward sloping.

8. The notion of compound interest is most familiar in terms of a savings account. Assuming you have $1,000 in a savings account, use the rule of

72 (Box 13.1) to determine how many years it will take to double that amount at an interest rate of

a. 2 percent
b. 7 percent
c. 12 percent
d. 18 percent

14

Determining the Level of Income and Output

*The celebrated optimism of traditional economic theory . . .
is . . . to be traced to . . . neglect . . . of the drag on prosperity
which can be exercised by an insufficiency of effective demand.*

JOHN MAYNARD KEYNES, *The General Theory of Employment, Interest, and Money*

Main Points

1. Aggregate demand depends on planned consumption spending by households *(C)*, investment spending by business firms *(I)*, government purchases *(G)*, and net exports *(X − M)*.

2. In a model with only households and business firms, equilibrium occurs where output and income equal planned spending for consumption and investment.

3. In a model that includes government, taxes reduce consumption while government purchases are another source of demand for output. In a model with a foreign sector, exports are a source of increased demand for do-

mestically produced output while imports are a reduction in demand.

4. Equilibrium income may be higher or lower than the desired level of income and output, which is the level at which full employment occurs.

5. When one component of planned spending shifts, the equilibrium level of income and output changes.

6. The relationship between the change in planned spending and the final change in income and output is given by the multiplier.

Households consume and save; businesses invest; governments tax and spend. Together the aggregate decisions of these three components of the economy determine the level of output. Changes in their decisions can change the level of output and, along with it, the levels of employment and prices.

The aggregate supply and aggregate demand model of Chapter 12 offers a very simplified explanation of the economy's level of output and prices. In this chapter and the three that follow, we will go behind the aggregate demand curve to see what determines its slope and what makes it shift.

Chapter 12 introduced the aggregate demand curve. We saw why it slopes downward from left to right and identified some of the factors that can cause aggregate demand to shift. However, the explanation of any demand curve—whether for particular goods or for aggregate real output—lies in the behavior of individuals as practical economists, responding to incentives and maximizing their satisfaction. You need to understand the aggregate demand curve in the same way you understand individual demand curves. Doing so requires exploring what makes consumers, businesses, and eventually government "tick," that is, what makes these practical economists choose to buy more or less total goods and services as well as what makes them buy more or less of a particular good or service. Policymakers are particularly concerned with identifying the causes of shifts in aggregate demand, or what makes buyers willing to buy more total output at every possible price. Knowing what makes aggregate demand shift will help policymakers identify demand management policy tools with which to change the levels of real output, employment, and prices in the desired direction. ■

CONSUMPTION, INVESTMENT, AND EQUILIBRIUM

To explore the effects of shifts in aggregate demand, we will hold the price level constant throughout most of this chapter. A fixed price level allows us to focus on changes in output (Y) and employment that result from shifts in aggregate demand. In Figure 14-1, the price level is fixed at P_1. Fixing the price level is equivalent to making aggregate supply horizontal. The position of the aggregate demand curve then is the sole factor that determines the level of real output, Y_1. When aggregate demand shifts from AD_1 to AD_2, the real quantity of output demanded at price level P_1 changes from Y_1 to Y_2.

FIGURE 14-1

If the price level is fixed—that is, aggregate supply is horizontal—a shift in aggregate demand from AD_1 to AD_2 will increase real output from Y_1 to Y_2, with no effect on the price level.

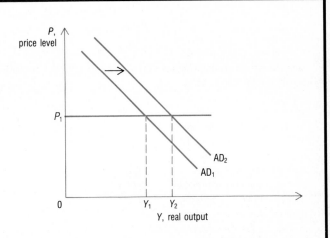

CHECKLIST : Temporary and Convenient Assumptions

1. No government
2. No foreign sector
3. Fixed price level (horizontal aggregate supply)

The Circular Flow Revisited

The circular flow model introduced in earlier chapters provides a good starting point for developing a model of how the level of output *(Y)* is determined when the price level is fixed.

The circular flow model in Figure 14-2 includes only households and business firms. In this two-sector economy, consumers receive an income from selling the services of the productive resources they own. They use part of that income to buy goods and services (consumption). The rest of their income flows into saving, which is a **leakage** out of the circular flow.

Leakage Income received by households that is not spent on consumption and therefore leaks out of the circular flow.

Investment is an **injection** back into the circular flow. Investment consists of business purchases of plant and equipment, inventory, and residential construction. Since the business sector in this model has no income to call its own, business firms must borrow the income saved by households to finance their investment spending.

Injection Spending by businesses (or other economic actors except for households), which do not earn income from production.

In this simplified version of the circular flow, consumption and saving are the only possible uses of income, and consumption and investment account for all the sales of final output. More elaborate models, which we will examine later in this chapter, add government and a foreign sector. A macroeconomy with

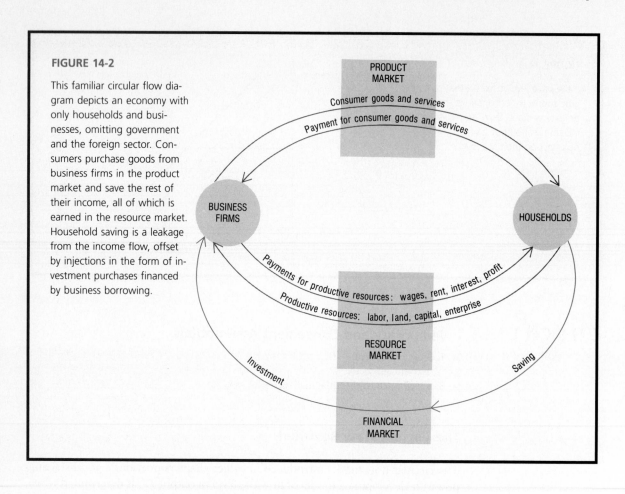

FIGURE 14-2

This familiar circular flow diagram depicts an economy with only households and businesses, omitting government and the foreign sector. Consumers purchase goods from business firms in the product market and save the rest of their income, all of which is earned in the resource market. Household saving is a leakage from the income flow, offset by injections in the form of investment purchases financed by business borrowing.

only two actors—households and business firms—makes it easier to see how the macroeconomy works and what determines the size of the flow of economic activity.

Consumption and Income

Households spend most of their incomes on consumption. Some consumers even spend more than their current incomes on consumption by borrowing. Consumption consists of almost everything that consumers purchase, including services such as medical care and recreation; nondurables like gasoline, food, clothing, and textbooks; and durable goods, such as VCRs and cars. The only exception is the purchase of new houses, which is counted as investment.

If you reflect for a moment on what affects a household's consumption, you can probably come up with a long list. Your list will likely include prices, interest

In Practice 14-1

. . . .

How Keynes Came to America

In 1933 Keynes wrote "An Open Letter to President Roosevelt," which was published in *The New York Times*. In this letter, he urged President Roosevelt to borrow money and spend it on public sector activities to increase income and output. The letter was not particularly well received.

In 1936 Keynes published *The General Theory of Employment, Interest, and Money,* setting forth the elements of the Keynesian model and the case for using deficit-financed government spending under depressed economic conditions to try to raise the level of output and employment. Looking at these dates, there is a widespread impression that New Deal policies were based on Keynesian economic theories.

According to Keynes's biographer, Robert Lekachman, Keynesian ideas about stimulating aggregate demand had little effect on the Roosevelt administration's circle of advisers until 1938.[1] The economic policies of the first eight years of the Roosevelt administration consisted of modest deficits, experiments, and various kinds of emergency actions. There was no coordinated plan of action based on economic theory.

The path by which new economic ideas find their way into policy is much slower and more indirect than one might think. Keynes's theories traveled from Cambridge, England, to Cambridge, Massachusetts, where they were adopted by members of the economics faculty at Harvard University in the early 1940s. These ideas spread from Harvard economists to the rest of the profession and appeared in undergraduate economics texts for the first time in the mid-1940s. Finally, Keynesian ideas were embraced by the general public with the passage of the Employment Act of 1946. This act committed the federal government to promote full employment, stable prices, and steady economic growth and created the Council of Economic Advisers to assist the president in carrying out that task.

This slow movement from theory to practice is the usual case. An accepted economic model usually holds sway until real-world experience clearly contradicts it. In response to that contradiction, new ideas begin to emerge. Some of the seeds of the full-blown economic model of *The General Theory* are found in Keynes's 1919 work on the Versailles peace treaty entitled *The Economic Consequences of the Peace.* It took 17 years to clearly develop these theories. Once new ideas appear, it takes time for them to win acceptance in the economics profession. Following that stage, those ideas have to be distilled into a form that the public and politicians can understand. The ten years from *The General Theory* to the Employment Act of 1946 is actually a rather quick passage from theory to policy! ■

[1] Robert Lekachman, *The Age of Keynes* (New York: McGraw-Hill) 1975, p. 112.

rates, ages of family members, expectations, debts, assets, and the age of the car or the TV. But surely the most important influence on any household's consumption is its income. If the Jones family is making twice as much as the Smith family, you would expect (other things equal) the Joneses to buy more goods and services—perhaps a newer car, more nights out at the movies, or more steak and less ground beef. Increase the Smiths' income, and they will be better able and more likely to keep up with the Joneses (increase their consumption). Thus, reasoning from the behavior of individual households to households in the aggregate, you might expect household consumption to be positively related to the aggregate level of income and output in the circular flow, or GDP.

British economist John Maynard Keynes called this relationship between con-

Consumption function The stable and predictable relationship between total consumption and the level of income (output), or $C = C_0 + (MPC \times Y)$.

Marginal propensity to consume *(MPC)* The fraction of an additional dollar of aggregate income *(Y)* that households will spend on consumption.

sumption *(C)* and income *(Y)* the **consumption function.** This function describes the total of decisions of countless households full of practical economists, responding to incentives and opportunities. The most important influence on households' consumption is income.

The consumption function is based on the idea that consumption rises as income increases and falls as income decreases, but the change in consumption in response to a change in income *($\Delta C/\Delta Y$)* is less than 1. When income rises by $1, consumption rises by less than $1. For example, an increase in income of $1.00 may drive consumption up by $0.80. In this case, the change in consumption divided by the change in income is 0.8. The fraction of an additional dollar of income spent on consumption is called the **marginal propensity to consume (MPC).** The MPC is equal to the change in consumption divided by the change in income, or $\Delta C/\Delta Y$.

Keynes believed the MPC for households in the aggregate would be very stable. When income increased by $1 (or $100, or $1000), different individuals might respond differently because of their ages or other factors. But Keynes predicted that for the economy as a whole, the fraction of an additional amount of income spent on consumption would be stable from month to month and from year to year.

Keynes also believed a part of consumption would be independent of the level of income. If the chief earner in a household gets sick, becomes unemployed, or goes back to school, the household's income may temporarily fall to zero, but borrowing or drawing on past saving will enable the household to keep its consumption close to the same level as before, even with no current income.

The same is true of aggregate consumption and aggregate income. If aggregate income falls, households can sustain most of their consumption spending by drawing on past saving or borrowing against future saving. If the part of consumption that is independent of the level of income is called C_0, the relationship between consumption and income can be written as

$$\text{Consumption} = C_0 + (MPC \times \text{Income})$$

or

$$C = C_0 + (MPC \times Y).$$

The $MPC \times Y$ term represents the effect of income on consumption. The C_0 term picks up all of the other influences on consumption to which practical economists might respond, such as changes in household debt, expectations, and interest rates. The zero subscript in this term means some fixed, or constant, value. If C_0 is $60 billion and the MPC is 0.8, the consumption function is

$$C = \$60 + 0.8Y,$$

where C, C_0, and Y are all in billions of dollars.

Table 14-1 gives both a consumption schedule and a saving schedule. The consumption function is graphed in Figure 14-3. The consumption function is

TABLE 14-1 Income, Consumption, and Saving ($billions)

Income	Consumption	Saving
$ 0	$ 60	$ – 60
100	140	– 40
200	220	– 20
300	300	0
400	380	20
500	460	40
600	540	60

a straight line because the slope, or the MPC, is constant. Note that at an income of $300, households consume all of their income. At lower levels of income, saving is negative; above that income level, saving is positive.

You can use the data in Table 14-1 to compute the values of C_0 and MPC in the consumption function, $C = C_0 + MPC \times Y$. The value of C_0 is the level of consumption when income is zero, or $60. The value of the MPC is the change in consumption divided by the change in income. Since the MPC is constant, its value can be measured between any two points in Table 14-1. For example, when income rises from 400 to 500 (change in income = 100), consumption rises from 380 to 460 (change in consumption = 80). Dividing the change in consumption by the change in income gives a value of 80/100, or 0.8, for the MPC. Thus, the consumption function describing the data in Table 14-1 and the graph in Figure 14-3 is the familiar one,

$$C = 60 + 0.8Y.$$

The Keynesian consumption function describes planned household spending. To account for all spending, however, we also need to look at the determinants of planned investment, which is the only other source of demand in an economy with no government and no foreign sector.

Investment Demand

You might expect that investment, like consumption, would depend on the level of income or output (Y). An increase in sales or final demand depends on Y. When Y rises and sales of consumer goods increase, firms may require more capital goods to produce those goods. However, investment goods generally last much longer than other kinds of final output. Often an existing stock of plant and equipment is being used at less than capacity. Thus, a rise in final demand will sometimes have no immediate effect on demand for investment

FIGURE 14-3

The consumption function shows a positive relationship between consumption and income. The slope is equal to the marginal propensity to consume (= 0.8) and is less than 1; thus, the consumption line is flatter than the 45° reference line. The intercept is the level of consumption at zero income, $C_0 = \$60$.

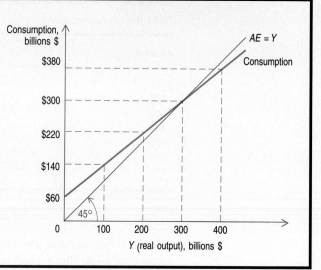

goods. At other times, a rise in final demand will lead to a flurry of investment activity to build up the stock of investment goods needed to produce for final buyers. Thus, the relationship between investment and income is complex and hard to predict. In addition, investment demand is also affected by changes in interest rates, expectations, and other factors. Because there is no simple way to relate investment demand to either consumption or income, for now we will treat it as a given amount, I_0.

What happens when investment is combined with consumption? Let's begin with the fact that production of $100 worth of goods generates $100 of income to households. Households spend part of that income—say, $80—and save the other $20. This leaves business firms with $20 in unsold goods. Some of those goods may be investment or capital goods—plant and equipment, new houses, or inventory—that other firms have ordered and want to buy. If investment demand happens to add up to $20, everything produced is sold to a willing buyer.

What happens if planned spending for investment does not equal $20? Suppose instead that planned spending by firms on capital goods, including inventory, is only $10. This level of investment demand means that $80 worth of goods are sold to consumers and $10 worth are sold to other firms. What happens to the other $10 worth of output?

Since this other $10 worth of goods is produced and not sold in the current year, according to the definitions in Chapter 11, it is an addition to inventory or, more precisely, **unplanned inventory investment.** Recall from Chapter 11 that inventory is one of the three components of investment, along with residential construction and business plant and equipment. These goods are added to

Unplanned inventory investment Increases in inventories resulting from the fact that planned consumption spending and planned business investment total less than actual current output.

FIGURE 14-4

Equilibrium income occurs where planned spending (aggregate expenditures, or *AE*) equal actual income or output, *Y*. This occurs at an output level of $400 billion. If income is $300 billion, planned spending will be less than output, and there will be an unplanned increase in inventories of $20 billion. If income is $600 billion, planned spending will be greater than output, and there will be an unplanned reduction in inventories of amount $60 billion.

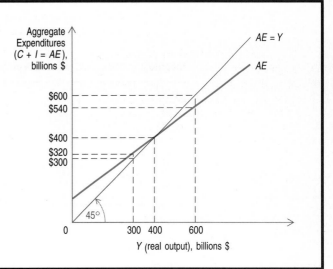

inventory because the firms that produced them were unable to sell them. The investment is unplanned because those firms did not *choose* to increase their inventory.

After the fact, everything produced is accounted for as either consumption or investment. Accounting deals with history; it describes and even explains what happened in the past. In this case, accounting tells us that last period's output *(Y)* equals consumption plus investment. Economics, however, is more like prophecy. On the basis of what just happened, economists attempt to predict what is going to happen next. To prophesy the events of the next time period, we need to introduce the concept of *equilibrium* in the context of macroeconomics.

Equilibrium and Aggregate Expenditures

In microeconomics, a market is in equilibrium when buyers and sellers exchange the same quantity at the same price each period. There is no tendency for that price and quantity to change until some outside force shifts the supply or demand curve. Similarly, in macroeconomics the level of output (and later prices) is in **equilibrium** when no tendency to change exists. That level will stay the same until something happens to shift the aggregate supply or aggregate demand curve.

Equilibrium (macroeconomics) A situation in which planned spending exactly equals current output, so no unplanned changes in inventories occur.

As long as households are not frustrated (that is, they are able to carry out their consumption and saving plans) and business firms are also satisfied (they are able to invest exactly as much as they planned), the economy is in equilibrium. Equilibrium occurs when *planned* consumption plus *planned* investment exactly

TABLE 14-2   Income and Aggregate Expenditures ($billions)

Income	Consumption	Investment	Aggregate Expenditures
$ 0	$ 60	$20	$ 80
100	140	20	160
200	220	20	240
300	300	20	320
400	380	20	400
500	460	20	480
600	540	20	560

Aggregate expenditures (AE) The sum of planned consumption and planned investment.

equal the level of output being produced. The sum of planned consumption and planned investment is called **aggregate expenditures (AE).** If planned investment, I_0, equals $20 billion, AE equals C plus I_0. Aggregate expenditures are graphed against real output in Figure 14-4, using the data in Table 14-2. The 45° line is a reference line. Where the aggregate expenditure line crosses the 45° line, planned spending on the vertical axis equals total income or output on the horizontal axis.

Inventories and Equilibrium   If aggregate expenditures exceed total output, firms must draw down on inventories to meet consumption demand, and business investment plans are frustrated. In Table 14-2, aggregate expenditures are greater than total output at income levels of less than $400 billion. For example, when income equals $300 billion, planned consumption and planned investment total $320 billion. The result is a drawdown of inventory of $20 billion, or unplanned inventory investment of − $20 billion. This gap between planned spending and output at an income of $320 billion is shown in Figure 14-4. The difference between AE and the 45° line in the diagram is the amount of unplanned inventory investment.

If aggregate expenditures are less than total output, business firms will find themselves piling up more inventory (investment) than planned (when output exceeds $400 billion). In Table 14-2, aggregate expenditures are less than total output at income levels greater than $400 billion. For example, when income equals $600 billion, total planned spending *(AE)* is only $560 billion and unplanned increases in inventory come to $40 billion. The difference between AE and the 45° line in Figure 14-4 is the amount of unplanned inventory investment.

Only at $Y = $400 billion do aggregate expenditures equal total output and no plans are frustrated. $Y = 400$ is the equilibrium level of income. You can find the equilibrium level of income from the numbers in Table 14-2 or from the point where AE crosses the 45° line in Figure 14-4. Note that AE equals

Y at a level of \$400 billion in Table 14-2 and AE crosses the 45° line at $Y =$ \$400 billion in Figure 14-4.

Disequilibrium What does the term *disequilibrium level of output* mean? In macroeconomics, *disequilibrium* corresponds to the surpluses and shortages in the microeconomic model of supply and demand. Consider the market for wheat. Even if there is a surplus or a shortage in the market for wheat, after the fact the quantity actually purchased by buyers will always equal the quantity sold by producers. The surplus or shortage means one of these groups is frustrated. If there is a surplus, sellers wanted, planned, or intended to sell more wheat at that price than they actually sold. If a shortage exists, buyers wanted, planned, or intended to buy more wheat at that price than they were able to find for sale. In both cases, the frustration of buyers' or sellers' plans calls forth a response that leads the market back toward equilibrium.

In macroeconomics, economists usually assume most of the burden of adjustment falls on inventories and production. At output levels below equilibrium, such as Y_2, producers find their inventories are being depleted as customers empty the shelves. They respond by expanding output in the next period, which increases output and income, moving closer to equilibrium output Y_1. At output levels above equilibrium, such as Y_3, shelves are full of unsold output. Firms will reduce production, moving output and income back toward Y_1. Only at Y_1 is there no tendency for the level of output to change.

Equilibrium and the Circular Flow

Saving (S) Income of households not spent on consumption, or $Y - C$.

Another way to think about equilibrium is in terms of the leakages and injections in the circular flow. Recall that **saving** is income minus consumption ($S = Y - C$). If equilibrium occurs where

$$AE = Y = C + I,$$

equilibrium can also be found where

$$Y - C = S = I,$$

or where leakages equal injections.

The concept of equilibrium in the circular flow diagram means the size of the flow is stable. Some economists prefer to visualize the circular flow somewhat more graphically, in terms of a bathtub. Injections, such as investment, flow into the tub as fresh water from the tap, while leakages, such as saving, are like water flowing out of the tub and down the drain. If leakages are greater than injections, the water level in the bathtub falls. If leakages are less than injections, the water level in the bathtub rises. When the flow out of the tub (leakages) exactly equals the flow into the tub (injections), there is a stable level of water in the tub, with no tendency to change. Likewise, only when leakages (saving) equal injections (investment) does the economy experience a stable level of total output and income, with no tendency to change.

CHECKLIST : **Basic Macroeconomic Relationships**

Consumption: $C = C_0 + (MPC \times Y)$
Saving: $S = Y - C = -C_0 + (1 - MPC) \times Y$
Investment: $I = I_0$
Aggregate expenditures: $AE = C + I = C_0 + (MPC \times Y) + I_0$

When

$AE > Y$, there is unintended inventory reduction: Y rises.
$AE < Y$, there is unintended inventory accumulation: Y falls.
$AE = Y$, the equilibrium level is reached.

THE SIMPLE KEYNESIAN MODEL

If we pull together the pieces we have developed, the result provides a simple explanation of what determines the economy's level of output and income. Households, consuming and saving in response to income and other influences, and business firms, investing according to their investment demand function, together determine the equilibrium level of income. These relationships are the building blocks of the *Keynesian model of income determination*, based on the work of John Maynard Keynes.

Basic Relationships: Consumption, Investment, and Equilibrium

The equilibrium model developed thus far consists of three relationships:
1. The consumption function, with a constant term and a positive marginal propensity to consume
2. The investment demand function, with planned investment, *I*, equal to some given value, I_0
3. The equilibrium condition that aggregate expenditures, *AE*, the sum of planned consumption and planned investment, must equal *Y*, the level of output

Shifting Consumption and Investment

If the equilibrium level of income occurs where output equals planned spending, *AE*, a change in planned consumption or planned investment leads to a change in equilibrium income. Consumption can shift in response to changes in consumer assets or debts, taxes, interest rates, prices, expectations, and the size or age distribution of the population.

Figure 14-5 shows two such shifts. The original equilibrium is found where AE_0 crosses the 45° line, which occurs at Y_0. Now assume consumers choose to consume more out of their incomes. The consumption function shifts upward, and so does the aggregate expenditures function, which is the sum of planned consumption and planned investment. With the new, higher AE function AE_1, there is also a new, higher equilibrium income, Y_1, due to increased consumer spending.

How did the economy get to this new level? At the old equilibrium level of output and income, planned spending for consumption plus investment is now greater than total output. Firms find their inventories falling below desired levels as they scramble to meet the demand of consumers on a spending spree. (This "shortage" of output is comparable to the temporary shortages in individual markets that occur after demand or supply has shifted and before price has had time to adjust.) Responding to market signals, the practical economists who manage firms increase output, moving in the direction of equilibrium. As output rises, so does income. Consumption rises as income increases, but by less than the rise in income. The gap between aggregate expenditures and output gets smaller and smaller and finally disappears.

The same process could result from a change in planned investment. Earlier in the chapter, we identified some influences that can shift investment demand, including changes in expectations, interest rates, technology, prices, business taxes, changes in final demand, or the size and age of the capital stock. Assume business firms become pessimistic and expect a recession. As they try to reduce inventories and cut back on spending for new plant and equipment, planned investment and aggregate expenditures fall.

FIGURE 14-5

When a change in consumption or investment occurs, there will be a shift in planned spending (aggregate expenditures, or *AE*) that changes the equilibrium level of output *(Y)*. If *AE* shifts upward from AE_0 to AE_1, equilibrium output will increase to Y_1. If *AE* shifts downward from AE_0 to AE_2, equilibrium output will decrease to Y_2.

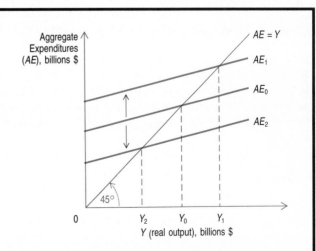

In Figure 14-5, this change in planned investment is drawn as a fall in aggregate expenditures from AE_0 to AE_2. This shift in planned investment means aggregate expenditures or planned spending for consumption and investment, is now less than output at the original equilibrium level of income (Y_0). Inventories start to pile up. Firms cut back on production to reduce inventories, and as production falls, so does income. As income falls, consumers spend less. The new equilibrium is reached at Y_2, where there is less consumption spending, less investment spending, and lower levels of income and output.

Equilibrium Income and Full Employment Income

The basic components of this model of how planned consumption and investment spending determine the level of income and output was developed by Keynes in the 1930s. For the first time planned, or desired, spending took center stage in macroeconomics analysis. In addition to consumption and investment, the simple Keynesian model contains two other important elements. One is the notion of a full employment level of income that can differ from the equilibrium level of income. The other is the multiplier.

There is nothing special about the equilibrium level of income. In particular, there is no reason to assume this level of income will be associated with full employment of labor (or of capital, either). Once practical economists have decided how much they want to consume and invest, those decisions will determine the equilibrium level of income and output. The equilibrium level of output, in turn, determines how many workers firms need to produce that output. Demand for workers determines the levels of employment and unemployment of the labor force.

Full employment output (Y^*) The level of total output (income) associated with full employment of the labor force.

In Chapter 11, we defined full employment as employment of 95 percent of the labor force (the other 5 percent are temporarily unemployed for frictional or structural reasons). Given the size of the labor force, there is some number of jobs, N^*, that constitutes full employment. For example, assume 100 million workers are in the labor force; then N^* equals 95 million. To create 95 million jobs, the **full employment output** has to be Y^*, or perhaps \$800 billion. This level of output may or may not be the same value as Y_e, the equilibrium level of output. Figure 14-6 illustrates this dilemma. Unless the consumption or investment function shifts, output will be stuck at the equilibrium level, Y_e, even if the economy is experiencing considerable unemployment.

How can a nation of practical economists, acting in their own self-interest, arrive at an unsatisfactory aggregate output? Keynes answered that the whole is not simply the sum of its parts, an idea known as the *fallacy of composition*. Each household or firm acts to maximize its own well-being, without regard for the effects of its decisions on others. The total level of output is a public good, and each household's influence on that total is so negligible that it is not taken into account in household decisions.

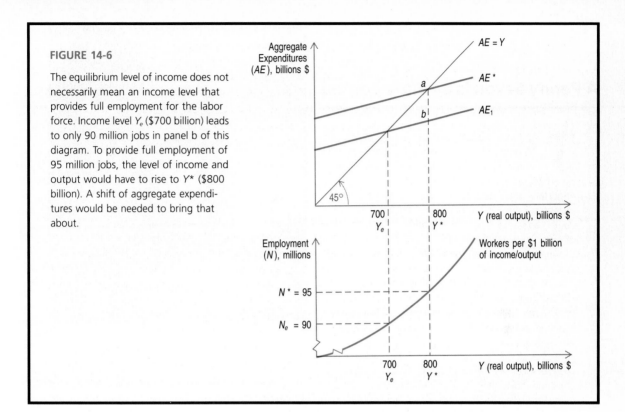

FIGURE 14-6

The equilibrium level of income does not necessarily mean an income level that provides full employment for the labor force. Income level Y_e ($700 billion) leads to only 90 million jobs in panel b of this diagram. To provide full employment of 95 million jobs, the level of income and output would have to rise to Y^* ($800 billion). A shift of aggregate expenditures would be needed to bring that about.

The Recessionary Gap

If Figure 14-6 has successfully explained why unemployment can occur and persist, it also points to a solution. If policymakers can shift either *C* or *I* upward so that the new AE^* crosses the 45° line at Y^*, output will rise to Y^* and create enough additional jobs to get employment to N^*. Now you can see why Keynes stressed the importance of planned spending and stimulation of spending as a way to get to full employment!

How much must planned consumption investment shift to get the economy to Y^*? In Figure 14-6, consumption *(C)* or investment *(I)* needs to shift upward by the vertical distance *ab* between *AE* and *AE**. The **recessionary gap** (*ab* in Figure 14-6) measures the difference between current aggregate expenditures *(AE)* and the level of *AE* needed to move the equilibrium levels of income and output to the full employment level.

The opposite problem could also occur, with Y^* below equilibrium income Y_e. Since Y^* is by definition the maximum the economy can produce, it is not possible to produce a level of Y_e greater than Y^*—but that does not stop consum-

Recessionary gap
The amount by which planned spending must be increased to bring the economy to the full employment level of output.

Myth 14-1

A Penny Saved Is a Penny Earned

The famous quotation from Benjamin Franklin, "A penny saved is a penny earned," seems to imply that some personal and civic virtue is associated with saving rather than consuming. However, an important implication of the Keynesian model is that increased saving is not necessarily the best thing that could happen to an economy operating at a low level of output and employment.

Suppose a collective attack of thrift has hit the United States and all citizens have decided to save a larger fraction of their incomes. As saving shifts upward, the consumption function and aggregate expenditures shift downward. At the old equilibrium level of Y, aggregate expenditures are less than output, and unsold inventories start to pile up. What happens? Falling sales of consumer goods lead firms to cut back output, which reduces incomes. As incomes fall, households reduce consumption further. This process continues until income has fallen to the point where households' new (lower) consumption plus investment *(AE)* is again equal to the new, lower level of income and output *(Y)*. Civic virtue has made the recession worse!

Increased saving is often appropriate and desirable for both individuals and societies. Saving provides the resources that can be used for investment. Most of the time, the U.S. economy does not save enough. But simply because saving is good, more saving is not always better. A penny saved may be a penny earned, but when the economy is in the doldrums, there may be more to be said for a penny spent than a penny saved. ■

ers and business investors from trying! The excess demand for output puts upward pressure on prices. To cool down an overheated economy, it would be desirable to reduce consumption or investment demand, shifting *AE* downward so that it crosses the 45° line at Y^*. More commonly, however, policymakers are concerned about situations where a recessionary gap requires an increase in planned spending to get to full employment.

The Multiplier

If you look carefully at both Figures 14-5 and 14-6, you will notice something very interesting: The shift in the aggregate expenditure function is always smaller than the resulting change in equilibrium income. In Figure 14-5, the distance between AE_0 and AE_1 (or between AE_0 and AE_2) is much smaller than the corresponding change in the level of Y. In Figure 14-6, when AE shifted from AE_1 to AE^*, equilibrium income rose from Y_e to Y^*. Again, the change in Y was much larger than the shift *(ab)* in aggregate expenditure. What appears to happen is that a relatively small change in consumption or investment demand has a much larger total effect on equilibrium income or output. This effect is known as the **multiplier.** The multiplier measures the relationship between a change in planned spending and the resulting total change in output and income.

Multiplier The ratio of changes in total output (income) to the initial shift in planned spending, or $1/(1 - MPC)$

How does the multiplier work? Suppose investment demand increases. Firms might be anticipating good times, or a new technological breakthrough might require new equipment. Planned investment I_0 rises from $100 to $150. This increase in spending then sets off a chain reaction.

The first effect is that business firms see a rise in demand for investment goods of $50. They can be expected to respond by expanding output by $50 to meet that demand. However, when output expands by $50, household income also rises by $50. The consumption function tells us that consumers will spend 80 percent of that increase, or $40. In the next round of production and income, there is an additional $40 in demand on top of the continuing demand of $50 for new investment goods. Producers increase output by another $40, which increases consumption spending (by $32), which increases output and income, and on and on. The chain reaction will eventually run its course because, as you can see, the increased spending gets a little smaller in each successive round. Table 14-3 shows the successive rounds of spending. They sum to an increase in income and output of $250. A $50 increase in planned spending has led to a $250 increase in income and output.

In general, the multiplier should be greater than 1. More precisely, the value of the multiplier is $1/(1 - MPC)$. In this example, the MPC is 0.8, so the

---

TABLE 14-3   Successive Rounds of Spending: The Multiplier

The initial increase in investment, $50, plus the increase in induced consumption, $200, sum to the increase in total spending, $250 (all figures in billions).

Round	Increase in Income	Increase in Consumption
1	$ 50.00	$ 40.00
2	40.00	32.00
3	32.00	24.80
4	24.80	19.80
5	19.80	16.00
All other rounds	80.40	67.40
Total	$250.00	$200.00

multiplier is $1/(1 - 0.8)$, or 5. A larger MPC means a larger multiplier, because more spending occurs in later rounds. A smaller MPC means a smaller multiplier.

Actual values of the multiplier for the U.S. economy are in the range of 2 or 3. A large multiplier is not necessarily good or bad; it depends on the circumstances. If there is a rise in aggregate expenditures *(AE),* a large multiplier will cause a large increase in income and output. On the downside, a relatively small drop in *AE* will result in a much larger fall in income and output. Thus, an economy with a smaller multiplier will tend to be more stable. On the other hand, if the government is trying to stimulate output and employment, a large multiplier would be convenient. Less additional spending would be needed to generate the same effect on output, income, and employment.

Limitations of the Simple Keynesian Model

The simple two-sector model developed in this chapter is one of the most basic in the "junior economist's tool kit," but it is also very far from the real world. Because this model of determining the level of output and employment is so "stripped down," you can see some relationships that might otherwise get lost in the forest of labor and financial markets, prices and interest rates, and government and the foreign sector. Many of these insights are still powerful even when the model is made more elaborate and more realistic. More elaborate and more realistic versions of the model explore other influences on consumption and investment and add the government and the foreign sector.

Other Influences on Consumption   In this model, consumption depends primarily on current income. Income is a very important influence on consumption, but it is not the only factor. Sometimes other influences are even more important. For instance,

1. After World War II economists expected a sharp drop in income, but it did not materialize because consumption was much higher than predicted. Why? Consumers' liquid *assets* were at an all-time high relative to income, because households had spent four years working hard and stashing away war bonds. Also, the stock of consumer durables (autos, washing machines, furniture) was worn out. Practical economists attempted to rebalance their mix of financial assets (higher than desired) and their physical assets (lower than desired) by cashing in bonds to buy consumer goods. In the late 1980s, the opposite was true: Households had ample consumer durables, but they also had high levels of *debt.* The recession that began in 1990 was followed by a slow and gradual recovery until consumers paid down their debt and wore out their cars and refrigerators.
2. During the early 1980s, the housing and auto industries were severely depressed. High *interest rates* had put the monthly payments for new cars and houses out of the reach of many families. High interest rates meant monthly

payments on existing mortgages with adjustable rates rose, leaving less to spend on other consumption. Consumption falls when interest rates rise and rises when interest rates fall.

3. In the 1970s, in contrast, housing enjoyed an exceptional and sustained boom due to increased demand for housing services. (Remember, although new houses are classified as investment, the services of housing are part of consumption.) Why did this increase occur? The changing *age distribution of the population* meant far more young families were setting up households.

Even though consumption is much more stable than investment, it too can shift. Consumption shifts in response to changes in debt and assets, the stock of consumer durables, the size and age distribution of the population, taxes, interest rates, and price expectations.

Investment, Interest Rates, and Final Demand   Like the consumption function, the investment demand function is much more complex than the simple I_0 used in the *AE* function. Investment depends on both interest rates and the demand for final output.

A large share of investment is financed by borrowing. At higher interest rates, some firms drop out of the market. At lower interest rates, more inventory and new factories and equipment look more attractive. Thus, higher interest rates tend to discourage investment spending. Remember, even if the firm does not need to borrow, the practical economists in charge could have put the funds spent on new plant and equipment into interest-bearing accounts or bonds of other firms. Only if the investment looks profitable enough to forgo the high rate of interest available on other assets will a practical economist in charge of a firm choose to invest in plant, equipment, and inventories.

Investment is also influenced by final demand. Firms purchase capital goods to produce goods and services to sell to consumers, including export sales to other countries. More consumer and export demand should call forth more demand for capital goods with which to produce them. If final demand increases, the capital stock must expand to produce those final goods. A rise in consumer or export demand of $1 might require from $2 to $5 in additional capital to produce it. Once the new capital is there, however, investment can drop back to its old level. Thus, a small change in final demand will generate a *temporary* large rise in investment, followed by a fall back to the old level. Because investment depends on the *change* in income and output *(ΔY)* rather than on the level of income and output, it is not possible to write a simple relationship between I and Y as we did for C and Y.

Another determinant of total investment is the size and age of the present stock of capital. New investment is a change in the capital stock. Replacement investment is also an important source of demand, however. As existing capital wears out, part of investment is devoted to replacement and part to increases in the stock. The larger the existing stock of capital, the more regular need for replacement capital there will be.

New technology and new products also influence investment demand, because they usually require new capital. In the 1980s, the semiconductor industry was a major purchaser of new capital that reflected new technology. Industrial robots and computers were other technological advances that led to purchases of new capital. In the 1990s, one area experiencing a great deal of technological advance is health care, with more sophisticated patient-monitoring devices and life support equipment. Technological advances in consumer products can also require investment in new capital. To produce the new, energy-efficient refrigerators unveiled in 1993 after years of development, General Electric and other manufacturers had to refit their refrigerator factories with new equipment.

Government can also try to encourage investment, primarily through special tax breaks, discussed in Chapter 13. These tax provisions may allow firms to write off the cost of equipment before the equipment actually wears out or grant firms tax credits for new investment. An investment tax credit for new investment was a part of both parties' platforms in the 1992 presidential election.

Because so many influences can change investment and investment is related to changes in Y rather than to Y itself, investment is difficult to capture in a simple relationship that is comparable to the consumption function. Much of the instability in the private sector that generates business cycles appears to originate in changes in business investment.

ADDING GOVERNMENT AND THE FOREIGN SECTOR

Adding government purchases (G) and taxes (T) will bring this simple model closer to reality. For simplicity, we will assume all government spending is to purchase goods and services from business firms and all taxes are paid by households. We will also assume, for now, that both taxes and government spending are independent of the level of income.

Government purchases (G), like investment, are an addition to planned spending or AE. Taxes (T) are a little more complicated. Taxes do not enter the equation for AE directly. Instead, they work through reducing consumption. Consumption depends not simply on Y as GDP or national income but on the income received by households. This measure of Y is disposable income, or Y_d, which is equal to income minus taxes $(Y - T)$.

Government Spending and Aggregate Expenditures

Like investment, government purchases of goods and services (G) are simply added to the list of planned expenditures (AE). G is probably somewhat related to the level of output and income, but not in a systematic or predictable way. For that reason, government purchases are treated as a given quantity, G_0. A change in government spending will have a multiplier effect on final output and income just like a change in C_0 or a change in I_0. An increase in government spending will increase income and output by a larger amount—determined by the size of the multiplier—and a reduction in government spending will reduce the equilibrium level of income and output.

Recall from Chapters 3 and 11 that government purchases of goods and services are only part of total government spending. These government purchases consist of the services of judges and members of Congress; construction of government buildings; purchases of paper clips, missiles, computers, and other ordinary goods and services used to provide the government services described in Chapters 9 and 10. Most of the rest of the government budget consists of transfer payments to individuals. These transfer payments are like negative taxes. Thus, they are grouped with T, which is defined as *net taxes*, or taxes minus transfer payments.

Taxes and Consumption

With government in the picture, households now have three ways to use their income. They must pay taxes *(T)*, and they can use the rest of their income to consume *(C)* and save *(S)*. An increase in taxes will reduce both consumption and saving, while a decrease in taxes will increase both consumption and saving.

Taxes work indirectly through household income to influence consumption. Taxes are not a part of planned spending, but when taxes go up, practical economists will reduce planned consumption as well as saving, because an increase in taxes is equivalent to a reduction in income. Thus, if taxes rise by T dollars, consumption falls by $MPC \times T$ dollars. Since the MPC is less than 1, the fall in consumption is smaller than the rise in taxes. This fall in consumption is then multiplied by the multiplier to find the effect on the level of income and output. For example, if the MPC is still 0.8, an increase in taxes of $10 billion would reduce consumption by $8 billion. The other $2 billion would come out of saving. The multiplier of 5 would then indicate that Y would fall by 5 times the fall in consumption spending, or $40 billion. In contrast, an equal change in government purchases *(G)* of $10 billion would add to planned spending *(AE)* directly and, through the multiplier, increase income and output by $50 billion.

Equilibrium with Government

Adding government purchases to aggregate expenditures and reducing consumption to reflect the effect of taxes determine a new equilibrium level of output. Taxes will shift consumption and AE downward, whereas increased government purchases will shift AE upward. How much AE shifts depends on the sizes of the changes in both G and T. If G is larger than T, AE shifts upward and equilibrium Y increases, if G is smaller than T, Y will fall. This model suggests a tool for attempting to control the levels of income, output, and employment. Government could use taxes and/or government spending to shift AE so that it crosses the 45° line exactly at Y^*. How and when such a policy works and why it may fail is the subject of the next chapter.

Exports and Imports

Exports, like government purchases, are added to planned spending, or AE. Exports are another source of demand for output produced in the United States. Imports are subtracted from planned spending because they represent a leakage, or a diversion of income from domestic use to make purchases outside the economy. Usually exports and imports are grouped together as net exports (the $X - M$ of the GDP accounts). If net exports are positive—that is, if the country exports more than it imports—AE will rise and so will equilibrium output and income. If net exports are negative, with imports exceeding exports, AE and Y will be lower than they would be if there were no foreign trade at all. In Chapter 18, we discuss some of the links among exports, imports, and the domestic economy.

 CHECKLIST : **Sources of Changes in Equilibrium Income**

Changes in equilibrium income result from a shift in planned spending, or *AE*. *AE* will shift if there is a change in

Consumption resulting from changes in interest rates, consumer debt or assets, population, expectations, stock of consumer durables, or taxes

Investment resulting from changes in tax policy, interest rates, technology, age of capital stock, expectations, or final demand

Government purchases resulting from changes in government policy

Net exports resulting from changes in exchange rates, events in other countries, changes in tastes, and other factors.

THE KEYNESIAN MODEL AND AGGREGATE DEMAND

The Keynesian model is not an alternative to the aggregate demand and supply model; rather, it is a look behind the aggregate demand curve. The Keynesian model is developed for a given price level. Each price level corresponds to a different amount of consumption and investment at each level of real income *(Y)*.

Thus, the equilibrium level of income in the Keynesian model is for one particular price level, P_1, and corresponds to a specific point on the aggregate demand curve (P_1, Y_1). At a lower price level (P_2), consumption would be lower.

Consumers, who are net asset holders, will feel wealthier and increase their spending. Even if a lower price level has no effect on net taxes, investment demand, government purchases, and net exports, it will affect consumption. *AE* will be lower at a higher price level and higher at a lower price level.

This relationship between consumption and the price level is shown in panel a of Figure 14-7. $AE_1(P_1)$ corresponds to price level P_1 and is associated with equilibrium income and output, Y_1. $AE_2(P_2)$ corresponds to a lower price level, P_2, and a higher equilibrium income level, Y_2. A whole range of price level choices will trace out a family of *AE* curves corresponding to each price level and will generate a set of *P, Y* points on the aggregate demand curve, *AD*, in panel b of Figure 14-7.

A shift in planned spending *(AE) for any reason other than a change in the price level* will shift the whole family of *AE* curves and thus shift the aggregate demand curve. Remember all the consumption-saving shifters—prices, interest rates, expectations, population, assets, and debts? Since changes in these factors can shift the *AE* function, they will also shift the aggregate demand curve.

FIGURE 14-7

Since consumption will vary at different price levels, each price level is associated with a different consumption function and thus also with a different *AE* curve in panel a. The price level, *P*, associated with a given *AE* curve and the equilibrium level of output, *Y*, determined where that *AE* curve crosses the 45° line, are one point on an aggregate demand curve, shown in panel b. Different price levels will be associated with different *AE* curves and thus with different levels of *Y*. These *AE* curves trace out the points on the aggregate demand curve in panel b.

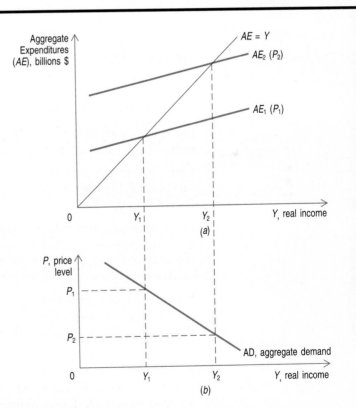

Changes in taxes *(T)* by government will also change planned spending through their impact on consumption.

Similarly, the investment component of *AE* can be shifted by changes in interest rates, technology, wearing out of the capital stock, expectations, and other variables. Government policy changes will shift government purchases, and changes in exchange rates and other factors can change net exports. A change in any one of these components of planned spending will shift the *AE* curve and will also shift the aggregate demand curve, changing not only equilibrium income but also the price level.

In the next chapter, we will explore how policymakers can use *G* and *T* as tools to change the levels of income, output, and employment. In this chapter and in Chapter 15, we largely ignore the effects of price changes. We will return to the issue of price level changes after you have a clearer grasp of the tools the government has to influence economic activity and how it uses those tools.

Summary

1. To understand shifts in aggregate demand, it is necessary to understand the behavior of the major economic "actors"—households, businesses, and government.

2. Households earn an income *(Y)* that they can either spend on consumption *(C)* or save *(S)*. Consumption is a positive function of income. In the Keynesian model, an increase in income will generate a predictable rise in consumption that is some fraction of the rise in income. That fraction is the marginal propensity to consume (MPC).

3. Saving is income that is not consumed. The saving function is a "mirror image" of the consumption function.

4. Consumption will shift in response to changes in the price level, price expectations, interest rates, consumer assets and debt, size and age distribution of the population, and taxes.

5. Planned investment spending for plant and equipment, residential construction, and inventories is I_0. Investment can shift in response to changes in consumer demand, interest rates, technology, size of the existing capital stock, expectations, taxes, and other influences.

6. Consumption plus investment equals aggregate expenditures *(AE)*. In equilibrium, aggregate expenditures must equal income and output *(Y)*. At any other level of output, unplanned increases or decreases in inventories will occur.

7. Equilibrium income may differ from the desired level, which is the full employment level of income and output. The change in planned spending needed to get to the full employment level is the recessionary gap.

8. A shift in consumption or investment will change the equilibrium level of income by a multiple amount. The relationship between the change in planned spending and the change in final income or output is given by the multiplier.

9. Government and net exports can be added to the Keynesian model. Government expenditures *(G)* and net exports are additions to aggregate expenditures. Taxes *(T)* work indirectly through changes in consumption. Economic policymakers can change the levels of government spending and taxes to change the equilibrium level of income and output.

10. The simple Keynesian model does not take interest rates or prices into account, but it does help explain how shifts in consumption, investment, or government spending translate into shifts in aggregate demand.

Key Terms

aggregate expenditures
  (AE)
consumption function
equilibrium
  (macroeconomics)
full employment output
  (Y*)

injection
leakage
marginal propensity to
  consume (MPC)
multiplier
recessionary gap

saving *(S)*
unplanned inventory
  investment

Questions and Problems

1. Suppose the marginal propensity to consume is 0.7, C_0 is 200, and investment *(I_0)* is 400. What is the equilibrium level of income?

2. If investment falls to 300 in Problem 1, what will happen to the equilibrium level of income? What is the value of the multiplier?

3. If the part of consumption that is independent of the level of income *(C_0)* increases from 200 to 250 in Problem 1, what will happen to the equilibrium level of income?

4. If an economy without a government suddenly creates one, and the government spends much more than it collected in taxes, in which direction would equilibrium income change? Why? Suppose the government started with large tax collections for future government spending but did no actual spending right away. What would happen to the level of income?

5. How would each of the following, by shifting consumption or investment, affect the equilibrium level of income?

   a. An increase in interest rates
   b. An increase in population

      c. Expectations of a recession

      d. A major natural disaster that destroyed a large part of the capital stock

6. Assume the marginal propensity to consume is 0.75. Investment spending increases by $200, which immediately increases output and income by $200. In the next period, how much does consumption increase? In the period after that? Trace through the effects on output and employment through the first five rounds in a table, as follows:

Change in Income	Change in Consumption
Period 1	
Period 2	
etc.	

7. Suppose you were put in charge of macroeconomic policy. If you could choose the value of the economy's marginal propensity to consume (meaning you get to select a multiplier), would you choose a high or a low value? Why?

8. The stock market is booming, and consumers are cashing in. The value of their portfolios has increased so that the average household now has $2,000 more than before. Is this an increase in income or an increase in wealth? How will it be reflected in the consumption function?

9. Suppose the price level rose by 5 percent last year. How will that affect the equilibrium level of real output in the Keynesian model? In the aggregate demand model?

15

Fiscal Policy and Deficits

The larger is the national debt, the greater is the burden to be borne by future generations. . . . In effect, we are stealing from our grandchildren in order to satisfy our desires of today.

FORMER PRESIDENT DWIGHT D. EISENHOWER, 1963

Main Points

1. The tools of fiscal policy are taxes, transfer payments, and government purchases. All three tools can be used to change the levels of output, employment, and prices by shifting aggregate expenditures and aggregate demand.

2. Fiscal policy includes automatic changes in tax collections and transfer payments as income rises or falls, as well as deliberate actions to shift aggregate demand by changing the levels of taxes and government spending.

3. Fiscal policy suffers from long lags between recognizing economic problems, developing policy responses, and seeing the effects of those policies on the economy.

4. Some of the impact of fiscal policy falls on the price level and interest rates rather than on the primary targets of output and employment.

5. Expansionary fiscal policy tends to result in budget deficits and to increase the national debt. Budget deficits affect the level of income, interest rates, and private investment, as well as the inflation rate, the distribution of income, and the size of the public sector.

I n this chapter, we examine how the government can use its power to tax and spend to influence the levels of output, employment, and prices in an aggregate supply and demand model. The tools of fiscal policy are taxes, transfer payments, and government purchases of goods and services. Policymakers can use various combinations of these three tools to try to increase or decrease aggregate demand. Fiscal policy involves some practical problems, including timing, the choice between tax changes and spending changes, the role of transfer payments, and the relationship between fiscal policy and monetary policy.

The difference between the government's income from taxes and its expenditures each year is the budget deficit or surplus. The sum total of accumulated deficits over the years is the national debt. The deficit and the national debt affect interest rates, the rate of inflation, and the distribution of income. A large deficit limits the government's ability to respond to recessions. Large deficits may also permit excessive growth of government. The deficit has been the most pressing macroeconomic policy issue in recent years. ■

FISCAL POLICY, THE BUSINESS CYCLE, AND AGGREGATE DEMAND

Fiscal policy The deliberate use of taxes, transfer payments, or government purchases to try to affect the levels of output, income, and employment in the economy.

If output is below the full employment level, resources are going to waste. Practical economists may want the government to take appropriate action to shift the level of planned spending to attain full employment. On the other hand, planned spending can be so high that it creates inflationary pressures. As the general price level rises, practical economists find it hard to interpret the market signals on which they rely to make sound choices about spending, earning, and saving. They may want the government to act to reduce the level of its planned spending to control inflation.

Fiscal policy consists of changes in taxes, transfer payments, or government purchases undertaken for the specific purpose of changing levels of output, employment, and prices. Note that the fact that government spends more than it collects in tax revenues does not in itself constitute fiscal policy. To determine what the government's fiscal policy is, one needs to know *why* taxes and spending are at their current level.

Suppose a war begins. The government increases spending for soldiers, airplanes, and military hardware. This increase in defense spending, however, is not fiscal policy. However, if, in response to the war effort, the government decides to cut spending in other areas so that additional defense spending will not drive up demand and prices, that action *is* fiscal policy. If instead the government raises taxes to keep higher defense spending from creating a larger deficit, driving up demand and prices, that tax increase too is fiscal policy. It is not only *what* the government does but also *why* it alters its levels of spending or taxes that make those changes fiscal policy.

Fiscal Policy and the Business Cycle

The purpose of fiscal policy is to reduce fluctuations in the levels of output, employment, and prices so that the economy's output grows at a steady rate that provides a high level of labor employment. One way to envision the role of fiscal policy is in terms of the business cycle. Recall that this cycle consists of an upturn followed by a downturn in economic activity. In Figure 15-1, the vertical axis represents real output or income *(Y)* and the horizontal axis measures time. If the economy grew at a nice, steady rate, it would follow the straight line in the diagram. Instead, however, the level of output and income tends to grow rapidly, reaching a peak at *a*, followed by a downturn or recession that continues until the economy "hits bottom in the trough" at *b*. Then the economy turns up again. A "trough-to-trough" time period measures one complete business cycle.

Expansionary fiscal policy Changes in taxes, transfer payments, and government purchases intended to shift aggregate demand to the right and increase output and employment.

The dashed line in Figure 15-1 represents the goal of fiscal policy. That goal is to reduce the fluctuations in the level of output. When output is more stable, growing along a steady growth path, employment and the price level are also more stable. Downturns, or recessions, represent high unemployment as well as lost income and output. A recession calls for **expansionary fiscal policy** to increase the levels of output and employment. The upswings, or expansions, are

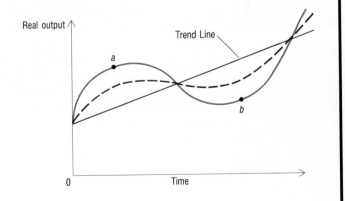

FIGURE 15-1

The purpose of stabilizing fiscal policy is to reduce the magnitude of the swings in the business cycle so that the ups and downs of output, as well as prices and employment, are more like the dashed line than the solid line.

Contractionary fiscal policy Changes in taxes, transfer payments, and government purchases intended to shift aggregate demand to the left and reduce output and employment.

usually accompanied by rising price levels. Upswings may require **contractionary fiscal policy** to reduce upward pressure on the price level. A contractionary policy would call for tax increases or spending cuts.

Keynes developed his ideas about the use of fiscal policy during an unusually severe downturn in the business cycle, the Great Depression of the 1930s. Keynes assumed the aggregate supply curve was close to horizontal. With plenty of unemployed resources, output could be expanded with no upward pressure on the price level. The fiscal policy model we will examine in the first part of this chapter will use that Keynesian assumption.

Government Purchases and Aggregate Demand

Government purchases are one of several tools policymakers can use to try to move the equilibrium level of real income and output closer to the full employment level of output. In terms of the model in Chapter 14, an increase in government purchases will increase aggregate expenditures. An increase in aggregate expenditures will shift aggregate demand to the right. In Figure 15-2, increased government purchases shift aggregate demand from AD_2 to AD_3. Since aggregate supply is horizontal, the level of income and output will rise from Y_2 to Y_3. If Y_2 were below the full employment level of output, this shift should move the economy toward full employment.

Note that the difference between Y_2 to Y_3 is greater than the difference between AD_2 to AD_3. Real output (Y) will increase by more than the rise in government spending alone because of the multiplier effect. Increased government spending raises the incomes of consumers, who then increase their consumption spending. Higher consumption spending leads to an increase in output, which further raises income and consumption, and so forth. Thus, the increase in government spending needed to get to the target level of income

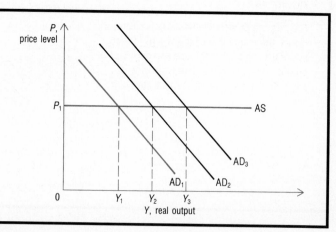

FIGURE 15-2

Fiscal policy works by shifting aggregate demand. Expansionary fiscal policy—tax cuts or increases in government purchases—would shift aggregate demand from AD_2 to AD_3, driving up Y to Y_3 with no change in the price level. Contractionary fiscal policy would shift AD from AD_2 to AD_1, reducing Y from Y_2 to Y_1.

and output is smaller than the gap between actual output and the full employment level of output *(Y*)*.

Reduced government spending, with everything else unchanged, will shift aggregate demand to the left (from AD_2 to AD_1). The level of real output will fall, and so will employment. Such a policy is used when there are severe pressures on the capacity of the economy to produce, such as during a war. This policy is not called for in the context of Figure 15-2, because the horizontal aggregate supply curve implies ample idle resources and therefore no need for contractionary fiscal policy.

Taxes, Transfer Payments, and Aggregate Demand

Balanced budget Results when government revenues (taxes) exactly equal outlays (government purchases plus transfers) in a given year.

Usually governments pay for at least part of their spending by collecting taxes. Taxes reduce consumers' disposable incomes and thus reduce planned spending, aggregate expenditures, and aggregate demand. Some kinds of taxes, such as personal income taxes, sales taxes, social security taxes, and personal property taxes, are paid directly by households. Since households own business firms, households ultimately also pay any taxes levied on those business firms, such as corporate income taxes or business property taxes.

Surplus An excess of government revenues (taxes) over outlays (government purchases plus transfers) in a given year.

If taxes *(T)* equal government purchases *(G)*, the government has a **balanced budget.** If *T* is greater than *G*, there is a **surplus;** if *T* is less than *G*, there is a **deficit.** Deficits have been the usual case for the last 30 years. Taxes and government spending can be raised or cut together or moved in opposite directions, or one can be changed and the other held constant. Changes in taxes are generally the preferred tool of fiscal policy, because government officials can usually put such changes into effect more quickly and easily than spending changes.

Deficit An excess of government purchases plus transfer payments over revenue in the form of taxes in a given year.

Like changes in government spending, changes in taxes shift aggregate demand, but indirectly. Since taxes reduce the disposable incomes of households, these practical economists respond by adjusting their consumption and saving. An increase in taxes will reduce consumption spending at every possible price level. The *AE* curve will shift downward and aggregate demand will shift to the left, reducing the equilibrium level of income. A reduction in taxes will increase consumption spending at every possible price level. The *AE* curve will shift upward and aggregate demand will shift to the right, raising the equilibrium level of income.

In addition to government purchases and taxes there is yet a third tool of fiscal policy. This third tool is transfer payments, introduced in Chapter 11. **Transfer payments** are payments such as welfare, scholarships, veterans' benefits, social security, and so forth, for which no production is expected in return. Transfer payments work exactly like taxes in reverse. Both taxes and transfer payments work indirectly on aggregate expenditures and aggregate demand by affecting consumption spending. An increase in transfer payments raises the disposable income of households without changing *Y*. These households react

Transfer payments Payments to individuals, usually by government, from whom no productive services are expected in return, such as welfare or social security benefits.

like practical economists by increasing their consumption relative to *Y*, that is, shifting consumption and *AE* upward and *AD* to the right. A reduction in transfer payments will reduce consumption, shifting *AE* downward and *AD* to the left, reducing output and the price level.

CHECKLIST : **Fiscal Policy Tools and Aggregate Demand**

The tools of fiscal policy are:

Government purchases
  Directly increase or decrease aggregate demand
  Higher *G* shifts *AD* right
  Lower *G* shifts AD left
Taxes
  Indirectly increase or decrease aggregate demand through changing consumption
  Higher *T* shifts *AD* left
  Lower *T* shifts *AD* right
  Less impact, dollar for dollar, than *G*
Transfer payments
  Indirectly increase or decrease aggregate demand through changing consumption
  Higher transfers shifts *AD* right
  Lower transfers shift *AD* left
  Less impact, dollar for dollar, than *G*
  Same impact, dollar for dollar, as *T*

THE CHOICE AMONG SPENDING, TAXES, AND TRANSFERS

Government purchases, taxes, and transfer payments can all be used, separately or in combination, to shift the aggregate demand curve so that it intersects the aggregate supply curve at the desired (full employment) level of income and output. However, there are, several important differences between changing taxes (or transfers) and changing government spending.

Differences in Impact

From a theoretical standpoint, there are two considerations. First, taxes and spending work in different directions. An increase in government spending or transfer payments shifts aggregate demand to the right, whereas an increase in taxes reduces demand, that is, shifts aggregate demand to the left. Second, changes in taxes or transfer payments have less of an impact on aggregate demand and real output, dollar for dollar, than changes in government purchases. An increase in government spending of $10 billion has an immediate and direct impact on spending. An equal reduction in taxes or increase in transfer payments starts with consumers. They will spend most of the increase in disposable income from lower taxes or higher transfers, but will save at least part of it. Thus, part of the $10 billion will not show up immediately as additional demand for goods and services. If, for example, consumers decide to save 20 percent of an income tax cut or an increase in social security benefits, the initial impact on aggregate demand will be only $8 billion instead of $10 billion.

Balance Between Public and Private Sectors

The choice between these two kinds of tools reflects philosophical differences over the appropriate balance between the public and private sectors. Economists and politicians who believe the government is doing too little will usually argue that expansionary fiscal policy should concentrate on increasing government purchases *(G)* rather than on reducing taxes *(T)*. Those who favor tax cuts will argue that the public sector is already too large and that practical economists can make wiser decisions about spending priorities than the government can. At least once in each decade since World War II, a recession has occurred that called for some kind of policy response. The choice always comes down to more spending or less taxes or, occasionally, more transfer payments. Almost always the tax cutters win. Tax cuts were approved in 1975 and 1981 in response to recessions. In 1991, in a rare exception, Congress enacted an increase in transfer payments in the form of extended unemployment benefits in response to the 1990–1991 recession.

Controlling the Budget

One advantage of government purchases over both taxes and transfers is that *G* can be controlled directly. Once the budget has been passed, the amount of potential spending has been decided. Tax collections and transfer outlays differ. In those cases, Congress establishes a set of rules consisting of eligibility requirements, tax rates, deductible expenses, and personal exemptions. Once those rules are set, the decisions of practical economists determine exactly how much tax the government collects and what level of transfer payments it makes. For example, if the government creates a tax credit for contributions to charity, the public decides how much tax revenue is given up by its decisions about how much to contribute to charity. If it is important to control the deficit and the size of the budget, government purchases are a better fiscal policy tool.

The biggest risk in changing government spending to influence output and employment is that those programs are hard to eliminate. Using spending programs as a fiscal policy tool will tend to expand the size of government relative to the private sector. Taxes, on the other hand, are easier to change in both directions, although tax cutting is always politically easier than raising taxes!

Thus, if policymakers rely more on taxes than on transfer payments or government purchases for fiscal policy, the public sector will grow less rapidly.

Winners and Losers

Any public policy change creates gainers and losers, and fiscal policy is no exception. The gains from additional spending initially go to suppliers, such as workers and firms in the defense industry, potential workers for the postal service, NASA, or other government agencies. Benefits then reach the other sectors of the economy indirectly as this initial group spends its earnings, driving up consumer demand for a variety of goods and services. Little, if any, in the way of benefits may reach the hard-core unemployed, elderly persons, or others not tied into the market economy.

Tax changes also have greater initial impact on middle- and upper-income groups, because changes in the structure of the federal income tax have already cut most of the poor off the tax rolls. Among major federal taxes, only changes in social security taxes have any impact on the poor, and then only on the working poor. Fiscal policy aimed directly at the poor comes in two forms: transfer payments and in-kind services such as public housing, rent supplements, health clinics, and food stamps.

If policymakers are concerned mainly about distributional effects, taxes and transfer payments are a better tool than government purchases. Policymakers can target particular groups—not only the poor or the rich but groups such as farmers, the elderly population, or families with children.

DISCRETIONARY FISCAL POLICY

Discretionary fiscal policy Deliberate changes in tax rates, eligibility rules for transfer payments, or government purchases to influence the levels of output and employment.

Discretionary fiscal policy refers to any deliberate changes in tax rates or spending programs intended to influence the levels of output and employment. This kind of fiscal policy really got its start in the United States with the Employment Act of 1946. This landmark legislation made it an obligation of the federal government to pursue full employment, stable prices, and steady economic growth. To assist the president in formulating fiscal policy, a three-member Council of Economic Advisers was created. The president was required to submit an annual economic report (the *Economic Report of the President*, published each January) to describe economic conditions and propose policies to deal with them. The Clinton administration has added another group of advisers called the Economic Security Council, which includes the secretary of the Treasury and the director of the Office of Management and Budget, to provide advice on a wide range of economic matters, including discretionary fiscal policy.

Although fiscal policy remains important, the period of greatest faith in fiscal policy occurred during the Kennedy and Johnson administrations in the 1960s. Their economic advisers firmly believed it was possible to "fine-tune" the economy (a phrase popularized by chairman of the Council of Economic Advisers Walter Heller); that is, policymakers could select a target combination of inflation rate, growth rate, and unemployment rate and carefully manipulate fiscal policy to achieve those targets. Fiscal policy went into eclipse in the 1970s, to be revived in the 1980s and 1990s in a somewhat different form. In the 1990s, the growth policies described in Chapter 13 play a bigger role than demand management policies.

Who Makes Fiscal Policy?

Responsibility for fiscal policy is shared between the executive and legislative branches of government. In the executive branch, there are several partners in the process. The budget is developed by the Office of Management and Budget, an agency of the executive branch, using input from the various departments and agencies. The director of that agency has been an important fiscal policy adviser since the early 1980s. Tax policy is the province of the Treasury; thus, the secretary of the Treasury is another important fiscal policy player. The Council of Economic Advisers has played an important fiscal policy role in some administrations and a lesser role in others. Under President Clinton the Council has played a smaller role than it has in some earlier administrations, because some power has shifted to the Economic Security Council.

In the 1970s, Congress became increasingly frustrated with relying on statistics and analyses from the executive branch for decisions about taxing and spending. In 1974 Congress created its own agency, the Congressional Budget Office, to provide both houses of Congress with technical analyses of various fiscal alternatives. With a second set of numbers, projections, and proposals provided by this agency instead of just one from the Office of Management and Budget, Congress has been able to play a more active role in fiscal policy.

Timing Fiscal Policy and Lags

Looking at this list of players, it is easy to see that implementing a fiscal policy change is a slow process. A major problem with fiscal policy is that long delays can occur between perceiving a need for action and getting a policy through Congress and the president. By the time the policy is actually in place and working its multiplier effects on the economy, it may no longer be the appropriate policy!

A visual image of this problem is presented in Figure 15-3, which sketches a typical business cycle like those presented earlier in this chapter and in Chapter 12. The fact that the economy is sliding into recession is perceived at point *b*. The executive branch analyzes, Congress debates, and finally a tax cut or a

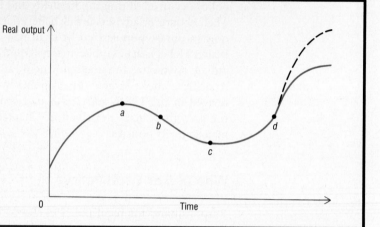

FIGURE 15-3

The ability of fiscal policy to reduce fluctuations in income and output is hampered by time lags. The downturn begins at *a*, is recognized at *b*, and calls forth a policy response at *c* that is finally felt (impact) at *d* just as the economy is pulling out of the recession on its own. Now the expansionary policy is inappropriate, increasing instead of decreasing the magnitude of fluctuations.

spending increase is enacted at point *c*. By the time the effects are felt, the economy has moved along to point *d*, having weathered the recession with very little help from the federal government. In fact, by point *d*, the expansionary fiscal policy is totally wrong: It sets off an inflationary episode that makes the economy follow the dotted path instead of the solid line it had been on. Thus, some economists argue that the existence of time lags makes fiscal policy *destabilizing* rather than stabilizing.

This issue of timing played an important role in the 1992 election. President Bush argued that the economy was beginning to recover from the 1990–1991 recession and therefore it was not necessary to pursue an expansionary policy of spending increases and tax cuts. In fact, he claimed, such policies would fall victim to the same bad timing described in Figure 15-3. The impact of the policies would be felt just as the expansion was in full swing, when restraint would be needed to hold down inflation. As a candidate, President Clinton argued that a stimulus was necessary because unemployment remained high even though other indicators seemed to say the recession was indeed over. Between the election and the inauguration, economic indicators improved enough that the new administration proposed only a very small stimulus (spending for roads, bridges, and Head Start) to ensure that the recovery continued to stay on course. Even that modest stimulus package failed to pass Congress, however. The result was that no discretionary fiscal policy took place during this recession except for the single action of extending unemployment benefits.

Recognition lag The time that elapses between the occurrence of a macroeconomic problem and its diagnosis by public officials.

There are three kinds of time lags in fiscal policy (and similar lags in monetary policy, which we will address in Chapters 16 and 17). The first is the **recognition lag**, the time that elapses until policymakers discover the existence and scope of the economic problem. In the Figure 15-3, the recognition lag is the distance from the upper turning point, *a*, to point *b*.

Statistics take time to gather, compile, and distribute. Even if the numbers

- -

Myth 15-1

- -

The United States Is a Land of "Big Government"

Government is big business in the United States. Federal, state, and local governments combined spent about 39 percent of GDP in 1993. That figure is a significant increase over historical levels. In 1930, government spending was only 11 percent of GDP. First the Great Depression, then World War II, then expanding grant and transfer programs drove that figure upward. Increases in the 1980s reflected higher defense spending and a growing interest on the national debt.

Critics of government growth argue that it reduces reliance on the market, which is a more efficient way to ensure efficiency in production and allocation. Defenders point out that a larger public sector makes an economy more stable, because government spending does not rise or fall as sharply as exports, imports, private investment, and some components of consumption. It is these latter shifts that generate most recessions.

A similar pattern of growth in government has been observed in many other industrial countries. Both the absolute size and the relative share of government tend to rise as both income and population increase. Rising income means more affluent citizens want more and better public services to go with their private consumption—better roads in front of their more expensive houses, better police protection for their increased possessions, more public recreation facilities for their leisure time. Increased population means people are living closer together, generating more conflicts over property rights and negative externalities. Government is expected to resolve those property rights issues and correct the nega-

tive externalities of crime, noise, congestion, and litter that result from packing people closer together.

One way to think about the size of government is to look at the government budgets of other developed countries. By this standard, the size of government in the United States doesn't look so impressive. Government spending does take a larger share of GDP in the United States than in Japan, whose government spends only 25 percent of total output. But in other industrial countries such as Canada, the United Kingdom, France, Germany, Italy, Sweden, and the Netherlands, a larger share of GDP flows through government than in the United States, ranging from 40 percent (Canada) to nearly 60 percent (Sweden). Thus, although the public sector has grown in the United States in the last 60 years, it still manages a smaller share of economic activity than the governments of many other developed market economies. ∎

are readily available, it is hard to discern a trend in output, employment, and prices from the data for a single quarter (a three-month period). It takes at least two quarters (six months) of falling real output *(Y)* to officially declare a recession and two quarters of a steady increase in *Y* to declare a recession over. With up to a two-month lag in data, it would be eight months from the start of a recession before its existence was even officially noted! The 1990–1991 recession actually ended just about the time when it was officially declared a recession. At the other end, this cycle was more than a year past its lower turning point before the recession was officially declared over. Even as the nation was in recovery, the indicators did not give a clear signal about whether the economy would continue to improve or fall back into recession, as happened in 1980–1982.

The second time lag is the **implementation lag,** or the time between recognizing the problem and legislating a policy change to address it. Such a change requires action by Congress, which can be extremely slow. The single action by Congress during the 1990–1991 recession was extended unemployment compensation benefits, which were finally passed in 1992 after the recession had ended (although unemployment still remained high). Various presidents, beginning with Kennedy, have asked Congress to delegate some limited authority to change spending or taxes to the executive branch to reduce this lag. Thus far, Congress has been unwilling to transfer that kind of power to the president.

The third time lag is the **impact lag,** or the time between the change in spending or taxes and the actual effects on economic activity. Taxes, especially personal income and social security taxes, have fairly short time lags in terms of initial impact on disposable income and consumption, although the secondary effects achieved through the multiplier process can take up to two years to completely run their course. The choice of extended unemployment benefits for the 1990–1991 recession was a good one because the impact was fairly quick, as income flowed directly to the unemployed.

The impact lags for changes in government purchases depend on the nature of the purchase. New government employees in agencies such as the Internal Revenue Service or the Social Security Administration can be hired fairly quickly. New roads, post offices, and public buildings, however, are long-term projects that involve design, acquiring land, and getting bids from contractors. Thus, such projects are less suited for use as fiscal policy except in the case of a long recession. The only major effort to use such projects as expansionary fiscal policy occurred during the Great Depression of the 1930s, when the Public Works Administration gave the nation a whole generation of post offices, hiking trails, and sewer systems.

BUILT-IN FISCAL POLICY: AUTOMATIC STABILIZERS

Discretionary fiscal policy is a relatively rare event. Most of the burden of stabilization falls on certain built-in factors that operate to dampen fluctuations in consumption and, through consumption, fluctuations in planned spending and equilibrium national income. These built-in anticyclical factors are called **automatic stabilizers.** They are stabilizers because they reduce fluctuations in income and output. They are automatic because they are a part of the tax

Implementation lag
The time that occurs between the recognition of a macroeconomic problem by public officials and the enactment of policies or programs to address it.

Impact lag   The time that elapses between the enactment of a program to address a macroeconomic problem and the program's actual effects on the economy.

Automatic stabilizer
A change in taxes and transfer payments that occurs automatically in a direction that stabilizes disposable income, and thus saving and consumption, without requiring formal action by Congress.

code and the eligibility requirements for transfer payments. No congressional legislation or executive order is required to trigger these stabilizers. Automatic stabilizers play a major role in economic stabilization; according to some estimates, they reduce fluctuations in income and output by one-third.

Recall from Chapter 11 that disposable income equals GDP or national income less taxes plus transfer payments. When the tax system is progressive, a decrease in income and output leads to a proportionally larger decline in tax collections. A fall in income and output will also trigger a rise in transfer payments. Thus, when real income *(Y)* falls, disposable personal income falls by a smaller proportion.

If disposable personal income falls by less than national income, the decline in consumption will also be proportionally smaller. Remember, disposable income rather than total real income determines consumption spending. This cushion under consumption allows people to maintain their standard of living during downturns. The fact that consumption demand remains relatively strong reduces the decline in total output.

Similar forces operate during an upturn. Taxes rise more than in proportion to rising income and output *(Y)*, and transfer payments fall as output and employment rise. The rise in disposable income is modest relative to the rise in output and income. The smaller rise in disposable income means a smaller increase in consumption. Whatever sets off the recession or expansion, the multiplier is much smaller when taxes and transfer payments depend on the level of income.

Taxes and Income

Since the Great Depression, the most important automatic stabilizer has been the progressive federal personal income tax, which is also the largest single revenue source at the federal level. A progressive income tax takes a higher *percentage* of income in taxes as the taxpayer's income rises. This kind of tax has a schedule of rates that are higher on additional dollars of income. The tax due on the extra dollar of income is called the **marginal tax rate.** Although marginal rates were greatly reduced during the 1980s, the federal income tax is still progressive.

Marginal tax rate The rate paid on the next dollar or last dollar of earnings.

In the 1992 federal income tax rate schedule, a single taxpayer paid no tax (tax rate = 0%) on the first $5,700 of income, because he or she could subtract one personal exemption of $2,300 and a standard deduction of $3,400 before calculating taxable income. After $5,700, the tax rate on the next $16,000 of income was 15 percent. This taxpayer then paid 28 percent on any additional income up to about $35,000 and 31 percent on income above that amount. At an income of $20,000, this taxpayer would be paying $2,145 in federal income tax. The average rate is *T/Y*, or $2,145/$20,000 = 10.7 percent. The marginal rate, however (the rate this taxpayer pays on the dollars from $5,701 to $20,000) is 15 percent. An extra dollar of income would be taxed at 15 percent. If this taxpayer's income jumped to $50,000, his or her marginal rate would be 31 percent. Some income would still be taxed at 0 percent (the first $5,700), some would still be taxed at 15 percent, some at 28 percent, and the last $15,000 at 31 percent. The total tax bill would be $11,300, and the taxpayer would pay 26.5 percent of his or her income in taxes.

Stabilization was not the original goal of progressive income taxes. The reasons offered for high marginal tax rates have always been expressed in terms of equity, or fairness. High marginal rates have also been criticized for creating the wrong kinds of incentives. Marginal rates are important, because practical economists decide at the margin. High marginal rates discourage people from working more, earning more, producing more, and investing more. A tax rate of 50 percent on the next dollar of income (the top rate before 1986) certainly discouraged working harder and earning more. Instead, it encouraged spending more time searching for tax shelters and tax dodges, or tax "avoision" (somewhere between legal tax avoidance and illegal tax evasion). Thus, one argument advanced for the tax reforms of the 1980s was that the lower rates would encourage more productive use of resources.

In any case, a side effect of these tax reductions was a reduction in the automatic stabilizing impact of progressive taxes. The more progressive the tax system is, the more stabilization it will generate. The reduction in income tax rates in the last decade, which had many beneficial effects, had the side effect of reducing the impact of this important automatic stabilizer.

Another important tax stabilizer is the corporate income tax, which is a tax on corporate profits. Corporate profits after taxes are either reinvested in the corporation or paid out as dividends to stockholders, increasing their income and consumption spending. Corporate profits are very sensitive to changes in the level of output and national income. Profits rise and fall more than in proportion to those changes. During recessions, corporate profits drop sharply, and so do corporate profit taxes. Corporate after-tax profits do not fall as much; thus, the impact on investment and consumer income is smaller because of the corporate income tax. During expansions, corporate profits rise rapidly and result in more investment spending by business firms, or more consumer spending by stockholders if the profits are paid out in dividends. When part of the extra profit must be paid in federal and state corporate income taxes, the impact on private spending is smaller.

Transfer Payments and Income

The other group of automatic stabilizers consists of those transfer payments tied to the level of income and output. The major stabilizers in this category are

1. Unemployment compensation benefits
2. Welfare, food stamps, and other antipoverty programs
3. Social security benefits
4. Farm price supports

In Practice 15-1

· ·

Can "It" Happen Again?

The Great Depression of the 1930s left a lasting mark on those who lived and worked during those times. Farm foreclosures, bank failures, 25 percent unemployment, bread lines, and shantytowns called "Hoovervilles" were the unforgettable signs of severe economic distress. Toward the end of the decade, economic conditions had improved, but the experience left many people concerned that "it" might happen again. Steps were taken during and after the Depression to ensure that future recessions would be less severe or less prolonged.

There is no guarantee that *any* disaster will not recur, but several signals suggest that the U.S. economy today is more stable and less vulnerable. Economic "safety nets" that date from the 1930s include

1. Automatic stabilizers
2. Greater regulation of stock markets and banks (although not enough to prevent crises in both in recent years)
3. An increase in the relative importance of consumer nondurables and government purchases (all fairly stable components of planned spending)
4. The willingness of the government to undertake discretionary fiscal policy when it appeared necessary

Most automatic stabilizers were put in place during the Great Depression, including unemployment compensation insurance, social security, and welfare programs. The federal income tax became much more progressive in the postwar period, although recent changes have reduced its progressivity.

The 1929 stock market crash reduced people's assets and therefore their ability to consume. It also shook their expectations and confidence. Today securities market regulations are much more strict. Bank failures also shook confidence and shrank the money supply, a process discussed in Chapters 16 and 17. Since the 1930s, deposit insurance and other safeguards have made the banking system somewhat more secure and less vulnerable to runs and panics, although the late 1980s and early 1990s saw some serious bank safety problems (discussed in Chapter 17).

Finally, policymakers in the 1930s were still greatly influenced by classical ideas, believing the economy would eventually correct itself. They were also very reluctant to deliberately run budget deficits. Today policymakers are much more willing to respond to recessions with discretionary fiscal policy and much less reluctant to run deficits.

There is no way to make the economy risk free. Nevertheless, Americans can feel somewhat more secure about the stability of their economy than they could 60 years ago at the start of the Great Depression. ∎

Unemployment compensation consists of temporary payments to laid-off workers who are covered by unemployment insurance. Most workers in the private nonfarm sector are insured. Unemployment benefits lasting up to 26 weeks are available to workers who are laid off, usually because of a decline in demand for the products they produce. These benefits tend to keep disposable income from dropping at the same rate as aggregate output and income and help unemployed workers keep their consumption near prerecession levels. Sometimes during recessions the benefit period is extended to 39 or 52 weeks, thus converting an automatic stabilizer into discretionary fiscal policy.

Welfare and food stamp applications rise during downturns. Unemployed workers are often eligible for food stamps. Workers whose unemployment benefits expire or who were ineligible for unemployment benefits turn to welfare programs when they lose their jobs. As the economy turns up, many of these workers are employed again or are working full time instead of part time, and welfare and food stamps payments fall. During the downturn, welfare and food stamps allow families to keep closer to their old levels of income and consumption, just as falling taxes and unemployment benefits do.

Social security payments tend to rise during recessions and fall during expansions. Workers can receive reduced benefits from social security at age 62, but many workers choose to work to age 65 or beyond. During recessions, some workers may be forced or encouraged to retire earlier than they had planned. During expansions, firms may encourage older, more experienced workers to stay on past normal retirement age because such workers are difficult to replace.

Federal farm price supports are tied to the prices of agricultural products. When these prices fall during recessions, support payments rise. During expansions, prices of farm products rise and support payments fall. Thus, farm price supports, although not enacted for fiscal policy reasons, do provide another automatic stabilizer.

The combined effects of these automatic stabilizers is to reduce fluctuations in output and employment without requiring any specific congressional action. In minor recessions and expansions, these stabilizers may be all that is needed. If a major or prolonged recession or a period of persistent inflation occurs, however, bigger changes in spending or taxes in the form of discretionary fiscal policy may be needed.

FISCAL POLICY, DEFICITS, AND THE NATIONAL DEBT

Expansionary fiscal policy calls for increasing spending by more than any increase in tax revenue. If the government deliberately uses its purchases, transfers, and taxes to try to raise the level of output and employment, deficits will result. If fiscal policy is an important priority for the government, some decision has to be made about whether and how to try to balance the budget.

The Deficit and Automatic Stabilizers

Net taxes Taxes collected less transfer payments to households.

The deficit equals government purchases minus net taxes collected $(G - T_n)$. **Net taxes** are collections minus transfer payments. The relationship between the surplus or deficit and the level of income or output is complex because of the automatic stabilizers. While T_n and G both affect the level of output, Y, net taxes (T_n) are in turn affected by Y. When income rises, the government collects more taxes, especially income and sales taxes. When income falls, tax collections decrease and transfer payments increase as more people become eligible. When income rises, some people get jobs, pay more taxes, and have less need for transfer payments such as welfare, unemployment benefits, and food stamps. These automatic changes in taxes and transfer payments are sound fiscal policy, but they do increase the deficit during recessions.

The Deficit and Discretionary Fiscal Policy

The problem of balancing the budget with automatic stabilizers is even more serious when the government also pursues a discretionary fiscal policy. Since the economy seems to spend more time below Y^* than above it, policymakers usually try to push the economy toward Y^* with the help of a budget deficit. Now and then demand is so high that the economy is straining at capacity, which calls for a budget surplus to reduce inflationary pressures. Most of the time, however, the economy seems to call for deficit spending as the appropriate policy. On rare occasions the levels of spending, taxing, and transfers called for in terms of fiscal policy may be a balanced budget. Most often, however, the budget that meets the needs of fiscal policy will not be in balance. There will be either a surplus or a deficit—most of the time a deficit.

Fiscal policy is not the only reason for budget deficits. It is painful for politicians to raise taxes and pleasant to cut them. Citizens and special-interest groups put a lot of pressure on Congress to pass spending programs they want and fiercely resist any cuts in those programs. These political forces have little to do with fiscal policy but everything to do with deficits. Once the pressure to balance the budget is eased, politicians are very tempted to spend more than they take in, even when economic conditions do not call for expansionary fiscal policy.

Why a Balanced Budget?

Supporters of a balanced budget argue that it is the only way to control the growth of the public sector. When citizens and taxpayers have to pay for public programs out of taxes, they are forced to be better practical economists, weighing the benefits of the services against the pain of taxes. When these programs are partly financed by borrowing, the pain is less immediate and obvious. Thus, the public sector may grow larger than citizens would really choose if they had to shoulder the costs in an immediate and visible fashion.

Another argument for balancing the federal budget concerns the effects of an unbalanced budget on private borrowing and spending. Proponents argue that when the federal government increases its borrowing to finance a deficit, interest rates rise. Private borrowers, who want to borrow for business investment or to purchase consumer durables, cannot compete for funds. Thus, the increased government spending displaces private spending.

If the government runs a deficit and its borrowing drives up interest rates, business spending for investment or consumer demand (especially for cars and houses, financed by borrowing) may both decline. As a result, the net increase

Crowding out The displacement of higher spending by government by lower private spending because interest rates rise as the government borrows more.

in planned spending is smaller than the change in *G*, and the shift in aggregate demand is also very small. The displacement of private spending by government borrowing through higher interest rates is called **crowding out.** The increase in government spending could drive up interest rates so high that an equal decline in spending for consumption or investment occurs. In this case, there will be no shift in aggregate demand and no increase in income and output at all. Crowding out is most likely to occur when the economy is at or near full employment and less likely to be a problem during recessions.

The High Employment Balanced Budget

High employment balanced budget A budget in which tax rates, purchases, and transfer payments are established so that the budget would be in balance at the full employment level of income.

These two arguments about crowding out and managing the growth of government led economists to seek a compromise approach to fiscal policy and deficits that recognized the conflict between the goal of a balanced budget and the needs of fiscal policy. This compromise was the **high employment balanced budget.** This budget calls for setting the levels of *G* and T_n such that the budget would be in balance at the full employment level of income. The high employment balanced budget represents a policy goal. It also measures whether fiscal policy is neutral, expansionary, or contractionary. If the budget is balanced at high employment income *(Y*)*, fiscal policy is neutral. If the budget is in deficit at *Y**, fiscal policy is expansionary. If the budget is in surplus at *Y**, fiscal policy is contractionary.

In Figure 15-4, the high employment balanced budget balances at an income level of *Y**. Net tax revenues are positively related to the level of income. Government purchases are largely independent of the income level. In this diagram, Congress has set the tax rates and transfer levels such that the budget will balance not at the actual level of income but at the full employment level

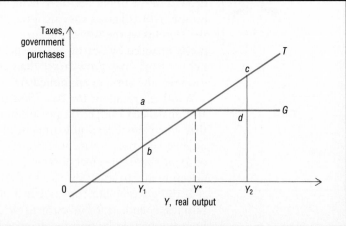

FIGURE 15-4

The high employment balanced budget calls for a budget that is in balance not at the actual level of income (Y_1 or Y_2) but at the full employment level, *Y**. Taxes, transfers, and spending would be set to create a deficit at output levels below *Y** and a surplus at output levels above *Y**.

of income, Y^*. Above full employment income, the surplus *cd* will depress demand and head the economy in the right direction. If actual income *(Y₁)* is below Y^*, the resulting deficit *ab* will increase demand and push the economy toward full employment. Any deficit in excess of *ab*, or any deficit that persists at Y^*, is called a **structural deficit.**

Structural deficit The portion of the deficit that would persist even if the economy were at the full employment level of income.

Deficits and Debt Since 1980

In the 1980s, tax cuts combined with increases in spending, especially for defense, contributed to rising structural deficits. Automatic stabilizers kicked in during the two recessions of the early 1980s and early 1990s, compounding the actual deficit. Once deficits began to grow, government borrowing at high interest rates increased the share of the budget going to interest payments on past borrowing. Table 15-1 shows the growth of the deficit and debt from 1980 to 1992.

In fiscal 1992, the federal government ran a deficit of about $290 billion. This deficit set a new record for a single year. Despite a budget agreement in 1990 to hold the line on spending and to increase taxes, the recession of 1990–1991 meant the automatic stabilizers drove up the deficit by more than the budget agreement could reduce it.

TABLE 15-1   Debt and Deficits Since 1980*

Year	Deficit (billions)	National Debt (billions)	Deficit/GDP	Debt/GDP
1980	$ 73.8	$ 908.5	2.8%	34.5%
1981	79.0	994.3	2.7	34.0
1982	128.0	1,136.8	4.1	36.4
1983	207.8	1,371.2	6.3	41.6
1984	185.4	1,564.1	5.0	42.2
1985	212.3	1,817.0	5.4	46.2
1986	221.2	2,120.1	5.2	49.8
1987	149.8	2,345.6	3.4	53.2
1988	155.2	2,600.8	3.2	53.6
1989	152.5	2,867.5	2.9	54.5
1990	221.4	3,206.3	4.0	57.9
1991	269.5	3,599.0	4.8	64.1
1992	290.2	4,002.7	4.9	67.6

*For fiscal years, October 1st to September 30th.

Source: *Economic Report of the President, 1993* (Washington, D.C.: U.S. Government Printing Office, 1993).

National debt   The accumulated obligations of
the central government,
representing the sum
of past deficits and
surpluses.

Each year the federal government runs a deficit, the national debt increases. The **national debt,** which was more than $4 trillion in 1992, is the cumulative total of deficits and surpluses from past years. It consists of Treasury bonds held by the public, the banking system, and foreign investors.

Do Debts and Deficits Matter?

Is the national debt "bad?" Should we try to pay it off? How did it get so large? These questions have been around for a long time, but they became particularly acute during the 1980s. Record deficits tripled the national debt from $1 trillion to $3 trillion between 1981 and 1990. The large deficit made the president and Congress reluctant to undertake any discretionary fiscal policy during the 1990–1991 recession. The question of how important the debt and the deficit are provokes more disagreement among economists and among politicians than almost any other issue. This question also troubles practical economists as citizens, taxpayers, and voters, because they find it difficult to assess the impact of the debt and the deficit on their personal lives and futures.

Most economists today agree that the national debt is not a burden on our grandchildren in the sense that former President Eisenhower implied in the quotation that opens this chapter. If there is a burden due to borrowing, it falls on those who were alive and paying taxes and earning income at the time the funds were borrowed. The transfer of these resources to the government meant a sacrifice of the other uses for those resources. If those resources were idle, as many were during the Great Depression or during recessions in the last 40 years, the opportunity cost (and the burden) was very low. In fact, to the extent that the practical economists in charge put those idle resources to work to build roads, hospitals, post offices, and schools, our grandchildren are the gainers, because they inherit a larger capital stock.

On the other hand, it is possible that those borrowed resources would otherwise have been used more productively in the private sector. In that case, the opportunity cost of those resources is very high. This effect is more likely if deficits are incurred while the economy is close to full employment. Then our grandchildren would inherit less capital and have a lower level of income and output than they would in the absence of borrowing. Thus, the effect of borrowing on future generations depends on the conditions under which the government borrowed and the uses to which the funds were put.

It is true that our grandchildren will have to make the interest and principal payments on the debt. Most of the debt, however, is also held by those same grandchildren; thus, interest and principal payments mean funds will be transferred from taxpayers to bondholders. If the bondholders are rich and the taxpayers are poor, it will be possible (although politically difficult) to devise a tax system to counteract the distributional effects of these interest and principal payments. In simple terms, for the most part Americans owe the debt to themselves, or at least to other Americans. A growing fraction of the debt (about 18 percent) is being held by non–U.S. citizens. Repaying that part of the debt may represent a burden on the next generation, who will have to give up real resources to make those payments. But since most of the debt is owed by Americans to other Americans, the effects of paying interest and repaying principal are mainly a matter of income distribution.

Another disadvantage of large budget deficits is that they make the president and Congress much more reluctant to undertake any discretionary fiscal policy during a recession. In fact, the Reagan and Bush Councils of Economic Advisers raised this problem in the annual *Economic Report of the President* in the late 1980s in anticipation of the coming recession.

By 1993, as the economy emerged from recession and began to grow again, the deficit became the major focus of macroeconomic policy. Support for some kind of aggressive deficit reduction program was strong, driven in part by projections from both the executive branch and the Congressional Budget Office of large and growing deficits for the foreseeable future. Reductions in defense spending, tax increases, and caps on transfer payments were the elements of the plan Congress approved. There was some concern that these policies might slow down the recovery from the 1990–1991 recession, but they would also bring down long-term interest rates and stimulate investment. Lower interest rates would, in turn, reduce the growth of the deficit, which was growing in part because of the rising interest payments on the accumulated debt. In 1993 interest payments were $187 billion, or about 13 percent of federal government spending. Whether this strategy will succeed remains to be seen.

FISCAL POLICY AND AGGREGATE DEMAND

Most of the description of fiscal policy in this chapter assumes unemployment is high and the aggregate supply curve is horizontal, so there is no problem of driving up the price level with expansionary policy. In a more realistic model, aggregate supply would slope upward from left to right. When expansionary fiscal policy shifts aggregate demand to the right and the aggregate supply curve slopes upward, both prices and real output rise. Because expansionary policy usually involves deficits and borrowing, interest rates may also rise.

Output, Prices, or Interest Rates?

The effects of a shift in aggregate demand due to expansionary fiscal policy depend on the slope of the aggregate supply curve. In Figure 15-5, aggregate demand shifts to the right. If aggregate supply is horizontal (panel a), as it is likely to be when output levels are very low, the only impact is on the level of output. As the economy gets closer to full employment, aggregate supply is more likely to be upward sloping. The impact of expansionary fiscal policy (such

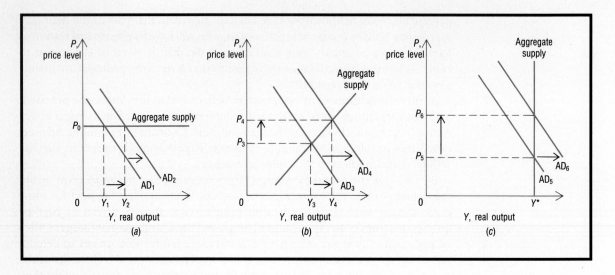

FIGURE 15-5

Expansionary fiscal policy is most effective in panel a, where aggregate supply is horizontal and only real output is affected; less effective in panel b, where aggregate supply is upward sloping and both output and prices rise; and least effective in panel c, where aggregate supply is vertical and expansionary fiscal policy only drives up prices.

as shifting from AD_3 to AD_4 in panel b) falls partly on income and output and partly on prices. In this case, much of the effect of expansionary fiscal policy falls on rising prices rather than on higher output, income, and employment. Finally, in panel c, the vertical aggregate supply curve at full employment output, Y^*, means attempts at expansionary fiscal policy at this income level will result only in a higher price level.

Now three variables can be affected by expansionary fiscal policy. The target variable is real output (and employment), but some of the impact of fiscal policy is dissipated by higher interest rates, and still more of the impact may be reduced by higher prices. In extreme cases, where aggregate supply is vertical and/or crowding out is severe, fiscal policy will have no impact at all on real output.

Suppose government purchases *(G)* increase by $10 billion, with no increase in taxes. Increased government borrowing drives up interest rates and chokes off $5 billion in private spending (crowding out). The net increase in aggregate demand will be smaller due to crowding out. In Figure 15-6, the initial shift in aggregate demand that reflects only an increase in *G* is from AD_1 to AD_2. As crowding out occurs, aggregate demand drops back to AD_3. Part of the impact of expansionary fiscal policy has been lost through crowding out.

Instead of the horizontal aggregate supply curve AS_1, suppose now that the new aggregate demand curve, AD_3 encounters a very steep aggregate supply curve, AS_2, so the price level rises from P_1 to P_2. Thus, output *(Y)* finally winds up at Y_4, which is a much smaller increase than the increase from Y_1 to Y_2 that

FIGURE 15-6

The effects of fiscal policy may be weakened by crowding out and/or dissipated in a rising price level rather than rising real output. The increase in government spending shifts aggregate demand from AD_1 to AD_2, but it is partly offset by a decline in investment spending due to higher interest rates. As a result, aggregate demand rises only to AD_3, and even with horizontal aggregate supply curve AS_1, income rises from Y_1 to Y_3 instead of to Y_2. If aggregate supply is upward sloping (AS_1), some of the effect of rising aggregate demand is reflected in a rise in prices to P_3, so that real output rises only to Y_4.

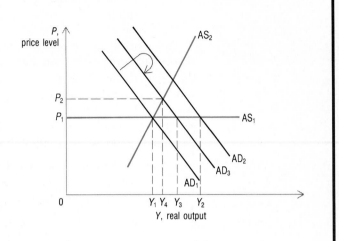

would have occurred with no change in interest rates (or crowding out) and no price level changes (inflation).

CHECKLIST : Fiscal Policy, Interest Rates, and Inflation

1. The effect of fiscal policy is divided among real output, interest rates, and price level changes.
2. The effect of expansionary fiscal policy on real income will be
    a. Largest when aggregate supply is horizontal and there is no crowding out
    b. Smaller if aggregate supply is upward sloping
    c. Smaller if there is crowding out
    d. Zero if aggregate supply is vertical
3. The effect of expansionary fiscal policy on the price level will be
    a. Zero if aggregate supply is horizontal
    b. Larger if aggregate supply is upward sloping
    c. Largest if aggregate supply is vertical

Does Fiscal Policy Work?

These two considerations, crowding out and rising prices, make fiscal policy a much less powerful tool than it appeared to be at first. Under some conditions, fiscal policy could be very effective. When substantial unemployment and very low interest rates exist, it is more likely that the aggregate supply curve is very flat and interest rates may rise little in response to expansionary fiscal policy.

Even if interest rates do rise, they may not get high enough to discourage much private spending. These are the conditions of a severe or prolonged recession or depression.

Under other conditions, however, the impact of expansionary fiscal policy will be blunted by crowding out and inflation. Exactly how much of the effect shows up in interest rates (and reduced private spending), how much in prices, and how much in real output depends on the slope of the aggregate supply curve and the sensitivity of private spending to interest rates.

Many economists do not expect fiscal policy to be very effective in increasing the level of income and output. Their critique of fiscal policy goes like this:

1. If expansionary fiscal policy consists of equal increases in taxes and government spending, it will have little effect. The tax increase will largely cancel the effects of the spending increase.
2. If expansionary fiscal policy consists of a reduction in taxes with no reduction in spending, or an increase in spending with no increase in taxes, the government will have to increase its borrowing, that is, run larger deficits. If the deficit is financed by borrowing, rising interest rates will discourage an equal amount of private spending (crowding out). The result is no net increase in aggregate demand.
3. Even if fiscal policy succeeds in shifting aggregate demand, the aggregate supply curve may still be very steep. In this case, the effect of shifting *AD* through fiscal policy would be mainly to raise the price level rather than output and employment.

Thus, some critics of fiscal policy argue that it is not effective in shifting aggregate demand whether spending increases are financed out of taxes or out of borrowing. Others claim that shifting aggregate demand has no impact on output because aggregate supply is very steep. If we assume, however, that aggregate supply is less than vertical, another possibility may salvage the effectiveness of fiscal policy: that of expanding the money supply to finance borrowing without driving up interest rates. In this case, fiscal policy may shift aggregate demand to the right, but only because of the cooperative role of monetary policy. In the next two chapters, we will explore the roles of money and the Fed in influencing output, employment, interest rates, and the price level.

Summary

1. Fiscal policy consists of changes in government spending, taxes, and transfers intended to influence the levels of output, employment, and prices.

2. Changes in government purchases and taxes, including transfer payments as negative taxes, shift the aggregate demand curve and change the equilibrium level of income and output. Dollar for dollar, taxes and transfers have less impact on output and demand than government purchases.

3. The goal of fiscal policy is to reduce fluctuations in output, employment, and prices and to push the economy in the direction of the full employment level of income and output.

4. An active fiscal policy means the budget—taxes minus transfers, and government purchases—is likely to be unbalanced. The surplus or deficit is sensitive to the level of income, because tax collections rise and transfers fall when the income level goes up.

5. Discretionary fiscal policy, or deliberate changes in taxes, transfers, and government purchases, is carried out by the president and Congress. The president is aided by the Council of Economic Advisers, the Office of Management and Budget, the secretary of the Treasury, and the Economic Security Council. Congress has the assistance of the Congressional Budget Office.

6. Fiscal policy is subject to recognition lags, implementation lags, and impact lags. Time lags can make fiscal policy destabilizing rather than stabilizing in its effect on output, employment, and prices. Taxes have shorter impact lags than government spending does.

7. The choice of fiscal policy tools affects the size of government, the distribution of income, and the degree of control over the budget.

8. Automatic stabilizers consist of progressive income taxes, corporate taxes, welfare and other transfers programs, and farm price supports. They tend to stabilize economic activity without a need for deliberate policy.

9. As a result of many years of deficits, the United States has a large and growing national debt. Some economists advocate a budget that would balance at full employment (the high employment balanced budget).

10. The U.S. national debt is owed mainly to its own citizens. It is a burden on future generations only if the resources transferred to the government would have increased the nation's stock of capital and given future generations a higher level of income and output.

11. Fiscal policy affects interest rates and prices as well as output. To the extent that government borrowing drives up interest rates and discourages investment (crowding out), fiscal policy has less effect on output. To the extent that the increase in aggregate demand from expansionary fiscal policy drives up prices rather than output, fiscal policy is less effective.

Key Terms

automatic stabilizer
balanced budget
contractionary fiscal
   policy
crowding out

deficit
discretionary fiscal
   policy
expansionary fiscal
   policy

fiscal policy
high employment
   balanced budget
impact lag
implementation lag

marginal tax rate   recognition lag   transfer payments
national debt   structural deficit
net taxes   surplus

Questions and Problems

1. Suppose the economy is operating substantially below full employment. What policy options are available? Which one would you choose? Why?

2. Suppose you implement the policy you chose in Question 1. How might crowding out or inflation erode the impact of your policy? Under what circumstances would your policy be most effective?

3. Is the national debt a burden on future generations? Why or why not?

4. How does a high employment balanced budget address the conflict between a balanced budget and fiscal policy?

5. In 1985 Congress passed the Gramm-Rudman-Hollings Act, which mandated that Congress move toward a balanced budget by 1991. Exceptions were allowed for periods of poor economic conditions. What do you think those poor economic conditions might be, and why does the law provide that exception?

6. Many states in the United States have "rainy day" funds, or surplus funds they keep in reserve in case a recession occurs and their revenues fall. When economic conditions improve, the rainy day fund is replenished by running a surplus. Is this fiscal policy? If so, is it discretionary or automatic?

7. In each of the following cases, explain whether fiscal policy is expansionary, contractionary, or neutral.

   a. An actual budget surplus, but a balanced budget at high employment; equilibrium income above the full employment level
   b. An actual budget deficit, but a balanced budget at high employment; equilibrium income below the full employment level
   c. A budget in deficit at both actual and full employment output; equilibrium income below the full employment level
   d. A budget in deficit at both actual and full employment output; equilibrium income above the full employment level

8. Why do taxes and transfers have relatively less impact on aggregate demand and output than government purchases do?

9. You are the chief economist for your country's government, and the country is in a recession. The proposals your staff has brought you are (a) a tax cut across the board (same percentage for all taxpayers); (b) increased government spending for construction of low-income housing; and (c) an increase in food distribution to the poor, combined with a reduction in the payroll tax, which falls mainly on lower- to middle-income taxpayers. Which would you favor, and why?

16

Money and Other Financial Assets

Money is only important for what it will procure.

JOHN MAYNARD KEYNES, 1924

Main Points

1. Money is anything that can serve as a unit of account, a medium of exchange, and a store of value. A desirable form for money is something that is scarce, durable, divisible, uniform, and portable.

2. The use of money developed to replace barter because money makes it easier to specialize and trade.

3. Money has evolved from full-bodied coins to token money, fiat money, and demand deposit money. The U.S. money supply consists primarily of demand deposits and secondarily of currency or Federal Reserve notes.

4. Individuals hold money to meet their day-to-day transactions needs. Money is one among many financial assets. Other important financial assets are stocks and bonds.

5. Demand for money by individual households and by the economy as a whole is related to money income and interests rates.

6. Changes in the money supply tend to lead to changes in prices and real output. The quantity theory of money is one way to describe this relationship. The aggregate demand and aggregate supply model also helps explain how changes in the money supply affect output and the price level.

I n Chapters 14 and 15, we largely ignored the money supply to examine the Keynesian model and the workings of fiscal policy. Now we will complete the picture of macroeconomic theory and policy by exploring the role of money demand and money supply.

Most economists expect that changes in monetary policy, like fiscal policy changes, will affect not only the level of real output but also prices and interest rates in various combinations. Monetary policy, or changes in the money supply and interest rates, can be used to enhance the effects of fiscal policy or to offset fiscal policy. Often monetary policy can be more effective in containing inflation, whereas fiscal policy is more useful in recessions. The relative effectiveness of monetary and fiscal policy has been a subject of continuing debate among economists.

In this chapter and Chapter 17, we explore what money is, how it is linked to other financial assets like stocks and bonds, where money comes from, why people hold it, and how it relates to the basic macroeconomic model of aggregate supply and demand. ■

WHAT IS MONEY?

"What is money?" may sound like a rather silly question. Surely everyone knows what money is. Money is nickels, dimes, quarters, and dollar bills. If you think a little harder, you might also consider the balance in your checking account to be money. But what about your savings account or the spending limit on your credit card? What about those government bonds stashed in safe deposit boxes that can be quickly liquidated (that is, turned into cash)? Are these things money? Is money what people can use to make payments on the spot, or is it any financial asset that can be converted quickly and easily into cash? Is there really a difference between the balance in a checking account and the balance in a money market account, a mutual fund, or a stack of Series E bonds?

Money has taken a variety of forms at different periods in history. Today money is generally defined as consisting of currency (including both coins and bills) and checking account deposits, both of which can be used directly to purchase goods and services. Later we will look at how these types of money came to be the standard forms in the twentieth century.

Money and Barter

Barter The exchange of one commodity or service directly for another without the use of money.

To understand what money is and what it does, consider a world without money in which all trade must take place through **barter**. Suppose you grow apples, and you want a shirt, a knife, and a loaf of bread. Like Jack and his cow in the nursery tale *Jack and the Beanstalk*, you trudge off to town with your wheelbarrowful of apples, looking for people who sell what you want and want what you sell.

Jack got lucky. He traded the cow for beans, which grew a beanstalk to the castle of the giant, who owned the goose which laid the golden eggs. So Jack finally got money—gold in the days of nursery tales—that he could use to buy whatever he wanted.

Chances are you would not be so lucky. It takes a long time to find the right trading partner, one who wants apples and who is selling knives, shirts, or bread. It takes even longer to price everything you want in apples. Are they McIntosh or Golden Delicious, wormy or blemish free? Is the shirt the right size and the cloth of good quality? A shirt may be worth three Golden Delicious apples or five McIntoshes, depending on the seller's tastes. A different shirt may command a still different set of apple prices. What a way to run a railroad!

After a day of bartering apples you, as a practical economist, would likely return home in disgust, having wasted a lot of time and effort in trading and haggling, searching for information and prices, and trying to match up sellers and buyers. Chances are you would decide that it just doesn't make sense to specialize in apples and exchange what you produce best for what other people can produce more efficiently than you can. It would take less time to grow your own wheat, sew your own shirt, and maybe even forge your own knife than to barter and bargain in a world in which there is no standard of payment and sellers and buyers have to match up their trades on a one-to-one basis. How much simpler life would be with money! And how much more specialization and exchange would take place!

What Money Does

Unit of account The function of money that refers to its use as a measure of value and a standard for comparing values of different goods and services.

This nursery tale suggests some of the functions money performs. Money provides a way to translate apples into shirts, knives, and loaves of bread, as well as to translate shirts into knives and knives into loaves of bread. This function of measuring the value of all goods (and services) in terms of some single measuring rod is called the **unit of account** function of money. With money, it is easy to measure the relative values of a pizza and a movie ticket. If one pizza (large, pepperoni) costs \$10 and a movie ticket costs \$5, 1 pizza = 2 movie tickets. You can even add pizzas and movie tickets; 1 pizza plus 2 movie tickets = \$20.

Medium of exchange The function of money as a vehicle for carrying out transactions.

A second function of money that appears in our story of the apple seller is the **medium of exchange** function of money. If you, the imaginary apple seller, could have sold your apples to a wholesaler for currency, you could have gone off to market with no more of a load than a fat wallet, exchanging dollar bills (or gold coins, or lira, or francs) for a knife, a shirt, and a loaf of bread. You would not have needed to find apple buyers to make your transactions. Money thus provides a convenient way to trade generalized purchasing power, which the recipient can use to buy any good or service.

Store of value   The function of money that consists of storing wealth, or purchasing power, for future use.

Money serves yet another function, one not implied in either the apple seller story or *Jack and the Beanstalk*: Money is a handy way to store purchasing power for future use. This function is called the **store of value**, or the *asset function* of money. Apples rot, knives rust, and bread gets moldy, but most of the forms in which people hold money can be stored indefinitely, in a small space, until it is needed. You can sell your apples for money today and wait to buy shirts next week or next month. Your money stores the value from the apple sale until you are ready to use it.

The medium of exchange and store of value functions of money require some concrete, tangible form of money, such as coins, bills, or at least a checkbook with some numbers written in it, that provide some way to measure how much there is. The unit of account function, unlike the other two functions, does not require you to actually have any dollars (or lira or francs). This function requires only that you know what the money measure is, just as you can know what an inch or a centimeter is without actually having a ruler or a meter stick in your hand.

 **CHECKLIST** : **What Money Does**

Money serves as a:

Unit of account	Means of comparing the value of goods
	Means of adding up the value of goods
Medium of exchange	A generalized item that can be exchanged for any good, replacing barter
Store of value	A means of storing purchasing power for future use

Desirable Properties of Money

Money has been a part of human history since (and probably before) history was first recorded. There are shekels in the Old Testament and records of coinage in the ancient kingdom of Lydia in Asia Minor. Most early forms of money did double duty. The king or other ruler would designate some particular commodity to serve as money. That item, whatever it was, had a value or use as money, and also had a value or use as a commodity. Gold money could be used for jewelry and other decorative purposes, and cow money (the Latin word for money, *pecunia*, is derived from the word for cow) could provide a nice steak barbecue.

Commodity money, full-bodied money Money that has value as a commodity as well as in its role as money, such as precious metals, cows, tobacco, or other tangible goods.

The commodity value of money made money more acceptable to skeptics because they could always find another use for their money in addition to its uses as a medium of exchange and a store of value. Thus, throughout most of human history, money was **commodity money** or **full-bodied money;** that is, money with a value in other, nonmonetary uses that are roughly equal to its monetary or purchasing power value.

Although a commodity value is no longer high on the list of desirable properties, certain other features of money have always been and still are desirable. Convenience dictates that money be *portable* and *divisible*, or easy to carry around and make change. Money in the form of bricks would be hard to carry around, and cows would present some serious problems in making change. Apples too would be a poor choice, because *uniformity* and *durability* are also important qualities. Gold is gold and lasts forever, but apples vary in size and taste and tend to rot over time.

Finally, it is important that money be *scarce*—but not too scarce. Sand would be a poor currency in the desert, where anyone could pick up a bucket of money any time she or he wished. Sand would be equally unsatisfactory at the North Pole, where money would be so scarce and difficult to find that Eskimos would probably resort to barter. Enough money should be available to meet day-to-day transactions needs, but not so much that the currency becomes worthless.

HOW MONEY EVOLVED

The production of money is one of only two production activities specifically reserved for the federal government by the U.S. Constitution (the other is the postal service). Governments have had a monopoly or near monopoly over the production of money since ancient times.

Coinage

Although all kinds of commodity moneys have been used—fishhooks, wampum, tobacco, teeth—the use of coins goes back to ancient history. Kings and other rulers in all parts of the world from China to Asia Minor to Europe made coins out of precious metals such as gold, silver, and copper. Precious metals passed all the tests for good commodity moneys discussed earlier. They were scarce, uniform, portable, durable, and divisible. They could be used in trading among different tribes or nations. Precious metals very quickly took hold as the universal form for money in the countries around the Mediterranean.

The only problem with precious metals as money is that it is difficult to verify their purity. Alloys can be made with baser metals, making a piece of metal appear to be all silver when it is actually a less valuable combination of, say, silver and tin or silver and lead. Weighing could verify the metallic content, and this was common practice. A simpler process, however, was to have the sovereign certify the metallic content by stamping it into coins with his (or occasionally her) likeness on it. Thus, coined money originated as a simple and inexpensive way to verify the value of full-bodied money.

Kings and other rulers, who pursued their own self-interest like all practical economists, found they could make a profit from coining money. A coin that was supposed to consist of, say, 100 grains of silver would contain only 96 grains. The rest was paid to the king for coining services, or seignorage. Kings, like other mortals, were also subject to temptation, and they were known to mix in baser metals and make more coins than they were supposed to from a given amount of gold or silver, a process known as *debasing the currency*. Debasing the currency also meant expanding the money supply, which tended to be inflationary. Another practice was to pare or shave coins to get a little of the precious metal. The ridges on the sides of quarters, dimes, and half-dollars are designed to prevent this kind of paring.

The Goldsmiths and Fractional Reserve Banking

Goldsmith   A member of a medieval guild of artisans who worked in gold, lent gold, and became the Western world's first bankers.

Coined money was the major form of money until the last five centuries, when paper money emerged in various forms. The credit for the first paper money goes to a group of medieval artisans known as **goldsmiths**. Goldsmiths were workers in gold and other precious metals. They also provided storage facilities for other people's gold, issuing "warehouse receipts." For many people who deposited their gold for safekeeping with the goldsmiths, it was simpler to use the paper receipts as money than to convert them to gold to make transactions. Thus, the receipts issued by goldsmiths began to circulate as paper money, fully backed by (and redeemable in) gold or silver. The size of the money supply did not change, but paper claims offered greater convenience than carrying around large quantities of gold or silver.

The important transition from storage to banking came when goldsmiths discovered how infrequently these paper claims were presented for payment. There sat the gold, waiting to be redeemed, and at any given time the owners were likely to claim only a very small portion of it. Goldsmiths gradually branched out into the lending business, first lending their own gold and eventually also lending a portion of the gold left with them for safekeeping. Only a fraction of the gold deposits needed to be kept to meet day-to-day withdrawals. Usually, by the time a claim showed up, the loan had been repaid with interest. This discovery was the origin of the modern principle of **fractional reserve banking,** or keeping only a portion of deposits on reserve and lending the rest. We examine this topic much more closely in the next chapter.

Fractional reserve banking   The practice of holding only a fraction of deposits in reserves and lending the rest.

The word *bank* itself comes from *banco,* the Italian word for "bench." One account of the origin of the term goes back to the medieval fairs, when visitors would leave their gold and silver with a guard, who placed it inside his bench for protected storage. Like the goldsmith, these "bench sitters" issued receipts that could be used to make purchases at the fair—a shorter-term version of the goldsmith, minus the lending function. If the bench sitter was caught lifting a little of the bullion for his own use (paring the bullion or scraping the gold dust), depositors would rush the bench (*banco*) and destroy it (*ruptura*)—a very literal kind of bankruptcy, or breaking of the bench.

Checking Account Money

Demand deposit Deposit at a bank that can be spent by writing a check.

Bank notes Currency issued by banks and redeemable in gold or silver; no longer in common use.

It was a fairly short step from the fractional reserve banking of the goldsmiths to checking account deposits, or **demand deposits**, which originated in fifteenth-century Italy. These deposits simply allowed the depositor to withdraw any portion of the gold on deposit rather than circulate receipts for the whole sum. At the same time, **bank notes** were available. If you deposited 1,000 francs with a goldsmith in Paris, you had three choices; a standard "warehouse receipt" for 1,000 francs; a set of "warehouse receipts" in denominations of 50 to 200 francs each (bank notes), which were easier to spend; or a checking account on which you could draw odd sums such as 33.25 francs. Bank notes, along with U.S. Treasury gold and silver certificates, were the biggest component of the money supply in the United States until the Civil War, when checking accounts replaced bank notes.

Fiat money Money that has no commodity value but is accepted as money because the government declares it to be money and regulates its scarcity.

The development of paper money was a long and slow process. At first, paper money was fully backed by precious metals. Then it was partly backed by precious metals. Today the only guarantee paper money carries is the health of the banking system and the faith and credit of the government. Money that is not redeemable in gold, silver, or other commodities, like the dollar bills in your wallet, is called **fiat money**. (*Fiat* is a Latin word that simply means "it shall be.") Fiat money is money by government decree. People accept fiat money in payment for goods and services because other people will accept it in payment for goods and services, not because it has a commodity value. Money has a usefulness of its own: as a medium of exchange and as a store of value. That usefulness depends not on its commodity backing but on careful control of the amount of money in circulation (scarcity). As long as money is scarce enough, and as long as it is accepted, at least by the government, practical economists will demand money for its own usefulness, even if it has no redemption value.

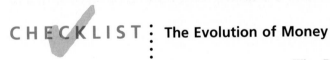 C H E C K L I S T **The Evolution of Money**

Form	When Developed
Coins	Prehistory, as guarantee of full-bodied value
Bank notes	Middle ages (goldsmiths), as full-bodied money
Checkable deposits	Fifteenth-century Italy (came to U.S. in 1860s)
Federal Reserve notes	1914 (creation of the Federal Reserve System)

The Money Supply in the United States

Currency Paper money such as bank notes or Federal Reserve notes; an important component of the money supply.

The money supply in the United States consists of coins, currency, and deposits at banks.

Coins and Currency. Coins are a relatively small part (about 3 percent) of the money supply. U.S. **currency** (paper money, or bills) consists solely of

· ·
Myth 16-1
· ·

The Dollar Is Backed by Gold

Since 1935, U.S. citizens have not been allowed to redeem their dollars for gold. Americans know there is gold in Fort Knox, and some may even be aware that the central bank, or the Federal Reserve, holds gold certificates (claims to gold owned by the Treasury). Since the Federal Reserve also issues dollar bills (Federal Reserve notes), these gold certificates may perpetuate the myth that some gold still lies behind the dollar.

The terms "backed by gold," "redeemable in gold," and "good as gold" originally meant the U.S. government would redeem currency in gold at a guaranteed price to anyone who requested it to do so. Until 1935, that price was $20.67 per ounce of gold. From 1935 to 1968, the U.S. government redeemed dollars held by non–Americans only (not Americans) at a price of $35.00 an ounce. After a brief period of redeeming U.S. dollars only when presented by foreign governments, the government closed the "gold window," that is, stopped redeeming dollars in gold.

Like any other fiat money, the Federal Reserve notes in your wallet are money because the government says they are money, the government accepts them in payment of taxes, and the central bank carefully controls their supply so that there aren't so many dollars in circulation that they become worthless. You can use your dollars to buy gold, but not from the government and not at any guaranteed price. The dollar is backed by nothing except the faith and credit of the government. ■

Federal Reserve notes. All U.S. currency is issued by the central bank and is not redeemable in either gold or silver. The green pieces of paper in your wallet with pictures of presidents and signatures of public officials and labeled "Federal Reserve Note" across the top are fiat money.

In 1992 there was $290 billion in coins and Federal Reserve notes in the money supply. Currency, including coins, is about 29 percent of the U.S. money supply. Only currency (including coins) outside banks is counted in the money supply.

Checkable deposits
Money in the form of checking account balances; the largest component of the M₁ money supply.

Checkable Deposits.   The largest single component of the U.S. money supply is **checkable deposits**, or checking account money. These deposits were once

M₁   A narrow definition
of the money supply, in-
cluding mainly coins, currency, and checkable
deposits.

available only at commercial banks. Recent changes in banking laws have made checkable deposits or very similar accounts available through savings banks, savings and loan associations, credit unions, and other financial institutions.

The narrowest definition of the money supply, M_1, consists of coins, currency, and checkable deposits. In 1992, M_1 was $1,019 billion, consisting of $299 billion in currency and $720 billion in checkable deposit accounts.

Near Money and Other Definitions of the Money Supply.   Remember the question at the beginning of the chapter about what is money? By now you probably understand why some of the items listed are not part of the money supply. Credit cards are not a store of value. Financial assets such as savings accounts, money market mutual funds, and bonds cannot be spent directly and therefore are not a medium of exchange. However, some of these highly liquid financial assets can be converted to money very easily.

Figure 16-1 shows a continuum of assets, placed along the line according to their liquidity, or how easily they can be converted to cash. This list is not exhaustive, but it includes the most common financial assets. Where should the line be drawn to separate money and near money? M_1 is a very conservative definition of the money supply. The measure of the money supply one chooses depends on how it will be used. If economists want to use changes in the money supply to forecast changes in prices and output, they probably should use the definition of the money supply that has the best track record in forecasting the price level *(P)* and real output *(Y)*. That definition is M_2, which adds savings deposits, time deposits, and money market mutual funds to M_1. M_2 is about four times as large as M_1.

M₂   A broader definition
of the money supply that
adds savings deposits,
time deposits, and money
market mutual funds to
M₁.

If economists want to define money in terms of liquidity, money is what can be spent immediately in its present form. For this purpose, the narrow M_1 definition is best. Broader definitions include large time deposits and short-term financial assets such as savings bonds, Treasury bills, commercial paper, and European deposits, all of which are part of the very inclusive concept of the money supply called *L* (for liquid assets).

CHECKLIST ⠿   **Measures of the Money Supply**

Measure	Amount (1992) (billions)	Includes
M₁	$1,019	Coins, currency, checkable deposits, traveler's checks
M₂	$3,508	M₁ plus savings and small time deposits, money market accounts, and a few other items
L	$5,051	M₂ plus various other liquid assets

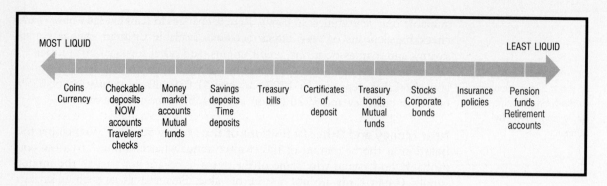

FIGURE 16-1

Financial assets range from the very liquid (coins and currency) through the somewhat less liquid (such as Series E savings bonds) to the very illiquid, such as pension funds and retirement accounts.

Other Financial Assets

Households typically hold a mix of assets, called a *portfolio*. Different assets have different desirable features. Money is liquid but earns little or no interest. Certificates of deposit earn more interest, but there is a penalty for early withdrawal. Bonds have a price risk and may require a minimum of $1,000 or even $10,000, but they usually offer higher interest rates. Mutual funds involve management fees and sometimes sales charges. Stocks are riskier than bonds, but they also have greater potential for increases in value. A practical economist will hold a variety of assets, including currency and checkable deposits, to take advantage of the desirable qualities of each asset and reduce the risk of the overall portfolio. Two of the most important nonmoney assets are bonds and common stocks.

Bonds and the Bond Market

Bond A note, issued by a government or a corporation, that carries interest and represents a loan or promise of repayment.

Bond market A network of buyers and sellers in which bonds are traded and bond prices are determined.

Bonds are the form in which most large loans are made to corporations and governments. Bonds include Treasury bills (short-term federal government borrowing), Treasury notes and bonds (longer term), corporate bonds (issued by incorporated firms), and municipals (bonds issued by state or local governments). Typically bonds come in units of $1,000 or $10,000. They earn interest from time of issue to time of maturity, when the original amount borrowed is repaid to whoever holds the bond at that time. If you own bonds, you can sell them in the **bond market**, an organized exchange in both newly issued and outstanding bonds that matches buyers and sellers through bond brokers. Stockbrokers, banks, and other financial institutions buy and sell bonds. You can also buy bonds through a mutual fund, which pools the funds of many lenders to purchase a diversified portfolio of bonds. Special, small-denomination government bonds, called Series E bonds, can be bought and sold with no sales charge at banks or through payroll deductions. Series E bonds can be bought in units as small as $50.

Interest and Yield. Bonds carry an interest rate that is determined by market forces when the bond is issued. For example, if XYZ corporation decides to issue $10 million in bonds, it will employ a professional firm to market the bonds. That market will offer bonds for sale at various interest rates until a rate that clears the market is settled on. That rate will reflect general economic conditions as well as the financial health of the particular issuer. Bonds are rated based on the risk of default, that is, of not getting payments of interest or principal when scheduled. The least risky bonds are rated Aaa. High-risk bonds, which carry high yields but have a higher probability of default, are also known as *junk bonds.*

Once the bond has been issued, the dollar amount of interest per bond is fixed until maturity. However, the interest yield to a particular holder depends on the price that person pays for the bond. For example, if you buy a bond at a price of $950 and the annual interest payment is $65, your interest yield is $65/$950, or 6.8 percent. If the bond cost you $1,060, the current yield would be $65/$1,060, or 6.1 percent.

Most of the bonds you are likely to own are listed in the bond market pages of major daily newspapers. For example, if you looked for bonds issued by AT&T on February 19, 1993, you would have found 13 bonds listed, maturing between 1996 and 2024. Here is the listing for one of those bonds:

	CurYld	Vol	Close	Net Chg.
ATT 7s01	6.0	382	100-3/4	− 1/8

This bond carries an official interest rate of 7 percent and matures in 2001. A $1,000 bond pays interest of $70 a year, which is 6.9 percent of its current (closing) price of $1007.50, the number in the close column multiplied by 10. On that date, 382 of these bonds were sold. The price fell by ⅛ of a dollar multiplied by 10, or $1.25, from the previous day's price.

Bond Prices and Interest Rates. Suppose Exxon issued a 20-year bond with a face value of $1,000 in 1992, when long-term interest rates were relatively high. The yield was 8 percent, which simply means Exxon agreed to pay the bond's owner $80 in interest each year. When the bond matures in 2012, Exxon will pay the current owner (who is probably not the original buyer) the $1,000 it borrowed 20 years earlier.

Now suppose that in 1993 the interest rates on newly issued bonds fell to 6 percent, and Coca-Cola issued some new bonds that year. Coca-Cola bonds issued in 1993 with a $1,000 face value will offer the buyer only $60 a year in interest. Meanwhile, the original buyer of the 1992 bond receives $80 a year. If the owner of the 1992 Exxon bond decides to sell it, she or he will find it easy to locate a buyer. This bond is far from maturity (16 years), so its value will rise. A bond with a very long time to maturity would rise as high as $1,333, at which price its yield of $80 would be 6 percent, the same as the newly issued Coca-Cola bond. A bond with a shorter time to maturity would rise less, because it would have only a few years of relatively high interest payments before being redeemed for $1,000.

As long as the interest rate on other bonds is below 8 percent, the value of the 1992 bond will be greater than its original issue price of $1,000. The rule to remember is this: Rising interest rates reduce the price of outstanding bonds, whereas falling interest rates raise the price of outstanding bonds. The prices of outstanding bonds and the current rate of interest move in opposite directions.

Stocks and the Stock Market

Another popular asset in many practical economists' portfolios is stock in corporations. **Stocks** are ownership shares. If the corporation makes a profit, stockholders share in the profit either directly (by receiving dividends) or indirectly (the stock rises in value when the corporation invests its profit in productive assets). Newly issued and outstanding shares of stock are traded in stock markets. **Stock markets** consist of brokers and dealers who match buyers and sellers of stocks through organized exchanges such as the New York Stock Exchange. Traders must pay a commission every time they buy and sell.

Stock   Ownership share in a corporation that earns dividends.

Stock market   A network of buyers and sellers who exchange shares of stocks on organized exchanges.

Although there are safe stocks (called *blue chips*) and risky bonds (including junk bonds), on average stocks are riskier than bonds. Corporations must pay the claims of bondholders first before stockholders are entitled to any dividends. If anything is left after bondholders have been paid, stockholders are next in line. The price of a share of stock reflects all the information people have about the health and prospects of the firm. Good news drives a stock's price up, and bad news drives it down. The average price of stocks also rises and falls with the economy, generally turning up about six months before an economic recovery and turning down about six months before the start of a recession.

Stock market quotations are also available in your daily newspaper. Here is the report on McDonald's stock on February 19, 1993:

		P-E	Sales	High	Low	Last	Change
McDonld	.40	19	11179	49-1/2	48-5/8	49-1/2	+ 7/8

After the abbreviated company name, the first figure is the annual dividend, in this case 40 cents a share. The P-E column shows the ratio of the price of the stock to the earnings or profits per share, which may be more or less than the dividend. In this case, a P-E of 19 and a price of 49.5 indicate that earnings per share for the most recent year were $2.61. The sales volume is in hundreds; thus 11,179 means 1,117,900 shares traded hands on that date. The highest price at which the share was traded that day was $49.50, the lowest price was $48.625, and the price when the exchange closed for the day was $49.50. That price represented an increase of ⅞, or $0.875, from the closing price the day before.

Like bonds, stocks can be purchased through mutual funds. Stock ownership is an important aspect of a market system, which spreads ownership of the nation's capital widely among its citizens. In the post-communist nations of Eastern and Central Europe, establishing a stock exchange and selling shares of stock in formerly state enterprises have been a major step toward establishing a market economy.

Money Supply and Money Demand

Although money is unique in many ways, the demand for money does not really differ from the demand for other financial assets or for other useful goods and services such as cars, scissors, and telephones. There is a demand for money to serve as a medium of exchange and as a store of value. There is also a supply of money. Unlike the supply of cars, scissors, and telephones, the supply of money in the United States and most other countries is controlled by the government. The government has a monopoly in the production of some forms of money (coins and currency) and substantial control over other forms of money through regulation of the banking system.

In equilibrium, the quantity of money demanded should equal the quantity supplied. We discuss exactly how money is created and how the supply is controlled in Chapter 17. For now, let's assume a given money supply determined by the government and not worry about how it is changed. This assumption makes it possible to focus on money demand and how the quantity of money demanded by practical economists responds to a change in the supply.

DEMAND FOR MONEY

Practical economists choose to hold money for two of its three functions: as a medium of exchange and as a store of value. The demand for money to serve as a medium of exchange is called the **transactions demand for money** (M_T). The demand for money to serve as a store of value is known as the **asset demand for money** (M_A). It is convenient to think of individuals as holding two "piles" of money. One pile meets their day-to-day transactions needs (buying groceries, paying the electric bill, filling the car's gas tank). The other consists of their

Transactions demand for money   The desire to hold money for the purpose of making purchases or expenditures in the near future.

Asset demand for money   The desire to hold money as one of many kinds of financial assets; negatively related to interest rates.

monetary assets, or the amount of their wealth they choose to hold in the form of money rather than of bonds, stocks, mutual funds, certificates of deposit, or other financial assets. Actually, a given dollar can perform both functions at the same time. Separating the individual's money balances into two components, however, makes it easier to explore the two sources of money demand separately.

Transactions Demand

The transactions demand for money is a demand for dollars to hold to meet day-to-day spending needs. People keep some balances on hand because they receive money at infrequent intervals but have to make payments fairly often. Suppose you are paid once a month with a check for $1,500. By the end of the month you expect to spend it all, leaving a transactions balance of zero. In the meantime, you will have a balance in your checking account until the last of the month's bills are paid and the last groceries are bought. That balance is your transactions balance. If you spend your paycheck at a steady rate throughout the month, your average transactions balance for the month should be about $750.

What determines the transactions demand for money? For an individual, the answer is easy: money income. If your income doubled from $1,500 to $3,000 a month, you would probably increase your average balance in your checking account and the amount of cash you carry in your wallet. You may not double both of those figures, but both will likely be higher because you buy more goods and services each month.

The same response holds true for the nation as a whole. The most important factor is nominal or money income, or PY (the price level times real income or output). As total money income rises, a corresponding increase occurs in the average amount of transactions balances households keep on hand. People need higher money balances to purchase the larger money value of goods and services that a higher money income can buy. Money balances demanded are some fraction of nominal money income. Thus, the relationship among the transactions demand for money (M_T), the price level, and real output is

Transactions Demand for Money = Constant × (Nominal Income),

or

$$M_T = k \times PY.$$

Note that an increase in either the price level or real output will produce a larger transactions demand for money because both increase nominal income, PY.

Other factors in addition to money income can shift the transactions demand for money. For example, suppose your employer switches from a monthly to a biweekly paycheck. Your average transactions balance will drop even though your money income is the same. If banks stay open longer hours or offer money machine cards, those institutional changes will reduce demand for money for transactions purposes. The size and age distribution of the population, price expectations, and other factors can also affect M_T. But the most important influences on the total or aggregate transactions demand for money are still changes in real income (output) and the price level.

Asset Demand and Interest Rates

The second source of demand for money balances is based on money's store of value function. In this function, money is one way to store purchasing power for future use, along with stocks, bonds, certificates of deposit, and other financial assets. The **liquidity** of various kinds of assets is measured by how quickly those assets can be converted into spendable forms. Monetary assets are very liquid, because they either are already a means of payment or can be quickly converted to a means of payment and used to purchase goods and services.

Opportunity Cost of Holding Money.   Holding financial assets in the form of money instead of stocks, bonds, or other assets also has some drawbacks. One is that holding money as an asset has a price risk, namely inflation. If the price level rises, the value of money (and other assets whose value is fixed in money, such as certificates of deposit and bonds) will fall. Real assets such as houses, cars, gold, jewelry, stamp collections, and stocks usually appreciate (increase) in value when prices rise. Thus, if prices are expected to rise, practical economists will shift their assets away from money and related assets toward assets whose value normally rises with increasing prices. These assets are known as **inflation hedges**, because they provide some protection of asset values against expected inflation.

Another cost of holding money is the interest forgone. Some forms of money, such as currency and coins, earn no interest; other forms, such as checking account balances, earn much lower rates of interest than such assets as certificates of deposit or government and corporate bonds. The interest one could have earned on other financial assets is the opportunity cost of holding money as an asset.

The most important influence on the asset demand for money is the market rate of interest and expectations about changes in the interest rate. When interest rates rise, money becomes less attractive because most forms of money earn little or no interest. On the other hand, if practical economists expect interest rates to rise on other financial assets in the near future, they may wait to buy those assets until they can tie down a higher interest rate. In the meantime, they will choose to hold more money and fewer bonds or other nonmoney financial assets. Thus, as interest rates rise, the asset demand for money falls because its opportunity cost is higher.

As interest rates fall, the asset demand for money (M_A) rises. The opportunity cost of holding money decreases because practical economists are giving up less interest on other kinds of assets. Thus, asset demand for money and interest rates are negatively related.

Liquidity   The property of financial assets that measures how easily they are converted to a form in which they can be spent, that is, how close they are to serving directly as money.

Inflation hedge   Any asset people purchase in the hope that its value will keep pace with expected inflation.

CHECKLIST : **Influences on the Demand for Money**

If	Then
Interest rates rise	Asset demand falls
Interest rates fall	Asset demand rises
Price level rises	Transactions demand rises
Price level falls	Transactions demand falls
Real income *(Y)* rises	Transactions demand rises
Real income *(Y)* falls	Transactions demand falls
Price expectations rise	Both demands fall
Price expectations fall	Both demands rise
Population increases	Both demands rise
Population falls	Both demands fall

Market (nominal) interest rate The actual interest rate charged on a particular loan, consisting of the real interest rate plus a default risk premium plus compensation for expected inflation.

Interest Rates, Bond Prices, and Money Demand.   Another reason for this negative relationship between asset demand for money and interest rates is the link between interest rates and bond prices discussed earlier. Bonds are a substitute for money. As in any substitute relationship, a change in the price of bonds will affect the demand for money.

Consider a world with only two assets, money and bonds. Bonds pay interest; money pays little or no interest. Suppose interest rates are very low relative to past experience; thus, investors expect those rates have no place to go but up. What is a practical economist to do? *Hold money, not bonds.* Why? First, the opportunity cost of holding money is low because interest rates are low. Second, bonds have a serious price risk that money does not carry in this situation. If practical economists buy bonds right now at low interest rates, as soon as interest rates rise the value of their bonds will fall. It therefore makes more sense to hold cash now and wait to buy bonds later, when interest rates rise and prices of outstanding bonds fall.

The opposite is true when interest rates are high relative to past experience. Asset demand for money almost disappears at high interest rates. Not only is the opportunity cost of holding cash high and the yield on bonds attractive; if interest rates fall, the value of bonds will rise above their original purchase price! At high interest rates, investors will dump their money to buy bonds, hoping to profit when interest rates fall.

Real Interest Rates and Market Interest Rates.   What interest rate do practical economists consider in making decisions? There are two kinds of interest rates: real interest rates and market interest rates. **Market** (or **nominal**) **interest rates** have three components:

1. The **real interest rate**, which is the price lenders (or buyers of bonds) demand to forgo present consumption in order to consume later. Even if there is no risk or uncertainty, money now is worth more than money later.

Real interest rate The interest rate that reflects only the preference for income and consumption right now rather than in the future; no component for expected inflation.

Risk premium The part of the market interest rate that reflects the probability that the borrower will fail to repay all or part of what was borrowed.

Treasury bill rate The interest rate on short-term federal government borrowing; reflects the real rate of interest plus expected inflation, but no default risk.

2. *Default risk*, or the possibility that the borrower will fail to pay the interest or even part or all of the principal. Default risk is very low on government bonds and Aaa corporate bonds, but can be very high with small companies or some local governments. The risk of default is reflected in a **risk premium**, or the additional interest paid by higher-risk borrowers.

3. The expected rate of inflation. Lenders want the dollars paid back to be equal in value or purchasing power to the ones they lend. If expected inflation over the life of a bond or loan is 4 percent, lenders will demand an additional 4 percent in interest over and above the first two items—the real interest rate and the default risk premium—to compensate them for lost purchasing power.

The market, or nominal, rate of interest is the sum of these three components. A 5 percent real rate plus 4 percent expected inflation gives a market rate of 9 percent to a zero-risk borrower, such as the U.S. government. Riskier borrowers pay higher rates. Look at the interest rates for 1980 through 1992 in Figure 16-2. You can see that the rate on Treasury bills is always the lowest rate, because the term of the loan is short and the U.S. Treasury is a risk-free borrower.

Market interest rates are those rates actually charged borrowers, such as the **Treasury bill rate** (the rate on short-term Treasury borrowing) or the mortgage rate charged home buyers. The real interest rate must be estimated from the market rate by correcting for default risk and expected inflation; thus, it is difficult to measure. In 1992, for example, the yield on Treasury bills was 3.5 percent and the inflation rate was about 1.9 percent. The inflation-adjusted interest rate on risk-free Treasury bills of 1.6 percent is a fairly good estimate of the real rate of interest for short-term borrowers. At the same time, the rate on Treasury bonds (long-term but low-risk) was about 7.5 percent, making the

FIGURE 16-2

This chart shows the relationship among various interest rates from 1981 through 1992. Short-term rates (Treasury bills) are lower than long-term rates (Treasury bonds), and interest rates are higher for riskier borrowers (corporate Aaa versus Baa rates).

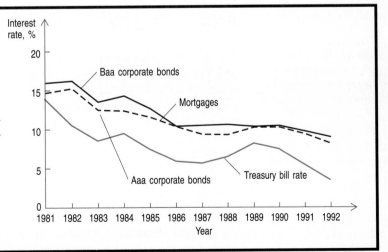

real rate about 5.6 percent. This spread between short-term and long-term rates was very high, reflecting uncertainty about longer-term prospects for inflation.

Interest Rates and Planned Spending.   The impact of interest rates on economic activity is felt mainly through investment and, to a lesser degree, consumption spending. As we noted in Chapter 15, when interest rates are high, firms are more reluctant to borrow. They may even put some of their own retained profits into interest-bearing accounts instead of into new plant and equipment. Retailers keep inventories low because they have to borrow money to buy those inventories, repaying the loan after the goods are sold. Consumers put off buying houses and cars when interest rates on mortgages and auto loans are high. Thus, interest rates are important not only for money demand but also for planned spending and aggregate demand.

MONEY, OUTPUT, AND THE PRICE LEVEL

In addition to the link between money and planned spending through interest rates, there is a direct link among money supply, money demand, the level of output, and the price level. We have already noted prices, output, and income as important influences on the demand for money. Fear of rising prices (inflation) reduces demand for money as an asset. Higher money income, which is partly real income and partly a higher price level, increases demand for transactions balances. The relationship among money, output, and prices also goes the other way, however. Money demand and money supply play an important role in determining the price level and the level of real output. One way to describe that relationship is in terms of the quantity theory of money.

The Quantity Theory of Money

Quantity theory of money   The relationship between the money supply and the price level; based on the equation of exchange, $M_s \times V = P \times Y$.

Velocity of money   The number of times an average dollar in the money supply is spent each year.

The **quantity theory of money** emerged in the nineteenth century as an explanation of how changes in the money supply affect the price level and real output. The quantity theory was expressed in shorthand as the *equation of exchange*, which describes the link between the money supply and total spending, or *GDP*.

   The basic idea behind this equation is that the money value of what the participants in a market economy buy has to equal what they spend. What people buy is *GDP*, or $P \times Y$. What do people spend? They spend the money supply. However, the dollar bills and checking account balances in the money supply can be spent more than once during the year. Some dollars turn over a dozen times, especially on college campuses! Other dollars sit in checking accounts, or under mattresses or in dresser drawers, and are not used at all during the year. The number of times the average dollar in the money supply passes from one hand to another is called the **velocity of money**. Velocity is fairly stable in the long run, although it fluctuates over the course of the business cycle. Using M_1 as a measure of the money supply, velocity is about 5 to 6. (In 1992, *GDP*

In Practice 16-1

When Money Becomes Worthless: Hyperinflation

The value, or purchasing power, of money depends on how much money there is relative to the amounts of goods and services available. The quantity theory of money says that either a sharp drop in the amount of real goods and services available or a sharp rise in the supply of money will drive up the price level. When the price level rises, the purchasing power of money falls.

In the late 1970s and early 1980s, U.S. price levels rose at annual rates of 11 to 13 percent. Some people feared inflation would accelerate to rates like those experienced in Brazil, Israel, and Argentina and more recently in Poland and Russia. In 1992 inflation raged at 1,200 percent in Russia; in other countries, inflation has exceeded 100 percent a year. Instead, however, a combination of recession, contractionary monetary policy, cheap imports (due to the high price of the U.S. dollar), and falling oil prices brought the inflation rate back down to normal levels. Inflation rates remained quite low into the 1990s, with some assistance from the 1990–1991 recession.

A rate of inflation in excess of 100 percent a year is called *hyperinflation.* Two of the most famous instances of hyperinflation took place in Germany after World War I and Hungary after World War II. After World War I, Germany had little productive capacity left, but was required to pay reparations to other countries. A weak government turned the printing presses loose, and the number of marks in circulation began to soar. From a base of 100 in 1913, the wholesale price index in Germany rose to 73 trillion by 1923. The rate of inflation was 600 percent per *month!*

This inflation was very costly in many respects. There was no incentive to save, because money quickly lost most of its value. People were paid daily and spent their salary on the way home, because its value would fall sharply by morning. Barter was commonplace. Owners of money or of assets with fixed money values, such as bonds and insurance policies, were wiped out. This disastrous experience is often credited with the rise of the Nazi party. Lesser episodes of hyperinflation took place in Hungary, Poland, Russia, and Austria after World War I and in Hungary after World War II. The most recent episodes, mostly quite brief, again occurred as part of a major economic transformation in the aftermath of the collapse of communism in Central and Eastern Europe. In 1992, Russia recorded 1,200 percent inflation for the year. At that rate, something that cost 1 ruble at the end of 1991 would sell for 1,200 rubles at the end of 1992.

Hyperinflation is rare. Most often it accompanies weak governments and the devastation of war. In Argentina, Brazil, and Israel, where conditions were much less severe, the government was able to bring the rates of inflation down to more acceptable levels fairly quickly. The likelihood of hyperinflation in the United States or other major industrial nations, in the absence of World War III or some other major disaster, is very small. ∎

was \$5,979 billion and M_1 was \$1,019 billion; velocity $= GDP/M_1$, or 5.87.) When the money supply is measured as M_2, velocity is only about 1.7.

If the number of dollars in the money supply (M_s) is multiplied by the number of times the average dollar is spent (V), the product of money supply and velocity is total spending on output. Since what is spent must equal the dollar value of what is bought, spending $= GDP$, or

$$M_s \times V = P \times Y = GDP.$$

This simple equation can help explain how an increase in the money supply is translated into changes in *GDP*. Suppose velocity is relatively stable, governed by habits such as how often people are paid and how often they shop and pay bills. Suppose also that Y is at the full employment level, Y^*. What do you think will happen if the money supply increases? If V and Y are fixed—and the equation must hold true by definition any increase in the money supply must lead to a proportional increase in the price level. Double the money supply, and the price level will also double.

This interpretation of the equation of exchange is sometimes referred to as the *crude quantity theory of money*. It is crude for two reasons. First, it assumes V and Y are fixed and unchanging. Second, it does not explain *how* the increase in money balances leads to a rise in the price level.

Let's address the *how* issue first. Suppose you were satisfied with the size of your money balances relative to your spending and your money income, and suddenly you have more money in your checking account. In the next chapter we will find out how it got there, but for now we have just magically increased the money supply. What will you do? You will *spend* it!

As households get rid of their excess money balances by spending them, they compete for a limited quantity of real goods and services *(Y)* and drive up the price level. At the higher price level, households find they require a higher average level of transactions balances to make their daily purchases and pay their monthly bills. The process of spending continues until the price level has increased enough that people "need" the higher level of cash balances for transactions purposes at a higher price level. (Remember, money demand for transactions purposes depends on money income.) At this point, the economy is at a new equilibrium. There are a larger money supply and higher average money balances, a higher level of prices, and no change in real output *(Y)* or velocity *(V)*. This explanation focuses on M_T, or the transactions demand for money.

Money and Aggregate Demand

How does this relationship work when either Y or V is not fixed? Suppose Y can change with a change in aggregate demand; that is, the aggregate supply curve is upward sloping rather than vertical. Figure 16-3 shows the familiar aggregate supply and aggregate demand curves, in equilibrium at Y_0, P_0.

Now the money supply increases. People try to "unload" their excess cash balances; they want to spend more at every level of real income *(Y)*. Aggregate demand shifts to the right to AD_1. Excess demand drives up income and prices to Y_1 and P_1. In terms of the quantity theory of money, increasing the money supply drives up both prices and output until equilibrium is restored. The equation changes from

$$M_S^0 \times V = P_0 Y_0$$

to

$$M_S^1 \times V = P_1 Y_1.$$

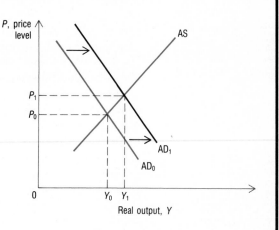

FIGURE 16-3

When an increase in the money supply shifts aggregate demand to the right, both the price level and real output will tend to rise as long as aggregate supply slopes upward.

An increase in the money supply, by shifting aggregate demand to the right, will drive up prices and/or output. How much of the increase in PY is real output and how much is prices depends on the slope of the aggregate supply curve. A decrease in the money supply will shift aggregate demand to the left and reduce prices and/or output in some combination.

Velocity and Interest Rates

What about velocity (V)? Is velocity really fixed, constant, and a product of habit? Velocity is constant only if one ignores the effect of interest rates on the asset demand for money.

Suppose once again the economy is in equilibrium in terms of the quantity theory equation:

$$M_s^0 \times V = P_0Y_0.$$

Now the money supply increases. The practical economists who hold the increased money supply now have two choices; *spend* it or *lend* it. Some of the excess money balances will go directly into increased demand for goods and services, driving up P and Y until households are satisfied with higher money balances. Households may not choose to spend it all, however. They may choose to save and lend some of it (through banks or by purchasing stocks or bonds) to business firms and others to use for new plant and equipment or housing. When households save, depositing unspent funds in banks and other lending institutions, the supply of loanable funds increases.

The market for loanable funds is like any other market. There are a supply from lenders, a demand by borrowers, and a price which is "the" interest rate as in Figure 16-4. There are many different interest rates, but as already noted, they tend to rise and fall together. The interest rate in Figure 16-4 is some representative interest rate, such as the Treasury bill rate or the Aaa corporate bond rate. When the supply of loanable funds increases, the interest rate falls, inducing more firms to borrow and invest.

The story does not end here, because the interest rate also affects the asset demand for money. As interest rates fall, the opportunity cost of holding money also falls. Practical economists respond to that signal by holding larger cash balances at every level of income. In terms of the quantity theory, velocity *(V)* falls. To the extent that *V* falls, a given increase in the money supply will mean a smaller rightward shift in aggregate demand. The resulting increase in the price level and/or real output will also be smaller.

CHECKLIST  : **Effects of Monetary Policy**

An increase in the money supply can

- Increase real output *(Y)* if the economy is operating below the full employment level *and* velocity is stable
- Increase the price level *(P)* if the economy is at or close to the full employment level of output *and* velocity is stable
- Reduce velocity if interest rates fall

or

- Increase real output and the price level and reduce velocity in some combination

FIGURE 16-4

In the market for loanable funds, an increase in supply (resulting in this case from an increase in the money supply) will tend to lower market rates of interest and increase the amount of borrowing from i_1 to i_2.

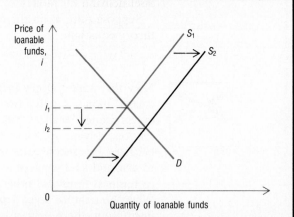

The Monetary Transmission Mechanism

Monetary transmission mechanism The process by which changes in the money supply work through the decisions of households and businesses to influence output and prices.

The process by which an increase in the money supply is translated into changes in output, prices, and interest rates is called the **monetary transmission mechanism**. The quantity theory describes a simple "spend it" transmission mechanism that leads the economy directly from an increase in the money supply to an increase in prices.

The "lend it" route goes through the market for loanable funds. When more loanable funds are available, interest rates fall and investment rises. More investment will have a multiplier effect on income and output, shifting aggregate demand to the right. Either route means an increase in the money supply increases aggregate demand, but the first mechanism stresses consumption and the second emphasizes investment, including housing and automobiles.

Figure 16-5 sketches the monetary transmission mechanism. The straight line route across the top part of the diagram is the "spend it" route of the simple quantity theory. The longer path through interest rates is the "lend it" route. With all these steps in the process, there are possibilities of failure. When the government increases the money supply to increase real income, some of the impact may be lost in interest rate changes, velocity changes, and a higher price level instead of affecting the level of real income and output. In Chapter 17, we will explore this process more closely to see where the route from an increase

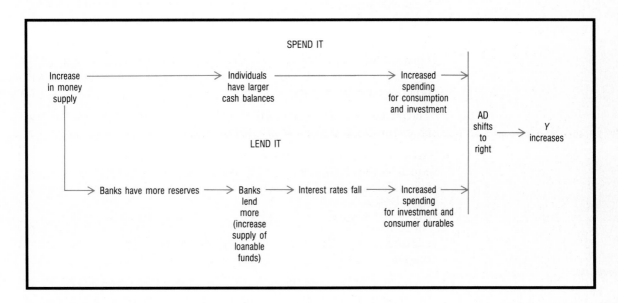

FIGURE 16-5

An increase in the money supply can work directly through spending (the upper series of arrows) or indirectly through interest rates and borrowing. In either case, an increase in the money supply will ultimately increase aggregate demand, the price level, and real output.

in the money supply to an increase in income and output might fail. Before we can do that, however, we need to look more closely at the supply side of the money picture, a task that will occupy most of the next chapter.

Summary

1. Money was an improvement over barter because it was no longer necessary to find someone who sells what you want *and* wants what you sell.

2. The functions of money are to serve as a unit of account, a medium of exchange, and a store of value. Demand for money as a medium of exchange is transactions demand, which depends on the level of money income *(PY)*. Demand for money as a store of value is asset demand, which is negatively related to the rate of interest.

3. Desirable properties of money are scarcity, durability, uniformity, divisibility, and portability. Money that also has value in nonmonetary uses as commodity money or full-bodied money. Money whose only value is as a medium of exchange or a store of value is fiat money.

4. The U.S. money supply consists of coins, currency, and primarily checkable deposits. Different definitions of the money supply include other liquid assets.

5. Among the other financial assets that share some of the properties of money are bonds and stocks. Bonds are loan instruments that represent ownership shares involving a greater voice in management and somewhat greater risk.

6. A rise in the rate of interest will reduce the value and the selling price of outstanding bonds. Because of this risk, low-interest rates encourage holding cash, whereas high rates induce a switch from money to bonds and other interest-bearing assets.

7. The market interest rate consists of the (unmeasured) real interest rate plus premiums for default risk and inflation risk.

8. According to the quantity theory of money, the money supply times velocity equals nominal *GDP*, or $P \times Y$. An increase in the money supply will increase P and/or Y, reduce velocity, or produce some combination of those effects.

9. An increase (decrease) in the money supply will tend to shift aggregate demand to the right (left), driving up (down) the price level and/or real output.

10. An increase in the money supply can also lower interest rates and stimulate investment. If this occurs, velocity will fall and the effect on prices and/or output will be smaller.

11. The monetary transmission mechanism describes the process by which a change in the money supply is translated into a rise in output and/or prices,

partly a direct process through higher spending and partly an indirect process through increased lending and lower interest rates.

Key Terms

asset demand for money
bank note
barter
bond
bond market
checkable deposits
commodity money
currency
fiat money
fractional reserve
  banking
full-bodied money

goldsmith
inflation hedge
liquidity
M_1
M_2
market (nominal)
  interest rate
medium of exchange
monetary transmission
  mechanism
quantity theory of
  money

real interest rate
risk premium
stock
stock market
store of value
transactions demand for
  money
Treasury bill rate
unit of account
velocity of money

Questions and Problems

1. Under which of the following circumstances would you choose to increase your cash balances in your checking account? When might you decrease them?

   a. You receive a 10 percent salary increase.
   b. Last year's inflation rate was 10 percent.
   c. You expect an increase in inflation next year.
   d. Interest rates are higher than they were last year.
   e. You expect interest rates on other assets to go up very soon.

2. In question 1, which events change the transactions demand for money, and which change the asset demand for money?

3. To compute the real rate of interest, you need to know the expected rate of inflation, but the only information available is the after-the-fact actual rate of inflation. Here are some actual data for the inflation rate (using the *GDP* deflator) and the Treasury bill rate for 1989–1992:

Year	T-Bill	Inflation Rate
1989	8.12	4.36
1990	7.51	4.45
1991	5.42	3.39
1992	3.45	1.93

Compute the real rate of interest for each year. What happened to real interest rates as the rate of inflation fell? Why do you think that happened? (Hint: What do you think happened to expected inflation compared to actual inflation?)

4. Look again at the monetary transmission mechanism in Figure 16-5. At each arrow is a point where the process can fail. For example, in the top line at the first arrow, consumers may choose not to spend if they are pessimistic about their future income. Try to identify something that might keep the transmission process from working at each of the other arrows.

5. Using a good U.S. history book, identify as many different kinds of money used in this country as you can, starting with wampum and tobacco. Which were full-bodied? Token? Fiat money?

6. Suppose the expected inflation rate rose, but at the same time individuals were optimistic about the future of the economy, so the perceived default risk for most borrowers fell. What would you expect to happen to the interest rate on Treasury bills? On Baa (relatively risky) corporate bonds? On mortgages? Explain your answers.

7. Discuss what is wrong with each of the following commodities serving as money in terms of the desirable characteristics of money.

    a. Houses
    b. Bananas
    c. Cats
    d. Kryptonite
    e. Coffee mugs
    f. Safety pins

8. If the price level is 2.0, real *GDP* is $1,000, and the money supply is $400, what is velocity? If real *GDP* rises to $2,000, the price level does not rise, and the money supply is unchanged, what must the new value of velocity be?

9. Given the following data, compute velocity for each year.

Year	M₁ (billions)	GDP (billions)	Velocity
1985	$ 620.2	$4,038.7	
1986	724.6	4,268.6	
1987	750.0	4,539.9	
1988	786.9	4,900.4	
1989	794.1	5,250.8	
1990	826.1	5,522.2	
1991	898.1	5,677.5	
1992	1019.0	5,978.5	

17

Money, the Banking System, and
Monetary Policy

A banker is a fellow who lends his umbrella when the sun is shining and wants it back the minute it begins to rain.

MARK TWAIN

Main Points

1. Changes in the money supply take place when commercial banks and other financial institutions make loans and create checkable deposits.

2. The banking system can lend more than it has in reserves (currency plus deposits at the central bank). The amount banks can lend, given their reserves, is smaller when the required reserve ratio is higher and larger when the required reserve ratio is lower.

3. The major responsibility of the Federal Reserve System, the central bank of the United States, is to conduct monetary policy through changes in the money supply and/or interest rates. The Fed also clears checks for banks and provides the banking system with a lender of last resort.

4. The Fed's monetary policy tools are open market operations, changes in reserve requirements, and changes in the discount rate.

5. A change in the money supply affects output and prices by changing one or more components of aggregate demand, usually consumption or investment.

6. The impact of monetary policy on real output depends on whether banks hold excess reserves, whether interest rates change very much in response to changes in the money supply, and how sensitive investment and consumption demand are to changes in interest rates.

I n this chapter, we complete the story of money begun in Chapter 16, shifting from the demand side to the supply side of the money market. Banks play a key role in creating money and thus changing the money supply. The process of money creation is the missing first step in the monetary transmission mechanism, which shows how changes in the money supply are translated through the "spend it" and "lend it" processes into changes in aggregate demand, the price level, and real output.

Banks are the most important component of a network of financial institutions. Banks are linked to one another through the U.S. central bank, or the Federal Reserve System. The Fed plays an important role in controlling the amounts banks can lend to customers. Through controlling lending, the Fed has considerable control over the supply of money. The Fed's actions to influence the money supply and interest rates (monetary policy) are the other half of the two-part team of fiscal and monetary policy that can be used to shift aggregate demand. ■

COMMERCIAL BANKS AND THE CREATION OF MONEY

Commercial bank   A firm that issues checkable deposits along with other services and engages in fractional reserve banking.

The most familiar part of the banking system to the average citizen is the local commercial bank. **Commercial banks** are where people keep checkable deposits, have safe deposit boxes, obtain car loans and student loans, buy savings bonds, get coins and currency for day-to-day transactions, maintain their savings accounts and, increasingly, even buy and sell stocks and bonds. The commercial bank is a direct descendant of the medieval goldsmiths. Like goldsmiths, commercial banks engage in fractional reserve banking.

Until about 1978, commercial banks were unique among financial institutions in the United States. They were the only private financial agencies allowed to issue "money" (checkable deposits, or checking account money). Practical economists could keep deposits elsewhere—in mutual savings banks, savings and loan associations, credit unions, or mutual funds. But commercial bank deposits differed from deposits in other kinds of institutions in two important ways. First, to be able to spend deposits kept in nonbank institutions, depositors had to convert those deposits to currency or transfer them to a deposit account in a commercial bank. Deposits in commercial banks could be spent directly. Second, these other deposits paid interest to depositors; checking accounts paid no interest.

Since 1980, legislative changes have blurred these distinctions between deposits at commercial banks and the various types of nonmoney deposit accounts. As a result of regulatory changes, checkable deposit accounts at commercial banks now pay some modest amount of interest. At the same time, other financial institutions now offer checkable accounts that can be used as money. Today it is almost impossible to tell the difference among commercial banks, savings banks, credit unions, and other financial institutions. Thus, the term *bank* now refers to any financial institution that issues deposit accounts on which checks can be written.

What Banks Do

Financial intermediary
A firm, such as a bank, credit union, mutual fund, or other financial institution, that collects the savings of households and channels them to borrowers.

Commercial banks and related institutions are the financial intermediaries at the bottom of the circular flow diagram. **Financial intermediaries** collect the savings of households and lend them to borrowers in the forms of consumer loans, business loans (including bonds, which are long-term loans), and government loans (bonds, Treasury bills, and Treasury notes). Banks and other financial intermediaries pay interest on the funds deposited with them and charge higher rates of interest on the funds they lend. The difference between the two rates, called the *spread*, covers their operating costs and hopefully—since bankers are also self-interested practical economists—leaves something for profit.

Market for loanable funds (credit market)
The sum total of the demand for funds by borrowers and the supply of funds by various lenders; determines the quantity of lending and the prices of loans (the interest rate).

Banks and other financial intermediaries make up the **market for loanable funds**, or the **credit market**. The credit market links lenders and borrowers and ensures a smooth flow of saving into investment. In this market, quantity is the amount of funds lent and borrowed, and price is the interest rate. Different borrowers pay different interest rates depending on default risk, the size and duration of the loan, and other factors. Deposits also come in different forms and sizes. Banks pay higher interest rates on larger, longer-term deposits and lower rates on small, short-term deposits.

The basic function of banks is to channel saving into investment, as well as noninvestment borrowing by consumers and government. Financial institutions that issue checkable deposits which can be used as money have a second important role: They create money or, more precisely, they are partners in the money creation process with the central bank.

Balance sheet A financial statement of a firm's assets (items of value), liabilities (obligations to repay), and net worth at a particular point in time.

The Bank's Balance Sheet

The best way to describe a commercial bank is in terms of its balance sheet. A **balance sheet** is a financial planning tool for a household, business firm, or public agency. It lists the value of the firm's various assets and liabilities, or debt obligations. The difference between assets and liabilities is called **net worth**. Net worth is what a firm or agency would have left if it went out of business, selling its assets and paying off its liabilities.

Net worth The difference between the market value of a firm's assets and the amount of liabilities the firm owes.

Assets are listed on the left and liabilities and net worth on the right. The totals in the two columns must be equal. Table 17-1 shows the simplified balance sheet for Farmers' National Bank. Some of these items are more familiar than

TABLE 17-1   Balance Sheet, December 31, 1993 Farmers' National Bank (in millions of dollars)

Assets (millions)		Liabilities and Net Worth (millions)	
Reserves	$ 800	Checkable deposits	2,000
Vault cash	120	Savings deposits	700
Deposits at the Fed	680	Borrowings from the Fed	300
Bonds	1,200	Other liabilities	900
Loans to public	3,000	Total liabilities	3,700
Building	50		
Other assets	30	Net worth (Assets − liabilities)	1,380
Total assets	5,080	Total liabilities + Net Worth	5,080

others. A building is obviously an asset; it can be sold for its market value. Vault cash (coins and currency on the bank premises) is also a well-known asset (just ask any would-be bank robber where to find cash!).

Bonds, which are interest-earning assets to the bank, are liabilities of governments or business firms. When a bond reaches maturity, the bank can redeem it for the face value. The bank can also sell bonds to other banks or individuals before the bonds mature. Likewise, loans to the public are assets to banks because they represent a claim to payments from borrowers in the future. Commercial banks keep some of their assets in the form of deposits (reserves) at the central bank, the Federal Reserve.

Checkable deposit A bank account that allows the holder to write checks for payment of deposited funds on demand.

The largest single liability for most banks is the sum of **checkable deposit accounts**. The bank is obligated to repay the money in those accounts any time a customer demands it by writing a check. When you deposit a check drawn against Hometown Bank into your account in State University Bank, those two banks clear your check by transferring reserves from Hometown Bank's reserve account at the Fed to the reserve account of State University Bank.

The bank's remaining liabilities are mostly other kinds of deposits, such as savings accounts, certificates of deposit, and money market accounts. Banks can also borrow from the Federal Reserve. Loans to the bank by the Fed are liabilities, because the bank will eventually have to pay them back.

One of the most important things to observe about the balance sheet in Table 17-1 is that it balances. Total assets of $5,080 equal total liabilities plus net worth. This means that if any item on the balance sheet changes, something else must change to keep it in balance. For example, suppose the bank sells a bond for cash. The sale of the bond reduces the asset item labeled *bonds*. There has to be another part to this transaction. The bank receives a cash payment for the bond. This increase in cash assets offsets the reduction in bond assets. If the bond were sold to a depositor, the payment might be in the form of a check, reducing the bank's checkable deposit liabilities. The important point is that

Myth 17-1

Banks Create Loans, Not Money

The myth "Banks create loans, not money" is popular with your neighborhood banker. Just ask him or her next time you are in the bank, "Do you create money?" The answer will be "Of course not. We just gather deposits and make loans." Most local bankers firmly believe they do not create money.

Since a particular bank has no printing press, issues no banknotes, and coins no coins, it does not look like it is creating money. But if you trace what happens to the deposit in your checking account, you will find your bank indeed creates money, and the banking system as a whole creates money on an even larger scale.

When Arthur deposited $100 in Federal Reserve notes in his checking account in Camelot Bank, his $100 was money (currency). It is still money (checkable deposits). This deposit is money because Arthur can use it whenever he wishes to purchase goods and services (medium of exchange) or just keep it handy for future use (store of value). So far, the money supply has not increased.

The complication arises when Camelot Bank lends Lancelot part of the money that Arthur is counting as his, sitting in his checking account. If the bank cautiously keeps a 25 percent reserve, Lancelot borrows $75.

Lancelot has $75 in his demand deposit account, and Arthur still has $100 in his account. Now there is $175 where before there was only $100. The only possible explanation for the appearance of the extra $75 is that the bank created money. The banker may think she only lent Lancelot Arthur's money, but Arthur does not think so. Arthur knows he still has the right to spend the money sitting in his checking account. For banks, whose deposit liabilities are money, the process of making loans and the creation of money are one and the same. ∎

Reserves Funds that banks hold on deposit at the Federal Reserve, or in the form of currency and coins, to meet withdrawals by depositors and meet legal reserve requirements.

any transaction, whether bond sales or purchases, deposits, or loans, must leave the balance sheet in balance.

Another interesting fact indicated by the balance sheet is the close relationship between this bank and the Fed. Like the goldsmiths of Chapter 16, this bank holds **reserves** against deposits. Also like the goldsmiths, its reserves are smaller than checkable deposits (that is, the bank engages in fractional reserve banking). A small amount is held in vault cash (the part that interests bank robbers). Most of the bank's reserves are held as deposits at the Fed. This bank has borrowed from the Fed (under *liabilities*), and will have to repay that amount at some future date. After exploring how banks create money, we will examine their links with the central bank more closely.

How Banks Create Money

Banks, like the goldsmiths in Chapter 16, acquire assets from depositors. Modern bank reserves, however, are not gold but coin, currency, and deposits at the central bank. These deposits are the bank's reserves. When banks acquire more reserve assets, they can make more loans, creating additional checkable deposits (also money). These additional checkable deposits are an increase in the money supply.

Why do banks make loans when they acquire more reserves? Consider a typical bank, Farmers' National, which—like most banks—is in business to make a profit. The practical economists who run this bank have to pay their expenses and also pay interest on their customers' deposits. Any idle reserves in vault cash or deposits at the central bank earn no interest to pay their tellers, pay depositors' interest, and cover any of their other costs, let alone turn a profit. They want to lend part or all of their reserves.

How much can (or should) this bank lend? Assume Farmers' Bank chooses to keep reserves equal to about 20 percent of its checkable deposit liabilities. For simplicity, we will ignore the need for reserves against other deposits, such as savings deposits. This percentage ratio may be legally required, or it may be Farmers' choice based on its past experience with withdrawals. If Farmers' National has $800 in reserves against $2,000 in checkable deposits, it has more reserves than it needs. This bank can lend up to $400 of its reserves and still have a 20 percent reserve (the remaining 400) against deposits.

If you have ever borrowed money from a bank, you may know that the most common way borrowers receive these funds is in the form of a deposit in their checking accounts. Farmers' National makes a $400 loan to the next acceptable borrower, Sam, by depositing funds in his checking account.

The process of money creation is easiest to understand in terms of changes in the bank's balance sheet. Since the balance sheet balanced to start with, we can list just those items that change as transactions occur. As long as the changes balance, the balance sheet as a whole will remain in balance as well. Partial balance sheets—those that list only changes—are called **T-accounts**, because they are in the form of a large *T*.

After the loan to Sam, the T-account of Farmers' National looks like this:

T-account A partial balance sheet showing the changes in a balance sheet resulting from a particular transaction or series of transactions.

Farmers' National Bank

Assets		Liabilities + Net Worth	
Loans	+400	Checkable deposits	+400

Is this the end of the story? Not quite. Sam will spend his loan by writing a check to Julie's Hardware, and that check will probably wind up in some other bank. When Sam spends his borrowed money on hardware, Julie deposits the check at Mechanic National Bank. Mechanic presents Sam's check to Farmers' for payment. Farmers' has to pay Mechanic out of its reserves, which will fall by $400. Farmers' also deducts $400 from its checkable deposits on the liability side. After all these transactions, the T-account for Farmers' National Bank looks like this:

Farmers' National Bank

Assets		Liabilities	
Loans	+400	Checkable deposits	+400
Reserves	−400	Checkable deposits	−400

When all the dust has settled, Farmers' National has traded $400 in reserve assets for $400 in additional loans (to Sam). The bank has only a 20 percent reserve behind its checkable deposits and can make no additional loans until more reserves come from somewhere. In short, Farmers' is "all loaned up."

Mechanic Bank, however, now has additional reserves and deposits of $400 on each side of its balance sheet. This bank can repeat the lending process on a smaller scale. Mechanic's T-account for this new deposit looks like this:

Mechanic National Bank

Assets		Liabilities	
Reserves	+400	Deposits	+400

Mechanic Bank can now make additional loans, because it has additional reserves. It cannot lend the entire $400, because it has to keep a reserve behind Julie's Hardware's new deposit. If Mechanic keeps a reserve of 20 percent of the $400 deposit, or $80, then $320 of the new reserves is available to lend. When Sandra comes in to borrow some money to buy a new air conditioner, Mechanic lends her the entire $320 (putting this sum in her demand deposit account). Mechanic's T-account now looks like this:

Mechanic National Bank

Assets		Liabilities	
Reserves	+400	Deposits	+400
Loans	+320	Deposits	+320

Naturally, Sandra will spend the $320 immediately. No practical economist would borrow money and pay interest on a loan just to let it sit in a checking account! When Sandra writes her check and that check is deposited in yet another bank, Mechanic's final T-account will look like this:

Mechanic National Bank			
Assets		**Liabilities**	
Reserves	+400	Deposits	+400
Loans	+320	Deposits	+320
Reserves	−320	Deposits	−320
Reserves	+80	Deposits	+400
Loans	+320		

The summary below the line simply combines changes in reserves and deposits to show net changes. After all the changes are accounted for, Mechanic has $400 more in assets, in the form of $80 in additional reserves, and $320 in additional loans. There are additional deposits of $400, the T-account is in balance, and Mechanic has a 20 percent reserve behind its additional deposits. Like Farmers' National, Mechanic is now all loaned up.

If you trace this series of loans and deposits through many banks, a series of changes will occur in reserves, deposits, and loans (with a 20 percent reserve ratio) as shown in Table 17-2. Farmer's National Bank's decision to lend its excess reserves set off a chain reaction. That $400 in reserves was able to support $2,000 in new loans and checkable deposits. As banks receive additional reserves, they lend any reserves that exceed the amounts they need or want to keep on hand.

The amount of reserves that banks are required to keep by law are called **required reserves**. Reserves over and above what banks are required to keep are called **excess reserves**. Excess reserves are what banks can lend. When all the excess reserves have been "nailed down" as required reserves behind newly

Required reserves The amount of reserves, as a fraction of checkable deposits, that banks are required by law to keep.

Excess reserves Reserves held by banks in excess of the amounts required by law.

TABLE 17-2 Summary of Stages in the Money Expansion Process

Bank	Change in Reserves	Change in Deposits	Change in Loans
Farmers'	−400	—	+ 400
Mechanic	+ 80	+ 400	+ 320
Bank 3	+ 64	+ 320	+ 256
Bank 4	+ 51.2	+ 256	+ 204.8
Bank 5	+ 40.96	+ 204.8	+ 163.84
. . . . .			
Total	0	+2,000	+2,000

created checkable deposits (resulting from loans), the process of money creation grinds to a halt until additional reserves come into the system. A change in the required reserve ratio will free up additional reserves for bank lending. In the case of Farmers' National, a reserve ratio of 15 percent of deposits instead of 20 percent would have meant $500 in excess reserves available to lend rather than $400. Each bank along the line would have been able to lend more, and total lending and money expansion would have been greater.

In this example, the increase in bank loans and checkable deposits in the banking system came about because one bank, Farmers', had excess reserves. The same process could have occurred if the banking system started with no excess reserves and Farmers' National somehow acquired $400 in additional reserves. When we introduce the Federal Reserve System, you will see how banks acquire new excess reserves.

There are two other ways banks can be in a position to make new loans. First, assume you have both a checkable deposit and a loan at Grand Bank. You write a check on your account to pay off the balance of your loan, which is $2,000. The bank now has $2,000 less in deposits and $2,000 less in loans. Because it has less in checkable deposits, a portion of the reserves it was keeping behind your deposit is now available to lend to someone else.

Second, banks can increase their lending if they are allowed to reduce their reserve ratio. In the case of Farmer's National, the required reserve ratio drops from 20 percent of deposits to 15 percent. In this case, $3,000 in reserves could now support $20,000 in deposits rather than $15,000.

From these examples you can see that the connection between such a change in reserves (R), the reserve ratio (r), and the resulting change in the money supply (M_S), or checkable deposits, can be expressed this way:

Change in Reserves = Reserve Ratio × Change in Money Supply,

or

$$\Delta R = r \times \Delta M_S.$$

In other words, when the money creation process is complete, all the new reserves will serve as required reserves behind new checkable deposits. The change in required reserves is the reserve ratio times the change in checkable deposits. Banks will continue to expand their loans until they have no more excess reserves, because reserves earn no interest and banks make a profit by lending at interest. This relationship is sometimes written as

$$\Delta M_S = 1/r \times \Delta R,$$

Money multiplier The ratio of a potential change in the money supply to an initial change in excess reserves; equal to 1/r, where r is the required reserve ratio.

which emphasizes the change in the money supply (ΔM_S) that can result from a given change in reserves (ΔR) for a given reserve ratio, r.

The term $1/r$ is called the **money multiplier**. The money multiplier is similar to the expenditure multiplier of Chapter 14, except that it shows the multiple change in the money supply that results from a given change in reserves.

CHECKLIST : **Banks and Money Creation**

A bank can create money if:

It acquires more reserves through
  Repayment of loans
  Selling bonds
  Receiving deposits

or

It reduces its deposit liabilities without reducing reserves

or

It is allowed to reduce its reserve ratio, freeing some reserves for lending

COMMERCIAL BANKS AND CENTRAL BANKS

As we have seen, reserves play a central role in the money creation process. But where do reserves come from, and how do they increase or decrease? To answer this question, we need to introduce the actor that has been lurking in the wings since the beginning of the chapter: the central bank.

In general, reserves in the commercial banking system are created (and destroyed) by the central bank, the **Federal Reserve System**. Most countries have a central bank to meet the needs of the banking system as a whole as well as a network of commercial banks to serve households and business firms. Although the specific functions differ from one country to another, a **central bank** is essentially a banker's bank. That is, a central bank is a government or government-designated private financial institution that controls bank reserves, makes loans to banks, and supervises the conduct of monetary policy.

The Evolution of Central Banking in the United States

Shortly after the U.S. Constitution was adopted, Secretary of the Treasury Alexander Hamilton led the move to create the nation's first central bank, the Bank of the United States. This bank's main role was to act as the banker to the Treasury. Tax revenues were deposited at the Bank of the United States, and the central government made withdrawals from this bank to pay its bills. This bank also had some supervisory powers over other banks and made loans to them, but its powers were more limited than those of modern central banks.

The Bank of the United States (1791–1811) was followed by the Second Bank of the United States (1816–1836). When renewal of the Second Bank's charter fell victim to political forces, the United States was without a central bank from 1837 to 1914. During that period, it became apparent that a central bank would be useful for several purposes: supervising bank safety, clearing

Federal Reserve System (Fed)   The central bank of the United States, which issues Federal Reserve notes and conducts monetary policy.

Central bank   A government bank or government-authorized bank that holds reserves of member banks, serves as a lender of last resort, issues currency, and supervises member banks.

Lender of last resort A financial institution—usually a central bank—at which commercial banks can borrow reserves to meet depositors' demands.

checks, and, most important at that time, providing a **lender of last resort** for the banks that made up the highly decentralized U.S. banking system.

Without a lender of last resort, individual banks may fail in response to temporary problems when those banks are actually quite sound; that is, their balance sheets may show that the value of their assets exceeds the value of their liabilities. This function of a central bank is particularly important if a number of banks are having problems at the same time and thus cannot solve their problems by borrowing from one another. If depositors suddenly appear in large numbers, demanding currency or making other withdrawals, the bank or banks may not have enough liquidity (reserves and other assets that can be quickly converted to cash) to meet those demands.

When a bank cannot pay of depositors promptly, its depositors will be concerned about the bank's safety. Such fear can trigger a **run on the bank**, in which many depositors demand payment at the same time. Even a bank that is sound cannot normally pay cash to all its depositors at once. A lender of last resort, however, can provide short-term funds to the bank to tide it over such a crisis.

Run on the bank A situation that occurs when many depositors demand repayment of their deposits in currency at the same time, creating a temporary shortage of bank reserves.

In the nineteenth century, runs on banks occurred during recessions. During expansionary periods, banks found borrowers plentiful and interest rates attractive and would lend as much as they thought they safely could (and then some). With no central bank to enforce reserve requirements, the practical economists who run the banks would be tempted to cut reserves to a bare minimum. When a downturn in economic activity occurred, some loans would go sour. Depositors would get nervous about whether the bank would be able to make good on deposits, and a run on the bank would follow.

The creation of the Fed in 1914 did not eliminate runs on banks. Many banks failed during the Great Depression, and people who lived through that experience are still much less trustful of banks than younger generations are. Runs on banks occurred in Ohio, Nebraska, and Maryland in 1984 and 1985 as word of impending bank failures among state-chartered banks spread and depositors grew concerned about recovering their funds. A rash of bank failures in 1988–1991 led to some similar panics among depositors. In general, however, runs on banks have been much less frequent since the creation of the Fed.

The Federal Reserve System in Operation

The Federal Reserve System was created as a cross between a government agency and a private agency—the government's bank and a private bank. The designers of the Federal Reserve System established a group of 12 regional Federal Reserve banks united under a board of governors in Washington, D.C. The Board of Governors conducts monetary policy and oversees the operation of the Fed. The board consists of seven governors from seven of the twelve Reserve district banks, appointed by the president for 14-year terms. All nationally chartered banks were required to join; state-chartered banks were allowed to join if they wished.

Originally, the Fed was designed to serve three functions: (1) check clearing, (2) lender of last resort, and (3) bank supervision. Controlling the money supply and monetary policy were not at the top of the original agenda. As the Fed developed, however, it became clear that these three functions were not nearly as important as controlling the money supply and influencing the level of interest rates, which together make up monetary policy. Today economists consider controlling the money supply to be the primary role of the Fed, but that is partly because they take the other functions for granted. In 1914, however, the functions of check clearing, lender of last resort, and bank supervision were essential needs of the banking system that no existing agency, public or private, was meeting.

Check Clearing.   Prior to the arrival of the Fed, clearing a check was often a tedious process. When a check was written on a checkable deposit account in Bank A and the person or firm to whom it was written deposited or cashed the check at Bank B, Bank B had to present the check to Bank A for payment. In the absence of a central clearinghouse, the process of moving a check from one bank to another could be very slow; the bank at which the check was deposited had a long wait before the funds were transferred. The Fed simplified that process. Since all banks must maintain reserve accounts at the Fed, when the Fed receives a check written by a depositor on an account in Bank A that was deposited in Bank B, it simply transfers reserves from Bank A to Bank B.

Lender of Last Resort.   Originally envisioned as the major function of the Fed, the lender of last resort role has become less important over time. The congressional committee that created the Fed used the Bank of England as its model. In England, the lender of last resort function was very important. When a country has a lender of last resort to which banks can turn, runs on banks and other financial panics are less likely. Banks that find themselves short of reserves do turn to the Fed, although they are more likely to turn to other banks first.

Federal Deposit Insurance Corporation (FDIC)   An agency created in 1935 to insure deposits at commercial banks.

Resolution Trust Corporation   An agency created in the 1980s to dispose of the assets of banks that failed during the savings and loan crisis.

Bank Supervision and Bank Safety.   The Fed shares responsibility for supervising banks with the Comptroller of the Currency for national banks and with the **Federal Deposit Insurance Corporation (FDIC),** created in 1935. State agencies supervise those state-chartered banks that are not members of either the Federal Reserve System or the FDIC. Banks that are no longer solvent fall under the jurisdiction of the **Resolution Trust Corporation**, created in response to the banking crisis of the 1980s. This agency tries to sell the assets of failed banks to recover some of the funds for depositors or for the FDIC.

The question of bank safety has seldom been raised since the Great Depression, when a wave of bank failures led to the creation of the FDIC. Deposits are insured up to $100,000. Note that the FDIC does not insure *banks*; it insures *deposits*. This agency does not protect banks or their stockholders against failure.

In Practice 17-1

. . . .

The Savings and Loan Crisis

The first signs of a problem in the U.S. banking system appeared in 1984 and 1985 when state-supervised banks failed in Ohio and Maryland. Depositors at these banks could not withdraw their funds. However, the banks were taken over by the federal government, most depositors got their money back, and the crisis appeared to have passed. In fact, though, these bank failures were the first wave of a series of doomed banks that wound up costing taxpayers more than $180 billion between 1987 and 1993.

Although commercial banks have had problems, more difficulties plagued savings banks and savings and loan associations. These banks traditionally had not issued checkable deposits or made many short-term loans before the 1980s. Most of their deposits were savings accounts, and most of their lending was for home mortgages. The reforms of 1980 and 1982 allowed these banks to issue checkable deposits and offer more kinds of loans. These reforms took place in a period of high market interest rates, although some of the loans and bonds behind those rates carried a high risk of default.

It's easy to see how tempting this situation was for bankers. Pay high interest rates on deposits to lend at even higher rates. Even if the loans are risky, depositors are protected by deposit insurance. The 1980s became the era of "go-go" banking. But in the mid-1980s, interest rates began to fall and property values in the over-built residential and commercial real estate markets began to slide. Banks found the value of the many loans they had made was less than the value of their deposit liabilities.

The value of a real estate loan depends on the value of the collateral. Suppose a bank lends $90,000 for a mortgage on a property with a market value of $100,000. The bank is certain the borrower will continue to make payments, because if he or she does not, it can foreclose (take over the property and sell it to collect the money owed). Now suppose real estate prices fall and the value of the property drops to $85,000. If the borrower walks away from the property and lets the bank take over, the bank is out $5,000. This story was repeated over and over on a large scale in the late 1980s. As banks became insolvent, they could not pay off their depositors.

Due to actual and potential bank failures on a massive scale, Congress had to bail out the FDIC, whose reserves were inadequate for the task. Congress created the Resolution Trust Corporation to come in and clean up failed banks by selling off their assets and using the funds to pay off deposit liabilities. The RTC has been selling loans and properties and merging failed banks with stronger banks. By 1992, most banks were in good shape again. In the process, however, the RTC cannot raise enough money to pay off depositors. The difference between the revenues from selling the assets and the payments to depositors has been made up by taxpayers—the cost of the bailout. ∎

Member banks pay a fee based on their insured deposits. These fees provide a fund with which to reimburse insured deposits if a bank fails (becomes insolvent). To minimize its losses, the FDIC examines the condition of a bank before accepting it for membership to ensure that it is solvent and reasonably well managed. A member bank gets to put the FDIC seal on its door, which until the mid-1980s served as an adequate guarantee of a safe bank.

The 1980s were a difficult period for banks. Deregulation meant banks could pay interest on checkable deposits. Banks were eager to attract deposits because interest rates were high and lending was profitable. As they paid high interest rates on deposits, they had to put those deposits to work, by making increasingly risky loans. Banks often made riskier loans than they might have otherwise because they knew their depositors were protected by the FDIC (and, in the case of savings banks, by the Federal Savings and Loan Insurance Corporation, or FSLIC). Savings and loans in particular became more adventurous as they were freed from the mortgage lending and savings account businesses to offer more kinds of deposits and make more kinds of loans. Inexperienced in the lending business, many of these banks made risky loans that later defaulted. When a bank had too many bad loans, it became insolvent and lacked the resources to pay off depositors when they showed up to claim their funds.

By 1987, it was clear that the reserves of the FDIC and FSLIC were grossly inadequate to meet the deposit insurance obligations of existing unsound banks. Many banks were allowed to continue to operate or were sold at a loss to other banks in "shotgun marriages" to save the FDIC or FSLIC from the burden of paying off depositors. A wave of bank failures between 1987 and 1991 exhausted the resources of the FDIC and necessitated a bailout by Congress.

Today banks are much less strictly regulated than they were prior to the reforms of 1979 and 1981. However, regulations intended to protect depositors by ensuring bank solvency and liquidity remain. These regulations tell banks what types of loans they can make or what kinds of assets they can acquire, how much they must keep in reserves, and what types of deposits they can offer.

CHECKLIST : **Responsibilities of the Fed**

The Fed's banking functions:
Banker for the Treasury
Check clearing
Lender of last resort
Depository for member bank reserves
Bank supervision
Issuer of currency (Federal Reserve notes)

The Fed's policy function:
Control the monetary base
    Change stock of Federal Reserve notes
    Increase or decrease stock of member bank reserves

The Fed and Member Bank Reserves

Over time, changing bank reserves to change the money supply has evolved into the most important single activity of the Federal Reserve System. Originally, controlling the money supply was a by-product of the Fed's more important activities: issuing currency and serving as a banker's bank. Today controlling the money supply occupies most of the attention of the Fed's Board of Governors

Monetary base Coins, currency, and member bank reserve deposits at the Fed; determines the maximum size of the money supply.

and its chairperson, who is widely regarded to be the second most powerful individual in Washington. The Fed does not directly control the money supply; rather, it controls the **monetary base**, which consists of member bank reserves and Federal Reserve notes (currency).

Earlier in this chapter, we saw how changes in reserves affect the ability of banks to make loans and create checkable deposits. What about changes in currency? Recall from Chapter 16 that the narrowly defined M_1 money supply consists of currency and checkable deposits. Changes in the supply of currency, or Federal Reserve notes, affect the money supply in two ways. First, if currency is in circulation in the hands of the public, it is part of the money supply. Second, if currency is in the hands of banks, it is part of reserves and can form the basis for multiple expansion of the money supply.

The money supply is at its maximum when banks have no excess reserves and all currency is in the hands of banks. In reality, the money supply is much smaller than the potential maximum, because the part of the potential monetary base that is in circulation is not available to support loans and deposits.

THE FED AND MONETARY POLICY

Monetary policy Use of Federal Reserve tools to change the money supply in order to change the levels of output and prices.

When the Board of Governors of the Fed deliberately changes the amount of Federal Reserve notes or member bank reserve deposits to try to influence the levels of income and prices, the Fed engages in **monetary policy**. Increasing the money supply is expansionary monetary policy, and decreasing it is contractionary monetary policy.

This important role of the Federal Reserve System first occupied the limelight in the late 1930s and has been the major focus of the Board of Governors since that time. Monetary policy may have several secondary targets as well, such as interest rates, particular sectors or markets such as the stock or bond market, housing or automobiles, or currency exchange rates. But the primary focus is on controlling the monetary base to control the money supply. The money supply, in turn, affects interest rates and aggregate demand, output, and prices.

How does the Fed "create" member bank reserves or Federal Reserve notes? You have already seen a part of the process of money creation from the perspective of a member bank. Now we will investigate how the Fed changes the monetary base to change the money supply.

The Tools of Monetary Policy

The Federal Reserve system has three tools for changing the monetary base: open market operations, changing the discount rate (the interest rate charged member banks when they borrow from the Fed), and changing reserve requirements. The first two work directly by changing the size of the monetary base, specifically by increasing or decreasing member bank reserves. Changing reserve requirements alters the relationship between the monetary base and the money supply by changing the value of r and therefore the size of the money multiplier.

Open Market Operations.

The largest asset in the Fed's portfolio is government bonds. The sale or purchase of government bonds by the Fed to change the monetary base is the most important single weapon at the Fed's disposal. These bond sales and purchases are called **open market operations**.

Open market operations Sales or purchases of government bonds by the Federal Reserve System made to change the monetary base and thus change the money supply.

When the Fed sells government bonds, member bank reserves fall. If member banks are "all loaned up"—that is, have no excess reserves—they must contract their lending to bring it into line with reduced reserves. When the Fed buys bonds, member bank reserves (and the monetary base) expand and banks can make more loans, increasing checkable deposits and the money supply. Let's take a closer look at this process.

Suppose the Fed offers to buy a $1,000 bond from Bank A. The Fed pays for the bond by increasing the amount in Bank A's reserve account at the Fed for $1,000. The Fed remains in balance, because both its assets and its liabilities have risen by $1,000. Bank A is also still in balance, with an increase in reserve assets balanced by an equal decrease in bond assets. Bank A now has an extra $1,000 in reserves and, since there are no new checkable deposits on the other side of the balance sheet, all of these new reserves are excess reserves, free to be lent. Here is Bank A's T-account after the Fed bought one of its bonds:

Bank A	
Assets	**Liabilities**
Bonds − 1,000	
Reserves + 1,000	

This bond purchase by the Fed sets the money creation process in motion. If the reserve ratio is still 20 percent, the money supply can expand by as much as $5,000. Bank A begins this process with a $1,000 loan to Fred's Trucking. Bank A's T-account now looks like this:

Bank A	
Assets	**Liabilities**
Bonds − 1,000	
Reserves + 1,000	
Loans + 1,000	Checkable deposits + 1,000

You should be able to trace what happens next as Fred spends the $1,000 he borrowed. Bank A loses checkable deposits and reserves, which are transferred to Bank B to continue the money creation process.

Money contraction works the same way. When the Fed sells a bond to a bank, bank reserves fall. When banks lose reserves, they have to contract loans and deposits until the money supply is once again in line with the smaller monetary base. (Try tracing the effects on T-accounts of a Fed bond sale, reversing of the numbers in the T-accounts for the Fed's bond purchase.) In fact, when the Fed sells bonds and banks lose reserves, banks are under great pressure to reduce deposits and loans to rebuild reserves and meet their reserve requirements. When the Fed buys bonds and creates reserves, banks may choose to lend more and create more deposits, but they are under less pressure.

Suppose Bank A refuses to cooperate with the Fed by buying (or selling) bonds. The practical economists who run this bank might not want to buy a bond because doing so would deplete their reserves below the required level, forcing the bank to reduce loans and deposits. Can banks frustrate the Fed's attempt to control the money supply through open market operations? Not really. The Fed will simply sell bonds to members of the public (or buy bonds from the public). When the Fed deals with the public, individual buyers pay for bonds with checks drawn on their banks, reducing bank reserves and checkable deposits. When members of the public sell bonds to the Fed, they deposit their Federal Reserve checks in their accounts at banks. When the checks clear, member bank reserves will change—with or without the banks' cooperation.

Open market operations were the last of the Fed's tools to develop. Over the last 40 years, they have become the most valuable tool for monetary policy. Open market operations allow the Fed to target exactly by how much and how quickly the monetary base changes.

Open market operations also affect interest rates. When the Fed buys or sells government bonds, both prices and yields of bonds change. When the Fed sells bonds, the supply of bonds shifts to the right, depressing their prices and driving up interest rates. (Recall from Chapter 16 the relationship between bond prices and interest rates.) Higher interest rates then spread to other loans and financial assets. Expansionary monetary policy through open market purchases will drive down interest rates directly through the bond market as well as indirectly through increased bank lending.

The Discount Rate and Interest Rates.   Originally the creators of the Federal Reserve Act expected that the most important policy tool of the Fed would be the discount rate. The **discount rate** is the interest rate the Fed charges member banks on Fed loans. Such a loan directly increases member bank reserves, since the loan is put into the reserve account of the borrowing member bank.

When the Fed changes the discount rate, that change signals its intentions. A lower discount rate signals easy, or expansionary, policy. It is cheaper for banks to borrow from the Fed, and the lower rate is a signal that the Fed intends to expand the monetary base. A higher discount rate means tight, or contractionary,

Discount rate   The interest rate charged by the Fed on loans to member banks.

monetary policy. It is more expensive for banks to borrow from the Fed, signaling that the Fed intends to slow growth of the monetary base.

In practice, banks turn to other banks to borrow reserves before they turn to the Fed. Some banks may find themselves short of reserves, whereas others may have excess reserves. Banks lend and borrow these reserves on an overnight basis in the federal funds market. The rate banks charge one another to borrow excess reserves, called the **federal funds rate**, is just slightly lower than the Fed's discount rate.

Federal funds rate The interest rate banks charge one another for lending excess reserves.

Lending by the Fed and the discount rate are less important than open market operations in influencing market interest rates. Fed loans to member banks are not a major source of changes in reserves and the monetary base. Open market operations have a greater impact on interest rates by changing the monetary base. When the Fed changes the monetary base, interest rates charged by banks also change. An increase in the monetary base means banks have more funds available to lend, and therefore interest rates (as the price of loanable funds) should fall when the supply of funds increases.

Reserve Requirements.   When the Fed was created in 1914, one of its most important powers was setting and changing reserve requirements for various classes of banks and deposits. Reserve ratios are the same for checkable deposits of all sizes and at all banks, with a lower ratio for savings deposits. The average required reserve ratio for checkable deposits is about 12 percent (only 3 percent for the bank's first $25 million in deposits). Current law authorizes the Fed to change that ratio to as low as 8 percent or as high as 14 percent.

Changing reserve requirements appears to be a very attractive tool because its impact is more direct, immediate, and certain than that of the other tools. Open market operation can change the monetary base, but such changes may lead to a smaller change in the money supply than expected. Changing the discount rate encourages banks to borrow and may affect market interest rates, but this tool is also fairly indirect. Changes in reserve requirements, however, have direct effects on the money supply.

Consider an increase in the reserve requirement from the standpoint of the entire banking system. Suppose the initial required reserve ratio is 10 percent and the amount of reserves is $100 million. The maximum money supply would be $1,000 million, or $1 billion. (Recall that $R = r \times M_s$, or $100 million = 0.10 \times \$1,000$ million.) Now the Fed raises the required reserve ratio to 12.5 percent. With the same amount of reserves, the maximum size of the money supply falls sharply, to $800 million. Raising the required reserve ratio from 10 percent to 12.5 percent has cut the money supply by 20 percent!

The fact that this tool is too powerful is precisely the reason it is so rarely used. Open market operations can be fine-tuned to a fairly precise amount of change in reserves. Reserve ratio changes are more like a sledgehammer, even with fairly small changes. With a higher reserve requirement, every bank that was fully loaned up, or close to it, must scramble for a limited supply of reserves. Banks reduce their loans and sell bonds as they try to meet the new, higher reserve requirement. Thus, reserve requirements are changed infrequently and only by small amounts. Like changes in the discount rate, reserve requirement adjustments are used primarily as a strong signal about the direction of monetary policy.

CHECKLIST ⋮ **The Fed's Policy Tools**

Tool	*How It Works*
Open market operations	Changes bank reserves
Discount rate	Encourages bank borrowing to increase reserves
Reserve requirement	Changes the amount of money supply a given amount of reserves can support

Monetary Policy and the Transmission Mechanism

As you learned in Chapter 16, an increase in the money supply will increase spending either directly through higher spending or indirectly through higher lending. This process is called the *monetary transmission mechanism.* The monetary transmission process actually begins not with an increase in the money supply but with an increase in the monetary base or a reduction in reserve requirements. Either step will give banks excess reserves that they can lend. The first part of the monetary transmission process should be clearer now that you understand the money creation process.

The First Step in the Transmission Mechanism.   When the Fed buys bonds (open market operations) to increase the monetary base of reserves and currency, there is more money in the hands of banks or the public. If the Fed purchased the bonds from the public, the practical economists who sold them have two choices: They may choose to spend those funds on consumption, or they may lend them. They can lend directly by buying stocks and bonds or lend indirectly by depositing the funds in banks, which in turn will make those funds available to borrowers. It does not matter whether the Fed purchased the bonds from banks or from individuals who deposit the proceeds of the sale in banks. In both cases, banks find themselves with excess reserves.

Normally banks do not favor excess reserves. They have to pay interest on deposits and other expenses, and reserves earn no interest. Thus, the practical economists who run the banks will try to put the excess reserves to work, making more funds available in the market for loanable funds. This situation is depicted in panel a of Figure 17-1 with a shift in the supply of loanable funds from S_1 to S_2. The interest rate falls, and the quantity of loanable funds demanded rises from Q_1 to Q_2.

Borrowers will spend these funds on business plant and equipment, state and local government facilities, housing, consumer durables, and college tuition, all

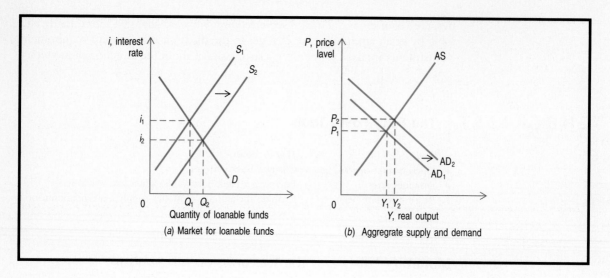

FIGURE 17-1

An increase in the supply of loanable funds in panel a lowers the interest rate and encourages more borrowing for investment or other spending. This additional spending means aggregate demand shifts to the right in panel b, driving up prices and real output from P_1 and Q_1 to P_2 and Q_2.

of which are forms of spending typically financed by borrowing. Aggregate demand will rise from AD_1 to AD_2 in panel b of Figure 17-1, driving up real output and the price level.

A reduction in the money supply brought about by the Fed's sale of government bonds (or by raising either the discount rate or reserve requirements) would reverse this process. Reserves would fall, reducing the supply of loanable funds, driving up interest rates, and lowering aggregate demand.

Breakdowns in the Transmission Process. This model makes monetary policy look very powerful. In fact, however, there are several points at which the transmission mechanism can fail so that the increase (decrease) in the money supply is not translated into the desired change in aggregate demand. In the transmission mechanism in Figure 17-2, the possible points of failure are marked with numbers.

Decline in Velocity. The number one point of failure in Figure 17-2 is in the direct process (along the upper line, or the "spend it" route). Suppose the Fed, responding to a recession, pursues an expansionary monetary policy. If the Fed purchases bonds from households, households may choose not to spend the funds but instead to hold onto those funds in the form of cash or checkable

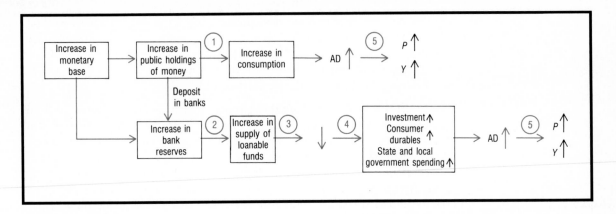

FIGURE 17-2

This monetary transmission mechanism, which shows how increases in the money supply are translated into increases in aggregate demand, prices, and real output, also stresses points at which the transmission process can fail. Points of failure are (1) the public holding more cash, (2) banks holding excess reserves, (3) interest rates failing to decline, (4) investment and other expenditures being unresponsive to lower interest rates, and (5) most of the effect falling on prices rather than on real output.

deposits. Perhaps these practical economists make this choice because interest rates are low and the opportunity cost of holding money is low, or perhaps they have high uncertainty and negative expectations.

In terms of the equation of exchange, a decision by the public to hold larger cash balances is a decrease in velocity. Money supply increases will then not be fully translated into changes in either the price level or real output.

Excess Reserves.   When households sell bonds to the Fed, they have to do something with the payments they receive. Most of those funds will go into checkable deposits, also increasing bank reserves. The increased bank reserves put the transmission mechanism on the "lend it" route in Figure 17-2. Here banks may frustrate monetary expansion by choosing to hold excess reserves at point 2 in the transmission process.

Like the public, banks are more likely to make this choice if interest rates are low and banks expect them to rise in the future. A prudent banker, as a practical economist, would not commit funds at low interest rates and forgo the chance to earn higher returns in the near future. (The development of some adjustable rate contracts, particularly for mortgages, over the last ten years has reduced some of this risk.) A decision by bankers to postpone lending would show up as a decline in velocity. The Fed can lead a banker to money, but it can't make him or her lend.

This kind of frustration is less likely to occur with contractionary monetary policy. Banks that lose reserves have little choice about reducing their lending. For this reason, the effects of contractionary monetary policy are generally considered to be more certain. If the Fed takes away banks' money, banks are forced to lend less, whether they want to or not.

Interest Rates and Investment Demand.   Even if banks choose to lend, they may not reduce interest rates very much. After examining their costs and the interest they are paying on deposits, they may be unwilling to cut interest rates dramatically. This hazard occurs at point 3 in the transmission diagram.

Even if interest rates fall, the demand curve for loanable funds may be so steep that only a very large drop in interest rates will stimulate much borrowing and spending. This problem occurs at point 4 in the transmission diagram and is illustrated in Figure 17-3. Even with a large drop in interest rates, the increase in borrowing (from Q_1 to Q_2) is quite small. A very large increase in the money supply may be needed to create a large impact not only on interest rates but also on investment spending and demand for consumer durables, and thus on aggregate demand. The same problem could plague contractionary monetary policy: A sharp rise in interest rates may be needed to curtail borrowing demand.

Real Output or Prices.   Finally, at point 5 on both routes in the transmission mechanism, the increase in aggregate demand may encounter a very steep aggregate supply curve, as in Figure 17-4. If this occurs, most of the increase in the

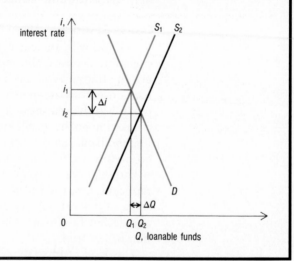

FIGURE 17-3

If the demand for loanable funds is relatively unresponsive to changes in interest rates, most of the effect of an increase in supply is felt on lower interest rates (i_1 to i_2) and relatively little on quantity (Q_1 to Q_2).

money supply will lead to rising prices rather than to rising real output. This possibility represents a problem for both monetary and fiscal policy.

Is Monetary Policy Effective?

In evaluating the effectiveness of fiscal policy, we considered what factors might limit its impact on output, employment, and the price level. The conclusions in Chapter 15 were that (1) the effects of fiscal policy can be weakened by crowding out, (2) fiscal policy is subject to a variety of lags that might make it less effective, and (3) fiscal policy may have a greater impact on prices than on real output.

Our discussion of the monetary transmission mechanism highlights some similar problems for monetary policy. Whereas fiscal policy is expected to be more effective in "curing" recessions, monetary policy appears to be more appropriate for containing inflation. Monetary policy is less effective in ending recessions, when people are more reluctant to spend and bankers are unwilling to lend. There are a number of points between the expansion of the monetary base and the ultimate effects on output and prices where the process could fail, or at least have less impact than the Fed expected.

In addition to the weaknesses highlighted in the monetary transmission diagram, monetary policy, like fiscal policy, is subject to time lags. The recognition lag—realizing that there is a problem to be addressed—is the same for both monetary and fiscal policy. Because the Open Market Committee meets weekly, the implementation lag is much shorter for monetary policy. The impact lag is estimated to be spread over about a two-year period.

FIGURE 17-4

If the shift in aggregate demand from an increase in the money supply (from AD_1 to AD_2) encounters a relatively steep aggregate supply curve, most of the impact may be on prices (P_1 to P_2) rather than on real output (Y_1 to Y_2).

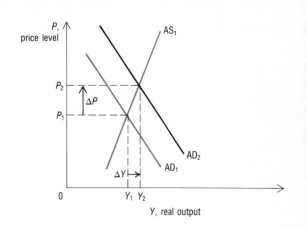

CHECKLIST : **Problems of Monetary Policy**

The effectiveness of money policy will be weaker if:

Expansionary Policy	*Contractionary Policy*
Velocity falls	Velocity rises
Banks hold excess reserves	Banks already have excess reserves
Interest rates do not fall	Interest rates do not rise
Demand is insensitive to interest rate changes	Demand is insensitive to interest rate changes
People choose to hold larger money balances	People choose to hold smaller money balances
Time lags are long	Time lags are long

Monetary and fiscal policy may be most effective when used together in a coordinated fashion. For example, expansionary monetary policy could be used to offset the crowding-out effect of expansionary fiscal policy, keeping interest rates from rising. Expansionary monetary policy could soften some of the negative effects of a contractionary fiscal policy on output and employment. An important aspect of President Clinton's deficit reduction proposals in 1993 was the promised cooperation of the Fed in offsetting tight fiscal policy with easy monetary policy.

The Fed has come under much criticism for several episodes in its history. Many critics believe monetary policy was too tight during the Great Depression, contributing to its duration and severity. After World War II, monetary policy was very easy as the Fed attempted to keep interest rates low for the Treasury on the large government debt accumulated during the war. The Fed has also been accused of allowing too much monetary growth in the 1960s and 1970s, resulting in persistent inflation. In the early 1980s, it was criticized for contractionary policies that helped to reduce inflation but also contributed to the severe 1982 recession. Tight money received at least part of the blame for the 1990–1991 recession.

Summary

1. The banking system consists of banks and other financial intermediaries and the central bank, or Federal Reserve System. Money is created through the banking system.

2. Banks operate on a fractional reserve principle. The amount banks can lend is a multiple of their reserves, which consist of currency and deposits at the Fed.

3. When banks lend excess reserves, they increase checkable deposits and therefore increase the money supply, or create money.

4. Banks and other financial intermediaries collect the savings of households and other sectors and channel them into the market for loanable funds, or the credit market, where the funds are borrowed by investors and others. The price at which funds are borrowed and lent in the loanable funds market is the interest rate.

5. The amount of money the banking system can create depends on the amount of reserves available and the required reserve ratio.

6. The Federal Reserve System, or central bank, is a banker's bank. It creates reserves through open market operations and discounting. It also regulates bank lending by setting reserve requirements. The Fed is a lender of last resort, is a supervisor of banks, and clears checks for banks.

7. The primary role of the Fed today is to carry out monetary policy designed to control the money supply and interest rates. Through its control of reserves and reserve requirements, the Fed controls the monetary base and, indirectly, the money supply. The discount rate also affects bank borrowing and the money supply.

8. Monetary policy works through changes in the money supply and interest rates to change the level of output and prices. Monetary policy is less effective in changing real output if (1) the public holds more cash or banks hold excess reserves, (2) loan demand is not sensitive to interest rates, or (3) aggregate supply is very steep so that changes in the money supply influence prices more than output.

9. Monetary policy is generally believed to be more effective in containing inflation than in ending recessions. Like fiscal policy, monetary policy is subject to recognition, implementation, and impact lags.

Key Terms

balance sheet
central bank
checkable deposit
commercial bank
discount rate
excess reserves
financial intermediary
Federal Deposit
   Insurance
   Corporation (FDIC)

federal funds rate
Federal Reserve System
  (Fed)
lender of last resort
market for loanable
   funds (credit market)
monetary base
monetary policy
money creation
money multiplier

net worth
open market operations
required reserves
reserve ratio
reserves
Resolution Trust
   Corporation (RTC)
run on the bank
T-account

Questions and Problems

1. Suppose the banking system is all loaned up, that is, banks have no excess reserves. The Fed then buys $10 million in bonds from banks. If the reserve ratio is 10 percent, by how much can the money supply expand? What if the reserve ratio is 25 percent? 50 percent?

2. Why does the Fed use open market operations in preference to changing reserve requirements or the discount rate?

3. The Fed really controls not the money supply but only the monetary base. Discuss why the ratio of the money supply to the monetary base is difficult to predict.

4. You are the manager of a bank that has $1,000 in reserves and $5,000 in checkable deposits. The Fed raises the reserve requirement from 20 to 25 percent. Explain your dilemma and what your options are for dealing with it.

5. Joe borrows $3,000 from Sand Bank to buy photographic equipment from Alice's Camera Shop for his private photography business. (Alice has her account at a different bank.) Show the effects of this transaction on the T-account of Sand Bank.

6. Every financial asset is someone else's liability. Whose liabilities are the following?

   a. Federal reserve notes
   b. U.S. government bonds
   c. Bank loans
   d. Checkable deposits
   e. Savings account deposits
   f. Fed loans to banks

7. Why is monetary policy generally believed to be more effective in controlling inflation than in ending recessions?

8. In which Federal Reserve District do you live? Look at the letter in the circle on the front of the Federal Reserve notes in your wallet to see which bank issues the currency you carry.

9. Obtain a year-end financial statement from the bank at which you have an account. Compare its assets and liabilities to those of Farmers' National Bank in this chapter.

IV

Special Topics in Economics

18

The Global Economy:

Trade and Foreign Exchange

There's nothing a tariff can do for a country that an earthquake can't do better.

JOHN MAYNARD KEYNES

Main Points

1. The law of one price states that price differences among markets tend to be reduced or eliminated by the flow of goods and resources from low-price to higher-price markets.

2. Individuals and nations trade to obtain the benefits of efficiency, competition, and economies of scale.

3. Nations restrict trade through tariffs, quotas, and non-tariff barriers. Most trade restrictions benefit particular groups of individuals at the expense of others.

4. Common markets and free trade areas expand the size of the market and offer some of the benefits of free trade to member countries.

5. The price of a nation's currency reflects foreign demand for its goods, services, and financial assets, as well as its citizens' demand for goods, services, and financial assets from other countries. Exchange rates are determined mainly by market forces.

6. A nation's balance of payments summarizes its international transactions in goods, services, and financial assets.

The United States and other countries operate in a global economy. Firms in Omaha compete with producers in Mexico and Taiwan. Plants in Chattanooga may belong to a British or Japanese multinational corporation. Immigrants enrich our labor force and our culture. The products you buy at your local retailer come from every part of the globe. A major share of U.S. farmers' sales are to foreign markets. Agricultural products account for about 18 percent of U.S. exports. Producers of high-tech goods, newly developed products, and goods with significant economies of scale also rely heavily on overseas customers for sales.

International trade is a substantial part of production, sales, and competition for the United States, both in the aggregate and for particular industries. Exports and imports are about 12 to 13 percent of *GDP*, up from about 5 percent 30 years ago. Your breakfast of bananas with coffee, tea, or hot chocolate is entirely imported! Chances are your car (or parts of it), many of your clothes, your camera, and your television set came from abroad as well. In fact, the notion of a domestic market for most industries is no longer valid, because firms are increasingly competing with other firms halfway around the world. In this chapter, we explore the costs and benefits of being a part of a global economy and some of the policy issues relating to the flow of goods, services, capital, and people from country to country.

When Americans trade with other countries, one partner has to convert to the other's currency to complete the sale. The price of a nation's currency is determined in foreign exchange markets. This price affects the nation's imports and exports of goods and resources. Thus, an introduction to currency markets and the balance of payments completes our look at how the United States operates in the global economy. ■

THE LAW OF ONE PRICE

Law of one price The tendency of goods and services to flow from markets in which their prices are lower to those in which their prices are higher, equalizing prices between the two types of markets.

A basic economic principle underlying many of the models in earlier chapters is the law of one price. The **law of one price** states that goods or services tend to flow from markets in which they are cheap to markets in which they are expensive. In the process, the difference in prices tends to be eliminated. If lettuce is selling for $0.50 in California and for $3.00 in Montana, some enterprising soul will rent a refrigerated truck, buy lettuce in California, truck it to Montana, and pocket a tidy profit. By doing so on a large enough scale, however, the entrepreneur will tend to drive up the price in California (where demand has increased) and drive down the price in Montana (where supply has increased). If it were costless to ship lettuce from California to Montana, the price would be the same in both states. Instead, the price will differ only by the cost of shipping.

This law also applies to trade among countries. In the absence of trade restrictions and shipping costs, goods and services would sell for the same price everywhere. International trade tends to equalize prices by bringing down the prices of goods that are relatively expensive and raising the prices of goods that are relatively cheap in each country. Each country exports those products that are relatively cheap at home. The export demand itself increases the prices of those products, raising them toward the world price. Each country imports those products that are expensive at home, lowering their prices in the home country and raising their prices abroad.

Experience offers many examples in which the law of one price appears not to hold. Restaurant meals are cheap in some countries and expensive in others. Tourists buy bargains in Mexico because those goods are so much cheaper there than in the United States. Some of these apparent violations of the law of one price are due to temporary problems in the price of the currency. Others are due to transport costs, trade barriers, or imperfect information. Without these obstacles, the law of one price would hold.

National Sovereignty and Obstacles to Trade

National sovereignty
The powers of a national government, particularly those that affect relations with other nations, including the powers to restrict international commerce and to issue its own currency.

National sovereignty refers to the control national governments exercise over the lives and actions of their citizens. It is expressed in various laws, regulations, and currencies, as well as in different languages and ways of doing business. If national sovereignty and cultural differences did not exist, trade among countries would be no different than trade between California and Tennessee or Tokyo and Kyoto. Shipping costs and access to information would still make international trade a little more difficult than domestic trade. But currency prices, tariffs, balance of payments accounts, and all the other special features of trading among citizens of different countries would disappear. Instead of national markets would be one world market, and the law of one price would hold to a much greater degree.

National sovereignty creates enough differences between California–Tennessee trade and United States–Japan trade to justify a separate chapter on international economics. Two of these differences are particularly important. One is that each country has its own national currency. California and Tennessee dollars always exchange one for one, but the prices of the U.S. dollar and the Japanese yen are not fixed in relation to each other. The other important difference is that each nation has its own commercial policy. **Commercial policy** is the set of rules, regulations, and taxes a nation applies to the flow of goods and services to and from other countries. Within the United States, the interstate commerce clause of the Constitution does not allow states to interfere with trade with

Commercial policy
The rules, regulations, and restrictions a nation applies to trade with other countries.

other states. The federal government, however, has the constitutional power to regulate trade with other countries.

The Law of One Price and Comparative Advantage

Individuals in different nations trade because it is in their self-interest to do so. The practical economist buys from sellers abroad because the foreign price is lower, the foreign quality is better, or the seller offers a product that is not produced in the home country. Nations encourage trade because their citizens can consume more with trade than without trade.

The principle of comparative advantage, discussed in Chapter 3, states that *both parties gain from trade.* These gains come from the fact that both traders can now specialize more heavily in those products in which they are relatively more efficient (in other words, in which their opportunity costs are lower). When individuals or nations specialize, total output increases. These gains from specializing can then be shared between trading partners so that each has at least as much of one product as before trade and more of the other product. In the process, the price of the cheaper good will rise and the price of the more expensive good will fall in each country.

Other Benefits of International Trade

Economists stress that the value of trade lies in allowing countries to specialize and increase total output. This benefit—more total output—is called the *efficiency gains from trade.* Two other kinds of economic benefits from international trade exist as well, both of which are linked to the law of one price: increased competition and economies of scale.

Competition.   One source of benefits is *increased competition.* Competition is an important reason for the existence of the law of one price. If one firm is making a profit in a market in which it faces no competition, and the price is lower in another market in which more competition exists, firms will rush in to fill the void in the first market. As new firms enter the market with fewer competitors, the price falls in that market until the difference is eliminated.

If an industry is monopolistic or oligopolistic within a country, foreign competition is especially important. Recall from Chapter 8 that the power of a monopoly or an oligopoly is limited by potential competitors. Not all potential (or actual) competitors are domestic firms. Foreign competition can limit a monopolist's ability to raise prices and restrict output.

Foreign competition has forced American automakers to respond to neglected markets for smaller, fuel-efficient cars and to adopt innovations such as electronic ignitions, fuel injection systems, and disk brakes. Foreign competition has shaken up a sleepy American steel industry and forced the U.S. textile industry to

Myth 18-1

Japan Has a Comparative Advantage in Everything

Some hand-wringers believe Japan can outproduce the United States in everything. Those who foresee gloom and doom—a flood of imports, increasing American unemployment, and "a nation of hamburger stands"—seem to suggest that the United States has a comparative advantage in nothing. It is quite possible that some countries have an *absolute* advantage in nothing; that is, there is no good or service they can produce with fewer resources than any other country. However, it is not possible for one country to have a comparative advantage in everything, while another has a comparative advantage in nothing. That is because comparative advantage is based on *relative* costs, and—except in the rare case when all relative costs for all goods are identical—if country A is relatively better at making watches than brooms, it is by definition relatively worse at making brooms than watches.

Comparative advantage is determined by looking at two countries' opportunity costs for two goods, such as brooms and watches. There are four pieces of information: the cost of brooms in country A, the cost of watches in A, the cost of brooms in country B, and the cost of watches in B. It is very possible that both brooms and watches cost less to produce in A than in B. In that event, A would have an absolute advantage in both goods, and B would have an absolute disadvantage.

But that is no reason for B to give up, go sit by the fire, and let A produce all of everything. B would lose and so would A, because world output would be lower when B's resources were left idle. B can still compete and sell brooms to A, if B's opportunity cost for brooms is lower; that is, B would have a comparative advantage in brooms.

A nation of hamburger stands whose citizens sell services only to one another while buying many products from abroad and selling nothing in return is simply not a logical possibility. The idea that any nation has nothing to offer confuses absolute advantage with comparative advantage. ■

---

modernize. Competition also expands the range of consumer choice in terms of quality and variety. Of course, none of this happens without pain; those who lose their jobs or see a decline in the value of the firms they own bear the costs of free trade. But in most cases, the long-term gains outweigh those losses.

Economies of Scale.   Another source of the benefits of trade comes through *economies of scale*. Recall from Chapter 6 that for many products, average costs fall as the scale of operations and the volume of output grow larger. To reach those low average costs, however, it may be necessary to serve an extremely large market. The largest possible market is the world market. For some industries, such as mainframe computers and jet aircraft manufacturing, the market needs to be worldwide to permit substantial economies of scale.

Economies of scale are closely related to the issue of competition. In industries with scale economies, there may be room for only one or two firms in a country or only half a dozen firms in the world. In a protected market, these firms would be monopolies with high prices and persistent profits. In an open, global market, the law of one price would bring their prices down to the world level.

CHECKLIST 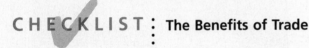 : **The Benefits of Trade**

Trade offers individuals and nations the following benefits:

From specialization	Increased total output
	Higher standards of living
From competition	Constraints on monopoly power
	Wider range of consumer choice
From economies of scale	Lower average production costs

HOW NATIONS RESTRICT FREE TRADE

Despite the benefits of free trade, most countries put some restrictions on the flow of goods into their home markets. These restrictions benefit some groups and hurt others. For example, restricting the flow of Japanese automobiles into the United States helped some U.S. auto manufacturers and autoworkers. At the same time, it hurt other groups. Consumers paid higher prices for cars and had fewer choices. Export firms found it more difficult to sell their products in Japan. As a general rule, the gains from imposing protection are less than the losses from reduced specialization and decreased competition. But the gains are concentrated on a few people and the losses are spread thinly over many consumers. The gainers from protection are likely to make a greater effort to get protection while the "silent majority" pays little attention.

The primary tools of commercial policy are tariffs, quotas, miscellaneous nontariff barriers, immigration rules, and capital controls. *Tariffs* are taxes on imported goods. *Quotas* are limits on the physical quantity or the dollar value of a good that can be imported. *Nontariff barriers* is a catchall category that includes all the national rules and regulations that make trade more difficult, including labeling requirements and electrical codes. All of these policies apply to the inflow of goods and services. Nations also have immigration laws that restrict the flow of labor and capital and controls that reduce the mobility of capital among countries. For the most part, lobbyists direct their efforts toward restricting trade in goods and services rather than movements of labor or capital.

Tariffs

A **tariff** is a tax on an imported good or service. Like other taxes, tariffs tend to increase the price the buyer pays and reduce the price the seller receives. Figure 18-1 illustrates how a tariff on wheat might work in one small country, Protectia. This country is small enough that its production and consumption of wheat has no influence on the world price.

This diagram is a simple supply and demand model, with one addition: Protectia can buy an unlimited quantity of imported wheat at a price of $4. Because foreign suppliers offer wheat at $4 a bushel, domestic suppliers cannot charge a higher price. The only decision for domestic firms is to choose the quantity on their combined supply curves that corresponds to a price of $4. They choose to produce 100 bushels. At that price, domestic consumers want to buy 400 bushels. The other 300 bushels are imported at $4, the world price.

Now Protectia puts a tariff of $0.50 a bushel on imported wheat. The price paid by the consumer in Protectia rises by the full amount of the tariff, from $4.00 to $4.50 a bushel. At the higher price of $4.50, domestic suppliers will offer 150 bushels of wheat instead of 100. Consumers will cut back their purchases from 400 bushels to 350. Now the gap between domestic supply and domestic demand, to be filled by imports, is only 200 bushels (350 − 150) instead of 300. Imports have fallen by 100 bushels. Domestic producers gain at the expense of foreign producers, who sell less, and at the expense of domestic consumers, who buy less and pay more per bushel.

There is one more party to the transaction. The government collects a tax of

FIGURE 18-1

Before the tariff, domestic producers supply 100 bushels of wheat, consumers purchase 400 bushels, and the remaining 300 bushels are imported. After the tariff the price rises to $4.50, domestic production rises to 150 bushels, domestic consumption falls to 350, and imports fall to 200.

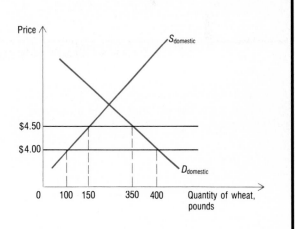

$0.50 per unit on the 200 units still imported under the tariff, or $100. Part of the higher cost to consumers becomes revenue to the government. Consumers hope the government will spend that revenue on valuable services like defense and highways. Even after allowing for the benefits of government services paid for with tariff revenue, however, consumers are still worse off. They are consuming less wheat and paying more. They are giving up consumption of 50 bushels of wheat that they valued at $4 a bushel, or $200, which alone is more than the tariff revenue. In addition, they are paying an extra $0.50 a bushel for the 350 bushels they still consume, or an extra $175. Thus, the $100 in tariff revenue is not offset by these two losses to consumers.

The United States imposes tariffs on a great variety of products, but the level of protection today is much lower than it was 20, 40, or 100 years ago. Today the average tariff on American imports is about 4 percent, down from 53 percent at its peak in 1930.

Quotas

Quota A physical or value limitation on the quantity of a particular good that can be imported.

Whereas tariffs work through price, quotas limit quantity. A **quota** sets a maximum physical quantity or a maximum dollar value of a good that can be imported into a country each year. The United States uses quotas less than tariffs, but there are quotas on sugar, textiles, steel, beef, and automobiles.

Figure 18-2 shows what happens when a small country imposes a quota on imports of cotton cloth. Without the quota, the equilibrium price is $2 and total consumption is 400 million yards. Domestic firms produce 200 million yards, and the other 200 million yards are imported. Now the government limits imports to 100 million yards. This quota causes the price to rise until domestic production plus imports under the quota just equal total quantity demanded.

FIGURE 18-2

A quota restricts the imports of cloth to 100 yards and drives up the price to $3. Under a quota, consumption falls, domestic production rises, and imports fall.

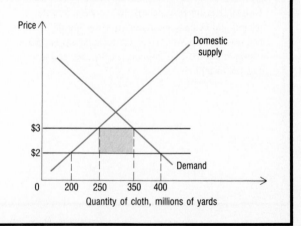

The gap between domestic quantity supplied and domestic quantity demanded is 100 million yards at a price of $3. At that price, quantity supplied is 250 million yards and quantity demanded is 350 million yards. The quota forces the price up from $2 to $3, encouraging more domestic production and discouraging domestic consumption.

Figure 18-2 looks very much like the tariff diagram (Figure 18-1). A quota, like a tariff, means price rises, total consumption falls, imports fall, and domestic production rises. Domestic producers gain at the expense of domestic consumers and foreign producers. However, some important differences exist.

First, there is no tariff revenue. There is something equivalent to tariff revenue in the shaded area of Figure 18-2, amounting to $100 million (the $1 rise in price times the 100 million yards of imports). But it no longer goes to the government. Who gets it? The importing wholesaler now gets to buy 100 million yards of cloth at the going world price of $3 a yard and resell it at the protected domestic price of $4 a yard. The wholesaler earns monopoly profits from a monopoly privilege created by the government, namely the right to import 100 million yards of cloth. The shaded area represents the monopoly profit.

The government could capture these profits by auctioning import licenses to the highest bidder. However, governments usually issue licenses on some other basis, such as first come, first served, or equal shares, and the monopoly profits remain in the hands of private holders of import licenses.

The second difference between a tariff and a quota does not show up until a change in demand occurs. This effect is shown in Figure 18-3. With a tariff, when demand increases from D_1 to D_2, more is imported at the going world price. Imports increase from AB to AC, and the price is unchanged. Domestic consumption is higher, but domestic production does not change. Under a

FIGURE 18-3

When demand shifts from D_1 to D_2 under a tariff, imports increase from AB to AC. Under a quota, the quantity of imports cannot rise. Therefore, domestic output rises to meet demand, driving the price up from P_1 to P_2.

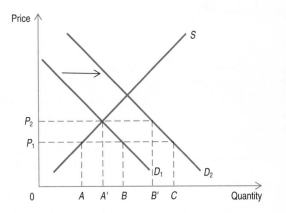

quota, however, price rises (to P_1) until the horizontal gap between domestic supply and domestic demand again equals the quota, *AB* (now A′B′). Thus, under a tariff the adjustment to increased demand falls on quantity, whereas under a quota the adjustment falls on price.

Given a choice, consumers would probably prefer tariffs for both these reasons. If there is money to be made from restricting imports, consumers would likely prefer those funds to go to the government as tariff revenue rather than to importing wholesalers as monopoly profits. Consumers would also prefer to see rising demand met by more imports rather than by higher prices. Import-competing producers (understandably) tend to prefer quotas, which give them more certainty than a tariff. Each group acts like a practical economist, promoting policies that are in its own self-interest.

CHECKLIST : Effects of Tariffs and Quotas

	Tariff	Quota
Raises price to consumers	Yes	Yes
Reduces volume of imports	Yes	Yes
Reduces domestic consumption	Yes	Yes
Stimulates domestic production	Yes	Yes
Revenue to government	Yes	No
Monopoly profits to favored importers	No	Yes
Import volume increases when demand increases	Yes	No
Price increases when demand increases	No*	Yes

*If the country is small. If its purchases are large enough to affect world price, price as well as import volume may rise when demand increases.

Nontariff Barriers

Nontariff barrier A rule, regulation, standard, or law that discourages trade in a particular commodity.

Nontariff barriers are a catchall category for various regulations, laws, and rules that restrict or discourage trade in goods and services. Some of these laws and regulations are intended for that very purpose. Some customs procedures involve excessive paperwork or delays. These procedures were probably designed for their nuisance effect in discouraging imports. Other nontariff barriers seem to be accidental by-products of national sovereignty. The fact that the United States is one of the few major countries not on the metric system affects trade in tools and other products for which measuring precision in millimeters or fractional inches is important. Labeling requirements, electrical codes, and various health and safety standards (especially for automobiles) make it difficult for firms to export. Different standards mean they will have to produce one set of goods for their domestic markets to meet those standards and another set of goods for foreign markets with different standards.

When governments negotiate to reduce trade barriers, they start with tariffs because tariffs are the most measurable entity. Nontariff barriers have proven a much more difficult problem in continuing efforts to reduce the level of protection in international trade.

WHY NATIONS RESTRICT TRADE

The primary reason for restricting free trade is that certain groups benefit greatly from trade restrictions, whereas the benefits of free trade are spread more thinly throughout the entire population. Thus, those few who stand to gain have a powerful self-interest motive for persuading Congress or the International Trade Commission to regulate trade on their behalf. Consumers are harmed by trade restrictions, and total losses to consumers usually exceed gains to protected producers. However, the cost per individual consumer is so low that there are really no incentives for consumers to organize to promote free trade. The practical economists who gain will work harder to secure their protection, because the practical economists who lose will not lose enough for the benefits of lobbying to outweigh the costs.

If you look carefully behind the rhetoric of protectionism, you will find a hidden battle over the distribution of income. The tariff and quota models in this chapter identified the various groups of gainers and losers from free trade and from protection. When product A receives protection, the factors of production in that industry—labor and capital—gain at the expense of consumers and foreign producers. Foreign producers, however, do not vote, and the loss to any individual consumer in this country is quite small relative to the gains to a particular worker or stockholder in the protected industry.

Consider a protective tariff on waffle irons. Perhaps 20,000 waffle irons are sold each year for wedding gifts. As a result of a tariff, the price might rise by $5. The 20,000 buyers are not likely, in the midst of the wedding festivities, to write their representatives in Congress about the extra $5, even if they were aware that the tariff caused the price to increase. To the 100 workers and stockholders in this small industry, however, the extra $100,000 in revenue (selling 20,000 waffle irons at a price $5 higher than before) is a substantial sum. Divided among 100 gainers, it comes to $1,000 each—an amount well worth writing a letter about or making a contribution to a lobbying association. Considered in these terms, it is surprising not that protection against import competition exists but that there is so little protection.

Once protection is entrenched, however, it is painful and costly to remove it. Practical economists have made decisions about careers and investments on the basis of the established order, and part of that established order was the tariff or quota that made that job or that investment attractive. Removing protection imposes substantial losses on workers, owners, investors, and even regions of the country. For this reason, battles over removing protection are usually more intense and painful that the arguments that led to implementing it in the first place.

HALFWAY TO FREE TRADE: FREE TRADE AREAS AND COMMON MARKETS

When a nation decides to move in the direction of free trade, it has two options. One is to reduce its barriers to free trade to all of its trading partners, either by itself or by negotiating with other countries. This approach dominated the world trade agenda from 1934 until the late 1980s. A series of negotiations under the General Agreement on Tariffs and Trade (GATT) produced substantial reductions in tariffs and other trade barriers over a half-century. That procedure is still going on and continues to reduce the trade barriers that built up in the period from the mid-nineteenth century through the beginning of the Great Depression.

At the same time, another movement began in the period after World War II that has gained momentum in recent years: the creation of free trade areas, customs unions, and common markets, a movement called **economic integration**. All forms of economic integration eliminate certain kinds of trade barriers with one or two specific trading partners, while maintaining existing trade barriers for the rest of the world.

Common Markets: The EC

Economic integration takes many forms. The two most widespread forms in recent decades have been common markets and free trade areas. A **common market** is an agreement among countries to eliminate barriers to trade and free movement of capital and labor among members while setting up a common barrier to external trade. The United States created a common market in the Constitution, which forbids barriers to interstate commerce and provides for the free movement of workers and capital among states.

The best-known example of a common market is the European Community (EC). The EC began in 1957 with six members and now has twelve members in Western Europe, with more countries waiting to join. The original six countries eliminated all barriers to trade in the 1960s, adopted a common tax system, and were working on a common currency and elimination of restrictions on migration when the decision was made to expand to include more countries. Bringing more countries in the EC slowed down the process of unifying them in other ways. By the late 1980s the integration process had picked up speed

Economic integration Any arrangement between two or more countries to eliminate trade barriers between themselves while maintaining some tariffs and quotas on outside countries.

Common market An agreement between two or more nations to eliminate all barriers to trade and factor movements within that group, while maintaining common barriers to trade with outside countries.

again, stressing free migration of labor and capital and elimination of nontariff barriers like labeling requirements.

Free Trade Areas: CUSTA and NAFTA

Free trade area An agreement between two or more nations to eliminate barriers to trade between them while maintaining their own barriers to trade with the outside world.

Many countries want the benefits of limited free trade but are unwilling to surrender as much national sovereignty as a common market would require. For these countries, a free trade area may be the best answer. A **free trade area** between two or more countries eliminates tariffs and other trade barriers between member countries, while each country maintains its own barriers to trade with outside nations. The biggest problem in a free trade area is enforcing one country's trade barriers when the other country has lower barriers for a particular good. Suppose countries A and B form a free trade area. Country A has a 15 percent tariff on bicycles to protect its domestic industry. Country B does not produce bicycles and has no tariff. What will happen? Foreign producers of bicycles will ship them to country B, which has no tariff. Once inside the free trade area, these bicycles could then be sold in A, avoiding the 15 percent tariff. To address this problem, free trade areas require that products have proof of origin. For a product to trade tariff free within the free trade area, 51 percent or more of its value must originate within the member countries.

In 1988, the United States and Canada joined in a free trade area to take advantage of the large North American market *(CUSTA)*. Canada and the United States were already each other's largest trading partners, so the change was not dramatic. But there were difficult problems to resolve, most of them centered around trade in agricultural products. Just as the United States–Canada free trade area was getting off the ground, a new initiative promoted expansion to include Mexico. This three-country area will be called the **North American Free Trade Area (NAFTA)**. The combined area will have almost as large a population as Europe and a larger total *GDP*. Despite objections from U.S. industries that fear competition from Mexico, supporters hope NAFTA will take shape and become one of the world's largest trading blocs in the next few years.

North American Free Trade Area (NAFTA) A free trade area developed in the 1980s and 1990s that includes the United States, Canada, and Mexico.

Effects of Economic Integration

Why do countries form free trade areas and common markets? For now, we will focus on free trade areas. Since a common market includes a free trade area as well as additional features, anything that is true of a free trade area will also apply to a common market.

A free trade area provides some of the same benefits as reducing trade barriers to all trading partners. There may be an increase in specialization based on comparative advantage. Consumers will benefit from more competition in the forms of lower prices and greater variety. In larger markets, some firms will enjoy greater economies of scale. However, a free trade area offers only partial free trade, because countries still maintain tariffs and quotas on trade with outside countries. In some cases, a free trade area may actually *reduce* efficiency, competition, and/or scale economies.

Trade creation   A shift from a higher-cost to a lower-cost supplier of imports as a result of a free trade area or common market.

Trade diversion   A shift from a lower-cost to a higher-cost supplier of imports as a result of a free trade area or common market.

Whether or not a country benefits from joining a free trade area depends on whether more trade creation or trade diversion occurs. **Trade creation** occurs when, as a result of a free trade area, a nation shifts from a higher-cost to a lower-cost supplier. **Trade diversion** occurs when, as a result of a free trade area, a nation shifts from a lower-cost to a higher-cost supplier.

Suppose a free trade area is formed between countries A and B. The rest of the world, or all the nations not in the free trade area, is represented by ROW. Now consider one particular product, such as soybeans. Suppose that before the free trade area was formed, A and B were supplying their own soybeans. Because its soybean farmers were relatively inefficient, A was protecting them with a tariff or a quota. In a free trade area, A's soybean farmers must now compete with B's more efficient soybean farmers without the benefit of protection. The result is that soybean prices will fall and A's consumers will enjoy lower prices. When this happens, the free trade area has led to trade creation for A.

Suppose, however, that A had been buying its soybeans from ROW before the free trade area because ROW was cheaper than B. After the free trade area is formed, B's soybeans will have an advantage in selling in A's markets. ROW producers have to pay a tariff, but B's soybeans enter duty free. If A switches from the cheaper, more efficient supplier ROW to B because of the free trade area, trade diversion has occurred. A's consumers will pay higher prices.

In any free trade area, there will be trade creation in some products and trade diversion in others. The important issue is whether there will be more trade creation or more trade diversion across the full range of products.

Before two countries form a free trade area, they should examine their patterns of production and trade to determine whether trade creation or trade diversion will dominate. In general, if countries are similar in terms of income level, range of products produced, and tastes, they will produce similar products. In this case, trade creation will dominate, because a cheaper supplier will be available for most goods within the free trade area. If the countries are very different, however, they will more likely divert their trade from the cheaper outside supplier to the free trade area partner. One concern expressed about the United States–Mexico free trade arrangement was that trade diversion was more likely than trade creation because each country produces very different kinds of products and services.

Even if trade diversion occurs, a free trade area offers other benefits. The market is larger, which allows firms to take advantage of economies of scale. There are more competing firms and more kinds of products available, giving consumers the benefits of competition. In general, enlarging the market is seen as a move in the direction of free trade. Like free trade among all partners, a free trade area will result in gainers and losers. Consumers will gain from increased output and competition. Exporters will gain sales to the new free trade area partner(s). Some import-competing industries will lose due to competition within the free trade area. As long as the balance of gains and losses is positive, the nation is made better off by joining a free trade area.

PAYING FOR INTERNATIONAL TRADE: INTERNATIONAL FINANCE

National sovereignty makes international trade differ from domestic trade in two important ways. One is commercial policy (tariffs, quotas, and nontariff barriers), which we considered earlier. The other is different national currencies. Because each country's currency is issued by the government, there is no truly international currency. Historically, gold served as an international money for many centuries, but it no longer fills that role. Thus, some other way must be found to settle accounts when the seller expects dollars, yen, or marks and the buyer offers francs, pounds, or pesos.

The Foreign Exchange Market

Foreign exchange market A network of banks and foreign exchange dealers that buy and sell national currencies.

These accounts are settled in the **foreign exchange market**—a network of banks and other traders that buy and sell currencies. Daily quotations for dollars, marks, yen, and pounds for immediate (or future delivery) can be found in most newspapers. If you travel abroad, you will find many financial firms ready to exchange your dollars for local currency. If you purchase something from abroad, your bank can usually convert your dollars to another currency.

It may be a little trickier to figure out increases and decreases in the prices of currencies than other commodities, because it depends on which prices you read. Consider the following actual exchange quotations for the U.S. dollar and the British pound:

Date	U.S. $ per Pound	Pounds per U.S. $
November, 1992	$1.51	0.66
March, 1993	$1.44	0.69

According to these figures, the price of the dollar rose from 0.66 pounds to 0.69 pounds in three months, or (equivalently) the price of the pound fell from $1.51 to $1.44. Note that the figures 0.66 pounds/$ and $1.51/pound are not two different prices; rather, they are two different ways of describing the same price.

Supply and Demand for Foreign Exchange   Figure 18-4 shows the international market for U.S. dollars. Foreigners demand American dollars with which to buy American exports, travel in the United States, and purchase stocks, bonds, and other financial assets issued in the U.S. market. This demand curve slopes downward from left to right for the same reasons any demand curve slopes downward from left to right. When the price of the dollar is lower, non–Americans can purchase more U.S. goods for the same amount of their currency (the income effect). They will also substitute cheaper American goods for domestic goods or goods from third countries (the substitution effect).

The supply of American dollars in the foreign exchange market slopes upward from left to right, but unlike most supply curves, it is not a marginal cost curve. The supply of dollars does not reflect costs of production. Americans supply dollars in trade for foreign currencies to purchase imports, travel abroad, and invest in foreign financial assets. The supply curve slopes upward because a higher price for the dollar is equivalent to lower prices for foreign currencies, making foreign goods and investments cheaper and more attractive. When the dollar is cheaper, foreign currencies are more expensive and Americans reduce their purchases of foreign goods. In the early 1990s, the price of the Japanese yen rose, and sales of Japanese-made cars began to drop in response.

Exchange rate The price of one country's currency in terms of another's.

The price of the dollar, or the **exchange rate,** can be quoted in any foreign currency. German marks (*DM*, which stands for "Deutsch mark") represent all foreign currencies in Figure 18-4. The equilibrium price of the dollar is 2 DM, and the equilibrium quantity is $100 billion. Any price other than 2 DM per

---

FIGURE 18-4

Demand for the dollar reflects the demand by non–Americans to purchase goods, services, and financial assets from Americans. Likewise, the supply of dollars offered by Americans is really a demand for foreign currencies (represented by the mark) to buy foreign goods, services, and assets. At the equilibrium price of the dollar (2 DM), quantity demanded equals quantity supplied. At a higher price, such as 2.3 DM, there is a surplus of dollars, and at a lower price, such as 1.7 DM, there is a dollar shortage.

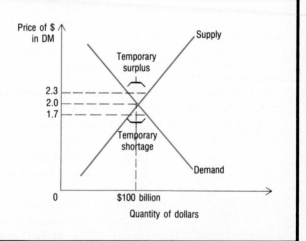

dollar would not clear the market. At 2.3 DM per dollar, the price of the dollar is too high, and a dollar surplus develops. At 1.7 DM per dollar, the dollar is cheap, and the rush by non–Americans to buy "bargain" U.S. products leads to a shortage of dollars. Left to itself, the foreign exchange market will correct those surpluses and shortages just as any other market would.

Shifts in Supply and Demand.   The foreign exchange market is a macroeconomic market. While there may be some shifts in supply or demand for foreign exchange due to changes in tastes or in relative prices of particular products, in general supply and demand for foreign exchange are most heavily influenced by changes in countries' incomes, price levels, and interest rates. Income affects total spending on everything, including imported goods. If the U.S. income level rises relative to Japan's, Americans will buy more Japanese goods, shifting demand for the yen to the right. Price levels abroad relative to the price level at home affect the demand for imported goods relative to domestic goods in both countries. Likewise, differences in interest rates between countries will increase demand for the currency of the high-interest-rate country and reduce the supply.

Figure 18-5 shows the effect of a decrease in demand for U.S. dollars. At the old price of 2 DM per dollar, a surplus of dollars occurs. If market forces are allowed to operate, the price of the dollar will fall to 1.5 DM. At this lower price, the quantity supplied will fall. The quantity demanded will rise a little, partly offsetting the initial effects of the shift in demand. The net effect is that quantity bought and sold will decline to $40 billion. Normal market forces will correct a disequilibrium when supply or demand shifts, bringing about a new equilibrium price and quantity.

FIGURE 18-5

When demand for the dollar declines from D_1 to D_2, a surplus of dollars develops at the old equilibrium price of 2 DM. The excess supply of dollars puts downward pressure on the price until equilibrium is restored at the new price of 1.5 DM and the new equilibrium quantity of $40 billion.

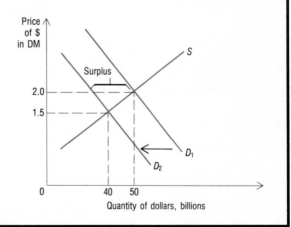

CHECKLIST :   **Sources of Shifts in Supply and Demand for**
            :   **Foreign Exchange**

Source of Shift	Effect on Dollar Demand	Effect on Dollar Supply
Foreign price level up	Increases	Decreases
U.S. price level up	Decreases	Increases
Foreign income *(Y)* up	Increases	No effect
U.S. income up	No effect	Increases
Foreign interest rates up	Decreases	Increases
U.S. interest rates up	Increases	Decreases

Floating exchange rates Exchange rates that are determined by market forces of supply and demand in the market rather than by governments.

Floating Exchange Rates   Since 1973, most governments in developed countries have let the market determine the prices of their currencies. A system of market-determined exchange rates is called **floating exchange rates**. In practice, even with floating rates governments occasionally step in, buying or selling currency on their own accounts to influence the exchange rate.

Some developing countries still practice exchange control. In such a system, all foreign exchange earnings must be sold to the government. People who need foreign exchange to make purchases abroad must buy them from the government. The formerly communist nations of Eastern and Central Europe are in transition from exchange control to market-determined, or floating, exchange rates. In general, government is far less involved in currency markets in the 1990s than it was 10 or 20 years ago.

The price of the dollar is important to firms that sell abroad or compete with imported goods and services. A high dollar price makes it more difficult to export. It also makes imports cheaper, increasing competition for domestic firms producing similar goods. On the other hand, a high dollar price means consumer dollars go farther when traveling abroad or buying imported goods. A cheap dollar has just the opposite effects.

The Balance of Payments

Balance of payments A statement that summarizes a nation's transactions with residents of other countries for a given year.

The **balance of payments** is a summary of the transactions that take place in the foreign exchange market for a country. The balance of payments is a financial statement that lists one country's total purchases and sales in goods, services, and financial assets with the rest of the world for one year. The balance of payments entries of exports, imports, and capital flows correspond to the various sources of supply and demand in the foreign exchange market. Table 18-1 presents a simplified form of the U.S. balance of payments for 1992.

TABLE 18-1   U.S. Balance of Payments, 1992 ($ billions)

Current Account

U.S. exports of goods	$439.3
U.S. imports of goods	(−) 535.5
Exports/imports of services (net)	57.6
Grants and transfers (net)	10.1
Investment income (net)	(−) 33.1
Balance on current account	(−) 62.4

Capital Account

U.S. purchases of foreign financial assets	(−) 44.9
Foreign purchases of U.S. financial assets	120.4
Balance on capital account	75.5
Statistical Discrepancy	**(−) $13.1**

Source: *Federal Reserve Bulletin,* July 1993

Exports, imports, and sales and purchases of financial assets are the items that create supply and demand in foreign exchange markets. These items are also the main components of the balance of payments.

Current Account.   Transactions in currently produced goods and services are entered in the current account. Export sales of merchandise or services are entered as a plus; imports are entered with a minus sign (see Table 18-1). The current account also includes grants and transfers. These items are foreign aid, private gifts and pensions, and other one-way transactions that lead to a flow of dollars abroad. (A flow of dollars abroad means a supply of dollars offered in trade for foreign currencies to pay the recipients in their own currencies.) The value of U.S. exports of goods and services (current account) in 1992 was less than the value of imports. The result was a negative balance on the current account of $62.4 billion.

Capital Account.   Transactions in financial assets such as stocks, bonds, bank deposits, and foreign currencies are listed under the capital account. When Americans make deposits in foreign banks or build plants in other countries, those items are treated as purchases of assets abroad. The effect of buying a share of foreign stock or building a plant abroad is exactly the same as the effect of buying foreign goods and services. These transactions are entered with a negative sign. When non–Americans make deposits in U.S. banks, buy U.S. stocks or bonds, or buy or build plants in the United States, those sales have the same effect on the balance of payments as an export of a good or service. In 1992 there was a positive balance in the capital account, more than offsetting the negative balance in the current account.

In Practice 18-1

· ·

What Is the "Right" Price for the Dollar?

Between 1980 and 1985, the price of the U.S. dollar rose 60 percent in terms of most other currencies. Following that rise, it dropped sharply. By the early 1990s, the dollar was back where it began in 1980. When the price of the dollar was rising, there were complaints that it was "too high"; as it fell, complaints changed to "too low!" Some complaints came from those who wanted to return to a fixed-rate system, but most came from those who had suffered losses from changes in the price of the dollar.

There is no "right" price for the dollar. The price of the dollar is determined by the forces of supply and demand. The U.S. government can modify that price slightly by entering the market on the demand side (buying dollars) to increase the price or entering the market on the supply side (selling dollars) to lower it. But most changes in the supply and demand for the dollar are outside the control of government.

The main factor in running up the price of the dollar in the early 1980s was very high interest rates in the United States. These high interest rates made U.S. financial assets attractive to investors abroad. The inflow of foreign funds to buy U.S. financial assets showed up in the foreign exchange market as a rightward shift in the demand for the dollar, driving up its price.

As the price of the dollar rose, it made U.S. exports less attractive and foreign products relatively cheap. Imports rose and exports fell. American tourist attractions like Disney World were finding fewer foreign tourists, while American tourists traveled abroad in search of bargains. U.S. exporters and import-competing firms, always on opposite sides of arguments over tariffs and quotas, were on the same side of this issue. Both were losing sales due to the rise in the price of the dollar. In fact, the automobile industry succeeded in getting quotas to protect it from foreign competition when the price of the dollar was rising in 1982–1984.

The fall in the price of the dollar since 1985 reduced complaints from exporters and import-competing industries, but it brought new problems. Americans could no longer afford foreign travel. At bargain prices, non–Americans were buying land, buildings, firms, and even whole industries and building plants in the United States. Whether the price of the dollar is high or low, there will always be those who would like it to move in the opposite direction. ∎

Balancing the Balance of Payments. The sum of these items—exports, imports, grants and transfers, and capital flows or financial assets sales and purchases—should come to zero. In most cases, the total is not zero. For 1992, the difference was $13.1 billion. If the balance of payments does not balance, the difference is called the *statistical discrepancy.* The reason for this account is that the government may miss some transactions, ranging from deposits in Swiss bank accounts to unrecorded tourist spending to drug smuggling.

The balance of payments provides a great deal of useful information. Changes in exports and imports affect aggregate demand and, through aggregate demand, influence output and the price level. The capital account provides information on how much the United States is investing in other countries relative to those countries' financial investments in the United States. Until the early 1980s, the United States usually had a surplus of exports over imports large enough to finance a net capital outflow of both private and public funds to other countries.

Since that time, the United States has had a deficit of goods and services financed by an inflow of capital from abroad.

The Budget Deficit and the Trade Deficit.   In the early 1980s, the growing federal budget deficit and the current account deficit were closely linked through interest rates and the price of the dollar. Budget deficits meant the government was borrowing heavily in the bond market, driving up interest rates. High real interest rates (interest rates adjusted for inflation) attracted an inflow of capital from abroad as non–Americans bought U.S. bonds and made deposits in U.S. banks. To buy bonds and make deposits, foreign investors had to buy dollars. The increase in demand for the dollar drove its price up. A higher price for the dollar made U.S. exports more expensive and imports cheaper. The result was a deficit in trade or the current account.

After 1985, real interest rates fell gradually. The price of the dollar declined, reducing the trade deficit (although less than some people had hoped). As long as budget deficits remain high, however, long-term interest rates will remain higher in the United States than in other countries, attracting a capital inflow and keeping the price of the dollar higher than it would be otherwise.

One lesson of this experience was that the United States cannot make monetary and fiscal policy in a vacuum. Tight monetary policy and budget deficits that lead to high interest rates also have an effect on exports, imports, and capital flows. A budget deficit that might otherwise increase output and employment will have less impact in an open economy in which much of the effect is blunted by falling exports and rising imports. A global economy puts some real limits on active monetary and fiscal policy.

Summary

1. The law of one price says that in the absence of transport costs, trade barriers, and imperfect information, the same product will sell for the same price in all markets.

2. International trade differs from domestic trade because national sovereignty leads to different national currencies and commercial policies.

3. Countries trade with one another to enjoy the efficiency gains from specialization as well as the benefits of competition and economies of scale.

4. Countries restrict trade in goods and services through tariffs, quotas, and nontariff barriers. A tariff is a tax on an imported good. A quota is a limit on the physical quantity or value of an imported good. Nontariff barriers restrict imports by imposing costly rules or requirements on goods to make them comply with domestic standards.

5. Tariffs raise prices, restrict imports and consumption, and increase domestic production at the expense of cheaper foreign production. Tariffs also raise revenue for the government.

6. Quotas raise the prices of protected goods, increase domestic output, reduce imports and domestic consumption, and create monopoly profits for those who receive import licenses. When demand increases, under a tariff the main effect is increased imports, whereas under a quota price will rise.

7. Nations often choose to reduce trade barriers with just a few trading partners in a free trade area or common market. NAFTA and the European Community (EC) are examples of this kind of economic integration respectively.

8. The foreign exchange market is the network of buyers and sellers who trade in national currencies. Demand for a country's currency reflects foreign demand for its exports and financial assets. Supply reflects its citizens' desire to buy foreign goods, services, and financial assets.

9. Supply and/or demand for a nation's currency shifts in response to changes in interest rates, price levels, and incomes in different countries.

10. The balance of payments is a summary of a country's transactions with the rest of the world. The categories are the current account (exports and imports of goods and services, plus grants and transfers), the capital account (purchases and sales of financial assets), and the statistical discrepancy.

Key Terms

balance of payments	foreign exchange	North American Free
commercial policy	market	Trade Area (NAFTA)
common market	free trade area	quota
economic integration	law of one price	tariff
exchange rate	national sovereignty	trade creation
floating exchange rates	nontariff barrier	trade diversion

Questions and Problems

1. As a practical economist, you are always alert to opportunities. You find that oranges are selling for 25 cents each in Townville and 50 cents each in Fairplay, only 20 miles away. What will you do? How will your actions affect the price of oranges in Townville and in Fairplay? Will there still be a price difference after you are through? If so, why?

2. Tarifia, a small country, produces and imports oranges. Oranges sell for 15 cents, and Tarifia produces 1,000,000 oranges, imports 400,000, and consumes 1,400,000 a year. Impose a tariff of 5 cents on oranges, and show the effects on a graph.

3. Suppose Tarifia decides on a quota instead. The quota is 300,000 oranges a year. How will the effects of the quota differ from the tariff in question 2?

4. You have persuaded your representative in Congress to sponsor legislation to provide protection for your industry. Do you prefer a tariff or a quota? Why?

5. You have been assigned as an economic adviser to Andaria, a small Central American country that produces a few tropical agricultural products (tropical hardwoods, bananas, and coffee) and imports most of its manufactured goods from the United States. Now Andaria is invited to join a free trade area with a large South American nation that will provide a market for its exports and supply many of the same kinds of products as the United States. Do you think trade creation or trade diversion will dominate in this free trade area? Should Andaria join?

6. Draw a supply curve and a demand curve for zerbas, the mythical currency of the African nation of Chadbabwe. Show the equilibrium price and quantity. Suppose there is an increase in demand for Chadbabwe's prime export, reeds for rafts. Show the effect on the supply and/or demand curve and the change in the currency's price.

7. How would a recession in Canada affect the price of the Canadian dollar if nothing else changed? Why?

8. If the United States succeeds in reducing the federal budget deficit, how should the price of the dollar be affected?

9. If the price of the dollar is 1.5 DM, what is the price of the mark in dollars?

10. Inland's government accountants have finally found all the pieces of their balance of payments. The balance on the current account added up to $100 million (surplus). The balance on the capital account came to $60 million (deficit). What is the statistical discrepancy, and where does it come from?

19

The Practical Economist:
Using Your Economics

Like theology, and unlike mathematics, economics deals with matters which men consider very close to their lives.

JOHN KENNETH GALBRAITH

Main Points

1. The basic concepts and models of economics include supply and demand, scarcity and opportunity cost, self-interest and maximizing behavior, and marginal analysis. These concepts can be applied to a wide range of issues in other disciplines, such as sociology, political science, business, and engineering. They are also useful in one's daily experiences as a consumer, worker, and citizen.

2. The practical economist must recognize not only the power but also the limitations of applying the economic way of thinking to daily decisions and public issues.

3. To keep one's human capital as a practical economist up to date, one should stay informed on current statistics and social issues and think about them in economic terms.

Remember the practical economist you met in Chapter 1 and encountered throughout this book? One aim of a course in economics is to help you better manage your personal resources and your community's collective scarce resources. Better management should result from being more tuned in to how those resources are allocated and the economic consequences of using them in alternative ways. Perhaps you recognized yourself in some of these pages—reaping the benefits of comparative advantage by specializing and trading, making a choice between two spending decisions (or job offers) on the basis of marginal benefits or marginal costs, being turned down for a loan because money (monetary policy) was tight, or trying to make sense out of changes in the tax law. In this chapter, we will leave you with some guidelines for continuing to use what you have learned in economics, not only in other courses but also in your daily life as a consumer, worker or entrepreneur, and citizen. ∎

WHY STUDY ECONOMICS? (REVISITED)

If you have ever seen a stage musical or rented a video or watched a late-night rerun of an old-time 1950s movie musical, you may recall that there is always a last song aimed at pulling the story together. That last song is called a *reprise*. College courses too often neglect the reprise. The last day and the last chapter should pull the concepts together so that the course is not merely another three or four credit hours completed. The reprise should also fit meaningfully into your curriculum and into your daily life. The first part of this chapter, like the final song in *Camelot, Oklahoma!* or *Cats!*, is a reprise of the concepts and models presented in this textbook.

Basic Economic Ideas

This textbook introduced some very basic economic ideas that have far-ranging applications. You should file these concepts in your permanent mental storage for quick and easy retrieval. Following is a short synopsis of the most widely used economic concepts that you will want to underscore, review, and be prepared to use over and over again.

Self-Interested, Maximizing Behavior.   The basic assumption of economics is that individuals maximize their satisfaction, resource owners maximize their incomes, and firms maximize profits. This view of behavior is a very useful description of how people approach economic problems. The assumption that people pursue their own self-interest predicts market behavior quite well.

The more aware you are of maximizing behavior, the more likely you are to get close to whatever you define your maximum satisfaction to be. Because economists spend much of their careers examining and talking about maximizing, they are more likely than many other people to consider a purchase, a move, or some other decision by drawing up a list of the costs and benefits of each alternative. Like a professional economist, you as a practical economist can sharpen your maximizing behavior to get the most satisfaction out of your scarce resources. All it takes is an effort to be a little more aware of what you are trying to maximize and of the costs and benefits of each option.

Scarcity and Opportunity Cost.   Remember, resources are limited whereas wants are unlimited. As a result, every choice has an opportunity cost. That cost is measured by the value of next best alternative given up. The lesson that resources are scarce but wants are unlimited is one that most people begin to learn before kindergarten and go on relearning for the rest of their lives.

One very practical application of the concept of scarcity and opportunity cost to both the household and the public sector is budgeting. A budget is simply a spending plan that reflects a set of choices among various kinds of expenditures made possible with a given income. On the income side, the budget also reflects choices about using productive resources in different ways to generate income or, alternatively, to use those resources for household production or leisure. On the spending side, the budget reflects some careful weighing of how much you value various goods in comparison to their different prices.

Beyond budgeting, the concept of opportunity cost is useful to anyone in learning to sharpen and improve one's management of scarce resources (time and money, labor and capital) by counting the opportunity cost of one's choices. Every action you take, every dollar you spend, every hour you use, and every course you take has an opportunity cost in terms of the alternative uses for the time and/or money spent. Self-interested, maximizing behavior implies that practical economists seek to know the opportunity costs of their choices to allocate their scarce resources wisely and well.

Marginal Analysis.   Practical economists make decisions about how to allocate scarce resources at the *margin*. Marginal analysis means making decisions about the next item to buy, the next dollar to spend, or how to use the next 15 minutes. Most meaningful choices are marginal rather than once-for-all decisions. Another slice of bread, another course this semester, another customer, another unit of output, another small increase or decrease in pollution are all examples of the kinds of marginal decisions that dominate people's private and public lives.

Consumers maximize satisfaction by comparing the extra satisfaction from the next purchase to the extra cost. Producers find maximum profits where marginal revenue equals marginal cost. Pollution is at the optimal level when marginal benefit equals marginal cost. Rarely do politicians get to make such all-or-nothing decisions as whether or not there will be public education. Instead, they must choose whether to spend the *extra* dollar on education instead of on highways, or on elementary education instead of on higher education, or on higher teachers' salaries instead of on more school buildings. In macroeconomics, policymakers weigh the impact of a marginal increase or decrease in government spending, taxes, or the money supply on output, employment, and the price level.

The law of diminishing marginal utility (Chapter 4) and the law of increasing marginal cost (Chapters 5 and 6) should help you understand marginal decisions that run the gamut from why you may not finish eating a pizza to why it is so hard to get that last five pounds of air into a bicycle tire.

Markets and the Law of One Price.   Markets are the arena in which prices send signals that coordinate and direct production and consumption. Prices ration scarce goods among consumers and allocate scarce resources to different productive uses.

Rarely does a day pass when practical economists do not participate in a market. You work in the job market, buy in the retail market, save and borrow in the credit market, and lend in the stock and bond markets. The price signals from these markets are your cues to buy, sell, substitute, produce, lend, or borrow. There are other ways to organize these decisions, but no system displaces the market entirely, and no system has a signaling device as effective as the market price.

The law of one price was developed in Chapter 18, but it fits in well with most of the micro models in earlier chapters. This law describes the relationship among markets that suggests that any price difference not based on costs of moving goods or buyers among markets will tend to be eliminated over time. This is a very powerful idea. Practical economists will take advantage of price differences in time or space to move goods from where they are in abundant supply to where they are in greater demand. These brokers make a profit, but they also tend to equalize prices among markets.

The law of one price also has macro implications. One of the most important macro implications is the equalization of interest rates among countries through the flow of funds from country to country in search of the highest rate of return. The fact that it is easier than ever before to transfer funds limits the ability of the central bank to control interest rates within a particular country.

Demand and Supply.   Demand reflects diminishing marginal utility and substitution, and supply reflects increasing marginal opportunity cost. Together, supply and demand are the most commonly used tool for analyzing microeconomic problems.

You have seen so many applications of demand and supply in this course that it is probably not necessary to point out the important role they play in daily decisions. Demand and supply determine the price of everything you buy, from cars and houses to gasoline and toothpaste. The demand and supply of workers in your chosen occupation determine the wage and the number of job openings. They also affect the number of persons available or in training for that occupation. Falling demand for middle managers as business firms downsized in the early 1990s quickly translated into fewer business majors in colleges and universities. The business plan essential for starting a new business is mainly a careful, detailed review of demand and supply conditions for both inputs and output in that line of business. In macro markets, the supply and demand of labor determine the market wage, and the supply and demand for loanable funds determine the interest rate.

Specialization and Comparative Advantage. This basic principle is the basis for exchange and an important source of higher standards of living (real output per person). Specialization occurs even in households or families. Traditionally Dad repaired the car and mowed the lawn, while Mom washed the clothes and cooked the meals, although in many modern households Dad cooks, Mom repairs the car, and the children do their own laundry. The particular pattern of who specializes in what is less important than the ability of the household to gain a higher standard of living (more consumption, more leisure, or more of both) through specialization. Even if the children have an absolute advantage in nothing, they have a comparative advantage in something. Parents try to figure out where that comparative advantage lies and assign chores accordingly.

When regions or nations specialize and trade, they face the conflict between the benefits of specializing in one or a few products and the risks of interdependence. These risks include vulnerability to changes in foreign markets as well as the threat of foreign competition. Specialization and comparative advantage are important in many public policy issues relating to regional economic development strategies as well as trade with other countries. Thus, as a member of a household or as a citizen interested in public issues, you will find that specialization and comparative advantage play an important role in many of your daily decisions.

Competition and Property Rights. These two basic features of a market system are critical to making markets responsive to consumers. Much of the explanation of why some markets work better than others rests on how competitive those markets are and how clearly defined the property rights are. When OPEC reduces the price of oil, why is the price cut reflected in large cities first and in small towns much later? Competition. Why are doctors so eager to limit the supply of new physicians entering the industry? Competition.

When you look for a job opening, you will hope there is much competition on the demand side of the market (prospective employers) and very little competition on the supply side (college graduates with degrees in the same field). People want competition for everyone else but not for themselves. Markets work faster and more effectively, with lower prices, larger quantities, and less likelihood of persistent economic profits, under conditions of competition.

Property rights too are essential to the effective operation of the markets in which you participate. You would not want to buy a house or a car unless it had a clear title, meaning the seller owns the property and has the unrestricted right to sell it to you. More complex kinds of property rights are embodied in the zoning and subdivision regulations that go with your house and the speed limits and license requirements that accompany your car. These kinds of rights are both protective and limiting for property owners, who are protected from undesirable activities by the same rules that limit their own freedom to change the way they use their property. The same local ordinance that forbids you to burn your leaves in the fall, polluting the air, also protects your air rights from the danger of your neighbor burning old tires in the backyard. It is difficult to go through a normal, middle-class adulthood without encountering at least one major conflict over local property rights. Many state and national issues are also, at bottom, battles over property rights.

Lack of competition means monopoly, resulting in less output at higher prices. If property rights are not clearly defined, production and consumption will create side effects, or externalities, for third parties, and output will be higher or lower than the socially desirable level.

Market Failure and Government Failure.   In a mixed economy, a primary economic role of government is to correct market failure. Market failure is not limited to monopoly and externalities; it also includes an unacceptable distribution of income, macroeconomic instability, and the failure of the private market to provide public goods. However, using government to correct for the failings of the private market creates a risk of government failure.

Market failures are everywhere. Pollutants from a hazardous waste dump endanger your vegetable garden. Despite hard work, some individuals never manage to earn a decent income. The market fails to provide a needed competitor for the local power company with its high electric rates and poor service. When the market fails, citizens expect the government to intervene.

Often government action is the best solution for market failure. Turning to government, however, also has some risks, since government too can fail. Sources of government failure include favoring special-interest groups, lack of market price signals, and problems with majority voting. All these problems mean the outcome of government action may make things no better than leaving markets alone.

Circular Flow.   This broad vision of the aggregate economy shows households, businesses, and government exchanging goods and services in product and resource markets. Flows of saving into investment pass through financial markets, including banks and other financial institutions. Each person is a part of the circular flow. As individuals, practical economists have no greater impact on the prices of what they buy and sell or on the aggregate level of output and prices than the individual wheat farmer does in the model of perfect competition.

Nevertheless, as with the wheat farmer, although *your* effect on the total flow is small, *its* effect on you is considerable.

The circular flow is a reminder of your links to other parts of the economy. Individuals and households are tied to business firms as sellers of labor services and buyers of goods and services. Households save and lend (and perhaps borrow as well). They pay taxes or receive transfers. Many people, including the authors of this textbook, are directly employed by some level of government. Your firm may sell part of its output abroad, and most households buy at least some foreign goods.

The circular flow is a broad picture that helps sort out what is going on without getting bogged down in the details. This picture helps you envision what happens when a change occurs in one of the components, such as labor supply, investment demand, or export demand, and how that change affects the size of the flow.

 The Role of Expectations. As individuals and as a society, practical economists make decisions about buying, lending, borrowing, and committing their resources. These decisions depend on their expectations about what will happen in the near future to particular prices and the price level and to their real incomes and the economy's real income.

A decision to postpone buying a house is based on a family's expectations about interest rates, housing prices, and its own future income. A decision to study computer programming instead of art reflects, among other things, expectations about future job opportunities and earnings in those two fields.

In the aggregate, the process by which people form and revise expectations determines whether policies to manage aggregate demand have any impact on the economy. Policymakers are very interested in expectations. So are business managers, who pay for surveys of consumer expectations, because those expectations affect sales and therefore influence production plans.

Practical economists can do a better job of allocating their scarce resources and maximizing their well-being if their expectations are correct. At the end of this chapter, we will identify some regular sources of information that can help predict the course of prices, output, employment, interest rates, and other important economic variables.

Aggregate Supply and Demand. This model is very useful for examining, explaining, and sometimes predicting macroeconomic events and policies and for understanding the relationships among output, employment, and prices and why those relationships change.

Aggregate supply and aggregate demand, like the circular flow, are not affected by any one person's decision making. But the changes in output, employment, and prices that emerge from shifts in aggregate demand and supply do affect your choices. Thus, to make wise saving, lending, earning, and spending decisions based on expected prices (and interest rates), the practical economist should follow the behavior of those factors that shift aggregate supply and demand. Those factors include tax and spending policy, monetary policy, changes in resource markets, development of new technology, and changes in government regulations.

The aggregate supply and demand model in this book has been around a long time, but is has only filtered into introductory economics textbooks in the last 12 years. The power of this model lies in the fact that a single, simple diagram can reflect a variety of monetary and fiscal policy changes and show the effects of those changes on the price level, real output, and employment. It is a particularly useful tool for the practical economist to use in understanding and evaluating public policy changes as they occur.

CHECKLIST : **Basic concepts and Their Uses**

Self-interested, maximizing behavior: Getting the most out of your personal and community resources

Scarcity and opportunity cost: Budgeting, making choices

Marginal analysis: Maximizing, minizing, making choices

Markets and the law of one price: Getting signals for decision, responding to profit opportunities

Demand and supply: Understanding market prices, predicting price changes, making career choices

Specialization and comparative advantage: Getting the most out of your resources, assigning tasks in a firm or household, choosing a career

Competition and property rights: Making markets work, understanding local government

Market failure and government failure: Weighing the costs and benefits of government intervention in markets at all levels

Circular flow: Seeing the big picture, envisioning the impact of macro changes on personal decisions

Role of expectations: Making informed decisions about the future

Aggregate supply and demand: Understanding macroeconomic events, evaluating public policy, providing input into your own expectations.

THE LIMITATIONS OF ECONOMICS

Both the practical economist and the professional economist need to keep the limitations of economics in mind. Imperfect information, sudden and unpredictable changes in population, tastes, or institutions, and other uncontrollable conditions make economics far from a laboratory science. Economists know much more about how both the microeconomy and the macroeconomy work than they did 50 years ago, but they have much more to learn. There are five important sources of limitations on the predictive powers of economics models: (1) the *ceteris paribus* (other things remaining unchanged) assumption, (2)

the emergence of new problems from old solutions, (3) self-fulfilling and self-negating prophecies, (4) imperfect knowledge, and (5) the difficulty of identifying how differences in values affect economic reasoning.

Ceteris Paribus

Most of the models in this textbook are very simplified. Many of the factors omitted or held constant can change. As a result, predictions from such simple models are inaccurate. More complete models make better predictions, but they are also much more complex and more difficult to use. For example, in the early 1990s economists and others were predicting sharp declines in college enrollments. These predictions were based on two factors from a simple supply and demand model. The population of high school graduates had been largely determined by the birth rate 18 years earlier. That pool of potential students declined each year from 1983 to 1994. Fewer potential students should have shifted the demand curve to the left. At the same time, the price (especially tuition and textbooks) of a college education were rising much more rapidly than other prices. Higher tuition should have reduced the quantity demanded. Both of these influences should have been reflected in the number of students enrolled.

The predicted large enrollment decline did not occur, however. There were small declines in some years, small increases in others. What happened? Some of the *ceteris paribus* conditions had changed. More members of the growing elderly population came back as nontraditional students. The small crop of high school graduates came from families with fewer children; thus, their parents could afford the cost of higher education for only one or two instead of three or four children. Incomes rose. Tastes changed. Opportunities for students without post–high school education looked less attractive. For all these reasons, the demand curve shifted to the right, confounding the forecast.

Self-Fulfilling and Self-Negating Prophecies

Self-fulfilling prophecy
An economic forecast that changes people's behavior so as to bring the forecasted change about, more quickly and sometimes more intensely.

Self-negating prophecy
An economic forecast that changes people's behavior so as to prevent the forecasted change from occurring or reduce the amount of change that occurs.

What do you think would happen if all economists predicted inflation? Everyone would rush out to buy before prices rose, which would drive prices up. This response is a good example of a **self-fulfilling prophecy**. On the other hand, consider a prediction that there will be a shortage of college professors in the late 1990s. The prediction becomes information. College students very quickly sense a new opportunity, and the number of students going on to graduate training will rise. The predicted shortage of professors fails to materialize, however, *because of the prediction*. In this case, there was a **self-negating prophecy**. Self-fulfilling prophecies make economists look more talented than they really are. Self-negating prophecies are a source of embarrassment for those economists foolish enough to make public forecasts.

Old Solutions Create New Problems

Economists and policymakers often devise solutions that appear to resolve a particular problem, only to create a new one. Yesterday's problems lead to today's solutions; today's solutions are the source of tomorrow's problems. For example, the solution to the high unemployment problem of the Depression era was Keynesian expansionary fiscal policies. Some economists blame these policies for contributing to the creation of a new problem, persistent federal budget deficits (although others would argue that at most, Keynesian economics provided an excuse for irresponsible budget management by presidents and Congress). Urban housing shortages in the 1960s led to building more low-income housing in the form of concentrated housing projects. These projects became "instant slums" with high concentrations of crime, drugs, and prostitution in many cases. Efforts to reduce infant mortality in less developed countries created unexpected pressures on food supplies and other resources. Floating exchange rates solved some of the problems of the old fixed-rate system, only to create new problems of uncertainty and wide swings in exchange rates. The "green revolution" of the early 1970s spawned new, high-yield rice varieties for developing countries, which led to self-sufficiency in some countries and caused U.S. farm exports to drop. It's hard to anticipate the new problems that will emerge from the old solution, but there are no costless answers.

Imperfect Knowledge

Imperfect knowledge plagues both microeconomics and macroeconomics. For example, economists do not know to what extent markets behave more like the contract model or the auction model, or whether expectations are more nearly rational or adaptive in nature. Thus, when policymakers fiddle with shifting the aggregate demand curve, they cannot really predict how the response will split between real output and prices or how large or how fast the response will be.

Some of the gaps in economists' knowledge can be corrected over time by patient and careful study and by building and testing better models. Some of the gaps are difficult to fill, because economists deal with the behavior of human beings, not atoms, molecules, or chemical compounds or even bees or apple trees, the subjects of the physical and biological sciences. Human behavior is too complex to fully capture in manageable models.

Positive Economics and Values

Because economics deals with choices, tastes, decisions, and the ordinary stuff of human life, it cannot ever be made truly value free, or positive. The analysis of real-world problems will always contain normative elements. Practical economists will put your personal values into your economic models, just as your instructors and the authors of your textbooks put their values into the models they use and teach.

Those macroeconomists who find rational expectations and auction markets a more "reasonable" view of the way things work are usually individuals whose personal values have led them to prefer a very limited macroeconomic role for government. Macroeconomists who really think expectations are adaptive and markets are contractual hold basic values and preferences that lead them toward a larger role for government in the first place.

Similarly, in microeconomics, some economists see competitive markets as the norm, externalities as uncommon, and the market's distribution of income as appropriate. These economists usually place higher values on freedom than on equity and translate those values into their view of how the real world is. Other microeconomists are more concerned about equity and less fearful of government intervention. They are more likely to look for, and find, abundant cases of monopoly power, negative externalities, and extremes of wealth and poverty. There is no effective way to divorce individual values from the use of models and policy pronouncements. The best economists can hope to do is make those values explicit.

CHECKLIST : **The Limitations of Economics**

Although economics is powerful, users of economic methods and tools need to be aware of their limitations and what those limitations imply. Categories of limitation are:

Ceteris paribus: The model's predictions may not be valid if other conditions change.

Old solutions create new problems: The solution to one economic problem may create new, unforeseen difficulties.

Self-fulfilling and self-negating prophecies: Predictions may be incorporated into expectations and alter outcomes.

Imperfect knowledge: Lack of adequate information about some aspects of a model in the real world limits the accuracy of predictions.

Positive economics and values: The formulation of a model may be influenced by the values of the economist who develops it.

This list of limitations is not exhaustive, but it does give some sense of the reason why economists are not always 100 percent correct 100 percent of the time, why economists disagree, and why economics cannot give you complete and unique answers to all of life's questions. Economics, like mathematics, is a tool. You would not want to use a hammer to kill a fly or a flyswatter to drive a nail. Used properly and with an awareness of its limitations, economics can be a very useful tool indeed.

USING ECONOMICS IN EVERYDAY LIFE

You should be prepared to use your economics in your daily life as a consumer (including lender and borrower), a worker (or entrepreneur), and a citizen. Many of these applications of economics appeared in the last few pages. Following is a brief summary of some of the relevant tools for each of these roles and the kinds of personal economic activity to which each can be applied.

Economics in the Household

Household production
The allocation of time and other resources to produce goods and services within the household rather than purchasing them in the market.

Economic activities in the household consist of budgeting, making purchases, lending (which includes buying stocks and bonds), and allocating time to household production. **Household production** consists of those production activities that take place within the household, such as cooking cleaning, yard work, house painting, child care, laundry, and similar activities, some of which can be purchased in the marketplace instead of produced at home. The choice of *where* to produce—at home or through firms—is a basic question for households, even if it is not one of the big three issues facing the macroeconomy. Different households will make different choices about home production versus market purchases depending on the opportunity costs and the preferences of household members.

Macroeconomic data, such as current and projected changes in the price level, interest rates, and employment, may be useful in making many household decisions. Most of the decisions, however, call for microeconomic tools. Household decisions about budgeting and making purchases involve maximizing behavior, evaluating opportunity cost, competition (especially in comparison shopping), and responding to changing prices by substituting.

Household production choices involve specialization based on comparative advantage and evaluating the opportunity cost of time. Lending and borrowing require some understanding of how markets for loanable funds work. Accurate expectations about interest rates help households to time borrowing and lending to earn the highest possible interest rates when they lend and pay the lowest interest rates when they borrow.

Economics on the Job

Economics on the job involves deciding what occupation to enter, how many hours to work, which employer to work for, and whether to go into business for yourself. Virtually every concept on the list, especially the microeconomic concepts, will enter into these decisions. Workers and employers have property rights that need to be spelled out in the contract. Getting employers to compete for your labor services should increase your wage. Markets send informational signals that you should seek out and use in your decisions. You need to identify your area of comparative advantage to gain the greatest benefit from specialization. The market supply and demand for workers with similar skills will determine your salary. And, of course, your ultimate goal is to maximize your earnings subject to some important constraints on job satisfaction, hours, and working conditions.

Economics at the Ballot Box

Economics in action is never more visible than when a citizen votes, lobbies, or participates directly in public decisions as a member of a city council, board, commission, or other public body. Similar skills are useful in governing private, nonprofit membership organizations such as a churches, clubs, and civic groups. You will have to analyze the self-interested, maximizing behavior of other practical economists as politicians, bureaucrats, leaders, or lobbyists to see the motives behind what they propose. Recognizing what markets do well will make you more inclined to limit the use of government power in some areas, especially price setting. Knowing the harmful effects of monopoly power, undefined or poorly defined property rights, or other forms of market failure may lead you to support more government intervention in other areas.

Your understanding of specialization and comparative advantage will affect your vote on downtown renewal, regional development programs, or (at the national level) restrictions on free trade. The public budget will appear to you as an exercise in maximizing and weighing opportunity costs, because scarce resources (tax revenues) have multiple competing uses. Finally, the macroeconomic tools of circular flow and aggregate supply and demand will be invaluable when you envision the impact of various macroeconomic policies on your state or community.

Being a practical economist will not necessarily make your role as a citizen easier. Like any knowledge, it will enable you to do a better job, but with a greater awareness of what you do not know that you probably need to know to make wise choices.

KEEPING UP: A GUIDE TO ECONOMIC INFORMATION

If you intend to function as a practical economist, you will need to keep your investment in human capital up to date. Part of the practical economist's human capital is the kit of tools that we have developed in this text and reviewed briefly here. These tools—supply and demand analysis, markets and prices, aggregate supply and demand, scarcity and opportunity cost—can be kept up to date with regular use. The more you use these models and concepts in daily decisions, the more polished and effective they will become.

However, economic models need raw material, usually numbers and other information. Much of the information you need as a householder, worker, or entrepreneur is at your fingertips. The prices of houses, socks, and carrots are readily available through advertising and word of mouth. Wage information is available in the help-wanted ads and in *Occupational Outlook Handbook*. The *Monthly Labor Review*, published by the U.S. Department of Labor, is another excellent source of information on labor market conditions, wages, fringe bene-fits, and price indexes.

Several excellent publications will help you keep abreast of current develop-ments. *The Wall Street Journal* is a popular and respected source of current information in all areas, but particularly for those who buy stocks and bonds, follow monetary and fiscal policy, or are otherwise interested in the world of business. Magazines such as *Money, Changing Times*, and *Consumer Reports* provide useful economic information for household management. *Business Week, Forbes*, and other business publications, as well as the business sections of weekly newsmagazines and daily newspapers, will keep you informed on new develop-ments in business, finance, banking, government, trade policy, and other areas. These publications will supply plenty of raw material for practice with economic models. The annual *Economic Report of the President* provides an update on macroeconomic policy and various problem areas in the economy. It is written in nontechnical language and accompanied by a wealth of statistics, including *GDP*, interest rates, prices, employment, unemployment, and other macroeco-nomic indicators.

One semester gives only a taste of economics, but you are leaving this course with some useful skills and tools that can last you a lifetime if you properly maintain them through regular use, keep them current with relevant and timely information, and keep them in good repair. We hope you will continue to function effectively as a practical economist in your household, your work, and your civic involvement for many years to come.

Summary

1. Certain basic economic ideas have applications to questions in daily life in the roles we play as consumers, workers, and citizens. These concepts are self-interested, maximizing behavior; scarcity and opportunity cost; marginal analysis; markets and the law of one price; demand and supply; specialization and comparative advantage; competition and property rights; market failure and government failure; circular flow; expectations; and aggregate supply and demand.

2. The limitations of economics mean its conclusions should be applied with caution. These limitations include the *ceteris paribus* assumption, new prob-lems arising from old solutions, self-fulfilling and self-negating prophecies, imperfect knowledge, and differences in values.

3. Economics offers useful insights into many household economic problems, including budgeting and the allocation of time.

4. Economics is useful to workers and entrepreneurs who want to earn the maximum return from the resources they control.

5. Economics is vital to citizens as voters, as lobbyists, or as public servants in legislative or administrative bodies as they allocate resources, correct market failures, and attempt to minimize government failures.

6. Practical economists can function more effectively by using economic skills regularly and keeping abreast of economic developments through a number of widely available publications.

Key Terms

household production   self-fulfilling prophecy   self-negating prophecy

Questions and Problems

1. If you have not yet checked out your intended occupation in *Occupational Outlook Handbook*, this would be a good time to do so. Summarize the prospects for earnings and employment and the amount of investment in human capital that this line of work will require.

2. If you wind up living in a household of more than one person, how will you and your partner decide on the division of responsibilities? What economic tools will enter into those decisions?

3. The headlines of the newspaper proclaimed, "Unemployment expected to rise this year." The following year, however, the unemployment rate was the same. Can you explain what might have gone wrong in terms of the limitations of economics?

4. How does the behavior of the practical economist contribute to self-fulfilling and self-negating prophecies?

Index